MODERN PROJECT FINANCE
A Casebook

Benjamin C. Esty

John Wiley & Sons, Inc.

Acquisitions Editor	Leslie Kraham
Project Editor	Cindy Rhoads
Marketing Manager	Charity Robey/David Woodbury
Production Editor	Sarah Wolfman-Robichaud
Designer	Madelyn Lesure
Cover Photos	Wernher Krutein/photovault.com
Author Photo	Catherine Walsh/HBC Communications

This book was set in 10/12 New Caledonia by Matrix Publishing and printed and bound by Hamilton Printing. The cover was printed by Phoenix Color.

Recognizing the importance of preserving what has been written, it is a policy of John Wiley & Sons, Inc. to have books of enduring value published in the United States printed on acid-free paper, and we exert our best efforts to that end.

Case material of the Harvard Graduate School of Business Administration is made possible by cooperation of business firms and other organizations which may wish to remain anonymous by having names, quantities, and other identifying details disguised while maintaining basic relationships. Cases are prepared as the basis for class discussion rather than to illustrate either effective or ineffective handling of an administrative situation.

ISBN 0-471-43425-6

Printed in the United States of America
10 9 8 7 6 5

Dedication

To my parents, John and Katharine,

and

my wife, Raquel

Acknowledgments

Writing a casebook is a collaborative endeavor and one that I could not have done without assistance from practitioners in the field of project finance, my colleagues at Harvard Business School, and numerous other people. First and foremost, I would like to thank the executives who helped write these case studies. Besides sharing their time, they shared their wisdom and experience. As Walter Wriston, the former head of Citicorp, once said (or is rumored to have said), "Good judgment comes from experience; experience comes from bad judgment." By studying these case studies, I hope others will learn important lessons about project finance in a far easier, shorter, and less costly way. I am grateful for their willingness to participate in the case-writing process and hope they know what an important contribution they have made to management education. Within this group of professionals, Bill Chew, Hal Davis, Chris Dymond, Cam Harvey, Robb Kneupfer, Frank Lysy, and especially Chris Beale and Jay Worenklein shared their insights into the practice of project finance, identified important case topics, and provided introductions to potential case protagonists.

My academic colleagues at Harvard Business School also helped create these case studies by refining the ideas contained in them. Mike Jensen originally got me interested in the incentive and valuation effects of leverage when I was a doctoral student at Harvard; Rick Ruback encouraged me to pursue these interests in the field of project finance. Bill Fruhan, Tom Piper, Rick Ruback, and Lou Wells each read many of my case studies and notes—in fact, far more than I had the right to ask any one of them to read. Many other people, including Jim Austin, George Baker, Carliss Baldwin, Joe Bower, Dwight Crane, Ron Fox, Pankaj Ghemawat, Sam Hayes, Carl Kester, Bill Sahlman, Mal Salter, Jim Sebenius, Deb Spar, and Peter Tufano, provided helpful comments on specific cases and notes. Tim Luehrman (Texas High-Speed Rail Corporation) and Peter Tufano (Bidding for Antamina) kindly allowed me to use their cases in this book. In addition to my academic colleagues, I want to thank the more than 500 students who have taken the Large-Scale Investment course, forced me to clarify my thinking and frameworks, and taught me about project finance through their insightful questions and required term papers, many of which subsequently became case studies in this book.

Besides providing a set of very helpful colleagues, Harvard Business School contributed to this book in many ways. The Division of Research generously funded my research, funding that allowed me to visit companies and projects around the world and to hire excellent research assistants (Carrie Ferman, Mike Kane, Mathew Millett, Fuaad Qureshi, and Aldo Sesia). It also allowed me to regularly and extensively use the school's research staff (Chris Allen, Sarah Eriksen, Erika McCaffrey, and Sarah Woolverton) and case services center (Jacqueline Archer, Aimee Hamel, Ele Jaynes, Jack McNamara, Lonya Turner, and Carol Sweet). Without this support, I could never have embarked on this line of research. I am also grateful for the many contributions Dee Luther has made to my research in general and to this book in particular. By managing all aspects of my academic life, she allows me to focus on research, teaching, and writing.

At John Wiley & Sons, I want to thank Leslie Kraham, Cindy Rhoads, and Sarah Wolfman-Robichaud who helped make this book a reality. Above all else, Leslie had the foresight and Wiley had the courage to publish an academic book about a very new and very practical subject. I hope their gamble pays off.

Last, but no means least, I want to thank my parents, John and Katharine Esty, and my wife Raquel. As former teachers and authors, my parents gave me an appreciation for learning and have shaped this book and my academic work in more ways than they will ever know. Raquel, for her part, has supported my work and been extremely understanding of the demands associated with research and travel. As my favorite traveling companion, I only wish she could have accompanied me on more of the trips. While her support made this book possible, her love and companionship make my life joyful.

About the Author

Benjamin Esty is a Professor of Business Administration in the Finance Group at Harvard Business School. He received his Ph.D. in Business Economics from Harvard University; his MBA with high distinction from Harvard Business School; and a B.A. degree in Economics with honors and distinction from Stanford University.

Professor Esty teaches courses on both project and corporate finance in the MBA program at Harvard. Five years ago, he developed a new course on project finance called Large-Scale Investment (LSI). This course analyzes how firms structure, value, and finance large capital investments, and serves as the intellectual foundation for this book. He also teaches in a variety of executive education programs and serves as the co-chairman of the program on Valuation. Professor Esty has received the Student Association Award for teaching excellence three times in recent years for both his corporate and project finance courses.

As a researcher, Professor Esty has published numerous articles in both academic and practitioner-oriented journals such as the *Journal of Financial Economics*, *Journal of Applied Corporate Finance*, and the *Journal of Financial and Quantitative Analysis*. In addition, he has written more than 70 case studies, technical notes, and teaching notes on project finance, emerging market investments, and valuation mechanics. He currently serves on the editorial board of the *Journal of Structured and Project Finance* and regularly advises investment banks, development institutions, government agencies, and project sponsors on a broad range of investment, financing, and valuation issues.

Table of Contents

1

Introduction to
Modern Project Finance

This book contains material for a case-based course on project finance. The course was designed to achieve two objectives: first, to provide an introduction to the field of project finance and a description of current practice; and second, to provide a new and effective setting in which to teach advanced principles of corporate finance. With regard to project finance, it is a large and rapidly growing subfield of finance, yet one where academic theory and research distantly lag current practice. This book is an attempt to bridge the gap and to provide institutional data that will facilitate future research. Chapter 2 introduces the field by defining project finance and describing its use over the past five years.[1] The data show that total project financed-investment grew at a compound annual rate of almost 20% through most of the 1990s and peaked at $217 billion in 2001. A slowdown in the global economy combined with various regional and sectoral crises (e.g., in U.S. power, global telecommunications, Asia, Russia, and Argentina) caused total project-financed investment to fall by 38% to $135 billion in 2002. Nevertheless, the long-term demand for capital and infrastructure investment remains large, which implies the long-term prospects for project finance remain strong. Given the magnitude of current investment and the prospects for future growth, financial managers, bankers, and government officials need to understand what project finance is, why it creates value, and how to structure transactions that have a high probability of succeeding both operationally and financially.

Besides the very practical reasons for studying project finance, this book provides a set of cases that can be used to illustrate core principles of finance ranging from capital structure theory to risk management, contracting, and corporate governance. The

Professor Benjamin C. Esty prepared this note to help instructors design and teach courses on project finance.

[1] There is no single, generally agreed upon definition of project finance. A recent article in *The Wall Street Journal* illustrates the confusion about what project finance actually is. The article defined project finance as "a term that typically refers to money lent to build power plants or oil refineries" (Pacelle et al., 2001).

central theme of the course is that "structure matters," which stands in sharp contrast to the neoclassical view of the firm as a "black box" production function and the assumption underlying Modigliani and Miller's first irrelevance proposition that financing and investment are separable and independent activities.[2] The cases illustrate how various aspects of project structure (e.g., capital, ownership, contractual, and organizational structures) affect managerial incentives to create value and manage risk. Ultimately, they illustrate how to create value through *both* investment and financing decisions.

The cases themselves analyze primarily *large* projects—those costing $500 million or more—because large, standalone projects provide a particularly clear window on how managers make important structural decisions and how these decisions, in turn, affect asset values.[3] Large projects are also interesting research subjects because many of them, at least historically, have encountered financial distress of one form or another (e.g., EuroTunnel, EuroDisney, Canary Wharf, Dabhol, and Iridium). Despite this track record, large projects are critical to economic growth and prosperity in both developed and developing markets. Chapter 3 describes these motivations for studying project finance in greater detail by answering two fundamental questions: why study project finance in general and why study large projects in particular? The rest of this chapter describes the course's (and the book's) key themes, structure, and content. The Appendix provides brief descriptions of each of the cases contained in the book.

KEY THEMES AND OBJECTIVES

Project companies exhibit many interesting and unique structural features. They are legally independent entities with very concentrated equity ownership: one to three sponsoring firms (or "sponsors") typically own all of the project's equity. By design, project companies have high leverage: the average book value debt-to-total capitalization ratio is 70%, which is roughly two to three times higher than the average leverage ratio of a typical publicly traded company. And finally, project companies are founded on a series of legal contracts. The typical project has 40 or more contracts uniting 15 parties in a vertical chain from input supplier to output purchaser.

At first glance, these structural features appear counterintuitive. For example, establishing a new and independent project company as part of the investment process involves greater transaction costs and, in most cases, higher debt rates than financing a comparable investment as part of an existing company. The use of high leverage, *ceteris paribus,* increases the probability of default, while the use of medium-term bank debt seems inappropriate for projects with lives ranging from 10 to 50 years. Moreover, the use of high leverage and extensive contracting severely restricts managerial discretion. For long-term projects with uncertain futures, it is not clear why sponsors would

---

[2] Modigliani and Miller (1958) show that corporate financing decisions do not affect firm value under certain conditions. Their "irrelevance" proposition, a cornerstone of modern finance and an important reason why they each won a Nobel Prize in economics (Modigliani in 1985 and Miller in 1990), is powerful because it highlights the factors that make financing and structuring decisions value relevant.

[3] From a research perspective, large projects represent what R.K. Merton (1987), the sociologist, defined as "strategic research sites." Merton described a strategic research site as a setting, event, or object "that exhibits the phenomena to be explained or interpreted to such advantage and in such accessible form that it enables the fruitful investigation of previously stubborn problems and the discovery of new problems for further inquiry." The fact that project-financed companies are newly created, standalone entities with unique, and often extreme, structural features makes them strategic research sites and an ideal laboratory in which to study corporate finance.

prefer rules (e.g., covenants, contracts, and forced cash distribution) over managerial discretion.

In practice, however, project finance provides an efficient way to finance certain assets—specifically, large, tangible assets with limited lives. By creating a project company, sponsors can transfer risk to debtholders and related parties who can bear the risks at lower cost and/or manage specific activities more effectively than they can themselves. But to preclude opportunistic behavior by these other parties—often the assets have transaction- or relationship-specific uses and are, therefore, vulnerable to opportunistic behavior—the sponsors write long-term contracts to dictate behavior and govern the allocation of cash flow.[4] While direct ownership of the project by a single firm would be a more effective way to prevent opportunistic behavior between related or connected parties, it would eliminate the benefits of risk sharing. The debtholders, in exchange for bearing project risk, impose tight discipline on management through contracts, oversight, and regular debt service payments (i.e., forced distribution of cash flow). High leverage, in turn, allows sponsors to reduce their equity commitments. This tightly integrated set of organizational, financial, and contractual features generates a low-cost financing vehicle for sponsoring firms and creates an effective governance structure for certain assets. One goal of this book is to highlight which assets are the best suited for project finance and which firms will benefit most from using it. A related goal is to understand the relationship between project structure and both managerial incentives and value creation.

To understand why structure matters (or why the Modigliani and Miller irrelevance proposition fails to hold in this context) requires a thorough understanding of market imperfections. These imperfections or deadweight costs, as they are known in finance, include the costs associated with agency or incentive conflicts, financial distress, structuring and executing transactions, asymmetric information between relevant parties, and taxes. The structural decisions surrounding project companies can be explained using an "imperfections framework" or lens, and the idea that structural decisions affect the existence and magnitude of deadweight costs. This framework helps explain why project finance creates value and why project companies represent optimal governance structures for certain kinds of assets. Given this pedagogical approach (the imperfections framework), the course's central theme becomes clearer: structure matters because it reduces the *net* cost of financing certain assets and improves their subsequent operating and financial performance (see Exhibit 1-1).

COURSE STRUCTURE

The course contains four modules: (1) Structuring Projects; (2) Valuing Projects; (3) Managing Risky Projects; and (4) Financing Projects. As shown in Exhibit 1-1, the modules correspond to different aspects of project structure. Module 1 analyzes *organizational* structure: sponsors must decide whether to finance assets jointly (corporate finance) or separately (project finance). This analysis focuses on the "project" nature of project finance. The next two modules (Modules 2 and 3) analyze *contractual* issues, with an emphasis on the allocation of returns, risks, and asset control. Successful structuring requires an ability to measure returns accurately (valuation analysis) and man-

---

[4] A good example is the decision to construct a coal-fired power plant next to an existing coal mine. The bargaining dynamics and balance of power that exists before the plant is built change dramatically once the plant is built (see Joskow, 1985; and Williamson, 1985). For example, the power plant's owners lose the ability to negotiate coal prices once the plant is built.

EXHIBIT 1-1

KEY THEMES

Course Theme: Project structure reduces the *net* cost of financing large, tangible assets and improves their subsequent operating and financial performance.

Pedagogical Approach: Analyze investment and financing decisions using a market imperfections framework; link the lessons from project finance to more general principles of corporate finance.

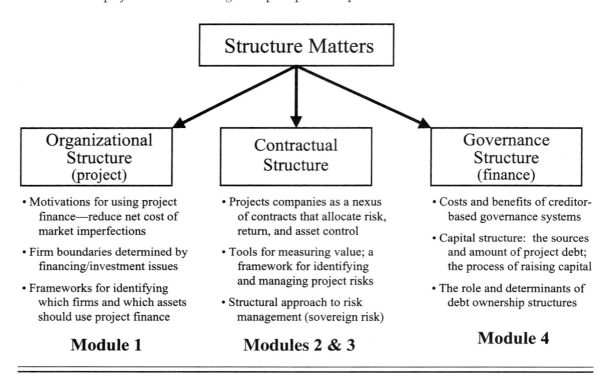

Organizational Structure (project)	Contractual Structure	Governance Structure (finance)
• Motivations for using project finance—reduce net cost of market imperfections • Firm boundaries determined by financing/investment issues • Frameworks for identifying which firms and which assets should use project finance	• Projects companies as a nexus of contracts that allocate risk, return, and asset control • Tools for measuring value; a framework for identifying and managing project risks • Structural approach to risk management (sovereign risk)	• Costs and benefits of creditor-based governance systems • Capital structure: the sources and amount of project debt; the process of raising capital • The role and determinants of debt ownership structures
Module 1	**Modules 2 & 3**	**Module 4**

---

age risks effectively. Module 4 analyzes *capital* structure, *debt ownership* structure, and project governance. In other words, it analyzes the "financial" aspects of project finance.

In terms of perspective, the cases are international, integrative, and managerial. Although several cases analyze projects in the United States and Western Europe, most of the cases analyze projects in developing markets. In fact, the cases analyze projects in 15 different countries including Azerbaijan, Mozambique, Venezuela, and Hong Kong, and were selected to reflect actual use of project finance in terms of geographic locations and industrial sectors (see the sector/geographic distribution of cases in Exhibit 1-2 and the statistics in Chapter 2 on actual use over the past five years). This range of applications will give readers a better sense of the overall field, a better understanding of how projects are similar, and a better appreciation for how they differ and why they differ.

The cases are integrative in that they require an awareness and understanding of other functional disciplines such as strategy, operations, ethics, and human resource management in addition to finance. Case analysis invariably incorporates these other disciplines, but they typically get less attention than the structuring and financing

EXHIBIT 1-2

CASE DISTRIBUTION BY INDUSTRIAL SECTOR AND GEOGRAPHIC LOCATION

Project Location	Industrial Sector						
	Transport	**Telecom.**	**Power**	**Oil & Gas**	**Mining**	**Industrial**	**Other**
North America	TX HSR	Iridium LLC	Calpine, MESC, PPL				
South America				Petrozuata	Antamina		
Europe	Airbus A3XX, A2 Motorway		Sutton Bridge	BP Amoco (A)			Basel II
Africa				Chad-Cameroon Pipeline		Mozal	
Middle East						Equate	
Australia/NZ		Australia Japan Cable			Bulong		
Asia				BP Amoco (B)		Nghe An Tate & Lyle	Hong Kong Disneyland

issues. Nevertheless, these nonfinance issues force one to adopt a more integrative perspective and wrestle with the interconnectedness of managerial decision making.

Finally, the cases are managerial; they present actual investment and financing situations. But rather than describing what happened and why (i.e., an *ex post* description of best practice), the cases focus on the critical decisions that faced deal participants during the investment process. This *ex ante* perspective replicates, albeit in a highly abbreviated fashion, the information available to the case protagonists when they had to make actual decisions. The goal of this pedagogical approach is to improve business judgment regardless of the context or setting. When used properly, the case method of teaching should help managers make better investment and financing decisions both inside and outside the realm of project finance. Cases are also designed to provide, in conjunction with classroom instruction, the necessary tools and frameworks to make important business decisions.

Module 1: Structuring Projects

The goal of the Structuring Projects module is to define project finance, describe the economic motivations for using it, and present frameworks to help identify the assets and the firms that are best suited for project finance. The theme of this module is that *organizational* structure matters, and the challenge is to understand why it matters. Stated more concretely, the goal is to understand why the combination of a firm plus a project might be worth more when financed separately with nonrecourse debt (project finance) than when financed jointly with corporate funds (corporate finance).[5] Using the imperfections framework, we see that the cases show how separate incorporation can reduce the *net* cost of financing large, tangible assets. Specifically, the cases illustrate the three primary motivations for using project finance:

- **Agency cost motivation:** Reduce costly agency (incentive) conflicts inside project companies and among capital providers.
- **Debt overhang motivation:** Reduce leverage-induced underinvestment in sponsoring companies, a phenomenon known as "debt overhang."
- **Risk management motivation:** Reduce underinvestment in positive net present value (NPV) projects due to distress costs and/or managerial risk aversion.

While the primary objective of this module is to describe why firms use project finance, the module must also, by virtue of coming first, introduce the field of project finance and provide basic terminology used throughout the rest of the book. The first case, The Chad-Cameroon Petroleum Development and Pipeline Project (Chapter 4 in Appendix 1-1), addresses issues in each of the four course modules: (1) Structuring Projects: why use project finance?; (2) Valuing Projects: how much is the oil field worth?; (3) Managing Risky Projects: how do you mitigate sovereign risks?; and (4) Financing Projects: how much leverage should the project have and who should finance it? The Chad-Cameroon Pipeline case also fits in the first module because it involves the choice between project and corporate finance: the sponsors (ExxonMobil, Chevron, and Petronas) plan to finance the $1.5 billion upstream project (oil field development) using corporate finance and the $2.2 billion downstream project (pipeline) using project finance. The fact they chose different financing strategies for different assets naturally raises the question of why project finance works in some settings but not in others.

The next three cases illustrate the three motivations for using project finance. The Australia-Japan Cable case (Australia-Japan Cable: Structuring the Project Company, Chapter 5) examines the range of agency conflicts associated with project companies—conflicts between ownership (sponsors) and control (managers), conflicts between sponsors and related parties, and conflicts between debtholders and equityholders—and shows how project structure can be used to mitigate these costly incentive conflicts. For certain kinds of assets, project finance is more effective and more efficient than corporate finance at resolving these conflicts. As a result, the expected cash flows are higher under the project structure.

The Calpine case (Calpine Corporation: The Evolution from Project to Corporate Finance, Chapter 6) illustrates the roots of project finance in the U.S. power industry and the recent evolution toward hybrid financing structures that contain elements of both project and corporate finance. Calpine, a relatively small firm with high leverage (a debt-to-total capitalization in excess of 80% and a subinvestment grade rating), has little spare debt capacity, yet uses project finance to finance its aggressive growth strategy. Project finance allows Calpine to avoid the opportunity cost of underinvestment in positive NPV projects. Yet project finance also has some very serious drawbacks—it is expensive to set up, it takes a long time to execute (i.e., the transaction costs are very high), and it is highly restrictive once in place—which force Calpine to consider alter-

---

[5] The costs and benefits of diversification appear in many contexts in the field of finance. On the one hand, the Capital Asset Pricing Model (CAPM) is built on the idea that diversification eliminates idiosyncratic risks, leaving only systematic risks to be priced in the market. On the other hand, diversification in operations is typically viewed as a disadvantage. In fact, there is evidence, albeit conflicting, that conglomerate firms trade at a discount relative to pure play firms.

native financing structures, namely, a hybrid structure that contains elements of both corporate and project finance.

Finally, the BP Amoco cases [BP Amoco (A): Policy Statement on the Use of Project Finance, Chapter 7; BP Amoco (B): Financing Development of the Caspian Oil Fields, Chapter 8] stand in sharp contrast with the Calpine case because they describe why a large, well-capitalized company uses project finance. The A case presents BP Amoco's policy statement on when to use project finance; the B case presents an opportunity to apply the policy to a real investment decision (the $8 billion Full-Field Development project in Azerbaijan). According to BP Amoco, the major benefit of project finance is that it provides a way to protect the corporate balance sheet from incremental distress costs caused by investing in a risky asset. The nonrecourse nature of project debt protects the sponsoring firm from risk contamination, the phenomenon whereby a failing project either drags an otherwise healthy sponsoring firm into default or imposes incremental distress costs on it (e.g., it disrupts an ongoing investment program). Project finance, therefore, provides an organizational approach to risk management, and one that is particularly effective when traditional financial approaches such as derivatives cannot be used to hedge exposures.

Taken together, these cases illustrate the full range of project finance users and applications. Both AAA-rated ExxonMobil and B-rated Calpine use project finance, but for very different reasons. At the same time, sponsors use project finance for both very safe assets such as independent power producers (IPPs) backed by contracts from creditworthy counterparties and for very risky assets such as merchant power plants (MPPs) facing market risks.[6] Finally, sponsors use project finance in both developed countries like the United States and developing countries like Chad and Azerbaijan. Given the range of sponsor types, asset types, and country settings, no single explanation can cover all of the motivations for using project finance. Instead, what is required is a broader set of economic rationales, which is exactly what is presented in this module.

		High Rated	Low or Un-rated
Project Location (Sovereign Risk Level)	**Developing Countries**	**BP Amoco** (Azerbaijan) **ExxonMobil** (Chad)	
	Developed Countries	**Telstra** (Australia and Japan)	**Calpine** (US)

Lead Sponsor Corporate Debt Rating

Module 2: Valuing Projects

After describing what project finance is and why firms use it, the rest of the course focuses on project-financed transactions.[7] The second module concentrates on the measurement of project returns, while the third module concentrates on the management

---

[6] IPPs are standalone power generating plants. They are financed based on the creditworthiness of the contracts used to create and operate them. In particular, the power purchase agreement (PPA—a long-term obligation to buy the power produced by the plant) is the key contractual agreement.

[7] Of course, the actual investment and financing process inside firms does not proceed in this fashion. Rather than deciding to use project finance and then analyzing the risks and returns, firms typically analyze the risks and returns under alternative financing structures and then pick the one that generates the highest value.

of project risks and the allocation of control. The theme of the second module is that complex valuation problems require complex tools. What makes project valuation so difficult is that projects are located in developing countries where they are exposed to nontraditional risks, have important embedded optionality, involve both subsidized and guaranteed cash flow streams, and have high and changing leverage ratios. Despite these complexities, most people value projects using relatively simple tools such as discounting free cash flow with constant or *ad hoc* discount rates. Unfortunately, these approaches can lead to serious valuation errors and result in poor decisions (see Esty, 1999). The goal of this module is to refine the basic valuation tools used in practice and to present new tools that are applicable to the field of project finance. In particular, this module covers three topics: cash flow estimation, equity cash flow valuation, and real options analysis.

- **Topic #1: Cash flow estimation** (including social cost/benefit analysis): This module begins with the Airbus A3XX case, which illustrates the economics of large projects, the difficulty of estimating long-term cash flows, and the role of social cost/ benefit analysis (Airbus A3XX: Developing the World's Largest Commercial Jet, Chapter 9).[8] The challenge in this case is to assess whether the market for very large aircraft (VLA—a plane that can hold 550 passengers in the standard three-class configuration) is sufficient to justify the $13 billion investment needed to develop the plane. Because four European governments are funding approximately one-third of the total cost in the form of "launch aid," the case naturally raises the issue of public versus private returns.

  Having raised the issue of public or social returns, the Tate & Lyle case [Nghe An Tate & Lyle Sugar Company (Vietnam), Chapter 10, and the accompanying note "An Economic Framework for Assessing Development Impact"] show how to conduct social cost/benefit analysis. This kind of analysis helps sponsors win concessions (the host government may select the project that generates the highest social returns), raise funds from development institutions such as the International Finance Corporation (IFC) or African Development Bank (AfDB) which require such analysis before they will consider making an investment, and mitigate the risk of expropriation. Even though a project generates a positive social return, there may be groups that experience a disproportionate share of the costs or a set of risks that are not commensurate with their returns. Identifying these groups and changing the allocation of risks and returns can help improve the probability of successful execution.

- **Topic #2: Equity cash flow (ECF) valuation:** The Texas High Speed Rail case (Texas High-Speed Rail Corporation, Chapter 12, written by T. Luehrman and A. Regan) illustrates and compares ECF valuation against the better-known, and more generally used, free cash flow (FCF) valuation approach. Although ECF valuation is widely used in practice, it is not taught in most introductory finance courses. This case provides an opportunity to explore the limitations of basic valuation tools and to present refinements that make the tools more appropriate for large projects. One of the most important refinements has to do with the inappropriateness of using a

---

[8] The Airbus case is one of two cases that is not directly about project finance *per se*. These cases are included in the book because they illustrate important points related to project finance. In the Airbus case, as in many projects, there is a need to assess long-term, and sometimes very uncertain, demand. The PPL Corporation case is about leasing, which emerged in the late 1990s as a very popular alternative to project finance.

single discount rate (e.g., a single weighted average cost of capital or WACC) to discount cash flows from a project with changing leverage and tax status.

- **Topic #3: Real options analysis:** The last two cases illustrate how optionality affects investment and strategic decisions. The first case (Contractual Innovation in the UK Energy Markets: Enron Europe, The Eastern Group, and the Sutton Bridge Project, Chapter 13, written with P. Tufano) provides an opportunity to value a project using real options analysis, while the second case (Bidding for Antamina, Chapter 14, written by P. Tufano and A. Moel) examines the sale of mining assets by the Peruvian government. In both cases, the goal is to recognize where the optionality exists and how to incorporate it into the analysis. For example, in the Sutton Bridge case, the key is to map the sponsor's investment and operating decisions into an option framework: to what extent does the decision to build or run a gas-fired generating plant resemble an option? These two cases show why advanced valuation tools are needed, particularly in project finance where the transformation of commodity inputs into commodity outputs (e.g., natural gas or coal into power) naturally fit into a real options framework. They also present opportunities for simulation analysis, another valuation tool that should be in the financial manager's toolkit.

Invariably, the analysis will broach other important topics such as the valuation of guarantees and the calculation of discount rates in developing countries. Despite the very real cost of providing completion guarantees or other forms of project support, most firms do not value the cost explicitly. By ignoring the very real cost of providing guarantees, they understate the total cost of a given project and, accordingly, overstate its value. Although there is not sufficient room in this book to describe the mechanics for valuing the many kinds of guarantees associated with project companies, the analysis is similar to the analysis used to value real options. As for calculating discount rates in developing countries, this topic comes up in many cases. Unfortunately, there is neither well-developed nor generally accepted theory for valuing assets in emerging markets. For further information on these topics, see the bibliographic references in the reference section at the end of this book.

Module 3: Managing Risky Projects

The third module on risk management provides a complement to the valuation module in that it explores the classic risk/return tradeoff. The module explores how risk management affects project value, describes a process of risk management, and presents a framework of strategies for managing various kinds of project risks. A key underlying assumption driving this analysis is that risk management is valuable because it reduces costly market imperfections. In contrast to the first module where the focus is on organizational structure as a form of risk management for sponsoring companies, the emphasis in this module is on managing risks *inside* project companies, particularly the costs associated with financial distress and incentive conflicts among deal participants.[9]

The first two cases, Petrozuata (Petrolera Zuata, Petrozuata C.A., Chapter 15) and A2 Motorway (Poland's A2 Motorway, Chapter 16) illustrate a four-stage process for risk

---

[9] One of the primary reasons why managers say they use project finance is to achieve better risk mitigation and improved risk allocation. Yet most of the same techniques used to mitigate project risk (e.g., offtake agreements, fixed-price construction contracts, etc.) and to allocate project risk could be replicated in a corporate-financed transaction. The intriguing question is which aspects of risk management cannot be replicated in a corporate setting.

management: identification, assessment, mitigation, and allocation. In the identification stage, the objective is to identify and classify project risks into four general categories: completion risks (completion on time and budget), operating risks (market demand, throughput, etc.), political/sovereign risks (expropriation, force majeure events, etc.), and financial risks (interest rate and exchange rate exposures).[10] After identifying the risks, the next step is to assess, often through sensitivity analysis, previous experience, or simulation, the most important risks, the risks that require active mitigation or management. The goal of risk mitigation is to reduce, in a cost effective fashion, cash flow variability, thereby increasing the project's debt capacity. By narrowing the distribution of possible returns, risk management allows projects to support leverage ratios in excess of 90%.

The final step is risk allocation where the goal is to allocate risks to the parties that are best able to control the risks and that can bear them at least cost. Typically, risk allocation is accomplished through long-term contracts. Invariably, however, these contracts end up being "incomplete": it is either impossible or too costly to describe all possible contingencies, and it may be costly to enforce them as well. When the contracts are incomplete, there is the potential for incentive conflicts between key decision makers. To induce optimal behavior, other governance mechanisms such as joint ownership are needed to solve or prevent conflicts. Some of the most important, yet most incomplete, contracts are with host nations. In this context, contractual incompleteness is due to an inability to enforce contracts rather than unforeseen or unspecified situations. When contracts are unenforceable, property rights are uncertain, and project cash flows are high, there is a serious risk of expropriation. Because so many projects are located in countries with nonexistent, untested, or unpredictable legal systems, managing sovereign risk becomes one of the most critical tasks for project managers.

Consistent with the course's overall emphasis on the importance of project structure, the cases illustrate the "newer" structural approach to managing sovereign risk and contrast it with the "older" financial approach. Under the financial approach, sponsors simply increase the company's hurdle rate and accept only those projects that generate sufficiently high returns. As Wells and Gleason (1995) point out, this approach can actually *increase* project risk because it makes the sponsors appear as if they are profiting excessively at the expense of local citizens. The idea that high returns can actually induce high risk is known as the "paradox of infrastructure investment." Recent examples of how this paradox plays out in practice can be seen in the Dabhol power project in India (allegation of excessive returns to Enron prompted the state government to abrogate the power purchase agreement) as well as in Calpine's power plants in California (the California state government unilaterally cut its contracted price for power when rates dropped). The idea that high returns can actually increase risk is a powerful, yet counterintuitive, concept.

After describing the process of risk management, the remaining cases focus on particular risk categories: the Bulong (Restructuring Bulong's Project Debt, Chapter 17), MESC (Mobile Energy Services Company, Chapter 18), and Mozal (Financing the Mozal Project, Chapter 19) cases analyze completion, operating, and sovereign risks, respectively. Although not covered directly in any single case, financial risks such as interest rate, exchange rate, funding, and default risks are addressed in almost every case. Capital structure decisions are viewed from a practical perspective in this module: can

---

[10] Technically, *force majeure* (French for "superior force") events come in two forms that fit in separate categories. The "Acts of God" (floods, earthquakes, or other natural disasters) are considered operating risks, while wars, strikes, riots, and expropriation are political/sovereign risks.

the project safely cover its debt service obligations, or should the repayment schedule be "sculpted" to provide higher coverage ratios. In the next module, however, capital structure decisions are analyzed more theoretically in an attempt to explain why projects employ such high leverage.

To illustrate the full range of project risks and risk management strategies, these cases involve different input and output configurations, and varying degrees of sovereign risk. One way to classify projects is by their type: "stock-type" projects involve a fixed resource that is depleted over time such as mines; in contrast, "flow-type" projects require use to generate value such as toll roads. Projects can also be classified as having either retail or wholesale customers. In the former, output is sold to end users (typically individuals); in the latter, output is sold to one or more intermediate producers or distributors. Given this classification scheme, the cases in this module span three of the four possible quadrants—the fourth quadrant (retail/stock type projects) is essentially nonexistent.

	Retail	Wholesale
Stock Type	(nonexistent)	**Petrozuata** (oil field) **Bulong** (nickel mine)
Flow Type	**A2 Motorway** (toll road)	**Mozal** (aluminum smelter) **MESC** (power plant)

Type of Project (vertical axis label)

Type of Customer

Module 4: Financing Projects

In contrast with venture-backed start-up firms, which are financed almost exclusively with equity, greenfield projects are financed largely with debt. As a result, the final module analyzes financing structures and the role of debt-based governance. The theme of this final module is that debt has benefits well beyond the interest tax shields that are discussed in most introductory finance courses. Understanding what these benefits are and how to increase them is the objective of this module.

Toward that end, the cases analyze both capital and debt ownership structures. With regard to capital structure, the cases analyze both the amount of debt and the types of debt. Unfortunately, basic capital structure theories have trouble explaining why projects have highly leveraged capital structures. For example, a tradeoff theory of capital structure, in which a firm trades off incremental interest tax shields against incremental distress costs as leverage increases, can explain why very safe projects use high leverage, but it cannot explain why other projects such as Iridium with several years of net operating losses and a low tax rate, Mozal with a permanent tax holiday, or Equate in a country (Kuwait) with no income taxes adopt highly leveraged capital structures. Nor can a tradeoff theory explain why projects with long-term cash flows use senior bank debt rather than long-term bonds for the majority of their capital. This module provides an opportunity to discuss and apply alternative capital structure theories.

The cases also analyze projects funded with many kinds of debt. Here the goal is to understand the various roles played by each type of debt and to recognize that "not all capital is created equal." Who provides the debt and in what form is a critical determinant of project performance. One of the most basic choices is between using bank loans and project bonds. Project bonds are a relatively new, but rapidly growing, form of project debt. If all debt provides an interest tax shield, then why choose one form over another? Several of the cases in Modules 3 and 4—Petrozuata, Bulong, MESC, and Iridium—analyze the choice between bank loans and bonds. The Hong Kong Disneyland case (Chase's Strategy for Syndicating the Hong Kong Disneyland Loan, Chapter 20) takes this analysis to an even deeper level by exploring the structure of debt ownership: what are the benefits of having a very concentrated syndicate of banks (few banks with large ownership positions) versus a very diffuse syndicate of banks (many banks with small ownership positions). In contrast, the Equate case (The International Investor: Islamic Finance and the Equate Project, Chapter 21) contrasts loans from local vs. foreign banks; traditional "Western" vs. Islamic financial institutions; senior vs. subordinated lenders; and banks vs. export credit agencies (ECAs) such as the United States Export-Import Bank (USExim). As described in the following table, these cases illustrate the full range of debt providers as well as the advantages and disadvantages of each type of debt.

		Type (Source) of Project Debt			
	Bank Loans	**Project Bonds**	**Agency Debt**	**Subordinated Debt (quasi-equity)**	**Other**
Module 3	A2 Motorway	Bulong MESC Petrozuata	Petrozuata Mozal	Mozal	
Module 4	HK Disneyland Equate	Iridium	Equate	Equate	PPL (synthetic lease)

The third case in the module is PPL Corporation (Financing PPL Corporation's Growth Strategy, Chapter 23), a U.S. firm with an aggressive growth strategy. Although PPL shares many similarities with Calpine, it adopts a very different financing strategy. Rather than using project finance to fund its growth strategy, PPL uses leveraged and synthetic leases. The case analyzes PPL's attempts to finance a portfolio of merchant power plants (MPPs—plants without fixed-price, fixed-quantity supply and purchase agreements) and its struggle to decide between a traditional and a limited-recourse synthetic lease. Like project finance, the limited-recourse synthetic lease reduces PPL's balance sheet exposure to the assets. One of the key objectives of the PPL case is to show that financial managers today must be familiar with a wide variety of financing tools ranging from corporate debt to project finance to synthetic leases.

The final two cases, Basel II (Basel II: Assessing the Default and Loss Characteristics of Project Finance Loans, case Chapter 24) and Iridium (Iridium LLC, case Chapter 25), are designed to wrap up the course. The Basel II case explores the performance of project-financed transactions in the context of bank regulators trying to establish new capital standards for international banks. The regulatory position, formed admittedly without quantitative performance data and with influence from some very prominent project defaults (e.g., EuroTunnel, EuroDisney, Dabhol, Iridium, Canary Wharf, and Globalstar), is that project loans are very risky and, therefore, should have large capital requirements. The Basel II case presents new and previously unavailable data on the performance of project loans and compares that performance against various types of corporate loans. This case not only serves as an initial foray into the unexplored realm of project performance, but it also helps identify key risk factors for project loans.

Finally, Iridium is a comprehensive review case that, like the Chad-Cameroon Pipeline case that begins the course, addresses important topics in each of the course modules: (1) Structuring Projects: why did Motorola use project finance for this project?; (2) Valuing Projects: how do you value a highly leveraged project with cyclical investment needs and uncertain future demand?; (3) Managing Risky Projects: which risks are the most important and how should they be managed?; and (4) Financing Projects: how much (is a target capital structure of 60% debt optimal?) and what kinds of debt (should Iridium use bank loans or project bonds, cash-pay or zero coupon bonds, secured vs. unsecured debt, etc.) should the project use?

The case also provides a nice way to circle back at the end of the course and reiterate the role of market imperfections, but this time in the context of raising capital. The imperfections framework helps explain how and why the sponsors raised capital in the order they did—the project raised almost $6 billion of debt and equity over the course of five years. This ability to examine the sequencing of capital in a newly created, standalone firm is yet another example of the benefits of studying project companies rather than other kinds of firms or corporations with multiple assets. The "cleanness" of the setting makes the analysis more powerful and the lessons more transparent.

In conclusion, the Financing Projects module provides a rich setting in which to discuss project governance and a unique laboratory in which to study contracting, agency, and capital structure theories. The cases show how the various structural attributes work together to produce a very effective, and low-cost governance system for tangible assets that generate high cash flows, but have limited lives.

Supplementary Material

The final section of the book contains a note on data sources related to project finance and a glossary of terms and acronyms. The note on data sources is intended to be a reference guide for students, researchers, and practitioners seeking additional information about the field of project finance. It contains bibliographical references for hundreds of books and articles on project finance; provides information about software available to analyze projects; and provides a list of multilateral agencies and export credit agencies (ECAs). The glossary contains a list of more than 300 definitions for terms commonly used in the field of project finance, a list of more than 150 acronyms, and a description of financial ratios used by project finance lenders. Most of this material as well as additional information about the field and practice of project finance is available on the Harvard Business School Project Finance web portal at www.hbs.edu/projfinportal/.

CONCLUSION

The gap between theory and practice in the field of project finance has been growing over the last 25 years. These cases help close the gap by describing current practice, presenting new frameworks and theories, and challenging readers to analyze the structural choices in great detail. One of the reasons so little academic research has been conducted on project companies is that detailed information is very difficult to obtain. These cases provide detailed information, much of which is held confidentially by deal participants. By presenting projects at different stages of development and in a wide variety of geographic and industrial settings, this book should improve the way managers structure, value, and finance large projects. Given the enormous sums currently being financed through project companies and the growing need to finance global infrastructure investment in the years ahead, even small changes in practice can generate large economic and social benefits.

But the course covers much more than project finance. It presents a wonderful opportunity to study core principles of corporate finance in a rich and relatively unexplored setting with major implications for value creation and economic development. The unique structural features of project companies show how project structure affects managerial incentives and asset values. Few settings offer such a transparent and relatively uncontaminated window into how managers make important structural decisions and how those decisions, in turn, affect performance.

REFERENCES

ESTY, B.C., Spring 1999, Improved techniques for valuing large-scale projects, *Journal of Project Finance* 5(1), 1–19.

JOSKOW, P., Fall 1985, Vertical integration and long-term contracts: The case of coal-burning electric generating plants, *Journal of Law, Economics, and Organizations* 33, 32–80.

MERTON, R.K., 1987, Three fragments from a sociologist's notebooks, *Annual Review of Sociology* 12, 1–28.

MODIGLIANI, F., and M. MILLER, June 1958, The cost of capital, corporation finance and the theory of investment, *American Economic Review* 53, 261–297.

PACELLE, M., M. SCHROEDER, and J. EMSHWILLER, December 13, 2001, Enron has one-year restructuring target, *The Wall Street Journal*, A3.

WELLS, L., and N. GLEASON, September/October 1995, Is foreign infrastructure investment still risky? *Harvard Business Review*, 1–12.

WILLIAMSON, O.E., 1985, *The Economic Institutions of Capitalism*, Free Press, New York.

CASE DESCRIPTIONS

MODULE 1: STRUCTURING PROJECTS

C-1: The Chad-Cameroon Petroleum Development and Pipeline Project (A), HBS no. 202-010

On June 6, 2000, the World Bank's Board of Directors was scheduled to vote on whether to approve funding for the $4 billion Chad-Cameroon Pipeline project. The project was a unique opportunity to alleviate poverty in Chad, one of the poorest countries in the world. Chad, however, had a president who had been described as a "warlord" and had been associated with various human rights violations. One of the most contentious issues in structuring the deal was how Chad would handle its newfound wealth—the project would increase Chad's annual government revenues by more than 50% (up to $125 million per year). To address this issue, the Bank had proposed a novel Revenue Management Plan (RMP) that would isolate Chad's project revenues and target them for poverty reduction programs. Whether this plan would work and what would happen if it did not were two questions that the directors had to resolve before they could approve the deal. Faced with a high-risk, but potentially high-return opportunity to improve conditions in Chad and Cameroon, students, as World Bank Directors, must decide whether to approve the funding.

C-2: Australia-Japan Cable: Structuring a Project Company, HBS no. 202-115

The lead sponsor in this project, Telstra (the Australian telecommunications firm), had just gotten the results from the feasibility study it commissioned on the proposed Australia-Japan cable project. The general conclusion was that this $520 million project could withstand the competition in the rapidly changing telecom market and still generate attractive returns. It was now up to Telstra to structure the project company. To do so, it had to select an ownership structure (which sponsors, how many, and what share allocations?), a financial structure (should it use project finance or corporate finance, and what kind of debt?), and a governance structure (the size and composition of the board, the nature of managerial compensation, etc.). These choices would affect managerial incentives as well as the project's subsequent operating performance.

C-3: Calpine Corporation: The Evolution from Project to Corporate Finance, HBS no. 201-098

In early 1999, Calpine Corporation's CEO Pete Cartwright adopted an aggressive growth strategy with the goal of increasing the company's aggregate generating capacity five-fold in five years to capture a fleeting opportunity to re-power America. To achieve the goal, Calpine will have to build 25 power plants at a total cost of $6 billion. For a company with assets of $1.7 billion, a subinvestment grade debt rating, a debt-to-capitalization ratio of 79%, and an after-tax cash flow of $143 million in 1998, funding this business strategy was going to be a formidable challenge. The case opens with Calpine's finance team trying to decide how to finance four power plants currently under development. Should they use project finance, corporate finance, or a new hybrid structure with elements of both project and corporate finance? Knowing the importance of speed, feasibility, and efficiency, the finance team must select a financial strat-

(Continued)

egy that not only supports the company's high-growth competitive strategy, but also maximizes firm value.

C-4: BP Amoco (A): Policy Statement on the Use of Project Finance, HBS no. 201-054

Following the BP/Amoco merger in December 1998, CFO David Watson asked Bill Young, the head of BP/Amoco's Specialized Finance Group, to recommend when and under what circumstances the firm should use external, project finance instead of internal corporate funds to finance new capital investments. As part of this assignment, Young and his team had to review each firm's current policy regarding project finance and evaluate the various rationales used to justify its use. Young and his team created a new policy statement recommending that BP Amoco finance capital expenditures using corporate funds except in three special circumstances. The three exceptions were: mega projects, projects in politically volatile areas, and joint ventures with heterogeneous partners. Whether the general rule of using corporate funds and whether the specific exceptions to the rule are appropriate for the merged entity are subjects for class discussion.

C-5: BP Amoco (B): Financing Development of the Caspian Oil Fields, HBS no. 201-067

British Petroleum and Amoco were the two largest members of the Azerbaijan International Oil Consortium (AIOC), an 11-firm consortium that was spending $10 billion to develop oil fields in the Caspian Sea. As of March 1999, AIOC had completed the $1.9 billion Early Oil project. The two companies, however, had financed their shares of this project in different ways: BP used internal funds (traditional, on-balance sheet corporate finance) while Amoco was one of five AIOC partners that raised $400 million of project finance. Following the BP/Amoco merger in December 1998, managers in the combined firm's Finance Group had to reassess the Early Oil financing strategy and determine the best way to finance its share of the $8.0 billion Full Field Development Project. Should it use internal funds, project finance, or a mixture of the two? This case allows students to apply BP Amoco's newly created policy statement on the use of project finance (described in the A case) to a real investment opportunity.

MODULE 2: VALUING PROJECTS

C-6: Airbus 3XX: Developing the World's Largest Commercial Jet (A), HBS no. 201-028

In July 2000, Airbus Industrie's Supervisory Board was on the verge of approving a $13 billion investment to develop a new super jumbo jet known as the A3XX that would seat from 550 to 1,000 passengers. Having secured approximately 20 orders for the new jet, the Board had to decide if there was sufficient long-term demand for the A3XX to justify the investment. At the time, Airbus was predicting that the market for very large aircraft (VLA) would exceed 1,500 aircraft over the next 20 years and would generate sales in excess of $300 billion. According to Airbus, it needed to sell 250 aircraft to break

(Continued)

even, though internal projections estimated sales of 750 aircraft over the next 20 years. Boeing, however, was predicting that the VLA market would be less than 500 aircraft over the next 20 years and that its 747 would capture a large share of the market. The case explores the two sets of forecasts, and asks students whether they would proceed with the launch given the size of the investment and the uncertainty in long-term demand. The case illustrates the role and impact of government intervention in financing large projects. For governments, project benefits extend well beyond cash flows, NPVs, and IRRs to other factors such as employment, trade, and strategic considerations like national defense.

C-7: Nghe An Tate & Lyle Sugar Company (Vietnam), HBS no. 202-067

In September 1998, Tate & Lyle asked the International Finance Corporation (IFC) to consider lending up to $45 million to finance a $90 million sugar mill in northern Vietnam. Ewen Cobban, an IFC agricultural specialist, was in charge of reviewing the proposal and making a loan recommendation to senior management. Cobban was concerned whether the plant would be able to obtain a sufficient amount of cane from local farmers and whether the government would follow through on its commitment to build new roads and bridges in the region. He was also concerned that world sugar prices were falling and that sugar was a protected commodity. All these issues affected the project's commercial viability, and he has to understand whether they were temporary or permanent problems. Cobban also had to assess the project's developmental impact before he could recommend loan approval. The IFC only supported projects that contributed to sustainable development, and one of the key determinants of sustainability was the degree to which the project was "fair" to all parties involved. Thus, Cobban needed to assess not only the private returns, but also the social returns as measured by the project's economic rate of return (ERR).

C-8: Texas High-Speed Rail Corporation (by T. Luehrman and A. Regan), HBS no. 293-072

The finance director of the Texas High-Speed Rail Corporation (THSRC) is considering modifications to the financing program designed to support the development, construction, and operations of THSRC's planned high-speed rail system. The current plan achieves many objectives, including raising $6.5 billion from private sources, but a few issues still need to be addressed. These include temporary overfunding, unutilized tax losses, and certain important contingencies. The case is designed to highlight the shortcomings of simple valuation tools in a static analysis when applied to a dynamic project. The class discussion should isolate specific analytical issues, which may then be addressed in subsequent class sessions.

C-9: Contractual Innovation in the U.K. Energy Markets: Enron Europe, The Eastern Group, and the Sutton Bridge Project, HBS no. 200-051

In December 1996, Enron Europe and The Eastern Group are on the verge of signing an innovative financial transaction. Eastern wants to buy a long-term option to convert natural gas into electricity from Enron, thereby giving it the economic right to

(Continued)

operate a "virtual" power station. Enron plans to hedge its exposure under this contract by constructing an actual power station and by trading in the gas and electricity markets. While Eastern's right to receive power proceeds and Enron's right to operate the plant were similar in character, there would be no legal or physical connection between Enron's physical plant and Eastern's virtual plant. This structure was vastly different from the traditional independent power plant (IPP) structure, and the executives involved had to convince their superiors of its wisdom before they could proceed. This case illustrates a new paradigm in the electric power industry: the creation of *virtual* power stations backed by *physical* power stations with merchant exposure. It allows students to value the spread option between gas and electricity, known as a "spark spread," and to appreciate the complexity involved with valuing real options in the rapidly evolving gas and electricity markets.

C-10: Bidding for Antamina (by P. Tufano and A. Moel), HBS no. 297-054

In June 1996, executives of the multinational mining company RTZ-CRA were contemplating bidding to acquire the Antamina copper and zinc mine in Peru. The Antamina project was being offered for sale by auction as part of the privatization of Peru's state mining company. RTZ-CRA had to determine what the mine was worth, and to recommend whether and how RTZ-CRA should bid in the upcoming auction. The bidding rules put in place by the Peruvian government dictated that each company's bid contain two components: an up-front cash amount and the amount the bidder will invest to develop the property, if development was warranted after further exploration was completed. The case introduces students to real option valuation of a natural resource project. The auction rules also force bidders to approach the problem as a real option.

MODULE 3: MANAGING PROJECT RISK

C-11: Petrolera Zuata, Petrozuata C.A., HBS no. 299-012

Petrolera Zuata, Petrozuata C.A. (Petrozuata) is a proposed $2.4 billion oil-field development project in Venezuela. The case is set in January 1997 as the project sponsors (DuPont and PDVSA) are developing the project's financing structure. According to the current plan, the sponsors hope to raise at least a portion of the $1.5 billion debt financing in the capital markets using project bonds. To facilitate a bond offering in the Rule 144A market, the deal must secure an investment-grade rating, yet neither PDVSA nor Venezuela is investment-grade. The key questions facing the sponsors are whether the project will achieve an investment grade rating and, if not, how to finance the deal so that it remains economically and operationally attractive to the sponsors. The case illustrates an extremely well-crafted deal that "pierced the sovereign ceiling" (achieved a higher project rating than the home country's sovereign rating).

C-12: Poland's A2 Motorway, HBS no. 202-030

Autostrada Wielkopolska S.A. (AWSA) was a consortium of 18 firms that won the concession to build and operate a Polish toll road in 1997. In June 2000, AWSA's chief financial officer, Wojciech Gebicki, was preparing for a meeting with the project's lead bankers regarding concerns they have over traffic forecasts and revenue projections. Based on their concerns, the bankers were asking the sponsors to inject an additional €60 million to €90 million of equity into the deal, a sizeable increase given the project's total cost of €934 million and the sponsor's current equity commitment of €235 million. This request presented a serious problem for Gebicki (AWSA) because the concession is scheduled to expire in six weeks if financing had not closed, and he had very few financing alternatives available this late in the game. Facing these constraints, Gebicki's best option was to convince the bankers that the deal should proceed as currently structured. The case describes the deal structure and invites students to accept or dispute Gebicki's view that the major risks have been identified, assessed, and mitigated in such a way that the senior lenders are adequately protected without further equity support.

C-13: Restructuring Bulong's Project Debt, HBS no. 203-027

In July 1998, Preston Resources bought the Bulong nickel mine and financed it with a short-term bridge loan. In December 1998, it issued a 10-year, $185 million project bond as part of the permanent financing. Although it purchased a "completed" mine, the processing facility still had to complete the commissioning phase (ramp-up of production to full capacity). A variety of operating problems and other mishaps delayed the ramp-up and caused cash flows to fall below expectations. As a result, Bulong defaulted on the bond one year after issuance. This case analyzes the choice between bank loans and bonds as sources of project funds, the credit decision underlying the original underwriting, and the means by which project companies emerge (or do not) from default situations.

C-14: Mobile Energy Services Company (MESC), HBS no. 203-061

When Al "Chainsaw" Dunlap became CEO of the Scott Paper Company in 1994, Scott owned a large, vertically integrated production facility in Mobile, Alabama, that included a track of timberlands, a pulp mill that supplied a tissue mill and a paper mill with raw materials, and a cogeneration energy complex that used byproducts from pulp production to generate electricity. In December 1994, Dunlap sold the energy complex to the Southern Company (Southern) for $350 million. Southern financed the acquisition with a bridge loan and formed a new limited liability company called Mobile Energy Services Company to own and operate the facility. The case is set in August 1995, as MESC was arranging permanent financing by issuing two bonds worth $340 million. Potential bond investors must consider the risks associated with an "inside the fence" energy complex (e.g., a generating plant whose revenues come exclusively from local sources—the three mills—rather than from sales through a power grid). In particular, they must consider how the transformation from a vertically integrated to a vertically segregated facility will affect the power plant's creditworthiness, and whether the contractual agreements that bind the parties and govern the operations will be as effective as uniform ownership.

C-15: Financing the Mozal Project, HBS no. 200-005

The case is set in June 1997, with a project team from the IFC recommending that the board approve a $120 million investment in the Mozal project and a $1.4 billion

(Continued)

aluminum smelter in Mozambique. Several factors make this investment controversial: it would be the IFC's largest investment in the world, it was approximately the size of Mozambique's gross domestic project (GDP), and it came closely on the heels of a 20-year civil war. Despite these concerns, the sponsors want to structure a limited recourse deal with IFC participation. After reviewing deal, the IFC team is recommending the investment, but the board must decide whether it is the right time and the right project to make such a large investment. The case presents an extreme example of political risk in a developing country setting and contrasts the older, financial approach to risk management against a newer, structural approach. The case also highlights the various roles multilateral development institutions, in general, and the IFC, in particular, can play in financing major projects.

MODULE 4: FINANCING PROJECTS

C-16: Chase's Strategy for Syndicating the Hong Kong Disneyland Loan (A), HBS no. 201-072

In late 1999, the Walt Disney Company and the Hong Kong government agreed to develop Hong Kong Disneyland, a $3.6 billion theme park and resort complex. As part of the total financing package, the sponsors decided to raise $423 million of nonrecourse bank loans for construction and working capital, and selected Chase Manhattan Bank to underwrite and syndicate these facilities. The case analyzes the process by which Chase successfully competed to lead this transaction. The key questions facing Chase were whether to bid at all, how to bid, and how to structure the syndication to meet the borrower's needs, its own profit objectives, and the market's expectation for an attractively priced credit. The case includes a generic section about the process, participants, and economics of syndicated lending for students who are unfamiliar with syndicated lending. It also illustrates the key issues in designing a syndication strategy as well as the costs and benefits of having a concentrated lending syndicate.

C-17: The International Investor: Islamic Finance and the Equate Project, HBS no. 200-012

Equate Petrochemical Company is a joint venture between Union Carbide and Petrochemical Industries Company (PIC) for the construction of a $2 billion petrochemical plant in Kuwait. The sponsors began construction in August 1994 using a bridge loan and are in search of permanent, nonrecourse finance. As part of the permanent financing, the sponsors want to use a tranche of Islamic finance—funds that are invested in accordance with Islamic religious principles known as *Sharia*. The sponsors hired Kuwait Finance House, which, in turn, approached The International Investor (a Kuwaiti investment bank) to assist in placing the Islamic tranche. The case is set in early December 1995, as members of The Institutional Investor's Structured Finance Group are deciding whether the proposed deal structure makes sense and how large a commitment to make on behalf of their investors. This case provides an introduction to Islamic finance in general and Islamic project finance in particular. It describes the primary instruments used by Islamic investors and challenges students to develop a

(Continued)

financing plan that is consistent with *Sharia*'s prohibition against the payment of interest (*riba*) while at the same time appropriate for a large, long-term capital project. The case also explores the complications of integrating Islamic and conventional Western financial instruments in a single transaction as well as some of the possible solutions.

C-18: Financing PPL Corporation's Growth Strategy, HBS no. 202-045

PPL Corporation, an electric utility in Pennsylvania, needed to finance $1 billion of peaking plants as part of its new growth strategy. After considering all the options, Finance Director Steve May decided that a synthetic lease was the best option, but he had to decide whether to recommend a traditional or a limited-recourse synthetic lease, and how to structure the specific terms. The advantages of the limited recourse structure were that it required a smaller corporate guarantee on the assets and received greater off-credit treatment by the ratings agencies, which was important given the company's growth objectives and limited debt capacity. However, finding investors willing to accept greater project risk would cost more and take more time. Timing was an issue for May because he had only two months to close the financing, or PPL would lose a valuable option to buy turbines for its peaking plants. Failure to exercise the option would delay the company's construction schedule, something PPL wanted to avoid given the nationwide race to build new generating plants.

C-19: Basel II: Assessing the Default and Loss Characteristics of Project Finance Loans, HBS no. 203-035

In June 1999, the Basel Committee on Banking Supervision announced plans to revise the capital standards for banks. The Basel Committee believed that project loans were significantly riskier than corporate loans and, therefore, warranted higher capital charges under the new proposal (known as Basel II). Bankers, fearing that higher capital charges would damage project lending by lowering profits and driving borrowers to nonbank competitors, formed a consortium to oppose the proposal by studying the actual default and loss characteristics of their combined portfolios of project loans. The study showed that project loans were not riskier than corporate loans. Armed with this data, the consortium sent a letter to the Basel Committee in August 2002 trying to convince them to lower the proposed capital charges on project finance loans. This case challenges students to examine the new capital Accord, understand the differences between project and corporate loans, and critique the statistical analysis conducted by the consortium. The case not only presents entirely new data on the performance of project loans, but it also describes the regulation of bank capital and the process of setting new capital standards.

C-20: Iridium LLC, HBS no. 200-039

This case is set in August 1999, just after Iridium, a global satellite communications firm, declared bankruptcy. Although the case describes Iridium's creation, development, and commercial launch, it concentrates primarily on the firm's financial strategy and execution as it raised more than $5 billion of capital. The case describes the specific securities Iridium issued, the sequence in which it issued them, and the firm's financial performance prior to bankruptcy. Using analyst forecasts, students can also value the firm prior to bankruptcy, but will recognize how difficult it is to value technology start-ups given the uncertainty in demand. The Iridium case is intended to challenge existing theories of capital structure. Is Iridium's target capital structure of 60% debt optimal? The case helps students understand the benefits and limitations of issuing different kinds of securities (e.g., cash-pay vs. zero coupon bonds, bank debt vs. public bonds, etc.), and the complexity of sequencing different kinds of securities. The overall objective is to help students understand the relevant issues in financing large, greenfield projects.

2

An Overview of Project Finance—2002 Update

This note provides an introduction to the field of project finance and a statistical overview of project-financed investments from 1998 to 2002. Recent examples of project-financed investments include the $4 billion Chad-Cameroon pipeline, $6 billion Iridium global satellite telecommunications project, €900 million A2 Toll Road in Poland, and the $1.4 billion aluminum smelter in Mozambique known as Mozal. Globally, firms financed $135 billion of capital expenditures using project finance in 2002, down from $217 billion in 2001. (These figures include both the debt and equity invested in project companies.) In the United States, firms financed $19 billion of capital expenditures using project finance in 2002, down from $68 billion in 2001 largely due to a sharp downturn in the power sector. By way of comparison with other financing mechanisms in the United States in 2002, the project finance market was smaller than the $612 billion corporate bond market, the $397 billion asset-backed security market, and the $205 billion equipment leasing market. It was approximately the same size as other financing vehicles for start-up firms: firms raised $27 billion through initial public offerings (IPOs) and $26 billion from venture capital funds in 2002.[1]

Private sector firms have historically used project finance to finance industrial projects such as mines, pipelines, and oil fields. More recently, however, private firms have begun to finance infrastructure projects (toll roads, power plants, telecommunications systems, etc.) as well.[2] According to the World Bank, the need for infrastructure investment is enormous: Asian countries alone, which historically have accounted for only 15% of the project finance market, will require $2 trillion of infrastructure investment over the next decade to maintain their current rate of economic development.[3] Like-

---

Research Associate Aldo Sesia, Jr. prepared this note under the supervision of Professor Benjamin C. Esty as the basis for class discussion. This note revises and updates previous versions written by Irina L. Christov (MBA '01), Suzie Harris (MBA '99), and Kathy Krueger (MBA '99).

[1] Thomson Financial SDC database. All figures are for 2002.

[2] Infrastructure includes investments in water, transportation, electricity, natural gas, and telecommunications projects.

[3] Boey Klt Yin, Reality Bites—A Quieter PF Horizon, *PFI Asia Pacific Review: News and Comment* (1998): 2–3.

wise, Latin America countries need $50 billion of infrastructure investment per year over the next decade.[4] Most studies on economic development find that infrastructure investment is associated with one-for-one percentage increases in gross domestic product (GDP).[5] Similar country-specific studies of development find that inadequate infrastructure severely hinders economic growth. For example, insufficient or irregular power supply reduces GDP by 1% to 2% in India, Pakistan, and Colombia.[6] Despite the growing demand and opportunities for private sector involvement in building infrastructure, private firms still provide only a small fraction of the total amount invested.

This note focuses exclusively on private sector investment in industrial and infrastructure projects, and contains four sections. The first section defines project finance and contrasts it with other well-known financing structures. The second section describes the evolution of project finance from its beginnings in the natural resources industry in the 1970s to the U.S. power industry in the 1980s and a much wider range of industrial sectors and geographic locations in the 1990s and 2000s. The third section provides a statistical overview of project-financed investment over the last five years—from 1998 to 2002—in terms of industry, project, and participant data. The final section discusses current and likely future trends. For further information on project finance, see the Harvard Business School Project Finance Portal at www.hbs.edu/projfinportal (Appendix 2-1 shows the portal's front page). This portal is intended to be a reference guide for students, researchers, and practitioners seeking to obtain information about project finance. In addition to bibliographical references to books, articles, and case studies, the portal contains more than 900 links to related sites.

DEFINITION AND USE OF PROJECT FINANCE

There is no single agreed upon definition for project finance. For example, Finnerty (1996, p. 2) defines project finance as:

> the raising of funds to finance an economically separable capital investment project in which the providers of the funds look primarily to the cash flow from the project as the source of funds to service their loans and provide the return of and a return on their equity invested in the project.

while Nevitt and Fabozzi (2000, p. 1) define it as:

> A financing of a particular economic unit in which a lender is satisfied to look initially to the cash flow and earnings of that economic unit as the source of funds from which a loan will be repaid and to the assets of the economic unit as collateral for the loan.

Although neither definition uses the term *nonrecourse debt* explicitly (i.e., debt repayment comes from the project company only rather than from any other entity), both

---

[4] "Latin Report: Project Trends," *ProjectFinance* (June 2000).

[5] The World Bank, *World Development Report: Infrastructure for Development* (New York: Oxford University Press, 1994), pp. 2–4. The endogenous nature of investment creates an econometric problem: does increased infrastructure result in economic growth, or does economic growth result in increased infrastructure spending? Other studies note very high rates of return from infrastructure investments (see pp. 13–16).

[6] International Finance Corporation, "Lessons of Experience #4: Financing Private Infrastructure" (Washington, DC: The World Bank, 1996), pp. 43–44.

recognize that it is an essential feature of project finance.[7] The following definition, albeit slightly more cumbersome, allows one to distinguish project finance from other financing vehicles, something the previous two definitions cannot do:

> **Project finance** involves the creation of a legally independent project company financed with nonrecourse debt (and equity from one or more sponsors) for the purpose of financing a single purpose, industrial asset.

This definition recognizes three key decisions related to the use of project finance. First, there is an *investment decision* involving an industrial asset. Here, the term *industrial asset* is meant to include infrastructure projects as well. Bruner and Langohr (1992, p. 2) differentiate between stock and flow-type projects. In stock-type projects, firms extract resources like oil or copper, sell the output, and use the proceeds to service debt and generate equity returns until the resource is depleted. In contrast, flow-type projects—toll roads, pipelines, telecommunications systems, and power plants—rely on asset use to generate returns for capital providers. The definition also highlights an *organizational decision* to create a legally independent entity to own the asset. As a result, project finance can represent a form of off-balance sheet finance, meaning that project assets and liabilities do not appear on the sponsor's balance sheet. The exact accounting treatment, however, is a function of the chosen organizational form (corporation, partnership, etc.) and the sponsor's fractional interest in and control over the project. In many cases (e.g., when there is only one sponsor), project assets and liabilities appear on the sponsor's balance sheet. Finally, there is a *financing decision* involving nonrecourse debt. Because the project company is legally independent, the debt can be structured without recourse to the sponsors. Legal independence also ensures that capital providers have a clear claim on the project assets and cash flows without concern for the sponsor's financial condition or for preexisting claims on its assets.

This formal definition stipulates a number of qualifications that may seem unimportant, but are needed to distinguish project finance from other financing structures. For example, the difference between asset-backed securities and project finance—a portfolio of financial assets vs. a single industrial asset—has ramifications for how you finance the assets: The portfolio of assets in an asset-backed security exhibits greater statistical regularity and can, therefore, support more debt. The nature of the assets also affects how you manage them because industrial assets require active management, whereas financial assets (e.g., receivables) require oversight but few day-to-day operating decisions. To clarify the definition, it helps to compare project finance with other financing structures. Consider the following financing structures—which could be considered project finance.

- **Secured debt:** No, because the debt has recourse to corporate assets.
- **Vendor-financed debt:** No, because the debt has recourse to corporate assets (vendor finance is a kind of secured debt in which the manufacturer of the goods provides the debt).
- **Subsidiary debt:** Not if it the debt has recourse to corporate assets.

---

[7] Limited recourse debt—debt that carries a repayment guarantee for a defined period of time, for a fraction of the total principal, or until a certain milestone is achieved (e.g., until construction is complete or the project achieves a minimum level of output)—is a subset of nonrecourse debt. The distinguishing feature is that at least some portion of the debt becomes nonrecourse at some point in time.

- **Lease:** No, because the obligation has recourse and it does not involve asset ownership.
- **Joint ventures:** Not unless funded with nonrecourse debt (*note*: many projects are structured as incorporated joint ventures).
- **Asset-backed securities (ABS) or real estate investment trusts (REITs):** No, because they hold financial, not single-purpose industrial assets.
- **Privatizations or municipal development:** No, because they lack a corporate sponsor.
- **Leveraged buyouts (LBOs and MBOs):** No, because they lack a corporate sponsor.
- **Commercial real estate development:** Yes, but real estate tends to have different institutional arrangements.
- **Project holding companies:** Maybe, but as the number of projects increases, it begins to look more like a corporation with cross-collateralized debt obligations.

Despite the fact that one can distinguish project finance from these other financing structures, the boundaries between them are not precise. For example, building power plants resembles commercial real estate development except that projects often involve more relationship or transaction-specific assets (i.e., the assets are more valuable to certain transacting parties or in certain business relationships than in other settings). Other projects such as satellite telecommunications systems resemble venture-backed start-up companies, while LBOs and project companies share highly leveraged capital structures and concentrated equity ownership. Because of these and other similarities, research on real estate finance, LBOs/MBOs, securitization, secured debt, and leasing provide insights into project finance and how it creates value. At the same time, research on project finance yields new insights for these and other related fields, such as risk management, corporate governance, development economics, and organizational economics.

HISTORY OF PROJECT FINANCE

Most people think of project finance as a relatively recent phenomenon, yet its history goes back hundreds, if not thousands of years. One of the earliest recorded applications of project finance dates back to 1299, when the English Crown enlisted a leading Florentine merchant bank to aid in the development of the Devon silver mines. The bank received a one-year lease for the total output of the mines in exchange for paying all operating costs without recourse to the Crown if the value or amount of the extracted ore was less than expected.[8] Today, this type of loan is known as a production payment loan. Early trading expeditions in the seventeenth and eighteenth centuries were also financed on a project basis. Investors provided funds to the Dutch East India Company and the British East India Company for voyages to Asia, after which they were repaid according to their share of the cargo when it was sold.[9] Over time, as other forms of more permanent capital became available, firms curtailed their use of voyage or project-specific financing.

[8] J.W. Kensinger and J.D. Martin, "Project Finance: Raising Money the Old-fashioned Way," *Journal of Applied Corporate Finance* (1988): 69–81.

[9] David K. Eiteman, Arthur I. Stonehill and Michael H. Moffett, *Multinational Business Finance*, 8th ed. (Reading, MA: Addison-Wesley Publishing Co., 1998), pp. 606–607.

Some of the earliest applications of project finance in the United States were in the natural resources sector and real estate. In the 1930s, "wildcat" explorers in Texas and Oklahoma used production payment loans to finance oil-field exploration.[10] Similarly, real estate developers built and financed standalone commercial properties through much of the twentieth century on a project basis. In both cases, the creditors had recourse to the project only.

During the 1970s, project finance began to develop into its modern form, partly in response to several large natural resource discoveries and partly in response to soaring energy prices and the resulting demand for alternative energy sources. British Petroleum raised $945 million on a project basis in the early 1970s to develop the "Forties Field" in the North Sea. At roughly the same time, Freeport Minerals project-financed the Ertsberg copper mine in Indonesia, while Conzinc Riotinto of Australia project-financed the Bougainville copper mine in Papua New Guinea.

The advent of modern project finance really began, by most accounts, in the early 1980s as the United States scrambled to build new power plants. The persistence of high energy prices during the 1970s motivated the U.S. Congress to pass the Public Utility Regulatory Policy Act (PURPA) of 1978 as a way to encourage investment in alternative (nonfossil fuel) energy generators. This act required local utilities to purchase all of the output from qualified power producers under long-term contracts. Project finance became the structure of choice for financing new generating plants with long-term power purchase agreements. Equity investors created new, standalone companies to own power plants and financed them with nonrecourse debt. These plants were known as independent power producers (IPPs).

Exhibit 2-1 shows a typical project structure involving up to 15 parties united in a vertical chain from input supplier to output buyer through 40 or more contractual agreements. To develop an IPP, a developer typically needed to sign four primary contracts: (1) a construction and equipment contract, usually on a fixed-price, turnkey basis with an experienced contractor; (2) a long-term fuel supply contract; (3) a long-term power purchase agreement with a creditworthy public utility; and (4) an operating and maintenance contract. After signing these, and numerous other contracts, sponsors could finance the "contractual bundle" on a project basis. Because of the extensive use of contracts, some people refer to project finance as "contractual finance."

Project finance was particularly attractive for IPPs because it offered high leverage with limited or no recourse to the sponsor's balance sheet. Lenders became comfortable with terms that were aggressive by conventional standards because IPPs had long-term, steady streams of cash flow from creditworthy counterparties. During the 1980s, power projects accounted for more than two-thirds of total project-financed investment.[11] For this reason, project finance was essentially synonymous with U.S. power finance until the early 1990s.

A separate, but concurrent, antecedent of modern project finance was the public sector's use of tax-exempt municipal bonds to finance roads, water treatment plants, and other infrastructure projects. Municipalities and other government entities originally financed these projects using general obligation bonds backed by their full faith and credit. Over time, they began to use revenue bonds backed by profit-specific cash flows.

---

[10] Smith, Roy C. and Ingo Walter, *Global Financial Services: Strategies for Building Competitive Strengths in International Commercial and Investment Banking* (New York: Harper Business, 1990), Chapter 9, pp. 214–219.

[11] A.H. Chen, J.W. Kensinger, and J.D. Martin, "Project Financing as a Means of Preserving Financial Flexibility," University of Texas working paper, 1989 (as cited in Finnerty, 1996, p. 1).

EXHIBIT 2-1

TYPICAL PROJECT STRUCTURE FOR AN IPP

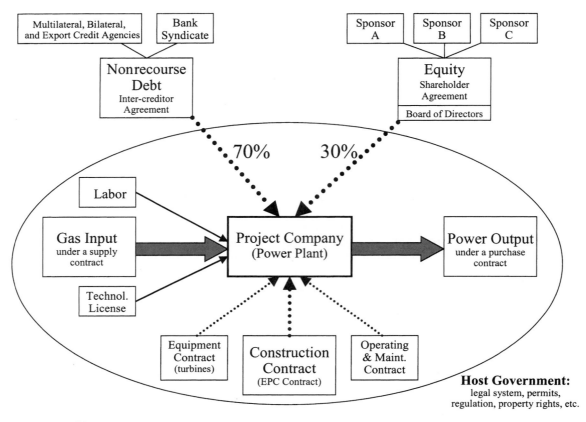

Source: Created by casewriter.

By the early 1990s, municipalities began to marry project finance with private sector involvement. While the stated objective was to encourage better management and promote more efficient risk sharing, these public/private structures could also be used to expand the pool of available funds in the face of limited government budgets.

Public private partnerships (known by the acronym PPP) have become more formalized in recent years. For example, the United Kingdom established the Private Finance Initiative (PFI) in 1992 to involve the private sector in financing and managing infrastructure projects. By 1999, the United Kingdom had signed agreements for more than 250 PFI projects with a total value of £16 billion. Based on its early success, the UK government has identified over 1,000 other projects for possible inclusion in the PFI program, including proposals for hospitals, schools, and prisons.[12] In recent years, many countries including Australia, Ireland, Italy, and South Africa have established similar PFI programs.

[12] Arthur Andersen and Enterprise LSE, Value for Money Drivers in the Private Finance Initiative, a report commissioned by the UK Treasury Task Force, January 17, 2000.

Since the early 1990s, privatization, deregulation, and globalization have spurred the use of project finance in both developed and developing countries. Privatization of state-owned companies became much more common, particularly in developing countries. From 1990 to 1996, privatization revenues in emerging markets totaled more than $155 billion, reaching $25 billion in 1996 alone.[13] As governments exited businesses, private sector companies stepped in to fill the void. Newly privatized companies such as YPF (the former state-owned oil and gas company in Argentina) have used project finance to fund much of their growth. Concurrent deregulation of key industrial sectors, such as power and telecommunications, has also created new opportunities for investment by the private sector. In many cases, project finance has been the vehicle of choice to finance large capital investments. And finally, globalization of product markets has increased the minimum efficient scale for many industries, while depletion of existing natural resources has forced firms to search in increasingly remote locations to find new reserves.

As a result of these changes, sponsors have begun to use project finance for a much broader range of assets in a much broader range of countries. No longer is project finance confined to power projects in the United States. Examples of the reach and versatility of project finance are the $3.7 billion Paiton power plants in Indonesia (1996), the $217 million Centragas pipeline in Colombia (1994), the $57 million Andacollo gold mine in Chile (1994), the $1.6 billion FLAG telecommunications project (1995), and the $3.4 billion Malaysian North-South expressway (1994).[14]

PROJECT FINANCED-INVESTMENT OVER THE LAST FIVE YEARS (1998–2002)

This section provides an overview of project-financed investment over the last five years. Using data from the trade journal *Project Finance International* and from the Thomson Financial Securities Data Project Finance database, this section contains three parts: industry data, project data, and participant data.

Industry Data

The total global project finance market in 2002 was approximately $135 billion, including both debt and equity invested in project companies (see Exhibit 2-2). This number represents private sector investment in the form of commercial bank loans and bonds as well as investments made by international financial institutions (development institutions and export credit agencies). Total project-financed investments declined by 38% in 2002, down from $217 billion in 2001. Investor interest waned as economic growth slowed, capacity utilization fell, and more projects, particularly merchant power plants and telecommunications projects, faced excess supply and rapidly falling prices. The conditions were so unfavorable that industry analysts referred to this confluence of events as the industry's "perfect storm"—a reference to the rare convergence of meteorological conditions that unleashed a ferocious ocean storm, which claimed the lives of Gloucester (Massachusetts) fishermen in 1991.

---

[13] Ira W. Lieberman and Christopher D. Kirkness, *Privatization and the Emerging Equity Markets* (Washington, DC: World Bank, 1998), p. 23.

[14] Henry A. Davis, *Project Finance: Practical Case Studies* (London: Euromoney Publications, 1996), pp. 47–199.

EXHIBIT 2-2

PROJECT-FINANCED INVESTMENT, 1994–2002

Total Project-Financed Investment (US$ billions)

	1994	1995	1996	1997	1998	1999	2000	2001	2002	5-Year CAGR 1996–2001	1997–2002
Bank loans	$13.68	$23.33	$42.83	$67.43	$56.65	$72.39	$110.89	$108.48	$62.20	20%	-2%
Bonds	3.99	3.79	4.79	7.50	9.79	19.97	20.81	25.00	13.80	39%	13%
Total project lending	17.67	27.12	47.62	74.93	66.44	92.36	131.70	133.48	76.00	23%	0%
Year-to-year change in lending		53%	76%	57%	-11%	39%	43%	1%	-43%		
MLA/BLA development agencies[a]	11.25	17.59	18.96	22.05	20.97	16.62	17.69	18.75	18.75	0%	-3%
Equity financing (estimate)[b]	12.39	19.16	28.54	41.56	37.46	46.70	64.02	65.24	40.61	18%	0%
Total private sector investment (including debt and equity)	$41.31	$63.88	$95.12	$138.54	$124.87	$155.68	$213.40	$217.47	$135.36	18%	0%

Percent of Lending by Type of Debt

	1994	1995	1996	1997	1998	1999	2000	2001	2002
Bank loans	77%	86%	90%	90%	85%	78%	84%	81%	82%
Bonds	23	14	10	10	15	22	16	19	18
Total	100%	100%	100%	100%	100%	100%	100%	100%	100%

Number of Projects and Average Amount of Debt

	1994	1995	1996	1997	1998	1999	2000	2001	2002
Number of projects:									
with bank loan financing	NA	NA	341	407	419	559	594	314	284
with bond financing	NA	22	19	25	43	78	86	79	53
Average amount of debt per project:									
projects with bank loans ($ millions)	NA	NA	$126	$166	$135	$130	$187	$345	$219
projects with bonds ($ millions)	NA	$172	$252	$300	$228	$256	$242	$316	$260

[a] Private sector investment made by bilateral development agencies (BLA), multilateral development agencies (MLA), export credit agencies (ECA), and export financing institutions. Adapted from "The Private Sector Financing Activities of International Financial Institutions: 1991–1997" and the 1998 and 2001 Updates (Washington, DC: International Finance Corporation). The numbers for 1994, 2001, and 2002 are casewriter estimates. Some of the reported total is for guarantees; we assume 75% of the total is for equity and debt investments.

[b] Assumes a total debt/total capitalization ratio of 70%.

Source: Adapted from Project Finance International (London: IFR Publishing), 3/2/95, 2/28/96, 1/29/97, 1/28/98, 1/27/99, 1/26/00, 1/24/01, 1/23/02, and 1/22/03.

The decrease in 2002 came after a sharp rise in recent years: project-financed investment increased from $95 billion in 1996 to $217 billion in 2001. Consequently, the compound annual growth rate (CAGR) of 0% from 1997 to 2002 is misleading. By comparison, the five-year CAGR from 1996 to 2001 was 18%. The decline in project-financed investment in 2002 was, in fact, the first since 1998 when the Asian financial crisis decreased global investment particularly in developing countries. Although the total investment of $135 billion in 2002 fell short of levels achieved in 1999, 2000, and 2001, total investment still exceeded 1998 levels by 8% or $11 billion.

Reflecting the rapid rise during the 1990s and the 2002 downturn, project loans had a negative CAGR of 2% from 1997 to 2002 but a positive CAGR of 20% from 1996 to 2001. Similarly, project bonds grew at a compound annual rate of 39% from 1996 to 2001. Total project bond issuance reached $25 billion in 2001 before declining 45% to $14 billion in 2002. Whereas bonds accounted for 10% of total project debt in 1996, they now account for almost 20% of total project debt. Despite the increased use of bond finance, project bonds are a relatively new kind of security. The Midland Cogeneration Project, an IPP in Michigan, issued the first project bond in 1991, which S&P rated subinvestment grade.[15] The following year, S&P issued its first investment grade rating for a project, the $560 million Coso Funding Corporation, and its first rating for a project in an emerging market country, the $200 million Toluca Toll Road refinancing in Mexico.

In 2002, bank loans financed 284 projects, while bonds financed 53 projects for a total of 337 projects. (An undisclosed number of projects used both bank and bond finance and are, therefore, double counted.) The total number of projects financed was the lowest number since 1996—the first year Thomson Financial reported the number of project deals. Notwithstanding the drop in the number of projects, the size of the deals in both 2001 and 2002 was larger than they had been in previous years. In 2001, the average debt per project reached a peak of $339 million. Although the average debt per project dropped to $225 million in 2002, it was still higher than that in any of the years between 1998 and 2000.

Exhibits 2-3, 2-4, and 2-5 show the distribution of bank lending by region, sector, and region/sector, respectively. From 1998 to 2002, 60% of all lending went to finance projects located in Western Europe and North America (see Exhibit 2-3). While each region received 30% of the total bank debt during this period, they are trending in opposite directions. Since 1999, loan volume in Western Europe, as a percentage of total loan volume, has increased from 22% to 38%. Over the same period, North America's volume has declined from 42% to 17%. Asia's four-year CAGR of 30% indicates that the region is recovering from the financial crisis of 1997. In fact, bank lending in Asia slightly exceeded North America in 2002, giving Asia second place in terms of project lending for the year.

With regard to industrial sectors, bank lending remains concentrated in power, telecoms, and infrastructure (see Exhibit 2-4). Since 1998, these three sectors have received 39%, 24%, and 14%, of all project lending, respectively. The power sector's four-year CAGR from 1998 to 2002 was 4%—a positive growth rate notwithstanding the sector's sharp decline in 2002 (from $47.3 billion to $20.2 billion). The telecoms sector experienced a negative four-year CAGR of 15% and suffered a reduction in project lending for the second year in a row. Project lending to the telecoms sector was $7.3 billion in 2002, down nearly 80% from its high of $34.7 billion in 2000. Infrastructure, however, experienced its second year of growth; the sector's CAGR from 1998 to 2002 was 17%,

[15] Ibid., pp. 18–20.

EXHIBIT 2-3

PROJECT FINANCE LENDING BY REGION, 1998–2002

Amount of Project Lending by Region (US$ billion)

Region	1998 $B	%	1999 $B	%	2000 $B	%	2001 $B	%	2002 $B	%	Total 1998–2002 $B	%	4-Year CAGR
Western Europe	$14.67	26%	$15.76	22%	$ 33.61	30%	$ 37.35	34%	$23.36	38%	$124.76	30%	12%
North America	12.66	22	30.69	42	36.10	33	31.88	29	10.32	17	121.64	30	–5
Americas	12.46	22	6.84	9	16.70	15	15.60	14	6.22	10	57.82	14	–16
Asia	3.67	6	4.40	6	7.79	7	7.17	7	10.61	17	33.63	8	30
Australia/New Zealand	6.16	11	8.05	11	4.30	4	4.17	4	6.06	10	28.74	7	0
Middle East	3.26	6	3.95	5	6.25	6	8.28	8	2.75	4	24.49	6	–4
Eastern Europe	2.13	4	0.62	1	4.59	4	1.06	1	1.32	2	9.73	2	–11
Africa	1.65	3	2.07	3	1.56	1	2.97	3	1.54	2	9.78	2	–2
Total	**$56.65**	**100%**	**$72.39**	**100%**	**$110.89**	**100%**	**$108.48**	**100%**	**$62.18**	**100%**	**$410.58**	**100%**	**2%**

Source: Adapted from *Project Finance International* (London: IFR Publishing), 1/28/98, 1/27/99, 1/26/00, 1/24/01, 1/23/02, and 1/22/03.

EXHIBIT 2-4

PROJECT FINANCE LENDING BY SECTOR, 1998–2002

Sector	Amount of Project Lending by Sector (US$ billion)													4-Year CAGR
	1998		1999		2000		2001		2002		Total 1998–2002			
	$B	%	$B	%	$B	%	$B	%	$B	%	$B	%		
Power	$17.21	30%	$29.99	41%	$44.59	40%	$47.26	44%	$20.20	32%	$159.24	39%		4%
Telecoms	14.06	25	19.70	27	34.70	31	23.96	22	7.29	12	99.71	24		−15
Infrastructure	7.70	14	9.00	12	13.36	12	11.28	10	14.20	23	55.54	14		17
Oil & Gas	9.34	16	4.97	7	9.27	8	8.83	8	6.44	10	38.84	9		−9
Petrochemicals	3.13	6	4.68	6	3.34	3	3.90	4	5.71	9	20.76	5		16
Leisure & Property	0.37	1	1.27	2	1.64	1	6.53	6	4.76	8	14.57	4		90
Industrial	2.64	5	1.40	2	3.36	3	3.65	3	0.82	1	11.87	3		−25
Mining	2.21	4	1.38	2	0.63	1	2.32	2	1.00	2	7.54	2		−18
Other	0.00	0	0.00	0	0.00	0	0.76	1	1.75	3	2.51	1		n/a
Total	**$56.65**	**100%**	**$72.39**	**100%**	**$110.89**	**100%**	**$108.48**	**100%**	**$62.18**	**100%**	**$410.58**	**100%**		**2%**

Source: Adapted from *Project Finance International* (London: IFR Publishing), 1/28/98, 1/27/99, 1/26/00, 1/24/01, 1/23/02, and 1/22/03.

EXHIBIT 2-5

PROJECT FINANCE BANK LOANS BY SECTOR AND REGION (US$ BILLION), 1998–2002[a]

Sector	Americas	Europe, Middle East, and Africa	Asia Pacific	1998–2002 Total	Percent of Total
Power	$100.84	$ 38.35	$20.06	$159.25	38.8%
Telecoms	27.52	62.67	9.52	99.71	24.3
Infrastructure[b]	7.36	35.62	12.56	55.54	13.5
Oil & Gas	19.87	10.67	8.30	38.84	9.5
Petrochemicals	7.69	8.46	4.60	20.76	5.1
Leisure & Property	6.14	6.96	1.48	14.57	3.5
Mining	5.32	3.09	3.46	11.87	2.9
Industrial	4.46	1.32	1.74	7.53	1.8
Water & Sewage	0.01	0.35	0.56	0.92	0.2
Other	0.25	1.30	0.05	1.60	0.4
Total	**$179.46**	**$168.78**	**$62.33**	**$410.58**	**100.0%**
Percent	**43.7%**	**41.1%**	**15.2%**	**100.0%**	

[a] Shaded boxes show market segments with the largest amount of bank financing.

[b] Infrastructure includes roads, bridges, and other transportation projects.

Source: Adapted from *Project Finance International* (London: IFR Publishing), 1/28/98, 1/27/99, 1/26/00, 1/24/01, 1/23/02, and 1/22/03.

which reflects greater involvement by private companies in infrastructure projects. Although project lending to the leisure and property sector remains relatively small (i.e., only 4% of total project lending from 1998 to 2002), the sector's CAGR over the last four years has been a notable 90%, largely because it started with such a low base.

Exhibit 2-5 shows the distribution of bank lending by both region and sector over the 1998 to 2002 period. The most active sectors/region combinations appear shaded in the exhibit: power in the Americas ($100.8 billion), telecoms in Europe/Middle East/Africa—EMEA ($62.7 billion), power in EMEA ($38.4 billion), infrastructure in EMEA ($35.6 billion), telecoms in the Americas ($27.5 billion), power in Asia Pacific ($20.1 billion), oil and gas in the Americas ($19.9 billion), and infrastructure in Asia Pacific ($12.6 billion). These eight sector/region pairs accounted for 77% of all bank lending over these five years. The top sector alone—power in the Americas—accounted for a quarter of the total bank lending to projects.

Turning to the bond market, Exhibits 2-6 and 2-7 show the distribution of bond financing by country and sector. Project bond issuance has largely been concentrated in the United States, which accounted for 53% of total bond financing over the last five years (see Exhibit 2-6). The remaining 47% of bond volume is spread among 33 different countries; note that the countries listed as "other" vary from year to year. One noticeable change is that project bonds have become more common in developing countries such as Brazil, Chile, and Malaysia. Indeed, project bond volume in Mexico exceeded the volume in the United Kingdom, Australia, and Canada over the past five years.

EXHIBIT 2-6

PROJECT FINANCE BONDS BY COUNTRY (US$ MILLIONS), 1998–2002

Country	1998	1999	2000	2001	2002	1998–2002 Total	Percent of Total
United States	$4,018	$11,944	$11,313	$16,334	$ 3,422	$47,031	52.6%
Mexico	770	892	1,831	1,250	2,966	7,709	8.6
United Kingdom	1,034	1,212	2,498	240	1,330	6,314	7.1
Australia	1,160	492	1,293	460	2,884	6,289	7.0
Malaysia	0	0	0	1,709	1,904	3,613	4.0
Canada	335	1,863	489	0	0	2,687	3.0
Chile	362	0	430	1,289	405	2,486	2.8
Brazil	0	0	875	1,050	250	2,175	2.4
Argentina	513	296	625	363	0	1,797	2.0
Venezuela	850	0	200	500	0	1,550	1.7
Puerto Rico	0	1,000	195	0	0	1,195	1.3
Spain	0	728	0	340	0	1,068	1.2
South Korea	0	132	0	652	0	784	0.9
Israel	0	250	175	0	104	529	0.6
Other	750	1,157	887	816	523	4,133	4.6
Total	**$9,792**	**$19,966**	**$20,811**	**$25,003**	**$13,788**	**$89,360**	**100.0%**
Total Countries	**12**	**16**	**16**	**17**	**9**		

Source: Adapted from *Project Finance International* (London: IFR Publishing), 1/28/98, 1/27/99, 1/26/00, 1/24/01, 1/23/02, and 1/22/03.

EXHIBIT 2-7

PROJECT FINANCE BONDS BY SECTOR (US$ MILLION), 1998–2002

Sector	1998	1999	2000	2001	2002	1998–2002 Total	Percent of Total
Power	4,458	$ 7,270	$11,920	$17,273	$ 4,315	$45,236	50.6%
Infrastructure	1,307	3,676	3,394	2,430	6,471	17,278	19.3
Oil & Gas	1,330	2,822	3,285	3,813	2,632	13,882	15.5
Telecoms	2,212	5,227	2,036	1,487	0	10,962	12.3
Petrochemical	0	672	0	0	0	672	0.8
Mining	485	0	0	0	0	485	0.5
Leisure	0	299	0	0	120	419	0.5
Industrial	0	0	176	0	250	426	0.5
Total	$9,792	$19,966	$20,811	$25,003	$13,788	$89,360	100.0%

Source: Adapted from *Project Finance International* (London: IFR Publishing), 1/28/98, 1/27/99, 1/26/00, 1/24/01, 1/23/02, and 1/22/03.

Like bank lending, project bonds are used extensively in the power sector (51% of the total bond financing over the last five years), although they have also been used regularly to finance infrastructure and oil and gas projects (see Exhibit 2-7). In 2002, infrastructure unseated power as the number one sector receiving bond funding, a position that the power sector had held from 1998 to 2001. The volume of bond financing for power projects dropped from $17.3 billion in 2001 to $4.3 billion in 2002—a 75% reduction. This decline occurred largely in the United States as merchant power plants began to default, causing sponsors to curtail construction spending. Although bond investment in power projects declined, power remains a strong sector: it still accounted for 31% of total bond financing in 2002.

Continuing with the bond market, Exhibit 2-8 shows the distribution of Standard & Poor's (S&P) ratings for project bonds over the last seven years. Since 1996, the volume of S&P rated bonds has increased at a compound annual rate of 33%, reaching $106 billion in 2002. The number of rated bonds increased from 57 in 1996 to 230 in

---

EXHIBIT 2-8

STANDARD & POOR'S RATED PROJECT DEBT DISTRIBUTION, 1996–2002

	Percent of Total Ratings by Number of Bonds						
S&P Rating	**June 1996**	**June 1997**	**August 1998**	**August 1999**	**June 2000**	**June 2001**	**August 2002**
AAA	2%	1%	2%	7%	9%	9%	10%
AA+, AA, or AA−	4	4	2	4	2	2	2
A+ or A	7	5	4	6	6	7	7
A−	9	6	8	7	7	6	6
BBB+	4	5	4	3	4	4	3
BBB	7	14	11	12	12	12	10
BBB−	51	41	31	29	22	26	27
BB+	2	4	5	6	12	10	7
BB	7	6	11	14	9	10	10
BB−	5	9	11	5	5	6	4
B+	0	1	2	1	1	1	2
B	1	1	2	2	1	3	1
B−	0	1	2	1	0	1	1
CCC and below	2	1	4	4	8	5	8
Total	**100%**	**100%**	**100%**	**100%**	**100%**	**100%**	**100%**
Total rated volume (US$ billion)	**$19.6**	**$27.6**	**$37.5**	**$50.4**	**$62.5**	**$81.3**	**$106.3**
Number of bonds	57	78	113	152	161	196	230
% investment grade	83%	77%	63%	67%	64%	65%	66%

Note: Bonds rated BBB− or higher are considered investment grade.

Source: Adapted from Standard & Poor's *Infrastructure Finance: Criteria and Commentary*, 9/98 and 9/99, 10/00, 10/01 and 10/02; *Global Project Finance*, 7/96; casewriter estimates.

2002. Over these five years, the percentage of project bonds with an investment grade (an S&P rating of BBB− or higher) ranged between 63% and 67% of all rated bonds. Most of these bonds have "negotiated" ratings, which means the sponsors adjust leverage, covenants, and deal structure until the projects achieve an investment grade rating, at least at issuance. The reason for targeting an investment grade rating is that the largest advantage in pricing and liquidity occurs at the BBB− threshold due to institutional restrictions against investing in subinvestment grade securities. For this reason, the general rule of thumb is that bonds must be investment grade in order to sell in the market. As a result, sponsors with projects in emerging markets may find it prohibitively expensive, if not impossible, to use project bonds

Project Data

The Thomson Financial Securities Data Project Finance database contains information on almost 1,200 deals financed between 1997 and 2001. A cursory review of 2002 data shows a decline in total volume but otherwise no clear changes in the statistics compared to the data from 1997 to 2001. For this reason, and because not all of the 2002 data has been reported yet, this analysis uses data from 1997 to 2001 only. The database permits detailed analysis of project size, leverage, and contractual maturities. This analysis reveals that projects tend to be larger than $100 million in size, have highly leveraged capital structures, and have long, but limited, lives.

Exhibit 2-9 shows the size distribution of projects by year and by sector. When broken down by the number of projects, Exhibit 2-9a shows that 27% of the projects by number are under $100 million in size. At the other end of the size spectrum, 26% of the projects are larger than $500 million in size, but they account for 74% of total lending volume (see Exhibit 2-9b). The majority of expenditure comes from the projects greater than $1 billion in size: they account for 12% of projects by number and 53% by total cost over the last five years. According to the breakdown by sector shown in Exhibit 2-9c, the petrochemical, telecoms, and oil and gas sectors have the greatest number of large projects (i.e., with total cost greater than $1 billion). When measured in terms of value, these sectors show even greater concentration in large deals. As shown in Exhibit 2-9d, the oil and gas, petrochemical, and telecoms sectors have 74%, 67%, and 59% of their total volume, respectively, in deals greater than $1 billion.

Exhibit 2-10 analyzes project leverage ratios from 1997 to 2001. The mean and median debt-to-total capitalization ratio has been 70%, though the ratios vary over time as a function of the mix of projects in any given year. Only 10% of projects have leverage ratios less than 50%, which is still much higher than the typical publicly traded company. The most noticeable fact is that leverage ratios vary by project sector. The median leisure and property deal has a leverage ratio of 85% compared to 73% for power deals and 60% for mining deals (see Exhibit 2-10b). Other sectors fall somewhere in between the two extremes.

Because project finance relies heavily on contractual agreements, Exhibit 2-11 provides some data on project contracts. Despite a limited number of observations—not all variables are reported in the database for each deal—the data reveal several interesting facts. Exhibit 2-11a shows the distribution of construction contracts by the number of years to complete the project. The mean and median numbers are both 2.0 years. The long construction period increases uncertainty and project risk; it also means that projects may not break even for three to six years or more. Exhibit 2-11b shows the distribution of offtake agreements in years (the number of years with output purchases under contract). The mean and median numbers are both approximately 20 years,

EXHIBIT 2-9

SIZE DISTRIBUTION OF PROJECTS, 1997–2001
(INCLUDES PROJECT DEBT AND EQUITY)

EXHIBIT 2-9A

SIZE DISTRIBUTION BY YEAR (NUMBER OF PROJECTS)

Size	1997	1998	1999	2000	2001	Total
< $50 million	6%	14%	12%	19%	13%	14%
$50–$100	12	11	13	15	13	13
$100–$500	44	48	51	46	47	47
$500–$1 billion	21	15	12	11	15	14
> $1 billion	16	11	12	9	12	12
Total	**100%**	**100%**	**100%**	**100%**	**100%**	**100%**

EXHIBIT 2-9B

SIZE DISTRIBUTION BY YEAR (VALUE OF PROJECTS)

Size	1997	1998	1999	2000	2001	Total
< $50 million	0%	1%	1%	1%	1%	1%
$50–$100	1	2	2	3	2	2
$100–$500	15	27	28	25	27	24
$500–$1 billion	23	25	18	17	23	21
> $1 billion	60	46	51	55	47	53
Total	**100%**	**100%**	**100%**	**100%**	**100%**	**100%**

EXHIBIT 2-9C

SIZE DISTRIBUTION BY SECTOR (NUMBER OF PROJECTS, INCLUDES ALL PROJECTS FROM 1997 TO 2001)

Sector	< $50 million	$50–$100 million	$100–$500 million	$500 million– $1 billion	> $1 billion	Total	Number Projects	% of Total
Power	8%	12%	52%	16%	12%	100%	408	34%
Leisure & Property	36	16	41	3	5	100	160	13
Telecoms	5	8	45	24	18	100	154	13
Transportation	15	13	44	17	11	100	142	12
Industry	10	12	52	18	8	100	83	7
Oil & Gas	10	14	46	14	16	100	80	7
Mining	27	20	38	3	13	100	64	5
Petrochemical	2	11	43	17	26	100	53	4
Water & Sewage	17	24	54	5	0	100	41	3
Other	33	11	56	0	0	100	9	1
Total	**14%**	**13%**	**47%**	**14%**	**12%**	**100%**	**1,194**	**100%**

(Continued)

38

EXHIBIT 2-9 (Continued)

EXHIBIT 2-9D

SIZE DISTRIBUTION BY SECTOR (VALUE OF PROJECTS, INCLUDES ALL PROJECTS FROM 1997 TO 2001)

Sector	< $50 million	$50–$100 million	$100–$500 million	$500 million– $1 billion	> $1 billion	Total	Project Value ($M)	% of Total	Mean Size	Median Size
Power	0%	2%	29%	24%	45%	100%	$202,003	34%	$495	$279
Telecoms	0	1	16	24	59	100	113,269	19	736	361
Transportation	1	2	18	22	58	100	82,139	14	578	210
Oil & Gas	0	1	13	12	74	100	70,090	12	876	250
Petrochemical	0	1	15	16	67	100	40,741	7	769	420
Leisure & Property	5	6	43	9	38	100	33,849	6	212	91
Industry	1	2	32	34	31	100	32,795	5	395	271
Mining	3	5	30	6	57	100	19,711	3	308	125
Water & Sewage	4	13	64	19	0	100	5,685	1	139	120
Other	12	5	83	0	0	100	959	0	107	120
Total	**1%**	**2%**	**24%**	**21%**	**53%**	**100%**	**$601,241**	**100%**	**$504**	**$234**

Source: Calculated using data from the Thomson Financial Securities Data Project Finance database and casewriter estimates.

EXHIBIT 2-10

PROJECT LEVERAGE (DEBT-TO-TOTAL CAPITALIZATION RATIOS)

EXHIBIT 2-10A

**DISTRIBUTION OF INITIAL DEBT-TO-TOTAL
CAPITALIZATION RATIOS BY YEAR, 1997–2001**

Debt/Total Capital	1997	1998	1999	2000	2001	Total
< 50%	12%	9%	7%	8%	20%	10%
50%–59%	13	12	13	9	10	11
60%–69%	21	22	24	16	15	20
70%–79%	26	28	23	28	23	26
80%–89%	16	18	21	20	20	19
> 90%	12	12	12	19	12	14
Total	**100%**	**100%**	**100%**	**100%**	**100%**	**100%**
Mean	**68%**	**69%**	**70%**	**73%**	**66%**	**70%**
Median	**70%**	**70%**	**70%**	**75%**	**70%**	**70%**

(Continued)

though 20% of the agreements are longer than 25 years. Having long-term offtake contracts makes project revenues more predictable and reduces lender risk as long as the counterparties are creditworthy. Concession agreements—agreements that govern project management and operations—typically run for 25 to 30 years, although there is a clear difference between projects in low-rated countries and projects in high-rated countries. Exhibit 2-11c shows the distribution of concession agreements in years. The median concession contract in high-rated countries (AAA to A−) is 30 years compared to 21.5 years in low-rated countries (BBB+ to B−). Debt maturities provide a final way to analyze project lives. According to Exhibit 2-11d, banks provide shorter-term financing (over 60% of bank loans mature in less than 10 years), while bonds provide longer-term financing (over 75% of bonds mature in more than 10 years). The median term for bank loans is 8.0 years, which is much shorter than the median bond maturity of 13.3 years.

Participant Data

Exhibit 2-12 provides "league tables" from *Project Finance International* (PFI) showing the major participants in four areas of the project finance market: lead arrangers, lead managers, advisors, and lawyers. In the 2002 Global Lead Arrangers category (the institutions responsible for arranging bank financings), Citigroup remained in the top spot for the third year in a row, followed by Société Générale, the Royal Bank of London, WestLB, and Barclays (see Exhibit 2-12a). The Royal Bank of Scotland rose up to #3 from #15 in 2001, HypoVereinsbank AG jumped to #8 from #26, and Mitsubishi Tokyo Financial Group finished #10 up from #17. The league tables provide an example of where the various industry data sources can differ. In contrast to the PFI rankings shown in Exhibit 2-12a, Dealogic's *Project Finance Review* ranks ABN AMRO #7, which did not make PFI's top ten, and Deutsche Bank AG #15, which PFI ranked #9.[16]

---

[16] Dealogic ProjectWare, "Project Finance Review," projectfinancereview.com (March 2003).

EXHIBIT 2-10 (Continued)

EXHIBIT 2-10B

DISTRIBUTION OF INITIAL DEBT-TO-TOTAL CAPITALIZATION RATIOS BY SECTOR, 1997–2001

Sector	Debt/Total Capitalization Ratio									Debt/Total Capital	
	< 50%	50%–59%	60%–69%	70%–79%	80%–89%	> 90%	Total %	Total Number	% by Number	Mean	Median
Power	9%	8%	17%	37%	21%	8%	100%	254	35%	70%	73%
Transportation	8	8	22	24	22	16	100	97	13	72	72
Leisure & Property	8	7	12	15	19	39	100	95	13	78	85
Telecoms	13	15	32	18	14	9	100	79	11	66	65
Industry	12	19	33	19	14	3	100	58	8	63	64
Oil & Gas	16	14	18	16	27	9	100	44	6	65	70
Mining	14	35	19	16	9	7	100	43	6	63	60
Petrochemical	6	9	30	27	15	12	100	33	4	70	70
Water & Sewage	4	7	11	37	15	26	100	27	4	76	77
Other	0	0	17	33	33	17	100	6	1	81	81
Total Number	**72**	**84**	**148**	**192**	**139**	**101**		**736**		**70**	**70**
Total %	**10%**	**11%**	**20%**	**26%**	**19%**	**14%**	**100%**		**100%**		

Note: Tables exclude projects with debt-to-total capitalization ratios of 100%. These projects are typically additions to existing projects.

Sources: Calculated using data from the Thomson Financial Securities Data Project Finance database and casewriter estimates.

EXHIBIT 2-11

CONTRACT LENGTH, 1997–2001

EXHIBIT 2-11A

DISTRIBUTION OF CONSTRUCTION CONTRACTS BY NUMBER OF YEARS

	Number of Years							
	≤1.0	1.1 to 2.0	2.1 to 3.0	3.1 to 4.0	4.1 to 5.0	>5	Mean	Median
Number	56	178	79	20	11	7	2.0	2.0
Percent	19%	60%	27%	7%	4%	2%		

Note: The construction period is the number of years to construct the project.

EXHIBIT 2-11B

DISTRIBUTION OF OFFTAKE AGREEMENTS BY NUMBER OF YEARS

	Number of Years							
	≤5	6 to 10	11 to 15	16 to 20	21 to 25	>25	Mean	Median
Number	6	15	45	71	40	45	19.5	20.0
Percent	3%	7%	20%	32%	18%	20%		

Note: The offtake period is the number of years with contracted purchase of output.

EXHIBIT 2-11C

DISTRIBUTION OF CONCESSION AGREEMENTS BY NUMBER OF YEARS

	Number of Years							
	≤10	11 to 20	21 to 30	31 to 40	41 to 50	>50	Mean	Median
Number	14	70	166	18	13	15	28.3	25.0
Percent	5%	25%	59%	6%	5%	5%		
Projects by Sovereign Rating								
AAA to A−	3%	11%	64%	8%	5%	8%	31.5	30.0
BBB+ to B−	5%	45%	44%	3%	2%	1%	23.5	21.5

Note: The concession period is the number of years the project sponsor will operate a given project.

EXHIBIT 2-11D

DISTRIBUTION OF DEBT INSTRUMENT MATURITIES BY NUMBER OF YEARS (1998 DATA ONLY)

	Number of Years							
	<5	5 to 9.9	10 to 14.9	15 to 19.9	20 to 24.9	≥25	Mean	Median
Bank Loans	16%	47%	18%	11%	4%	4%	9.4	8.0
Bonds	6%	18%	44%	9%	21%	3%	13.6	13.3
# of deals	25	72	41	19	13	6		

Source: Calculations in Exhibits 2-11a, 2-11b, and 2-11c use data from the Thomson Financial Securities Data Project Finance database. Calculations in Exhibit 2-11d use Dealogic ProjectWare database and casewriter estimates.

EXHIBIT 2-12

PROJECT FINANCE 2002 LEAGUE TABLES

EXHIBIT 2-12A

GLOBAL LEAD ARRANGERS—BANK LOANS (US$ MILLIONS)

2002 Rank	Name	2001 Rank	2002		
			Number of Facilities	Amount Underwritten	Percent of Total
1	Citigroup SSB	1	43	$ 6,248	10.0%
2	Société Générale	4	21	3,589	5.8
3	Royal Bank of London	15	23	3,257	5.2
4	WestLB	2	29	2,894	4.7
5	Barclays	10	13	2,556	4.1
6	Mizuho Financial Group	11	17	2,367	3.8
7	BNP Paribas SA	3	15	1,666	2.7
8	HypoVereinsbank AG	26	19	1,639	2.6
9	Deutsche Bank	9	12	1,608	2.6
10	Mitsubishi Tokyo Financial Group	17	21	1,493	2.4
	Other		71	34,855	56.1
	Total Market		**284**	**$62,172**	**100.0%**

EXHIBIT 2-12B

LEAD MANAGERS—BONDS (US$ MILLIONS)

2002 Rank	Name	2001 Rank	2002		
			Number of Issues	Amount Underwritten	Percent of Total
1	Lehman Brothers	1	8	$ 2,186	15.9%
2	Citigroup SSB	2	10	2,146	15.6
3	ABN AMRO	7	4	1,472	10.7
4	JP MorganChase	17	4	1,405	10.2
5	BNP Paribas SA	—	1	595	4.3
6	CDC Ixix	—	1	523	3.8
7	Goldman Sachs	4	1	500	3.6
8	Barclay's Capital	—	1	439	3.2
9	Bank Muamalat	21	1	438	3.2
10	KAF Discount	22	1	438	3.2
	Other		21	3,646	26.4
	Total Market		**53**	**$13,788**	**100.0%**

(*Continued*)

EXHIBIT 2-12   (Continued)

EXHIBIT 2-12C

GLOBAL ADVISORY MANDATES

2002 Rank	Name	2002 Number of Mandates	2002 Percent of Total	2001 Number of Mandates	2001 Percent of Total
1	PricewaterhouseCoopers	131	16.6%	98	15.4%
2	Macquarie	120	15.2	72	11.3
3	Ernst & Young	105	13.3	83	13.1
4	David Wylde Project Finance	42	5.3	n/a	n/a
5	KPMG	38	4.8	33	5.2
6	Grant Thornton	36	4.6	n/a	n/a
7	Citigroup SSB	32	4.1	18	2.8
8	Sumitomo Mitsui	30	3.8	10	1.6
9	Fieldstone	26	3.3	21	3.3
10	ABN AMRO	25	3.2	24	3.8
	Other	202	25.7	276	43.5
	Total for all firms	**787**	**100.0%**	**635**	**100.0%**

Source: Adapted from *Project Finance International* (London: IFR Publishing) January 24, 2001 and January 23, 2002.

EXHIBIT 2-12D

GLOBAL PROJECT FINANCE LAW FIRMS, 1998–2002[a]

2002 Rank	Firm Name	Location	Number of Financings Closed
1	Allen & Overy	U.K.	44
2	Clifford Chance	U.K.	33
3	Shearman & Sterling	U.K.	29
4	Millbank, Tweed, Hadley & McCloy	U.S.	26
4	Latham & Watkins	U.S.	26
6	Linklaters & Alliance	Global	23
7	Skadden, Arps	U.S.	22
8	Allens Arthur Robinson	Australia	17
9	Sullivan & Cromwell	U.S.	16
10	White & Case	U.K.	14

[a] Includes only deals over $500 million and counts only the lead advisor.

Source: Adapted from *Project Finance International*, November 27, 2002.

Exhibit 2-12b shows the league table for lead managers (the institutions responsible for managing bond issues). Lehman Brothers topped the list in 2002, the second straight year, with a 15.9% share of total volume, followed closely by Citigroup with 15.6% of the market. ABN AMRO, JP MorganChase, and BNP Paribas round out the top five. Collectively, the top five institutions control nearly 60% of the bond market, which is significantly more concentrated than the bank loan market where the top five institutions control 30% of the total market. The bond market rankings are also more dynamic than the bank market rankings. There were six new entrants to the top 10 in 2002, compared to four new entrants in the bank market.

Exhibit 2-12c ranks firms based on advisory mandates, defined as paid contracts for advisory services won in 2002. PricewaterhouseCoopers has garnered the top spot in the Global Advisory Mandates league table for the past five years. It is important to note, however, that this exhibit ranks firms by the *number* of mandates, not the dollar value or profitability of specific mandates.

Finally, in the legal advisory role in terms of the number of "major" deals—those with total value over $500 million—the top five law firms are Allen & Overy, Clifford Chance, Shearman & Sterling, Millbank Tweed, and Latham & Watkins (see Exhibit 2-12d). What is most striking about the law firm league table is that eight of the top ten law firms are from either the United States or the United Kingdom. Whereas German, French, and Dutch firms play prominent roles in the arranger market—and there are many projects in Western Europe (see Exhibit 2-3)—they are less of a factor in the legal advisory markets.

Exhibit 2-13 identifies the major international financial institutions (IFIs) and details their investment in private sector projects from 1991 to 1998. There are two types of IFIs: development finance institutions (DFIs) and export credit agencies (ECAs). The DFIs try to foster economic development, while the ECAs try to help domestic firms export their goods and services into international markets. According to the International Finance Corporation (IFC, 1998), these institutions invested $24.7 billion in *private sector* projects around the world in 1998. Of this amount, medium to long-term loans and equity accounted for an estimated $19 billion, while guarantees and insurance products accounted for the remaining $6 billion.

CURRENT AND FUTURE TRENDS

Through the early to mid-1990s, project deals were typically highly structured and involved extensive contracting. Yet as project finance evolved into new applications and new geographic settings in the mid- to late 1990s, lenders loosened covenants, extended maturities, and reduced lending spreads. These recent deals were much more exposed to market risks because they were often financed without long-term, fixed-priced supply and offtake contracts.

Although total project-financed investment grew through 2001, several crises in recent years have dramatically reduced total investment. The Asian crisis in July 1997, the Russian crisis in August 1998, and the Brazil devaluation in January 1999 decreased sponsor interest in emerging markets. The financial crisis in Argentina in 2001 furthered heightened investor concerns. And in the United States, the energy crisis in California and the collapse of Enron in late 2001 decreased sponsor interest in the traditionally strong U.S. power sector.

These crises have highlighted the dangers of market, currency, and soverign risks. Of the three risks, market risk has been the most severe. Merchant power plants have been hammered in the past few years and vividly illustrate what can happen when a

EXHIBIT 2-13

PRIVATE SECTOR INVESTMENT VOLUME IN DEVELOPING COUNTRIES
(MEDIUM/LONG-TERM LOANS, EQUITY, GUARANTEES, AND INSURANCE) IN $US MILLIONS

Type Name	Acronym	Country	1991	1995	1996	1997	1998
Multilateral Development Agencies							
Asian Development Bank	ADB	Regional, based in Manila	$ 174	$ 174	$ 263	$ 119	$ 198
African Development Bank	AFDB	Regional, based in Abidjan	8	13	24	50	157
European Bank for Reconstruction and Development	EBRD	Regional, based in London	43	1,863	1,920	2,002	2,121
European Investment Bank	EIB	Regional, based in Luxembourg	422	780	468	760	1,896
Inter-American Development Bank	IDB	Regional, based in Washington, DC	0	146	198	320	576
The Inter-American Investment Corporation	IIC	Regional, based in Washington, DC	102	37	72	150	223
Nordic Investment Bank	NIB	Regional, based in Helsinki	0	73	118	67	141
Subtotal			**749**	**3,085**	**3,063**	**3,467**	**5,313**
Bilateral Development Agencies							
Agence Francaise de Development	AFD	France	254	420	329	278	312
Commonwealth Development Corporation	CDC	United Kingdom	156	411	447	474	365
Deutsche Entwicklunge Gesellschaft	DEG	Germany	189	329	446	404	399
Finnish Fund for Industrial Cooperation Ltd.	Finnfund	Finland	9	21	14	25	70
The Netherlands Development Finance Company	FMO	Netherlands	105	333	333	363	415
The Industrialization Fund for Developing Countries	IFU	Denmark	16	54	52	48	28
The Investment Fund for Central and Eastern Europe	IO	Denmark	4	53	54	58	43
The Investment Fund for Emerging Markets	IFV	Denmark	0	0	0	0	3
Kreditanstalt fur Wiederaufbau (fin. coop. only)	KfW	Germany	35	153	299	172	195
Overseas Economic Cooperation Fund	OECF	Japan	88	190	60	10	6
Overseas Private Investment Corporation	OPIC	United States	290	1,911	2,255	709	695
Swedfund International AB	Swedfund	Sweden	11	9	40	31	11
Subtotal			**1,157**	**3,884**	**4,328**	**2,573**	**2,543**
International Finance Corporation	IFC	International, Washington, DC	1,300	2,112	2,398	2,699	2,800
Total for Development Agencies			**3,206**	**9,081**	**9,789**	**8,739**	**10,655**

(Continued)

EXHIBIT 2-13 *(Continued)*

Type Name	Acronym	Country	1991	1995	1996	1997	1998
Export Credit Agencies/Export Financing Institutions							
The Export-Import Bank of the United States	USEXIM	United States	500	2,179	2,932	3,193	599
The Export-Import Bank of Japan	JEXIM	Japan (now JBIC)	424	2,386	3,142	3,894	3,766
Compagnie Francaise d'Assurance pour le Commerce Exterieur	COFACE	France	373	2,519	1,480	1,586	931
Export Credits Guarantee Department	ECGD	United Kingdom	300	600	700	729	811
Export Development Corporation	EDC	Canada	300	700	808	1,130	1,369
Hermes Kraditvorsicherungs-AGS	Hermes	Germany	3,122	5,388	5,404	6,831	3,793
Kreditanstalt fur Wiederaufbau (w/out fin. coop. & w/out Hermes cover)	KIW	Germany	500	500	833	1,826	1,544
Sezaine Speciale per l'Assicurazione del Credito all'Esportazione	SACE	Italy	0	121	183	1,272	1,243
Total for Export Financing Institutions			5,519	14,393	15,482	20,461	14,056
Grand Total			$8,725	$23,474	$25,270	$29,200	$24,711

Source: Adapted from Appendix A in, "The Private Sector Financing Activities of International Financial Institutions: 1991–1997" (Washington, DC: International Finance Corporation, 1998).

project is exposed to market risk.[17] In the United States, power prices fell dramatically, sending many merchant plants into default. For example, plants owned by NRG Energy and Entergy Corporation defaulted and were seized by their creditors. By one estimate, at least $30 billion of power plants defaulted in 2002.[18] Market risk affected the telecoms sector as well. Flag Telecomm Holdings Ltd. and Global Crossing Ltd. filed for bankruptcy protection in 2002. In total, over 60 telecom companies filed for bankruptcy in the last two years as overcapacity led to price wars, and customer volumes failed to live up to wildly optimistic projections.[19] Similarly, in the infrastructure sector, sponsors appear to have had unrealistic expectations of customer volume for toll projects. Recently, S&P published a study revealing nearly 90% of toll projects overestimate traffic volumes—an indication toll projects may be highly vulnerable to market risk.[20]

Set against this unflattering backdrop, analysis of future trends can be divided in two parts: the nature of project assets and the financing of project assets. A practical starting point in assessing what types of assets will attract interest in the future is to look at the power sector—the sector that helped fuel the growth in project finance over the last five years. Despite the recent downturn, the long-term need for new power plants in both developed and developing countries is clear. According to one estimate, the United States needs to build between 1,300 and 1,900 new generating plants in order to meet projected demand over the next two decades and to avoid crises like what occurred in California.[21] Infrastructure, as a whole, remains an area of opportunity, especially in developing nations. In the short term, however, investors are likely to favor projects in developed countries. While the geographic location may narrow in the short term, one thing we have learned over the past few years is that the project finance model can be applied to a very broad range of assets.

As far as financing is concerned, sponsors are likely to revert to more structured deals, as they did in the early 1990s, as a way to shift market risk from project companies back to the buyers of the project's output. More extensive contracting will partially address the problem of having inappropriate parties bear project risks. In lieu of purchase contracts, sponsors may utilize various hybrid structures to mitigate market risks. Hybrid structures are better suited for certain types of assets, solve some of the disadvantages of using project finance (i.e., they help reduce transaction costs), and have the potential to expand the boundaries of project finance into new asset classes. Examples of hybrid structures include project holding companies and revolving construction facilities for power plants. Rather than financing single merchant power plants, firms like

---

[17] According to Worenklein (2003), the equity market capitalization of leading power companies (AES, Williams, El Paso, Calpine, Dynegy, Mirant, Aquila, and Reliant) fell from $145 billion to $11 billion in less than two years. The debt ratings on 10 of the leading companies fell from an average of BBB+ in 2001 to B− in 2003.

[18] Jeffery Ryser, "Bad to Worse: Defaults, Bankruptcies Seen Further Crippling Trading Market," *Power Markets Week*, November 18, 2002.

[19] Dennis Berman, "Innovation Outpaced the Marketplace," *The Wall Street Journal*, September 26, 2002, p. B1.

[20] Robert Bain, and Michael Wilkins, "Road Risk," *ProjectFinance* Transport Report, September 2002. Flyvbjerg, Bruzelius, and Rothengatter (2003) analyze the performance of large transport infrastructure projects (toll roads, bridges, railroads, etc.) and conclude that, "over-optimistic forecasts of viability are the rule for major investments rather than the exception."

[21] Report of the National Energy Policy Development Group, U.S. National Energy Policy (May 2001), p. 11.

Calpine have financed portfolios of merchant plants.[22] Because lenders do not have recourse to Calpine itself, the structure has an element of project finance. Yet because there is more than one asset in the portfolio, the structure also resembles corporate finance. A second example is the 1.4 billion Energias Eolicas Europeas project, which included 31 separate wind farms in a single transaction (this deal closed in 2001). These structures not only diversify project risk, but they also reduce the time it takes to structure a deal, increase flexibility, and reduce up-front financing costs.

Public private partnerships (PPPs) are another example of a hybrid structure that is becoming more common. PPPs use private capital and private companies to construct and then operate project assets, such as roads, prisons, and schools, which historically have been financed with public resources and operated on a not-for-profit basis. Through PPP structures, governments shift construction and operating risks to the private sector, which is usually more efficient in building and then running the assets. However, governments assume the market risk (e.g., in the case of a toll road, the risk associated with traffic volume revenue). A government or municipality is better suited than a private company to bear many large, long-term risks. As PPPs are used in the future, the role of the government and the private sector in developing and operating project assets for public use will continue to be defined.

Projects that are being financed in nontraditional sectors (i.e., outside of the power industry) or in emerging markets are utilizing greater support from IFIs and other forms of insurance. Investors are looking for new ways to mitigate sovereign risk and manage exposure to macroeconomic risks, in part because the protection afforded by multilateral agency participation is weaker than sponsors once believed. Instead, sponsors are using political risk insurance (PRI) to cover currency devaluation, expropriation, and breach of contract.[23] As one might expect, pricing for PRI is increasing as demand is beginning to outstrip the available supply. In addition, standard business interruption and other forms of commercial insurance are becoming more expensive as well. In particular, insurers have dramatically increased the price for terrorism coverage after the tragic events of September 11. Since then, insurance companies have demanded separate coverage for terrorist events, which previously was included in the general property and casualty insurance. This additional cost has made it more difficult to finance many kinds of projects as well as refinance existing projects. Another particularly troublesome risk has been currency or foreign exchange risk; this risk is especially problematic in developing countries and with "retail" projects (i.e., those projects with individuals as the customer such as toll roads, power, water). Increasingly, projects will use local currency financing and guarantees against currency devaluation. A relatively new innovation is currency devaluation insurance. In 2001, the Overseas Private Investment Corporation (OPIC) and Bank of America introduced a new form of protection against currency devaluation. Used in the $300 million bond financing for AES Tiete, a Brazilian hydropower project, currency devaluation insurance along with PRI helped to make the financing the first investment grade power deal in a noninvestment-grade country.[24]

---

[22] For more information, see "Calpine Corporation: The Evolution from Project to Corporate Finance," (Chapter 6 in this book).

[23] Kenneth Hansen, "Spotlight on Political Risk Insurance," *Infrastructure Journal* (January 2002).

[24] Hal Davis, "Down, but far from out: while there are plenty of brakes on the Latin American project finance market, ground-breaking deals are still coming out of the region with bankers offering creative solutions for a tougher credit market," *Latin Finance*, December 1, 2001, p. 40.

For their part, banks are looking for ways to minimize their exposures as well. For example, banks are developing capital market capabilities to securitize project loans, thereby creating a new asset class for institutional investors. CSFB started this trend when it securitized the first portfolio of project loans in 1998. Other banks have followed suit with similar collateralized debt obligation securities (CDOs). Some of the more recent deals have been open-ended funds (i.e., pools of money not yet earmarked for specific projects). For instance, CSFB launched a $5 billion Project Finance Program, and Chase launched a $3 billion Global Project Finance Fund in 2001. Sponsors benefit from securitization by gaining quicker access to funds, which improves execution, while banks benefit by increasing the velocity of lending and improving liquidity in the project loan market. Despite these benefits, there have been very few securitized transactions in recent years.

Another important influence on the prospects for project finance is the impact of bank regulation. The Basel Committee on Banking Supervision, established by the Bank for International Settlements (BIS) to create international banking standards, is developing new capital standards for banks. This accord, known as Basel II, is expected to be in place by 2006.[25] With regard to project finance, the regulators believe that project loans have higher default and loss rates than commercial loans and, therefore, deserve higher capital charges. As a result, most project loans will require additional capital which, in turn, may increase project loan rates. Chris Beale, Global Head of Project Finance at Citibank Salomon Smith Barney, said:

> The Basel II accord poses a major threat to the project finance industry. It has the potential to drive banks out of the business of project finance, and could dramatically curtail lending in both developed and emerging markets.[26]

What eventually happens will depend on bankers' ability to influence the process. In fact, early evidence from both S&P and several leading project lenders shows that "project loans perform better than corporate loans, especially when going down the credit spectrum."[27] Whether the bankers will be able to assemble credible evidence to support their point remains to be seen.

Project finance is, in a sense, going through its adolescent years, a period of adjustment after a period of rapid growth and experimentation. The difficulties in some industrial sectors and in certain geographic regions combined with the failure of several high-profile projects have been, if you will, evidence of the industry's growing pains. Sponsors, lenders, and other deal participants must now analyze and learn from what happened over the past few years. The logical conclusion is not that the concept of project finance is inherently flawed, but rather that we need to improve our understanding of how to use it. Like any new tool or concept, there is a natural tendency towards overuse in the early days. Invariably, the result is some kind of crisis or failure. Looking forward, investors need to learn more about which structures are most appropriate for which assets. Certain assets can bear merchant exposure, while others will require extensive contracting or will need to be financed as part of a portfolio of projects.

---

[25] For more information, see "Basel II: Assessing the Default and Loss Characteristics of Project Finance Loans," (Chapter 24 in this book).

[26] B.C. Esty and Aldo M. Sesia Jr., "Basel II: Assessing the Default and Loss Characteristics of Project Finance Loans," HBS Case No. 203-035 (Boston: Harvard Business School Publishing, 2002), p. 1.

[27] "React or Die," *Project Finance* (February 2002), p. 40.

Sponsors will recognize when to incorporate the public sector and when it will be optimal to go it alone. The end result will be a much more varied set of structures applied to an equally varied set of assets. This improved matching of structures and assets should lead to better operating and financial performance in the years ahead.

In conclusion, in the short term, investors will focus on safer locations, more traditional assets, and more structured deals. However, in the longer term, project finance will continue to expand into new regions and nontraditional assets because of the enormous need for global investment. Sponsors will continue to structure, and investors will continue to finance, large-scale projects such as the $3.7 billion Caspian oil pipeline, China's $2.5 billion Nanjing ethylene plant, and the £13 billion London underground PPP project. Given the trends in the global marketplace and the ever-growing demand for private capital to finance new infrastructure and services, project finance will continue to play an important role in both developed and developing markets.

REFERENCES

BRUNER, R., and H. LANGHOR, 1992, Project financing: an economic overview, Darden School Case no. 295-026-6, University of Virginia.

ESTY, BENJAMIN C., 2003, The economic motivations for using project finance, Harvard Business School mimeo, February.

FINNERTY, JOHN D., 1996, *Project Finance: Asset-Based Financial Engineering*, John Wiley & Sons, New York.

FLYVBJERG, B., N. BRUZELIUS, and W. ROTHENGATTER, 2003, *Megaprojects and Risk: An Anatomy of Ambition*, Cambridge University Press, Port Chester, NY.

HOFFMAN, SCOTT L., 1998, *The Law and Business of International Project Finance*, Kluwer Law International, London.

International Finance Corporation, 1998, The private sector financing activities of international financial institutions: 1991–1997, World Bank Group (Washington, DC). See also the 1998 Update.

NEVITT, P.K., and F.J. FABOZZI, 2000, *Project Financing*, 7th ed., Euromoney Books, London.

WORENKLEIN, J.J., 2003, The global crises in power and infrastructure: lessons learned and new directions, *The Journal of Structured and Project Finance* 9(1), 7–11.

PROJECT FINANCE PORTAL (WWW.HBS.EDU/PROJFINPORTAL/)

Project Finance Portal

RESEARCH, DATA, AND
INFORMATION SOURCES

This portal is intended to be a reference guide for students, researchers, and practitioners seeking to obtain information about project finance. In addition to bibliographical references for books, articles, and case studies, the site contains more than 900 links to related sites.

Research and Publications

Articles, Notes and Book Chapters
Books and Monographs
Case Studies and Notes
Courses
Rating Agency Information
Related Finance Books and Articles
Trade Magazines and Journals
Software
Legal and Regulatory Issues
Glossary of Terms

Project Finance Links

General Project Finance Sites
Project Finance Data
Rating Agency Information
Publications
Country Data
Emerging Markets Data
Development Banks
Export Credit Agencies (ECAs)
Law Firms
Private Finance Inititative (PFI/PPP)
Bankers and Advisors
Project Sites
Related Finance Sites

If you have any suggestions for additional content,
please contact Professor Benjamin C. Esty.
Last updated March 20, 2003.

HBS Home   Search   Index   Faculty

3

Why Study Large Projects?

Project finance involves the creation of a legally independent project company financed with nonrecourse debt for the purpose of investing in an industrial asset.[1] The most common applications of project finance are in the natural resource (mines, pipelines, and oil fields) and infrastructure (toll roads, bridges, telecommunications systems, and power plants) sectors. This book focuses primarily on *large* investments, where large is defined in terms of absolute cost (typically greater than $500 million) and investment refers to capital assets (see Exhibit 3-1). Rather than emphasizing the strategic decisions such as which assets to invest in and why, the cases focus on the financing and structuring decisions involved with capital budgeting.

This note explains why large projects represent an interesting and managerially relevant subset of total capital investments and why they merit separate academic research and instruction. The short answer is that project companies are strategic research sites[2] for people interested in learning more about how structural attributes such as high leverage, separate legal incorporation, and concentrated equity ownership affect managerial incentives and asset values. Large project companies are attractive research sites because they provide a relatively clear window into the process by which managers make important financing and structuring decisions. Whereas many corporate decisions are made for reasons of expediency, the structuring decisions associated with large projects reflect conscious attempts to increase value or manage risk. The more practical reasons to study large projects are that they can generate significant financial, developmental, and social returns when they succeed. Yet many of the largest projects have encountered financial distress in one form or another (e.g., EuroTunnel, EuroDisney, Dabhol, Iridium, etc.). As a result, there may be significant opportunities to improve the way managers make major investment decisions, and then structure and finance them.

Professor Benjamin C. Esty prepared this note as the basis for class discussion.

[1] For more information about the history and use of project finance, see Esty (2002).

[2] R.K. Merton (1987) defines a "strategic research site" as a setting, event, or object "that exhibits the phenomena to be explained or interpreted to such advantage and in such accessible form that it enables the fruitful investigation of previously stubborn problems and the discovery of new problems for further inquiry."

EXHIBIT 3-1

PROJECTS ANALYZED IN THIS BOOK

Project	Type	Location	Amount (in millions)	Case Number[a]
A2 Motorway	Toll road	Poland	$ 900	202-030
Airbus A3XX (A380)	Super jumbo jet	Europe/France	$13,000	201-028
Antamina	Copper mine	Peru	$2,300	297-054
Australia-Japan Cable	Undersea cable	Australia-Japan	$ 520	203-029
Bulong	Nickel mine	Australia	$ 200	203-027
Calpine Credit Facility	Power plants	United States	$ 1,000	201-098
Caspian Oil Fields (BP Amoco)	Oil field development	Azerbaijan	$10,000	201-054
Chad-Cameroon Pipeline	Oil field and pipeline	Chad/Cameroon	$ 4,000	202-010
Equate	Petrochemical plant	Kuwait	$ 2,000	200-012
Hong Kong Disneyland	Theme park and resort	Hong Kong	$ 1,800	201-072
Iridium	Telecommunications	Global	$ 6,000	200-039
Mobile Energy Services Co.	Power plant	United States	$ 400	203-061
Mozal	Aluminum smelter	Mozambique	$ 1,400	200-005
Nghe An Sugar Company	Sugar processing plant	Vietnam	$ 90	202-054
Petrozuata	Oil field development	Venezuela	$ 2,400	299-012
PPL Corporation	Power plants	United States	$ 1,000	202-045
Sutton Bridge (Enron)	Power plant	United Kingdom	$ 500	201-051
TX High Speed Rail	High-speed train	United States	$ 7,000	293-072

[a] All case studies are from Harvard Business School except Westmoreland Energy, which is from the University of Virginia (Darden Graduate School of Business Administration).

Source: Casewriter.

In addition to describing the reasons for studying large projects, this note presents empirical data on the use of project finance. The data show that total project-financed investment is large (it reached $217 billion in 2001) and has, until a sharp decline in 2002, been growing rapidly (the compound annual growth rate from 1996 to 2001 was 18%). The data also show that approximately 10% to 15% of total capital investment is financed through project companies. While this fraction may seem low, it masks the importance of project finance as a financing tool for large capital investments. In the United States, firms financed more than half of their largest capital investments through project companies. Viewed in this light, the relative importance of project finance is much more pronounced. Moreover, in the years ahead, the use of project finance is likely to grow as globalization, deregulation, and privatization create new demands for capital investment.

WHY STUDY PROJECT FINANCE?

Modigliani and Miller (1958) show that corporate financing decisions do not affect firm value under certain conditions. Their "irrelevance" proposition, a cornerstone of modern finance and an important reason why each won a Nobel Prize (Modigliani in 1985 and Miller in 1990), is powerful because it highlights the factors that make financing decisions value relevant. One of the key assumptions underlying their irrelevance proposition is that financing and investment decisions are separable and independent. When this assumption holds, various financing decisions such as the firm's organizational, capital, and ownership structures do not affect firm value or investment decisions. Building on this theoretical foundation, much of the empirical research in corporate finance over the last 25 years has attempted to show that financing structures do, indeed, matter.

The primary reason to study project finance is because it provides an attractive setting in which to illustrate why structure matters. Project companies are attractive research subjects because they possess unique structural attributes. For example, project companies have highly leveraged capital structures (the average project company has a debt-to-total capitalization ratio of 70% compared to 35% for public companies) and concentrated equity ownership (the typical project has two or three shareholders compared to hundreds or thousands of shareholders in public companies). The cases in this book examine these and other structural attributes in great detail to understand why they exist and what benefits they provide. In fact, the central theme of this book is that "structure matters" because it affects investment decisions and subsequent cash flows available to capital providers.

A second reason why project companies make attractive research sites is that we can observe the determinants and impacts of various financing decisions in a cleaner and more transparent way than in corporate settings. Whereas the vagaries of history, past profitability, and previous strategic commitments limit the range of structural choices available to managers of existing companies, these factors have less impact on managers as they design new project companies. While it is true that project structures result from complex, multiparty negotiations, the final structures must be attractive to the sponsoring firms or else they would not proceed with the transactions. The fact that project companies are standalone entities is also beneficial from a research perspective because it means the structural details and the performance outcomes are more readily observable to outsiders. When structural decisions are made inside diversified corporations, both the decisions and the subsequent outcomes can become obscured by other corporate activities. For these reasons, project companies provide a new and, potentially, very powerful laboratory for research on financing decisions, structural attributes, and value creation.

One example of a unique structural attribute is leverage. The extensive use of leverage in project companies provides new insights about debt finance in the same way that the extensive use of equity in venture-backed organizations provides new insights about equity finance.[3] By studying companies in the tails of the leverage distribution, we can test the boundaries of existing capital-structure theories and see which ones do a better job of explaining extreme observations. In the case of project companies, leverage plays an important disciplinary role: it prevents managers from wasting or misallocating free cash flow and deters related parties, including host governments, from trying

---

[3] See, for example, the research done by Sahlman (1990), Gompers and Lerner (1999), or Kaplan and Strömberg (2003) on venture-backed firms.

to appropriate it.[4] Because leverage mitigates these costly incentive conflicts, it increases expected cash flows available to capital providers, thereby establishing a link between project structure and project value. As it turns out, it is difficult and often undesirable or impossible for companies to replicate the structural attributes of project companies within a corporate setting.

Whereas leverage affects expected cash flows available to capital providers, other structural attributes affect the investment decisions made by managers. The ability to create a stand alone project company and finance it with nonrecourse debt reduces the probability that managers will forgo valuable investment opportunities.[5] For example, managers are particularly reluctant to invest in large, risky assets. By segregating risky assets in a project company, managers can prevent a failing project from dragging the firm into default. When the risk of a bad outcome is sufficiently high, a manager may choose to forgo even positive net present value (NPV) investments. Project finance allows the firm to isolate asset risk in a separate entity where it has limited ability to inflict collateral damage on the sponsoring firm. This example shows how organizational structure—the choice between project finance (financing assets separately) and corporate finance (financing assets jointly)—affects firm value by helping firms avoid the opportunity cost of underinvestment in positive NPV projects.

In summary, this book focuses on project companies because they have the potential to shed new light on existing theories of capital structure, corporate governance, and risk management. At the same time, analysis of project companies can illustrate in a very clear way how financing structures affect managerial decisions and asset values.

WHY STUDY *LARGE* PROJECTS?

Within the broader context of project companies, this book focuses on large projects—those costing $500 million or more. While there has been some academic research on project finance and some on large capital investments, relatively little research has been done on the joint subset of *large* projects.[6] The research on project finance does not differentiate between large and small projects—Box 1 vs. Box 3 in Figure 3-A. At the same time, the research on large capital investments does not differentiate between project and corporate finance—Boxes 1 and 2. In contrast, LSI focuses on how managers structure and finance *large* projects—Box 1.

This book focuses on the subset of large projects for academic, managerial, and pedagogical reasons. As before, the academic reasons relate to the ability to conduct research in a productive and illustrative environment. From a research perspective, large projects are more attractive than small projects because they allow us to observe

---

[4] The capital structures observed in project companies support agency-based theories of capital structure in the presence of incomplete contracts (Jensen and Meckling, 1976; Jensen, 1986; Stulz, 1990; and Hart, 1995). In essence, forced cash distributions help ensure that parties fulfill their contractual obligations.

[5] See Stulz (1984) on the role of managerial risk aversion and its effect on investment decisions. More importantly, project finance also reduces the opportunity cost of leverage-induced underinvestment. Myers (1977) refers to the inability or unwillingness of managers in highly leveraged firms to make positive NPV investments as the "debt overhang" problem.

[6] Finnerty (1996) and Fabozzi and Nevitt (2000) study project finance without regard to project size. In contrast, Fox (1984), Merrow et al. (1988), and Miller and Lessard (2000) study large investments without emphasizing their financing structures.

Type of Financing

	Project Finance	Corporate Finance
Large	Box 1	Box 2
Small	Box 3	Box 4

Investment Size

Figure 3-A Distribution of Capital Expenditures by Investment Size and Type of Financing

managers as they make very conscious and deliberate decisions. When managers make large investment and financing decisions, they have the ability and the economic incentive to make careful, value-enhancing decisions. They have the ability because large projects require at least one and up to five years to structure; they have the incentive because significantly more money is at stake—both their personal wealth and their professional reputations are on the line as well as substantial amounts of capital from other investors.

Some of the most interesting managerial decisions reflect attempts to mitigate costly capital market imperfections. These imperfections—agency conflicts, asymmetric information, distress, and so on—impose "deadweight" financing costs on firms. Research on large projects necessarily means that small relative costs become large absolute costs, thereby increasing the probability of detecting their existence and observing managerial responses to them. For example, an agency conflict that causes a deadweight cost of 5% of asset value is worth only $1 million in a $20 million investment, but is worth $100 million in a $2 billion investment. Facing a $100 million loss in value, capital providers willingly undertake costly actions, such as using project finance and changing organizational form, to achieve a *net* reduction in total financing costs. The cases analyze when capital providers respond, what steps they take, and how much they are willing to spend to mitigate these costly imperfections. These expenditures provide a lower bound estimate of the magnitude of deadweight costs.

Of course, there are alternative ways to interpret managerial decisions—they can have no effect on value, or they can be manifestations of incentive conflicts between managers and capital providers (i.e., the decisions reflect value destroying actions). For the very largest projects, where powerful political agendas and numerous influential parties inevitably enter the decision-making calculus, the structural decisions may not reflect true value maximization. One of the very important constraints on managerial discretion in the investment process is the need to raise *external* funds, usually in the form of bank debt. Convincing debtholders that a particular investment and financing structure makes sense, particularly risk-averse bankers who supply the majority of the capital and bear downside risk without the benefit of upside payoffs, is not easy. For this reason, it seems reasonable to assume that the financing and investment decisions do, in fact, reflect careful and deliberate attempts to increase value.

At a more practical, managerial level, deciding to make a "mega" investment turns out to be a defining moment for most companies. It is, in Ghemawat's (1991) terminology, an act of "commitment" that can establish (or destroy) a trajectory of sustainable competitive advantage. A good example is Airbus Industrie's decision to develop a new super jumbo jet, the A380, at a cost of $13 billion.[7] For a company with $17 billion in sales when it decided to launch the plane, developing this plane represents a "bet-the-company" type of investment. History contains several examples of plane manufacturers that went bankrupt after failed product launches. This development effort will have major ramifications for both Airbus as a company and its senior management for many years to come.

Asset size has a particularly important effect on a manager's incentive and ability to finance new investments. With regard to incentives, asset size clearly affects a manager's willingness to bear risk. For example, when the amounts at stake are small, people typically exhibit risk-seeking behavior (e.g., they buy lottery tickets). Yet when the amounts at stake are large, they often exhibit risk-averse behavior (e.g., they buy car insurance) and, ultimately, they even reject positive NPV investments if the project is sufficiently risky. Thus, in contrast to the prescription taught in most introductory finance classes—accept all positive NPV investments—managers often reject large, risky investment opportunities, especially if they have the potential to bankrupt the firm. Size also affects a manager's ability to finance a particular investment. In the extreme, a manager trying to finance a large project in an emerging market will quickly encounter capital constraints. Local capital providers are likely to be small and have limited resources, while international capital providers may have limited interest and, in the extreme, be forbidden by internal credit policies from investing in specific countries.

Large projects not only affect key decision makers and the companies in which they work, but they also affect the communities and nations where they are located. When large projects succeed, they can dramatically improve the social and economic conditions in a given region. The Mozal project, notwithstanding Easterly's (2001) criticism of World Bank and International Finance Corporation (IFC) activities, is a wonderful example of how a mega project can change a country, in this case Mozambique, for the better.[8] The aluminum smelter cost $1.4 billion to build, a sum that was approximately equal to the country's gross domestic product (GDP) at the time. The success of the initial investment led to a follow-on investment of another $1 billion, as well as several other infrastructure and industrial investments. For a developing country like Mozambique, with a per capita GDP of less than $100 per year, large-scale investments can dramatically change the business climate and economic conditions for local citizens.

Unfortunately, the anecdotal and limited quantitative evidence that exists on the performance of large projects is not particularly favorable.[9] Industrial projects such as the EuroTunnel, EuroDisney, Enron's Dabhol power plant, Iridium, ICO Communications, Global Crossing (the Atlantic Crossing and Pacific Crossing cables), Globalstar, and Murrin Murrin (an Australian nickel mine) as well as real estate projects such as the Millennium Dome and Canary Wharf have all encountered financial distress or been restructured in recent years. Of course, this unscientific sample of large projects is not

---

[7] B.C. Esty, "Airbus A3XX: Developing the World's Largest Commercial Jet," Chapter 9 in this book.

[8] B.C. Esty, "Financing the Mozal Project," Chapter 19 in this book.

[9] According to Cassidy (2000), several post-Depression public works projects in the United States turned out to be "success stories." The Hoover Dam cost $151 million, took five years, and was completed in 1935 (vs. projections of $155 million and seven years) and the Golden Gate Bridge cost $35 million, took four years, and was completed in 1937 on budget. The Panama Canal, completed in 1914, also came in well under budget.

necessarily representative of the project finance market as a whole. The few empirical studies that have been done on the performance of large projects, however, corroborate the anecdotal evidence.

- Miller and Lessard (2000) studied 60 large engineering projects with an average size of $1 billion undertaken between 1980 and 2000. They found that almost 40% of the projects performed very badly and were either abandoned totally or restructured after experiencing some kind of financial crisis.
- Merrow et al. (1988) studied 47 "megaprojects" and found that only four of them came in on budget—the average cost overrun was 88%. Of the 36 projects that had sufficient data, 26 of them (72%) failed to achieve their profit objectives. Based on this analysis, they conclude that projects with a greater fraction of public ownership as well as larger, first-of-a-kind, and one-of-a-kind projects exhibit worse performance.
- Flyvbjerg, Bruzelius, and Rothengatter (2003) analyze the performance of large transport infrastructure projects (toll roads, bridges, railroads, etc.) and conclude that "over-optimistic forecasts of viability are the rule for major investments rather than the exception." Cost overruns of 50% to 100% and revenue shortfalls of 20% to 70% are common. In a related study of 258 large transportation projects worth $90 billion, Flyvbjerg et al. (2002) found that nine out of ten projects experienced cost overruns; actual costs were 28% over estimated costs (in real terms); and cost overruns have not decreased over time.

The general conclusion from these studies, although none of them analyzed project-financed investments specifically, is that large investments frequently fail to achieve their intended financial and operating objectives. Determining whether these findings are, in fact, valid for large project-financed investments will require additional research. It is important to note, however, that the results for large projects do not appear to reflect the performance of all project-financed investments. The most comprehensive study on the performance of project loans done to date was recently completed by four of the leading project finance banks and S&P Risk Solutions, a division of Standard & Poor's Corporation. Their analysis shows that project loans have lower default rates and higher recovery rates than corporate loans.[10] While more research and data are clearly needed, there is sufficient evidence to suggest that large projects may be a unique subgroup with different performance characteristics. Analysis of large projects, therefore, has the potential to not only generate new academic insight, but also improve current practice.

Finally, there are important pedagogical reasons for studying large projects. To make optimal investing, financing, and operating decisions, senior executives must possess functional expertise across a broad range of disciplines. In addition to the financing issues, managers must understand issues related to competitive strategy (should one enter the aluminum smelting industry?), business-government relations (how do you enlist sovereign support and reduce the probability of expropriation?), marketing/sales (how do you estimate demand for a new super jumbo airplane?), negotiations (how do you conduct and resolve multiparty negotiations?), ethics (should you fund projects in countries with oppressive political regimes?), and human resources management (how

---

[10] See B.C. Esty and A. Sesia, "Basel II: Assessing the Default and Loss Characteristics of Project Finance Loans," Chapter 24 in this book.

do you hire and organize 5,000 people in a developing country in only one year?). These cases invariably broach these and other topics, but they get less attention than the structuring and financing issues. Nevertheless, this range of issues forces readers to adopt a more integrated perspective and wrestle with the interconnectedness of managerial decision making. In essence, a course on project finance can be an ideal capstone class for an MBA program because it both sharpens finance skills and broadens perspective.

LARGE PROJECTS AS A SUBSET OF TOTAL CAPITAL INVESTMENT

Having described the reasons to study large projects, this section presents some empirical data on project-financed investment as a subset of total capital investment. This analysis proceeds in two parts: it first analyzes capital expenditures (the investment side of the equation) and then financing decisions (the financing side of the equation). The goal is to give readers a better sense of how important project finance is as a financing vehicle particularly for large capital investments.

Exhibit 3-2 shows the number of firms in the Standard & Poor's Compustat Global database (known as Global Vantage) and the total dollar value of capital expenditures made by these firms from 1996 to 2002.[11] Unfortunately, the coverage is incomplete prior to 1997; even after 1997, it still only covers the largest public companies in most countries. As a result, these figures represent a *lower* bound on total global capital expenditure. The 13,686 firms in the database as of 2001 recorded capital expenditures totaling $1.6 trillion. Of these firms, 554 invested more than $500 million in 2001 (4% of the total number of firms). Collectively, the 554 firms invested over $1.2 trillion, or 73.9% of the total amount invested by all firms in 2001.

Similarly, Exhibit 3-3 presents an analysis of capital expenditures, but by U.S. firms from 1991 to 2002. It excludes financial firms and foreign firms with traded American Depositor Receipts (ADRs). In 2001, 6,303 firms reported total capital expenditures of $619 billion.[12] Thus, capital expenditure by U.S. firms represents approximately 38% (= $619 billion/$1,644 billion) of total global capital expenditure. Like the global data, a small fraction of the firms (3.6%) accounted for more than 75% of the total amount invested in 2001.

Turning now from investment to financing, Exhibits 3-4a and 3-4b analyze the subset of project-financed investments. This analysis assumes that all capital expenditures are financed with either project finance or corporate finance of one form or another (e.g., corporate debt, equity, retained earnings, etc.). Exhibit 3-4a shows that total global project-financed investment was $135 billion in 2002, down from $217 billion in 2001 and $213 billion in 2000. The five-year compound average growth rate (CAGR) from 1997 to 2002 was 0%, compared to 18% from 1996 to 2001. Exhibit 3-4b shows that approximately 14% of total investment in 2002 was for projects located in the United States. As a basis of comparison, the total amount invested in U.S. projects in 2001,

[11] Standard & Poor's Global Vantage provides financial and market data on more than 13,000 international companies in more than 80 countries around the world. The Compustat database provides in-depth financial information on publicly traded companies in the United States and around the world. It contains data on more than 10,000 actively traded companies and 13,000 inactive U.S. companies (see www.compustat.com).

[12] According to the U.S. Census Bureau (January 2003), which tracks private firms as well as public companies, total capital expenditure in the United States in 2001 was $1,110 billion, well above the $619 billion Compustat number. Of this amount, $361.9 billion (32.6%) was for "structures," while the rest was for "equipment."

EXHIBIT 3-2

CAPITAL EXPENDITURES (CAPEX) BY FIRMS IN GLOBAL VANTAGE, 1996–2002

Year	All Firms Listed in Global Vantage		Global Vantage Firms with Capital Expenditures > $500 million in Current Year			
	Number of Firms	Total CapEx in billions	Number of Firms	Percent of Total	Total CapEx in billions	Percent of Total
1996	12,370	$ 944,302	383	3.1%	$ 597,436	63.3%
1997	14,196	1,160,142	487	3.4	730,456	63.0
1998	14,786	1,200,446	496	3.4	769,605	64.1
1999	14,901	1,353,345	528	3.5	889,048	65.7
2000	14,515	1,523,067	557	3.8	1,053,741	69.2
2001	13,686	1,644,625	554	4.0	1,214,743	73.9
2002[a]	3,586	612,915	202	5.6	487,725	79.6
5-year CAGR (1996 to 2001)	**11.7%**			**15.2%**		

[a] Partial-year results.

Source: Adapted from Global Vantage; casewriter analysis.

EXHIBIT 3-3

CAPITAL EXPENDITURES (CAPEX) BY U.S. FIRMS IN COMPUSTAT, 1991–2002[a]

Year	All Firms Listed in Compustat		Compustat Firms with Capital Expenditures > $500 million in Current Year			
	Number of Firms	Total CapEx in billions	Number of Firms	Percent of Total	Total CapEx in billions	Percent of Total
1991	5,728	$303,104	123	2.1%	$187,749	61.9%
1992	6,055	304,381	112	1.8	176,565	58.0
1993	6,376	317,729	128	2.0	183,019	57.6
1994	6,667	356,224	133	2.0	204,812	57.5
1995	7,389	408,281	156	2.1	241,228	59.1
1996	7,527	462,888	180	2.4	284,240	61.4
1997	7,340	517,779	196	2.7	331,073	63.9
1998	7,503	553,042	216	2.9	360,276	65.1
1999	7,452	592,862	219	2.9	410,408	69.2
2000	7,021	667,394	228	3.2	479,647	71.9
2001	6,303	619,150	226	3.6	464,710	75.1
2002[b]	2,679	300,481	114	4.3	229,371	76.3
5-year CAGR (1996 to 2001)	**6.0%**			**10.3%**		
10-year CAGR (1991 to 2001)	**7.4%**			**9.5%**		

[a] Excludes non-U.S. firms, financial firms, and firms with traded ADRs.

[b] Partial-year results.

Source: Adapted from Compustat; casewriter analysis.

EXHIBIT 3-4A

GLOBAL PROJECT-FINANCED INVESTMENT, 1994–2002

	Total Project-Financed Investment (US$ billions)									5-Year CAGR	
	1994	1995	1996	1997	1998	1999	2000	2001	2002	1996–2001	1997–2002
Bank loans	$13.68	$23.33	$42.83	$ 67.43	$ 56.65	$ 72.39	$110.89	$108.48	$ 62.20	20%	–2%
Bonds	3.99	3.79	4.79	7.50	9.79	19.97	20.81	25.00	13.80	39%	13%
Total project lending	17.67	27.12	47.62	74.93	66.44	92.36	131.70	133.48	76.00	23%	0%
Year-to-year change in lending		53%	76%	57%	–11%	39%	43%	1%	–43%		
MLA/BLA development agencies[a]	11.25	17.59	18.96	22.05	20.97	16.62	17.69	18.75	18.75	0%	–3%
Equity financing (estimate)[b]	12.39	19.16	28.54	41.56	37.46	46.70	64.02	65.24	40.61	18%	0%
Total private sector investment (including debt and equity)	**$41.31**	**$63.88**	**$95.12**	**$138.54**	**$124.87**	**$155.68**	**$213.40**	**$217.47**	**$135.36**	**18%**	**0%**

[a]Private sector investment made by bilateral development agencies (BLA), multilateral development agencies (MLA), export credit agencies (ECA), and export financing institutions. Adapted from "The Private Sector Financing Activities of International Financial Institutions: 1991–1997" and the 1998 and 2001 Updates (International Finance Corporation, Washington, DC). The numbers for 1994, 2001, and 2002 are casewriter estimates. Some of the reported total is for guarantees; we assume 75% of the total is for equity and debt investments.
[b] Assumes a total debt/total capitalization ratio of 70%.

Source: Adapted from *Project Finance International* (London: IFR Publishing), 3/2/95, 2/28/96, 1/29/97, 1/28/98, 1/27/99, 1/26/00, 1/24/01, 1/23/02, and 1/22/03).

EXHIBIT 3-4B

PROJECT-FINANCED INVESTMENT IN THE UNITED STATES, 1994–2002

					Project-Financed Investment in the United States (US$ billions)					5-Year CAGR	
	1994	1995	1996	1997	1998	1999	2000	2001	2002	1996–2001	1997–2002
Bank loans	n/a	$4.31	$5.71	$ 5.30	$ 9.63	$27.61	$33.57	$31.25	$ 9.81	40%	13%
Bonds	n/a	n/a	1.14	2.55	4.02	11.94	11.31	16.33	3.42	70%	6%
Equity financing (estimate)[a]	n/a	n/a	2.94	5.35	5.85	16.95	19.23	20.40	5.67	47%	1%
Total	**n/a**	**n/a**	**$9.79**	**$13.20**	**$19.50**	**$56.50**	**$64.11**	**$67.98**	**$18.90**	**47%**	**7%**
U.S. investment as a percent of total investment	n/a	n/a	10.3%	9.5%	16.0%	36.3%	30.0%	31.3%	14.0%		

[a] Assumes a total debt/total capitalization ratio of 70%.

Source: Adapted from *Project Finance International* (London: IFR Publishing), 3/2/95, 2/28/96, 1/29/97, 1/28/98, 1/27/99, 1/26/00, 1/24/01, 1/23/02, and 1/22/03).

EXHIBIT 3-5

SIZE DISTRIBUTION OF PROJECTS, 1997–2001
(INCLUDES TOTAL CAPITAL)

EXHIBIT 3-5A

SIZE DISTRIBUTION BY YEAR (NUMBER OF PROJECTS = 1,194)

Size (in millions)	1997	1998	1999	2000	2001	Total
≤ $50	6%	14%	12%	19%	13%	14%
$50 < X ≤ $100	12	11	13	15	13	13
$100 < X ≤ $500	44	48	51	46	47	47
$500 < X ≤ $1,000	21	15	12	11	15	14
> $1,000	16	11	12	9	12	12
Total	**100%**	**100%**	**100%**	**100%**	**100%**	**100%**

(Continued)

$68 billion, was approximately twice the amount raised in IPOs or invested by venture capital firms in 2001 but substantially less than the $354 billion and the $434 billion invested in asset-backed securities and corporate bonds, respectively.[13]

Combining the data on capital expenditures (Exhibit 3-2) with the data on project-financed investment (Exhibit 3-4a) shows that 13% of total global capital investment was financed on a project basis in 2001 (= $217 billion/$1,645 billion).[14] For the United States, project-financed investment accounted for 11% of the total investment in 2001 (= $68.0 billion/$619.2 billion). This percentage is understated because the amount of project-financed investment includes only projects located in the United States, whereas some fraction of the total capital expenditure by U.S. firms was invested abroad and, therefore, should be excluded from the total to give a fair U.S.-to-U.S. comparison. According to this analysis, firms finance approximately 10% to 15% of their total capital expenditures using project finance.

Moving from the industry level to the project level, Exhibits 3-5a, 3-5b, and 3-5c present the distributions of projects based on total cost. A subset of 1,194 projects, with a total cost of $601 billion, drawn from the Thompson Financial Securities Data Project Finance database,[15] reveals that 26% of the projects by number and 74% by value

---

[13] The total amount raised in IPOs in 2001 was $37.5 billion according to Thompson Financial Securities Data (TFSD); the total amount invested by venture capital firms was $36.4 billion according to VenturExpert. Both were down sharply in 2001 compared with 2000. The amounts invested in asset-backed securities and corporate bonds are also from TFSD.

[14] A fraction of the $217 billion of project-financed investment is not counted in the $1,645 billion of global capital investment because Compustat tracks only publicly traded firms and not all project sponsors (equity investors) are public companies. In addition, many sponsors hold (and control) less than 50% of the total project equity, which allows them to account for the transaction using the equity method of reporting. Under this method, an investment in a project company shows up as an equity investment rather than as a capital investment. As a result, the total amount of investment is understated.

[15] Thomson Financial Securities Data Project Finance database goes back to 1992 and covers more than 1,700 transactions (see www.tfsd.com). This sample includes projects that were financed over the past five years (1997 to 2001) and that provide full information about their capital structure (debt-to-total capitalization), size (total cost), and financing date.

EXHIBIT 3-5 *(Continued)*

SIZE DISTRIBUTION OF PROJECTS, 1997–2001
(INCLUDES TOTAL CAPITAL)

EXHIBIT 3-5B

SIZE DISTRIBUTION BY YEAR (VALUE OF PROJECTS = $601 BILLION)

Size (in millions)	1997	1998	1999	2000	2001	Total
≤ $50	0%	1%	1%	1%	1%	1%
$50 < X ≤ $100	1	2	2	3	2	2
$100 < X ≤ $500	15	27	28	25	27	24
$500 < X ≤ $1,000	23	25	18	17	23	21
> $1,000	60	46	51	55	47	53
Total	**100%**	**100%**	**100%**	**100%**	**100%**	**100%**

EXHIBIT 3-5C

DISTRIBUTION OF PROJECT SIZE BY NUMBER OF PROJECTS
(NUMBER OF OBSERVATIONS = 1,194)

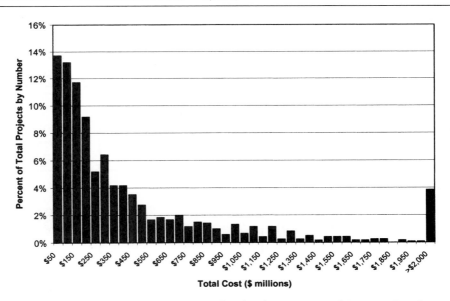

Source: Calculated from a subset of projects reported in the Thomson Financial Securities Data Project Finance database. The subset includes all projects that report capital structure (debt-to-total capitalization), size (total cost), and financing date.

cost $500 million or more (i.e., they are "large" projects). At the other end of the spectrum, only 14% of the projects by number and 1% by value cost less than $50 million. So while the number of large projects is relatively small (approximately 60 projects per year), the total investment in large projects is very large.

Using the data on U.S. capital expenditures contained in Exhibit 3-3, the data on project-financed investment contained in Exhibits 3-4b and 3-5b, and a few additional assumptions, it is possible to calculate the distribution of U.S. capital expenditures by size (large vs. small investments, where large is defined as costing $500 million or more and small defined as the remainder) and by type of financing (project finance vs. corporate finance)—see the matrix in Exhibit 3-6. According to the data in the matrix:

- Project-financed investment accounts for 11.0% of total U.S. capital investment (Boxes 1 and 3).
- Within the subset of project-financed investments, large projects account for 74.0% of the total investment (Box 1 vs. Box 3).
- Large investments account for 14.8% of total U.S. capital investment (Boxes 1 and 2).
- Within the subset of large investments, project-financed investments accounts for more than half (54.7%) of the total investment (Box 1 vs. Box 2).

In conclusion, this analysis highlights several important facts about project finance. First, the total value of project-financed investment is large and until recently, has been growing. More and more firms are discovering that project finance allows them to raise

---

EXHIBIT 3-6

DISTRIBUTION OF U.S. CAPITAL EXPENDITURE BY INVESTMENT SIZE AND TYPE OF FINANCING

Total US Capital Expenditure in 2001 = $619.2B

	Project Financed = $68.0B	Corporate Financed (not project financed) = $551.2B
Large Investments (≥$500m) = $91.9B	① $50.3B (8.1% of total)	② $41.6B* (6.7% of total)
Small Investments (<$500m) =$527.3B	③ $17.7B (2.9% of total)	④ $509.6B (82.3% of total)

Assumptions: Firms investing $500 million or more in CapEx account for 75.4% of total investment. Of this amount, 10% is for "large" investments.

Source: Casewriter.

funds that they could not otherwise raise on their own balance sheet through corporate finance, or could not raise as cheaply. Developing countries, too, are discovering that it is easier to raise funds through project companies than it is to finance projects using the national balance sheet. Second, the percentage of total capital investment financed on a project basis is relatively small, but it accounts for an important and growing subset of total capital investment. And finally, project finance is an especially important financing vehicle for the largest capital investments.

CONCLUSION

The question posed in the title of this note—why study large projects?—can best be answered by breaking it into two related questions: why study projects (project finance) and why study large projects. We study project finance because it illustrates important principles of corporate finance, it has the potential to extend and develop new financial theories, and it is an increasingly important financing vehicle used in practice. Just as securitization, leasing, and joint ventures are important financing tools, project finance is, too, and should be included in the financial manager's toolkit. The answer to the second question—why study large projects?—is because they provide a clean setting in which to analyze how managers make important structuring and financing decisions in response to capital market imperfections.

Studying large projects, however, can be difficult, which partially explains why there is not much academic research and only a few project finance courses in MBA programs today.[16] First, and foremost, there are relatively few large projects, they have long lives, and they have idiosyncratic features. As a result, statistical tests are weak and the lessons are not readily applicable across projects. Second, studying projects requires significant up-front investment to understand the institutional details. Moreover, obtaining data can be exceedingly difficult because most project companies are private. This combination of few observations, complex institutional details, and private information necessarily implies that the primary research methodology will be in depth and field based rather than broader and large sample statistical analysis.

Although large projects present a research challenge, the barriers to research have been falling in recent years. There is now a growing body of scholarly research on project finance, including numerous case studies and an increasing number of books. The LSI course collects, summarizes, and presents this research with the goal of improving the way managers make financing and investing decisions. After all, and unlike the Modigliani and Miller irrelevance proposition, financing and investment are *not* separable and independent activities. How you finance an asset directly affects whether it gets financed and how much it is worth. Because the concepts covered in the course have applications to the broader field of finance, it is appropriate for people interested in deepening their understanding of financial theory. Project finance, as it turns out, happens to be a particularly interesting and effective setting in which to study financial theories and analyze managerial decisions.

---

[16] In fact, only one article on project finance has been published in the four leading finance journals in the last 20 years and not more than 15 articles in all finance journals over the same period. Arguably, the four top journals are: *Journal of Financial Economics* (JFE), *Journal of Finance* (JF), *Review of Financial Studies* (RFS), and *Journal of Financial and Quantitative Analysis* (JFQA). Similarly, the coverage of project finance in corporate finance textbooks is very thin compared to other financing mechanisms such as IPOs, venture capital, and leasing.

REFERENCES

CASSIDY, T., 2000, Officials defend big dig as unique; reject parallels to historic projects, *The Boston Globe*, February 28, p. A1.

EASTERLY, WILLIAM, 2001, *The Elusive Quest for Growth: Economists' Adventures and Misadventures in the Tropics*, MIT Press, Cambridge, MA.

ESTY, B.C., 2002, An overview of project finance—2002 update, HBS Case No. 202-105, Harvard Business School Publishing, Boston.

FABOZZI, F. and P. NEVITT, 2000, *Project Financing*, 7th ed., Euromoney Publications, London.

FINNERTY, J.D., 1996, *Project Financing: Asset-Based Financial Engineering*, John Wiley & Sons, New York.

FLYVBJERG, B., N. BRUZELIUS, and W. ROTHENGATTER, 2003, *Megaprojects and Risk: An Anatomy of Ambition*, Cambridge University Press, Port Chester, NY.

FLYVBJERG, B., M.K. HOLM, and S.L. BUHL, 2002, Underestimating costs in public works projects: error or lie, *Journal of the American Planning Association* 68(3), 279–295.

FOX, J.R., 1984, The management of large, complex projects: a synthesis of observations from the literature, HBS Working Paper No. 1-784-004, 1984.

GOMPERS, P., and J. LERNER, 1999, *The Venture Capital Cycle*, MIT Press, Cambridge, MA.

GHEMAWAT, P., 1991, *Commitment: The Dynamic of Strategy*, Free Press, New York.

HART, O., 1995, Firms, contracts, and financial structure. Oxford University Press, Clarendon Lectures in Economics, Oxford, UK.

JENSEN, M.C., 1986, Agency costs of free cash flow, corporate finance, and takeovers. *American Economic Review* 76: 323–329.

JENSEN, M.C., and W.H. MECKLING, 1976, Theory of the firm: managerial behavior, agency costs, and ownership structure, *Journal of Financial Economics* 3: 305–360.

KAPLAN, S.N., and P. STRÖMBERG, 2003, Financial contracting theory meets the real world: An empirical analysis of venture capital contracts, forthcoming, *Review of Economic Studies*, February.

MERROW, E., L. MCDONNELL, and R. ARGÜDEN, March 1988, Understanding the outcomes of megaprojects: A quantitative analysis of very large civilian projects, The Rand Corporation Publication Series #R-3560-PSSP.

MERTON, R.K., 1987, Three fragments from a sociologist's notebooks, *Annual Review of Sociology* 12: 1–28.

MILLER, R. and D.R. LESSARD, 2000, *The Strategic Management of Large Engineering Projects*, MIT Press, Cambridge, MA.

MODIGLIANI, F., and M. MILLER, June 1958, The cost of capital, corporation finance and the theory of investment. *American Economic Review*, 53: 261–297.

MYERS, S.C., 1977, Determinants of corporate borrowing. *Journal of Financial Economics* 5: 147–175.

SAHLMAN, W.A., 1990, The structure and governance of venture-capital organizations. *Journal of Financial Economics* 27: 473–521.

SMITH, C.W., and R. STULZ, 1995, The determinants of firms' hedging policies, *Journal of Financial and Quantitative Analysis* 20: 391–405.

STULZ, R., 1984, Optimal hedging policies, *Journal of Financial and Quantitative Analysis* 19: 127–140.

STULZ, R., 1990, Managerial discretion and optimal financing policies, *Journal of Financial Economics* 26: 3–27.

U.S. Census Bureau, April 2002, U.S. Department of Commerce, Annual Capital Expenditures.

STRUCTURING PROJECTS

4

The Chad-Cameroon Petroleum Development and Pipeline Project (A)

On June 6, 2000, the Boards of Directors of the World Bank and International Finance Corporation (IFC) were scheduled to vote on whether to approve funding for the $4 billion Chad-Cameroon Petroleum Development and Pipeline Project. The project presented a unique opportunity to stimulate economic development in Chad, one of the poorest countries on earth, yet it entailed substantial environmental and social risks. Compounding these risks was an unstable political structure: Chad had been in various states of civil war since gaining its independence in 1960 and was currently run by a president who had a history of oppressing people and violating human rights.

Although heated debate surrounded this project, the most contentious issue was how Chad would use its share of project cash flows. According to the projections, Chad would receive up to $125 million per year from the project, an amount that would increase government revenues by more than 50%. Critics argued that the revenues could be used to fund further oppression. To address this concern, the World Bank Group had proposed an innovative revenue management plan that would isolate Chad's share of project revenues and target them for poverty reduction programs. Whether this plan would work and what would happen if it did not were two questions that the directors had to resolve before they could approve the deal. Yet the alternative, rejecting the proposal, seemed to run against the Bank's mission of alleviating poverty around the world, especially given Chad's impoverished condition and limited opportunities for development.

Research Associate Carrie Ferman prepared this case under the supervision of Professor Benjamin C. Esty. This case was developed from published sources. HBS cases are developed solely as the basis for class discussion. Cases are not intended to serve as endorsements, sources of primary data, or illustrations of effective or ineffective management.

THE PROJECT

A consortium of oil companies, including Conoco, Chevron, Exxon, and Royal Dutch/ Shell, discovered oil in Chad in the early 1970s but suspended development of the fields in 1979 due to increasing civil unrest. Frustrated by the situation, Conoco withdrew and Chevron sold its stake to Elf Aquitaine. Almost 15 years later, a reorganized consortium began conducting economic and environmental feasibility studies for an oil-field development project in Chad connected to the coast via a pipeline through Cameroon (see Exhibit 4-1). After the studies yielded positive results, the consortium signed memoranda of understanding (MOU) with the two countries' governments in February 1996.

In November 1999, Shell and Elf unexpectedly dropped out of the consortium citing concerns over project economics (oil was at $10.00 per barrel); analysts also cited friction with ExxonMobil.[1] Six months later, Petroleum Nasional Berhad (Petronas) and Chevron joined the consortium with 35% and 25% stakes, respectively. ExxonMobil remained the leading shareholder with 40%.

With total revenues of $185 billion, a AAA debt rating, and operations in more than 100 countries, ExxonMobil was one of the "super majors" in the oil industry. (Exhibit 4-2a and 4-2b show summarized financial statements.) Like other large oil companies, ExxonMobil operated four major divisions: (1) Upstream Operations explored for and produced both crude oil and natural gases; (2) Downstream Operations transported and sold these products; (3) Chemicals manufactured and marketed petrochemicals; and (4) Coal, Minerals & Power did mining and power generation. Despite the range of activities, ExxonMobil was known for its strength in Upstream Operations, which accounted for three-fourths of its earnings. With 58 major exploration projects under way in 1999, the company had one of the strongest upstream portfolios in the industry.

In all of its businesses, ExxonMobil made environmental responsibility a priority:

> A core value of ExxonMobil is to conduct its operations safely and in an environmentally sound manner. ExxonMobil's policy is to conduct its business in a manner that is compatible with the balanced environmental and economic needs of the communities in which we operate. We are committed to continuous efforts to improve environmental performance throughout our operations.[2]

The company, however, had a tainted environmental record largely due to the *Exxon Valdez* oil spill in 1989. The single-hulled tanker hit a reef spilling 11 million gallons of oil along the pristine Alaskan coastline. Following the spill, ExxonMobil paid $1 billion in damages, began using double-hulled tankers for most of its fleet, and significantly enhanced its environment control systems to the point where many viewed it as an industry leader in setting and enforcing environmental standards. Nevertheless, critics pointed to a recent speech by Chairman Lee Raymond to the World Petroleum Congress as a reason for concern. While arguing for a sensible tradeoff between environmental protection and economic development, he warned developing countries to avoid excessive environmental controls that could discourage foreign investment and hinder development.[3]

---

[1] P. Rosenblum, "Pipeline Politics in Chad," *Current History* (May 2000): 199.

[2] See the ExxonMobil Corporation Summary Annual Report 1999.

[3] I. Johnson, "Exxon Urges Developing Nations to Shun Environmental Curbs Hindering Growth," *The Wall Street Journal*, October 14, 1997, p. A17.

EXHIBIT 4-1

CHAD-CAMEROON PETROLEUM DEVELOPMENT AND PIPELINE PROJECT

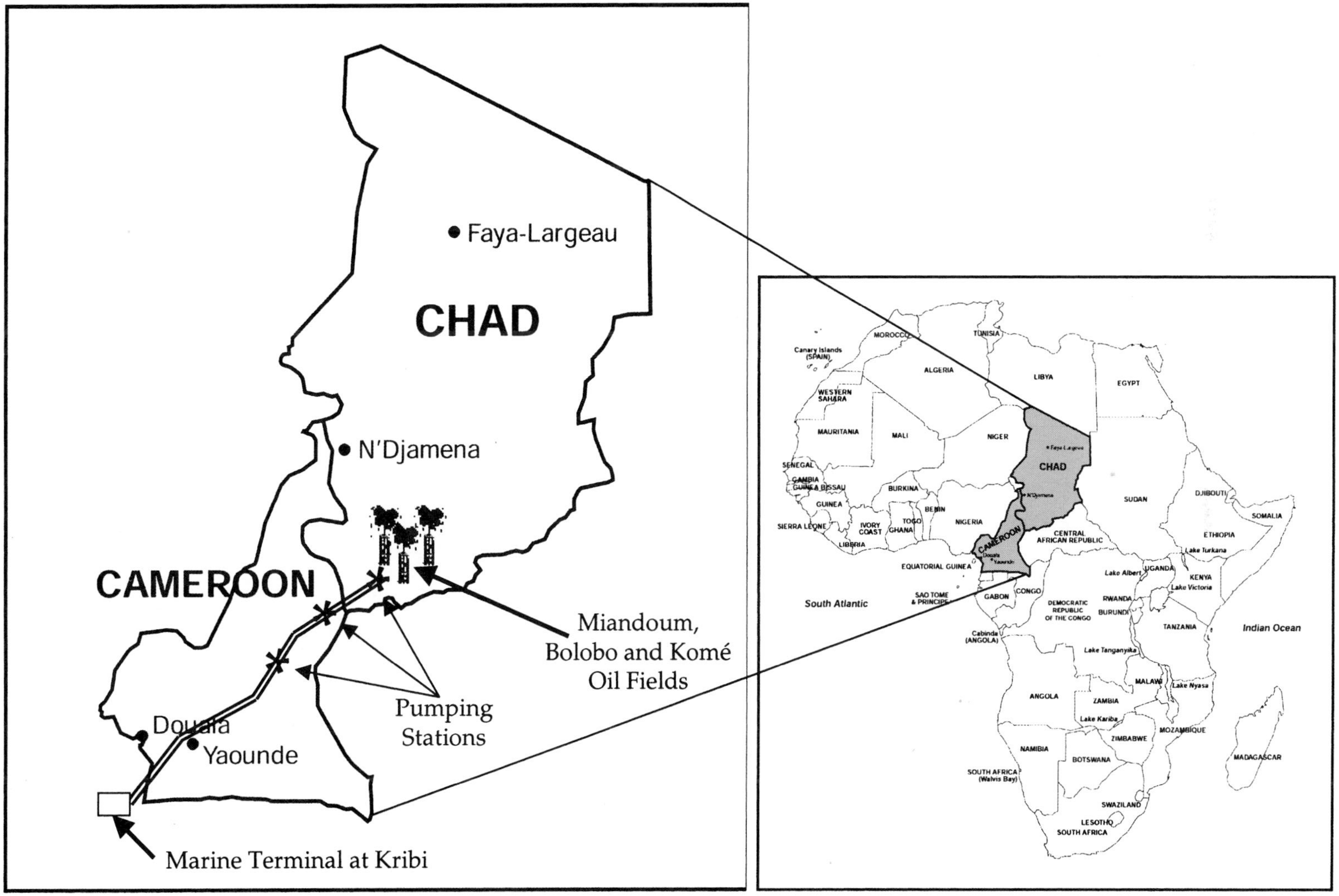

Source: Casewriter.

EXHIBIT 4-2A

SUMMARIZED INCOME STATEMENTS FOR PROJECT SPONSORS ($US IN MILLIONS)

	ExxonMobil[a]	Chevron[a]	Petronas[b]
Revenues	$185,527	$36,586	$15,955
Costs and other deductions	165,678	29,600	9,207
Depreciation, deletion, and amortization	8,304	2,866	937
Interest and debt expenses	695	472	657
Total costs	174,377	32,938	10,801
Income before income taxes	11,150	3,648	5,154
Incomes taxes	3,240	1,578	1,837
Net income	**7,910**	**2,070**	**3,317**

EXHIBIT 4-2B

SUMMARIZED BALANCE SHEETS FOR PROJECT SPONSORS ($US IN MILLIONS)

	ExxonMobil[a]	Chevron[a]	Petronas[b]
Assets			
Current assets	$ 31,141	$ 8,297	$13,379
Fixed assets less depreciation and depletion	94,043	25,317	15,988
Other assets	19,337	7,054	2,621
Total assets	**144,521**	**40,668**	**31,994**
Liabilities			
Current liabilities	28,163	5,455	8,377
Total debt	18,972	8,608	10,455
Other liabilities	33,920	8,856	2,567
Total liabilities	81,055	22,919	21,399
Shareholders' equity	63,466	17,749	10,595
Total liabilities and shareholders' equity	**144,521**	**40,668**	**31,994**
Number of employees	80,000	31,000	18,500
Numbers of common shares outstanding (mil.)	3,477	713	n/a
Stock price as of December 31, 1999	$80.56	$86.63	n/a
S&P Debt Rating	AAA	AA	BBB

[a] As of December 31, 1999.

[b] As of March 31, 2000, exchange rate US$1.00 = Malaysian Ringgit (RM) 3.80.

Source: Company Annual Reports.

Petronas, the second largest shareholder, was owned by the Malaysian government and was responsible for developing the country's oil and gas resources. Since its incorporation in 1974, Petronas had become a fully integrated oil and gas company engaged in upstream and downstream operations. At the time, the company operated 40 fields in 24 countries throughout Asia and Africa.

The third sponsor, U.S.-based Chevron, engaged in a broad range of energy-related activities. The company relied on its upstream business for current revenues and income as well as long-term growth. Chevron was especially active in Africa with projects in Nigeria, Angola, and the Republic of the Congo. The company also owned a 50% stake in Caltex, a downstream operator active in over 60 African, Asian, and Middle Eastern countries.

Project Description

The sponsors planned to develop the $3.7 billion project in two parts: a $1.5 billion Field System to extract oil from the Doba Basin in Chad, and a $2.2 billion Export System to transport oil to the coastal city of Kribi (see Exhibit 4-1). The Field System would consist of 300 wells in three fields, a treatment facility to upgrade the oil, and an operations center to support production. Geologic studies confirmed by independent consultants estimated that the fields contained total proven plus probable reserves of 917 million barrels and could produce up to 250,000 barrels per day using known technologies.[4] The Export System would consist of a 670-mile (1,070 km) pipeline buried 1 meter (3.3 feet) underground. It would contain a monitoring system to detect leaks and be connected to a floating storage and offloading vessel, a stationary, single-hulled tanker capable of holding two million barrels of oil. The sponsors agreed to buy all of the output at market prices in proportion to their ownership shares. Production would end by 2032, and the project would end.

According to the plan, an unincorporated joint venture known as the Upstream Consortium would own and finance the Field System. (Exhibit 4-3a contains a diagram of the corporate structure.) Tchad Oil Transportation Company (TOTCO), a special-purpose entity incorporated as a joint venture between the Upstream Consortium and the Chad government, would own the Chad portion of the pipeline. Cameroon Oil Transportation Company (COTCO), an incorporated joint venture between the Upstream Consortium and the Chad and Cameroon Governments, would own the Cameroon section of the pipeline. EssoChad, a wholly-owned subsidiary of ExxonMobil, would be responsible for project coordination and upstream operations.

Assuming construction began in 2000, and the contractors met the schedule approved by independent consultants, the project would be completed in 2004. During construction, the project would employ as many as 7,000 people; it would employ 500 to 800 people once operations began. Most of the skilled workers would be foreigners, but ExxonMobil hoped that 80% of the employees during operation would be local citizens with extensive training and other skills enhancement.[5]

[4] Based on geological and engineering data, *proved* reserves are expected to be recovered with reasonable certainty; *probable* reserves are more likely than not to be recovered (at least 50% probability); *possible* reserves are less likely to be recovered (at least 10% probability). These definitions are from the Society of Petroleum Engineers and World Petroleum Congress.

[5] N. Onishi, "The Perils of Plenty: A Special Report," *The New York Times*, May 16, 2001, p. 1.

EXHIBIT 4-3A

CORPORATE STRUCTURE

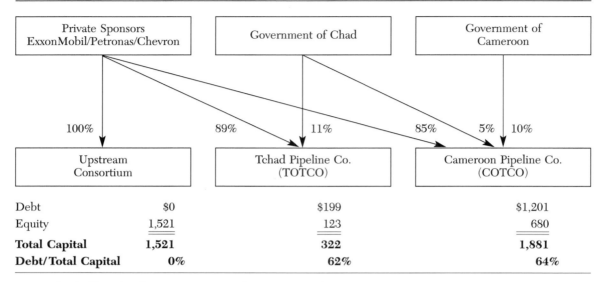

	Upstream Consortium	Tchad Pipeline Co. (TOTCO)	Cameroon Pipeline Co. (COTCO)
Debt	$0	$199	$1,201
Equity	1,521	123	680
Total Capital	**1,521**	**322**	**1,881**
Debt/Total Capital	**0%**	**62%**	**64%**

Source: The World Bank and IFC Project Appraisal Document, April 13, 2000.

EXHIBIT 4-3B

SOURCES AND USES OF CASH ($US IN MILLIONS)

Uses of Cash			Sources of Cash		
Field System			Debt:		
Chad	$1,521	40.8%	Capital markets bond	$ 400	10.7%
			IFC A—Loan	100	2.7
Export System			IFC B—Loan	300	8.1
Chad	229		Export credit agencies loans	600	16.1
Cameroon	1,338		**Total**	**1,400**	**37.6**
Subtotal	1,567	42.1			
			Equity:[a]		
Interest and finance costs	458	12.3	ExxonMobil	883	
			Petronas	772	
Debt service reserve fund	177	4.8	Chevron	551	
			Subtotal	2,206	59.2
Project Total	**3,723**	**100.0**	Chad Government		
			IBRD	33	
			EIB	15	
			Subtotal	47	1.3
			Cameroon Government		
			IBRD	44	
			EIB	27	
			Subtotal	70	1.9
			Total	**2,323**	**62.4**
			Project Total	**3,723**	**100.0**

[a] Portions of equity financing to be provided as subordinated loans and other forms of quasi-equity.

Source: The World Bank and IFC Project Appraisal Document, April 13, 2000, Annex 3.

Financial Projections[6]

The sponsors chose to use corporate finance for the Field System and project finance for the Export System. This structure facilitated equity participation by the host governments and issuance of limited-recourse debt by the pipeline companies (the sponsors would guarantee debt repayment through, but not after, completion). The Treasurer of Exxon Exploration Company explained the firm's policy:

> (We) most often borrow centrally. This has minimized borrowing costs by capitalizing on deep, efficient markets, and drawing on the cash flow support of our global operations . . . despite our predilection for funding most projects from central sources, we believe project finance can make a constructive contribution to managing risk of projects in a number of areas. . . . However, project finance is not a panacea. We need to assess whether the added costs entailed are worth the various risk mitigation steps achieved.[7]

The proposed structure included $2.3 billion of equity, of which $2.2 billion would come from the private sponsors (see Exhibit 4-3b). The International Bank for Reconstruction and Development (IBRD) and the European Investment Bank (EIB) had agreed to lend the host countries funds to finance their equity stakes. IBRD, a member of the World Bank Group, would lend $77 million, while the EIB, the financing institution of the European Union, would lend $42 million.

The $1.4 billion of project debt would come from three sources: the International Finance Corporation (IFC), two export credit agencies (ECAs), and the capital markets. IFC, also a member of the Bank Group, would make a $100 million "A loan" for its own account and up to a $300 million "B loan" for syndication to other institutions. The two ECAs, Coface from France and the US Export-Import Bank (US Exim), would arrange $600 million of bank financing. ECAs agreed to arrange financing in exchange for commitments to buy French and U.S. equipment for the project. Finally, COTCO and TOTCO would issue $400 million in bonds. When all the financing was in place, TOTCO and COTCO would have leverage ratios of 62% and 64%, respectively (see Exhibit 4-3a).

The base case financial projections assumed that the fields would produce 883 million barrels of salable crude oil out of the 917 million barrels of reserves. With an average price of more than $15 per barrel, total revenues would be $13.7 billion (see Exhibit 4-4a). Distributions to Chad, Cameroon, and the private sponsors would come in the form of royalties, taxes, and dividends (see Exhibit 4-4b). Because the majority of Chad's distributions would come in the form of royalties, its returns were closely tied to project revenues. In addition, it was scheduled to receive a $25 million payment from Chevron and Petronas at financial close, a payment for tax benefits received when they joined the consortium.[8] As a pipeline owner, Cameroon's returns would be a function

---

[6] "Project Appraisal Document on Proposed International Bank for Reconstruction and Development Loans in Amount of US$ 39.5 Million to the Republic of Chad And US$ 53.4 Million to the Republic of Cameroon and on Proposed International Finance Corporation Loans in Amount of US$ 100 Millions in A-Loans and Up To US$ 300 Million In B-Loans to the Tchad Oil Transportation Company, S.A. and Cameroon Oil Transportation Company, S.A. for a Petroleum Development and Pipeline Project" (hereafter referred to as: The World Bank/IFC Project Appraisal Document, April 13, 2000), The World Bank and International Finance Corporation, Report No: 19343 AFR, April 13, 2000, see Annexes 3 and 4.

[7] A.L. MacDonald, Treasurer, Exxon Exploration Company, "Challenges in the Financing of International Oil Operations," in *Managing International Political Risk*, ed. T.H. Morgan, (Malden, MA: Blackwell Publishers, 1998), pp. 121–123.

[8] "Work Starts on the $3.5B Chad Pipeline; Pres Causes Concern," Dow Jones International News, Dow Jones Newswires, 12/19/00. Officially, the payment was compensation for tax benefits received when they bought into the deal when Shell and Elf left the consortium.

EXHIBIT 4-4A

PROJECT FINANCING AND CASH FLOWS[a] (NOMINAL, $US IN MILLIONS)

	Financing						Project Cash Flow							
Year	Private Sponsors Equity	Chad Equity	Cameroon Equity	Total Debt	Total Debt & Equity[b]	Capital Invest.[b]	Volume (mm bbl)	Price Per Barrel	Total Rev.	Operating Costs	Other Uses of Cash[a]	Total Operating Cash Flow	Total Debt Service	Debt Service Coverage Ratio
2000	$ 24	$ 9	$13	$ 315	$ 361	$ 304	0	$ 0	$ 0	$ 0	$ 0	$ 0	$ 0	—
2001	298	6	10	312	626	736	0	0	0	0	0	0	0	—
2002	611	9	15	467	1,102	1,101	0	0	0	0	0	0	0	—
2003	559	8	14	283	864	864	0	0	0	0	0	0	0	—
2004	409	11	18	23	461	519	42	14.29	600	100	67	433	205	2.1×
2005	305	4	0	0	309	137	81	14.64	1,186	184	108	894	348	2.6
2006	0	0	0	0	0	16	81	14.78	1,197	174	16	1,007	337	3.0
2007	0	0	0	0	0	13	81	14.94	1,210	175	33	1,002	249	4.0
2008	0	0	0	0	0	13	81	15.05	1,219	182	13	1,024	191	5.4
2009	0	0	0	0	0	1	79	15.20	1,201	181	1	1,019	148	6.9
2010	0	0	0	0	0	1	65	15.28	993	166	1	826	106	7.8
2011	0	0	0	0	0	1	51	15.57	794	151	1	642	83	7.7
2012	0	0	0	0	0	1	39	15.59	608	137	1	470	66	7.1
2013	0	0	0	0	0	1	32	15.88	508	131	1	376	57	6.6
2014	0	0	0	0	0	1	28	16.07	450	125	1	324	46	7.0
2015	0	0	0	0	0	1	25	16.20	405	122	2	281	37	7.6
2016	0	0	0	0	0	1	23	15.87	365	120	1	244	29	8.4
2017	0	0	0	0	0	1	20	16.55	331	119	0	212	8	26.5
2018	0	0	0	0	0	1	19	16.11	306	150	2	154	0	—
2019	0	0	0	0	0	1	17	16.53	281	115	2	164	0	—
2020	0	0	0	0	0	1	15	16.93	254	113	2	139	0	—
2021	0	0	0	0	0	1	14	16.79	235	111	2	122	0	—
2022	0	0	0	0	0	1	13	17.08	222	109	2	111	0	—
2023	0	0	0	0	0	1	12	17.33	208	109	1	98	0	—
2024	0	0	0	0	0	1	11	17.45	192	106	2	84	0	—
2025	0	0	0	0	0	1	10	18.10	181	106	1	74	0	—
2026	0	0	0	0	0	1	9	17.33	156	101	1	54	0	—
2027	0	0	0	0	0	1	7	18.00	126	95	2	29	0	—
Total	**2,206**	**47**	**70**	**1,400**	**3,723**	**3,722**	**855**		**13,228**	**3,182**	**263**	**9,783**	**1,910**	
Stated Total (2000–2032)						3,737	883		13,721	3,183	n/a	9,857	1,909	

[a] These figures ignore some early oil cash flows from 2000 to 2004 and some final cash flows from 2028 to 2032. In addition, the World Bank released only summary data, which means some elements of cash flow are missing. As a result, certain annual cash flows may exhibit discrepancies, and the calculated total cash flows across all years may not match the stated totals in the exhibit or the case. The "Other Uses of Cash" column is an attempt to eliminate some of these discrepancies—it is based on casewriter estimates.

[b] Excludes $15 million of project preparation costs.

Source: The World Bank and IFC Project Appraisal Document, April 13, 2000, Annex 5; and casewriter estimates.

EXHIBIT 4-4B

PARTICIPANT REVENUE PROJECTIONS[a] (NOMINAL, $US IN MILLIONS)

Year	Cash Flow Available to Distribute	Chad Returns					Cameroon Returns				Private Sponsors Returns		
		Royalty	Upstream Tax	Pipeline Tax	Share of ROE[b]	Total	Transit Tax	Pipeline Tax	Share of ROE[b]	Total	Upstream Cash Flow	Share of ROE[b]	Total
2000	$ 0	$ 0	$ 0	$ 0	$ 0	$ 0	$ 0	$ 0	$ 0	$ 0	$ 0	$ 0	$ 0
2001	0	0	0	0	0	0	0	0	0	0	0	0	0
2002	0	0	0	0	0	0	0	0	0	0	0	0	0
2003	0	0	0	0	0	0	0	0	0	0	0	0	0
2004	405	22	0	1	8	31	17	0	12	29	19	166	185
2005	547	55	0	14	11	80	33	1	18	52	141	243	384
2006	670	70	0	8	10	88	33	0	16	49	369	218	587
2007	774	81	0	5	10	96	33	0	15	48	448	214	662
2008	833	89	0	2	10	100	33	0	15	48	498	209	707
2009	871	96	0	22	8	125	32	1	14	47	543	179	722
2010	720	78	0	26	6	110	27	11	12	50	425	149	574
2011	559	59	0	22	6	87	21	10	11	42	304	135	439
2012	404	41	0	19	5	65	16	8	10	34	189	121	310
2013	319	32	0	17	5	54	13	7	9	29	132	110	242
2014	277	39	70	9	1	119	12	3	3	18	113	32	145
2015	244	39	74	4	0	117	10	2	1	13	112	6	118
2016	215	36	66	4	0	106	9	1	1	11	101	6	107
2017	204	35	62	2	0	99	8	1	1	10	95	8	103
2018	154	28	43	2	0	72	8	1	0	9	66	7	73
2019	164	29	47	2	0	78	7	1	0	8	72	7	79
2020	139	26	39	1	0	66	6	1	0	7	60	6	66
2021	122	24	33	1	0	59	6	0	0	6	52	6	58
2022	111	22	30	1	0	53	5	0	0	5	46	6	52
2023	98	20	25	1	0	47	5	0	0	5	40	5	45
2024	84	18	22	1	0	41	4	0	0	4	33	5	38
2025	74	17	20	1	0	39	4	0	0	4	25	5	30
2026	54	14	16	1	0	31	4	0	0	4	15	4	19
2027	29	11	5	1	0	17	3	0	0	3	5	3	8
Total	**8,071**	**981**	**552**	**167**	**80**	**1,780**	**349**	**48**	**138**	**535**	**3,903**	**1,850**	**5,753**

[a] These figures ignore some early oil cash flows from 2000 to 2004 and some final cash flows from 2028 to 2032. In addition, the World Bank released only summary data, which means some elements of cash flow are missing. As a result, certain annual cash flows may exhibit discrepancies, and the calculated total cash flows across all years may not match the stated totals in the exhibit or the case. For example, the "Cash Flow Available to Distribute" column does not equal the sum of the total distributions to each of the three sponsors in every year.

[b] The share of dividend distributions received as an equity holder in COTCO and/or TOTCO.

Source: The World Bank and IFC Project Appraisal Document, April 13, 2000, Annex 5; and casewriter estimates.

EXHIBIT 4-5

PROJECTED RETURNS[a]

	Net Present Value (NPV)[b] (in $US millions)			Internal Rate of Return (IRR)		
	Chad	**Cameroon**	**Private Sponsors**	**Chad**	**Cameroon**	**Private Sponsors**
Reserves: 595 mm bbl						
Price = $12.00/bbl	$ 108	$ 92	$(917)	42%	34%	< 0%
Price = $15.25/bbl	205	104	(344)	60	35	< 0
Price = $18.50/bbl	330	101	235	75	35	13
Reserves: 917 mm bbl						
Price = $12.00/bbl	271	148	(98)	56	39	9
Price = $15.25/bbl	463	144	706	70	39	18
Price = $18.50/bbl	822	141	1,361	84	39	25
Reserves: 1,038 mm bbl						
Price = $12.00/bbl	337	162	198	60	41	12
Price = $15.25/bbl	603	158	1,045	75	40	21
Price = $18.50/bbl	1,170	156	1,614	90	40	27

[a] Project benefits are generated through the sale of the project's crude oil in international markets. Calculated returns may vary from stated returns because of early (2000–2004) and late (2028–2032) cash flows.

[b] Discounted at 10% to year-end 1999.

Source: The World Bank and IFC Project Appraisal Document, April 13, 2000, Annex 4.

of pipeline volume. Exhibit 4-5 provides a matrix of returns given various oil price and volume scenarios.

Sensitivity analysis revealed that project returns were driven by oil price and volume assumptions. The Bank's technical staff and independent consultants confirmed that actual reserves could vary from 595 million barrels of proven reserves to 1,038 million barrels of proven, probable, and possible reserves. Price assumptions were based on Brent Crude prices, which had ranged from $9 to $42 per barrel over the last 18 years, with an average price of $20 per barrel (see Exhibits 4-6a and 4-6b). Given the acidic, corrosive nature of Doba Basin oil, analysts expected it would sell at a discount of 10% to 20% below Brent Crude.[9] Even with the discount, the price was well above the project's finding and development costs of $5.20 per barrel.

Chad (Tchad)

Shortly after gaining independence from France in 1960, Chad erupted in a civil war, with rebel groups in the north fighting against the government in the south. Conflict raged through most of the 1960s and 1970s, and escalated through the 1980s. According to a government study, over 20,000 people were killed, and thousands more were tortured during this period.[10]

[9] The World Bank and IFC Project Appraisal Document, April 13, 2000, p. 27.
[10] P. Rosenblum, "Pipeline Politics in Chad," *Current History* (May 2000): 195.

EXHIBIT 4-6A

BRENT CRUDE PRICES FROM JUNE 1982–JUNE 2000 ($US PER BARREL)

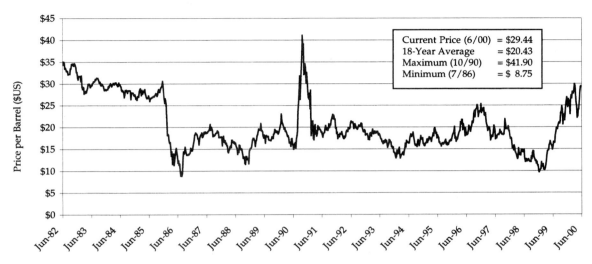

Current Price (6/00)	= $29.44
18-Year Average	= $20.43
Maximum (10/90)	= $41.90
Minimum (7/86)	= $ 8.75

Source: Adapted from Datastream data.

EXHIBIT 4-6B

CAPITAL MARKETS DATA AS OF JUNE 2000

Maturity	U.S. Treasury Yields	Brent Crude Futures Prices ($ per bbl)	Light Sweet Crude Futures Prices ($ per bbl)	Projected Prices for World Oil ($ per bbl)[a]
1 month	—	$29.19	$29.01	—
3 months	5.70%	26.34	27.89	—
6 months	6.24	25.26	26.47	—
1 year	6.30	22.91	24.21	$23.81
2 years	6.58	20.09	21.13	21.80
3 years	—	18.56	19.46	20.98
4 years	—	—	18.43	20.73
5 years	6.43	—	18.17	20.57
7 years	—	—	—	20.58
10 years	6.19	—	—	20.88
20 years	—	—	—	21.76
30 years	5.94	—	—	—

[a]Based on projections from the Energy Information Administration's *Annual Energy Outlook, 2001* (in constant 1999 $US). The world oil price is an annual average acquisition cost of imported crude oils to U.S. refiners.

Sources: Bloomberg and casewriter analysis.

General Idriss Déby, a French trained army officer and opposition leader, came to power in 1990 after staging a coup against the government. One political analyst described him this way:

> Chadian President Idriss Déby is a warlord . . . few credible analysts would argue that Déby is anything other than an African strongman, whose weapons purchases dwarf levels of social spending in one of the world's poorest countries, where incidents of political violence continue.[11]

As recently as 1998, Déby's troops had massacred 100 unarmed civilians and imprisoned Ngarléjy Yorongar, a member of Parliament and leading opposition figure, after he criticized the pipeline project.[12] That year, Amnesty International and the U.S. State Department criticized Déby's regime:

> State security forces continue to commit extrajudicial killings, and they torture, beat, abuse and rape persons. Prison conditions remain harsh and life threatening. Security forces continue to use arbitrary arrest and detention. Although the Government detains and imprisons . . . it rarely prosecutes.[13]

Many years of political instability severely hampered Chad's economic development. Since Déby seized power, output levels had declined, the government had consistently run budget deficits, and the external debt had more than doubled (see Exhibit 4-7). Whereas public aid and foreign investment came largely from international development institutions such as the World Bank and the International Monetary Fund (IMF), the war had significantly reduced overall investment.

As of 1999, Chad was one of the poorest and least developed nations in the world, and showed few signs of reversing its slow decline (see Exhibit 4-8). Approximately 80% of the 7 million citizens lived on less than $1.00 a day.[14] Except for oil, the landlocked country had few natural resources and lacked even rudimentary infrastructure needed for development: there were only 267 kilometers (166 miles) of paved roads in a country almost three times larger than France, no railways, poor tele-communications (two phones per 1,000 people), and irregular electricity supply.[15] In terms of living conditions, poor nutrition and unsafe water—less than 25% of the population had access to clean water—contributed to a life expectancy of 49 years and an infant mortality rate of 115 deaths per 1,000 births, compared to 78 years and 3 to 6 deaths per 1,000 births in developed countries.[16] In fact, more than 20% of children born in Chad died by age five. Based on these conditions and other similar statistics, the United Nations ranked Chad 167 out of 174 counties in terms of development.

---

[11] "The Chad/Cameroon Pipeline: A Question of Governance," *African Energy* 19/31 (October 1999).

[12] "Problem Project #2: Chad Cameroon Pipeline Project," Bank Information Center, October 2000, Bank Information Center Website: www.bicusa.org/africa/ppa_chad1.htm.

[13] "1999 Country Reports on Human Rights Practices: Chad," Bureau of Democracy, Human Rights, and Labor, U.S. Department of State, February 25, 2000, State Department Website: www.state.gov/www/global/human_rights/1999_hrp_report/chad.html.

[14] N. Onishi, "Pygmies Wonder If Oil Pipeline Will Ease Their Poverty," *The New York Times*, July 10, 2000, p. A3.

[15] Economist Intelligence Unit, Chad Country Profile 2000, pp. 72–74.

[16] "Environmental Assessment Executive Summary & Update," Chapter 2, Table: Socioeconomic Conditions in Chad, EssoChad Website: http://www.essochad.com/eaff/essochad/documentation/english/summary/index.html.

EXHIBIT 4-7

CHAD COUNTRY DATA, 1990–1999

	1990	1991	1992	1993	1994	1995	1996	1997	1998	1999
Government Finances										
Total revenue ($US, millions)[a]	$293	202	269	279	158	197	216	221	196	175
Total expenditures ($US, millions)	$379	352	509	360	306	289	407	333	306	266
Net revenues ($US, millions)	($87)	(150)	(241)	(81)	(148)	(91)	(191)	(112)	(110)	(91)
Budget balance (% of revenue)[b]	−29.6%	−74.1	−89.6	−29.0	−93.8	−46.2	−88.5	−51.0	−56.5	−52.3
External debt (current $US, millions)	$524	629	723	768	828	902	997	1,026	1,092	1,142
External debt/Gross Domestic Product	30.1%	33.5	38.4	52.5	70.2	62.7	62.1	68.0	64.9	74.6
Output										
Gross domestic product (current $US, millions)	$1,739	1,877	1,882	1,463	1,179	1,438	1,605	1,508	1,682	1,531
Gross national product/capita (constant 1995 $US)	$226	242	255	206	215	210	212	215	224	216
Interest and Monetary Rates										
Inflation (Consumer Price Index)	−0.17%	4.19	−3.14	−7.07	40.43	9.06	12.39	5.62	12.14	−6.80
Lending rate	18.50%	18.15	17.77	17.46	17.50	16.00	22.00	22.00	22.00	22.00
Deposit interest rate	7.50%	7.50	7.50	7.75	8.08	5.50	5.46	5.00	5.00	5.00
Exchange rate (CFAfr per $US)	272.26	282.11	264.69	283.16	555.20	499.15	511.55	583.67	589.95	615.70
Other										
Aid per capita (current $US)	$54.61	44.82	39.47	35.95	32.96	35.24	42.92	32.12	22.98	25.08
Current account balance (% of GDP)	−2.62%	−3.49	−4.55	−7.97	−3.20	−2.53	−4.69	−5.56	−5.99	−10.49
Foreign direct investment (% of GDP)	0.00%	0.21	0.11	1.04	2.30	0.90	1.12	0.99	0.95	0.98
Illiteracy rate (% of population 15 and over)	72.31%	71.04	69.72	68.33	66.92	65.39	63.89	62.29	60.62	59.00

[a] Chad currency is the CFA Franc, which has fixed parity with the French Franc: CFA100 = FFr 1.00.

[b] Does not include financial grants or other forms of assistance.

Sources: The World Bank's World Development Indicators 2001 and IMF International Financial Statistics.

EXHIBIT 4-8

AFRICAN DEVELOPMENT, MACROECONOMIC, AND POLITICAL RISK DATA (1999 UNLESS OTHERWISE NOTED)

Country	Population (000)	Life Expect. (years)	Access to Improved Water Sources (% of pop.)	United Nations Develop. Rank[a] 1998	Gross National Product ($ mil.)	GNP per Capita ($)	GNP per Capita Growth 1989-99 (%)	Total Debt (% of GDP)	Gov't Surplus or Deficit (% of GDP)	Euromoney Country Credit Rating[b] Sept. 1999	ICRG Composite Risk Rating[c] May 2000	Corruption Perception Rank[d]	Country Credit Rank[e] March 2000
Chad	**7,500**	**49**	**24%**	**167**	**$ 1,600**	**$ 200**	**−0.7%**	**74.6%**	**−10.6%**	**27.2**	**NA**	**NA**	**132**
Cameroon	**14,700**	**56**	**44**	**134**	**8,500**	**580**	**−2.5**	**83.6**	**−3.2**	**28.1**	**59.9**	**99**	**115**
Algeria	30,000	71	70	107	46,600	1,550	−0.9	58.6	−0.5	32.3	55.5	NA	91
Angola	12,400	46	32	160	27,000	220	−9.9	194.7	−13.1	24.4	45.5	NA	130
Benin	6,100	53	50	157	2,300	380	1.7	58.8	−2.3	29.7	NA	NA	118
Botswana	1,600	46	70	122	5,100	3,280	1.6	10.8	−2.6	51.1	83.0	24	39
Burkina Faso	11,000	44	—	172	2,600	230	0.9	54.9	−10.9	31.4	62.3	NA	107
Burundi	6,700	42	—	170	800	130	−4.5	157.6	−7.6	NA	NA	NA	136
Central African Rep.	3,500	44	—	166	1,000	290	−0.8	83.4	−8.7	25.6	NA	NA	NA
Congo Republic	2,900	48	—	139	1,900	670	−6.6	245.3	−8.1	25.0	48.8	NA	142
Dem. Rep. of Congo	49,800	49	—	152	—	—	−7.6	—	−7.4	20.0	44.8	NA	139
Cote d'Ivoire	14,700	46	72	154	10,600	720	1.5	132.2	−0.8	31.2	55.8	75	97
Gabon	1,200	53	67	123	3,800	3,090	−0.8	88.4	1.2	33.4	67.5	NA	102
Ghana	18,900	60	56	139	7,500	390	1.9	81.0	−6.0	38.8	57.5	63	82
Libya	5,400	70	90	72	—	—	—	—	—	16.1	68.5	NA	80
Malawi	10,800	42	45	163	2,000	180	1.2	131.4	−11.1	30.3	61.3	45	104
Mali	10,900	50	37	165	2,600	240	0.2	118.6	−8.1	31.9	65.8	NA	119
Niger	10,500	46	53	173	2,000	190	−1.3	80.1	−6.6	28.0	62.3	NA	125
Nigeria	123,900	53	39	151	38,400	310	0.4	92.8	−7.4	31.2	55.5	98	112
Sudan	29,000	55	50	143	9,400	330	—	218.3	−0.8	19.0	NA	NA	140
Togo	4,600	49	—	145	1,500	320	−0.8	89.3	−5.8	29.7	59.5	NA	117
Sub-Saharan Africa	2,417,000	49	—	—	—	500	—	—	—	—	—	—	—
World	6,000,000	66.5	78	—	—	5,130	—	—	—	—	—	—	—

[a] The United Nations Human Development Index (HDI) provides a rating of health, education, and income across 174 countries. The rank ranges from 1 (high) to 174 (low).

[b] Euromoney's country rating assess the risk of investing in an economy based on nine analytical, credit, and market indicators. The scores ranges from 0 (most risky) to 100 (least risky).

[c] The International Country Risk Guide (ICRG) provides a rating composed of 22 variables in three subcategories of risk: political (100 points), financial (50 points), and economic (50 points). The composite risk rating equals the sum of the individual ratings divided by two: 0.0 to 49.5 is very high risk; 80.0 to 100.0 is very low risk.

[d] Transparency International's Corruption Perception Index (CPI) score relates to perceptions of the degree of corruption as seen by businesspeople, risk analysts, and the general public. Transparency International ranks 99 countries from highly clean (1) to highly corrupt (99).

[e] Institutional Investor ranks 145 countries based on information provided by economists at global banks and securities firms. Higher numbers represent a greater chance of country default.

Sources: World Bank, United Nations, African Development Indicators, Transparency International, and Institutional Investor Online Edition.

Cameroon

Cameroon gained its independence from France in 1960. The country developed its oil resources and agricultural sector, but a severe drop in commodity prices in the mid-1980s threw the country into a decade-long recession. Gross domestic product (GDP) fell by more than 60% from 1986 to 1994.[17] The government, with support from IMF and the World Bank, implemented several reform programs in an effort to improve accelerate growth and alleviate poverty.[18] The economy responded favorably and grew at an average rate of 5% per year during mid- to late 1990s.[19]

Despite the improvement and favorable relative position vis-à-vis other African countries, Cameroon was still a very poor nation, ranking 134 out of 174 countries on the UN Development Index and 99 out of 99 countries in terms of corruption according to Transparency International, a nongovernmental organization (NGO). (See Exhibit 4-8.) In addition, activists criticized President Biya's administration for its human rights record. Amnesty International reported:

> Large numbers of people were extrajudicially executed in the north of the country. Torture and ill treatment by the security forces remained routine, and prison conditions amounted to cruel, inhuman and degrading treatment, resulting in high mortality rate. Critics of the government . . . were harassed, arrested and imprisoned. Thirty-six were convicted after an unfair trial before a military tribunal.[20]

WORLD BANK INVOLVEMENT

By any measure, Chad was one of the riskiest places on earth to invest. The sponsors had stated, and commercial bankers had concurred, that they would not invest without some kind of protection against political risk.[21] The sponsors considered including one or more multilateral development agencies as partners in the deal. The Treasurer of Exxon Exploration Company explained:

> Political risk associated with large-scale projects in the developing world is a reality that must be thoughtfully assessed and carefully addressed in project planning. . . . While the involvement of multilateral institutions and other lenders adds complexity, their presence can enhance country commitment and mitigate political risk.[22]

The World Bank was a logical choice to approach because it had extensive lending and policy experience with developing countries, and had been working in Chad and Cameroon for many years.

Founded in 1944, the World Bank Group's mission was to stimulate economic development and alleviate poverty in its 183 member countries. Under the leadership of President James D. Wolfensohn, the Bank was the largest source of development assistance in the world, providing more than $15 billion in loans to developing countries

---

[17] "Background Notes: Cameroon," U.S. Department of State, Bureau of African Affairs, December 1999, www.state.gov/www/background_notes/camerron_9912_bgn.html.

[18] The World Bank and IFC Project Appraisal Document, April 13, 2000, p. 8.

[19] IBRD/IDA Project Information Document, Project ID TDPA 534, April 4, 1995, p. 3.

[20] "Annual Report 2000: Cameroon," Amnesty International Website: www.web.amnesty.org/web/ar2000web.nsf/countries/c51a5e1ec565cc52802568f20055290f?OpenDocument.

[21] "Pipeline Closes Oversubscribed," *Project Finance International* 220, June 27, 2001, p. 45.

[22] MacDonald, "Challenges in the Financing of International Oil Operations," pp. 121–123.

in 1999 alone. With operations in more than 100 countries, the Bank invested in development projects and acted as the lender of last resort for countries with no other borrowing options. It carried out its operations through five distinct entities, each of which focused on a different aspect of development:

- **International Bank for Reconstruction and Development** (IBRD) provided market-based loans and development assistance to help governments in middle-income countries.
- **International Development Association** (IDA) provided subsidized loans, technical assistance, and policy advice to the poorest countries.
- **Multilateral Investment Guarantee Agency** (MIGA) provided investment guarantees.
- **International Center for Settlement of Investment Disputes** (ICSID) helped resolve investment disputes between foreign investors and host countries.
- **International Finance Corporation** (IFC) advised investors and was the largest source of debt and equity financing for private sector projects in developing countries. The IFC had a reputation for acting as an "honest broker" between the public and private sectors and for structuring fair deals.

Over the previous 25 years, the Bank had been involved with numerous projects around the world, including at least 10 major pipelines. Besides earning an average pretax financial return of 22%, more than 70% of the Bank's investments achieved their development objectives according to the Bank's Operation Evaluations Department.[23] However, projects in Africa and in the oil and gas sector experienced lower returns and greater problems than other projects in the Bank's portfolio.[24]

When the sponsors first approached the Bank about participating in the deal, senior management was immediately intrigued by the idea of a major development project in Chad. First, the project was commercially viable, and it would be the Bank's responsibility to ensure that the host countries received returns that were commensurate with the risks they would bear. Second, the project could help jump start Chad's listless economy. President James Wolfensohn wrote:

> We think that the project provides the best, and perhaps only opportunity for Chad to reduce the severe poverty of most of its population. . . . Chad's development prospects can only be improved significantly through the use of this traditional energy source. . . . We know this undertaking will involve significant risks. Translating Chad's oil revenues into services which will help the poor directly will be a difficult challenge—as it has been in many countries. But we believe it is a challenge which a development institution like the World Bank Group must take up.[25]

And third, the Bank could play an important role in protecting the environment as well as indigenous people. On its route to the coastline, the pipeline would cross 17 rivers

[23] The World Bank 2000 Annual Report, III. Evaluation of Operations, The World Bank Group Website: www.worldbank.org/html/extpb/annrep/operate.htm.

[24] Letter from K. Horta et al., Environmental Defense Fund, to James D. Wolfensohn, President, The World Bank, 1818 H Street, N.W., Washington, DC 20433, July 9, 1998. Environmental Defense Fund Website: www.environmentaldefensefund.org/prog . . . International/Africa/a_ChadCameroon.html.

[25] Letter from James D. Wolfensohn to Honorable James P. McGovern, United States House of Representatives, Washington, DC 20515, June 28, 1999.

and five habitat zones. These zones were home to rare plant life and endangered species. The forest regions were also home to more than 11,000 Bakola people, known as pygmies. As hunters and gatherers, and the region's oldest known inhabitants, the pygmies depended on the vegetation, land, and wildlife for survival.

While Bank participation had clear benefits, there were risks if it chose not to participate. For example, the sponsors might abandon the project and look to invest in safer countries. A World Bank economist recognized this possibility:

> Chad is not the only country with untapped petroleum reserves. Exploration is underway right across the continent to find new oil sources—which could prove cheaper and more accessible. If Chad does not seize this opportunity, it may well pass the country by.[26]

Another, and potentially worse, outcome might be if the Chadians developed the oil fields with other neighboring countries. The Sudanese government had recently financed a pipeline without the Bank and was using revenues to fund a civil war.[27] In addition, Libya's president Muammar Qaddafi had been urging President Déby to drop his deal with the Westerners and ship oil through Libya.[28] Although the U.S. State Department classified both Sudan and Libya as terrorist nations, they were, nevertheless, potentially feasible options for exporting oil.[29] Because much of the rebel opposition and fighting was based in northern Chad, these routes would entail considerable risk.

After weighing the opportunity against the alternatives, the Bank agreed to work with the sponsors in 1995. They began with an extensive consultation process that included meetings with both supporters and opponents. During this process, the Bank, sponsors, and host governments enlisted advice from 45 scientists and environmental engineers, hosted 145 meetings with 250 international NGOs, and held nearly 900 village meetings. An Esso-Chad spokesperson commented:

> The public consultation process for the Chad Export Project has been one of the most extensive consultation efforts ever undertaken in Africa for an industrial development project. Few similar projects in Europe or North America have held so many village-level public consultation meetings over such a wide area.[30]

The Bank insisted, and the governments and sponsors agreed, that the process should be conducted in an open and transparent way. Towards this end, they posted data collected from environmental surveys on the Web, placed project-related information in 17 reading rooms in and around affected areas, and distributed nearly 700 copies of the draft Environmental Assessment (EA). After five years of review and public debate, the sponsors published the final 3,000-page EA for comment. The 19-volume study contained contingency plans for almost every aspect of the project. There were plans for, among other things, waste management, oil spills, regional development, indigenous peoples, offsite environmental enhancement, community health,

---

[26] "World Bank Group Approves Support for the Chad-Cameroon Petroleum Development and Pipeline Project," World Bank, News Release No. 2000/AFR, p. 2.

[27] "Sudan: Oil and Gas Industry," Mbendi Information For Africa, Mbendi Website: www.mbendi.co.za.

[28] P. Rosenblum, "Pipeline Politics in Chad," *Current History* (May 2000): 199.

[29] Foreign Terrorist Organization Designation 1999 Annual Report, U.S. Department of State, Office of the Coordinator for Counterterrorism, www.state.gov/www/global/terrorism/1999report/sponsor.html.

[30] EssoChad Website: www.essochad.com/eaff/essochad/index.html.

compensation and resettlement, induced access management, decommissioning, cultural properties, environmental monitoring and management.

The analysis and contingency planning addressed three key topics—environmental impact, indigenous people, and long-term sustainability—and led to numerous changes to the sponsors' original plans. For example, after careful analysis using satellite imagery and aerial mapping, the sponsors changed the pipeline route in Cameroon to protect the natural habitat and human settlements in the Mbere Rift and Deng Deng forests. The sponsors also increased the benefits for indigenous people under the Compensation and Resettlement Plan. Following these and many other changes, a World Bank report concluded:

> although there is uncertainty in estimating incremental environment and social costs, most of these potential costs will be mitigated and/or compensated for by the Private Sponsors, and any remaining impacts are expected to be negligible in comparison to the large benefits that Chad and Cameroon stand to gain from the project.[31]

To address sustainability, the Bank established capacity-building programs in both Chad and Cameroon. Through these programs, the Bank hoped to develop the fiscal, legal, regulatory, and managerial infrastructure needed to develop the country's petroleum sector and minimize the project's adverse impact.[32] Concern regarding this last point generated the greatest opposition and led the Bank team to propose a Revenue Management Plan (RMP), something that had never been tried before.

REVENUE MANAGEMENT PLAN

Based on previous experience, the Bank had learned that a large influx of oil revenues could lead to economic distortion, corruption, and waste. With almost $14 billion in revenues and $8 billion in total distributions, the Bank feared Chad would be susceptible to these same problems. To prevent history from repeating itself, the Bank designed, with input from the Chadian government, a Revenue Management Plan. World Bank President Wolfensohn commented:

> Natural resource "booms" are difficult to manage. This is why our knowledge of other countries' experience has been crucial to designing the project. In Chad, in particular, we want to make certain that the country's new wealth will be invested for the well-being of all Chadians. With our help, the Chad Government has developed a revenue management program that targets oil revenues to key development sectors that are at the heart of its poverty alleviation strategy.[33]

According to projections, Chad would receive $1.8 billion of cash flow from the project in the form of income taxes, royalties, and dividends. Over the first 10 years of production (2004 to 2013), income taxes would represent 16% of total, while royalties and dividends would represent the remainder. Under the RPM, the government would have discretion over how to spend the income tax revenues as long as they were used

---

[31] The World Bank and IFC Project Appraisal Document, April 13, 2000, Annex 4, p. 76.

[32] "Project Appraisal Documentation on a Proposed Credit in the Amount of SRD 17.4 Million to the Republic of Chad for a Petroleum Sector Management Capacity-Building Project," The World Bank, Report No: 19342 CD, March 30, 2000, p. 5.

[33] Letter from James D. Wolfensohn to Honorable James P. McGovern, June 28, 1999.

for general development purposes. In contrast, the royalties and dividends would be deposited into a Special Petroleum Revenue Account and distributed in the following way: 10% would be deposited in foreign financial institutions and used to finance poverty reduction programs for future generations. Of the remaining 90%, 85% would be deposited in Chadian commercial banks and used to finance development programs in five high-priority sectors: education, health and social services, rural development, infrastructure, and environment and water resources.[34] The other 15% would go to the government budget and programs in the Doba region. The $25 million payment from Chevron and Petronas was not covered under the RMP.

Oversight and control of the RMP would occur at several levels. The World Bank and Chadian government would approve a detailed annual expenditure program that had to be reviewed by a newly formed oversight committee. The committee's nine members—seven from government and two from civil society (one from an NGO and one from a trade union)—would be appointed for terms of three to five years. Each year the committee would publish a review of operations that was subject to an external audit. The World Bank would monitor the full program and retained the right to review all expenditures. To ensure acceptance of the plan, the Bank made implementation of the RMP a contractual obligation under the proposed IBRD and EIB loans. As an added incentive, the Bank explicitly linked the government's performance under the RPM to future World Bank lending.[35]

In 1998, the Chadian government took the first step toward implementation by passing a law that supported key elements of the plan including provisions to establish the oversight committee and various auditing procedures.[36] To further demonstrate its commitment to economic reform and development, the government privatized 45 out of 50 state-owned enterprises, cut the size of the army in half, and reallocated public expenditures to increase development efforts.[37]

OPPOSITION

Right from the start, critics attacked the project on all fronts. An official from a Chadian environmental agency complained:

> There is not one example in Africa where oil has led to development. Look at Nigeria, Angola, the two Congos, and Gabon. They all have an overabundance of oil, and what do they have to show for it? We can even say that the exploitation of oil has retarded their development. What are the chances that things will be any different in Chad or Cameroon?[38]

A report from the Environmental Defense Fund criticized the World Bank for participating:

> The World Bank's involvement . . . sets a disturbing precedent of public support for oil development which experience and analysis show has detrimental social and environmental impacts with few development benefits. . . . The project as currently designed has little

[34] The World Bank and IFC Project Appraisal Document, April 13, 2000, Appendix 11, p. 96.
[35] Ibid., p. 98.
[36] Ibid.
[37] EssoChad Website: www.essochad.com/eaff/essochad/index.html.
[38] N. Onishi, "Pygmies Wonder If Oil Pipeline Will Ease Their Poverty," p. A3.

chance of delivering the claimed benefits to sustainable development while carrying major risks of irreparable environmental and social disruption.[39]

In particular, environmental groups such as Friends of the Earth, the Sierra Club, and the Rainforest Action Network pointed to deforestation and oil spills as serious risks. The potential for the greatest damage was in the Atlantic Littoral Forest zone in Cameroon where it would be necessary to clear land to make room for roads, storage depots, and worker housing, not to mention the pipeline itself. The decision to bury the pipeline only increased the chances of groundwater contamination and made it more difficult to repair damage. An environmentalist noted:

> Even with the latest state-of-the-art technology, oil leaks in pipelines can go undetected until a huge amount of damage has been done. The most sophisticated technology has a detection capacity of a leakage of 0.002% of the oil passing through. [T]his means that under the best of circumstances 2,000 gallons could leak a day without being detected.[40]

And when the oil reached the coast, it would threaten two national reserves containing endangered marine life and the Lob Waterfalls, one of the few waterfalls in the world that flowed directly into the ocean. An oil spill in this area could cause irreversible environmental damage.

Social activists, too, joined the chorus of criticism. They claimed the Indigenous Peoples Plan was incomplete because it did not create a specific agency to oversee social issues as required under Bank policy, nor did it establish on-going programs to address future social issues.[41] They also condemned the implementation strategy described in the Compensation and Resettlement Plan. According to one activist:

> there are numerous examples in Africa and throughout the world, where the Bank has not been able to implement this provision and where poor and vulnerable groups, which are the ones who usually have to be forcibly resettled, suffer greatly as a result of resettlement and are unable to re-establish their livelihoods.[42]

The most vehement opposition, however, centered on the Revenue Management Plan. While one study described it as "massively flawed,"[43] another from Harvard Law School said, "The law is vague in essential parts and lacks the detail necessary to ensure effective oversight. . . . As it is, the law can be seen at best as only a first, and clearly insufficient, step."[44]

Critics were particularly concerned about the allocation of funds. Whereas the RMP spelled out broad categories for expenditure, it did not give specific details regarding permissible expenditures by type and region. Funds directed to one region could be used entirely for infrastructure rather than addressing serious social or health prob-

---

[39] "The Chad Cameroon Oil and Pipeline Project: Putting People and the Environment at Risk," Environmental Defense Fund, U.S.A. (New York) September 1999, p. 3.

[40] K. Walsh, "World Bank Funding of Chad/Cameroon Oil Project," Environmental Defense Fund, March 17, 1997, www.hartford-hwp.com/archives/32/031.html.

[41] "Putting People and the Environment at Risk," pp. 11–12.

[42] Walsh, "World Bank Funding of Chad/Cameroon Oil Project."

[43] "Putting People and the Environment at Risk," p. 18.

[44] L. Lampriere et al., "Managing Oil Revenues in Chad: Legal Deficiencies and Institutional Weaknesses," Human Rights Clinical Program Harvard Law School, October 13, 1999, pp. 6–7.

lems.[45] An even greater concern was the fact that the government could change the revenue allocation every five years.

Luc Lampiere, a visiting fellow at Harvard Law School's Human Rights Program, and co-authors noted several problems with the local support needed to make the plan work:

> While the law itself represents a remarkable breakthrough in linking private investment, development, and human rights, it has little chance of succeeding without the will of the authorities or the confidence of the population. . . . According to one high ranking diplomat in Chad, the authorities understood that the law was necessary for World Bank support, but have little intention of allowing it to affect local practice.[46]

The Lampiere report continued:

> Oil will not lead to development in Chad without real participation, real transparency, and real oversight, none of which currently exists. The proposed revenue management plan and the law that was essentially imposed on the Chadian authorities is, at best, a first step in that direction."[47]

Criticism also focused on the oversight committee's composition and powers. Only two of the nine members were from civil society, and there were no stipulations to guarantee that they remained faithful to their organizations.[48] Moreover, the RMP did not specify how decisions would be made or how voting power would be determined.[49] Finally, the committee did not possess the right to obtain information (e.g., subpoena power), authorize distributions, or publish opinions on the project.[50]

On a more fundamental level, critics attacked the RMP as an infringement of sovereign rights. Peter Rosenblum, associate director for Harvard Law School's Human Rights Program, commented:

> At the core is a challenge to the sovereignty of undemocratic rulers. . . . Previously, no one would have interfered in the relations between an oil company and an African state. He who ruled the state controlled its resources. . . . There is still hope of a delicate balance, where the World Bank strengthens loan conditions that reinforce the democratic process in Chad and enable the Chadian people to better determine how their resources should be spent. That would still threaten the sovereignty of leaders, but would also empower the people.[51]

In the opposition's eyes, the project was not going to benefit the people of Chad and Cameroon. Instead, the most likely beneficiaries would be the project sponsors. Korinna Horta, an economist and environmentalist from Environmental Defense (a U.S.-based nonprofit organization), expressed her concern:

> The private sector—the oil companies and the commercial banks—are taking cover behind publicly funded or guaranteed institutions, be they the World Bank group or the

---

[45] Ibid., p. 3.

[46] Ibid., pp. 2, 5.

[47] P. Rosenblum, quoted in "Putting People and the Environment at Risk," p. 5.

[48] Lampriere et al., "Managing Oil Revenues in Chad," pp. 3, 4.

[49] "Putting People and the Environment at Risk," p. 19.

[50] L. Lampriere et al., "Managing Oil Revenues in Chad," p. 4.

[51] Rosenblum, "Pipeline Politics in Chad," pp. 195, 199.

export-credit agencies of individual countries. . . . What we have is a financial structure where private sector risk is comfortably cushioned by public funds intended to help the poor in a politically unstable area of Sub-Saharan Africa. What emerges is a case of corporate welfare.[52]

CONCLUSION

On June 6, the Bank and IFC directors would have to decide whether to approve the funding request. After studying the project for five years, it seemed that they had addressed and corrected the most serious concerns. Though committed, World Bank officials still expressed some concerns:

> One can say it is a bit of an experiment, but it is not a choice between not doing it or doing it. . . . If we don't do it today, somebody will develop (the project) without the safeguards (we are putting into the deal).[53]

As an institution dedicated to poverty alleviation, how could the World Bank turn its back on the only opportunity to effect change in one of the poorest, most underdeveloped nations in the world? Mr. Madavo, a Bank vice president, stated, "It's very, very important that the World Bank, as an economic institution, not become so risk adverse that it would only do the sure thing."[54] He went on to say, "If it succeeds, wouldn't that be wonderful for a story to be written 20 years from now . . . that the World Bank stood up, did its homework, supported something that made a tremendous difference to Africa?"[55]

---

[52] K. Horta, "Corporate Welfare Disguised as Aid to the Poor?" Environmental Defense Fund, March 1997, http://www.environmentaldefense.org/pubs/Reports/c_chadcam.html.

[53] World Bank representative quoted in "Pipeline Closes Oversubscribed," *Project Finance International*, 220, June 27, 2001, pp. 46.

[54] N. Onishi, "Pygmies the Focus of Pipeline Politics," *The New York Times*, July 29, 2000, www.smh.com.au/news/0007/29/text/world15.html.

[55] N. Onishi, "Pygmies Wonder If Oil Pipeline Will Ease Their Poverty," p. A3.

5

Australia-Japan Cable: Structuring the Project Company

John Hibbard, Telstra's managing director of Global Wholesale, entered a conference room where representatives from Japan Telecom and Teleglobe sat waiting to discuss the next steps for the Australia-Japan Cable (AJC) project, a $520 million submarine telecommunication cable system. Hibbard had developed the idea in 1997 and had been working with colleagues on the design, business model, and financing for the past two years. Having decided to use project finance, Hibbard and his team approached the market in early 1999 looking for strategic partners. Several telecom carriers expressed an interest in the project and agreed to commission a joint feasibility study. The study, completed in August 1999, confirmed the project's technological and commercial viability. The next month, Telstra, Teleglobe, and Japan Telecom signed a memorandum of understanding (MOU) to develop the project and arrange the financing.

The sponsors were excited by the prospects but needed to move quickly. Demand for broadband capacity was growing rapidly in Australia, and market forecasters were predicting a capacity shortfall within three years.[1] Although projected demand justified investment in a cable system, rapid improvements in cable technology and corresponding price declines of 25% or more per year made commitment to such a large investment a risky proposition. As carriers in the Australian market, the sponsors needed the capacity to serve their customers; as submarine cable system owners, they hoped to capitalize on the expected capacity shortfall before competitors developed alterna-

---

Research Associate Carrie Ferman prepared this case under the supervision of Professor Benjamin C. Esty and with assistance from Masako Egawa, executive director of the Japan Research Office. HBS cases are developed solely as the basis for class discussion. Cases are not intended to serve as endorsements, sources of primary data, or illustrations of effective or ineffective management.

[1] P. Russel, A. Begun, and D. Reingold, "Merrill Lynch Equity Research Report (Australasia/Telecommunications) on Southern Cross Cable," April 22, 1999, p. 1.

tive systems. The need to move quickly in the face of such technological and competitive uncertainty made the tasks of creating a project company and closing a $520 million financing even more daunting.

THE SUBMARINE CABLE SYSTEMS INDUSTRY

For over 150 years, slow, cyclical growth and incremental technological changes characterized the market for submarine cables.[2] But in the 1990s, explosive growth and rapid advances in cable technology radically changed the telecommunications industry. Worldwide deregulation, growing international business, new voice and data applications, and the introduction of the Internet reshaped the industry. As a result, customers needed more transmission capacity quickly, and submarine cables offered the possibility of a low-cost solution.

Submarine Cable Technology

Submarine cable systems first transmitted telegraph, then voice and, more recently, data signals across large bodies of water. Telegraph & Construction Maintenance Company (British) built the first submarine telegraph cable system between England and France in 1850. Over time, a global network of telegraph cables slowly developed. There were few technological innovations in evidence until the introduction of the coaxial (telephone) cable almost 100 years later. The first coaxial cables could handle 90 simultaneous phone calls.[3] The next major innovation, the development of fiber-optic cables in the late 1980s, allowed cables to carry both voice and data signals. The first submarine fiber-optic cable, Trans-Atlantic Telephone-8 (TAT-8), could handle 16,000 simultaneous phone calls and transfer data speeds of 280 megabits per second (Mbit/s).[4] (A megabit (Mbit) is a million binary pulses, or "bits"; a gigabit (Gbit) is a billion binary pulses.)

During the 1990s, transmission capacity steadily increased with the introduction of new technologies. The most recent innovation, dense wavelength division multiplexing (DWDM), occurred in 1995. DWDM allowed data to be transmitted on multiple wavelengths within a single fiber. Before DWDM, a fiber-optic wire could transmit up to 2.5 gigabits of data per second (Gbit/s) on a single wavelength, equivalent to 470,000 simultaneous phone calls.[5] With DWDM, that same fiber could transmit 10 Gbit/s per wavelength on eight different wavelengths.

Submarine cable systems consisted of the physical cable, repeaters, and transmission equipment. Each cable contained from two to six optical-fiber pairs, with each fiber transmitting data in only one direction. To send an intercontinental signal, a carrier transmitted the signal from the point of origin to its local router (a transmission and reception hub). The carrier then sent the signal through a "backhaul" cable to a landing station, where it was compressed and sent through the undersea cable. Because optical signals could travel only about 400 kilometers before becoming attenuated, cable operators had to install repeaters to reshape and boost the signals if they wanted to

---

[2] Frost & Sullivan, *1999 World Submarine Cable Transmission Systems*, Chapter 1, p. 1.

[3] Frost & Sullivan, *1999 World Submarine Cable Transmission Systems*, Chapter 2, p. 2.

[4] Ibid.

[5] Ibid.

transmit signals across greater distances.[6] At the other end of the cable, another landing station received the signal, decompressed it, and sent it to its final destination via another router. Several cable systems, often owned by different companies, could be housed in a single landing station. At the same time, carriers could connect to one or more cable systems within a single landing station. Because the transmission equipment, not the cable, determined the capacity, cable systems could be equipped to support only the number of wavelengths needed to meet current or near-term demand. When there was sufficient demand, the transmission equipment could be upgraded to handle additional capacity for a fraction of the original cost.

Specialized cable ships laid the cables on the ocean floor in deep water and buried them one meter deep in shallow water to avoid damage from anchors, fishing nets, and ocean currents. Most cables were durable and reliable; a typical cable lasted 25 years and suffered as few as one device failure during its lifetime. To prevent delays or lost traffic due to device failures, system owners generally designed cable networks in loops. They laid two cables hundreds of kilometers apart, linked them to separate landing stations, and completed the loop with terrestrial lines running between the landing stations. Cable operators routed traffic around the loop in one direction but could reroute traffic in the opposite direction if the cable was damaged. An alternative configuration, known as a "collapsed ring," had been discussed but not yet implemented. Rather than running two cables through deep water, collapsed ring systems had just one under the assumption that device failures were far less common in deeper water. In shallow water, where device failures were more common, this single cable branched into two cables connected to separate landing stations. By eliminating the second deep water cable, system operators could theoretically lower their capital costs.

The Demand for Submarine Cable Systems

From 1990 to 1999, the global telecommunications market grew at a compound annual rate of 10.2%, from US$348 billion to $835 billion.[7] Submarine cable systems became the primary medium for transoceanic transmission because the alternative, satellite transmission, had limited capacity, poorer quality, and higher prices. As demand for submarine cable transmission grew in the late 1990s (see Exhibit 5-1), faster growth in capacity caused prices to fall at a rate of 20% to 40% per year (see Exhibit 5-2). In fact, over the previous 10 years, prices had fallen at a compound annual rate of 25%.[8] Ovum, a leading telecommunications consulting company, predicted that the cost of an STM-1 in the Northern Hemisphere,[9] which had been US$10 million in 1998 and had fallen to US$5 million by the end of 1999, would be US$1 million by 2003.[10] As a result, system owners faced front-loaded revenue and cash flow streams.[11] For example,

---

[6] D. Williams, "An Over-simplified Overview of the Undersea Cable System," version 2.3, 1998, at ⟨http://davidw.home.cern.ch/davidw/public/SubCables.html⟩.

[7] *U.S. Industry and Trade Outlook*, Telecommunication Services, 1999.

[8] S. Hardy, "Undersea Bandwidth Prices Submerge," *Lightwave*, November 1, 1999.

[9] STM-n (Synchronous Transfer Module) is the basic unit in which broadband capacity is sold. The unit is defined in increments of 155.2 megabits per second (Mbit/s), where n is a multiple of the increment. For example, STM-1 equals 155.2 Mbit/s, and STM-64 equals 9,933 Mbit/s (64 times 155.2), or 9.9 Gbit/s (9,933 divided by 1,000).

[10] R. Braddell, "Cable delays raise Telecom debt load," *New Zealand Herald*, November 25, 1999.

[11] Here, "revenue" refers to cash receipts, not accounting receivables, which are typically amortized over the life of the cable.

EXHIBIT 5-1

TRANSOCEANIC SUBMARINE CABLE CAPACITY DEMAND (GIGABITS)

Submarine Cable Route	1997	1998	1999E	2000E	2001E	2002E	2003E	2004E	2005E
North America to Europe	17.5	42.1	81.9	154.3	281.6	489.4	812.5	1,287.6	1,975.0
Growth rate	—	141%	95%	88%	83%	74%	66%	58%	53%
North America to Asia	14.3	20.2	29.7	48.9	86.3	160.6	314.1	638.5	1,350.0
Growth rate	—	41%	47%	65%	76%	86%	96%	103%	111%
North to South America	3.9	6.2	10.6	19.2	36.6	72.4	149.5	327.9	760.0
Growth rate	—	59%	71%	81%	91%	98%	106%	119%	132%
Europe to Asia	4.0	7.3	13.7	26.3	51.1	100.5	199.7	401.3	810.0
Growth rate	—	83%	88%	92%	94%	97%	99%	101%	102%
Europe to South America	1.0	1.6	2.8	5.1	9.7	19.2	39.4	83.3	180.3
Growth rate	—	60%	75%	82%	90%	98%	105%	111%	116%
Africa to Middle East	0.2	0.3	0.5	1.0	2.1	4.2	9.0	20.1	46.7
Growth rate	—	50%	67%	100%	110%	100%	114%	123%	132%
Total Demand	**40.9**	**77.7**	**139.2**	**254.8**	**467.4**	**846.3**	**1,524.2**	**2,758.7**	**5,122.0**
Growth rate	**—**	**90%**	**79%**	**83%**	**83%**	**81%**	**80%**	**81%**	**86%**

Source: Created from data contained in Chapter 3 of the 1999 Submarine Industry Report, Frost & Sullivan (Report #5902-60).

EXHIBIT 5-2

TRANSOCEANIC SUBMARINE CABLE COSTS AND PRICES (US$ MILLIONS PER STM-1)

Transatlantic Pricing

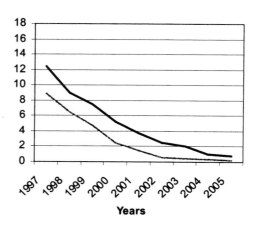

Transpacific Pricing

━━━ Unit Cost per STM-1   ━━━ Market Price per STM-1

Source: Casewriter estimates based on data contained in "Capacity to Change: The New Bandwidth Sales Models," by K. Richards, in Lightwave Fiber Exchange, January 2000, available at ⟨www.fiber-exchange.com⟩.

with 30% price declines, a project would realize 75% of the present value of total revenue within the first three years of operation (see Exhibit 5-3).

The Financing of Submarine Cable Systems

Sponsors financed cable systems using one of three structures: clubs, private deals with carrier sponsors, and private deals with noncarrier sponsors. Prior to the explosion of growth in the submarine cable systems market, carriers owned and operated submarine cable systems. To finance, a new cable, they formed large *clubs* comprised of as many as 90 sponsors who participated to obtain capacity. The club formed committees to resolve issues concerning capacity, ownership percentages, and governance. With so many carriers involved in the process, projects often took five to seven years to complete. The club model fit the carrier's needs at the time for two reasons. First, submarine cable systems were expensive to build. To limit their exposure on any given cable, many carriers contributed small amounts of equity. Second, slow and predictable growth in demand meant that it took years before a carrier would use all the capacity available on a cable.

EXHIBIT 5-3

IMPACT OF DECLINING PRICES ON THE PRESENT VALUE OF REVENUE

Annual Rate of Price Declines	Cumulative Present Value of Revenue as Percent of Total 10-Year Revenue (by Year)			
	Year 1	Year 3	Year 5	Year 7
0%	15%	40%	62%	79%
10%	21%	52%	73%	87%
20%	28%	64%	83%	93%
30%	37%	75%	91%	97%
40%	46%	84%	95%	99%
50%	55%	91%	98%	100%

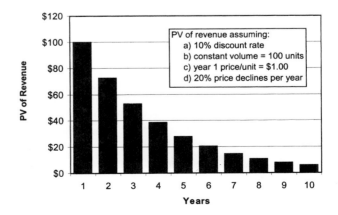

PV of revenue assuming:
a) 10% discount rate
b) constant volume = 100 units
c) year 1 price/unit = $1.00
d) 20% price declines per year

Source: Casewriter analysis.

But by the mid-1990s, industry evolution had changed the way sponsors financed cables. Carriers suddenly needed much larger blocks of capacity and quicker execution. To be competitive, they needed to build cables faster than their competitors and sell as much capacity as possible before new technology forced market prices below their costs. In response, system owners (carriers) adopted a new business model, known as the *private carrier* deal structure. A small number of carriers (usually two to four) formed limited partnerships to finance cables using both debt and equity. With fewer parties involved, carriers could make decisions more quickly. Although carriers needed larger blocks of capacity, they could not use all the new capacity themselves. So they began to sell capacity to other carriers.[12] The proceeds offset some of the costs and helped secure more favorable financing terms. Cable & Wireless and WorldCom formed the first "private carrier" deal in 1995 to build Gemini—a 20 Gbit/s submarine cable that ran between the United States and the United Kingdom. The sponsors completed the cable in just two years.

The private carrier structure created a new wholesale market for capacity. A carrier could now be another carrier's competitor, business partner, customer, or supplier. Strategy experts, recognizing the complementary roles of competing firms, referred to this interaction as co-opetition:

> Business is cooperation when it comes to creating a pie and competition when it comes to dividing it up. . . . You can compete without having to kill the opposition. If fighting to the death destroys the pie, there'll be nothing left to capture—that's lose-lose. By the same token, you can cooperate without having to ignore your self-interest. After all, it isn't smart to create a pie you can't capture—that's lose-win.[13]

The private carrier structure demonstrated the willingness of carriers to buy capacity on cables they did not own, opening up ownership of cable systems to noncarriers such as private investors and giving rise to a third business model. In 1996, the Pacific Group, a private investment firm, completed the first *private noncarrier* deal when it raised equity to build Atlantic Crossing-1 (AC-1), a cable from the United States to the United Kingdom. Rather than using the capacity, the Pacific Group built the cable and sold capacity to carriers. The Pacific Group completed AC-1 in just over two years.

Building Submarine Cable Systems

Building submarine cable systems involved several critical steps. First, system owners needed to choose equipment suppliers and sign supply contracts for the production of the cable, repeaters, and landing station equipment. In the 1990s the equipment market consisted of only a handful of manufacturers, with 80% of the market dominated by the top-three suppliers.[14] Suppliers competed for business on several levels, including technology, delivery time, and cost. Second, system owners hired cable ships to install the cable and repeaters. Like the equipment market, the cable ship industry was highly concentrated. Because cable ships also provided ongoing maintenance, system owners looked for companies that were responsive, flexible, and efficient. One late

---

[12] Carriers signed indefeasible right to use (IRU) contracts. Under the IRU contract, the carrier made an upfront cash payment for the right to unlimited access to a designated block capacity, typically for 15 years.

[13] A.M. Brandenburger and B.J. Nalebuff, Co-opetition (New York, NY: A Currency Book, Doubleday, 1996), pp. 4–5.

[14] Frost & Sullivan, *1999 World Submarine Cable Transmission Systems*, Chapter 1, p. 3.

delivery anywhere in the process could push the entire installation schedule back six months to a year, or more. System owners had to sign supply contracts and book cable ships as much as two years in advance, and even then they often encountered delays in delivery.

To bring the cable onshore, system owners had to have access to a landing station, right-of-way permits, and harbor clearance from local governments. System owners could either build their own landing stations or sign contracts, known as "landing party agreements," to use preexisting stations. The ability to get a right-of-way permit granting permission to bring a cable onshore often determined which approach firms used. Governments granted permits sparingly, and the application process could take years to complete. In some countries, governments only gave out permits for paths where cables and landing stations already existed, which meant dealing with the owners of existing landing stations. After obtaining a permit and access to a landing station, system owners had to get clearance from local fishing and government authorities. With a desire not to disrupt fishing activities, authorities granted clearances for only short periods, often once or twice a year.

AUSTRALIAN SUBMARINE CABLE INDUSTRY

Australia's telecom carriers needed greater access to Asia, Australia's largest trading partner, and the United States, where 80% of all Internet hosts were located.[15] In 1999 there were three cables for Australian traffic (see Exhibit 5-4). SEA-ME-WE3 offered access to the United States from the west coast of Australia via Japan or China. Although SEA-ME-WE3 had excess capacity, it was not an ideal route for traffic destined for the United States or Northern Asia, and it was prone to cable failures because of extensive shipping, dredging, and fishing activities in the relatively shallow Java Sea and the Singapore coast. PacRim East and PacRim West offered access to the United States from Australia's east coast, but both cables were operating at full capacity. Telecom Corporation of New Zealand, Cable & Wireless (Australia), and MCI WorldCom (United States) were in the process of building Southern Cross Cable Network (SCCN)—a 29,600-kilometer loop configuration system linking the east coast of Australia, New Zealand, and the United States. According to demand forecasts, however, it would reach full capacity by 2002 (see Exhibit 5-5).

Southern Cross Cable Network (SCCN)

SCCN was a US$1.2 billion cable network that would initially be equipped with 40 Gbit/s of capacity (with possible upgrades to 120 Gbit/s). Three sponsors provided all 10 of the landing stations and financed the project in the fall of 1998 using US$920 million in senior secured loans—the project had a debt-to-total-capitalization ratio of 85%. The syndication was significantly oversubscribed due to the strength of presales commitments from creditworthy sponsors and the potential returns.[16] Merrill Lynch analysts conducted an independent analysis of the project assuming SCCN presold some capacity to its sponsors and sold the rest over a 10-year period. They further assumed

---

[15] Cable & Wireless Optus Prospectus, 1998, p. 25.

[16] "The Southern Cross Cable Submarine Fibre-optic Cable," *Project Finance International Yearbook 1999*, p. 78.

EXHIBIT 5-4

TELECOMMUNICATIONS MAP

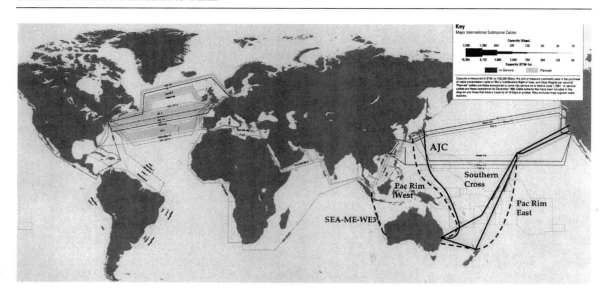

Source: Telegeography, Inc. ⟨www.telegeography.com⟩.

that prices would decline 10% per year, which translated into a total price decline of 60% over 10 years. Their downside scenario assumed a 70% price decline over 10 years, while their upside scenario assumed a 35% decline (see Exhibit 5-6). The report concluded:

> Our 10-year DCF model is generating a base case market value of equity for Southern Cross of US$1.12 billion (using a discount rate of 13%) . . . which compares with book equity of just US$150 million. . . . Southern Cross has confirmed purchase agreements for US$640 million of capacity. Long term, value is driven by incremental sales of spare

EXHIBIT 5-5

AUSTRALIAN DEMAND AND SUPPLY FOR CAPACITY (GIGABITS)

	1999E	2000E	2001E	2002E	2003E	2004E	2005E
Existing Capacity	27	27	27	27	27	27	27
Southern Cross Cable	0	120	120	120	120	120	120
SEA-ME-WE3 Upgrade	0	20	20	20	20	20	20
Total Existing & Planned Capacity	**27**	**167**	**167**	**167**	**167**	**167**	**167**
Forecast Demand	**10**	**25**	**63**	**129**	**209**	**320**	**470**

Source: Company documents.

EXHIBIT 5-6

MERRILL LYNCH'S FINANCIAL PROJECTIONS FOR SOUTHERN CROSS CABLE NETWORK (US$ MILLIONS)

	1998	1999	2000	2001	2002	2003	2004	2005	2006	2007	2008
Base Case											
Presold Capacity	$0.0	0.0	20.0	40.0	40.0	40.0	40.0	40.0	40.0	40.0	40.0
Anticipatory Sales	$0.0	0.0	0.0	16.2	30.8	43.9	55.7	66.3	85.5	119.9	150.9
Total Revenue	$0.0	0.0	20.0	56.2	70.8	83.9	95.7	106.3	125.5	159.9	190.9
Net Operating Costs	$0.0	0.0	10.0	11.0	12.2	13.6	15.4	17.4	19.9	22.9	26.5
EBITDA	$0.0	0.0	10.0	45.2	58.6	70.3	80.3	88.9	105.6	137.0	164.4
EBITDA Margin	—	—	50%	80%	83%	84%	84%	84%	84%	86%	86%
Depreciation	$0.0	0.0	47.5	47.5	47.5	47.5	47.5	47.5	47.5	47.5	47.5
Net Interest	$3.8	11.3	52.5	25.3	9.6	0.0	0.0	0.0	0.0	0.0	0.0
Profit Before Tax	($3.8)	(11.3)	(90.0)	(27.6)	1.5	22.8	32.8	41.4	58.1	89.5	116.9
ROE (on US$150 million)	-2.5%	-7.5%	-60.0%	-18.4%	-0.8%	12.1%	17.5%	22.1%	31.0%	47.7%	62.3%
Cash Flow											
Cash Receipts[a]	$0.0	0.0	300.0	493.0	268.7	236.8	177.1	159.4	287.0	516.6	464.9
Capital Expenditures	($50.0)	(100.0)	(700.0)	(100.0)	(47.5)	(47.5)	(47.5)	(47.5)	(47.5)	(47.5)	(47.5)
Free Cash Flow	($50.0)	(100.0)	(550.0)	363.0	209.0	175.7	114.3	94.5	219.5	446.1	338.4
Dividends	$0.0	0.0	0.0	0.0	0.0	47.7	114.3	94.5	219.5	446.1	338.4
Downside Scenario											
Total Revenue	$0.0	0.0	20.0	54.0	66.7	77.2	86.0	94.5	110.5	140.9	169.8
EBITDA	$0.0	0.0	10.0	43.5	54.5	63.5	70.7	77.0	90.6	118.0	143.3
Net Income	($3.8)	(11.3)	(90.0)	(31.3)	(7.1)	9.6	18.5	23.6	34.5	56.4	76.7
ROE (on US$150 million)	-2.5%	-7.5%	-60.0%	-20.9%	-4.7%	6.4%	12.4%	15.8%	23.0%	37.6%	51.1%
Upside Scenario											
Total Revenue	$0.0	0.0	20.0	56.9	72.5	101.2	153.9	214.5	250.9	287.3	323.7
EBITDA	$0.0	0.0	10.0	45.9	60.3	87.5	138.5	197.1	231.0	264.4	297.2
Net Income	($3.8)	(11.3)	(90.0)	(26.0)	4.1	32.0	72.8	119.7	146.8	173.5	199.7
ROE (on US$150 million)	-2.5%	-7.5%	-60.0%	-17.4%	2.7%	21.3%	48.9%	79.8%	97.9%	115.7%	133.2%

[a] Cash receipts reflect front-loaded sales of capacity.

Source: Adapted from the Merrill Lynch Equity Research Report (Australasia/Telecommunications) on Southern Cross Cable, by P. Russel, A. Begun, and D. Reingold, April 22, 1999.

capacity, which we expect to snowball as data traffic out of Australasia to the USA skyrockets. A critical valuation issue is the impact of competing cables on pricing of Southern Cross' spare capacity.[17]

SCCN began construction in 1998 with a scheduled completion date in late 1999. However, the project ran into permitting problems that threatened to delay completion by as much as six months. As a result, SCCN canceled its financing in August 1999 and obtained alternative funding until the project could be refinanced. An article in *Project Finance International* described the situation this way:

> In what is considered a first for Australia, the sponsors of the Southern Cross fiber-optic cable project signed an agreement . . . to buy back the deal and return the funds. . . . The reason cited for this dramatic turn was the sponsors' inability to satisfy a crucial condition precedent within the given time frame in the loan financing documents. . . . The CP relates to the requirement on the sponsors being able to obtain certain U.S. environmental clearances. . . . [The lenders thought meeting this CP was] a mere formality and that none of this had really been foreseen.[18]

Shortly after canceling the financing, SCCN decreased prices to induce greater demand. The cost of an STM-1 from Australia to the United States fell from $37.8 million in mid-1998 to $12.9 million in September 1999.[19] To compensate customers who had already bought capacity on the cable, SCCN provided additional free capacity so that they would have the same cost per unit of capacity.[20]

The Australia-Japan Cable (AJC)

With A$17 billion (US$11 billion) in revenues in 1998, Telstra was Australia's leading telecommunications and information services company (see Exhibits 5-7a and 5-7b). Its fixed telephone network extended across Australia, serving virtually all Australian homes and businesses, and its broadband network ran past 2.5 million homes. Telstra's international transmission infrastructure included both satellite and submarine cable transmission. Owning substantial submarine capacity in the Asia Pacific region and around the world and partly owning and managing several cable landing stations on Australian shores, Telstra provided customers with a full range of data and online services. The company's major submarine cable investments included SEA-ME-WE3, China-U.S. cable, and Japan-U.S. cable.

Telstra commissioned a $6 million feasibility study in mid-1997 for a new cable system from the east coast of Australia to Japan via Guam (a U.S. territory, see Exhibit 5-8). There were two reasons to go through Guam: it was more efficient to surface and repower the signal than to send it all the way to Japan and it could connect with other cables running through Guam. Hibbard, the project's leader, explained:

> AJC grew out of my vision for a triangular communication system running between Australia, Japan, and the U.S. At the time (mid-1997), the sponsors of the Southern Cross

---

[17] Merrill Lynch Industry Report, Southern Cross Cable, April 22, 1999, p. 1.

[18] *Project Finance International*, August 25, 1999, pp. 10–11.

[19] S. Hardy, "Undersea Bandwidth Prices Submerge," *Lightwave*, November 1, 1999.

[20] For example, a customer who already bought one STM-1 would now receive an additional 1.93 STM-1s for free, for a total of 2.93 STM-1s. The original price of $37.80 divided by the new capacity of 2.93 yielded the new price of $12.90 per STM-1.

EXHIBIT 5-7A

1998 SUMMARIZED PROFIT AND LOSS STATEMENTS (US$ MILLIONS)

	Original Sponsor Group				Potential Sponsors		
	Telstra	Japan Telecom	Teleglobe	AT&T	NTT	MCI WorldCom
Net Sales	$10,741	$3,117	$1,701	$53,223	$71,591	$17,678
Cost of Goods Sold	(3,878)	(1,706)	(1,107)	(25,578)	(29,313)	(8,416)
Other Expenses	(2,254)	(888)	(268)	(15,529)	(11,543)	(8,037)
Operating Income	4,609	523	326	12,116	30,735	1,225
Nonoperating Income	0	17	11	1,247	143	41
Amortization & Depreciation	(1,441)	(278)	(112)	(4,629)	(24,129)	(2,200)
Interest Expense	(394)	(35)	(32)	(427)	(1,783)	(637)
Pretax Income	2,774	227	193	8,307	4,966	(1,571)
Taxes	(911)	(106)	(63)	(3,072)	(3,169)	(876)
Extraordinary and/or other expenses	2	(60)	(173)	1,163	(172)	(222)
Net Income	1,865	61	(43)	6,398	1,625	(2,669)

Source: Company annual reports, Global Access, and casewriter estimates.

103

EXHIBIT 5-7B

1998 SUMMARIZED BALANCE SHEETS (US$ MILLIONS)

	Original Sponsor Group			Potential Sponsors		
	Telstra	Japan Telecom	Teleglobe	AT&T	NTT	MCI WorldCom
Current Assets	$ 2,800	$1,091	$ 886	$14,118	$ 19,731	$10,639
Noncurrent Assets	13,634	3,152	5,021	45,432	111,728	75,762
Total Assets	**16,434**	**4,234**	**5,907**	**59,550**	**131,459**	**86,401**
Current Liabilities	5,305	1,404	921	15,442	26,104	16,029
Noncurrent Liabilities	4,250	839	832	18,586	63,961	25,369
Shareholders' Equity	6,879	2,000	4,154	25,522	41,394	45,003
Total Liabilities & Shareholders' Equity	**16,434**	**4,243**	**5,907**	**59,550**	**131,459**	**86,401**
Home Country	Australia	Japan	Canada	United States	Japan	United States
S&P Senior Debt Rating	AA+	AA	BBB+	AA−	AA+	A−
Landing Stations on AJC Route	Australia (2)	Japan (1)	none	Guam (2)	Japan (3)	none

Source: Company annual reports, Global Access, and casewriter estimates.

104

EXHIBIT 5-8

AUSTRALIA-JAPAN CABLE ROUTE

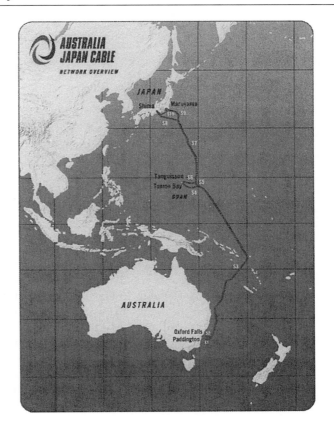

Source: Company documents ⟨www.ajcable.com⟩.

Cable Network were building a full loop link between Australia and the U.S. We suggested modifying the project by removing the parallel path direct to the U.S.A., creating a link from Australia to Japan, and acquiring capacity across the North Pacific. But the sponsors of the Southern Cross project were not persuaded by our proposal. So we decided to build a cable system between Australia and Japan using a collapsed ring configuration. By taking advantage of the cost savings inherent in a collapsed ring and the low-cost capacity available across the North Pacific, we knew we could meet or beat Southern Cross's prices to the U.S. And at the same time, we would have access to an even larger market because of our link to Asia and other cables that surfaced in Guam.

As he developed the business model, Hibbard had a simple but critical philosophy for AJC:

I did not believe AJC should compete with its customers [large telecom carriers]. That meant it would sell shore-to-shore service on a wholesale basis, not point-to-point service to retail customers. AJC should be a producer of basic capacity services with wholesale and retail sellers between AJC and the end users.

EXHIBIT 5-9

EXPECTED SOURCES AND USES OF FUNDS (US$ MILLIONS)

Uses of Funds			Sources of Funds[a]		
System cost	$425	75%	Equity (maximum)	$ 85	15%
Construction contingency	40	7%			
Other development costs	30	5%	Debt		
Interest, financing, & closing costs	25	4%	Tranche A, presales (up to)	337	59%
Total Budget Costs	520	91%	Tranche B, market sales	145	26%
Delay contingency	47	9%	Total Debt	482	85%
Total Uses of Funds	**$567**	**100%**	**Total Sources of Funds**	**$567**	**100%**

[a] Sources assume $85 million of equity and 70% of total debt ($482) in Tranche A according to information contained in "AJC Financed," *Project Finance International* 208, January 10, 2001, p. 23.

Source: Casewriter estimates based on public documents and company information.

The 12,500-kilometer cable system would initially be equipped with 40 Gbit/s of capacity. The system would use Telstra's two landing stations near Sydney. In Guam, the project could contract with AT&T to use its landing stations or try to get approval from the government to build new ones; like in other countries, obtaining permits to build new stations could be very difficult and time consuming. Obtaining access to landing stations in Japan would be even more complicated. There were approximately a dozen landing stations in the country,[21] and the government was not likely to approve construction of new stations in the near future. The project would, therefore, have to partner or contract with one or more companies to gain access to landing stations in Japan.

Telstra's preliminary estimate to build the system was $520 million, up to $567 million if there was a major delay (see Exhibit 5-9). It anticipated at least two 40 Gbit/s upgrades during the first five years—funded by cash flow from operations—and had the ability to increase capacity to 320 Gbit/s if demand materialized. Upgrades to the system would cost approximately $25 million per 40 Gbit/s and would take approximately 12 to 15 months to implement. The company expected the system would have a useful life of 15 years and intended to sell IRUs for that period.

Telstra envisioned a private carrier deal using a project finance structure to fund construction. Peter Keating, project finance manager for Telstra, explained:

> We decided to use project finance as a way to conserve scarce capital. For Telstra, that meant limiting the amount of equity we had to invest in the project. We wanted to hold around 40% of the equity to ensure that we had a significant role in running the company. At the same time, we wanted to leave enough equity so that our partners would have meaningful equity positions and large enough shares to justify board representation. Without using any debt, we would be looking at an investment of approximately US$200 million—

[21] Of the existing landing stations, Kokusai Denshin Denwa (KDD) owned five, Nippon Telegraph and Telephone (NTT) owned three, Global Access Limited (an affiliate of Global Crossing) owned two, Japan Telecom owned one, and Cable & Wireless IDC owned one.

40% of a US$520 million project. However, with high gearing (leverage) and a project finance structure, we could reduce our investment to US$30–$40 million, a much more acceptable size.

Telstra engaged ABN AMRO, which had led the SCCN financing, to advise on the financing strategy. Brian Tellam, director of project finance at ABN AMRO, believed the project could support a highly leveraged capital structure. Tellam commented on the project's capitalization ratio:

> We recommended a gearing ratio of 85% for AJC, which we believed would be accepted by financiers as long as we had identified and mitigated the major risks. For AJC, market risk was the major concern. To mitigate this risk, we needed pre-sales capacity contracts from high-rated companies covering approximately two-thirds of the total cost. We were less concerned about physical construction because cable suppliers have been laying submarine cables for 150 years. Another important risk, especially recently, has been completion delays due to environmental approvals and other permitting. To mitigate this risk, we needed to incorporate procedures that would allow AJC to draw funds for construction even if there were delays in some other aspect of the project.

As part of the target capital structure, Telstra envisioned raising two debt tranches. Tranche A would be secured and repaid (probably within five years) with presale commitments to purchase capacity, while Tranche B would be repaid from future sales of capacity to other parties, also within five years. Telstra approached the market in early 1999 looking for strategic partners. Hibbard explained his objectives:

> I can't emphasize enough how important sponsor selection is. Creating a joint venture like AJC is a lot like a marriage. There is a preliminary courtship in which the partners check each other out. Then there is a commitment and a long-term relationship. You really want to avoid divorces, which are very mean and nasty and can totally disrupt the business. For this reason, we wanted to spend time with each of the potential sponsors to make sure there was a good fit on both the company and the personal level, to understand their objectives, and to understand how they made decisions. If we don't have complete compatibility, then we don't want to be in the relationship.

Several telecommunications companies expressed an interest in the project and agreed to commission an independent feasibility study. The study concluded that there was "more than sufficient capacity demand" and reaffirmed Telstra's belief that the expected cash flows could support a highly leveraged capital structure. Based on these results, Japan Telecom, which owned a landing station in Japan, and Teleglobe, a major carrier that could bring significant volume to the project, agreed to sign an MOU with Telstra and proceed with structuring the project company.

STRUCTURING THE PROJECT COMPANY

The first thing the sponsors did was lay out a timeline, complete with intermediate milestones that would result in a "ready-for-service" (RFS) date of June 30, 2001. Because construction would take approximately one year, they needed to have the financing in place by June 2000, less than a year away. To close the financing in June, the sponsors had to release the information memorandum, sign landing-party agreements, and sign a cable supply contract by April 2000. Under the project finance structure, the sponsors had to create a separate legal entity (the project company) that would obtain financing and control operations. Based on these deadlines, the sponsors had to finalize the ownership structure, sign a shareholders agreement, and structure the project company in the next six months (by March 2000). To achieve this timetable, the sponsors needed to resolve several issues quickly. Keating explained:

> Before we could raise any money, we needed to develop our story. First, we had to show there was demand for a new cable. That meant getting a believable forecast of market demand. The key was to present a realistic business case, not one built on "blue sky" assumptions. Second, we had to show AJC had advantages relative to existing cables. It would be bigger, safer, and cheaper than SEA-ME-WE3 for traffic to the U.S., and it would be roughly the same cost as Southern Cross for traffic to the U.S. Third, we needed to attract a group of high-quality sponsors who would sign presale capacity agreements. Project finance bankers look very carefully at the revenue line, and capacity agreements from high-rated sponsors are the key to achieving high gearing ratios and raising project debt with the least restrictive financial and operating covenants.

The sponsors had to decide whether to invite other equity investors into the deal and, if so, whom. Hibbard noted:

> Originally, we were looking for four sponsors to simplify management of the project company. In selecting partners, there had to be, first and foremost, good chemistry between the firms and the individuals. After that, we wanted partners who would be investors as well as users [capacity buyers] in roughly the same proportion. The key was to find partners who were strong financially so that their presales capacity contracts would support the project and give us credibility with bankers. Finally, we wanted to find partners that would bring something to the project. That meant bringing significant volume and/or access to landing stations.

The sponsors had recently met with NTT Communications, which had expressed an interest in joining AJC and raised the possibility of using its landing station in Japan. Yoshiro Takano, vice president of NTT's international network, commented:

> We did not have cables directly connecting Japan and Australia and wanted to obtain additional capacity on that route. We compared the cost of other options and concluded that AJC would offer the lowest cost if the dividend to shareholders was taken into consideration. But we wanted more than capacity. We thought AJC would be an attractive addition to the business in our existing cable stations. It seemed like a good partnership because we wanted low-cost capacity and they needed landing stations in Japan.

After selecting the new sponsors, the original sponsors would have to discuss and resolve ownership shares, voting rights, transfer restrictions on shares, and board membership before they could write the shareholders agreement. Keating knew that the issue of transfer restrictions would be contentious:

> Resolving when and how sponsors could exit the business was clearly going to be an issue. As a private deal, sponsors will have liquidity concerns, which meant we needed a process for valuing and selling shares. But having such a process in place worries bankers who make credit decisions based on the composition of the sponsor group. They agree to lend because the purchase commitments come from high-rated sponsors and could get very concerned if low-rated sponsor became owners.

The shareholders agreement would also describe the size and composition of the project company's board of directors. The board would be responsible for setting strategic goals, approving pricing decisions and capacity expansions, and hiring and firing senior management. Thus, the sponsors also had to decide how many directors there should be, who they should be, and how they should be paid. Hibbard explained the sponsors' objectives for the project's board of directors:

> Good will permeated this project right from the start. The idea was that we would be equal partners regardless of our individual ownership shares. The project was to be built on a foundation of cooperation and collaboration. The goal was to avoid dogfights on the board and to achieve unanimity on all decisions. By linking ownership and cable use—by requiring the sponsors to sign purchase agreements—we hoped there would be greater harmony in the decision-making process.

Next, the sponsors needed to design the organizational structure and select the senior management team. In the short term, there would be an interim management team comprised of people from the sponsoring firms. Eventually, however, they would hire a permanent management team that worked exclusively for the project company. Besides identifying candidates for the interim and permanent management teams and ensuring some continuity between the two, they needed to design a compensation package for the CEO and other senior managers. Hibbard explained:

> We wanted a solid management team that would be good at execution. This is a single-asset company with limited, and well-defined, expansion opportunities. It's not a multifaceted business, nor one with lots of varied, high-cost growth opportunities. As a result, we had to get the execution right on the core asset. We wanted people with project management experience, preferably with an undersea cable. The challenges were to convince someone to take this job and do it properly. Like all aspects of the deal, good relationships and good chemistry were critical.

Finally, the sponsors had to decide about the project financing. They had already decided to use bank debt, but they needed to discuss the finer details. ABN AMRO had suggested an 85:15 debt-to-equity capital structure, but the sponsors wondered if they needed so much leverage. They also needed to think about the optimal maturity (short vs. medium term) and repayment schedule (bullet vs. amortizing) for the loans, as well as the covenant package and reporting requirements they would be willing to accept. With regard to the loan syndication, they had to select a lead arranger (or arrangers) for the syndication and decide how many banks to invite to participate. Keating commented:

> We took the perspective that the banks should be our partners. All projects develop problems of one kind or another that require waivers or amendments. When these problems arise, as they invariably do, you want to work with a banking group that will solve the problem and move forward as quickly as possible. Based on my experience, the smaller the lending group the better. For exactly this reason, we did not want to issue a project bond—trustees don't provide the same kind of flexibility.

Once they had made all these organizational and managerial decisions, the sponsors could write the information memorandum to raise the debt.

EXHIBIT 5-10

PROJECT GOVERNANCE AND RELATED ARRANGEMENTS FOR THE AUSTRALIA-JAPAN CABLE PROJECT

Project Period	Project Body	Governing Agreement	Tasks	External Contracts
Planning Period	Equity investors consortium consisting of committed equity investors.	Memorandum of understanding (MOU).	• Structure and negotiate project financing. • Capacity sales promotion as preconstruction commitment. • Procurement activities. • Institutional arrangement for cable operation. • Write information memorandum.	• Contract with the financial arranger. • Contracts necessary for route survey (desktop and marine).
Incorporation of Special Purpose Vehicle (SPV)	Equity investors consortium to establish special purpose vehicle.	Shareholders agreement among the equity investors.	• Establish special purpose vehicle with a corporate constitution.	• Capacity sales agreements with capacity purchasers who made preconstruction capacity purchase commitments.
Financial Closure	Special purpose vehicle.	Corporate constitution (or equivalent, depending on the jurisdiction of the country where the SPV is founded) established based on the shareholders agreement.	• Finalize project financing. • Finalize supply contracts. • Finalize institutional arrangement for cable operation. • Complete capacity sales agreement.	• Syndicate facilities agreement with financiers. • Security documents with financiers (as required). • Supply contract with the selected supplier • Agreement of institutional arrangements with the operation providers (cable station providers, ship operators, etc.). • Capacity sales agreement.
Implementation Period	Special purpose vehicle.	Corporate constitution established based on the shareholders agreement.	• Construct the cable. • Manage the cable and the business. • Continue capacity sales.	• Restoration agreement with other cable systems. • Any other contract to acquire service from outside suppliers

Source: Company documents.

CONCLUSION

With just six months to go before they needed to release the information memorandum, the sponsors had a lot to accomplish. Finding additional strategic partners, if any, and drawing up a shareholders agreement would take several months. In addition, the sponsors needed to solicit bids for a lead arranger, which could also take several months. And there was still the task of creating a governance structure for the project company. While they had some preliminary ideas on how to govern the project (see Exhibit 5-10), they needed to flesh out the details. The sponsors would have to work quickly if they were going to close the financing by June 2000 and achieve their target "ready-for-service" date of June 2001.

6

Calpine Corporation: The Evolution from Project to Corporate Finance

Right from the start, Calpine Corporation's Senior Vice President of Finance (SVP) Bob Kelly and Vice President (VP) of finance Rohn Crabtree knew 1999 was going to be a difficult year. Chief Executive Officer (CEO) Pete Cartwright had recently announced a bold ramp-up in Calpine's growth strategy, raising the five-year target for generating capacity from 6,300 to 15,000 megawatts (MW).[1] While Kelly and Crabtree strongly supported the high-growth strategy given the changes taking place in the U.S. power industry, the financing requirements were formidable. Adding 12,000 MW to Calpine's current 3,000 MW portfolio would mean building or acquiring 25 new plants, or an average of five plants per year compared to one or two per year in recent years. Moreover, at a cost of roughly $500,000 per MW, they would need to raise more than $6 billion, which, for a BB-rated company with total assets of only $1.7 billion and a debt-to-capitalization ratio of 79%, was not going to be easy. And if Cartwright ratcheted up the five-year target next year to 25,000 MW, as many suspected he might, Calpine would need an additional $5 billion. Knowing they would be responsible for raising the funds, Kelly and Crabtree wondered if Calpine's historical practice of project financings with periodic takeouts in the debt capital markets would be adequate for the new growth model and, if not, what the alternatives were? Cartwright had been encouraging them to come up with creative solutions, but as of May 1999, there were still no obvious answers.

Dean's Research Fellow Michael Kane and Professor Benjamin C. Esty prepared this case. HBS cases are developed solely as the basis for class discussion. Cases are not intended to serve as endorsements, sources of primary data, or illustrations of effective or ineffective management.

[1] One MW was sufficient to power 1,000 households.

THE U.S. ELECTRIC POWER INDUSTRY

With annual revenues of $296 billion and assets of $686 billion, the U.S. electric power industry was the country's third largest after automobiles and health care. Over the years, the industry had become increasingly segregated into three principal functions: generation, bulk transmission, and distribution. Approximately 170 investor-owned utilities controlled 72% of the industry's total generating capacity of 733,000 MW; the federal government, municipal and cooperative electric companies, and other kinds of producers controlled the remaining 28%. Most observers projected long-term growth rates of 2% p.a.,[2] which implied a need to add 15,000 MW of new capacity annually at a cost of more than $7 billion.[3] Substantial investment also was needed to replace aging plants in operation. Ron Walter, a Calpine senior vice president, pointed out that 45% of U.S. generating capacity was over 25 years old and that 90% of the installed base would have to be replaced by 2015.[4]

Despite the increasing demand for new power plants, capital spending had declined sharply over the previous two decades primarily because utilities and other developers feared deregulation might limit their ability to recover the cost of building new plants. As a result, the benchmark "reserve margin" between peak electricity demand and generating capacity had declined from 35% in 1985 to under 12% in mid-1999.[5] Industry experts generally believed that a reserve margin of 15% to 20% was a comfort zone below which there could be blackouts and other problems in periods of peak demand. The fact that electricity, for the most part, could not be stored meant that sufficient generating capacity had to be available to meet demand.

A Changing Industry Model

Since the early twentieth century, the production and delivery of electricity had been dominated by vertically integrated public utilities with exclusive rights to serve specific markets. Federal regulation dating back to the 1930s created restrictions on multistate operation, which meant the power industry became a collection of regional markets rather than a single national market. State regulation set retail prices (the price per kilowatt-hour or kwh) in a way that allowed utilities to cover their operating costs and earn a market rate of return on their invested capital. In return for this cost-plus revenue stream and protection from competition, utilities had an obligation to serve their local market, requiring them to build and operate generating plants, transmission lines, and local distribution systems as needed.

This regulated industry structure precluded the development of competitive wholesale (bulk power sales by or to utilities) or retail (sales to end users) markets. During the 1970s and 1980s, deregulation eliminated or weakened the monopoly service rights and fixed-price systems that defined the industry. Congress, responding to concerns about U.S. dependence on foreign oil and environmental damage resulting from burning fossil fuels (oil, gas, and coal) to produce electricity, passed the Public Utilities Regulatory Policies Act (PURPA) in 1978. The Act encouraged the creation of small power plants using nontraditional fuels such as geothermal, solar and wind power, and larger plants burning traditional fuels such as coal, oil, and natural gas, provided they quali-

[2] Standard & Poor's, *Industry Surveys-Electric Utilities*, February 2001, p. 5.

[3] H. Hiller and G. McIsaac, "Talkin' 'Bout Their Generation," Part II, Salomon Smith Barney Research Report, December 1, 2000, p. 7.

[4] C.W. Thurston, "Merchant Power: Promise or reality?" *Public Utilities Fortnightly*, January 1, 1999, p. 14.

[5] H. Hiller and G. McIsaac, "Talkin' 'Bout Their Generation," p. 14.

fied as cogenerators, meaning they produced both electricity and heat. As long as these nonutility generators (known as qualifying facilities or QFs) met PURPA standards, local utilities had to buy all of their electrical output. In response to this new opportunity, independent power producers (IPPs) began to build new plants.

To develop a power plant, an IPP typically had to complete the following steps: (1) acquire the site; (2) sign a long-term power purchase agreement with a creditworthy public utility; (3) sign construction and equipment contracts, usually on a fixed-price, turnkey basis with an experienced contractor; (4) sign a long-term fuel supply contract; (5) sign operating and maintenance contracts, if needed; (6) obtain the necessary approvals from state utility, environmental, and other regulatory agencies; and (7) arrange financing. Exhibit 6-1a illustrates a representative project structure used by Calpine and other developers.

The instrument of choice for financing this "contractual bundle" was project finance, in which the project company borrowed on a nonrecourse basis (i.e., the parent corporation was not responsible for repaying subsidiary borrowings, see Exhibit 6-1b). Prior to the 1970s, project financing was used primarily to finance the development of natural resources, including mines and oil fields. It was particularly attractive to IPPs because it offered high leverage with limited or no recourse to the sponsor's balance

EXHIBIT 6-1A

TYPICAL PROJECT STRUCTURE FOR AN INDEPENDENT POWER PLANT (IPP)

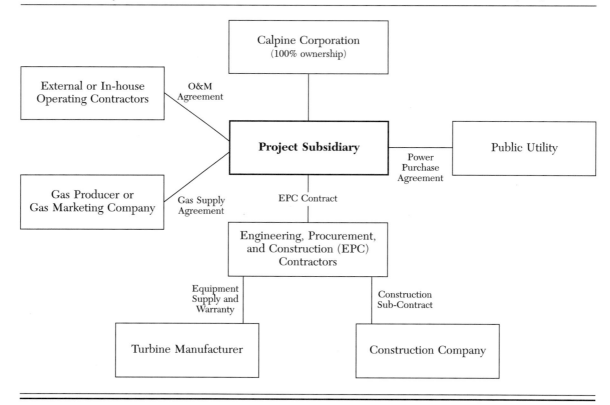

EXHIBIT 6-1B

TYPICAL PROJECT FINANCE STRUCTURE (CASH AND COLLATERAL FLOWS)

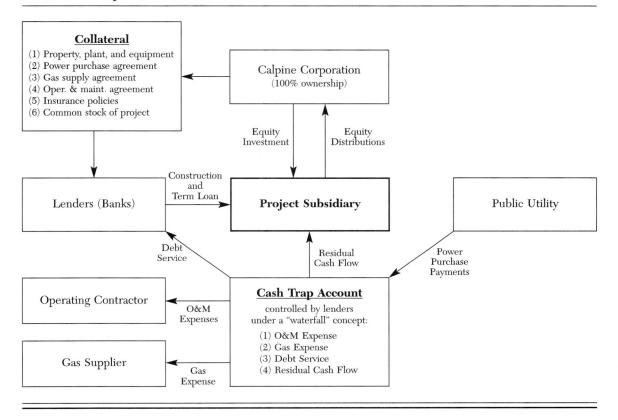

sheet. Project finance lenders became comfortable with terms that were aggressive by the standards of conventional bank lending because IPPs had steady streams of long-term cash flow and were ring-fenced from other risks associated with the parent company. Bob Kelly summarized the IPP project finance world this way:

> If you look at the old business model, the IPP, you were basically financing long-term power contracts. It was an arbitrage in financing that yielded greater interest tax shields because the average IPP had a debt-to-capital ratio of 80% to 95% compared to 40% to 50% for the average utility. IPPs could support higher leverage without a large penalty in funding cost because the asset, the power contract, was relatively safe. And since IPPs had little need for additional investment, they did not need spare debt capacity.

Deregulation combined with technological advances in power generation spurred the growth of IPPs. For example, combined-cycle gas turbines (CCGT) were capable of generating power at significantly lower cost and in an environmentally cleaner way than existing technologies. In fact, the marginal cost of operating a CCGT plant, as determined by its heat rate,[6] was 25% to 35% lower than existing technologies, and they cost less to build: approximately $500,000 per MW compared to $750,000 per MW or more for coal and nuclear plants.

In 1992, 14 years after PURPA, Congress introduced further competition by passing the National Energy Policy Act (NEPA), an Act that allowed IPPs to sell power at wholesale prices over the existing transmission systems and protected them against discriminatory rates and access. NEPA also removed the cogeneration requirement, thereby allowing IPPs to build larger and more efficient plants, but left the issue of retail competition in distribution up to individual states. By early 1999, over 30 states had passed or were considering legislation to introduce retail competition.

As these changes took effect, it became clear that the industry was transitioning to a competitive structure in which IPPs and unregulated utility affiliates would have to build power plants without the benefit of long-term power purchase agreements. In fact, IPPs accounted for half of all power plant construction during the 1990s and represented almost 7% of total U.S. generating capacity by 1998.[7] Forecasters predicted that by 2002, these merchant—or competitive transactions—would account for anywhere from 0% to 90% of wholesale transactions depending on the region. Forecasters also predicted increases in generating capacity, though the predictions on the amount of new generating capacity varied widely (see Exhibit 6-2).

CALPINE CORPORATION

Headquartered in San Jose, California, Calpine was founded in 1984 as a wholly-owned subsidiary of Electrowatt, a Swiss industrial corporation affiliated with Credit Suisse Banking Group. The name Calpine reflected its California location and its Swiss parentage (*Cali*fornia + *Alpine* = Calpine). From 1984 through 1998, Calpine pursued the construction and operation of QF power plants on the IPP model, creating a new subsidiary to finance each plant, as well as acquisitions of other IPPs. As of March 31, 1999, it had 22 plants with a combined capacity of 2,729 MW operating in seven states, and another 12 plants in various stages of development. In recent years, Calpine had gradually been increasing its growth rate. Between 1994 and 1998, consolidated assets increased from $421 million to $1,712 million, revenues grew from $94 million to $556 million, and net income from $6 million to $46 million (see Exhibit 6-3a). The company's goal was to earn a return on equity of 18% to 22% and a return on invested capital of 10% to 12%.

During its first 10 years, Calpine used project finance to construct new plants but had recently changed its financial strategy. In 1994, the company began a policy of retiring subsidiary-level project debt with parent-level, corporate debt issues (Exhibit 6-3b). Between 1994 and 1999, Calpine issued five corporate bonds as its debt rating improved from B1/B to Ba2/BB. CEO Pete Cartwright hoped Calpine would achieve an investment grade rating by 2003, which would require a consolidated debt-to-capitalization ratio of 65% or less according to Kelly.

---

[6] The heat rate was the key industry measure of generating efficiency and referred to the quantity of fuel, expressed in British Thermal Units (BTUs), required to generate one kilowatt-hour (kWh) of electricity. Because the fuel cost was roughly equal to the marginal operating cost of a power plant, the difference between the cost of fuel and the price of power, known as the spark spread, served as a proxy for the gross margin. The U.S. industry average heat rate was a little over 10,000, though in several regions such as New England and in states like California and Texas, the average heat rate approached 12,000 or more.

[7] Hagler Bailly Consulting, 1996 Global Power Market Forecast, p. 3; Standard & Poor's, *Industry Surveys—Electric Utilities*, February 1999, p. 20.

EXHIBIT 6-2

U.S. POWER INDUSTRY (GENERATING CAPACITY IN MEGAWATTS)

North American Electric Reliability Council (NERC) Region		States in Region	Market Size in 1999[a]	Percent Merchant Power in 2002 (est)	Projected New Development by 2002	
					Salomon SB	Resource Data
Northeast Power Coordinating Council	NPCC	ME,VT,NH,CT,MA, RI,NY	59,000	68%	7,000	20,322
Mid-Atlantic Area Council	MAAC	PA,NJ,MD	58,000	90	5,000	11,714
East Central Area Reliability Coordination	ECAR	MI,IN,OH,KY,WV	106,000	26	5,000	19,895
Mid-America Interconnected Network	MAIN	MO,IL,WI,MI	52,000	59	4,000	14,777
Mid-Continent Area Power Pool	MAPP	MT,ND,SD,NE,MN, IA,WI	33,000	0	0	1,501
Southeastern Electric Reliability Council	SERC	LA,AR,MO,MS.AL, GA,SC,NC,VA,TN	150,000	17	14,000	39,250
Florida Reliability Coordinating Council	FRCC	FL	38,000	0	0	8,499
Southwest Power Pool	SPP	TX,OK,KS,LA,AR	43,000	3	2,000	9,124
Electric Reliability Council of Texas	ERCOT	TX	60,000	89	13,000	22,122
Western Systems Coordinating Council	WSCC	CA,NV,NM,CO,UT, WA,OR,ID,MT,WY	136,000	35	9,000	21,487
Total			733,000		57,000	168,681

[a] Of this total amount, coal accounted for 51.0%, nuclear for 19.7%, natural gas for 15.3%, hydroelectric for 8.3%, oil for 3.2%, and other for 2.4% according to the U.S. Department of Energy.

Source: H. Hiller and G. McIsaac, "Talkin' 'Bout Their Generation," Part II, Salomon Smith Barney Research Report, December 1, 2000.

EXHIBIT 6-3A

CALPINE CORPORATION—SUMMARY CONSOLIDATED FINANCIAL DATA ($ MILLIONS)

	1994	1995	1996	1997	1998	3/31/99
Income Statement						
Total revenue	$94.8	$132.1	$214.5	$276.3	$555.9	$145.9
EBITDA	53.7	69.5	117.4	172.6	255.3	46.3
Deprec./amort. expense	20.3	25.9	36.6	46.8	74.3	19.0
Interest expense	23.9	32.2	45.3	61.5	86.7	21.0
Net income	6.0	7.4	18.7	34.7	45.7	3.9
Earnings per Share—Basic[a]	n/a	n/a	$1.45	$1.74	$2.27	$0.19
Earnings per Share—Diluted	n/a	n/a	1.22	1.65	2.16	0.18
Dividends per Share	n/a	n/a	$0.00	$0.00	$0.00	$0.00
Balance Sheet						
Total assets	$421.0	$554.5	$1,030.2	$1,380.9	$1,728.9	$2,562.6
Short-term debt	27.3	85.9	37.5	113.0	5.5	5.5
Project finance debt	196.8	190.6	278.6	182.9	114.2	115.2
Total debt	334.4	407.7	601.1	855.9	1,071.4	1,786.5
Total equity	18.6	25.2	203.1	240.0	287.0	470.3
Leverage/Capitalization						
Debt ratings (Moody's/S&P)	B1/B	Ba3/B+	Ba3/BB−	Ba2/BB−	Ba2/BB	Ba2/BB
EBITDA to interest expense	2.23X	2.11X	2.41X	2.60X	2.74X	2.20X
Total Debt/Capitalization	95%	94%	75%	79%	80%	79%
Total debt to EBITDA	6.23X	5.87X	5.12X	4.96X	4.20X	n/a
Common shares outstanding at year-end (millions)	n/a	n/a	19.8	20.1	20.2	26.3
Period-end share price	n/a	n/a	$20.00	$14.88	$25.25	$36.44
Operations						
Number of operating plants	5	8	10	18	22	22
Capacity-gross (MW)	221	349	589	2,194	2,729	3,018
Capacity-net (MW)	141	268	508	1,268	2,064	2,064

[a] Basic and fully diluted earnings per share in the first quarter of 1998 were ($0.15) and ($0.15), respectively.

Source: Calpine Corporation Annual Reports.

In addition to the debt issues, Calpine also decided to raise public equity. Credit Suisse First Boston (CSFB) led an initial public offering (IPO) in September 1996, which raised $317 million at a price of $16.00 per share (Exhibit 6-4 shows the performance of Calpine's stock since the IPO). Of this amount, $109 million went to Calpine and the rest went to Electrowatt, which sold all of its shares. Commenting on the IPO, *Barron's* wrote:

> In this year's first half, Calpine's pro forma $28 million interest expense was far greater than its $20 million cash flow. Eight of its 16 plants sell electricity to Pacific Gas & Electric for fixed prices under agreements that expire in 1998 through 2000. . . . Maybe that's why Electrowatt is willing to sell all its Calpine shares and cease its financing of Calpine. Electrowatt's decision gives the public the chance to invest in a highly-leveraged company whose fundamentals may be about to deteriorate. If that's not enough to discourage the

EXHIBIT 6-3B

CALPINE CORPORATION'S ISSUANCE OF PUBLIC CAPITAL, 1984–1999 ($ IN MILLIONS)[a]

	1994	1995	1996	1997	1998	3/99
S&P Debt Rating	B	B−	BB−	BB−	BB	BB
Debt[b]	$105.0	—	$180.0	$275.0	$400.0	$600.0
Net proceeds to Calpine	101.0	—	175.0	265.0	392.0	589.8
Underwriter discounts (bp)	262.5		250.0	195.0	190.0	162.5
Common Stock	—	—	$317.0	—	—	$213.9
net proceeds to sellers	—	—	298.0	—	—	203.8

[a] Prior to 1994 there were no capital markets issues.

[b] Debt issues consisted of Calpine Corporation senior unsecured fixed-rate notes with either seven- or ten-year bullet maturities. Underwriter discounts and other fees represent the difference between gross and net proceeds to Calpine.

[c] Combined initial public offering by Calpine and secondary offering by its parent Electrowatt; proceeds—$109 million for Calpine IPO and $189 million for Electrowatt. Offering price was $16 per share.

Source: Calpine Corporation Annual Reports; casewriter estimates.

over-enthusiastic, the multiples may; Calpine's market value will be 1.5 times revenues, and 26 times earnings.[8]

The Pasadena Power Plant

In 1996, Phillips Petroleum requested bids for a 20-year, fixed-price contract on 90 MW of power for a chemical plant in Pasadena, Texas. Having lost out on a previous request for proposal (RFP) from Phillips, Calpine was determined to win this proposal. The Calpine team analyzed the Texas power market and recognized that NEPA's open-access rulings meant Calpine could sell power to any wholesale buyer connected to the Texas power grid. The wholesale market price, they reasoned, had to be driven by the economics of existing gas-fired generating plants, which had an average heat rate of approximately 11,000. Calpine's CCGT plant, on the other hand, would have a heat rate of 7,500 or less, assuming they used a larger, more efficient turbine package capable of producing 240 MW of output. This difference in generating efficiency would be an advantage in a competitive market for a commodity product. Assuming a natural gas price of $3.00 per million BTU (mmBTU), the extra 150 MW of "merchant" or competitively priced output would have an annual fuel cost of $29.6 million [= 150MW * 8,760 hours/year * $22.50/MWh; where $22.50/MWh = ($3.00/mmBTU) * (7,500 BTU/kWh) * (1 mmBTU/1,000,000BTU) * (1,000kWh/MWh)]. Yet the market price would reflect the market's average heat rate of 11,000, which implied a generating cost of $43.4 million.[9] This cost advantage would last until new, more efficient

[8] "Offerings in the Offing," *Barron's*, September 16, 1996, p. 46.

[9] The calculations assume that the plants operate continuously throughout the year. In industry terminology, they have an "availability factor" of 100%. The average availability factor for CCGT plants was 89%, though it ranged from a high of 97% down to 80% or less depending on a plant's age and quality.

EXHIBIT 6-4

CALPINE CORPORATION STOCK PRICE FROM ITS IPO IN SEPTEMBER 1996 TO MAY 1999 (NYSE:CPN)

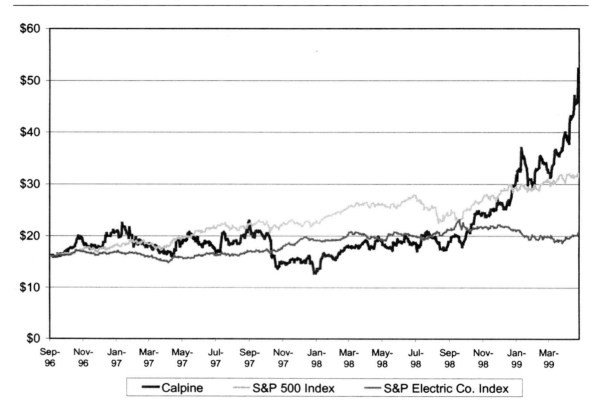

Source: Adapted from Datastream.

marginal capacity drove down the market's average heat rate. Exhibit 6-5 illustrates the economics for a typical CCGT power plant.

After reviewing this analysis, Calpine senior management assembled to prepare their final proposal. In that meeting, they decided to oversize the plant and aggressively bid on the deal. With hindsight, Kelly saw this Sunday afternoon meeting as a turning point in the company's history because Calpine was leaving its IPP roots and entering the unexplored world of merchant power.

Ultimately, Calpine won the contract. They began construction in February 1997, financed with a $152 million project loan from ING (U.S.) Capital. Although it was the first loan to a U.S. power plant with merchant risk, the syndication was oversubscribed in the bank market. Calpine completed the Pasadena plant three months ahead of schedule and $21 million under budget. Since completion, the plant had achieved an average availability of 95.1%.

EXHIBIT 6-5

REPRESENTATIVE ECONOMICS FOR A COMBINED-CYCLE GAS FIRED POWER PLANT

Key Assumptions

Output (megawatts)	1,000	
Capacity Factor (availability)	90%	
Electricity Price ($ per MWh)		
In 1999	$31.00	assuming a market heat rate of 11,000
In 2009	$24.00	assuming a market heat rate of 7,500
Fuel (Gas) Price ($ per MMBtu)	$2.20	note: 1 MMBtu = 1,000,000 Btu
Plant Heat Rate (Btu per kWh)	7,500	note: 1000 kWh = 1 MWh
O&M Expense ($ per MWh)	$3.50	
Capital Costs (millions)	$500	note: construction period = 2 years
Depreciable Life (years)	30	
Debt-to-Capitalization Ratio	65%	
Debt Interest Rate	7.75%	
Inflation Rate	2.00%	
Tax Rate	38%	

	Total For the Plant ($000)	Dollars Per MWh Produced
Production (MWh)	**7,884,000**	
Revenue	**$ 244,404**	**$31.00**
Expense		
Fuel	130,086	16.50
O&M Expense	27,594	3.50
Depreciation	16,667	2.11
Total Expense	174,347	22.11
Gross Profit	70,057	8.89
Interest Expense	25,188	3.19
Profit before Tax	44,870	5.69
Taxes @ 38%	17,051	2.16
Net Income	**27,819**	**3.53**

Source: Company documents and casewriter estimates.

Calpine's New Strategy

Following the Pasadena decision, the company's strategy changed dramatically. Kelly explained:

> Pete Cartwright sensed that the world was going towards large, gas-fired generating units selling power into competitive markets. Rather than being reactive and answering RFPs, Pete wanted to be proactive and re-power America. With a cost advantage of this

magnitude and a market where demand was exceeding supply, we didn't see how we could lose. The only questions were how quickly could we build plants and how long could we sustain an advantage?

The components of the new strategy quickly fell into place. The goal was to become one of the largest and most profitable power generators in the United States. Although Cartwright believed the strategy was exportable as well as scaleable, the initial focus was on the United States where the opportunity was the greatest. Calpine could achieve this goal by using environmentally friendly, high-efficiency gas turbines and building a vertically integrated company with engineering, construction, operating, fuel supply, power marketing, and financing capabilities in a single firm. The concept of a vertically integrated power system was predicated on a belief that being the low-cost producer was the only way to win in a business where both the primary input (natural gas) and the primary output (electricity) were commodities. This structure meant that Calpine had to reduce costs in all of the other aspects of the value chain if it were going to become the low-cost producer.

Kelly described the first component of the strategy, reducing construction costs:

> We want to commoditize the physical product—a power plant. We ask how much did it cost to build the last one, and then say the next one should be less. The key, however, is that we focus on life-cycle costs, not just construction costs. As the contractor, owner, and operator of plants, we have the ability and the incentive to reduce life-cycle costs in ways that independent contractors or operators do not.

Kelly believed they could reduce the cost of a $300 million plant by at least 25% by using a standardized plant design, buying turbines and other equipment in bulk, and using experienced management who could benefit from learning curve efficiencies. Rather than relying on outside general contractors and turnkey contracts, Calpine would manage construction itself under the "Calpine Construct" method. Besides eliminating costly and time-consuming negotiations with contractors, this approach eliminated the cost of the general contractor's margin and contingency reserves. In October 1998, Calpine acquired the Walsh Construction Power Division of the Guy Atkinson Corporation, a Sacramento-based construction management firm, and folded it into a new subsidiary named Calpine Construction Corporation to manage plant construction.

Next, Calpine focused on reducing operating and maintenance costs, a major factor given the expected life of a power plant was 35 years or more. By avoiding myopic decisions during construction that lowered construction costs but increased operating costs, and by having system operators rather than duplicative plant operators, Calpine could reduce operating costs. In terms of maintenance costs, Calpine planned to develop an in-house maintenance group, which would enable it to forgo costly turbine warranties as well as after-sale maintenance contracts. At the same time, it could have a single inventory of spare parts for the entire system rather than an inventory for each plant. These and other savings might reduce operating and maintenance costs by 10%.

To operate a system of merchant power plants in a competitive market also required active management of the fuel supply and power marketing functions. Neither of these activities was a core competency in the company's former mode of operating single power plants with long-term contracts covering 100% of the output. In a competitive market, Calpine would either own or buy gas in bulk, and would sell power to multiple customers under spot, medium, and long-term contracts. In addition to diversifying the credit risk inherent in power sales, there was an opportunity to improve the product offering by enhancing reliability. For customers, reliability was a critical purchase criteria because electricity had to be available without interruption and at a specific voltage when needed. For these reasons, a multiplant operator had a significant advantage over a single-plant operator. Calpine expected to save 5% in gas supply costs and power marketing costs and might even get a price premium for its power. Like the construction and maintenance functions, Calpine began staffing new subsidiaries to handle these functions.

Although the senior management team believed the power system approach made sense and would allow them to win in a competitive environment, they knew the opportunity to re-power America was, at best, likely to be a five-year opportunity. As new, more efficient capacity came on line, the industry's average heat rate would gradually decline to 7,500—a process they thought would take 10 to 12 years. In fact, as of year-end 1998, developers had announced plans to build 109 plants in the United States with generating capacity of 56,368 MW, prompting one journalist to proclaim "Merchant power plants are emerging en masse . . . thanks to deregulation and fearless developers."[10]

Recognizing that speed was of the essence, Calpine carefully considered the options for developing barriers to entry, of which they saw two. First, they had to secure the best plant sites in markets where existing plants had high heat rates and regulation favored merchant plants. Locating sites was not difficult because gas-fired plants needed to be near the intersection of a gas pipeline and a high-voltage transmission line. On the other hand, getting permits and locking in customers was more complicated. If Calpine was able to get the most attractive sites and begin construction, it might discourage others from entering particular markets. Second, Calpine needed combined-cycle gas turbines. Siemens-Westinghouse and General Electric (GE) were the only substantial domestic manufacturers of high-efficiency gas turbines, and both had limited production capacity. Neither had increased capacity over the past 20 years due to the dropoff in construction of new power plants. Calpine believed neither was likely to increase capacity much in the next several years because adding new capacity was expensive, could hurt pricing, and might end up idle once the building spree was over. Recognizing the strategic importance of turbines, CEO Pete Cartwright had recently decided to increase the company's turbine orders from six at the end of 1998 to 60 or more with deliveries scheduled over the next five years. Total cost for the turbines would exceed $3 billion.[11]

FINANCING THE NEW STRATEGY

Kelly and Crabtree realized that the same pressure for cost reductions would be applied to the finance function as well. Whereas reductions of 10% to 25% were set as goals for other functions, the opportunities for reducing financing costs were less clear, especially if speed was critical. On the one hand, the capital markets set the price of debt and equity issues. (Exhibits 6-6a and 6-6b show current financial and power market data.) On the other hand, they could choose the specific instruments and the sequence in which to use them. If they could save even a small amount on issuance costs, it might turn out to be a significant amount given the financial need.

To get to 15,000 MW in five years, they needed to raise at least $4.5 billion from the debt and equity markets assuming Calpine generated $1.5 billion of cash from operations as projected. In the near term, however, they needed to finance four merchant plants with a total capacity of 2,365 MW—Magic Valley (Texas), Sutter (California),

[10] Thurston, "Merchant Power: Promise or reality? p. 14.
[11] Calpine Corporation, 1998 Annual Report, p. 61.

EXHIBIT 6-6A

SELECTED FINANCIAL MARKET DATA

	May 17, 1999
Yields on U.S. Treasury Bills, Notes, and Bonds	
1-year	4.90%
2-year	5.31
5-year	5.53
10-year	5.66
30-year	5.91
Yields on 10-year Corporate Bonds (by S&P Rating)	
AAA	6.27%
AA	6.34
A	6.53
BBB	6.84
BB	7.76
B	9.12
C	10.21
Interest Rates	
3-month LIBOR	5.03%
6-month LIBOR	5.13
3-month CD	4.94
Prime Rate	7.75
Calpine Corporation	
Equity Beta (calculated using 2 years of daily data)	0.60
Asset Beta (calculated using 2 years of daily data)	0.20

Source: Federal Reserve Bulletin, Bloomberg, and Datastream.

EXHIBIT 6-6B

ASSUMED GAS AND ELECTRICITY PRICES IN CERTAIN REGIONAL MARKETS

	1999	2000	2001	2002
Electricity ($/MWh)				
California/Arizona	$24.69	$26.50	$27.73	$29.54
Texas	25.22	26.21	26.00	26.36
New England	35.18	36.48	37.86	40.15
Gas ($/mmBTU)				
California/Arizona	$ 2.24	$ 2.19	$ 2.28	$ 2.38
Texas	2.19	2.14	2.23	2.33
New England	2.84	2.94	2.99	3.07
Hypothetical Heat Rates[a]				
California/Arizona	11,024	12,101	12,164	12,413
Texas	11,515	12,246	11,661	11,314
New England	12,400	12,409	12,658	12,678

[a] Assuming 100% availability and fuel (gas) costs only.

Source: Morgan Stanley Dean Witter, US Investment Research on Calpine Corp., June 18, 1999.

Westbrook (Maine), and South Point (Arizona)—at a cost of approximately $300 million each. Kelly and Crabtree believed they had three options: use project finance at the subsidiary level, raise corporate debt at the parent level, or, perhaps, try a hybrid option with elements of both project and corporate finance.

Project Finance

Project finance had worked well for Calpine, and the company could count on support as well as reasonable terms from a broad group of banks. The process and players were familiar to Kelly and his team, and vice versa. As a result, it seemed the most certain source of funding. But Kelly had reservations about whether the traditional approach was going to fit with the company's new growth strategy. For example, if each plant were in a separate collateral package with a different group of lenders, could Calpine operate the plants as a power system? Would the lenders to plant A allow power to be diverted to plant B's customers when plant B went down for maintenance? An even greater source of concern was the time and cost of structuring individual deals—historically, it had taken six months or more per deal. With four plants under development, they would have to manage four sets of contracts, four sets of loan negotiations, and four bank groups, all in parallel. Finally, they were concerned about both the total size and the absorption capacity of the project finance market. In Kelly's words:

> There are only 50 or so banks in the project loan market at any one time, and they all have per-customer credit limits. If we want to finance a $6 billion portfolio, that's over $100 million per bank, which is going to be a stretch number for many of them. Size limitations in the bank loan market were the reason why we migrated to the bond market back in 1994. The bond market is huge.[12]

Crabtree added, "You just can't put that many deals into the bank market at one time, at any price. I don't think we can do more than three or four deals at a time without competing against ourselves."

Despite these concerns, Kelly and Crabtree opened discussions with Calpine's project finance lenders, hoping to discover new ways to finance the growth. While the bankers were willing to lend on a single-plant basis, they showed little flexibility when Kelly described his desire to finance a power system. Kelly explained:

> We sat down with a couple of banks and explained our objectives. They told us you can't do this and you can't do that, and said the idea of financing a group of plants was like trying to put a square peg in a round hole. It sounded like a nice concept, but the bankers didn't think it would work in practice.[13]

Following these discussions, Calpine's banks submitted term sheets for each of the four plants assuming the traditional project finance model. The term sheet for the Sutter plant was representative (see Exhibit 6-7). It offered 100% construction financing for two years but required Calpine to repay half the debt, $150 million, once construction was complete. Except for this obligation, the debt was nonrecourse to Calpine. The remaining $150 million construction loan would then convert to a three-year term

[12] Adapted from "My Way," an interview with Calpine Senior Vice President for Finance, Robert D. Kelly, in the November 2000 issue of *Project Finance*, p. 29. Supplemented with information from a personal interview with the casewriters.
[13] Ibid.

EXHIBIT 6-7

PROPOSED TERM SHEET FOR PROJECT FINANCING OF SUTTER COUNTY (CALIFORNIA) PLANT

Borrower:	Special Purpose Project Company, wholly owned by Calpine Corporation.
Use of Proceeds:	Construction and operation of 500 MW natural gas-fired, combined–cycle, fully merchant power plant located in Sutter County, California.
Project Cost:	$300 million (estimate).
Equity Contribution:	Calpine will contribute 50% of the Project Cost on the Conversion Date.
Credit Facilities:	Senior secured construction loan and senior secured term loan.
Security:	Lenders will have a senior security interest in all Project assets including plant and equipment, contracts, contract rights, and bank accounts.
Construction Loan Amount:	100% of a predetermined and agreed Project Cost.
Term Loan Amount:	The amount of the Construction Loan outstanding after application of the Equity Contribution (expected to be 50% of the Project Cost).
Conversion Date:	The earlier of the Project Completion Date or two years after the Closing Date.
Maturities:	The Construction Loan will mature on the Conversion Date; the Term Loan will mature three years after the Conversion Date.
Repayment:	The Construction Loan will be repaid from the proceeds of the Term Loan and the Equity Contribution. The Term Loan will be repaid over three years in quarterly installments to be negotiated.
Arranger:	A Leading Project Finance Bank (to be determined).
Underwriting:	The Arranger will underwrite 100% of the Credit Facilities, with the expectation that funds will be provided by lenders in a syndication led by the Arranger.
Underwriting Fee:	1.50% of the Construction Loan, payable on the Closing Date. The Arranger will pay up-front fees to the lenders at its discretion.
Interest Rates:	Construction Loan: LIBOR +1.375%. Term Loan: LIBOR +1.375% in Year 1, 1.500% in Year 2, and 1.625% in Year 3.
Interest Rate Hedging:	Borrower required to hedge or fix all or a portion of the Construction Loan and the Term Loan.
Commitment Fee:	The Borrower will pay 0.375% p.a. on Undrawn Construction Loan Amounts.
Drawdowns:	Construction Loan Drawdowns monthly according to an agreed plan of construction and subject to approval by the Lenders' independent engineer.
Distributions of Operating Cash Flow:	The Borrower may distribute cash flow during the term loan period only after payment of operating expenses and debt service, funding of a 6-month debt service reserve account, and subject to maintaining a Debt Service Coverage Ratio (DSCR) to be determined. All excess cash will be swept into debt repayment if the DSCR falls below a level to be agreed.
Conditions Precedent:	Usual and customary, including technical evaluation reports from the lenders' independent engineer, gas consultant, electricity market consultant, and other consultants as reasonably required by the Arranger.
	The Arranger shall have received and approved the Construction Budget, drawdown schedule, and financial projections.
	The Arranger shall be satisfied that the financial projections, under sensitivity analysis, show an average DSCR of 2.75X-3.00X and a minimum DSCR of 2.25X-2.50X.
	The Arranger shall have received a satisfactory power marketing plan identifying potential buyers under a full output assumption and a satisfactory fuel plan that addresses the Project's natural gas requirements.

Source: Company documents.

loan with a yet to be negotiated principal payment schedule. If the lenders insisted on rapid repayment, it would reduce Calpine's internal rate of return (IRR); if the lenders allowed a big balloon payment, it would expose Calpine to refinancing risk at the end of the three years. In terms of rates, the banks proposed an underwriting fee of 150 bp and a spread of 137.5 bp to 162.5 bp over LIBOR—the spread increased over time as a way to encourage early refinancing. In addition, the banks requested market flex and clear market provisions, which would allow them to increase fees and rates if necessary to syndicate the deals. Although not stated explicitly, Kelly expected the banks to require a floating-to-fixed rate swap contract that could add as much as 75 bp to the spread. Finally, the term sheets included standard project finance covenants, conditions precedent, and reporting requirements. Through these loan agreements, the banks would have a lien on the plant and control over cash flows. (Exhibits 6-1a and 6-1b illustrate the legal and transaction structures of the project finance proposals.)

Corporate Finance

A second option was a public offering of senior notes by Calpine Corporation. Calpine had achieved a Ba2/BB rating on its most recent debt issue, a $350 million offering of senior notes in March 1999, putting it at the upper end of the subinvestment grade or high-yield market. Except for the interest rate, Kelly expected future senior note issues would have similar terms (see Exhibit 6-8). The March 1999 notes had a fixed coupon of 7.75% per annum that was some 250 bp over the 10-year Treasury yield at the time. The amortized underwriting discount (i.e., issuance cost) of 1.625% and legal fees resulted in an all-in cost of 8.10% per annum.

There were several advantages to issuing corporate notes. For example, based on Calpine's previous note issues, the market was receptive to 7- and 10-year bullet maturities, which fit well with Calpine's growth strategy. Moreover, a high-yield offering would not require collateral, would reduce legal fees, and would leave Calpine free to operate its plants as a system. Compared to project finance, the covenant package was liberal. The main restrictions were that Calpine could not issue any secured debt and could not issue unsecured debt if the ratio of EBITDA to interest expense fell below 2:1 on a consolidated basis. There were no restrictions on nonrecourse debt at the subsidiary level, leaving the project finance option open for new construction. Finally, the note holders had no rights to approve individual projects, monitor construction, or receive information beyond Calpine's normal SEC filings.

On the other hand, the high-yield market was thinner and more volatile than the investment grade market (Exhibit 6-9), making availability and pricing a risk from one month to the next. Another concern was the cost of negative arbitrage. During construction, Calpine would have to pay a long-term interest rate, yet earn only a short-term deposit rate, on unused funds. This spread could easily be 250 to 300 basis points.

Even if market conditions were receptive, a large debt issue might jeopardize its BB debt rating unless Calpine concurrently issued additional equity. However, Kelly believed that equity was the most expensive form of capital:

> The market sees equity sales prior to completion as highly risky and, therefore, demands venture capital returns. If we sell stock before the plants are built, it'll be priced at 12 times earnings, but if we sell stock after the plants are up and running, I think we can get 25 to 40 times earnings. The risk is that we dilute our earnings per share, which would have a devastating effect on our stock price as a high-growth company and hurt our ability to raise new capital for future growth.

EXHIBIT 6-8

SUMMARY OF TERMS FOR CALPINE CORPORATION'S $350 MILLION SENIOR NOTE ISSUE OF MARCH 29, 1999

Borrower:	Calpine Corporation
Issue Amount:	$350,000,000 Senior Notes Due 2009
Use of Proceeds:	Unrestricted
Underwriters:	Credit Suisse First Boston (Books), CIBC Oppenheimer, TD Securities, ING Barings, Scotia Capital Markets.
Repayment:	The Borrower will be obligated to repay the Notes on April 15, 2009.
Redemption:	The Borrower has no right to redeem the Notes prior to maturity.
Collateral:	The Notes are unsecured.
Ranking:	The Notes will rank equally with other senior indebtedness of the Borrower, consisting of approximately $952 million in other issues of senior unsecured long-term notes. The Notes are effectively subordinated to all liabilities of Calpine subsidiaries, including trade payables.
Interest Rate:	7.75% p.a., payable semiannually.
Underwriting Discount:	1.625% of the Issue Amount will be retained by the Underwriters.
Covenants:	Covenants impose limitations on the Borrower in regard to changing the nature of its business, incurring additional debt, incurring liens on its assets (but not assets of its subsidiaries), repaying subordinated debt (if any), and payment of dividends. Generally, covenants do not restrict the Borrower from incurring additional *unsecured* debt provided the consolidated EBITDA/interest ratio remains greater than 2:1; and do not restrict the subsidiaries from incurring additional *non-recourse* debt to acquire or construct assets; there are no financial covenants (required financial ratios, minimum net worth, etc.).
Events of Default:	Nonpayment of interest or principal; bankruptcy
Conditions Precedent:	Not required

Source: Company documents; casewriter summary.

Revolving Construction Facility

Through discussions with Credit Suisse First Boston (CSFB), Calpine developed a third option. Managing Directors Adebayo (Bayo) Ogunlesi and Ray Wood, who managed the Calpine relationship for CSFB, believed their firm could arrange a financing that met Calpine's needs. Ogunlesi said, "We've always thought there must be a more efficient way (to finance power plants) that could cut out the time spent sitting around a table, eating stale pizza and Chinese food, and re-inventing the wheel."[14] According to the plan, a new subsidiary named Calpine Construction Finance Company (CCFC) would borrow $1 billion in a secured revolving construction facility with a four-year maturity (see Exhibits 6-10 and 6-11). Calpine would invest $430 million of equity and guarantee completion of the four plants by investing as much additional equity as needed to finish the plants by a certain date. CCFC would also be able to use the funds to build additional power plants subject to approval by a committee comprised of lending banks.

[14] J. Keegan, "Building Calpine's Financing Future: Deregulation Breeds Innovation," *Investment Dealers Digest*, December 13, 1999.

EXHIBIT 6-9

U.S. CORPORATE BOND ISSUANCE BY S&P RATING AND PROJECT DEBT, 1990–1999 (IN $ BILLIONS)

	1985	1986	1987	1988	1989	1990	1991	1992	1993	1994	1995	1996	1997	1998
US Corporate Bond Issuance (by S&P Rating)														
AAA	$22.2	$63.8	$78.0	$79.3	$54.2	$119.2	$170.7	$188.4	$213.1	$207.9	$167.2	$242.3	$329.2	$517.1
AA	23.4	53.8	42.2	31.7	37.3	108.8	116.3	105.5	140.2	67.8	82.3	100.0	237.9	336.8
A	23.5	32.9	24.8	28.9	32.8	105.5	215.8	203.6	228.5	182.9	322.2	329.7	529.9	647.6
BBB	11.2	21.6	19.4	15.2	13.9	36.4	52.9	100.5	115.7	101.2	105.7	146.5	219.2	323.2
BB	3.3	6.0	5.7	2.9	4.5	7.2	20.6	23.0	33.4	21.0	26.6	40.9	82.6	104.9
B	5.9	20.2	21.5	18.5	20.0	1.5	6.2	27.9	39.8	23.7	20.0	44.6	82.9	92.8
CCC	2.0	5.2	5.2	5.9	1.0	0.0	0.5	1.0	1.6	1.9	1.0	1.8	3.0	9.4
Global Project Debt														
Loans	n/a	n/a	n/a	n/a	n/a	n/a	n/a	n/a	n/a	13.7	23.3	42.8	67.5	56.7
Bonds	n/a	n/a	n/a	n/a	n/a	n/a	n/a	n/a	n/a	4.0	3.8	4.8	7.5	9.8

Source: Securities Data Corporation, Project Finance International (various issues).

EXHIBIT 6-10

PROPOSED STRUCTURE FOR A REVOLVING CONSTRUCTION FACILITY

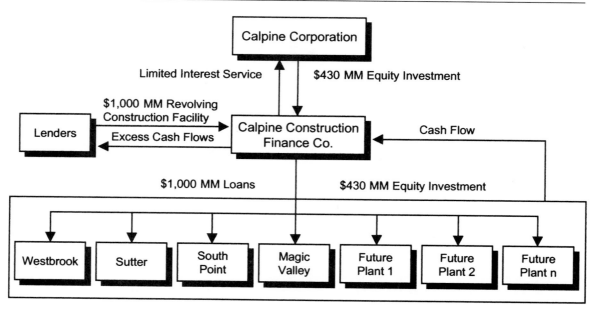

Source: Company documents, CS First Boston term sheet.

As a revolving facility, amounts borrowed and repaid could be re-borrowed for these additional plants, with no required repayment of principal due until 2003. Financing the four plants in one transaction was appealing from a process standpoint and would save legal and other fees. Kelly summarized the advantages as he saw them:

> In traditional project finance, when you pay down the loan, that's it. But here, we can re-borrow as we pay down the loan and bring in the next plant. So we are basically constructing plants in a circle. We can use the $1 billion of capital to finance eight or twelve plants instead of just four. Essentially, this structure allows us to increase the velocity of money with a single up-front fee. And it allows us to develop our program regardless of what's going on in the bank or bond markets because we have pre-approval to build plants.[15]

What was unique about the structure was that it combined elements of both project and corporate finance: in essence, Calpine would project finance a portfolio of plants rather than a single plant. Like project finance, CCFC would involve a nonrecourse loan, thereby allowing Calpine to raise a large amount of capital, which might not be possible at the parent level. In addition, the banks would have CCFC's assets as collateral and would control the cash flows. Yet like a corporate bond, it gave Calpine the flexibility to build plants using its in-house resources and manage them as part of a power system. Even though the structure gave Calpine more flexibility, they believed

[15] Adapted from "My Way," an interview with Calpine Senior Vice President for Finance, Robert D. Kelly, p. 27.

EXHIBIT 6-11

TERM SHEET FOR PROPOSED CSFB–CALPINE REVOLVING CONSTRUCTION FACILITY

Borrower: Calpine Construction Finance Company (CCFC), a wholly-owned subsidiary of Calpine Corporation.

Approved Plants: Magic Valley, South Point, Sutter, Westbrook, and future plants that are located in the U.S. and are approved by a Technical Committee of Lenders.

Credit Facility: 4-year secured revolving credit.

Equity Contribution: $430 million from Calpine prior to any loan disbursement.

Guarantor: Calpine guarantees additional equity, if required to complete construction of the plants on the agreed schedule.

Calpine guarantees obligations, if any, of its affiliates to Borrower.

Lead Arrangers: Credit Suisse First Boston and Bank of Nova Scotia.

Lenders: A syndicate of banks selected by the Lead Arrangers and Calpine.

Amount: $1,000,000,000

Purpose: Construction of the Approved Plants

Collateral: (i) all assets of the Borrower including the Approved Plants and assignment of the Borrower's rights under all Project Contracts.

(ii) all partnership or other ownership interests in the Borrower.

Interest Rate: Level I: LIBOR + 150bp if the Borrower has Debt/Capital ≤ 50%

Level II: LIBOR + 175bp if the Borrower has 50% < Debt/Capital ≤ 60%

Level III: LIBOR + 212.50bp if the Borrower has 60% < Debt/Capital ≤ 70%

Commitment Fee: 50 bp per annum payable on any committed but undrawn portion of the Revolver.

Upfront Fee: 150 bp payable to the Lead Arrangers at closing.

Activation Fee: 25 bp on subsequent borrowings

Conditions Precedent to First Funding: Including, but not limited to:
(1) All required equity contributions have been made;
(2) Independent Engineer's confirmation that costs incurred conform to approved construction plans and sufficient funds remain to complete construction;
(3) Calpine Corporation is rated no lower than Ba3 and BB, or Ba2 and BB−, by Moody's and S&P, respectively,
(4) projected Interest Coverage Ratio not materially different from projections;
(5) No Material Adverse Effect on Borrower or Calpine.

Priority of Cash Flow: Revenues generated at Approved Plants to be applied as follows:
(1) on a monthly basis to operating and maintenance expenses;
(2) on a quarterly basis to bank fees and interest;
(3) distributions to Calpine but only to fund interest on debt used to pay down this Revolver or equity investment in the Borrower;
(4) principal reductions on this credit facility.

Non-Recourse: All obligations (other than Calpine equity obligations and Calpine covenants) shall be obligations solely of the Borrower and the Banks shall have recourse only to the Borrower and the collateral with respect thereto.

Borrower Covenants: Maintain trailing four-quarter EBITDA/interest coverage of ≥ 2.25:1.00;

Maintain a maximum Debt/Capitalization ratio of 70% (60% if Calpine is not rated at least Ba2/BB).

Calpine Covenants: On a consolidated basis:
(i) Debt/Capitalization ratio ≤ 0.85;
(ii) EBITDA/Interest ≥ 1.75X;
(iii) Calpine (parent only) EBITDA/interest ≥ 1.60X.

Other: Calpine required to own 100% of the Borrower;

Borrower required to own 100% of Approved Plants until maturity of this Facility.

Source: Company documents.

the cost would be competitive with standard project financings. There was a 150 bp up-front fee plus a 25 bp activation fee on any borrowings associated with the future plants after the first four. Interest was on a floating-rate basis starting at 150 bp over LIBOR and ranging up to 212.5 bp over LIBOR as CCFC's leverage increased.

One area of concern, however, was the refinancing risk associated with the four-year maturity. Kelly and Crabtree identified four ways to address this risk. First, they could use operating cash flow from the first four plants to pay down the revolver balance to the point where CCFC would be an attractive borrower in either the bank or the public debt market—these plants would begin operations in 2001. Second, they could issue debt or equity at the Calpine level to repay the debt. Third, they could refinance the plants individually using project finance. Even if these options were not available, Kelly believed that CCFC's cash flow would pay off the $1 billion loan within a reasonable period after the maturity date. With so many options available, Kelly's main concern was not the refinancing:

> I just need the money and I don't care whose balance sheet it comes off. If I don't get the money up front, I don't have to worry about taking it out in four years. I also don't have to worry about building any power plants. So our philosophy has been, send the money first, then we'll talk about taking it out in the capital markets.[16]

CONCLUSION

Intrigued by the concept, Kelly and Crabtree invited the CSFB team out to San Jose so they could flesh out the details of the revolving credit facility. To avoid the anticipated tendency to hold on to traditional notions associated with project finance, Crabtree placed a glass bowl in the center of the conference table with a sign that read "No Project Finance." Every time someone harkened back to a project finance concept, he or she would have to put $5.00 into the bowl. As the dollars began to mount and various doubts began to emerge, Kelly added a second deterrent. Knowing Ogunlesi's confidence that some kind of deal could be done, he put Ogunlesi's phone number on the wall and referred to a willingness "to call Bayo" whenever the conversation hit a snag.

These tactics seemed to work because the group made steady progress throughout the day. As the details emerged, Kelly and Crabtree grew increasingly excited about the structure. But convincing them the deal was possible was not the hard part. The real problem would be to convince the market that the revolving credit facility made sense. After all, Calpine had pioneered the relatively new concept of financing single merchant plants, yet the CCFC proposal involved the concurrent construction of four merchant plants, plus a number of follow-on plants that were still not much past the conceptual stage. Would they be able to convince banks to finance a system of merchant plants? If bankers reacted with the same skepticism they did when Kelly first described the deal, it would never fly. Recent discussions with a team from Bank of Nova Scotia led them to believe they had other advocates for the deal. But to raise the full $1 billion, they would need to convince 20 or more banks that it was feasible. On a grander scale, Kelly and Crabtree wanted to understand how the revolving credit facility deal would affect Calpine's ability to finance the remaining $3 billion to $4 billion needed to reach the five-year target of 15,000 MW. Could they do more than one deal, or would they have to search for other solutions in the coming years?

---

[16] Ibid., p. 29.

7

BP Amoco (A): Policy Statement on the Use of Project Finance

As two of the largest oil and gas firms in the world, The British Petroleum Company p.l.c. (BP) and Amoco Corporation (Amoco) had a long history of competitive encounters. This rivalry continued into the 1990s in a variety of locations ranging from the United States to the North Sea to, more recently, the Caspian Sea—a region that had opened up to exploration by Western oil companies following the breakup of the Soviet Union in 1991. In describing this rivalry, one analyst wrote:

> Azerbaijan was an early battleground for BP and Amoco as these two companies competed for the oil riches of this newly independent country. During the period from 1990 until 1994, BP and Amoco were the two major players in the Azerbaijan oil rush. This competition extended to their respective governments, each of which was trying to support its country's commercial interests via BP and Amoco.[1]

Despite their historic rivalry, BP and Amoco agreed to a $48 billion merger in August 1998. Following shareholder approvals in December, they began the process of integration, which involved placement decisions for hundreds of executives and creation of a new organizational structure. Within the Finance Group, BP's John Buchanan and David Watson retained their positions as chief financial officer and treasurer, respectively. Bill Young, a 20-year Amoco veteran, became head of a unit known as Specialized Finance, with responsibility for advising the company's business units on project structuring, project finance, leasing, and other asset-backed transactions.

Dean's Research Fellow Michael Kane and Professor Benjamin C. Esty prepared this case. HBS cases are developed solely as the basis for class discussion. Cases are not intended to serve as endorsements, sources of primary data, or illustrations of effective or ineffective management.

[1] S.R. Sobhani, "BP-Amoco Oil Marriage May Force US-Iran vows, Too," *Houston Chronicle*, August 30, 1998.

Shortly after the merger, in March 1999, David Watson asked Bill Young to prepare a recommendation on when and in what circumstances the firm should use external project finance instead of its own internal, corporate funds to finance new investments. One challenging aspect of this assignment was the perception that BP and Amoco had somewhat different philosophies regarding project finance. To some observers, particularly those outside the firms, Amoco was viewed as more willing to use project finance than BP. Young disagreed with this characterization, though he acknowledged that he had little information on BP's financial policies prior to the merger. As background for his presentation, he and two colleagues from the Finance Group, Adam Wilson and Mike Wrenn, met with finance executives from both organizations and debated the merits of project finance with them.

Based on these discussions, Young, Wilson, and Wrenn proposed that BP Amoco should finance all projects with corporate funds, except in a few special circumstances. As they prepared for the upcoming presentation, they wondered whether they had fairly evaluated the costs and benefits of project finance, and whether senior management would concur with their recommendations.

THE BP/AMOCO MERGER

The British Petroleum Company p.l.c.

BP was the largest company in the United Kingdom and the third largest publicly held oil and gas company in the world. It had 56,000 employees, activities in more than 70 countries, and three principal lines of businesses: crude oil and natural gas exploration and production (E&P), refining and marketing (R&M), and petrochemical production. Its principal producing or "upstream" assets were oil and gas fields in the North Sea and on Alaska's North Slope, where it had been a leader in the development of the Prudhoe Bay oil field and the construction of the Trans Alaska Pipeline. BP's refining and marketing operations, the "downstream" assets, consisted of refineries, service stations, transportation and storage facilities, most of which were located in the United Kingdom, United States, and Europe. Besides oil and gas, BP was also a leading chemical producer with several proprietary technologies such as processes for making polyethylene and acetyls. Sir John Browne, a 22-year veteran of the company and former head of the E&P business, had been the group chief executive since 1995.

In 1997, BP earned $4.1 billion on revenues of $71.3 billion and assets of $54.6 billion. (Exhibits 7-1 and 7-2 include summaries of BP's financial statements.) Adjusted for exceptional items, exploration and production, refining and marketing, and petrochemicals accounted for 68%, 21%, and 11%, respectively, of consolidated 1997 earnings.

Amoco Corporation

Amoco was the sixth largest publicly traded oil and gas company in the world and, like BP, had vertically integrated global operations encompassing exploration and production, refining and marketing, and chemical production. Although it had significant exploration and development programs in over 25 countries, the United States and Canada accounted for over 80% of consolidated assets and 95% of operating profit. In fact, its corporate headquarters were in Chicago, Illinois, and most of its 43,000 employees were in the United States. H. Laurance (Larry) Fuller, whose career began as an engineer in Amoco's petrochemical business, had been the chairman and CEO since 1991.

EXHIBIT 7-1

SUMMARY INCOME STATEMENT (U.K. GAAP, IN US$ MILLIONS)

	BP 1997	Amoco 1997	BP Amoco 1997	BP Amoco 1998
Revenues	$71,274	$31,910	$91,760	$68,304
Cost of sales	58,702	26,380	73,928	56,354
Distribution/administrative expense	5,989	2,172	6,742	6,044
EBIT	6,985	4,177	11,094	7,287
EBITDA	10,247	6,550	15,175	10,850
Interest expense	486	401	908	1,053
Income taxes	1,915	1,056	3,066	1,520
Profit for the year	**$ 4,051**	**$ 2,720**	**$ 6,030**	**$ 3,260**
Dividends	2,070	1,382	3,452	4,121
Number shares outstanding (millions)	5,763	983	n/a	9,683
Stock price (12/31)	$13.28[a]	$85.13	n/a	$14.55[a]
Capital expenditures	$6,672	$3,943	$11,420	$10,362
Average revenue per barrel of crude oil			$19.05	$12.65

[a]The BP share price in 1997 is derived from the ADR price on the NYSE.

Source: BP, Amoco, and BP Amoco Annual Reports.

In 1997, Amoco earned $2.7 billion on revenues of $31.9 billion and assets of $32.5 billion. Adjusted for exceptional items, exploration and production accounted for 60% of 1997 consolidated earnings, refining and marketing 22%, and petrochemicals 18%. (Exhibits 7-1 and 7-2 present summaries of Amoco's financial statements.)

The 1998 Merger

In May 1998, Sir John Browne initiated a series of meetings with H. Laurance Fuller to explore ways of combining their companies. Browne's motivation for combining the firms was based on a belief that success in the capital-intensive oil and gas industry was becoming increasingly dependent on scale. They announced the deal, the largest cross-border transaction in corporate history, on August 11 and consummated the deal on December 31, 1998. The firm established its global headquarters in London with BP's Sir John Browne as group chief executive, and Amoco's H. Laurance Fuller and BP's Peter Sutherland as nonexecutive co-chairmen.

At the time, executives cited several reasons for the merger including scale and synergies. According to Amoco's management, "the best investment opportunities, in terms of rates of return on capital employed, will be ones that, because of location or complexity, will be available only to companies with the greatest financial resources."[2] Industry analysts concurred with this view:

[2] Amoco Corporation, Letter to Shareholders, October 30, 1998, p. 1.

EXHIBIT 7-2

BALANCE SHEET, DECEMBER 31 (U.K. GAAP, IN US$ MILLIONS)

	BP 1997	Amoco 1997	BP Amoco 1997	BP Amoco 1998
Assets				
Cash and investments	$ 276	$ 1,145	$ 1,422	$ 875
Inventory	4,284	1,174	4,923	3,642
Accounts receivable	11,532	3,585	14,381	12,709
Current assets	$16,092	$ 7,044	$20,726	$17,226
Fixed assets	32,601	22,543	52,263	54,465
Investments (joint ventures, net)	4,007	2,902	10,376	9,772
Intangibles	1,876	1,140	2,582	3,037
Total assets	**$54,576**	**$32,489**	**$85,947**	**$84,500**
Liabilities				
Current liabilities	$16,794	$ 6,044	$20,527	$18,166
Long-term debt	5,330	4,719	10,021	10,918
Other long-term liabilities	2,261	—	2,562	2,109
Deferred tax and provisions	6,672	5,276	9,989	10,449
Minority interest	93	131	1,100	1,072
Shareholders' equity	23,426	16,319	41,748	41,786
Total liabilities and shareholders' equity	**$54,576**	**$32,489**	**$85,947**	**$84,500**

Source: BP, Amoco, and BP Amoco Annual Reports.

The action nowadays is in such places as the deep waters off West Africa and in China, where the risks are high and the capital costs enormous—as are the potential riches if a huge oil field is discovered. Only well-capitalized firms that are big enough to afford the time, money, and risk required to play in this poker game can hope to thrive. Because the stakes are so high, finding that "elephant" of an oilfield has become the industry's obsession.[3]

Besides the need for scale, analysts cited potential cost savings of $2 billion annually and complementary commercial strengths—BP in upstream operations and Amoco in downstream operations—as reasons for the merger. In addition, executives highlighted "sustainable long-term growth" and "strongly competitive returns" as corporate objectives.[4] In terms of financial polices, they said the new firm would have a target debt-to-capitalization ratio of 30% and a target payout ratio of 50% of midcycle earnings.[5] As a result of the merger, BP Amoco became one of the world's three "super-majors" along with Exxon and Shell (see Exhibit 7-3).

[3] "Hunting the Big One," *The Economist*, October 21, 2000, p. 71.

[4] Amoco Corporation, S.E.C. Form 8-K dated August 26, 1998, pp. 4–5.

[5] The British Petroleum Company p.l.c., Notice of an Extraordinary General Meeting, Part I: Letter from the Chairman of BP, October 30, 1998, p. 7.

EXHIBIT 7-3

BP AMOCO PEER GROUP AND LARGEST U.S. COMPETITORS, FYE 1997 AND 1998 (AMOUNTS IN $US BILLIONS)

Company: Headquarters:	Royal Dutch Shell The Hague, London		The "Super-Majors" Exxon TX (USA)		BP Amoco London (UK)		Next Largest U.S. "Majors" Mobil VA (USA)	Chevron CA (USA)	Texaco NY (USA)
	1998	1997	1998	1997	1998	1997	1998	1998	1998
Assets	$114.0	$115.0	$ 93.0	$ 96.1	$84.5	$85.9	43.0	37.0	29.0
Revenues	138.0	172.0	118.0	137.2	68.3	91.8	54.0	30.0	32.0
Net Income									
Upstream (E&P)	(0.2)	4.3	2.7	4.4	1.7	4.1	0.6	1.1	0.3
Downstream (R&M)	2.0	2.7	2.5	2.0	1.0	1.1	1.0	0.6	0.8
Chemicals	(1.0)	1.0	1.2	1.3	0.5	0.8	0.2	0.1	n/a
Total[a]	0.4[d]	8.0	6.4	8.5	3.3	6.0	1.7	1.3	0.6
Debt to Capital Ratio	19%	15%	16%	16%	24%	23%	29%	31%	37%
S&P Debt Rating	AAA	AAA	AAA	AAA	AA	AA	AA	AA	A+
Capital Expenditures[b]	15.7	15.7	9.7	8.6	10.4	11.4	5.5	5.3	4.0
Market Capitalization	164.0	164.0	178.0	169.0	141.0	125.6	68.0	54.0	28.0
Oil & Gas Reserves (bn bbls)[c]	20.5	19.4	14.1	14.1	15.2	14.8	7.6	6.3	4.7
Production (mm bbls/day)[c]									
Crude Oil	2.4	2.3	1.6	1.6	2.1	1.9	0.9	1.1	0.8
Natural Gas (oil equivalent)	1.4	1.4	1.1	1.1	1.0	1.0	0.7	0.4	0.4
Refinery Output	3.4	4.3	3.9	4.0	2.7	2.6	2.1	1.3	1.6
Refined Product Sales	5.7	6.6	5.4	5.4	4.8	4.7	3.4	2.0	2.6

[a] Upstream, downstream, and chemicals segment earnings may *not* equal net income because of exceptional charges and corporate overhead expense.

[b] Includes exploration expense charged to income and acquisitions.

[c] One barrel of crude oil equals 42 U.S. gallons, 35 imperial gallons, or 159 liters.

[d] Would have been $5.1 billion, excluding special charges.

Source: Company Annual Reports, casewriter estimates.

137

Integrating the Finance Group

Shortly after consummating the merger, management began the process of integrating the two companies. Both companies had highly centralized finance functions, although BP did have regional finance offices in Asia and the United States. Both companies also tended to separate investment and financing decisions, and had organizational structures that reflected this approach. The business units valued proposed investments using the corporate weighted-average cost of capital (WACC), while the Finance Group determined the best way to finance proposed investments and executed approved transactions. Management decided to retain the centralized finance structure because it provided better cash management, risk management, and financial execution. One of the perceived disadvantages of this centralized structure was that decisions impacting financing opportunities were often made at a business unit level before the Finance Group had an opportunity to provide input, thereby creating on occasion the potential for missed opportunities and suboptimal financing solutions. Given this structure, the Finance Group had two distinct groups of customers for its services: the business units and senior management/shareholders.

To achieve the benefits of centralization without creating too much of an information gap between the business units and the Finance Group, management retained BP's central office in London to service the business units in Europe, Africa, the Middle East, and the former Soviet Union. BP's existing office in Singapore would provide financial services and support for business units in Asia/Pacific, while the U.S.-based finance staffs were consolidated in Amoco's Chicago headquarters with responsibility for supporting business units in the Americas. CFO John Buchanan and Treasurer David Watson ran the Finance Group, which consisted of three major divisions. (Exhibit 7-4 shows the organization chart for the new Finance Group.) Treasury Operations handled cash management, including short-term debt. Corporate Services managed all debt and equity at the parent level, as well as shareholder relations. Business Services had five major responsibilities: financial skills (training), business insurance, financial engineering, banking projects, and specialized finance. Bill Young, head of Specialized Finance, led a team of nine finance professionals based in London. Similar teams existed in Singapore and Chicago. All maintained close contact with the business units in the geographic areas and helped shepherd transactions through the headquarters approval process, financial negotiation, and closing.

THE ASSIGNMENT

As part of the integration process, David Watson asked Bill Young to review existing policy and recommend when and in what circumstances the firm should use project finance to fund new capital investments. Young knew this request was not just a matter of intellectual curiosity because the company invested heavily in fixed assets. In fact, BP and Amoco together had spent more than $10 billion per year on capital expenditures in each of the last three years. Expenditures of this magnitude were common among the major oil companies because their key assets, oil and gas reserves, were continually depleting (see Exhibit 7-5). By one estimate, total capital spending on exploration and development for the entire industry could reach $1.4 trillion in the decade leading up to 2005.[6] This assignment was also important because project finance was a

---

[6] "All about Money," *Energy Economist*, November 1, 1995, p. 8.

EXHIBIT 7-4

POST-MERGER ORGANIZATION CHART FOR BP AMOCO'S FINANCE GROUP (SIMPLIFIED)

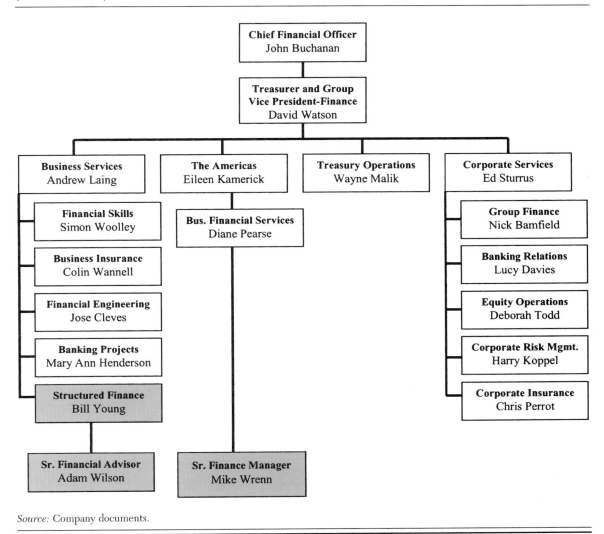

Source: Company documents.

well-established financial structure in the oil and gas industry, and many firms had used it successfully in the past.

Knowing the importance of the assignment, Young sought assistance from Mike Wrenn from the America's Finance Group in Chicago and Adam Wilson from the Specialized Finance Group in London (see Exhibit 7-4). The team began by defining project finance:

Project finance is the financing of a project which is arranged in such a way that lenders are totally reliant on the assets and cash flows of that project for interest and loan repay-

EXHIBIT 7-5

CAPITAL EXPENDITURE INTENSITY BY INDUSTRY

Industry (3 digit SIC code)	Number of Firms	Median Asset Size ($ millions)	1998 PPE as a % of 1998 Assets[a]	1998 Capital Expenditure as a % of 1997 Assets[a]	Return on Assets[a]
Auto Rental	7	$4,505	70.1%	44.6%	2.25%
Crude Petroleum, Gas (131)	165	65	71.5	20.3	(7.73)
Air Transport (451)	37	751	62.2	15.1	5.60
Grocery Stores (541)	41	582	49.1	12.0	4.31
Petroleum Refining (291)[c]	25	3,145	65.1	10.3	3.65
Cable/Pay TV (484)	28	1,175	25.8	8.6	24.54
Motor Vehicles and Bodies (371)	84	223	23.9	8.5	4.93
Railroads (401)	16	1,451	81.4	8.3	3.22
Industrial Chemicals (286)	16	991	46.0	7.8	4.61
Retail Stores (599)	20	73	27.5	7.6	1.91
Radio Broadcast (483)	37	753	14.4	7.1	4.43
Paper Mills (262)	13	3,627	65.1	7.0	4.16
Beverages (208)	34	100	30.4	6.8	8.41
Medical Laboratories (807)	26	65	20.4	5.8	0.92
Hospitals (806)	15	304	46.4	5.6	2.23
Aircraft and Parts (372)	25	174	26.3	4.5	5.48
Department Stores (531)	18	1,516	29.5	4.4	2.67
Newspaper (271)	22	1,704	24.2	4.2	11.31
Advertising (731)	26	161	15.7	3.2	3.66
Cigarettes (211)	4	9,815	17.0	2.5	6.39
Mortgage Bankers (616)	36	143	1.6	0.9	(2.14)
Life Insurance (631)	39	5,745	0.6	0.0	0.77
Median for all industries	**12**	**181**	**26.4**	**6.6**	**3.65**

[a] Figures represent weighted averages. PPE stands for property, plant, and equipment.

[b] Return on assets equals 1998 net income divided by 1997 total assets.

[c] SIC code 2910 contains firms such as Amerada Hess, Amoco, Chevron Conoco, Exxon, Getty, Mobil, Phillips, and Texaco.

Source: Compustat.

ment, as opposed to "corporate finance," where the lenders are not reliant upon any one project and can rely on the cash flows and financial strength of the entire corporate entity.[7]

While this definition was not perfect, because there was often some form of partial or temporary recourse to the project's sponsors such as a completion guarantee, it captured the critical distinction between corporate finance and project finance. Exhibit 7-6A presents a typical corporate transaction, while Exhibits 7-6B and 7-6C present pos-

[7] BP Internal Memorandum "Project Finance" (1990), p. 1.

EXHIBIT 7-6A

CORPORATE FINANCE MODEL

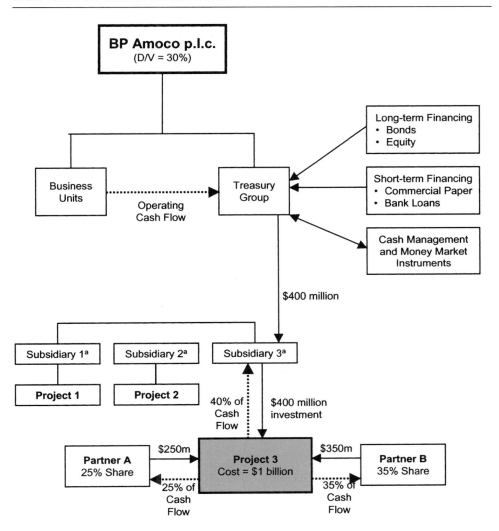

[a] BP typically created, for liability and/or tax reasons, a separate special purpose subsidiary to hold its investment in each project.

Source: Casewriter.

sible project finance structures. Exhibit 7-6B shows an *incorporated* joint-venture, which was more common in petrochemical and power projects. The *unincorporated* joint-venture structure shown in Exhibit 7-6C was more common for BP Amoco's upstream businesses (i.e., exploration and production projects). Under the project finance structure, a special purpose entity with limited liability borrowed funds directly and pledged its assets and cash flows to support the loan. With few exceptions, the lenders had no recourse to the project's beneficial owners, often called sponsors. The use of internal

EXHIBIT 7-6B

PROJECT FINANCE MODEL #1: PROJECT USES PROJECT FINANCE

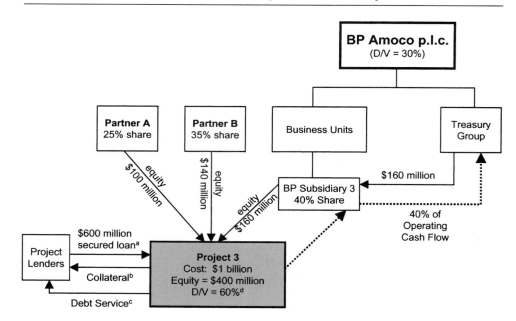

[a] Loan was the obligation of Project 3 Corporation; there was no recourse to the Partners.

[b] Collateral usually consisted of Project 3 Corporation's:
  (a) shares
  (b) Assets including, for example, cash, oil and/or gas produced, cash flow from exploration and production rights, drilling platforms, pipelines, storage and processing facilities, and rights under insurance policies, operating service, construction and other contracts.

[c] Debt Service—interest, principal installments, and operating expenses must be paid prior to distributions to shareholders.

[d] Assumes that projected cash flows, asset values, and financial market conditions will support 60% leverage.

Source: Casewriter.

funds, on the other hand, implied the use of the corporation's balance sheet to obtain the debt and equity needed to finance its share of a project. It also implied that all corporate assets and cash flows could be used to repay debt.

The next step in the process was to limit the scope of the assignment by considering the types of investments that could utilize project finance. Although BP Amoco could use project finance in any of its divisions, it used project finance most frequently in the downstream businesses, particularly for petrochemical plants and power-generating facilities. Project finance was more often appropriate for power plants because they were discrete, noncore assets; had, at least historically, cash inflows and outflows set by long-term contracts; and had lenders familiar with project finance. According to Adam Wilson:

The market expects developers to use project finance for power projects, and you can't underestimate the importance of precedent. The existence of investor clienteles familiar with

EXHIBIT 7-6C

PROJECT FINANCE MODEL #2: BP SUBSIDIARY USES PROJECT FINANCE

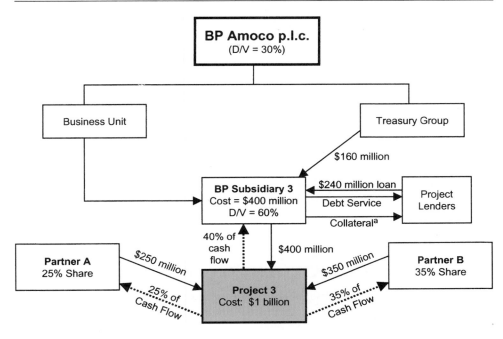

Notes:

[a] Collateral consisted of all of the assets in the BP subsidiary including the 40% interest in Project 3, related cash flows, and other contractual rights.

Source: Casewriter.

power plants tends to improve their valuation. The project finance structure also facilitates a sell-down of our position if and when we choose to do so.

With regard to the upstream businesses, the focus would be on production rather than exploration assets because banks were reluctant to lend on a project basis until reserves were proven and capable of production.

After defining project finance and bounding the scope of their assignment, the team conducted a series of meetings with executives from both organizations to understand their positions on project finance. Historically, BP had used project finance only sparingly based on a belief that the disadvantages in terms of costs, time, and rigidity outweighed the advantages in terms of risk management. Young's interviews led him to believe this position remained an accurate assessment of the views held by most BP executives. BP executives recalled only limited applications of project financing in recent memory. Examples included the financing of the North Sea Forties Field in the early 1970s. This deal, however, was more of a corporate financing because BP remained obligated to the lenders for all interest and principal, but could use the project financing structure as a tool for reshaping debt repayment obligations in line with project economic performance. Another example was the Kaltim Prima Coal Mine project in Indonesia. Here BP chose to use project finance as a way to manage Indonesian exposure. More recently, BP, as the operator of the Cusiana and Cupiagua oil fields in Colombia, had worked with partners to create a financial structure that facilitated project financing for the export pipeline. Ecopetrol, the state oil company, and some of the other sponsors, subsequently used this structure to raise project funds for the pipeline. Nevertheless, BP chose to fund its share of the pipeline using internal funds.

According to Young, Amoco also preferred corporate finance, even though it had used project finance on occasion. In the early 1980s, Amoco used project finance for the $1 billion Ok Tedi gold and copper mine in Papua New Guinea. It also used project finance for a variety of international joint ventures in the petrochemicals industry to accommodate partners who were unable to finance their shares through corporate borrowings. More recently, Amoco and others had financed the $1 billion Atlantic Liquified Natural Gas (LNG) plant in Trinidad and Tobago on a project basis because certain critical partners did not want to have such a large investment on their balance sheets. In contrast, Amoco, which was investing $600 million of internal funds to develop the offshore gas fields that would eventually supply the plant with natural gas, was prepared to finance its share of the LNG plant entirely with internal funds. The Atlantic LNG financing was widely syndicated in the bank loan market, and perhaps this fact accounted for the perception that Amoco was an advocate of project finance.

THE NEW POLICY STATEMENT ON PROJECT FINANCE

Following these meetings, the team concluded that BP and Amoco shared a common preference for using internal funds to finance capital expenditures, and that the combined firm should prefer internal funds as well. To justify this recommendation, the team carefully assessed the costs and benefits of using project finance they had discussed with their colleagues.

The Costs of Using Project Finance

When asked to describe the merits of project finance, Bill Young jokingly replied, "The only people who prefer project finance are the ones who've never done a deal using project finance." Without much hesitation, he cited four disadvantages of project finance: it cost more, took longer to arrange, restricted managerial flexibility, and required greater disclosure.

To begin with, nonrecourse project debt cost more than otherwise equivalent corporate debt due in part to greater risk and in part to greater leverage. Lenders typically demanded up-front fees ranging from 50 to 200 basis points of the amount financed and interest rate spreads ranging from 100 to 400 basis points over LIBOR depending on project type, location, and maturity. In contrast, BP Amoco would expect to pay slightly less than LIBOR for short-term borrowings under bank lines or through commercial paper programs, or 80 to 120 basis points over equivalent maturity treasuries for long-term, fixed-rate bonds (including fees). The ability to raise cheaper corporate funds was the direct result of having a strong balance sheet and lots of excess debt capacity. Prior to the merger, BP and Amoco had senior unsecured debt ratings of AA and AAA, respectively.

Besides the direct financial costs, project finance involved substantial third-party costs. Financial advisors, selected to help structure the financing, charged advisory fees on the order of 50 to 100 basis points of the amount eventually raised. Sponsors also had to pay for engineering reports certifying the quality of project design, the feasibility of the project schedule, and, in the case of oil and gas projects, the existence of hydrocarbon reserves. In addition, they had to pay legal fees incurred in structuring operating contracts and crafting loan documentation. While some of these costs would also be incurred in a corporate deal, the incremental cost associated with project finance could add an additional 100 basis points or more in fees, according to Mike Wrenn.

Structuring a project-financed deal, particularly a multiparty deal, took considerably longer than structuring a comparable corporate-financed deal. Decisions that could be made internally in a matter of days by only a handful of people, took significantly longer in a project-financed deal because more independent parties were involved in the process. Adam Wilson estimated that using project finance added a minimum of four to six months to a deal, and considerably more if one of the multilateral lending agencies was involved. Incremental time not only reduced a project's NPV, but it could also result in a missed opportunity.

A third disadvantage of project finance was the loss of managerial flexibility. The loan documentation imposed an extensive set of operating and reporting requirements on borrowers. These provisions restricted the sponsors' ability to change design, admit new partners, dispose of assets, or respond to any number of contingencies that invariably arose over the course of a project's life. As Young put it, "I think of corporate finance as a way to avoid the inflexibility associated with project finance. When you sign a project finance deal, you have to live with a giant stack of documents full of provisions that hinder your ability to respond to a changing environment."

A final factor weighing against the use of project finance was the occasional need to disclose proprietary information to lenders. For example, there could be tax or royalty reductions, or commitments to ancillary infrastructure investments intended to support the project that neither the owners nor the host governments wanted in the public domain. Yet lenders needed this information to make credit decisions. Depending on the size of the deal, scores of lenders could be involved, many of whom would have banking relations with BP Amoco's competitors. Despite the use of confidentiality agreements, the potential for leakage was troublesome.

The Benefits of Using Project Finance

The basic assumption behind the team's analysis was that BP Amoco was a portfolio of exploration, development, refining, and marketing assets. With less than perfect correlation among its various assets, it was able to eliminate idiosyncratic risks through diversification. Because it was particularly skilled at assessing business risks, had a strong balance sheet, and had a vertically integrated business model, it was more efficient to hold the assets collectively than individually. However, there might be instances in which it made sense to finance investments individually on a project basis. In these instances, project finance created value by improving risk management. Whereas risk management could take several forms—risk sharing, direct risk reduction, hedging (reducing a risk by giving up the opportunity for a gain), and insurance (reducing a risk by paying a premium)—the benefits were typically associated with risk sharing and risk reduction.

In terms of risk sharing, the project structure limited BP's exposure to downside risk. In essence, BP exchanged downside exposure for a price in the form of higher interest rates and loan fees. According to Wilson, using project finance was tantamount to buying a "walk-away" or put option for the project. Exhibit 7-7 presents this framework: the combination of holding an underlying asset (a project) and buying a put

---

EXHIBIT 7-7

**HYPOTHETICAL PAYOFFS TO PROJECT-FINANCED VERSUS
CORPORATE-FINANCED INVESTMENT**

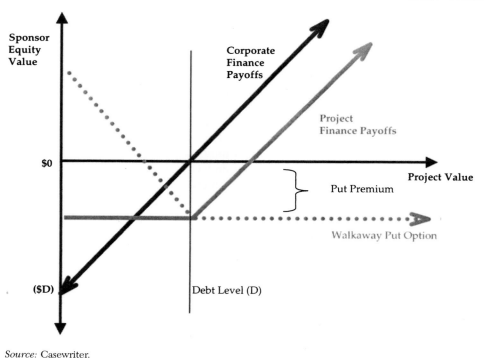

Source: Casewriter.

---

option on that asset created a payoff function that resembled a call option on the underlying asset. When BP Amoco used corporate finance, the firm was exposed to the full range of outcomes (NPVs); when it used project finance, it sacrificed some of the upside in exchange for truncating the downside. Such downside protection could be extremely valuable in certain settings. Whether the benefits of risk sharing outweighed the incremental structuring costs was the real question.

In deciding whether to make this exchange, BP had to consider both the price of the walk-away option and its willingness to exercise the option. For investments in its core businesses, BP was better equipped than most lenders to assess and bear the risks. As a result, it was not likely to get favorable, or even fair, pricing on the put option. Unlike a financial option with continuous prices, the downside scenarios in the investment business tended to be discrete events with highly uncertain, if not unknown, distributions. In these instances, history did not give you a good indication of the magnitude of potential losses or the probability of occurrence. Valuing such an option was not easy, and even informed parties could disagree on how much it was worth.

The value of the walk-away option also depended on BP Amoco's ability and willingness to exercise it. Prior to project completion, the ability to walk away from a loan could be constrained by support obligations and completion guarantees. Only after an independent third party certified completion, usually defined in terms of both financial and operational characteristics, did the loan become nonrecourse to the sponsors. Although BP Amoco could walk away at this point, it might be reluctant to do so for several reasons. For example, it might not be wise to abandon a project that was an integral part of a larger development, thereby turning over a key asset to a bank group. Alternatively, a sponsor might be reluctant to abandon a proprietary asset. Would the Walt Disney Company really abandon a theme park and let project lenders control Mickey Mouse and other Magic Kingdom characters? Finally, default could tarnish the firm's reputation and jeopardize important relationships with host governments, international agencies, and bankers. Such actions could preclude the firm's ability to gain access to or finance future projects. To the extent BP was either unwilling or unable to walk away, the put option had no value.

In addition to risk sharing, project finance had other benefits, even though Young believed most of them were illusory or nonexistent, at least for BP Amoco. Five such benefits came to mind. Some argued that project debt, particularly when accounting rules did not require project assets or liabilities to appear on the sponsor's balance sheet, expanded a firm's debt capacity. Of course, this assertion was true only to the extent that investors and rating agency analysts did not "see through" the financial statements and recognize continuing obligations to pay.

Another supposed benefit of project finance was that it generated additional interest tax shields because projects had a higher leverage ratios than sponsoring firms: the typical project had a debt-to-value ratio of 70% compared to 30% for a firm like BP Amoco. The difference in leverage existed, in part, because firms, but not projects, needed the flexibility and excess debt capacity to invest whenever attractive opportunities arose. Yet BP Amoco viewed its investments and payment obligations on a consolidated basis even if they were project financed. Thus, the decision to finance a given asset with 70% debt simply displaced corporate borrowing capacity. As a result, the total amount of debt did not depend on particular financial structures. Besides, equivalent debt tax shield benefits could be obtained by careful choice of project ownership vehicles and intragroup financing structures. In those instances where the firm could take on more leverage using the project finance structure, the incremental interest expense (and potential distress costs) usually outweighed the incremental interest tax shields, which meant that using project finance could reduce firm value. That said, there were other debt-related factors such as tax arbitrage, risk transfer, or managerial incentives that could easily offset the benefits of incremental interest tax shields.

Third, there might be tax benefits associated with reduced rates or tax "holidays" that made particular transactions attractive—host governments were often more willing to make one-off concessions to project companies than to make full-scale policy changes. Yet these benefits usually had a greater influence on site selection than on the choice between corporate and project finance.

Fourth, some argued that the project resulted in better risk allocation among the various parties to a deal. This argument rested on the assumption that you could not replicate or get pricing credit for the same allocation of responsibilities in a corporate-financed deal. Except for political risk—one of the key exceptions discussed below—this assumption appeared untrue. For example, BP could sign a fixed-price, turnkey construction contract, thereby transferring completion risk to an experienced contractor, regardless of how it financed the deal.

Finally, some firms used project finance for high-risk projects such as first-time investments in new industries, markets, or technologies. Here, project finance created value by introducing an added level of discipline to the process and by providing access to partners with greater or different previous experience. With the exception of investments in new countries, this rationale was not a major consideration for BP Amoco. Instead, it relied on its accumulated experience and largely restricted its investments to core assets, thereby limiting the technological and markets risks associated with new projects.

THE EXCEPTIONS

Based on the team's assessment of these costs and benefits, they were recommending that BP Amoco use internal corporate funds to finance new projects except in three very particular circumstances: (1) mega projects; (2) projects in politically volatile areas; and (3) joint ventures with heterogeneous partners. While other companies might weigh the costs and benefits differently and, therefore, reach different conclusions, the costs clearly outweighed the benefits in most situations for BP Amoco.

Exception #1: Mega Projects

Mega projects were those that were large enough to cause "material" harm to the company's earnings, debt rating, and, in the extreme, survival. Quantifying material harm was not easy to do. Instead, it was a more qualitative concept. Wilson defined mega as the size "where senior management begins to feel uncomfortable about the size and the level of risk." Prior to the merger, Amoco viewed investments of $2 billion and up as potential candidates for project finance; executives from BP estimated the number at closer to $3 billion. The key issue here was one of relative size and the firm's ability to hold a diversified portfolio, a concept that would surely change following the merger. In deciding whether a project qualified as mega, it was important to define it correctly. Many oil and gas developments proceeded in phases over several years. Whereas the first phase might not exceed a given threshold, the total investment across all phases could. In the event BP Amoco elected to use project finance, it would require a much smaller and more diversifiable investment (compare the $400 million investment in Exhibits 7-6A to the $160 million investment in Exhibits 7-6B and 7-6C).

Exception #2: Projects in Politically Volatile Areas

Projects exposed to a high degree of political risk, broadly defined as war, strikes, sabotage, lack of property rights, direct or "creeping" expropriation, or currency inconvertibility, were candidates for project finance because they benefited from the presence of outside lenders. The logic was that host governments would be less likely to take or tolerate hostile action against the project because such action could jeopardize access to future credit from the international financial community. In the most risky countries, commercial lenders would not even consider lending unless one of the multilateral lending agencies (MLAs) or Export Credit Agencies (ECA) was involved in the deal. Given their roles as development lenders and as lenders of last resort to highly indebted countries, MLAs such as World Bank Group, the European Bank for Reconstruction and Development (EBRD), and the Asian Development Bank (ADB) helped deter sovereign interference. Thus, they reduced the level of risk by reducing the probability of default. For this reason, MLA participation was said to confer a "halo effect" on projects.

Even in high-risk countries, however, relative size remained a critical factor in deciding whether to use project finance. According to Adam Wilson:

> The threshold for what constitutes mega in the United States or Canada is much higher than the threshold in an emerging country. For big projects in developed countries, we would prefer to use internal funds or to share the project with a well-capitalized partner before using project finance. At the same time, we would prefer to finance small and medium-sized projects in even the riskiest places using our own corporate funds.

The problem with using project finance was that outside lenders often required some form of political risk insurance (PRI), and the market for PRI in high-risk markets was very thin. As a result, it was expensive to buy, which created another factor arguing against the use of project finance.

Exception #3: Joint Ventures with Heterogeneous Partners

In certain joint ventures, BP Amoco might find it necessary to use project finance, even if unjustified on other criteria, as a way to manage the financial needs of partners with weaker credit capabilities. For example, host governments or their agencies sometimes wanted to participate in projects, yet did not want to use or did not have large amounts of funds available. At other times, partners with weaker balance sheets could not raise the required amounts on their own. In these instances, the project structure became the price of admission for BP Amoco to participate in the project. In other cases, BP Amoco might participate in a project financing so that it could negotiate with lenders rather than letting weaker partners negotiate for the group as a whole. Because BP Amoco's ability to make decisions could be compromised by partner debt covenants, it wanted as much say in the negotiations as possible.

Project Evaluation

If a particular project met one or more of these criteria, then it would be a candidate for project finance. Because the internal finance organizations and project approval processes were similar at both firms prior to the merger, they decided to retain a similar system in the new organization. The new process was designed to quantify the incremental costs and benefits of using project finance. After a business unit determined a project had a positive NPV using the predetermined corporate WACC assuming a debt-to-capitalization ratio of 30% (the "investment" NPV), it would forward the project to the Specialized Finance team, which would then assess various financing structures using an incremental cost analysis. They estimated the incremental, after-tax cash flows associated with fees, interest, and principal payments, and discounted these cash flows at the firm's marginal cost of debt for a comparable maturity. This "financing" NPV was typically negative. But when combined with the "investment" NPV and other possible benefits described above, the result could be positive. In these instances, the Finance Group could recommend using project finance and seek approval for the chosen structure.

CONCLUSION: PREPARING FOR THE PRESENTATION

As he put the finishing touches on his presentation, Young wondered why the public perception of differences between BP and Amoco existed. In particular, he thought of a recent comment made by an analyst at the Center for Global Energy Studies in London shortly after the merger. At the time, both companies were participating in the Azerbaijan International Operating Company (AIOC), an 11-firm joint venture created to develop oil fields in the Caspian Sea. The analyst wrote, "The BP-Amoco merger consolidates the ownership of AIOC a little bit. . . . The two will be speaking with one voice, whereas perhaps they haven't always been in the past."[8]

Bill Young saw things differently: "Contrary to the public view that we were on opposite ends of the project finance/corporate finance spectrum, we discovered that we really were reasonably well-aligned in our views and philosophies." His team, and the colleagues with whom he had discussed his recommendations, seemed to concur with the idea that BP Amoco should use corporate funds to finance new investments except in very special circumstances. Elaborating, he said:

> It's likely that project finance will continue to be used sparingly at BP Amoco. We have a big balance sheet and an ability to manage risks internally. Nevertheless, there are some projects for which it could be an effective risk mitigation tool and we will certainly consider using it in those instances, particularly if it helps us to implement a project with attractive economics.

---

[8] D. Stern, "BP-Amoco Alliance Set to Dominate Azerbaijani Oil Industry," *Agence France-Presse*, August 14, 1998.

8

BP Amoco (B): Financing Development of the Caspian Oil Fields

One of the many challenges facing the Finance Group after the BP Amoco merger in 1998 was to evaluate and, if necessary, restructure the company's global investment portfolio, including its 34% share of the Azerbaijani International Oil Consortium (AIOC). The 11-firm consortium was in the process of developing oil fields in the Azerbaijani sector of the Caspian Sea. (Exhibit 8-1 identifies the AIOC members.) As of March 1999, AIOC had completed the $1.9 billion Early Oil Project, which was producing 100,000 barrels of crude oil per day (bpd). The next three stages, known as the Full Field Development Project, were expected to cost an additional $8 to $10 billion and would bring total production to 800,000 bpd by 2005.[1]

Before the merger, BP and Amoco held the two largest interests in AIOC (17% each), yet they had chosen different strategies for funding their shares of the Early Oil Project. Whereas BP had used general corporate funds, Amoco was one of five AIOC partners that had raised $400 million of project finance with assistance from two multilateral agencies. Now, as a merged entity, the Finance Group had to reassess the firm's financial strategy for the Early Oil Project and determine the best way to finance the Full Field Development Project. While it was possible to continue with a dual financing strategy, such an approach could complicate BP Amoco's management of the asset as well as impair its effectiveness as the *de facto* leader of the joint venture.

Dean's Research Fellow Michael Kane and Professor Benjamin C. Esty prepared this case. This case was developed from published sources only. HBS cases are developed solely as the basis for class discussion. Cases are not intended to serve as endorsements, sources of primary data, or illustrations of effective or ineffective management.

[1] Dow Jones Newswires, "IFC Board Approves $200M Loan for Caspian Oil Project," July 27, 1998; A.M. d'Intignano, "Opening the Caspian Gateway," *Project Finance*, January 2000, p. 19; Dow Jones Energy Service, "IFC, EBRD to Invest $400M in Azerbaijan 'Early Oil' Project, February 17, 1999.

EXHIBIT 8-1

AZERBAIJAN INTERNATIONAL OPERATING COMMITTEE (AIOC) MEMBERS AS OF DECEMBER 31, 1998 (EXCEPT ITOCHU CORP—FYE MARCH 31, 1999)

Company	Country	AIOC Share	Assets (billions)	Net Worth (billions)	Debt to Total Capital	S&P Debt Rating[a]	Revenues (billions)	Net Income (billions)	Capital Expend. (billions)	Ownership	Reserves (barrels in billions)[b]
BP Amoco p.l.c[c] Amoco Corp. British Petrol.	**UK** USA UK	**34.1** 17.0% 17.1	**$84.5**	**$41.8**	**24.0%**	**AAA** AA	**$68.0**	**$3.3**	**$10.4**	**public**	**15.2**
Statoil	Norway	8.6	18.6	5.3	47.0	AA	14.1	0.0	2.8	government	4.6
Turkish Petroleum	Turkey	6.8	0.3	0.2	34.0	unrated	0.3	0.0	0.1	government	n/a
Amerada Hess	US	1.7	7.9	2.6	44.2	BB−	6.6	(0.5)	1.4	public	1.0
Unocal	US	10.0	7.6	2.2	54.3	A	5.0	0.1	1.7	public	1.6
Exxon	US	8.0	92.6	43.8	16.2	AAA	118.0	6.4	8.8	public	14.1
Pennzoil	US	4.8	n/a	n/a	44.9	n/a	1.8	0.0	n/a	public	n/a
Ramco PLC	UK	2.1	0.1	0.1	0.0	unrated	0.0	0.0	0.0	public	10.9
LUKoil	Russia	10.0	3.9	2.1	33.0	unrated	1.9	(0.1)	0.8	government	10.7
Itochu Corp.	Japan	3.9	56.9	2.6	85.0	unrated	108.7	(0.3)	0.7	public	n/a
Socar	Azerbaijan	10.0	n/a	n/a	n/a	unrated	n/a	n/a	n/a	government	n/a

[a] Senior unsecured debt rating, except in the case of Amerada Hess, which is an issuer rating.

[b] Reserves of crude oil and natural gas in billions of barrels or oil equivalent.

[c] British Petroleum plc and Amoco Corporation became subsidiaries of BP Amoco on December 31, 1998.

Source: Company Annual Reports.

CASPIAN OIL AND THE AIOC

The Caspian Basin (see the map in Exhibit 8-2) had been the site of significant oil production since the middle of the nineteenth century. Although the fields had, at one time, provided as much as 70% of the former Soviet Union's output, production had fallen to only 8% by the late 1980s.[2] Despite the decline, many industry experts believed the region held from 50 to 200 billion barrels of undeveloped oil and gas reserves, an amount equal to the reserves in the North Sea.[3]

EXHIBIT 8-2

MAP OF THE CASPIAN REGION

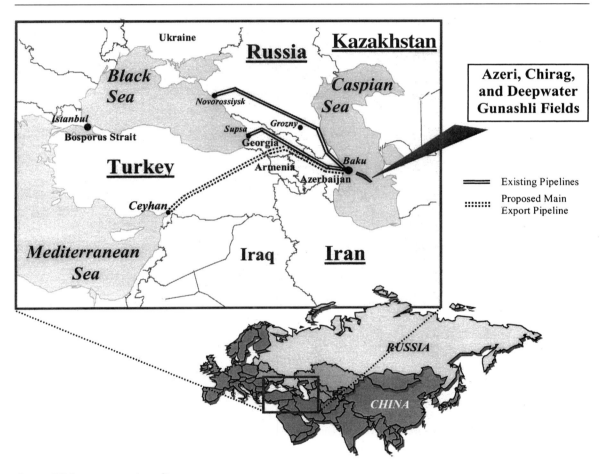

Source: BP Amoco, casewriter edits.

---

[2] d'Intignano, "Opening the Caspian Gateway," p. 18.

[3] H. Pope, "Azerbaijan's Top Oil Consortium Pulls in Horns," *The Wall Street Journal*, February 2, 1999, p. A16.

EXHIBIT 8-3

STATISTICS ON CASPIAN COUNTRIES AND
AIOC MEMBER COUNTRIES (1998)

Country	Population (millions)	GNP (billions)	GNP per Capita Rank	Euromoney Country Investment Risk[a]	S&P Sovereign Debt Rating[b]	Institutional Investor Risk Rating[c]
Armenia	3.8	$1.7	162	29.6	unrated	unrated
Azerbaijan	7.9	3.8	161	33.4	unrated	unrated
Georgia	5.4	5.3	139	25.7	unrated	10.8
Japan	126.4	4,089.1	7	90.9	AAA	86.5
Kazakhstan	15.6	20.9	126	40.3	B+	29.7
Norway	4.4	152.0	4	94.0	AAA	87.7
Russia	146.9	331.8	101	23.0	CCC	19.3
Turkey	63.5	200.5	89	48.5	B	38.9
Turkmenistan	4.7	n/a	n/a	31.8	unrated	unrated
United States	270.3	7,903.0	10	94.5	AAA	90.9
United Kingdom	59.1	1,264.3	22	91.2	AAA	90.2
Uzbekistan	24.1	22.9	141	28.8	unrated	18.9

[a] 27th Annual Rating, March 1999. The Euromoney risk rating measures the relative risk of investing in 180 countries, based on surveys of economists and analysts, and runs on a scale from 0 (high risk) to 100 (low risk).

[b] The S&P sovereign debt rating measures the capacity and willingness of host governments to repay their foreign currency debt when due.

[c] The *Institutional Investor* risk rating measures the risk of government default on debt and runs on a scale from 0 (high risk) to 100 (low risk).

Source: World Bank, *World Development Indicators*, 2000; Euromoney, Institutional Investor.

With the transformation of the Soviet Union into the Commonwealth of Independent States in 1991, Azerbaijan and the other Soviet republics became independent countries. Azerbaijan, on the western shore of the Caspian Sea, had a population of 8 million and a land area slightly smaller than the state of Maine. About 90% of the population were Azeri, an ethnic and linguistic group with mixed Turkish and Iranian heritage. In common with the other Caspian Sea littoral states, it had a majority Muslim population, a high unemployment rate, a low standard of living, and an economy that was dependent on oil. (Exhibit 8-3 provides data on Azerbaijan and other AIOC member countries.)

The years following independence were marked by coup attempts, terrorist activities, declining GDP—GDP fell by more than 60% between 1988 and 1994—and external conflicts with neighboring countries. In fact, Azerbaijan and Armenia had been fighting over disputed border provinces since the early 1990s. A 1994 cease-fire had ended the war, but other border conflicts with Russia to the north and Iran to the south remained a threat. As one author noted, the region "almost seems to have been made for war" with more than 50 ethnic groups living along the 900-mile Caucasus mountain range.[4]

Heydar Aliyev, a former head of the KGB in the Brezhnev administration, was elected president of Ajerbaijan in 1993. In 1994, he signed a Production Sharing Agreement (PSA) for Caspian oil as a first step toward developing Azerbaijan's natural resources. This "Deal of the Century," as it was called in the popular press, created a 30-year agreement between the Azerbaijani government and AIOC, a joint venture including SOCAR (the State Oil Company of Azerbaijan), BP, Amoco, Russia's and Turkey's national oil companies, and several other foreign oil companies. The PSA gave AIOC exclusive rights to develop three geologically connected oil fields—Azeri, Chirag, and deepwater Gunashli—in the western part of the Caspian Sea. SOCAR had discovered, but only partially developed, the fields between 1979 and 1987. According to AIOC, the fields contained between 4.5 and 5.0 billion barrels of oil.[5]

The diversity of AIOC's membership reflected Aliyev's development strategy. One industry analyst wrote, "President Heydar Aliyev's goal has been to attract as wide as possible a variety of oil companies to the tiny Caspian state, so as to anchor Azerbaijan firmly within the Western powers' interest and assure its political future."[6] By early 1999, Azerbaijan had signed 17 similar agreements with potential capital spending of $40 billion.[7] During this period, BP, Amoco, and other foreign oil companies were negotiating similar concessions with other Caspian states.

THE CASPIAN OIL FIELDS

AIOC had the exclusive right to develop the Azeri, Chirag, and deepwater Gunashli fields subject to certain conditions. It had to complete a seismic survey, an environmental impact study, and a series of test wells. Based on the findings, AIOC then had to submit a detailed plan of development to SOCAR. The actual development plan consisted of four parts: the Early Oil Project followed by the three-stage Full Field Development Project. Both AIOC and SOCAR had the right to approve each stage, based on the results of the previous stage. In addition to describing these rights and obligations, the PSA created a revenue-sharing agreement for the output and established a special tax regime for AIOC in lieu of other local taxes.[8]

The Early Oil Project involved developing the Chirag Field by refurbishing an offshore production platform, drilling new wells, and constructing a 105-mile subsea pipeline to an onshore terminal. It also involved rebuilding two export pipelines to the Black Sea—a 750-mile northern route to the Russian port of Novorossiysk and a 550-mile western route to the Georgian port of Supsa—and constructing an export terminal at Supsa. As of March 1999, Early Oil was complete except for the pipeline through Georgia. It was producing 100,000 bpd as planned and shipping the oil via the northern pipeline to Novorossisyk (see Exhibit 8-2). Originally estimated to cost

---

[4] C. Croissant, *Azerbaijan, Oil and Politics* (Commack, NY: Nova Science Publishers, 1998), p. 13.

[5] "Azerbaijan-Pipeline Knocked Back," *Project Finance International*, March 24, 1999, p. 45.

[6] D. Stern, "BP-Amoco Alliance Set to Dominate Azerbaijani Oil Industry," *Agence France-Presse*, August 14, 1998.

[7] H. Pope, "Azerbaijan's Top Oil Consortium Pulls in Horns," *The Wall St. Journal*, February 2, 1999 p. A16; "Azerbaijan Oil Contracts Signed," *Financial Times*, April 28, 1999, p. 4.

[8] Ramco Energy p.l.c. *Prospectus* dated March 10, 1997, pp. 41, 47.

$1 billion, the final cost came in at $1.9 billion primarily due to greater than expected expenditures on the western pipeline.[9]

Having essentially finished the Early Oil Project, AIOC began to concentrate on developing the rest of the field. The first stage, development of the Azeri field, would begin in early 2000, cost $2.6 to $3.1 billion, and bring total production to 300,000 bpd by 2003.[10] The second stage, planned for 2002, would develop the deepwater Gunashli field at an estimated cost of $3 billion. The third and final stage, planned for 2003 and 2004, targeted further development of the Azeri field at an estimated cost of $2 billion.[11] The final stages would increase production by 300,000 bpd and 200,000 bpd, respectively, for a total production rate of 800,000 bpd by 2005. The fields would produce at this rate until 2011, at which time output would gradually decline as the reserves were depleted.[12] According to the plan, the refurbished pipelines from the Early Oil Project could transport the production through Stage 1, but additional production would require a new pipeline that was not currently part of the AIOC investment budget.[13]

AIOC had recognized the need for a new pipeline since the very first PSA negotiations in the early 1990s because the Caspian Sea and the former Soviet republics of Azerbaijan, Kazakhstan, Turkmenistan, and Uzbekistan were landlocked. A banker from Citibank summed up the political and transportation issues this way:

> It is hard to find a more geo-politically challenging territory than the homes of Caspian Basin oil, and not surprisingly, investors have been reluctant to take the risky bet that the oil can be developed, produced and, crucially, transported to safer shores without wars or government action getting in the way.[14]

Driven by these concerns, oil companies and governments engaged in an active debate over the route, timing, cost, and financial responsibility for a Main Export Pipeline (MEP). The U.S., Turkish, Georgian, and Azerbaijani governments became advocates for a 1,080-mile pipeline from Baku through Georgia and Turkey to the Mediterranean port of Ceyhan, thereby avoiding both Russia and Iran (see Exhibit 8-2). With cost estimates ranging from $2.6 to $4 billion, additional reserves from other Caspian producers would be necessary to justify the investment.[15] By one estimate, the MEP would be economical only if there were at least 6 billion barrels of proven reserves to trans-

[9] The $1 billion estimate is from the Ramco Energy p.l.c. *Prospectus* dated March 10, 1997, p. 37; the final cost of $1.9 billion is from the EBRD's Website at: http://www.ebrd.com/english/opera/PSD.

[10] James M. Dorsey, "Pipeline Flap May Clog Expansion in the Caspian Sea," *The Wall Street Journal*, August 11, 1999, p. A14.

[11] Assumes a $10 billion total cost less $1.9 billion for Early Oil and $3.1 billion for Stage 1. The remaining $5 billion is split proportionally based on projected output—300,000 bpd in Stage 2 and 200,000 in Stage 3—given the similar geology. This reasoning implies Stage 2 will cost 60% of the total $5 billion or $3 billion; Stage 3 will cost 40% of the total or $2 billion.

[12] Dow Jones Energy Service, "IFC Board Approves $200M Loan for Caspian Oil Project," July 27, 1998.

[13] "Azerbaijan-Pipeline Knocked Back," p. 45.

[14] Stuart Brown, Director, Citibank Global Project Finance, London, quoted in "For & Against," *Project & Trade Finance*, February 10, 1999, p. 48.

[15] "Azerbaijan-Pipeline Knocked Back," p. 45; "Turkey Gets Tough in Its Push for Ceyhan Pipeline Project," *The Wall Street Journal*, November 9, 1998, p. A18.

port.[16] At the time, however, it was not clear who was going to build the MEP, where it would go, or when it would be completed.

Financing Early Oil

AIOC was organized as an unincorporated joint venture between subsidiaries from each member company.[17] Each subsidiary was responsible for funding a certain percentage of the capital expenditures and was entitled to receive an equivalent percentage of the output. The obligations to provide funds were several, meaning that members were responsible for only their shares of the total. Members achieved limited liability by incorporating special purpose subsidiaries as their investment vehicles and created centralized project management by forming a joint operating company with staff and funds contributed by the members.

Under this structure, each partner had a choice in how to finance its share of the $1.9 billion Early Oil Project. Six members with combined interests of 48.2% chose to use internal corporate funds. For example, BP contributed approximately $325 million to cover its share (17.1% * $1.9 billion). In contrast, five AIOC members (Amoco, Exxon, Unocal, LUKoil, and Turkish Petroleum) formed a Mutual Interest Group (MIG) for the purpose of obtaining a project loan with assistance from two multilateral agencies, the International Finance Corporation (IFC, a member of the World Bank Group) and the European Bank for Reconstruction and Development (EBRD).[18] The multilaterals not only provided access to long-term funds that banks were often unwilling to provide, but also helped mitigate political risks because of their roles as development banks and lenders of last resort. The MIG's creation surprised many analysts because "Exxon could clearly fund its 8% share comfortably on balance sheet, and Unocal could do the same with its 10% holding. (And the) appetite among banks for a non-recourse debt package for Russia's LUKoil and Turkish Petroleum . . . (was) likely to be limited."[19] According to a senior project finance banker:

> These are tougher countries from a political risk point of view than such countries as Chile and the Philippines. Some are quite new as autonomous countries, some harbor long standing border tensions, others have less than stable governments or economic policies. So it will not be an easy process for lenders to get comfortable.[20]

In February 1999, the IFC, EBRD, and MIG members closed a $400 million, limited-recourse project financing with an effective interest rate of less than 10%, representing a spread of 350 to 400 basis points over the current six-month LIBOR rate.[21] Traditionally, the multilateral agencies funded projects in one of three ways: direct lending ("A loans"), indirect lending as agent for a syndicated bank loan ("B loans"), or

---

[16] "Azerbaijan-Pipeline Knocked Back," p. 45; Jessica McCallin, "The Race Is On," *Project Finance*, October 19, 1998, p. 21.

[17] Summary of Project Information, International Finance Corporation (IFC), March 25, 1998, available at: http://wbln0018.worldbank.org/IFCExt/spiwebsite1.

[18] "Azerbaijan Oilfield to Get International Finance," BBC Worldwide Monitoring, Interfax News Agency, Moscow, February 18, 1999.

[19] "Azerbaijan-AIOC to Spend $2bn," *Project Finance International*, p. 37.

[20] Stuart Brown, Director, Citibank Global Project Finance, p. 48.

[21] Interfax News Agency, "LUKOil Gets $77.2MLN from EBRD to Finance AIOC Participation, January 22, 1999.

equity contributions. In this case, the financing was structured as ten A loans and ten B loans—each agency (IFC and EBRD) made an A and a B loan to special purpose subsidiaries at each of the five MIG partners.[22]

Syndication of the $200 million of B loans proved difficult, yielding commitments totaling just $75 million from three commercial banks. Concurrently, the IFC and EBRD funded $150 million out of the $200 million in A loans, yet hoped to raise the rest of the money once the appetite for emerging market debt improved.[23] Even though the financing was not complete, it was seen as an important milestone for the region in general and for AIOC in particular. The deputy director of the EBRD's natural resources group said:

> The kind of long-term financing that the EBRD and the International Finance Corporation (IFC) has provided . . . has not been previously made available to the region. The commitment of the EBRD and IFC will send a positive signal about financing projects in the region.[24]

THE FINANCE GROUP'S DECISIONS

In March 1999, BP Amoco's Finance Group needed to resolve two issues: first, whether to refinance Amoco's project loan from the Early Oil Project; and second, how to finance BP Amoco's share of the Full Field Development Project, currently estimated at approximately $2.8 billion ($8.1 billion of expenditures * 34.1% share). In deciding whether to prepay the IFC/EBRD loans, the Group had to consider the costs and benefits of prepayment. While BP Amoco could lower its funding cost by prepaying the loan, the total amount outstanding was only $73.8 million ($225 million of loans * 32.8%, representing BP Amoco's proportionate share of the MIG loans). In the past, BP had been able to issue medium-term bonds at 40 to 80 basis points over equivalent government bonds, issue long-term bonds at 80 to 120 basis points over government bonds, and obtain bank loans at or slightly below LIBOR. (In March 1999, the 10-year U.S. Treasury yield was 5.20% and the current 6-month LIBOR rate was 5.30%.) Because it had a cost advantage in raising corporate debt, BP preferred to use internal funds rather than project loans to finance its oil and gas investments. Prepayment, however, would not relieve BP of its administrative and reporting duties as the project operator. More importantly, it might send a negative signal to the other MIG members and could jeopardize AIOC's relationship with the IFC and EBRD.

The second decision, how to finance the Full Field Development Project, was more critical because capital expenditures for Stage 1 were projected to start in less than a year. BP Amoco could finance its $1.0 billion obligation (34.1% * $3.0 billion) for Stage 1 in several ways. Like the Early Oil Project, it could use a dual financing strategy, whereby half its commitment would come from internal funds and half from a project

[22] Assumes EBRD used the same structure that IFC used. The IFC's 10 loans are described in the Summary of Project Information, International Finance Corporation (IFC), March 25, 1998, available at: http://wbln0018.worldbank.org/IFCExt/spiwebsite1.nsf

[23] A. Cavenagh, "Caspian Oil Project Has a Slow Road to Syndication," *Project Finance International*, February 24, 1999, pp. 50, 51.

[24] "EBRD, The Show Must Go On," *Project & Trade Finance*, Euromoney Publications, April 10, 1999, p. 30.

loan. The advantage of this approach was that it gave them the best of both worlds; the disadvantage was that it also gave them the worst of both worlds.

Alternatively, BP Amoco could join some or all of the AIOC members and try to arrange a project loan following the IFC/EBRD model used for the Early Oil Project. This strategy allowed BP Amoco to leverage its investment with outside funds and extended the multilaterals' commitment to the project. The real question was how much protection was needed. Did the existing commitment provide sufficient protection against political risks, or did they need more? The main concerns associated with this option, particularly given the incomplete syndication, were the time needed to close a deal and the cost associated with project debt.

The third option for Stage 1 was to fund it entirely using internal funds. Like each of the options, this one had drawbacks. For example, by stepping away from the IFC/EBRD process, BP Amoco could be perceived as making it harder for the remaining members to negotiate a good deal—BP Amoco was, after all, the consortium's largest investor and project operator. Having weaker consortium members negotiate with lenders might result in a deal that unduly hindered BP Amoco's operational and managerial flexibility. More importantly, it could establish disadvantageous precedents for future financings. A related problem involved decision making at the consortium level. If, as expected, at least some partners participated in another project loan, would the dual financing strategy create an environment prone to disagreement? A final concern was that other AIOC partners might accuse BP Amoco of free riding on their efforts to set up and carry the more expensive financing, while sharing in the political risk protection it provided. Whether these arguments against the use of internal funds outweighed the advantages from BP Amoco's perspective was not clear.

A final, though not immediate, concern was how BP was going to finance later stages of the Full Field Development. Its ability to participate in project financings for later stages might be affected by how it decided to finance the earlier stages. Specifically, if by abstaining from an IFC financing for Stage 1, BP Amoco was perceived to make the financing more difficult, or if the financing actually failed, then the IFC might be unreceptive to later requests for financing. For the Finance Group, the question boiled down to one of perspective. Should they view the Full Field Development as a single project or a series of projects?

PROJECT RISKS

The oil industry was notorious for reserve, price, and, in certain cases like Azerbaijan, transportation risks. Compounding these risks was the fact that it was an especially volatile period for emerging market investments. As the Finance Group contemplated their options, they had to consider how these risks affected their current and future AIOC commitments, and the probability they would earn an acceptable rate of return. But they could not restrict their attention to AIOC assets alone because BP Amoco was, concurrently, the largest foreign investor in four unrelated exploration concessions in Azerbaijan alone.[25] As exploration projects, these investments were much smaller (e.g., $100 million) than the investment in a typical development project such as the Full Field Development Project (e.g., several billion dollars).

---

[25] Stern, "BP-Amoco Alliance Set to Dominate Azerbaijani Oil Industry"; d'Intignano,"Opening the Caspian Gateway," p. 20.

Political Risks

Political instability in Azerbaijan was an immediate concern because success hinged on local support for the project. Although the 76-year-old Aliyev was in control in early 1999, the Economist Intelligence Unit noted the precarious situation that existed at the time:

> The sudden departure of the president, Heydar Aliyev, for medical treatment in Turkey on January 17th (1999) reopens the issue of the succession in Azerbaijan. . . . There are real questions about whether a transition, especially one prompted by the sudden incapacitation of Mr. Aliyev, could be effected peacefully.[26]

A change in leadership could easily exacerbate existing disputes. For example, the ownership of oil and gas in the Caspian Sea was hotly contested between all of the countries bordering the Sea. Russia and Iran both rejected Azerbaijan's claims to reserves, contending that the Caspian was a lake and, therefore, its oil should be under international law. Without the Azeri government to enforce its claims, AIOC could lose its exclusive right to develop the fields. In addition, there was the smoldering dispute with Armenia, which could reignite at any moment.

Another dimension of political risk was the region's new and essentially untested legal infrastructure. Russia and the former Soviet republics had, to varying degrees, recently adopted new corporate, securities, and bankruptcy laws. Yet as one AIOC partner cautioned:

> Azerbaijan lacks a fully developed legal system, which could result in legal uncertainties and, ultimately, investment risks. . . . Effective redress in Azeri courts for a breach of law or regulation may be difficult or impossible to obtain, particularly against state agencies.[27]

BP Amoco had good reason to be concerned about these risks because of its $571 million investment OAO Sidanko, Russia's fifth largest oil and gas company. Sidanko had declared bankruptcy in January 1999, and was presenting a high-profile test case of Russia's new bankruptcy law. While some argued that the Russian legal system was plagued with asset stripping, tainted court rulings, and corruption, others argued that the new system might actually work in a fair and efficient manner, albeit with some growing pains.[28]

Financial Risks

The financial crisis that began in Thailand in 1997 and spread to Russia in the fall of 1998 was now affecting emerging markets around the world. A project finance banker said: "Everything has stopped in Russia. It is becoming increasingly difficult to open credit lines for Russian projects, even with the support of the multilaterals."[29] The crises would surely affect both the availability and cost of funds. As evidence, the MIG financing was the first significant syndication of long-term debt to the oil and gas sector

---

[26] The Economist Intelligence Unit, "Report on Azerbaijan, 1st Quarter 1999," p. 6.

[27] Ramco Energy p.l.c. *Prospectus* dated March 10, 1997, p. 15.

[28] A. Higgins, "Bankruptcy Court Deals BP Amoco Setback in Russia," *The Wall Street Journal*, March 3, 1999, p. A15.

[29] "EBRD, The Show Must Go On," p. 30.

in the former Soviet Union, and even this financing was incomplete.[30] Previous loans were small, short-term, and expensive, with rates up to 450 basis points over LIBOR.[31]

The Russian crisis also increased the likelihood that government–owned AIOC member LUKoil might have trouble raising the funds required for its 10% participation. If such an event occurred, it would create a difficult situation for the other partners in deciding how to proceed.

Transportation Risks

The northern and western pipelines to the Black Sea could handle the production levels projected through Stage 1 but presented operational and economic risks that made them an unsatisfactory long-term solution. The northern route was owned and operated by SOCAR on the Azerbaijan side and by Transneft, the Russian state-owned pipeline system, on the Russian side. Thus, Transneft controlled pricing and service decisions for a pipeline that was already more expensive to use than the western pipeline.[32] Perhaps even more troubling was the fact that the pipeline crossed through Chechnya where a civil war had been raging for years. Commenting on these risks, *The Economist* wrote: "Azerbaijan is worried that the Russians will have a stranglehold, and the oil companies fret about security: even with a bypass (around Chechnya), the pipeline will still be within shooting distance of the unpredictable Chechens."[33]

Even if the oil did reach the Black Sea, it still had to get through the Bosporus Straits before it reached western markets. As part of its ongoing campaign to bring the Main Export Pipeline through Turkey to Ceyhan, the Turkish government had taken an increasingly restrictive stance against tanker traffic through the Straits. The Turkish minister for maritime affairs had recently warned the Caspian oil producers that Turkey was ready to raise transit fees fivefold, and reportedly said, "Then they will see what happens to their dreams of cheap oil."[34]

Industry Risks

Like all upstream investment projects, the Caspian development projects were subject to reserve and commodity price risk. Both the level of actual reserves in the three fields and the ability to get them out of the ground were still largely unknowns. In fact, other exploration ventures in the Azeri sector of the Caspian had come up short:

> CIPCO, a consortium led by the U.S. company Pennzenergy, has decided to wind up operations next month after discovering an offshore field that was uneconomic. The North Absheron Operating Company led by Unocal and BP Amoco, which is drilling on the same structure, may not have found enough oil to justify exploiting the field.[35]

---

[30] Cavenagh, "Caspian Oil Project Has a Slow Road to Syndication," p. 50.

[31] "Deal Analysis, Leveling the Ground," *Project & Trade Finance*, May 10, 1998, p. 8.

[32] "Azerbaijan-AIOC Scales Back," p. 43.

[33] "Survey Central Asia," *The Economist*, February 7, 1998, p. 8.

[34] H. Pope, and B. Bahree, "Turkey Gets Tough in Its Push for Ceyhan Pipeline Project," *The Wall Street Journal*, November 9, 1998, p. A18.

[35] Pope, "Azerbaijan's Top Oil Consortium Pulls in its Horns," p. A16.

EXHIBIT 8-4A

**HISTORICAL PRICE PER BARREL OF BRENT CRUDE
(JANUARY 1982 TO MARCH 1999)**

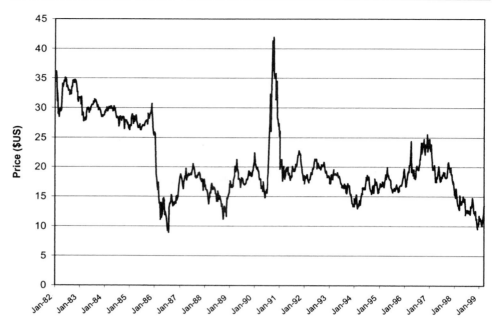

Source: Datastream.

EXHIBIT 8-4B

CAPITAL MARKETS DATA AS OF MARCH 15, 1999

Maturity	U.S. Treasury Yields	Brent Crude Futures Prices ($ per bbl)	Light Sweet Crude Oil Futures Prices ($ per bbl)	Projected Prices for World Oil ($ per bbl)[a]
1 month		$12.56	$14.49	
3 months	4.60%	12.61	14.40	
6 months	4.69	12.65	14.28	
1 year	4.75	12.83	14.31	$16.55
2 years	4.95	13.45	14.60	16.85
3 years	5.10	13.65	14.95	17.24
4 years			15.35	17.48
5 years	5.06		15.90	17.80
7 years	5.29			18.15
10 years	5.14			18.64
20 years				20.46
30 years	5.51			

[a] Based on projections from the Energy Information Administration's *Annual Energy Outlook, 2000* (in constant 1998 $US). The world oil price is an annual average acquisition cost of imported crude oils to U.S. refiners.

Sources: Datastream, *The Wall Street Journal*, and casewriter analysis.

EXHIBIT 8-5A

ESTIMATED PROJECT ECONOMICS FOR THE AZERI, CHIRAG, AND DEEPWATER GUNASHLI FIELDS

	Project Economics (per barrel)			
Oil price (assumed)	**$10.00**	**$15.00**	**$20.00**	**$25.00**
Production costs[a]	4.00	4.00	4.00	4.00
Transportation costs[b]	3.00	3.00	3.00	3.00
Gross profit	3.00	8.00	13.00	18.00
AIOC cost recovery[c]	1.50	4.00	6.50	9.00
Pretax profit	1.50	4.00	6.50	9.00
AIOC share[d]	1.05	2.80	4.55	6.30
Azerbaijani taxes[e]	0.26	0.70	1.14	1.58
After-tax profit to AIOC	0.79	2.10	3.41	4.72
Total available to AIOC for cost recovery and profit[f]	**$ 2.29**	**$ 6.10**	**$ 9.91**	**$13.72**

[a] Production costs are assumed higher than BP Amoco's world average of $3.05/bbl (Amoco Corp., Form 8K, August 12, 1998).

[b] The PSA contemplates transportation costs to the Mediterranean of $3.00/bbl (Ramco Energy Prospectus, March 10, 1997, p. 40).

[c] The PSA allocates 50% of gross profit for cost recovery (Ramco Energy Prospectus, March 10, 1997, p. 40).

[d] Initially, there is a 70/30 split between AIOC and SOCAR (Ramco Energy Prospectus, March 10, 1997, p. 40).

[e] The Azeri tax rate for the AIOC is 25% (Ramco Energy Prospectus, March 10, 1997, p. 47).

[f] Includes the AIOC cost recovery plus the after-tax profit to AIOC, but excludes certain bonus payments due to SOCAR. This number is approximately equal to the free cash flow AIOC could expect to receive per barrel.

Source: Casewriter estimates based on public information.

Besides reserve risks, AIOC also had to contend with volatility in crude oil prices. In early 1999, the price of oil had collapsed to $10.00 per barrel, a 25-year low. (Exhibit 8-4a shows historical prices for Brent Crude, a roughly comparable grade of oil.) Low oil prices in 1998 had dramatically affected the reported earnings, market values, and capital spending programs of oil companies around the world. For example, BP Amoco's net income was down by almost 50% (from $6.0 to 3.3 billion) and its capital expenditures were down by almost 10% (from $11.4 to 10.4 billion) in 1998. In response to falling oil prices, David Woodward, AIOC president, announced a 20% cut in the consortium's budget for the coming year and warned: "With oil prices hovering around the US$10 a barrel mark, the high cost of [getting and] shipping oil from the Caspian region—on average US$7 a barrel—is threatening the viability of much existing pro-

EXHIBIT 8-5B

ESTIMATED PRODUCTION VOLUMES FOR THE AZERI, CHIRAG, AND DEEPWATER GUNASHLI PROJECTS

Year		Average Daily Production (barrels of oil)	Production (millions of barrels per year)	Capital Expenditures ($ millions)
1998				$ 1,900
1999	Early Oil Complete	100,000	36.5	$ 1,000
2000		100,000	36.5	$ 1,000
2001		100,000	36.5	$ 1,100
2002		200,000	73.0	$ 1,000
2003	Stage 1 Complete	200,000	73.0	$ 1,500
2004	Stage 2 Complete	400,000	146.0	$ 1,500
2005	Stage 3 Complete	600,000	219.0	$ 1,000
2006		800,000	292.0	
2007		800,000	292.0	
2008		800,000	292.0	
2009		800,000	292.0	
2010		800,000	292.0	
2011		800,000	292.0	
2012		700,000	255.5	
2013		700,000	255.5	
2014		700,000	255.5	
2015		600,000	219.0	
2016		600,000	219.0	
2017		600,000	219.0	
2018		500,000	182.5	
2019		500,000	182.5	
2020		500,000	182.5	
2021		300,000	109.5	
2022		200,000	73.0	
2023		0	0.0	0.0
Total			**4,526.0**	**$10,000**

Source: Casewriter estimates assuming reserves of 4.5 billion barrels of oil and $10 billion total development cost.

duction, never mind new investment."[36] In its analysis of the Caspian oil projects, BP Amoco had used $14.00 per barrel as its benchmark price, well above the current price.[37]

According to traded futures contracts, however, market participants were expecting prices to rise in the coming years (see Exhibit 8-4b). Given the project's cost structure and expected production levels, AIOC's financial returns would clearly be a function of the existence of reserves and the price at which they could be sold. (Exhibits 8-5a and 8-5b present estimates of project economics and production levels, respectively.)

[36] "Azerbaijan: AIOC Scales Back," pp. 42–43.

[37] F. Demirmen, "Baku-Ceyhan: While the Pipeline Is Far from Certain, Turkey Should Act from a Position of Strength," *Turkish Daily News*, April 4, 2000.

VALUING PROJECTS

9

Airbus A3XX: Developing the World's Largest Commercial Jet (A)

Aviation is a great business to be in, provided you have limitless money at your disposal, limitless confidence in your ability to get everything right the first time, and limitless resolve and iron nerve.[1]

EADS (Airbus) is betting the company on this aircraft.[2]

On June 23, 2000, Airbus Industrie's Supervisory Board approved an Authorization to Offer (ATO) the A3XX, a proposed super jumbo jet that would seat from 550 to 990 passengers, have a list price of $216 million, and cost $13 billion to develop. Before the Board would commit to industrial launch, the point at which significant expenditures would begin, it hoped to secure orders for 50 jets from as many as five major airlines. While Airbus had been courting potential customers for many years—in fact, development had been underway since 1990—the ATO gave the sales force permission to begin taking firm orders for the plane with delivery starting in 2006.

Airbus management announced the first orders for the A3XX at the bi-annual Air Show in Farnborough, England, in July 2000. Noël Forgeard, Airbus's CEO, reported that Air France, Emirates Airlines, and International Lease Finance Corporation had agreed to order ten, seven, and five jets, respectively, and that another 30 orders were lined up.[3] The initial orders were a positive, though not unexpected, sign. The real question, however, was whether there was sufficient long-term demand to justify industrial

---

Dean's Research Fellow Michael Kane and Professor Benjamin Esty prepared this case with assistance from Research Associate Fuaad A. Qureshi. HBS cases are developed solely as the basis for class discussion. Cases are not intended to serve as endorsements, sources of primary data, or illustrations of effective or ineffective management.

[1] B. Gunston, *Airbus* (London: Osprey Publishing Limited, 1988), p. 10.

[2] "Chocks Away," *The Economist*, July 29, 2000, pp. 58–59.

[3] D. Michaels, "Airbus Scores Big as Industry Slump Holds Off," *The Wall Street Journal*, July 26, 2000, p. A21.

launch. Management believed they would break even on an undiscounted cash flow basis with sales of 250 planes and could sell as many as 750 over the next 20 years.[4] At the time, Airbus was predicting that demand for more than 1,500 super jumbos over the next 20 years that would generate sales in excess of $350 billion.[5] Given the fact that Airbus had booked more than half of the orders for new passenger aircraft for the first time in 1999, capturing more than half the very large aircraft (VLA) market with the A3XX would constitute an enormous financial success and would position Airbus as the commercial aviation industry leader.

THE COMMERCIAL JET AIRCRAFT MARKET

At year-end 1999, the world commercial jet fleet consisted of 12,000 passenger and 1,600 cargo planes operated by more than 400 scheduled passenger and cargo airlines.[6] In the passenger category, large aircraft (those with 70 or more seats) accounted for 90% of annual deliveries, while smaller, regional jets accounted for the rest. The largest aircraft, those seating more than 400 passengers or carrying more than 80 tons of freight, were known as very large aircraft (VLA).

With revenues of $56.5 billion in 1999, the manufacture and sale of jet aircraft was the biggest single segment of the $143 billion commercial aviation industry (see Exhibit 9-1). Two firms, Boeing Company and Airbus Industrie, dominated the manufacture of large aircraft. Although Boeing had recently announced a desire to expand into the $86.7 billion support services segment, both companies had historically focused on manufacturing and left support services to the airlines, component manufacturers, and other vendors. Airbus and Boeing were less active in this segment because the components that required the most maintenance and repair work, such as engines, landing gear, and electrical systems, were installed but not manufactured by them.

Combined, the two firms delivered 889 aircraft in 1999, ranging from single-aisle jets seating 100–200 passengers to the twin-aisle Boeing 747-400 seating more than 400 passengers. Exhibit 9-2 shows a market map of the Boeing and Airbus fleets. Boeing had built approximately 85% of the industry's current fleet and had regularly captured 60 to 70% of orders and deliveries until recently when Airbus had gained share. Exhibit 9-3 shows the delivery history and order status for select passenger aircraft.

The Boeing Company

Boeing had been at the forefront of civil aviation for over half a century. From the B17s and B29s of World War II through the B52s of the Cold War, Boeing had leveraged its manufacturing and defense experience to become the world's leading producer of commercial aircraft. Sales of commercial aircraft accounted for two-thirds of revenues; sales of military aircraft, missiles, and space systems accounted for the rest. Strong demand and improved operations led to a doubling of net income in 1999 compared to 1998. Exhibit 9-4A presents Boeing's recent financial statements.

Boeing's unique importance for the U.S. economy as a whole, underscored by its role as the supplier of Air Force One, F-15s fighter aircraft, and the Space Shuttle, provided a basis for its political strength. In addition to being the federal government's

---

[4] Credit Suisse First Boston, *Global Commercial Aerospace Monthly*, May 23, 2000, p. 20.

[5] Airbus Industrie, *1st Quarter 2000 Briefing*, p. 3; Credit Suisse First Boston, *Global Commercial Aerospace Monthly*, May 2000, reporting on a securities analysts' meeting held by Airbus Management in May 2000.

[6] Boeing, *2000 Current Market Outlook*, p. 42; Airbus Industrie, *Global Market Forecast 2000–2019*, July 2000, p. 4.

EXHIBIT 9-1

SALES OF COMMERCIAL AIRPLANE AND AVIATION SUPPORT SERVICES (1999, BILLIONS)

	1999 Annual Sales (Actual)	2019 Annual Sales (Estimate)	2000–2019 Cumulative Sales (Estimate)
Aircraft Deliveries			
Regional Aircraft	$ 3.8	n/a	n/a
Airbus	16.0	$ 60.6	$729.5
Boeing	36.7	56.9	692.5
Total Aircraft Deliveries	**$ 56.5**	**$117.5**	**$1,422.0**
Aircraft Support Services			
Airplane Servicing	13.8	32.3	441
Heavy Airplane Maintenance	18.5	43.0	588
Engine Repair (off wing)	8.4	19.6	268
Airframe Component Repair	12.3	28.8	394
Major Airplane Modification	1.8	3.5	43
Airframe and Engine Repair Parts	8.1	18.8	257
Flight Crew Training	1.7	3.4	49
Airport and Route Infrastructure	21.4	43.0	622
Used Airplane Remarketing	0.7	1.4	20
Total Support Services	**$ 86.7**	**$193.8**	**$2,682**
Total Deliveries and Services	**$143.2**	**$311.3**	**$4,104**

Sources: Boeing *Current Market Outlook*, 2000; *The Airline Monitor*, July 2000.

second largest defense contractor, Boeing was the largest single contributor to the United States balance of payments in terms of exports. In addition, it had 190,000 employees in the United States and indirectly accounted for at least as many jobs at its extensive network of vendors.

Boeing's fleet consisted of 14 models spread across five aircraft families, each with somewhat different technologies. The flagship of the Boeing fleet, the 747-400, held 420 passengers in the standard three-class configuration. There were, however, more than 30 so-called high-density models operating in Asia that could hold as many as 550 passengers. Boeing's decision to develop the 747 in 1965 was widely viewed as a daring, bet-the-company gamble on an untested product. The 747 was more than twice as big as the 707, the largest plane then operating, and Boeing had only 25 orders when it committed to build the plane. Yet when Boeing announced the initial 25-plane order, its stock price jumped 5.1%.[7] At the time, it predicted the launch would cost $1.5 billion and would generate sales of more than 700 planes by 1980.[8] Despite this optimism, the launch turned out to be very difficult and almost caused Boeing to fail:

> Boeing's problems with the 747 sounds like a litany of the damned . . . (and almost) threatened the company's survival. . . . Boeing not only had to pay penalty fees for late deliver-

[7] R.P. Cooke, "Pan Am to Buy 25 Giant Boeing 747s For Record Outlay of $525 Million," *The Wall Street Journal*, April 14, 1966, p. 3.
[8] "Boeing Co. Sells 10 More of Its 747s for $200 Million," *The Wall Street Journal*, September 29, 1996, p. 3.

EXHIBIT 9-2

LARGE COMMERCIAL AIRCRAFT: AIRBUS AND BOEING

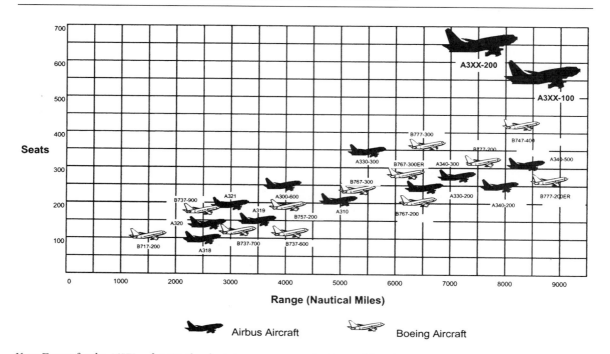

Note: Except for the A3XX and A318, the chart shows current production models only.

Sources: Lehman Brothers Aerospace & Defense Electronics Industry Update, June 23, 2000; Airbus Industrie; Boeing.

ies, but, far worse, didn't receive the large last installments until the deliveries were made. Deprived of an adequate . . . cash flow, Boeing found itself seriously short of funds yet obliged to finance a huge inventory of partly built 747s.[9]

More than three decades later, demand for the 747 was running strong. Boeing delivered 47 planes in 1999, at an average price of $150 million per plane, and had an order backlog for 74 more.

Airbus Industrie

Airbus was founded in 1970 as a consortium of the principal aerospace companies of Germany (Deutsche Aerospace, now a DaimlerChrysler subsidiary known as DASA), France (Aerospatiale Matra), England (Britain's Hawker Siddeley, later BAE Systems), and Spain (Construcciones Aeronauticas, CASA), and had its headquarters in Toulouse, France. Through the consortium, the partners combined their resources and technologies to produce a more competitive line of commercial aircraft. While Airbus functioned as a marketing organization, the partners developed and manufactured aircraft compo-

[9] J. Newhouse, *The Sporty Game* (New York: Alfred A. Knopf, 1982), pp. 166, 168–169.

EXHIBIT 9-3

ORDERS AND DELIVERIES FOR SELECT PASSENGER AIRCRAFT

	Boeing Aircraft					Airbus Aircraft				
	737	747-1/2/300	767-2/3/400	747-400	777-2/300	A-300	A-310	A-320	A-330	A-340
Average Number of Seats	140	390	220	410	350	265	220	150	310	300
Actual Deliveries										
1967	4									
1968	105									
1969	114	3								
1970	37	40								
1971	29	40								
1972	22	17								
1973	18	19								
1974	47	15								
1975	51	19				1				
1976	41	21				6				
1977	25	18				10				
1978	40	28				10				
1979	77	60				18				
1980	92	67				31				
1981	108	53				37				
1982	95	24	20			37				
1983	82	22	55			19	17			
1984	67	15	29			17	26			
1985	115	24	25			15	26			
1986	141	35	24			10	18			
1987	161	23	36			10	19			
1988	165	24	53			17	28	14		
1989	146	4	35	41		24	23	57		
1990	174	8	60	62		18	18	57		
1991	215	2	62	62		23	19	119		
1992	218	0	63	61		22	23	111		
1993	152		51	55		22	22	72	1	21
1994	121		40	40		23	2	48	9	25
1995	89		36	25	13	17	2	32	30	19
1996	76		42	25	32	14	2	38	10	28
1997	135		41	39	59	6	2	57	14	33
1998	274		47	53	74	13	1	80	23	24
1999	295		44	47	83	8	0	101	44	20
Total	3,531	581	763	510	261	428	248	786	131	170
Average Yearly Deliveries	107	25	42	46	52	17	15	66	19	24

(Continued)

nents individually. For example, BAE made the wings in Great Britain and DASA did final assembly in Hamburg. The host governments had significant interests in the consortium because it employed approximately 37,000 workers and provided military aircraft and space systems to them. In addition, the French and Spanish governments had direct financial interests in their member companies. As a partnership, Airbus did not

EXHIBIT 9-3   (Continued)

	Boeing Aircraft					Airbus Aircraft				
	737	747-1/2/300	767-2/3/400	747-400	777-2/300	A-300	A-310	A-320	A-330	A-340
Current Order Book by Scheduled Delivery Date										
2000	285	0	41	18	41	4	0	82	33	14
2001	255	0	34	24	54	8	0	139	49	21
2002	188	0	21	18	37	11	3	126	25	32
2003	125	0	10	6	18	9	1	96	14	31
2004	95	0	3	3	17	3	46	19	14	
2005	40	0	1	3	9	0	0	22	13	5
2006	25	0	0	1	8	0	0	8	0	1
2007	0	0	0	1	0	0	0	4	0	0
2008	0	0	0	0	0	0	0	0	0	0
Total	**1,013**	**0**	**110**	**74**	**184**	**35**	**5**	**523**	**153**	**118**

Note: The Boeing 737 includes three model versions: 737-200 (1967–1988), 737-3/500 (1984–present), and 737-6/900 (1997–present).

Sources: The Airline Monitor, May 2000 (deliveries); *CSFB Global Commercial Aerospace Monthly*, May 2000 (orders).

publish detailed financial statements, but analysts estimated it had sales of $16.7 billion and earnings before interest and taxes (EBIT) of $0.9 billion in 1999 (see Exhibit 9-4A).

Over time, the partnership structure had become increasingly cumbersome and limited the consortium's ability to reduce costs and finance growth. To address these problems, the three continental European partners merged into a new company known as European Aeronautic Defense and Space Company (EADS). The new company was launched in July 2000, with a €1.6 billion initial public equity offering (IPO). Exhibit 9-4B presents consolidated pro forma financial statements for EADS. The partners also planned to create a new French corporation called Airbus Integrated Company (AIC) which would assume all of the Airbus-related activities. When formed in January 2001, EADS and BAE Systems would own 80% and 20% of AIC, respectively.

From the beginning, Airbus had a reputation for innovative design and technology. Its first plane, the A300, served as the platform for several derivative models with varying range and capacity combinations. By 1999, it had a fleet of nine basic models (see Exhibit 9-2), a customer base of 171 operators, and an order backlog for 1,445 planes.[10] All Airbus planes employed "fly-by-wire" technology that substituted computerized control for mechanical linkages between the pilot and the aircraft's control surfaces. This technology combined with a common cockpit design permitted "cross crew qualification" (CCQ) whereby pilots were certified to fly similar aircraft. For example, pilots could fly and maintain certification in several planes including the A3XX, A340, and A330. The ability to schedule flight crews interchangeably on various models led to better pilot utilization and lower training costs. These features helped explain why Airbus had received over half of the total large aircraft orders for the first time in 1999, and why a leading industry journal had recently declared: "Airbus has won and will become the world's leading producer of commercial jets."[11]

[10] *The Airline Monitor*, January/February 2000, p. 7.

[11] Ibid., p. 1.

EXHIBIT 9-4A

FINANCIAL STATEMENTS ($ MILLIONS)

	The Boeing Company[a]					Airbus Industrie				
	1995	1996	1997	1998	1999	1995	1996	1997	1998	1999
Balance Sheet										
Cash and Short Term Investments	$ 3,730	$ 5,469	$ 4,420	$ 2,741	$ 3,554					
Total Assets	22,040	37,880	38,024	36,672	36,147					
Total Debt	2,615	7,489	6,854	6,972	6,732					
Income Statement										
Sales	32,960	35,453	45,800	56,154	57,993	$9,600	$8,800	$11,600	$13,300	$16,700
Depreciation and amortization	1,306	1,267	1,458	1,622	1,645					
EBIT	(316)	2,618	(355)	1,567	3,349	n/a	n/a	335	579	896[b]
Net Income	(36)	1,818	(178)	1,120	2,309					
Market Value										
Number of Shares (millions)	344	347	973	938	871					
Stock Price (year end)	$78	$107	$49	$33	$41					
Bond Rating	AA	AA	AA	AA−	AA−					
Market Share (% by Units)										
Deliveries	67.5%	68.1%	67.3%	70.7%	66.9%	32.5%	31.9%	32.7%	29.3%	33.1%
Orders	n/a	71.1%	56.1%	53.6%	45.2%	n/a	28.9%	43.9%	46.4%	54.8%

[a] Boeing acquired McDonnell Douglas on August 1, 1997. The income statement and balance sheet data (except for 1995 balance sheet) reflect the combined financial statements.

[b] EADS Offering Memorandum dated July 9, 2000, p. 48. Because launch aid was granted to the partners not to Airbus, the partners recognized the effects of launch aid on their own financial statements. In 1999, BAE Systems (a 20% owner) reported a loss of £42 million ($67 million) in its commercial aviation division after repayment of launch aid.

Sources: Boeing Annual Reports; Airbus Industrie Website; *The Airline Monitor*, July 2000, *The Wall Street Journal*, June 26, 2000, p. A28.

EXHIBIT 9-4B

AIRBUS PARTNERS AT YEAR-END 1999 (€MILLIONS)[a]

	BAE Systems PLC (UK)	EADS Participants			
		Aerospatiale Matra S.A.[b] (France)	DaimlerChrysler Aerospace AG (DASA)[b] (Germany)	Construcciones Aeronáuticas SA (CASA)[b] (Spain)	EADS[c] (pro forma)
Ownership of Airbus Industrie	20.0%	37.9%	37.9%	4.2%	80.0%
Balance Sheet					
Cash & ST Investments	€1,306	€759	€3,958	€570	€3,175
Fixed Assets	13,742	8,218	1,576	192	19,591
Total Assets	28,079	16,194	9,737	1,268	35,640
Total Debt	5,122	3,681	217	110	5,696
Stockholder's Equity	11,991	1,778	2,397	507	8,123
Income Statement					
Revenues	€14,381	€12,236	€7,455	€931	€22,553
Cost of Sales	8,823	(9,624)	(5,914)	(735)	(18,278)
Gross Margin	789	2,612	1,541	196	4,275
Income before income taxes	739	750	461	114	815
Net Income (loss)	522	(644)	(39)	74	(1,009)
Ownership	100% Public	48% French State 33% Lagardere 17% Public 2% Employees	100% Public[d]	100% Spanish State	
Market Capitalization (€B)	18.5	8.6	59.1[d]		
S&P Bond Rating	A	A−	A+[d]	NA	

[a] The €/$ exchange rate on 6/30/00 was €1.00 = $ 0.9545; the €/£ exchange rate on June 30, 2000 was €1.00 = £0.6209.

[b] Presented in accordance with International Accounting Standards (IAS).

[c] Unaudited, proforma consolidation of Aerospatiale Matra, DASA, and CASA after accounting adjustments and eliminations. Different forms of accounting recognition (full consolidation vs. equity method) prevent the amounts from summing across the EADS participants. EADS net loss is due to an extraordinary charge of €1.9 billion related to foreign currency hedging positions.

[d] These figures refer to the parent corporation, DaimlerChrysler AG.

Source: EADS Offering Memorandum, July 9, 2000; BAE Systems 1999 Annual Report.

Despite the gains in market share, Airbus still did not have a product to compete with Boeing's 747 in the VLA market. A senior executive at Aerospatiale complained: "The problem is the monopoly of the 747, which is a fantastic advantage. They have a product. We have none."[12]

THE AIRBUS A3XX

Airbus began exploring the possibility of creating a jumbo jet in 1990. Initially, Boeing and Airbus collaborated on a feasibility study for the plane, but Boeing withdrew in 1995 because the project was too expensive and too risky given the uncertainty in demand.[13] Airbus forged ahead with development and finalized the basic design in 1999. It proposed to offer a family of aircraft consisting of both passenger and cargo models. The first model would seat 550 passengers in the standard three-class configuration and could provide nonstop service from Sydney to Los Angeles, Singapore to London, or New York to Tokyo, the same routes currently served by the 747. A later, extended-range model could operate from the East Coast of the United States to either Sydney or Singapore. Both versions would have two full passenger decks and a third deck capable of accommodating baggage, cargo, and/or passenger amenities such as a cocktail lounge, an exercise room, or showers. Exhibit 9-5 presents an artist's rendition of the A3XX.

Compared to the 747, the A3XX would have more space per seat and wider aisles. Airbus believed these features would attract passengers especially on the longer routes. Other passengers, particularly on transpacific flights, would appreciate the safety of a four-engine plane compared to two-engine planes like the Boeing 777. From the airlines' perspective, the plane would have the same fly-by-wire technology, flight deck design, and performance characteristics that were common across the Airbus family. Although the A3XX would have a higher list price than the 747-400, Airbus claimed the combination of increased capacity and reduced costs would provide superior economics. The operating cost per flight would be 12% more than the 747's cost, but given the plane's 35% greater capacity, it would provide almost 25% more volume for free.[14] According to Airbus, the A3XX would need only 323 passengers to break even compared to 290 for the 747.[15]

Despite these advantages, the plane's size posed several problems. Yet based on continuing dialogue with its customers, airport authorities, and others, Airbus believed it had solved all of them and had begun the necessary procedures for regulatory approvals in the United States and elsewhere. The major issues were noise, emissions, turnaround time, taxiway movements, and evacuation. Airbus claimed that the noise levels would be below those of the 747 and emissions would be at the low end of the 747 range. Turnaround times would be held within the 747 envelope by using dual boarding bridges and taking advantage of the A3XX's wider aisles and double interior staircase.[16] Airbus claimed that the A3XX would operate within existing runways and

---

[12] J. Cole, "Airbus Prepares to 'Bet the Company' As It Builds a Huge New Jet," *The Wall Street Journal*, November 3, 1999, p. A1.

[13] K. West, "Boeing May Quit Large-Jet Venture Timing and Market Don't Appear Right," *Seattle Post-Intelligencer*, July 8, 1995, p. A1.

[14] *The Airline Monitor*, Editor Edmund Greenslet, remarks to casewriter on September 28, 2000.

[15] Airbus Industrie, *1st Quarter 2000 Briefing*, p. 9.

[16] Ibid., p. 7.

EXHIBIT 9-5

AIRBUS A3XX: PROFILE AND CROSS-SECTIONS

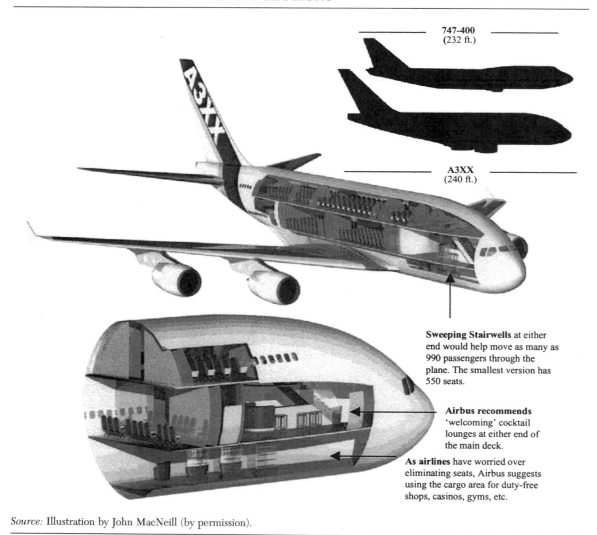

747-400
(232 ft.)

A3XX
(240 ft.)

Sweeping Stairwells at either end would help move as many as 990 passengers through the plane. The smallest version has 550 seats.

Airbus recommends 'welcoming' cocktail lounges at either end of the main deck.

As airlines have worried over eliminating seats, Airbus suggests using the cargo area for duty-free shops, casinos, gyms, etc.

Source: Illustration by John MacNeill (by permission).

---

airports because it had been designed to fit within an 80 square meter box as specified by the United States Federal Aviation Administration (FAA). In fact, the FAA had recently published an "Issues Document" identifying 102 technical, physical, and safety issues in connection with the operation of new large aircraft in the United States. One key hurdle, though again one Airbus believed that it had solved, was the requirement that the plane could be evacuated within 90 seconds even if half the exits were blocked.

Forecasting Demand

Because large jet aircraft took years to design and develop, required enormous up-front investment, and had useful lives of over 30 years (some thought the 747 would have a useful life of 50 years or more), Airbus and Boeing had to generate long-term demand projections. Each year they prepared 20-year forecasts for large commercial jet aircraft: Airbus published the *Global Market Forecast* (GMF), while Boeing published the *Current Market Outlook* (CMO). Exhibit 9-6 presents a comparison of the forecasts over the past six years.

The 2000 editions agreed that there would be significant growth in the air transportation industry. Worldwide passenger traffic would almost triple in volume by 2019—Airbus forecast an average annual growth rate of 4.9% while Boeing forecast growth of 4.8% per year. Although Boeing had, at one point, cut its growth forecasts for Asia because of the regional financial crisis in 1998, both manufacturers believed that Asia would register the world's highest growth rates over the next 20 years.[17]

To produce the GMF, Airbus predicted annual demand for new aircraft on each of 10,000 passenger routes linking almost 2,000 airports. The model assumed that cargo

---

EXHIBIT 9-6

COMPARISON OF BOEING AND AIRBUS 20-YEAR MARKET FORECASTS (BY YEAR OF FORECAST)

	1995	1996	1997	1998	1999	2000
Forecast Period	to 2014	to 2015	to 2016	to 2017	to 2018	to 2019
Passenger Traffic Growth (per year)						
Airbus	5.1%	n/a	5.2%	5.0%	5.0%	4.9%
Boeing	5.1%	5.1%	4.9%	4.9%	4.7%	4.8%
Commercial Aircraft in Operation (in 20 years)						
Airbus	16,588	n/a	17,184	17,920	22,506	22,620
Boeing (including regional jets < 70 seats)	20,683	23,080	23,600	26,200	28,400	31,755
Deliveries of New Comm. Aircraft (over 20 years)						
Airbus	12,933	n/a	13,758	15,518	15,500	15,364
Boeing	15,462	15,900	16,160	17,650	20,150	22,315
Value of 20-Year Market for New Aircraft ($ billions)						
Airbus	n/a	n/a	n/a	$1,170	$1,290	$1,310
Boeing	$1,000	$1,100	$1,100	$1,250	$1,380	$1,490
Deliveries of VLA Passenger Aircraft (≥ 500 seats)						
Airbus	1,374	n/a	1,442	1,332	1,208	1,235
Boeing	n/a	n/a	460	405	365	330
Deliveries of Large Cargo Aircraft[a]						
Airbus	n/a	n/a	n/a	n/a	301	315
Boeing	n/a	n/a	n/a	n/a	275	270

[a] Includes both the Boeing 747-400 and the Airbus A3XX.

Sources: Boeing Current Market Outlook, Airbus Global Market Forecast, and casewriter estimates. (Airbus did not issue a GMF in 1996 and did not publish data on the cargo market until 1999.)

---

[17] "The Size Equation," *Airline Business*, April 1999, p. 52.

EXHIBIT 9-7

REVENUE-PASSENGER-KILOMETER (RPK) GROWTH RATES, 1999–2019, FOR THE 15 LARGEST SUBMARKETS (WITH PERCENT OF 1999 WORLD RPK IN PARENTHESES)

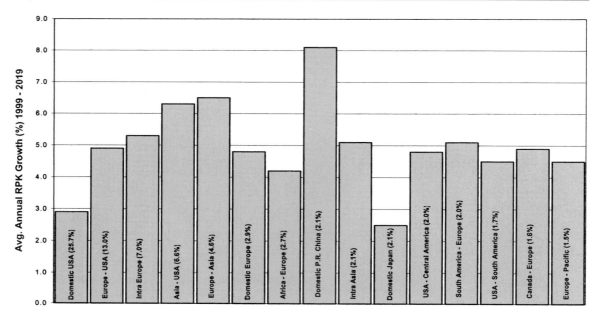

Source: Airbus Industrie 1999 Global Market Forecast.

and passenger demand would track GDP growth as they had for the past 50 years. For each airline, on each route pair, the model estimated the need for specific aircraft, and compared that number against the then existing supply of aircraft. The model calculated maximum feasible frequency limits for each route based on assumptions about airport capacity, airplane speed, distance, and other factors. It assumed that all airlines would attempt to maintain market share by adding capacity as demand increased, and by increasing aircraft size when it was no longer feasible to increase flight frequencies. Exhibit 9-7 presents forecast growth rates for the 15 largest air travel submarkets. Exhibit 9-8 illustrates a highly simplified example of this kind of analysis focused on the VLA segment. It shows how assumptions about growth, fleet retirement, and conversions to alternative planes (e.g., from the 747 to the larger A3XX) could be used to estimate the total demand for super jumbos.

Airbus forecast demand for 14,661 new passenger aircraft and 703 new air freighters over the 20-year period through 2019. It forecast demand for 727 new aircraft seating from 400 to 500 passengers—the mainstay of the 747 market—and 1,550 new aircraft seating 500 or more passengers.[18] Of this number, 1,235 would be passenger planes and 315 would be cargo planes. The GMF predicted that, by 2019, Asia-Pacific airlines

---

[18] The Airbus GMF defined the VLA market as consisting of passenger aircraft with 500 or more seats and cargo aircraft capable of handling more than 80 tons of freight (the size of the 747 or larger).

EXHIBIT 9-8

ESTIMATED MARKET FOR VERY LARGE AIRCRAFT (VLA, ≥ 500 SEATS) BY 2019

Aircraft	Seats in Commercial Fleet in 1999 (A)	Estimated Annual Growth (B)	Seats Needed in 2019 (C = A[1 + B][20])	Estimated Retirements and Conversions (D)	Total New Seats Required (E = C − A + D)	Assumed Conversion Rate to VLA Aircraft (F)	Potential Market for VLA Aircraft (G = E * F)	Seats Per VLA (H)	Estimated VLA Market (I = G/H)
A-330	40,300	5.00%	106,928	1,000	67,628	10.0%	6,763		12
A-340	48,300	5.00	128,154	1,000	80,854	10.0	8,085		15
777-2/300	90,650	5.60	269,554	1,500	180,404	10.0	18,040		33
747-1/2/300	134,550	6.00	431,520	127,697	424,667	35.0	148,633		270
747-400	191,907	7.00	742,620	34,935	585,648	85.0	497,800		905
Total	**505,707**		**1,678,776**	**166,132**	**1,339,201**		**679,323**	**550**	**1,235**

(D) Retirements are based on current fleet age and composition.

(H) The number of seats per VLA is a function of the mix of aircraft types.

Does not include VLA freighters, which could represent another 315 new aircraft to be delivered by 2019, according to Airbus.

Sources: Casewriter estimates; Lehman Brothers Equity Research Report, December 6, 1999; Airbus Industrie Global Market Forecast 2000.

would hold almost half the VLA passenger fleet, and that six of the top ten airports served by VLA aircraft would be in Asia.[19]

In contrast, Boeing forecast economic growth in 12 regions in its CMO. It then used these growth assumptions to forecast regional traffic flows in 51 intra- and inter-regional markets. For example, travel within China would grow at an average annual rate of 9.0% compared to 2.8% within North America. The CMO concluded there would be demand for 22,315 new aircraft through 2019. One reason for the difference between the two forecasts was that the CMO included demand for more than 4,000 regional jets.

Despite general agreement on overall growth, Boeing forecast a much smaller VLA market. The CMO stated bluntly: "The demand for very large airplanes is small."[20] It forecast total demand for only 1,010 new aircraft seating 400 passengers or more, 40% of which would be 747-400s (410 aircraft). Of the remaining 600 planes, 270 would be cargo planes, leaving demand for only 330 aircraft seating 500 passengers or more. More importantly, most of the demand for the larger planes would not materialize for at least 10 years.[21]

The disparity between the two forecasts could be traced to conflicting assumptions regarding the relative importance of flight frequency, new route development, and aircraft size. Airbus believed that increased frequencies and new routes would provide only short-term solutions to the problem of growing demand. Airport curfews, gate and runway capacity, and passenger arrival preferences would limit the ability to increase frequencies at many airports, including some of the world's busiest airports like London Heathrow, Tokyo Narita, Singapore, and Los Angeles International. As Airbus Senior Vice President John Leahy said, "The trouble is that on these long-distance flights, nobody wants to arrive at 3:00 a.m. and nobody wants to drive out to the airport for a 2:30 a.m. departure so that they can have more flights."[22]

At the same time, Airbus did not believe that the development of new routes would provide a feasible long-term solution. Adam Brown, vice president for strategic planning and forecasting, noted: "The pace of new route development has slowed sharply . . . between 1990 and 1995, the total number of routes grew by less than 700, an average increase of just 1.7% per year."[23] Part of the problem was the difficulty of opening new airports. In fact, only 10 major new airports were scheduled to open within the next 10 years, and only 18 airports had approved plans for growth.[24] An even bigger concern was the fact that new routes would not solve the problem of growth at the largest population centers, especially in Asia. Said Leahy, "if you want to go from Los Angeles to Tokyo . . . you aren't going to go to Denver, fly to Osaka, and then backtrack to Tokyo."[25] While Boeing and others cited the expansion of new routes in transatlantic markets as a model for growth in transpacific travel, Airbus pointed out that Asia lacked the secondary urban centers to support new destinations.[26] Thus, hub-to-hub transport would remain the industry standard in these markets.

---

[19] Ibid.

[20] Boeing, *2000 Current Market Outlook*, p. 34.

[21] Ibid.

[22] P. Flint, "A Quantum Change," *Air Transport World*, July 2000, p. 38.

[23] Ibid.

[24] Ibid.

[25] Ibid.

[26] Airbus Industrie, *Global Market Forecast 2000–2019*, July 2000, p. 61.

Like Airbus, Boeing assumed that increasing flight frequency at existing airports would absorb a certain amount of growth, but that congestion at the largest hubs would require an alternative solution which, according to Boeing, would be new point-to-point routes using medium-sized, long-range aircraft like its 777 or Airbus A340. In support of this view, a Boeing executive claimed: "60% of the airlines that bought the 1,000 or so 747s we've sold bought them for their range, not for their capacity."[27] To the extent there was demand for VLA aircraft, the 747-400 would be sufficient for most airlines.

Recent developments in the airline industry supported this assertion. In the United States, following airline deregulation in 1985, Southwest Airlines had prospered by introducing new service at secondary airports such as Providence, Rhode Island and Islip, New York. In Europe, Ireland-based Ryanair was copying Southwest's model and had achieved 25% annual passenger growth since 1989 by offering no-frills, economy service between secondary airports.[28] More recently, other European start-ups such as "buzz" and "easyJet" had adopted similar business models. Transatlantic, and to a much lesser but growing extent, transpacific travel reflected this trend toward fragmentation. Randy Baseler, a Boeing vice president, explained:

> Back in 1987, the only daily flight between Chicago and Europe was a TWA 747 to London. . . . In those days 60% of American carriers' transatlantic flights were in 747s operated by Pan Am and TWA in and out of big East-coast airports. Today, United and American Airlines operate 21 daily flights from Chicago to 11 different European destinations using smaller 767 and 777 aircraft.[29]

More recently, both Delta Airlines and American Airlines have introduced new point-to-point service across the Pacific, the Delta from Portland, Oregon, to Nagoya, Japan, and American from San Jose, California, to Tokyo.[30]

Related to the opening of new routes was a decline in the average seating capacity in many airline fleets. In fact, Boeing predicted that smaller jets such as its 777 and the Airbus 330 would provide 160 additional direct transatlantic routes in the coming years and that there would be similar fragmentation across the Pacific.[31] Boeing assumed these trends would continue because people seemed to favor timely and direct service over minimum cost as they became wealthier.[32] Another factor that would contribute to further fragmentation, though one that was exceedingly difficult to predict, was entry by new airlines. Nevertheless, Boeing believed entry by new airlines was likely.

Industry analysts made projections that fell somewhere in between the two companies' projections. *The Airline Monitor*, a leading industry journal, assumed that airlines would buy the A3XX for its operating advantages and passenger appeal. Based on this assumption, the journal forecast total demand for 735 A3XXs through 2019 (passenger and cargo planes).[33] Edmund Greenslet, the journal's editor, commented: "It is very likely that when the market actually sees the A3XX it will displace the 747 as the 'Queen of the Air' and that means that any airline which considers itself to be a top line

---

[27] D. Field, "Boeing Stock Flies after Jet Plan Scrubbed," *USA Today*, January 22, 1997, p. B1.

[28] D. Michaels, "No-Frills Irish Airline Flies High," *The Wall Street Journal*, September 6, 2000, p. B1.

[29] "Airbus Bets the Company," *The Economist*, March 18, 2000, p. 68.

[30] Cole, "Airbus Prepares to 'Bet the Company' as It Builds a Huge New Jet," p. A1.

[31] "Airbus Bets the Company," p. 68.

[32] Boeing, *2000 Current Market Outlook*, p. 26.

[33] *The Airline Monitor*, July 2000, p. 11 (Table S).

international carrier will feel the need to have it."[34] Particularly among "high-yield" (business and first class) passengers, flying on the newest and best aircraft held special appeal.

Major airlines, including the largest 747 operators (Exhibit 9-9 shows fleet composition for each of the 15 largest 747 operators), appeared equally divided regarding the need for a super jumbo aircraft. On the one hand, a spokesperson for United Airlines said, "We are of the school that a larger airplane with seating for 700 to 800 could make sense in the right circumstances because we have very strong hubs and we could consolidate traffic. But a lot depends on cost."[35] Similarly, a spokesman for Singapore Airlines said, "SIA has a definite need for some of the super jumbos particularly at congested, slot-constrained international gateways."[36] Other airlines, however, were less optimistic, especially in the short term. When asked if British Airways was interested in ordering the 3XX, CEO Robert Ayling said, "I'm a cautious person by nature . . . (and) I'm not inclined to go ahead unless it really can be demonstrated that this equipment can produce the kind of savings we need to justify it."[37] A spokesman for Japan Airlines was more emphatic, "JAL has no plans to buy the A3XX, at least until March 2003. After that, Airbus may have a chance, but even then some new purchases will go to Boeing."[38]

Despite the disagreement, Airbus felt confident in its analysis that capacity increases would eventually prevail. Adam Brown commented: "There may be some awful blunder in our forecasts that we have not spotted. But if there is one we haven't found it yet."[39] A sanguine John Leahy made the point more emphatically: "Just as the 747 introduced a new way of flying compared to what was in existence before that, we are absolutely convinced the A3XX will create that same quantum change in the way people fly."[40]

Financing the A3XX

Although Airbus had not publicized detailed cost estimates or financing plans for the A3XX, various details emerged through meetings with analysts, airlines, and journalists. The A3XX would cost approximately $13 billion to launch: $11 billion for research and development (including $10 billion to develop two passenger versions and $1 billion to develop a cargo version), $1 billion for property, plant, and equipment (tools, jigs, and factories which would be depreciated over 10 years on a straight-line basis), and $1 billion for working capital. Exhibit 9-10 shows the $13 billion investment over time but does not include an estimated $700 million that would already have been spent by the end of 2000.

Funding would come from three sources: $3.5 billion from vendors referred to as "risk sharing partners" (RSPs); $3.6 billion of "launch aid" from the partners' national governments; and $5.9 billion from the Airbus partners themselves in proportion to their ownership interests. There would also be early cash flows from progress payments

---

[34] *The Airline Monitor*, January/February 2000, p. 17.

[35] "Manufacturers Debate Future of Superjumbo Jet," *Advanced Materials & Composites News*, February 1, 1999.

[36] S. Chew, "Group Has 'Definite Need' for Super-large Jetliners," *Singapore Straits Times*, January 23, 1997.

[37] D. Field, "CEO Ayling Thinks International," *USA Today*, September 27, 1996, p. 4B.

[38] "Airbus Woos Mitsubishi for Jet Project," *The Wall Street Journal*, March 31, 2000, p. A3.

[39] "The Size Equation," *Airline Business*, April 1999, p. 52.

[40] Flint, "A Quantum Change," p. 38.

EXHIBIT 9-9

FLEET COMPOSITION FOR THE 15 LARGEST BOEING 747 OPERATORS IN 1997

	Airline	Headquarters' Location	1997 Widebody Fleet			2001 (expected) Widebody Fleet			1997–2001 Growth in Widebody Fleet Size
			747s	Total	747s as % of Total	747s	Total	747s as % of Total	
1	Japan Airlines	Asia	79	130	60.8%	73	136	53.7%	4.6%
2	British Airways	Europe	69	117	59.0%	71	140	50.7%	19.7%
3	United Airlines	U.S.	51	153	33.3%	45	161	28.0%	5.2%
4	Singapore Airlines	Asia	48	83	57.8%	53	104	51.0%	25.3%
5	Korean Air	Asia	45	86	52.3%	39	89	43.8%	3.5%
6	Air France	Europe	43	74	58.1%	33	86	38.4%	16.2%
7	Northwest Airlines	U.S.	43	80	53.8%	42	86	48.8%	7.5%
8	All Nippon Airlines	Asia	38	109	34.9%	34	113	30.1%	3.7%
9	Cathay Pacific	Asia	38	59	64.4%	33	68	48.5%	15.3%
10	KLM	Europe	32	51	62.7%	33	53	62.3%	3.9%
11	Qantas	Australia	30	60	50.0%	34	63	54.0%	5.0%
12	Lufthansa	Europe	30	67	44.8%	29	83	34.9%	23.9%
13	Saudi Arabian Airlines	Mid-East	28	65	43.1%	26	64	40.6%	−1.5%
14	China Airlines	Asia	18	34	52.9%	22	41	53.7%	20.6%
15	Air China International	Asia	18	31	58.1%	22	44	50.0%	41.9%
	Total		**610**	**1,199**	**50.9%**	**589**	**1,331**	**44.3%**	**11.0%**

Note: Widebody jets include Boeing's 747, 767, MD-11, L10–111, and 777, and Airbus's A300, A310, A330, and A340.

Source: Aviation Week and Space Technology Aerospace, *Sourcebook 2000.*

EXHIBIT 9-10

AIRBUS DEVELOPMENT EXPENDITURE BY YEAR ($ MILLIONS)

Investment	2001	2002	2003	2004	2005	2006	2007	2008	Total
R&D Expenditures	$1,100	$2,200	$2,200	$2,200	$1,320	$880	$660	$440	$11,000
Capital Expenditures	0	250	350	350	50	0	0	0	$ 1,000
Working Capital	0	150	300	300	200	50	0	0	$ 1,000
Total	**$1,100**	**$2,600**	**$2,850**	**$2,850**	**$1,570**	**$930**	**$660**	**$440**	**$13,000**

Source: Dresdner Kleinwort Benson, Aerospace and Defense Report, May 8, 2000.

made by airlines prior to delivery, but Airbus had not released the terms of these payments. The risk sharing partners agreed to bear the cost of development in exchange for the right to become exclusive suppliers for the A3XX. Airbus was prepared to share profits with risk sharing partners and had signed agreements with nine leading companies by mid-2000.[41] According to the contracts, the partners would be repaid on a per plane basis.[42] If Airbus did not sell any A3XXs, the RSPs would not recover any of their initial investments.

Launch aid, the second source of funds, had been the subject of past controversy between the United States and European governments. In 1992, the United States and the European Union (EU) agreed to limit launch aid to a maximum 33% of defined development costs. According to EU rules, launch aid had to be repaid within 17 years and had to earn a market rate of return. Historically, and like the risk sharing capital, launch aid repayment came through a per plane fee. For this reason, plus the fact that nonrepayment did not trigger default, launch aid more closely resembled cumulative preferred stock than debt. The British government had recently approved $835 (£530) million in launch aid to support BAE Systems' share of project, in part because the plane would create 8,000 new jobs and safeguard 20,000 more across the British aerospace industry.[43] Yet in reporting the story, *The Economist* noted, "The terms of the British government aid are suspiciously secret . . . (which) may indicate the rules have been stretched."[44]

Project Economics[45]

Assuming the development went as planned and the cost remained at $13 billion—skeptics cautioned that the total cost might reach $15 billion or more—Airbus expected to deliver the first planes in 2006. When it reached full production capacity of just over four planes per month in 2008, the A3XX would have an average realized price of approximately $225 million and operating margins ranging from 15% to 20%. These margins were based on earnings *before* repayment of launch aid and risk sharing capital. In other words, they were potential returns to all capital providers collectively. The project would likely have an effective tax rate equal to 38%, the standard French rate including "social contribution."

The analysts, however, disagreed in many areas. Besides total demand, they disagreed on the magnitude and composition of up-front investment (how much of the development cost was R&D that had to be expensed and how much could be capitalized and depreciated). They also disagreed on the appropriate tax rate, AIC's tax status (could the firm use the initial operating losses or would it have to use them to offset future income), and the project's operating margins. For example, Lehman Brothers and CS First Boston predicted that the A3XX would generate operating margins rang-

---

[41] Airbus, *First Quarter 2000 Briefing*, p. 12.

[42] Lehman Brothers, "Airbus Industrie," December 6, 1999, p. 24.

[43] "U.S. Questions U.K.'s Big Loans to British Aerospace for Airbus Jet," *The Wall Street Journal*, March 14, 2000, p. A27.

[44] "Airbus Bets the Company," *The Economist*, March 18, 2000, p. 67.

[45] This section is based on Aerospace/Defense analyst reports from Lehman Brothers (Airbus Industrie, December 6, 1999), CS First Boston (Global Commercial Aerospace Monthly, May 23, 2000), and Dresdner Kleinwort Benson Research (The Business Case for the Double Decker, May 8, 2000), plus casewriter estimates.

ing from 20% to 30% (again before repayment of launch aid and risk sharing capital). Both were well above the 15% to 20% operating margins Boeing was thought to earn on its 747s. In general, however, larger planes earned bigger margins, leading some analysts to claim that the companies made virtually all of their profits on wide body jets.

Among other factors, financial success depended on getting enough early sales to drive down costs through learning curve effects. The concept of the learning curve originated in the 1930s based on studies of aircraft assembly. The basic idea was that unit costs, such as direct labor, declined as a function of cumulative output. As a result, the faster Airbus could sell planes, the more profitable it would become. This was especially true in the early years when cumulative output doubled relatively quickly.

Based on these assumptions, Airbus had a target pretax IRR of 15% but thought the actual IRR might be as much as 20%.[46] As reference points, yields on long-term U.S. government bonds were approximately 6.0%, inflation was 2.0%, and aircraft manufacturers like Boeing and Canada's Bombardier had asset betas of 0.84 for their commercial aviation divisions. In addition to the direct profits from the A3XX, there were other sources of potential value. Foremost among them was the fact that the A3XX would eliminate Boeing's monopolistic control of the VLA market and its ability to cross-subsidize smaller jets in its product line. According to the Dresdner Kleinwort Benson, this benefit could add another 1.5% to the project's IRR. A final, though smaller source of income would be the support services related to the sale, maintenance, and repair of planes.

BOEING'S RESPONSE

In addition to forecasting demand, Airbus management had to assess how Boeing would respond to their entry into the VLA segment. Boeing had already said that it would challenge the launch aid by filing a complaint with the World Trade Organization (WTO).[47] The WTO had recently ruled against regional jet makers Bombardier of Canada and Embraer of Brazil for improper subsidies, indicating the WTO might be an effective weapon.[48] At least once before, however, Boeing had withdrawn a complaint to avoid offending foreign governments who owned some of Boeing's major customers such as Air France.[49] Even more troubling was the fact that Boeing itself might be vulnerable to WTO sanctions for alleged subsidies on its military contracts and its use of foreign sales corporations (FSCs). The WTO had recently ruled FSCs were illegal, a ruling that could jeopardize the estimated $150 million Boeing saved in taxes in 1998 by selling planes through such vehicles.[50]

Besides fighting the A3XX on legal grounds, Boeing would likely respond in one of four ways: it could develop a stretch version of the 747 (the 747X), cut prices on the 747, develop a competing super jumbo jet, or ignore the potential threat. Boeing had been planning a stretched, 520-seat version of the 747 since it withdrew from the A3XX project in 1995. Although it had the advantage of being ready several years ahead of

---

[46] J. Cole, "Airbus Board Is Seen Clearing Giant-Jet Plans," *The Wall Street Journal*, December 8, 1999, p. A7.

[47] "Super-jumbo Trade War Ahead," *The Economist*, May 6, 2000, pp. 63–64.

[48] Ibid.

[49] Ibid.

[50] "Airbus Bets the Company," p. 67.

the A3XX because it was a retrofit of an existing model, Boeing scrapped the idea in January 1997. Ronald Woodard, then head of Boeing's commercial airplane group, said "We were starting to spend a lot of money (but) we just did not see customers showing the interest."[51] The announcement prompted one analyst to raise Boeing's earnings target by 30% and triggered a surge in its stock price of $7.375, a gain of almost 7%.[52] Two years later in September 1999, Boeing's Chairman Phil Condit indicated the idea had been revived at a cost of up to $4 billion.[53] In response, Boeing's stock declined 1.7% on a day when the market was flat. Apart from the cost, there was the question whether the 747's older style and technology could stand up to the newer A3XX in terms of passenger comfort and operating efficiency. Alternatively, Boeing could cut the price of the 747. At the very least, this strategy might divert sales away from the A3XX; it might even deter launch completely by making the economics sufficiently unattractive. Third, Boeing could develop its own super jumbo jet to compete head on with the A3XX. This approach involved the greatest financial risk because Boeing would have to invest $13 billion only to share the VLA market with Airbus. While it seemed likely that Boeing would pick one of these options, one analyst suggested that no response might be the best option. Boeing had an opportunity to enhance profitability on its existing products while Airbus was tied up developing the A3XX.[54] In other words, Boeing could ignore the A3XX and concentrate on its existing product line.

Whichever option Boeing selected, it had to be consistent with the firm's renewed emphasis on shareholder value. After Boeing reported its first loss in more than 50 years in 1997, shareholder value had become a major priority. To further the company's stated goal of increasing its stock price five times in five years,[55] the Board instituted a new incentive program that linked compensation with stock price appreciation and established stock ownership guidelines for top executives.[56] The company highlighted this new objective in its 1998 Annual Report: "Our overriding goal is to return Boeing to the top quartile of companies both in profitability and in total return to shareholders. . . . Shareholder value is the single most important measure of our long term success."[57]

CONCLUSION

As the orders began to roll in, Airbus management faced a critical decision: should they commit to launch the A3XX? The risks, in terms of both the up-front investment and the uncertainty of demand, made this decision particularly daunting. While the early response from customers had been positive, initial orders were not always a reliable indicator of long-term demand because "launch" customers typically received substantial discounts. Yet given that delivery would not take place until 2006 or later and few airlines ordered planes more than five or six years in advance, Airbus was unlikely to secure more than 50 to 100 total orders before it had to make the launch decision. Exhibit 9-11 shows the order status as of July 2000.

[51] "Boeing's 747 Decision Shifts Rivalry with Airbus," *The Wall Street Journal*, January 22, 1997, p. A3.

[52] Ibid.

[53] Dresdner Kleinwort Benson Research, The Business Case for the Double Decker, May 8, 2000, p. 34.

[54] *The Airline Monitor*, January/February 2000, p. 17.

[55] D. Schenk, "Has Success Been Re-defined?" Paper presented at IPEC 2000 Conference, May 11, 2000, p. 5.

[56] The Boeing Company, Proxy Statement, May 11, 2000, pp. 29–30.

[57] The Boeing Company, 1998 Annual Report, Chairman's *Message to Shareholders*, pp. 3–4.

EXHIBIT 9-11

AIRBUS A3XX ORDERS AS OF JULY 26, 2000

	Orders	Options	Total
Announced Orders			
Air France	10	—	10
Emirates	7	5	12
International Lease Finance Corp. (ILFC)	5	5	10
Total	22	10	32
Probable Orders			
Atlas Air[a]	8	6	14
Federal Express[a]	10	5	15
Singapore Airlines	10	6	16
Virgin Atlantic	6	4	10
Total	34	21	55
Potential Orders			
Cathay Pacific	6	4	10
Cargolux[a]	6	4	10
Korean Air	6	4	10
Malaysian Airways	6	4	10
Qantas	6	4	10
Total	30	20	50
Total Potential Orders	**86**	**51**	**137**

[a] Denotes cargo operator.

Source: Lehman Brothers Aerospace & Defense Report, June 23, 2000; *The Wall Street Journal*, July 26, 2000, p. A21.

Commenting on the industry's need to gamble on new planes, one observer wrote: "In this business you have to put the company on the line every three or four years."[58] But if a launch failed, it could cause a company to exit the industry. In fact, several prominent companies, including the Glenn Martin Company, General Dynamics, and most recently Lockheed, were victims of failed launches.[59] Despite the apparent risk, Airbus management claimed that the "decision to proceed with the A3XX was not an extraordinary risk but rather a decision that was . . . very well thought through by a conservative, no nonsense team of people."[60]

[58] J. Newhouse, *The Sporty Game* (New York: Alfred A. Knopf, 1982), p. 7.
[59] Ibid., p. 4.
[60] Cole, "Airbus Prepares to 'Bet the Company' As It Builds a Huge New Jet," p. A1.

10

Nghe An Tate & Lyle Sugar Company (Vietnam)

In September 1998, Nghe An Tate & Lyle (NATL) had largely completed its $90 million sugar mill in northern Vietnam. The equity sponsors, Tate & Lyle, Mitr Phol (pronounced "Mit Pong") Sugar Company, the Vietnam Fund, and the Nghe An Sugar Company, had financed the project with their own equity, short-term loans, and a $40 million bridge loan from Rabobank, which was acting as an advisor and potential investor. The sponsors now wanted to refinance the loans with up to $45 million from the International Finance Corporation (IFC) and up to $20 million from other sources. They had originally approached the IFC in 1996, before construction had begun, but protracted negotiations over lending terms and uncertainties surrounding the Asian financial crisis prevented them from finalizing a deal. Now that the plant was essentially complete, Paul Cooper, Tate & Lyle's Divisional Commercial and Finance Director for international sugar investments, had asked the IFC to reconsider investing in the project.

Ewen Cobban, an IFC agricultural specialist, was in charge of reviewing the project and making a recommendation to IFC management regarding a possible loan. As he reviewed the request, Cobban had a number of concerns. First, he was concerned whether NATL would be able to obtain a sufficient amount of cane from local farmers. Second, he wondered whether the government would follow through on its commitment to build new roads and bridges in the region that would be needed to transport cane from the fields to the mill. And finally, he was concerned by the fact that world sugar prices were falling and that sugar was a protected commodity. Like most countries, Vietnam protected its domestic sugar producers, but it was not clear whether the

Research Associate Carrie Ferman prepared this case under the supervision of Professor Benjamin C. Esty and Frank Lysy, Senior Advisor at the International Finance Corporation. HBS cases are developed solely as the basis for class discussion. Cases are not intended to serve as endorsements, sources of primary data, or illustrations of effective or ineffective management. Participation by Dr. Lysy does not constitute an endorsement by the IFC, and the conclusions and judgments contained herein should not be attributed to, and do not necessarily reflect the views of, the IFC or its Board of Directors.

IFC should support a project that depended on trade protection for commercial viability. Despite these concerns, he was intrigued by the potential for large social benefits resulting from the project. In order to make his recommendation, Cobban had to assess the project's financial viability and quantify its development impact.

THE SUGAR INDUSTRY[1]

Although all green plants contain some sucrose, a type of sugar used as a sweetening agent, the primary commercial sources of sucrose were sugar cane and sugar beets. As of 1998, more than half of the world's sugar supply came from sugar cane, a grass that thrived in tropical and subtropical climates. Farmers produced sugar cane by planting cuttings from mature stalks. Sugar cane generally took 11 to 18 months to mature, growing 12 to 15 feet high and about one to two inches thick. When it was time to harvest, farmers cut the stalks leaving only a stubble that would re-grow and provide up to three or four more crops (known as ratoons). They sent harvested cane to processing mills, usually located near the farms to minimize transportation costs and decay because the sugar content began to decline as soon as the cane stalks were cut. At the mill, the stalks were crushed to extract juice, which was then clarified, boiled, and crystallized to produce raw or milled sugar. The milled sugar, usually 96% to 99% pure, could be consumed or processed further to produce fully refined or white sugar. Unlike harvesting, which was labor intensive, milling and refining were capital intensive. Significant economies of scale made high-capacity utilization a requirement for low-cost production.

Sugar was one of the few agricultural commodities where developed and developing countries competed against each other. In the late 1990s, the market consisted of four major exporters—Australia, Brazil, the European Union (EU), and Thailand—and a more diverse group of importing countries. Total world production of sugar reached 125 million metric tons in 1997, while consumption stood at 126 million tons.[2]

Historically, extensive government regulation affected the worldwide sugar trade. Particularly in developed economies, state action protected domestic production. Quotas and tariffs restricted low-cost imports from developing nations, while subsidies encouraged high-cost production in developed countries like the United States and Japan. Adding up all the various forms of subsidies, the OECD reported that total subsidies as a proportion of sugar producer receipts came to 41% in the United States, 43% in the European Union, and 61% in Japan in 1998.[3] Despite the fact that more than 100 countries had agreed to reduce tariff and nontariff barriers for sugar (a minimum of 15% for developed countries and 10% for developing countries) at the conclusion of the Uruguay Round of the General Agreement on Tariffs and Trade (GATT) in December 1993, such trade protection persisted.

Vietnam's Sugar Industry

With a population of 76 million and an average annual per capita income of $357 in 1997, Vietnam was a poor country that had spent the previous 15 years trying to recover from the ravages of war and the loss of financial support from the former Soviet

---

[1] M. Weston and N. Koehn, "The World Sugar Industry and Tate & Lyle," Harvard Business School Case No. 794-119 (Boston: Harvard Business School Publishing, 1996).

[2] 1 metric ton (tonne) = 2,204.62 pounds; all references to tons refer to metric tons.

[3] OECD, *Agricultural Policies in OECD Countries—Monitoring and Evaluation* (Paris, 1999).

Bloc.[4] Economic reconstruction had been slow, and the Communist Party continued to exercise monopoly powers across much of the economy. Unfortunately, the onset of the Asian financial crisis, as well as moves within Vietnam to a regime less open to foreign investment, led to a slowdown in growth (see Exhibit 10-1). At the time, the full extent of the crisis was unknown, but the Vietnamese government predicted that total foreign direct investment would decline by 40% in 1998 and that GDP growth would fall from 8.2% in 1997 to 5.8% in 1998.

Although the Vietnamese government had been promoting industrial growth during the 1990s, agriculture still accounted for nearly half of the country's income. Crop production included paddy rice, peanuts, maize, pineapples, rubber, coffee, and sugar. The majority of Vietnam's sugar production occurred in the south. While new, larger sugar mills existed, several thousand small, inefficient "handicraft" mills produced the majority of sugar in the north. These mills could process from 1.0 to 7.5 tons of cane per day depending on the kind of equipment used (a modern mill could process upwards of 5,000 tons of cane per day by comparison). "Handicraft" mills were also less efficient at extracting sugar from cane; extraction rates were approximately 50% versus about 90% for a modern mill.

In 1997, Vietnam produced approximately 360,000 tons of sugar, consumed more than 700,000 tons, and imported the rest. The Ministry of Agriculture Food Industry (MAFI) controlled Vietnam's sugar industry. Because demand for sugar was strongly correlated with economic development, MAFI expected domestic consumption to exceed one million tons annually by the year 2000. MAFI's objective was to increase domestic sugar production so that the country would become more self-sufficient. To protect domestic production, the Ministry had imposed high tariffs on imported sugar, which led to higher domestic prices for domestic producers as well as high tariff receipts for the government. The high tariffs, however, also led to high prices for domestic consumers. The tariff rates varied depending on the grade of the sugar (raw, mill white, or refined) but averaged about 30%.

TATE & LYLE PLC

With over £5 billion of total revenue in 1997, Tate & Lyle was one of the world's largest producers of white and raw sugar (see Exhibits 10-2a and 10-2b). The company produced a number of grain-based sweeteners, including high fructose corn syrup and citric acids used in beverages, food, and pharmaceuticals. Based in London since its formation in 1921, the company had expanded its geographical scope to include the United States, Canada, Latin America, Africa, and, most recently, Asia.

Sensing an opportunity to meet growing Asian demand, Tate & Lyle developed an expansion plan for Asia in 1990. In China, it invested a minority stake in a joint venture with a Thai partner (Mitr Phol) to acquire four small factories, and it invested $25 million more to acquire a majority stake in two more factories. At the same time, it began to consider investing in Vietnam. Paul Cooper explained:

> Vietnam was an attractive market for several reasons. First, it had a large population—approximately 70 million people and rising. Second, current sugar consumption was quite low, about 9 kilograms (kg) per person compared to 24 kg in Thailand and 32 kg in the United States, but we expected it to grow to 14 kg by 2005 as the country developed. Third, it was a deficit country, meaning that it imported sugar. Fourth, it had a strong, albeit

[4] Central Intelligence Agency Fact Book: ⟨www.odci.gov/cia/publications/factbook/geos/vm.html⟩.

EXHIBIT 10-1

MACRO-ECONOMIC STATISTICS FOR VIETNAM, 1990–1999

	1990	1991	1992	1993	1994	1995	1996	1997	1998	1999
				Actual					Estimate	
Government Finances										
Total revenue (US$, millions)	$1,199	1,116	1,885	2,885	3,845	4,835	5,655	5,587		
Total expenditures (US$, millions)	$1,674	1,241	2,054	3,471	4,117	4,992	5,828	6,629		
Net Revenues (US$, millions)	($475)	(125)	(169)	(586)	(272)	(157)	(173)	(1,042)		
Budget balance (% of revenue)	–39.6%	–11.2	–9.0	–20.3	–7.1	–3.2	–3.1	–18.7		
External debt (US$, millions)	$4,186	3,931	3,793	5,492	6,170	7,592	9,557	10,659		
External debt/gross domestic product	27.5%	24.4	21.7	29.0	30.0	33.7	38.8	40.0		
Output										
Gross domestic product growth	5.1%	6.0	8.0	8.1	8.8	9.5	9.3	8.2	5.2	5.0
Gross domestic product (US$, millions)	$15,208	16,114	17,505	18,921	20,586	22,550	24,657	26,667		
Gross domestic product/capita (US$)	$124	124	146	190	225	280	327	357		
Total exports (US$, millions)	$1,731	2,042	2,475	2,985	4,054	5,198	7,337	9,145	9,735	10,817
Total imports (US$, millions)	$1,373	2,049	2,540	3,532	5,250	8,381	11,644	11,592	11,670	12,651
Trade balance (US$, millions)	$358	(7)	(65)	(547)	(1,196)	(3,183)	(4,307)	(2,447)	(1,935)	(1,834)
Interest and Monetary Rates										
Inflation (Consumer Price Index)	36.4%	82.7	37.7%	8.4	9.3	16.9	5.6	3.0		
Lending rate (parent)	NA	NA	37.7%	28.3	28.3	28.3	20.1	12.0		
Exchange rate (Dong per US$)	5,133	9,274	11,150	10,640	10,955	11,038	11,033	11,706		
Country Risk Ratings										
Institutional Investor Country Risk Rank[a]	NA	NA	96	88	76	72	67	75	81	
Euromoney Country Risk Ranking[b]	NA	NA	128	103	84	69	63	77	98	
ICRG Risk Rating[c]	42.5	46.0	49.5	56.0	57.5	60.5	70.5	65.8	58.5	
Corruption Perceptions Index[d]	NA	NA	NA	NA	NA	NA	43/52	74/85		

[a] Institutional Investor ranks 145 countries based on information provided by economists at global banks and securities firms. Higher numbers represent a greater chance of country default.

[b] Euromoney ranks 167 countries based on the risk of investing in that country. The ratings are based on nine analytical, credit, and market indicators. Lower numbers indicate lower risks.

[c] The International Country Risk Guide (ICRG) provides a rating composed of 22 variables in three subcategories of risk: political (100 points), financial (50 points), and economic (50 points). The composite risk rating equals the sum of the individual ratings divided by two: 0.0 to 49.5 is very high risk; 80.0 to 100.0 is very low risk.

[d] Transparency International's Corruption Perception Index (CPI) score relates to perceptions of the degree of corruption as seen by business people, risk analysts, and the general public. Transparency International ranks countries from highly clean (1) to highly corrupt. Format equals Vietnam's number out of the number of countries ranked in that year.

Sources: Created from data contained in the Economist Intelligence Unit Country Data, Institutional Investor Online Edition, and Euromoney Online Edition.

EXHIBIT 10-2A

SUMMARIZED PROFIT AND LOSS STATEMENTS FOR TATE & LYLE FROM 1993 TO 1997 (£ IN MILLIONS)

	Tate & Lyle PLC				
	1993	1994	1995	1996	1997
Sales	£3,326	£3,715	£4,095	£4,896	£5,047
Operating profit	245	278	327	364	170
Profits from joint ventures	7	15	17	27	30
Total operating profit	252	293	344	391	200
Net interest expense	(46)	(43)	(43)	(58)	(56)
Net interest from joint ventures	(1)	(3)	(5)	(6)	(5)
Profit before taxation	205	247	296	327	139
Taxation	(53)	(65)	(81)	(84)	(39)
Profit after taxation	**152**	**182**	**215**	**243**	**100**
Minority interest	(21)	(22)	(29)	(34)	(14)
Dividends	(58)	(62)	(67)	(73)	(83)
Retained profit	**£ 73**	**£ 98**	**£ 119**	**£ 136**	**£ 3**

Source: Company annual reports.

EXHIBIT 10-2B

SUMMARIZED BALANCE SHEET STATEMENTS FOR TATE & LYLE FROM 1993 TO 1997 (£ IN MILLIONS)

	Tate & Lyle PLC				
	1993	1994	1995	1996	1997
Employment of Capital					
Fixed assets	£1,383	£1,366	£1,484	£1,718	£1,764
Working capital	242	324	320	454	326
Net operating assets	1,625	1,690	1,804	2,172	2,090
Net borrowings	(755)	(745)	(743)	(915)	(955)
Net (liabilities)/assets for dividends/tax	(49)	(63)	(66)	(36)	(4)
Total net assets	**821**	**882**	**995**	**1,221**	**1,131**
Capital Employed					
Called up share capital	116	115	115	116	116
Reserves	606	659	736	909	844
Minority interests	99	108	144	196	171
Total capital employed	**£ 821**	**£ 882**	**£ 995**	**£1,221**	**£1,131**

Source: Company annual reports.

informal, tariff system that would make domestic production more profitable. And finally, the project would be important enough to receive attention at the highest levels within the Vietnamese government, thereby ensuring decisions could be made rapidly. For instance, although we had to pass through a complex regulatory and approval system, we got a commitment to complete this project quickly during a meeting between the prime minister of Vietnam and the chairman of Tate & Lyle. High-level support was going to be vital if we were going to persuade farmers to expand cane production at the expense of cash crops before we had completed the incremental capacity needed to process it.

In late 1993, the company began negotiating to purchase the Lam Son Sugar Factory. Cooper described the deal:

> We wanted to participate in an existing plant rather than develop a greenfield site—it's much easier to buy existing assets than to build them from scratch in a country like Vietnam. And we wanted to do a joint venture with an experienced partner who knew Vietnam because we didn't really know much about operating inside the country. Having a local partner certainly helps in new markets.

Although a preliminary feasibility study concluded that the project would provide attractive financial returns, the local partner decided it did not want a foreign firm to invest in the plant. Instead, the Vietnamese government and MAFI invited Tate & Lyle to build a greenfield project in the Nghe An (pronounced "nay on") Province in northern Vietnam (see Exhibit 10-3).

After considering the offer, Tate & Lyle hired Booker Tate to conduct a feasibility study. At the time, farmers did not grow much cane in the Nghe An region, but interviews with farmers revealed a willingness to switch to cane cultivation if a plant were built. Optimistic about the potential returns, Tate & Lyle negotiated a joint-venture structure with a local partner, the Nghe An Sugar Company, and decided to proceed with the project in late 1995. The government of Vietnam issued an investment license in February 1996, and Bundaberg Foundry, a Tate & Lyle subsidiary, was appointed as the project manager with construction due to begin in September.

Nghe An Tate & Lyle Project History

Nghe An Province forms part of the North Central Coastal Region of Vietnam, one of seven regions in the country. The province was one of the poorest regions with a per capita income of about two-thirds the national average. Poor health services resulted in high sickness rates, but strong values placed on education resulted in a 91% literacy rate. The high literacy rate provided some comfort that agricultural extension work and training programs could succeed. Over 75% of the region consisted of farming households that relied on manual or ox-driven agricultural equipment. Independent farmers primarily grew rice, while a few state-owned farms located in the region grew tree crops like rubber, coffee, and tea. Infrastructure in Nghe An was undeveloped. The roads in the province were poor, and few bridges were available to cross the province's many rivers.

NATL designed a development plan consisting of three parts: (1) an integrated sugar mill and refinery with an ultimate capacity of 900,000 tons of cane per year (tc/y), (2) an outreach program to help local farmers convert to cane production, and (3) new transportation infrastructure including improved roads and bridges, which the Nghe An provincial government had agreed to build at a cost of $800,000. The company planned to complete the project by the start of the 1998/1999 harvesting season, which ran from

EXHIBIT 10-3

MAP OF VIETNAM AND PROJECT AREA

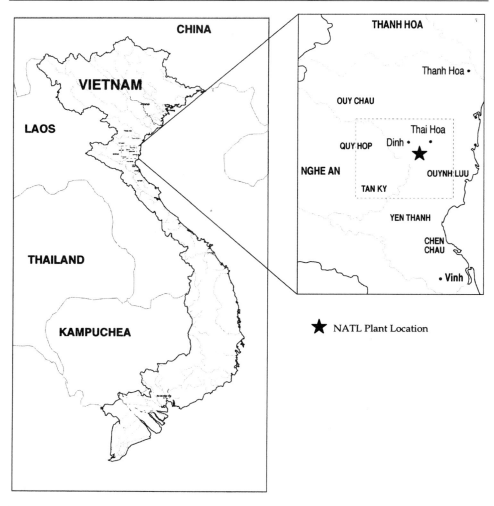

★ NATL Plant Location

Source: Casewriter.

November to April. It expected that the transportation infrastructure would also be completed by that date. NATL expected to process 330,000 tons of cane during the first season and reach full capacity by the 2002/2003 harvesting season. Depending on the specific variety grown, as well as weather and growing conditions, each metric ton of cane produced approximately 220 pounds of sugar, that is, about 10% of the cane by weight. Of the output, 75% would be mill white sugar (a standard in the Vietnamese marketplace) while the other 25% would be converted into fully refined sugar for bottlers and other industrial users. Most of the sugar would be sold in the north, particularly in Hanoi.

The company constructed the mill near the village of Dinh, which was located near a highway and a railway spur. During the crushing season, the facility would operate around the clock, seven days a week. The company expected to employ 725 people once the plant was operational. NATL would provide in-house training for most workers but would send some workers abroad to acquire certain operating and managerial skills.

Rather than grow its own cane, NATL planned to purchase cane from local farmers who lived within 50 kilometers of the plant. With an assumed yield of 50 tons of cane per hectare,[5] the plant would require a total of 18,000 hectares of cane from about 22,000 farmers to reach its full capacity—there was enough labor in the province and arable land nearby to grow the cane. NATL employees would encourage local farmers to convert to cane, help them gain access to seed cane and fertilizer, and advise them on cane production. NATL planned to pay the farmers for the cane in two installments. The first installment, approximately 75% of the total, would be made within 14 days of delivery. The balance would be paid at the end of the season and would reflect an adjustment for the cane's sugar content and the market price NATL received for the processed sugar.

During harvesting season, field officers would organize deliveries. The project would utilize private hauliers to transport cane from the fields to the factory. The transport price would be factored into the cane price; that is, cane farmers would receive a price net of transportation costs. The feasibility study indicated that the project would need roughly 300 lorries (trucks) during the harvest season.[6] NATL believed that the availability of six months of such work per year would induce people to purchase lorries or bring them to the region during the harvest season.

Financing the Project

Tate & Lyle originally envisioned a highly leveraged capital structure for the project funded by a small group of equity partners and bank debt. Tate & Lyle joined forces with three equity partners (see Exhibit 10-4): Mitr Phol Sugar Company, the Vietnam Fund Limited (VFL), and Nghe An Sugar Company (NASC). Mitr Phol was Thailand's largest domestic producer of sugar; VFL was an Irish-quoted asset management fund that invested in Vietnamese companies; and NASC was an investment vehicle created to hold the provincial government's share of the project. With a total cost of $90 million, the sponsors hoped to finance the project with up to 70% debt, most of it from commercial banks. Paul Cooper explained:

> I began with a parallel set of discussions with Western and Thai banks, but quickly ran into a brick wall. The Western banks liked the project, but said there was no way they would lend in Vietnam without some kind of multilateral support. Moreover, the high reserve requirements on loans in Vietnam, as dictated by the Basle Accord, made lending there unattractive unless the IFC participated in the deal, in which case the reserve requirements would be eliminated. The Thai banks were an option because they had established relationships with our Thai partner, but they wouldn't commit without some form of commercial support. Because of the risk exposure, we didn't want to provide an open-ended guarantee for 100% of the project. And finally, after the Asian Crisis hit in 1997, liquidity in this market just vanished. We also explored a combination of bilateral agencies. One agency withdrew its support because it wanted to finance telecom projects rather than agriculture projects. Another, Export Finance Insurance Corporation of Australia, was very supportive of the project because it used heavy machinery that was manufactured in Queensland, Australia. It was prepared to lend in conjunction with a multilateral such as the IFC.

[5] Hectare = a metric unit of area equal to 2.47 acres or 10,000 square meters.
[6] 900,000 tons per season/150 crushing days per season = 6,000 tons per day/5.5 tons of cane per trip = 1,091 trips per day/3.5 trips per day per lorry = 312 lorries.

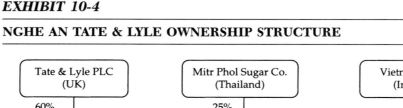

EXHIBIT 10-4

NGHE AN TATE & LYLE OWNERSHIP STRUCTURE

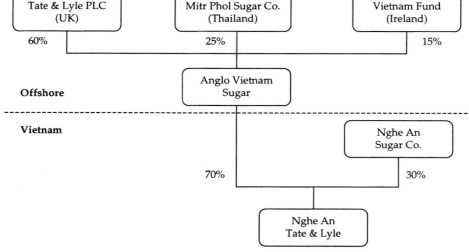

Source: Phu Quy Sugar Project Vietnam, Feasibility Study, August 1995, Annex III, p. 1.

For these reasons, NATL decided to approach the IFC. Cooper noted:

> IFC participation was an attractive option for several reasons. It would provide the protection we needed against political risks in Vietnam that we could only obtain through relatively expensive commercial insurance. It would also give us a tax advantage because IFC loans are exempt from withholding taxes. In contrast, payments to all other foreign banks would be subject to a 10% withholding tax on top of the interest element of debt service.

NATL hoped to secure $45 million from the IFC, $20 million in the form of an "A" loan on the IFC's own account, and $25 million in the form of a "B" loan that would be syndicated to other banks (see Exhibit 10-5). NATL envisioned bilateral agencies, and/or export credit agencies would supply the rest of the funding. These loans would be priced based on a spread over LIBOR.

IFC Participation

The International Finance Corporation (IFC), a member of the World Bank Group, promoted *private sector* investment in developing countries as a way to reduce poverty and stimulate economic growth. Founded in 1956 and owned by its 175 member countries, the IFC was the world's largest multilateral source of debt and equity financing for private sector projects. To be eligible for IFC funding, projects had to be privately owned, commercially viable, and environmentally sound. They also had to provide significant development benefits to the local economy.

Paul Cooper knew that the Bank Group had been providing development assistance to Vietnam for several years. He believed the proposed project was consistent

EXHIBIT 10-5

PROJECT SOURCES AND USES (US$ MILLIONS)

Uses of Cash			Sources of Cash		
Fixed Assets			**Senior Loans**		
Land	$ 1.5		IFC A—Loan	$20.0	22.1%
Buildings and Utilities	26.7		IFC B—Loan	25.0	27.6
Machinery and Equip.	33.0		Export Credit	5.0	5.5
Contingencies	7.4		Total Senior Loans	50.0	55.2
Total Fixed Assets	68.6	75.8%			
			Subordinated Bank Loan	15.0	16.6
Other Expenses					
Pre-operational	10.3		**Equity**		
Administrative	6.6		Tate & Lyle PLC	10.7	11.8
Working Capital	5.0		Mitr Phol Sugar Co.	4.4	4.9
Total Other Uses	21.9	24.2	Vietnam Fund	2.7	3.0
			Nghe An Sugar Co.	7.7	8.5
Total Uses of Funds	**$90.5**	**100.0%**	Total Equity	25.5	28.2
			Total Sources of Funds	**$90.5**	**100.0%**

Source: IFC Corporate Investment Committee, Initial Project Summary, October 7, 1996.

with the Bank Group's efforts, and in October 1996, he asked the IFC to participate in the deal. Ewen Cobban commented:

> Initially we were very excited about the project. The deal had strong international sponsors with deep pockets. Our major concern was the agricultural risk. I felt we were in danger of being in a situation where we had a great factory, but no cane. We also had some internal concerns about our total exposure in Vietnam. We had recently approved funding for a sugar mill in the south. The exposure created by funding two sugar mills in the same country was an early point of contention.

Although representatives from the IFC and NATL agreed to a term sheet in early 1997, there were complications related to the proposed security structure, conditions precedent, and completion tests, which prevented them from closing the deal. Nevertheless, NATL decided to proceed with construction because of the high-level commitment from Rabobank and because it needed to retain both credibility and momentum with local farmers and key suppliers. The sponsors financed construction through a combination of equity, local credits, and a $40 million bridge loan from Rabobank, but fully expected to close a project financing at some point in the future. By the fall of 1998, they had finished the plant ahead of schedule and under budget.

As the first crushing season approached, NATL management was concerned. The outreach program had not convinced enough farmers to plant cane. The problem worsened as the season got underway because farmers began selling their cane to local "handicraft" mills instead of NATL. Interviews with farmers revealed dissatisfaction with the complex payment system. Instead, farmers wanted to be paid in-full upon delivery, even if it meant less money. Similarly, fewer trucks than expected had appeared. And to make matters worse, the government had not completed all of the roads and bridges that it had promised to build. Given the resulting revenue shortfall, Cooper knew the project would require new subordinated loans or additional equity contributions. More importantly, the Rabobank bridge loan had already been rolled over more than once and had to be refinanced. After considering his options, he decided to ask the IFC to review the project again now that the plant was complete and operational.

As he reviewed the proposal, Cobban had several concerns. Both the Asian crisis and falling sugar prices (Exhibit 10-6) cast some doubt on the plant's commercial viability. He had to determine whether the effects were likely to be temporary or permanent problems. Cobban also knew he would have to make the case for the project from a developmental perspective if he was going to recommend approval. The IFC only supported projects that contributed to sustainable development, and one of the key determinants of sustainability was the degree to which the project was "fair" to all parties involved. Thus, Cobban had to assess not only the private returns to those financing the project, but also the returns to the key groups who might be affected by it and the overall social returns as measured by the economic rate of return (ERR). The ERR captured all of the project's costs and benefits from a social perspective rather than just the portion of returns that accrued to the project financiers (the private returns or financial rate of return, FRR). To be approved, the ERR would have to meet or exceed 10% in *real* terms—the customary threshold for approval.

EXHIBIT 10-6

MILL WHITE SUGAR PRICES (LONDON DAILY), JANUARY 1990–SEPTEMBER 1998 (US$ PER TON)

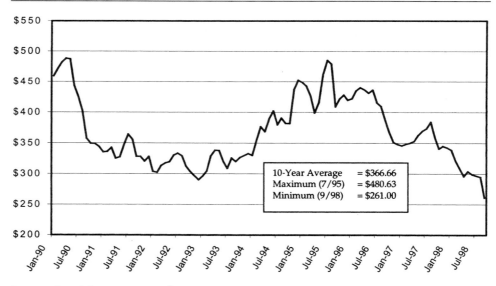

10-Year Average	= $366.66
Maximum (7/95)	= $480.63
Minimum (9/98)	= $261.00

Source: Adapted from Datastream data.

SOCIAL COST-BENEFIT ANALYSIS

Cobban began by calculating the sponsors' private return. With that as a base, he then began to add the net costs and benefits accruing to other groups, including employees, customers, producers of complementary goods, suppliers to the plant, competitors, new entrants, neighbors, and the rest of society (see Exhibits 10-7 and 10-8). The impacts on some of these groups would likely be significant, while for others the impacts might be quite small or even nonexistent. Cobban needed to think through each group to see if there was an impact and if so whether it was big or small, positive or negative. Where possible, he would attempt to quantify the impact.

Employees and Other Labor

NATL would employ approximately 525 workers year-round and an additional 200 during the crushing season. From the financial projections, Cobban could estimate wages, standard bonuses, and other labor costs (e.g., meals provided, etc.). For expatriate labor, it was reasonable to assume that recruitment was being done on a competitive basis. As a result, there would be no "extra" benefit to these employees above their opportunity cost (what they would have received elsewhere).

To estimate the economic benefit for the Vietnamese labor, Cobban needed to compare NATL's compensation package with what the workers could earn elsewhere in Vietnam. Technically, Cobban needed to compare NATL's compensation package to what the workers would have earned if the project had not been built. Economists referred

---

EXHIBIT 10-7

GROUPS AFFECTED BY PROJECT DEVELOPMENT (IFC FRAMEWORK)

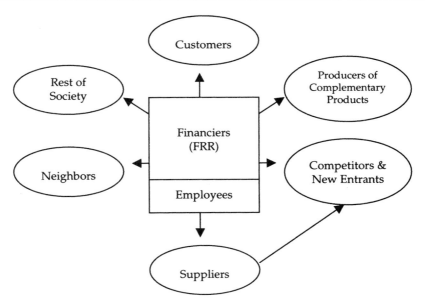

Source: Casewriter.

EXHIBIT 10-8

FINANCIAL PROJECTIONS ASSUMING THE IFC REFINANCES THE NATL PROJECT (US$ IN THOUSANDS)

	1996–1998[a]	1999	2000	2001	2002	2003	2004	2005	2006	2007	2008	2009	2010	2011	2012	2013	2014	2015
Production																		
Cane crushed (000 tons)	0	64	400	750	850	900	900	900	900	900	900	900	900	900	900	900	900	900
Yield of sugar/ton of cane (%)	0	10.3	10.3	10.3	10.3	10.3	10.3	10.3	10.3	10.3	10.3	10.3	10.3	10.3	10.3	10.3	10.3	10.3
Revenue																		
Sugar produced (000 tons)	0	6.6	41.2	77.3	87.6	92.7	92.7	92.7	92.7	92.7	92.7	92.7	92.7	92.7	92.7	92.7	92.7	92.7
World sugar price per ton[b]	0	300	314	331	348	366	385	405	417	426	435	444	454	459	463	468	472	476
Domestic sugar price per ton	0	390	409	430	453	476	501	527	542	554	566	578	590	597	602	608	613	619
Total revenue with VAT	0	2,857	18,701	36,920	44,024	49,045	51,603	54,294	55,853	57,043	58,258	59,499	60,765	61,496	62,049	62,607	63,171	63,739
Expenses																		
Admin., operating, and selling	0	5,712	3,109	2,587	3,244	3,500	3,605	3,714	3,825	3,940	4,058	4,180	4,305	4,434	4,567	4,704	4,845	4,991
Cost for cane[d]	0	853	5,333	10,000	11,333	12,000	12,360	12,731	13,113	13,506	13,911	14,329	14,758	15,201	15,657	16,127	16,611	17,109
Other cost of sales	0	1,099	1,788	2,550	2,858	3,017	3,107	3,200	3,296	3,395	3,497	3,602	3,710	3,821	3,936	4,054	4,176	4,301
VAT	0	(234)	1,329	3,188	3,784	4,236	4,472	4,720	4,855	4,952	5,051	5,151	5,254	5,303	5,332	5,362	5,391	5,421
Total expenses	0	7,429	11,559	18,325	21,220	22,753	23,544	24,365	25,089	25,793	26,517	27,262	28,028	28,759	29,493	30,248	31,024	31,822
EBITDA	0	(4,572)	7,142	18,595	22,805	26,292	28,059	29,929	30,764	31,250	31,741	32,237	32,737	32,736	32,556	32,360	32,147	31,918
Depreciation	0	0	3,307	3,472	3,642	3,818	3,999	4,185	4,376	4,574	4,777	4,986	5,202	5,424	5,653	5,889	6,132	3,075
EBIT	0	(4,572)	3,835	15,122	19,162	22,474	24,060	25,744	26,388	26,676	26,964	27,250	27,535	27,312	26,903	26,471	26,015	28,843
Interest expense[e]	0	4,500	5,600	5,594	5,419	4,798	3,807	2,719	1,632	544	0	0	0	0	0	0	0	0
Profit before taxes	0	(9,072)	(1,765)	9,529	13,743	17,677	20,253	23,025	24,756	26,132	26,964	27,250	27,535	27,312	26,903	26,471	26,015	28,843
Profit taxes @25%	0	0	0	0	0	0	0	0	6,189	6,533	6,741	6,813	6,884	6,828	6,726	6,618	6,504	7,211
Net income	0	(9,072)	(1,765)	9,529	13,743	17,677	20,253	23,025	18,567	19,599	20,223	20,438	20,651	20,484	20,177	19,853	19,512	21,632

(Continued)

EXHIBIT 10-8 (Continued)

	1996–1998[a]	1999	2000	2001	2002	2003	2004	2005	2006	2007	2008	2009	2010	2011	2012	2013	2014	2015
Free cash flow calculation																		
EBIT	0	(4,572)	3,835	15,122	19,162	22,474	24,060	25,744	26,388	26,676	26,964	27,250	27,535	27,312	26,903	26,471	26,015	28,843
Profit taxes @25%	0	0	0	0	0	0	0	0	6,597	6,669	6,741	6,813	6,884	6,828	6,726	6,618	6,504	7,211
EBIAT	0	(4,572)	3,835	15,122	19,162	22,474	24,060	25,744	19,791	20,007	20,223	20,438	20,651	20,484	20,177	19,853	19,512	21,632
Plus: Depreciation	0	0	3,307	3,472	3,642	3,818	3,999	4,185	4,376	4,574	4,777	4,986	5,202	5,424	5,653	5,889	6,132	3,075
Less: Capital expenditure	56,482	10,376	1,585	3,307	3,406	3,508	3,613	3,722	3,833	3,948	4,067	4,189	4,315	4,444	4,577	4,715	4,856	5,002
Less: Incr. net working capital	1,457	310	220	1,822	710	502	256	269	156	119	122	124	127	73	55	56	56	57
Terminal value[c]	0	0	0	0	0	0	0	0	0	0	0	0	0	0	0	0	0	196,485
Nominal free cash flow	(57,939)	(15,258)	5,337	13,466	18,688	22,282	24,189	25,938	20,178	20,514	20,811	21,111	21,412	21,391	21,198	20,972	20,731	216,133
Inflation Deflator	1.000	0.971	0.943	0.915	0.888	0.863	0.837	0.813	0.789	0.766	0.744	0.722	0.701	0.681	0.661	0.642	0.623	0.605
Real free cash flow	(57,939)	(14,814)	5,031	12,323	16,604	19,221	20,258	21,090	15,929	15,722	15,486	15,251	15,018	14,566	14,014	13,461	12,919	130,764

Note: Some numbers have been disguised to protect confidentiality. Assumes all cash flows from harvesting cane from November of year T to April of year T + 1 occur in year T+1; assumes no change in the $US/Dong nominal exchange rate; and ignores withholding taxes due to IFC participation.

[a] Numbers are present values as of year-end 1998.

[b] Price for mill white grade of sugar, which is close to the average price received for the mix of grades produced by NATL. Assumes a cyclical recovery in sugar prices by 2005.

[c] Terminal value equals a growing perpetuity based on final year free cash flow; [19,648 (1 + 3%)]/(13.3% − 3%) = 196,485, where the inflation rate is 3%, the real discount rate is 10%, and the nominal discount rate is 13.3%.

[d] Includes amounts paid to both farmers for cane and truckers for transportation.

[e] Assumes $65 million of debt at expected borrowing rates.

Source: Casewriter estimates.

to this opportunity cost as the "shadow wage" for the workers, and formally should be taken from society's point of view. However, the distinction between the opportunity cost to society and the opportunity cost to the individual worker was a distinction that Cobban was willing to ignore. NATL projected total payments to Vietnamese workers of $3 million per year during construction and $1.5 million during operations (including wages and benefits such as housing and meals, health insurance, and pensions). Cobban knew that NATL put a premium on its compensation package so it could be selective and retain good workers. He believed that NATL wages were eight or nine times as high as wages paid to workers with similar backgrounds and equivalent responsibilities in the nearby state enterprises. However, interviews with local workers revealed that state enterprises offered other benefits, which the formal wage scales did not capture. After valuing these benefits, Cobban assumed for the purposes of the analysis that NATL workers would be paid roughly double what they earned at alternative jobs such as the state-owned firms.

Customers

NATL would sell sugar that otherwise would be imported at a price that was close to the import price, inclusive of tariffs and taxes (i.e., the value-added tax (VAT)). As a result, consumers would pay the same price regardless of whether they bought NATL or imported sugar. Although the convenience of having domestic production of sugar with defined quality would appeal to customers, Cobban thought this benefit was probably small and would be difficult to assess.

Producers of Complementary Products

Complementary products are products whose demand increases if there is increased availability of related products. Because NATL would provide the same product at basically the same price as what customers could get currently from imports, there would be no impact on this group.

Suppliers

Cane farmers and truckers delivering cane would benefit from the project, as would any group that provided supplies directly to the mill or to the mill's suppliers.

The Cane Farmers

Cobban tried to estimate the economic gain to the farmers from conversion to cane, which was equal to the difference between the returns (revenues less costs) from growing cane and the returns from growing alternative crops. The difference was not only an indication of whether the farmers would convert, it was also a social benefit. To the extent the farmers earned more from growing cane than from growing alternative crops or holding alternative jobs, the project would be creating social value.

Using NATL's assumptions, Cobban computed the total revenues that cane growers would receive from the project per hectare. Through interviews with NATL, he estimated that an average of 10% of total revenues would be paid for haulage, which left the farmers with 90% of total revenues. The net return would require an estimate of costs, which Cobban found in Booker Tate's feasibility study and later confirmed with Cooper (see Exhibit 10-9). The cost estimates included both variable crop costs and required labor costs. Labor costs, assuming alternative employment opportunities existed

EXHIBIT 10-9

NET RETURNS TO FARMERS PER HECTARE (HA) FROM GROWING SUGAR CANE

Sugar Cane	Year 0	Year 1	Year 2	Year 3
In Dong (000):				
Revenue				
Tons per hectare	0	50	50	50
Price per ton	0	200	200	200
Total Revenue	0	10,000	10,000	10,000
Costs				
Labor[a]	3,000	3,000	3,000	3,000
Fertilizer	1,300	1,300	1,300	1,300
Seeds	1,700	0	0	0
Land preparation	1,200	0	0	0
Cane transportation	0	1,000	1,000	1,000
Total Cost	7,200	5,300	5,300	5,300
Net Return	**(7,200)**	**4,700**	**4,700**	**4,700**
In US$:[b]				
Total Revenue	$ 0	$667	$667	$667
Total Cost	480	353	353	353
Net Return	**($480)**	**$313**	**$313**	**$313**

[a] Assumes the opportunity cost of labor is 15,000 Dong per day.

[b] Exchange rate equals 15,000 Dong per US$1.00.

Source: Casewriter estimated based on the Booker Tate 1995 Feasibility Study and company documents.

in the region, were equal to US$1.00 or Vietnamese Dong (VND) 15,000 per day. After multiplying the estimated cost per hectare by the total number of hectares under cultivation, Cobban was able to calculate the net return from cane.

He followed a similar process to estimate the returns on both cash crops (crops grown for resale) and subsistence crops. The most common cash crops in Nghe An Province were pineapple, coffee, and rubber (see Exhibit 10-10). Cobban estimated the revenues and costs per hectare for each of the crops and then calculated the net return for each (see Exhibit 10-11). Cobban then compared the net returns from growing alternative crops against the net returns from growing cane. He conducted a similar analysis for subsistence crops such as rice, beans, peanuts, and maize, which farmers tended to grow in combination (see Exhibit 10-10 and 10-11). Although farmers did not receive cash for these crops, the crops had an implicit value. By comparing the explicit value of growing cane against the implicit value of growing subsistence crops, he could determine whether it made sense for farmers to switch to cane. As part of this analysis, he had to consider the risks as well as the returns of converting to cane.

Truck Haulers

Cobban also needed to understand the incentives for local people to purchase trucks or use their existing trucks to haul cane. Because NATL needed only 300 truckers at full capacity, the impact on the ERR would probably be relatively small. However, if it

EXHIBIT 10-10

**COMPARISON OF CROP ECONOMICS
(DONG PER HECTARE, UNLESS NOTED, IN THOUSANDS)**

		Cash Crops			Subsistence Crops[a]		
	Sugar Cane	Pineapple	Coffee	Rubber	Peanuts and Maize	Peanuts and Peanuts	Peanuts and Rice
Crop Life Cycle (years)	4	3	10	28	1	1	1
Labor Days per Hectare							
in a planting year	200	60	175	260	200/200	200/200	200/230
in a typical year	200	135	425	250	200/200	200/200	200/230
Years to Revenue	1	1	4	8	0	0	0
Revenue in a Typical Year	10,000	14,125	18,000	10,000	6,800	9,600	9,175
Total Costs							
in a planting year[b]	7,200	11,400	13,125	11,000	8,800	9,200	9,300
in a typical year[b]	4,300	5,925	11,175	5,925	8,800	9,200	9,300

[a] Partial year crops are grouped and can be grown during a single year. For labor days, 200/200 means that it takes 400 labor days to grow both crops.

[b] Total cost includes labor costs based on the required number of working days but *excludes* transportation costs. The total cost in a typical year is representative of the cost in all years except the planting year.

Source: Casewriter estimates.

was not a profitable activity for the truckers, no one would haul the cane to the mill. Cobban needed to estimate how profitable trucking would likely be.

He knew the expected revenue stream to the trucking industry as a whole. He also knew that NATL was under some pressure from local governmental authorities to give preference to the local population when they signed the trucking contracts. These people would probably be involved in local farming or similar work before, but would likely be towards the upper end of the local income scale and would likely need to borrow (formally or informally from family and friends) enough to buy a second-hand (i.e., used) truck. The feasibility study provided Cobban with the other assumptions needed to calculate the profit margin for a single truck driver for a representative season (including the opportunity cost of labor of a typical trucker, as well as the cost of capital he would face; see Exhibit 10-12). From this, he could work out the net returns the truckers would earn as a group.

Other Suppliers

The mill would utilize a variety of other suppliers. However, most of the supplies (e.g., spare parts, chemicals, and fuels) would come from competitive markets or from imports. As a result, the new mill would not have much, if any, impact on these suppliers. There would also be suppliers to the suppliers, such as fertilizer to the cane growers or fuel to the truckers. But again, these goods were sold in competitive markets or from imports (ultimately) and would not generate much of a social gain.

EXHIBIT 10-11

CROP CASH FLOWS (NOMINAL US$ IN THOUSANDS)

	1998	1999	2000	2001	2002	2003	2004	2005	2006	2007	2008	2009	2010	2011	2012	2013	2014	2015
Hectares under cultivation (000)	1.28	8.00	15.00	17.00	18.00	18.00	18.00	18.00	18.00	18.00	18.00	18.00	18.00	18.00	18.00	18.00	18.00	18.00
Opportunity Cost of Labor = $1.00/day:																		
Net Return from:[a]																		
Cane	(614)	(2,825)	(853)	3,740	4,599	4,341	4,611	5,911	6,201	5,696	6,007	7,349	7,682	7,222	7,578	8,968	9,349	8,939
Cash Crops (avg.)[b]	(1,010)	(5,474)	(6,636)	(3,948)	(3,427)	(303)	2,285	912	1,149	4,232	3,161	709	272	(1,837)	90	4,898	3,848	4,288
Pineapple	(973)	(4,557)	(1,581)	4,975	187	175	5,638	187	175	5,638	187	175	5,638	187	175	5,638	187	175
Coffee	(1,120)	(6,535)	(10,688)	(10,652)	(4,407)	4,557	6,857	8,190	8,190	8,190	6,488	(1,985)	(9,323)	(10,197)	(4,407)	4,557	6,857	8,190
Rubber	(939)	(5,329)	(7,640)	(6,167)	(6,060)	(5,640)	(5,640)	(5,640)	(4,919)	(1,133)	2,810	3,937	4,500	4,500	4,500	4,500	4,500	4,500
Combo A— peanuts & maize	(171)	(1,067)	(2,000)	(2,267)	(2,400)	(2,400)	(2,400)	(2,400)	(2,400)	(2,400)	(2,400)	(2,400)	(2,400)	(2,400)	(2,400)	(2,400)	(2,400)	(2,400)
Combo B— peanuts & peanuts	34	213	400	453	480	480	480	480	480	480	480	480	480	480	480	480	480	480
Combo C— peanuts & rice	(11)	(67)	(125)	(142)	(150)	(150)	(150)	(150)	(150)	(150)	(150)	(150)	(150)	(150)	(150)	(150)	(150)	(150)
Opportunity Cost of Labor = $0.00/day:																		
Net Return from:[a]																		
Cane	(358)	(1,225)	2,147	7,140	8,199	7,941	8,211	9,511	9,801	9,296	9,607	10,949	11,282	10,822	11,178	12,568	12,949	12,539
Cash Crops (avg.)[b]	(799)	(4,019)	(3,321)	400	1,160	4,382	7,063	5,579	5,834	9,010	7,722	4,834	4,466	2,664	4,691	9,676	8,515	8,973
Pineapple	(896)	(3,981)	(81)	7,024	2,038	2,080	7,822	2,038	2,080	7,822	2,038	2,080	7,822	2,038	2,080	7,822	2,038	2,080
Coffee	(896)	(4,815)	(6,063)	(3,927)	2,993	12,207	14,507	15,840	15,840	15,840	13,818	3,985	(3,423)	(3,047)	2,993	12,207	14,507	15,840
Rubber	(606)	(3,262)	(3,820)	(1,897)	(1,550)	(1,140)	(1,140)	(1,140)	(419)	3,367	7,310	8,437	9,000	9,000	9,000	9,000	9,000	9,000
Combo A— peanuts and maize	341	2,133	4,000	4,533	4,800	4,800	4,800	4,800	4,800	4,800	4,800	4,800	4,800	4,800	4,800	4,800	4,800	4,800
Combo B—peanuts and peanuts	546	3,413	6,400	7,253	7,680	7,680	7,680	7,680	7,680	7,680	7,680	7,680	7,680	7,680	7,680	7,680	7,680	7,680
Combo C— peanuts and rice	540	3,373	6,325	7,168	7,590	7,590	7,590	7,590	7,590	7,590	7,590	7,590	7,590	7,590	7,590	7,590	7,590	7,590

[a] Returns for each year are a function of the total number of hectares under cultivation, the year each hectare was planted, and the crop economics from Exhibit 10. The analysis ignores taxes (profit and VAT) and transportation costs.

[b] Assumes an equal proportion of each crop: pineapple, coffee, and rubber.

Source: Casewriter estimates.

EXHIBIT 10-12

TRUCKING (LORRY) ECONOMICS[a]

Exchange Rate (Dong per US$)	15,000
Revenue Assumptions	
Average travel distance round trip (km)	20
Cost to deliver (Dong per ton)	VND 23,000
Tons per load (payload)	5.5
Average trips per day	3.5
Number of days	150
Cost Assumptions	
Gasoline	
Lorry: kilometers per gallon	12
Fuel: US$ per gallon	$1.50
Labor	
Average wage per day	VND 30,000
Maintenance per season	VND 10,000,000
Lorry Costs	
Average cost per lorry	VND 100,000,000
Annual interest rate	12%
Deprecation per kilometer[b]	VND 625

[a] Ignores VAT and profit taxes.

[b] Assumes straight-line depreciation and a 160,000 km life for lorries.

Source: Casewriter estimates.

Competitors

Currently, local residents grew some sugar cane for home consumption and for small "handicraft" mills. Because these mills were relatively inefficient, NATL could pay a higher price for the cane, thereby giving an incremental gain to the farmers. Those residents who had money invested in "handicraft" mills would lose their investment if they chose to sell their cane to NATL. Presumably, they would only sell their cane to NATL if that was a more attractive option financially. Overall this impact would be quite small.

There were also other larger sugar mills in Vietnam that competed with NATL. Most of these mills, however, were much smaller and less efficient than NATL. These competitors might benefit in that they would learn how to operate more efficiently. It would be difficult to quantify the value of the demonstration effects, but Cobban would certainly highlight them to IFC management.

New Entrants

Should NATL be successful, it would provide a good example to other foreign investors of the possibilities that existed in Vietnam. Like the demonstration effects for competitors, coming up with an estimate of this value would be difficult, but he would note this benefit as well.

Neighbors

He had to consider two key impacts on neighboring residents: environmental impacts and transportation benefits from the improved roads and new bridges. Environment impacts could occur from the air emissions generated at the plant, the liquid effluent produced from crushing cane, and the solid waste generated by the process. Cobban analyzed the impacts carefully knowing that environmental impacts were a major concern for the IFC. He knew the mill was designed not only to meet, but also beat the World Bank's strict guidelines on air and water emissions. With regard to the mill's solid waste—the main byproducts were bagasse and filter mud—both would be used. The bagasse would be used as fuel at the mill, and the filter mud would be given to farmers as low-grade fertilizer. NATL also implemented a workplace health and safety policy commensurate with Tate & Lyle's worldwide procedures. Safety equipment and protective clothing would be issued to all personnel working in or around hazardous substances. Given the plant's design and the various environmental safeguards, it appeared that the environmental impacts would be negligible.

The value of the new transportation infrastructure to NATL was already captured in the private returns—the haulage fee paid to the truckers would have been higher if the roads and bridges had not been upgraded. However, the local residents could also use the same roads and bridges for their daily activities. The benefits would be difficult to assess but would certainly be positive. As an offset, however, the local authorities would need to spend the $800,000 to upgrade the roads and build the bridges, funds that could potentially go to other social uses. In the end, Cobban decided that it would be reasonable to assume that the extra benefits to the local residents would match, and hence, offset the costs.

Rest of Society

Finally, there would be other societal effects, principally increases in tax revenue paid by NATL and a decrease in tariffs from imported sugar. Cobban had to work through the effect on profit taxes, net receipts from value-added taxes (the VAT), and net receipts from import tariffs. The sum would be the project's net impact on the government and, by extension, the general taxpayer.

Profit Taxes

Like other foreign-invested companies in Vietnam, NATL would pay a 25% profit tax after a five-year tax holiday from the first operating profit. Whereas the profit tax was a cost from the company's perspective, the tax revenues were a benefit from society's perspective. Hence, the profit tax was simply a transfer of value from the private to the public sector. Because the tax was already subtracted from the private returns (the private investors receive a return after tax), it had to be added back to calculate the ERR.

To the extent the government spent these tax revenues in a way that benefited society, there could be second, third, or higher order benefits from the project. The creation of new wealth and expenditure of tax revenues would be especially important in a low-income country like Vietnam. Because quantifying these multiplier effects was very difficult to do and because they were likely to be small, Cobban decided to ignore them.

Value-added Taxes

NATL would pay VAT at the standard 10% rate on its gross revenues. It could deduct the VAT paid by its suppliers (including the sugar cane growers), which is what makes this a tax on value-added only. While the cane growers would pay VAT at a lower rate than the standard 10%, this just shifted the tax burden to NATL, which meant that total VAT collections would not change. The government would receive, from either NATL or the suppliers to NATL, a total VAT collection of 10% of NATL's gross revenues from sugar sales. However, the government also charged a VAT on gross revenues from imported sugar. Because of NATL's output, imported sugar would be expected to fall by an equal amount. That is, the mill would be substituting domestic production for imported sugar. Therefore, the VAT received by the government from NATL would offset the VAT lost as a result of the decrease in imports. This result would apply even if the sugar coming into the country was smuggled because the VAT was due and collected up to the retail level. In reality, of course, it could be a bit more complicated because some sales could evade the VAT system altogether such as smuggled imports (or production of sugar from the small "handicraft" mills) being sold directly to households and other end users. Cobban believed it was reasonable to assume that such effects would likely be very small because NATL production would be substituting for sugar sold through formal channels subject to VAT collection.

Tariffs on Imports

NATL expected to sell its sugar at a price equal to the world price plus a 30% tariff, to match what Vietnamese companies would have to pay for imported sugar. As a result, this investment neither helped nor hurt consumers; they would pay the same price for domestic or imported sugar. The Vietnamese government, on the other hand, would be affected because the amount it would receive from tariffs would decline. To calculate this reduction for a given year (say 2004), Cobban multiplied the expected world sugar price for that year ($385 per ton for the mill white grade of sugar) by the 30% tariff rate to get a local price. Cobban then multiplied the price by the expected number of tons (92,700) to get a total value of $10.7 million ($385/ton * 30% * 92,700 tons). Thus, the government would lose a little less than $11 million in tariff revenues that year. Across the project's life, this loss to the government could be substantial.

CONCLUSION

For Cobban to recommend loan approval, he had to do two things. First, he had to understand whether the project was commercially viable. Second, he had to assess the project's development impact as measured by the economic rate of return. In part, this meant determining whether the farmers were likely to switch to cane, and in part it meant determining whether the government would complete the transportation infrastructure. The higher the project's social returns, the more likely it was the government would invest in the region. With these answers, Cobban could prepare his recommendation on whether to proceed with a loan.

11

An Economic Framework for Assessing Development Impact

Multilateral institutions such as the International Finance Corporation (IFC) and multilateral development banks such as the European Bank for Reconstruction and Development (EBRD) provide support to private projects in developing nations with the goal of stimulating growth and reducing poverty. The institutions may lend funds directly, provide support indirectly though guarantees, or take equity positions in project companies. As a basis for participation, they need to understand a project's private and social returns. The private returns can be summarized by the project's financial rate of return (the FRR, also referred to as the internal rate of return or IRR). The social returns can similarly be summarized by the economic rate of return (ERR), sometimes called the social rate of return.[1] As a financial manager in a company seeking multilateral funding or negotiating with host governments, it is imperative to understand both calculations. By doing so, a financial manager will be better able to predict how a project will be received and, in some instances, will be able to modify the project or supply information that will promote outside assistance and encourage approval.[2]

This note draws on and extends several working papers by Frank J. Lysy, senior advisor at the International Finance Corporation. It was prepared by Research Associate Carrie Ferman under the supervision of Frank Lysy and Professor Benjamin C. Esty for the purpose of class discussion. Participation by Dr. Lysy does not constitute an endorsement by the IFC, and the conclusions and judgments contained herein should not be attributed to, and do not necessarily reflect the views of, the IFC or its Board of Directors.

[1] While there has been extensive discussion in the development literature on the differences between working in terms of net present values (NPVs) and rates of return (such as an ERR or FRR), for the purposes of this note, the differences are not important. At the level of generality of the issues being addressed here, working in terms of rates of return will not be a problem, yet it facilitates exposition.

[2] L.T. Wells, Jr., "Social Cost/Benefit Analysis for MNC's," *Harvard Business Review*, March–April 1975, p. 40.

This note discusses the differences between private and social returns, and describes an economic framework for assessing a project's ERR.[3] The framework begins by analyzing a project's impact from the perspective of the project financiers (the private return). The framework then identifies other stakeholders who might be affected, directly or indirectly, by the project, and examines the impact on each group. The overall development impact, the ERR, is the sum of the flows that are used to calculate the FRR and the individual net returns to each of the other stakeholders. This note assumes that readers have a working knowledge of cost-benefit analysis, microeconomics, and basic valuation mechanics.

PRIVATE VS. SOCIAL RETURNS

Adam Smith wrote in his 1776 classic, *The Wealth of Nations*, that a private businessman, worried only about the profitability of his investments, would be guided "as if by an invisible hand" to those actions that are best for society as a whole. If this is true, then why do we need to worry whether an investment is socially beneficial if we know that it is privately beneficial?

While Adam Smith's insight is the foundation of modern economics and a foundation to build on, Smith was also the first to note that the result does not *always* follow. There are several reasons why the profitability of an investment from society's perspective may differ from the private sector's perspective. For example, what a firm receives from the sale of its product may be less than the amount paid by the customer because a portion goes to taxes.

Where people are free to decide which transactions they wish to enter into, the social returns may differ from the private returns, for four main reasons:

- **Taxes, Tariffs, Subsidies, and Other Government Interventions:** Because governments collect taxes and provide subsidies, there is a difference between the return the private investor receives and the total returns generated by the project. Similarly, tariffs and other public sector interventions lead to differences between private and social returns.

- **Transaction costs:** Transaction costs may prevent the private investor from collecting a fee for services it provides, resulting in an unpriced benefit to society. For example, an investor may need to build a bridge or upgrade a road to provide access to a new plant. The improved infrastructure helps those who live in the area and use the bridge or road. However, the cost of collecting the toll may exceed the actual toll itself. Nevertheless, society benefits even if the toll is not collected.

- **Externalities:** Nonmarket effects are known as externalities, and they are not captured in private returns. Externalities include such things as a project's environmental impacts or its contribution to congestion on local highways. Network effects can also be considered externalities. A firm may work with a supplier to improve the quality of an input. While the improvement helps the firm, suppliers can provide these improved products to other customers. Demonstration effects are yet

---

[3] F.J. Lysy, "Assessing Development Impact," Working Paper, International Finance Corporation, Washington, DC, October 20, 1999. Available at: http://www.ifc.org/economics/pubs/AssessingDevImpact.pdf.
F.J. Lysy, "Stakeholder Analysis: An Economic Framework for Assessing the Development Impact of IFC Project," Results on the Ground: The Private Sector and Development, Vol. 4, International Finance Corporation, Washington, DC, 2000. Available at: http://www.ifc.org/economics/pubs/rog4/ROG4Framework.pdf

another type of externality. A project may demonstrate the viability of a new market, technology, or way of doing business, which others can then replicate.

- **Imperfect Markets:** In practice, especially in developing countries, there can be a significant difference between the price paid for a good and the opportunity cost of providing that good. For example, a worker may be paid much more in a modern factory than in a traditional occupation. Active and effective market competition should eliminate such differentials, but product, labor, and capital markets in developing countries do not always function smoothly. The markets can also be relatively "thin," in that the production of the new plant, or the demand by it for labor or other inputs, can have nontrivial effects on prices.

THE PROPOSED FRAMEWORK FOR ASSESSING DEVELOPMENT IMPACT

A useful approach to working out the overall development impact of a project on society is to sum the estimated net impact on each of the individual groups affected by the project. For a private sector project, the possible groups or "stakeholders" include the financiers (those who will earn the private return), employees, customers, producers of complementary products, suppliers, competitors and new entrants, "neighboring" residents, and the rest of society. This classification includes everyone who may be affected whether they are a domestic resident or a foreign entity. In other words, the project's impact is not limited by national boundaries.[4] The process of assessing the project's impact on each stakeholder provides a bridge between the traditional cost/benefit analysis and the social analyses utilized by development economists. In practice, projects are likely to affect only a few of the possible groups. One should focus on the groups where the impact is expected to be the greatest.

The list of affected groups helps break up the problem of the overall social impact into more manageable pieces. It also allows one to see the impacts on specific groups. While the overall social return of a project may be positive, the effect on any particular group may be negative. As a result, opposition from these groups may arise even though the total social return is positive. Finally, this analysis may suggest whether compensation programs are warranted for those groups hurt by a specific project.

People familiar with traditional economic (sometimes called social) cost/benefit analysis may wonder how the traditional approach, with its focus on shadow prices, relates to the one presented here. The answer is that both, if properly applied, will produce identical answers (see Exhibit 11-1). But we have found that the two-stage approach presented in this note is more intuitive, especially for students with a business background and those who do not have advanced training in economics.

In traditional economic cost/benefit analysis, the analyst works out the private return based on actual market prices, inclusive of taxes, and then calculates the social return using "shadow prices" whenever they differ from market prices. The shadow price reflects the opportunity cost to society of the good or service and may differ from market prices for any of the four reasons noted above (i.e., taxes and subsidies, transaction costs, externalities, and imperfect markets). In the proposed two-stage approach, one also uses shadow prices but calculates the social return in two stages. First, you

---

[4] Some people define a net return concept for only those people who reside within the national boundaries where the project is located. This concept, labeled the "return to the domestic economy" (RDE), is of particular interest for mining and other natural resource extraction projects. The stakeholder framework developed in this note can, in fact, serve as a first step toward working out the RDE.

EXHIBIT 11-1

TWO EQUIVALENT METHODS FOR CALCULATING SOCIAL RETURNS

Assumptions: Suppose a project produces a service that requires only one input, labor. Further assume that there is only one price (the price of labor), where the opportunity cost (the shadow price) differs from the market price observed.[a] Assuming there are no taxes and no other distortions in this simple example, we can calculate the private returns and then calculate the social returns in either of two ways: the traditional approach or the proposed two-step approach. Under both approaches, the private returns equal:

$$\text{Private Returns} = \text{Actual Revenues} - \text{Actual Wages Paid}$$

Method 1: *The Traditional Approach for Calculating Social Returns:*

$$\text{Social Returns} = \text{Actual Revenues} - \text{Wages at Opportunity Cost}$$

where:

$$\text{Wages at Opportunity Cost} = \text{Wages at Shadow Price of Labor}$$

Method 2: *The Proposed 2-Step Approach for Calculating Social Returns*

$$\begin{aligned}
\text{Social Returns} &= \text{Actual Revenues} - \text{Wages at Opportunity Cost} \\
&= \text{Actual Revenues} - \text{Wages at Opportunity Cost} \\
&\quad + (\text{Actual Wages Paid} - \text{Actual Wages Paid})
\end{aligned}$$

rearrange the terms:

$$\begin{aligned}
&= (\text{Actual Revenues} - \text{Actual Wages Paid}) \\
&\quad + (\text{Actual Wages Paid} - \text{Wages at Opportunity Cost}) \\
&= \text{Private Returns} + \text{Gain to Labor}
\end{aligned}$$

where:

$$\text{Private Returns} = \text{Actual Revenues} - \text{Actual Wages Paid}$$
$$\text{Gain to Labor} = \text{Actual Wages Paid} - \text{Wages at Opportunity Cost}$$

[a] This example assumes there is a difference between the market price of labor and the opportunity cost of labor, but that the opportunity cost to society equals the opportunity cost to the worker (see footnotes). It also assumes the output (the service) is sold in a competitive market.

---

calculate the private return, as before, with market prices. Then you calculate the additional return to each of the relevant stakeholder groups as the difference between the actual market prices and the opportunity costs.[5]

Exhibit 11-2 presents a graphical representation of stakeholders who may be affected by the project. The remainder of this section considers the possible impacts on each group. For each group, one must assess the net impacts of building the project relative to a scenario in which the project is not built (the "with investment" versus the "without investment" scenarios). It is very important to be clear and consistent when defining the "without investment" scenario.

The Project Financiers

The benefits and costs of the project from the private perspective are depicted in the center of Exhibit 11-2 as the square box for the project financiers. The stream of net private benefits is the annual total free cash flows generated by the project.[6] The internal rate of return on this stream of earnings is referred to as the FRR, where the FRR summarizes the returns to all capital providers including both debt and equity.

Employees

The employees are depicted in Exhibit 11-2 as part of the central square because they are directly employed by the project and provide a key input (labor to the project company). The net benefits to employees fall into two categories:

- The **increased wages** (including all benefits such as health, pension, meals, special housing, etc.) employees receive to the extent, and only to the extent, they are greater than what the employees would receive from alternative employment opportunities. In other words, the benefit equals the value above the opportunity cost of labor. Because employees chose to take these new jobs, we typically assume the benefit is positive, or at least not negative.[7]

---

[5] To be precise, one should distinguish between the opportunity cost to the individual stakeholder and the opportunity cost to society as a whole. For example, in the case of suppliers, one would distinguish between the opportunity cost to the individual supplier (what the supplier would have received by selling the input to someone else) and the opportunity cost to society of that input. In most cases, however, these costs will be equal, at least to the level of precision needed for this kind of analysis. When the costs are not equal, it is relatively easy to recognize and account for the difference (e.g., cases where a subsidy is provided if the product is sold to one category of user and not another). A more common example would apply in countries where there is a system of unemployment compensation paid by the government. If a worker who was previously unemployed and receiving unemployment compensation is hired by a project, then one should include the savings in unemployment compensation paid as a benefit to the government and the increase in wages above what the worker had been receiving in unemployment compensation as a benefit to the worker.

[6] Free Cash Flow (FCF) equals earnings before interest but after-tax (EBIAT) plus depreciation (noncash charges), less capital expenditures, and less increases in net working capital.

[7] The qualitative direction of these and the other impacts is important to keep in mind. When certain effects cannot be quantified, but are known to be positive, the calculated ERR will be a lower bound on the true return. That is, we know the economic return of the project is at least as high as the calculated return, and is in fact higher but by an undeterminable amount. As discussed below, the impacts on various groups (e.g., workers who choose to be employed at the plant, or consumers who choose to buy the product) are typically positive but difficult to quantify. The two possible exceptions, also discussed below, are impacts on neighbors from higher pollution levels or greater congestion, and the net impact of taxes, tariffs, and subsidies.

EXHIBIT 11-2

PROJECT STAKEHOLDERS: A FRAMEWORK FOR ASSESSING DEVELOPMENT IMPACT

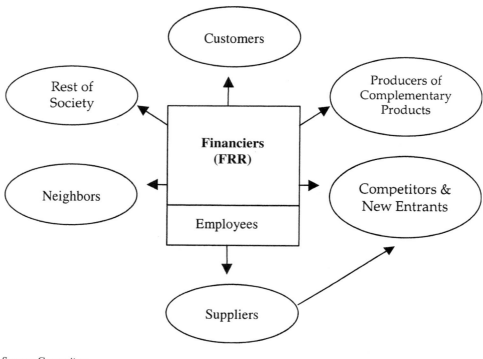

Source: Casewriters.

- The second benefit comes from **training** received as a consequence of employment in the project company. Part of this benefit goes to the company, which is providing the training in order to raise the worker's productivity. This higher productivity is captured in the private returns (the higher productivity leads to increased output or lower costs). The personal benefit to the worker stems from the increased skills gained from training that can be useful in other jobs. It may be difficult to measure this value, but a reasonable approximation is that the benefit to the worker is equal to the training cost. The benefit here should always be positive, or at least not less than zero.

Customers

Those who consume the project's goods or services may benefit from access to a product previously unavailable, of better quality, or for sale at a lower price.

- **New good or service:** Consumers benefit if a project provides a good or service that was previously unavailable in the market. The benefit to the consumer equals the price they are willing to pay for the good or service, that is, the total area under the market demand curve less what they have to pay for it (the market price).

Hence, the net benefit to the consumer (the consumers' surplus) is the triangular area below the demand curve and above the market price line in a simple diagram of supply and demand curves. Consumers' surplus can be quite significant for certain projects, but it can be difficult to estimate quantitatively because the demand curve is not directly observable.

- **Better quality product:** Consumers clearly benefit from an improved good or service that sells for the same price. This benefit can also be difficult to quantify.

- **Increased supply leading to a lower price for the good or service:** When a project increases the supply of a product facing a downward-sloping demand curve, the market price falls. These conditions may hold in developing countries for infrastructure projects or, more generally, for the production of nontradable goods. One would not expect it to apply to the production of goods that can be imported or exported because the demand curve in these cases is normally flat (the product can be imported or exported at a constant price). But where the conditions do apply, consumers benefit from a lower price. Incremental consumer surplus can be calculated as the area of a triangle equal to: ½ *times* the change in the price (a fall) *times* the increase in output due to of the project (area E in Exhibit 11-3).

Producers of Complementary Products

The project may also benefit producers of complementary goods. A complementary good is one whose value to the consumer increases as the supply of another good increases. For example, consider a gasoline station located near the exit of a new toll road. After building the toll road, demand for gasoline increases and the owner of the gasoline station benefits from increased sales. In general, it is difficult to quantify the value derived from this effect. (It depends on an estimate of how far the demand curve shifts upward, but the demand curve is not observable.) But, where relevant, the effect is positive.

There may be indirect benefits as well. For example, additional workers now employed in the production of the complementary goods benefit to the extent they receive a wage that is higher than what they were receiving before the project was built. How far one goes to calculate these indirect benefits depends on the project, and on how important they appear to be.

A question to address is why, if the producers of complementary goods benefit, don't the project sponsors vertically integrate to produce the complementary good? For toll roads, one in fact often sees such vertical integration (i.e., the toll road builder also gets the development rights around the road), and such integration can be critical to the project's financial success. If such integration exists, the benefits are already included in the FRR calculation. But if integration does not occur, and yet we believe the benefits are large, then why did it not occur? There may be good reasons for this outcome. For example, the organizers of the core project may not have special expertise (core competencies) or other advantages, which the producers of the complementary products might have. Alternatively, the lack of vertical integration may suggest that the benefits may not, in fact, be as large as initially estimated. In this case, it is worth rechecking the basic assumptions.

Suppliers

Suppliers to the project enjoy increased demand for the goods or services they provide, and often higher profits. Once again, because the supplier is choosing to sell to the project company, this impact should be positive or at least nonnegative. If the increased

---

EXHIBIT 11-3

GAIN TO CONSUMERS RESULTING FROM THE
INCREASED SUPPLY COMING FROM THE PROJECT

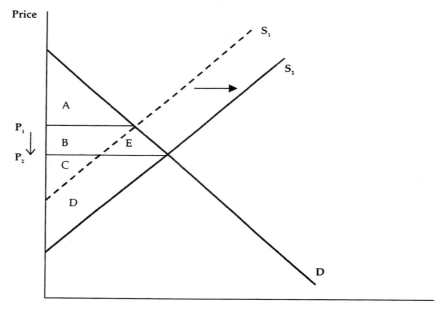

Consumer Surplus: Producer Surplus:
    Initial = A   Initial = B + C
    Final = A + B + E   Final = C + D
    Change = B + E   Change = D − B

Total Change = E + D

Area D = Value to Producer but is already included in the FRR flows

Area E = Gain in Consumer Surplus not offset by decline in Producer Surplus

Source: Casewriters.

---

demand for this particular input leads to a rise in its market price, an attempt should be made to estimate the size of the increased profits and to include these benefits in the social return. The impact is depicted graphically in Exhibit 11-4. The project's suppliers gain a net amount equal to the area E. This value is equal to the area of a simple triangle: ½ *times* the change in the price (a rise) *times* the amount purchased by the project of this input.

There may also be increased wages (again, beyond what they could receive under alternative employment) of the additional workers employed by the suppliers, which should be counted if significant. If there is information and it appears to be important, the chain can continue to the suppliers of the suppliers, and so on. In practice, however, such indirect impacts rapidly diminish in importance to the point where it is no longer worthwhile to estimate them.

EXHIBIT 11-4

GAIN TO SUPPLIERS RESULTING FROM THE INCREASED DEMAND FOR INPUTS BY THE PROJECT

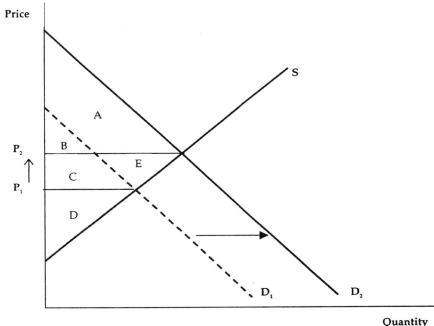

Consumer Surplus:
    Initial = B + C
    Final = A + B
    Change = A − C

Producer Surplus:
    Initial = D
    Final = C + D + E
    Change = C + E

Total Change = A + E

Area A = Value to Project Entity, but is already included in the FRR flows

Area E = Gain in Producer Surplus of the supplier not offset by decline in Consumer Surplus

Source: Casewriters.

    Aside from the simple increase in demand generated by backward linkages, project managers often assist their suppliers in producing better quality or cheaper products by providing assistance in managerial or organizational skills, technology, finance (e.g., trade credit), and so on. This assistance may be especially clear when the project entity is taking the initiative in developing a network of new suppliers (e.g., the suppliers of car parts to a car plant or of sugar cane to a sugar mill). The actions assist the core project (already reflected in the project's profits and its FRR) but benefit the suppliers as well. While it may be difficult to determine the value to the supplier of this benefit, one should try to estimate it if it is likely to be significant.

    The impact on suppliers is an example of a backward linkage, while the impact on customers (who may themselves be producers, using the product as an input to something they are making), as well as on producers of complementary products, are examples of forward linkages. Development economists have argued that linkages, both forward and backward, are among the most important sources of development impact.[8]

Competitors and New Entrants

In contrast to suppliers, competitors may see a reduction in demand and thus a lower price for their product as a result of a new project. Such increased competition is not a loss, however, from the point of view of society as a whole. Consumers benefit from the lower prices in an equal and offsetting amount.

On the other hand, competitors may benefit from demonstration effects and network effects. The project might demonstrate, for example, the feasibility and profitability of a new technology, a new way of managing or organizing business, or the viability of some market segment, which competitors can copy. These demonstration effects may also encourage new firms to enter the market. In addition, competitors may benefit from the network effects with suppliers. For example, a new hotel may work with local farmers to grow fresh fruits and vegetables of a type and quality needed in its restaurants. Competing hotels and restaurants may then benefit from the improved inputs.

Neighbors

The category "neighbors" refers to the impacts a project has on the surrounding community other than through some market-intermediated effect (i.e., an unpriced transaction). These impacts may result from environmental externalities, new or improved infrastructure, and other interactions the firm has with the community.

There is normally some impact on the environment. It may be positive or negative, depending on what would have happened in the "without investment" counterfactual case. For example, if the project involves building a new factory, the effects can be negative and should be taken into account. However, if the new factory is relatively clean (by utilizing new technology) and displaces an older, dirtier plant, the *net* environmental impact may be positive.

A new project may also lead to negative effects through infrastructure congestion. The cost of additional congestion imposed on the surrounding community should be counted as part of the project's social cost. Alternatively, a project may build or improve the availability of infrastructure such as roads, water, and power networks. Neighbors may benefit from the increased availability of this infrastructure and may either pay nothing for it (e.g., a new road with no toll) or pay a price that is below what it is worth to them. If the project paid for the new infrastructure, then the costs of the infrastructure as well as the benefits to the project itself are included in the FRR. However, for the ERR, the benefits to the neighbors should also be counted. Note that if the host government paid for the infrastructure, then the cost should be included in the project's costs, with the government expenditure counted as a subsidy if the project is not otherwise charged (see the discussion of subsidies in the the the next section).

Finally, there may be other impacts on the surrounding community. Large firms often contribute to the local community by funding scholarship or training programs, building schools or community centers, or making available on-site facilities and services (such as medical care) to community members. It is often difficult to measure the value of such community programs, but a reasonable assumption is that the benefits are

---

[8] A.O. Hirschman, *The Strategy of Economic Development* (New Haven, CT: Yale University Press, 1958); and A. O. Hirschman, *Development Projects Observed*, Washington, DC: The Brookings Institute, 1967). See Chapter Five, "Project Appraisal: The Centrality of Side-Effects."

at least equal to the cost of providing the services. This assumption helps bound the size of the potential benefits.

Rest of Society

Under the category "Rest of Society," one would include the effects of taxes, subsidies, tariffs, and other government interventions.

- **Profit Taxes:** The profit generated by a project equals the revenues minus the costs, but a portion of the profits goes to the government in the form of taxes. For the private return (the FRR), one calculates the free cash flows *after* any profit taxes due; for the social return (the ERR), one includes the profit taxes as part of the overall return. This calculation has nothing to do with what the government does with the tax revenues. To the extent taxes are redistributed in a way that benefits society, there may be second- or third-order effects that should be counted, if they are meaningful. The decision on whether to calculate these multiplier effects should be approached pragmatically.

- **Value-Added, Sales, and Excise Taxes:** Government collection of value-added taxes (VAT) will rise if overall sales increase. If, however, the product is imported, and the project simply leads to a substitution for imports, then total sales on the market (from domestic and imported sources) will be unchanged. Because value-added taxes are normally charged on imports (and at the final price of the import inclusive of any import tariffs charged), the mere substitution of domestic for imported supply has no effect on overall VAT receipts. However, if the increased supply on the market due to the project leads to an increase in overall sales, then VAT receipts will rise by an amount equal to the VAT rate times the increase in sales. This amount must be included in the ERR calculations. Sales and excise taxes should be treated similarly. Of course, this analysis assumes equivalent effectiveness in collecting taxes, which may not always be true if tax evasion is prevalent.

- **Subsidies:** The cost of providing subsidies to the project, while a benefit to the private owner (and hence included in the FRR), should clearly be subtracted in the ERR calculation. If the subsidies were used to construct associated infrastructure or if the infrastructure was provided in kind, then the costs should be subtracted in the ERR calculation, net of any associated benefits accruing to others (e.g., neighbors who enjoy access to the infrastructure).

- **Import Tariffs and Export Taxes or Subsidies:** If the project produces or makes use of goods that are subject to tariffs (or nontariff barriers), then the private prices will differ from the social costs. The cost to society is the world price at which the goods can be imported: the tariffs are a transfer to the government, and the domestic price will rise by the amount of the tariff due to competition (or, more precisely, the restriction on competition from potential imports). Thus for goods produced by the project, the social revenue stream should be reduced by the portion of the price that is accounted for by the tariff (or the tariff equivalent for nontariff barriers). For inputs, the costs should also be adjusted to reflect the existence of tariffs. Similar adjustments should be made to incorporate the effects of export taxes or subsidies.

CONSIDERATIONS WHEN APPLYING THE FRAMEWORK

The following list of issues should be considered when applying this framework:

- **Information Gap:** Not all the costs and benefits generated by a project can be qualified easily or accurately. For example, there may be no way to calculate the value of demonstration effects. And even when an estimation procedure is possible, the effort may not be worthwhile. In such cases, a description of the impact may be sufficient. In these instances, it is most important to understand the direction of the impact. If the nonquantified impacts are positive, then the actual ERR will be greater than the calculated ERR. And if the calculated ERR is already sufficient to warrant project approval, then one has the information required to make a decision.

- **Discount Rate:** This note does not discuss the appropriate discount rate for societal cash flows. The concept of one "social" discount rate may be too simplistic and does not properly weigh the risk associated with various flows. Yet assigning multiple discount rates to each component of flow can be arbitrary. Needless to say, there has been a lot of disagreements among development economists about what discount rates to apply and when. As a rule of thumb, the IFC generally uses a 10% *real* discount rate for social cost/benefit analysis.

- **Shadow Foreign Exchange Rates:** Traditional social cost/benefit analysis, as developed in the 1960s and 1970s, paid a great deal of attention to the proper determination of shadow foreign exchange rates. The shadow foreign exchange rate is an estimate of the opportunity cost to society of using or producing foreign exchange, and differs from the actual rate paid for foreign exchange when foreign exchange markets are subject to capital controls. Distortions of this kind were far more prevalent during the 1960s and 1970s than they are today. As a result, the issue is less important now. However, in certain countries and in certain circumstances, it may still be worthwhile to estimate and apply a shadow exchange rate. Probably more important today than adjusting the current market exchange rate for possible distortions is to use suitable projections of real movements in the market exchange rate over time to account for the possibility that the real exchange rate will depreciate or appreciate relative to current rates.

- **Efficiency Versus Equity:** The ERR calculation focuses on the *efficiency* of resource allocation, and treats the returns to each group equally. It does not address the question of whether society should place a higher value on the net benefits to certain groups (e.g., the poor) than the net benefits going to others (e.g., the rich).[9] The analysis outlined in this note provides a first step towards incorporating such distributional issues, as one could apply different weights to the net returns of the different groups identified. But determining the weights is fundamentally a political decision.

- **Accounting for the Future:** Project analysis is generally undertaken prior to the start of a project to assist in the decision on whether to proceed. It should incorporate any changes that are expected to take place, such as price changes (including expected changes in the real exchange rate or in the real wage rate). More fundamentally, standard project cost/benefit analysis is static in the sense that it takes into account only what is known or expected for the future as of a certain date. It does not take into account the fact that one will know more in the future. That is, standard cost/benefit analysis does not take into account the value of flexibility inherent in current actions. But taking account of the embedded optionality raises an entirely new set of issues that are beyond the scope of this note.

---

[9] L. Squire and H.G. van der Tak, *Economic Analysis of Projects*, A World Bank Research Publication, 8th ed. (Baltimore, MD: Johns Hopkins University Press, 1995).

12

Texas High-Speed Rail Corporation

The Texas cities of Dallas, Fort Worth, Houston, Austin, and San Antonio, through an unusual combination of geography and demographics, represented one of the most promising markets in the United States for an intercity high-speed passenger rail network. They were situated on a rough triangle with 250-mile-long legs. They had about 3.5 million households in 1988 and a combined population of about 10 million people. Residents and visitors traveled frequently between these cities. By the year 2000, they were expected to take about 20 million person-trips per year, of which 12 million would be by air. Most of the air travel would be to and from Dallas-Fort Worth, a major air traffic hub, and most of it would consist of business trips. The Texas High-Speed Rail Corporation (THSRC) was formed by the Texas TGV Consortium, a group of private investors, to construct and operate a rail network offering fast travel times and reliable, high-quality service connecting Texas's major centers of business, government, and tourism. In 1991, the Consortium had been awarded an exclusive franchise for such a system by the State of Texas.

Beginning in 1998, THSRC planned to operate trains at 200 miles per hour along the eastern leg of the triangle and offer door-to-door travel times comparable to existing air service (for example, $1\frac{1}{2}$ hours to/from downtown Houston from/to downtown Dallas) at prices competitive with airfares. By the end of 1999, service would commence along the western corridor from San Antonio to Austin and Dallas-Fort Worth. A southern corridor, connecting Houston and San Antonio, could be added later if sufficient demand materialized. Exhibit 12-1 presents a map showing routes under consideration by THSRC.

Professor Timothy A. Luehrman and Andrew D. Regan, Charles M. Williams Fellow, prepared this case. Certain facts and data have been disguised. HBS cases are developed solely as the basis for class discussion. Cases are not intended to serve as endorsements, sources of primary data, or illustrations of effective or ineffective management.

EXHIBIT 12-1

ILLUSTRATION OF POTENTIAL ROUTE ALIGNMENTS

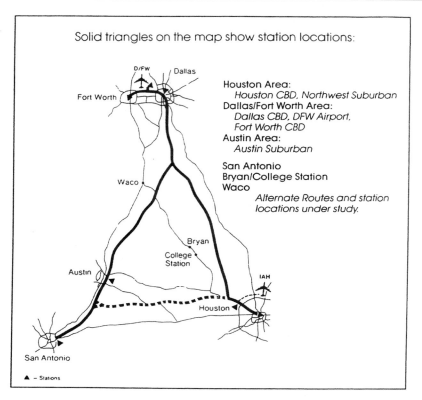

Solid triangles on the map show station locations:

Houston Area:
  Houston CBD, Northwest Suburban
Dallas/Fort Worth Area:
  Dallas CBD, DFW Airport,
  Fort Worth CBD
Austin Area:
  Austin Suburban

San Antonio
Bryan/College Station
Waco
  Alternate Routes and station
  locations under study.

▲ – Stations

Note: THSRC's franchise gave it exclusive rights to develop a route between Houston and San Antonio. The dashed line shows one route that was being studied in 1991. However, none of THSRC's cash flow projections in 1991 included future expenditures or operating revenues and costs for the southern corridor.

Source: Company documents.

With practically no delays due to equipment, weather, or peak-hour congestion, THSRC expected to have 97% on-time reliability compared to the airlines' 80%. Service would be scheduled from 6:00 A.M. to midnight daily, with departures every half hour during most of the day, and every 15 minutes during peak travel times. The trains would offer ample passenger space, with no center seats and complete freedom of movement. They also would provide amenities such as optional business- and first-class service, reserved seats, full at-seat meal service, at-seat cellular telephones with inward and outward dialing, car rental desks, and complete baggage handling services. THSRC would have a station adjacent to new departure gates at Dallas–Fort Worth Airport (DFW), and passengers departing or arriving on cooperating airlines could obtain reservations, seat assignments, and tickets in advance for both the air and rail portions of their trip. Travelers also would be able to check luggage through from an out-of-state airline departure point to a train destination within Texas, or vice versa.

Long before the first paying passenger boarded a train, however, THSRC had to raise more than $6 billion to build the system and begin operations. The Texas TGV Consortium had already developed a detailed financing plan that anticipated raising all the necessary funds from private investors. This plan had been described and submitted to the state with the Consortium's franchise application in January 1991. Now, in July 1991, a team of legal and financial professionals assembled in Boise, Idaho, to begin refining and implementing the plan.

The Morrison Knudsen Corporation (MK) was the Consortium's managing partner and largest shareholder. William Agee, chairman and chief executive of MK, led the meeting in Boise, which also included MK's chief financial officer and its senior vice president for strategic planning. Seven finance experts from Merrill Lynch, Credit Lyonnais, and Banque Indosuez also attended, along with three attorneys from the firm of Kelly, Hart & Hallman. Completing the group was James C. Gerber, one of THSRC's first employees and its director of finance. Gerber's job was to direct and coordinate the efforts of the financial team and oversee day-to-day financial affairs for THSRC as work progressed. He had been preparing and interpreting financial analyses of the project for nearly two years, longer than the Consortium itself had existed. As it stood in July 1991, the financing plan addressed several problems that Mr. Gerber's analyses had identified, but he and other team members were considering further modifications in it.

HISTORY OF THE TEXAS TGV PROJECT

In 1991, trains were not a popular mode of transportation between cities in the United States. Amtrak offered regular passenger service in the heavily traveled Boston–New York–Washington corridor in the northeast United States. Although Amtrak as a whole was government-owned and subsidized, many experts thought this particular route to be breakeven, if not profitable. It was not, however, particularly fast, nor was the twisted, heavily urban route likely to be cheaply adapted to the technologically advanced, very fast trains being developed outside the United States. Several other U.S. locations were more promising, and three in particular—California, Florida, and Texas—had been studied in some detail.

Four primary attributes could enhance the economic viability of high-speed rail in a given location. The first was good demographics, reflected in a large, steadily growing population of potential travelers. The second and third involved geography. The target cities had to be between 200 and 300 miles apart. If they were significantly closer, automobiles would dominate trains in both cost and convenience. If they were too far apart, airlines would dominate. Furthermore, the terrain between cities had to be hospitable. Mountains, valleys, rivers, and roads all presented obstacles that made construction riskier and more expensive. Sharp turns and changes in elevation slowed down average train speed. The last attribute involved politics and regulation. Routes that crossed state lines were subject to approval and regulation by the U.S. federal government to a far greater extent than intrastate routes. All else equal, intrastate routes were less subject to political uncertainty and were expected to be less costly to build and operate.

Texas began attracting serious attention in the early 1980s from a group of German engineering and rolling stock companies working on a similar project in Europe. The German group studied volumes and patterns of travel between Dallas-Fort Worth and Houston. Encouraged by their findings, they lobbied the Texas legislature to create a franchise for which private companies could compete. In April 1989, the legislators voted to create the Texas High-Speed Rail Authority and charged it with soliciting franchise applications to develop high-speed rail in Texas and overseeing any systems established as a result. The legislation permitted the Authority to grant exclusive franchises for particular routes and expressly prohibited state subsidies for either construction or operation of a privately owned system.

In the midst of the legislature's deliberations, Mannai Investment Company, together with Bradford C. Corbett and Ben Barnes, began exploring the possibilities for high-speed rail in Texas. Mannai was a privately held corporation whose principals were experienced real estate developers. Corbett was an experienced private investor, and Barnes was a former lieutenant governor of Texas. Following the creation of the Authority, Mannai, Corbett, and Barnes (Mannai/C&B) began circulating a private memorandum that described possible approaches to a Texas system and potential investment opportunities. Morrison Knudsen's William Agee was among those who received a copy of this memorandum in July 1989. MK's Engineering Group was already familiar with the opportunity, having been engaged by the Texas Department of Transportation to help investigate its feasibility. Agee agreed to attend a meeting with Mannai/C&B principals in New York. James Gerber, who had just received his MBA and joined MK as assistant to the president, accompanied an MK group president to the meeting.

Mannai/C&B proposed to license the French TGV (*train à grande vitesse*) technology that had been used since 1981 by SNCF, the French national rail company, on a 264-mile route between Paris and Lyon. The Paris–Lyon route was similar in many ways to a potential Dallas–Houston route. Based on the French experience, MK and Mannai/C&B felt they could develop reasonable estimates of construction and operating costs. A more difficult question was whether an unsubsidized high-speed line between Dallas–Fort Worth and Houston could both match competing airfares and realize high enough load factors to produce an adequate return on investment. Indeed, initial projections indicated that the project was uneconomic on this basis. Then MK planners conceived the idea of increasing rail traffic by cooperating with airlines to deliver air passengers from outlying parts of Texas to the DFW hub. The addition of this so-called interconnect traffic yielded projected load factors high enough to make the rail project appear viable. Based on these and other considerations, MK decided to participate in further discussions with Mannai/C&B.

In a second meeting in New York in September 1989, MK and Mannai/C&B agreed to form the Texas TGV Consortium to develop a proposal and submit a franchise application to the Texas High-Speed Rail Authority. Initially, MK contributed $500,000 cash and $500,000 in services, and Mannai contributed $500,000 cash and $500,000 in imputed services. Corbett and Barnes together contributed $700,000 in imputed services. A separate agreement was concluded with Bombardier, a Canadian manufacturer of rolling stock that owned the North American rights to the TGV technology. This agreement ensured the Consortium's access to the TGV technology for a Texas system.

In the next several months, many professional advisors were consulted in the process of preparing data and analyses to support the franchise application. In the spring of 1990, Merrill Lynch, a U.S. investment bank and brokerage house, and Credit Lyonnais, a French state-owned commercial bank, were hired as advisors. So was the Houston office of Wilbur Smith & Associates, a prominent engineering and transportation planning firm. Also in the spring, Gerber began meeting with American Airlines to describe some of the Consortium's plans involving DFW. In July, Banque Indosuez, a French merchant bank, joined the financing team. Earlier in the 1980s, the two French banks had helped arrange private financing for the $15 billion Eurotunnel project: Banque Indosuez had played a leading role in placing Eurotunnel equity, while

Credit Lyonnais had arranged a long-term bank credit facility. Finally, Gerber himself was seconded from MK to the Texas TGV Consortium in the summer of 1990 and began devoting all of his time to the project.

The Consortium's franchise application was tendered in January 1991. The only competing application came from a German group, which called itself Texas FastTrack, and it differed substantially from the TGV Consortium's. FastTrack proposed to use a different technology, one that lacked TGV's 10 years of proven reliable operation. It planned to serve only Houston and Dallas initially and relied only marginally on interconnect traffic in and out of DFW. Finally, FastTrack's financing proposal did not identify financing for all system costs, and it was essentially all debt, in contrast to the large amount of private equity that Texas TGV planned to issue. Hearings on the two proposals started in mid-March and lasted a month. In May 1991, the hearing examiner produced a draft order awarding an exclusive franchise to Texas TGV.

THE ECONOMICS OF HIGH-SPEED RAIL IN TEXAS

Revenues

Preliminary ridership studies had been prepared with help from several independent consultants, including senior managers from SNCF who had been in charge of ridership and marketing in France since 1981. THSRC planned to position its service primarily as an alternative to intrastate air travel, especially for business travelers. Market studies showed some two million (nonconnecting) plane trips per year between Dallas and Houston and nearly as many among San Antonio, Austin, and Dallas. An additional four million passengers per year traveled along THSRC's corridors to connect at Dallas's two major airports for destinations outside Texas. Both market segments were expected to grow at 3 to 4% per year through the end of the decade. Exhibit 12-2 summarizes THSRC's anticipated ridership, based on preliminary studies.

Interconnect Traffic

Interconnect passengers formed a crucial part of THSRC's business plan, accounting for approximately 38% of anticipated revenues. Currently, people beginning or ending a long trip in a smaller Texas city flew through a "hub," such as DFW or Houston Intercontinental Airport, where they had to switch planes. Major airlines operated their own short-haul routes into and out of the hub, or contracted with smaller commuter lines to do so. The TGV Consortium's analyses showed that short-haul routes were marginally profitable at best, and perhaps unprofitable, for the major airlines. Large airlines offered such service as a necessary adjunct to the more profitable long-haul routes, particularly trans- and intercontinental routes that originated in the hub. Studies also suggested that a high-speed train could deliver passengers to and from the hub at lower cost than could the airlines themselves. If correct, the Consortium's analyses pointed to a large potential market for high-speed rail services. In 1990, fully 70% of out-of-state passengers connecting to the Texas cities targeted by THSRC passed through the American and Delta gates at DFW. THSRC hoped eventually to reach formal, long-term agreements with American and/or Delta Airlines that would integrate the reservation and marketing systems of each with THSRC.[1]

---

[1] If traffic grew sufficiently, similar agreements could be discussed with Continental Airlines, which operated a hub at Houston Intercontinental Airport and short-haul routes to Austin, San Antonio, and Dallas.

EXHIBIT 12-2

PROJECTED RIDERSHIP AND REVENUE COMPOSITION

A. Projected THSRC Share of Targeted Airline Passenger Traffic

| | THSRC Market Share (%) | | | | | |
| | Dallas–Houston | | | Dallas–San Antonio | | |
	1998	1999	2000	1999	2000	2001
Target Air Market						
DFW—interconnect	27%	80%	80%	33%	100%	100%
DFW—local	13%	43%	65%	17%	48%	65%
Love Field—local	12%	30%	60%	16%	36%	60%
Love Field—interconnect	nil	nil	nil	nil	nil	Nil

B. Projected Composition of THSRC Ridership (in thousands of trips)

	1998	1999	2000	2001	2002	2003
Total Projected Market						
Interconnect air	5,169	5,339	5,516	5,698	5,886	6,080
Local air	5,064	5,231	5,404	5,582	5,766	5,957
Auto	6,667	6,849	7,041	7,238	7,441	7,649
Total trips (000s)	16,900	17,419	17,961	18,518	19,093	19,686
Projected THSRC Share						
Interconnect air	0.09	0.40	0.71	0.71	0.71	0.71
Local air	0.07	0.30	0.52	0.62	0.62	0.62
Auto	0.03	0.10	0.17	0.18	0.18	0.18
Projected Captured Riders						
Interconnect air	465.2	2,135.6	3,916.4	4,045.6	4,179.1	4,316.8
Local air	354.5	1,569.3	2,810.1	3,460.8	3,574.9	3,693.3
Auto	200.0	684.9	1,197.0	1,302.8	1,339.4	1,376.8
Commuters	336.6	1,815.9	3,541.6	4,030.6	4,143.4	4,259.4
Other induced	62.4	451.2	904.9	1,070.3	1,103.3	1,137.3
Total riders	1,418.7	6,656.9	12,369.9	13,910.2	14,340.1	14,783.7
Total inter-city	1,019.7	4,389.8	7,923.4	8,809.3	9,093.4	9,387.0

C. Projected Composition of THSRC Revenue

	1998	1999	2000
Former air traffic	72%	73%	73%
Former auto traffic	18%	11%	10%
Commuters	6%	11%	12%
Other induced	4%	5%	5%
	100%	100%	100%

Source: Company documents.

The TGV Consortium believed that American and Delta would find a cooperative arrangement with THSRC economically attractive, providing their passengers would accept it. Focus groups with airline passengers had so far suggested that they liked the concept. If it became a reality, the airlines could expect several benefits. Fast trains' very high (97%) schedule reliability and more frequent service would improve the airlines' own passenger management and help alleviate peak-hour congestion in terminals and on runways at DFW. Valuable departure gates and takeoff spots could then be shifted to more profitable long-haul routes. Travelers would receive better service within Texas and experience fewer delays and less frustration overall. In effect, by cooperating with THSRC, airlines could shift assets from lower- to higher-returning activities while offering their customers better service.

Local Traffic

Another 35% of THSRC's anticipated revenues came from local traffic, that is, non-connecting intrastate airline passengers. Many of these travelers were businesspeople currently served by Southwest Airlines, which operated inexpensive "no-frills" flights between many cities in Texas and throughout the southwestern United States.[2] These passengers would have to be induced to switch from air to train travel notwithstanding Southwest Airlines' desire to retain their business. THSRC believed it could match Southwest's fares, travel times, and departure frequencies, while offering more convenient and comfortable service. The targeted travelers were expected to be attracted by THSRC's downtown and suburban train stations, which eliminated arrival and check-in at congested airports, and by the availability of more comfortable workspace on the train.

Unlike Delta and American, Southwest Airlines was not using its Texas routes primarily as feeders for long-haul trips out of a hub. Instead, Southwest structured its operations to deliver high-frequency, short-haul, no-frills service at a profit. Its costs were thought to be the lowest in the U.S. airline industry, and it had been profitable in all but its first two years of operation. A loss of traffic to trains would be perceived by Southwest as a threat to its profitability and might spark a battle for market share on certain routes. The planned THSRC routes accounted for only 12% of Southwest's total traffic in 1991, so Southwest theoretically could survive an extended fare war on those routes by using non-Texas routes to subsidize them.

However, extensive analyses commissioned by THSRC suggested that protracted fare wars were unlikely. First, THSRC itself did not plan to use price as a marketing weapon, and in fact expected to charge the same or slightly higher fares than Southwest where the two competed directly. Second, it appeared that THSRC trains would not create excess intrastate capacity generally, assuming some major carriers diverted some capacity to long-haul routes. Indeed, THSRC expected to meet its projections without causing Southwest's load factors to drop below breakeven levels. Finally, THSRC's detailed comparison of cost structures showed that neither company could expect to harm its competitor more than itself by engaging in predatory pricing. Although Southwest was renowned in the industry as a tough competitor, it displayed no tendency to waste capital. Thus, THSRC officials fully expected Southwest's executives to comprehend the long-run futility of a price war. Nevertheless, Southwest had chosen to fight THSRC by filing lawsuits in state court challenging the franchise award. THSRC and its attorneys expected to prevail in all such procedural challenges.

Other Traffic

The remaining 27% of THSRC's expected revenue came from automobile traffic, both inter- and intracity, and from induced traffic. Targeted marketing and special fares would attract many of these passengers. For example, commuters could ride at peak hours

---

[2] Southwest served the Dallas–Fort Worth area with flights out of downtown Dallas's Love Field rather than DFW.

between suburban and downtown locations. Since some of these seats would otherwise be open, they could be sold at low prices to intracity travelers at virtually no marginal cost. Induced traffic was a small but important source of additional ridership, consisting of trips, mostly for pleasure, that otherwise would not be taken. In France, such traffic eventually accounted for about 10% of revenue, and it was expected to be even more significant in Texas.

Last, THSRC had identified several potential sources of ancillary revenues. For example, parking, package delivery, and advertising could generate stable, if modest, cash flows. In addition, some of THSRC's right-of-way and station sites would create opportunities for real estate development, though none of THSRC's current projections included costs or revenues from such projects. Similarly, THSRC planned to lay fiber-optic cables along its right-of-way. This would involve low incremental costs during the system's construction phase and create some immediate cash flow when the resulting telecommunications capacity was sold or leased.[3]

Operating Costs

To develop estimates of operating costs, the TGV Consortium had worked closely with Rail Transportation Systems (RTS), an Atlanta-based subsidiary of France's SNCF. Experienced RTS personnel assisted in the development of operations standards, structures evaluation, and operations and maintenance scheduling and costing. These analyses were performed based on independent assessments of the Texas market and extensive operating experience in France. To be conservative, planners assumed that operating costs would be stepped up as new departures were added, but would be otherwise constant, in real terms, once full-scale operations commenced in 1999. Although tracks and trainsets in Texas were to be engineered for speeds up to 250 miles per hour, they would operate initially at only 200 miles per hour. Over time, speeds would increase and higher speeds would actually improve efficiency.[4]

Construction and Startup Costs

THSRC anticipated spending a total of $5.8 billion over eight years to get its system built. Construction costs were estimated for 30 different cost categories over 12 separate geographic regions. Preliminary expenditures for overhead and for preliminary operating, engineering, construction, environmental, and financial studies were estimated at $40 million. Another $280 million would be spent in a development phase on preconstruction engineering, on environmental impact studies, and for all related permitting. At the same time, the necessary right-of-way would be acquired for an estimated $230 million. Infrastructure was to be constructed at a cost of $4.1 billion. Some "public" facilities, primarily urban and electrical infrastructure (approximately $1.6 billion), would qualify for tax-exempt financing. "Private" infrastructure (e.g., stations, maintenance depots, ancillary structures, and the actual right-of-way trackage) either did not qualify or carried valuable depreciation tax shields that would be lost if THSRC financed them with tax-exempt debt. Rolling stock, which also was ineligible for tax-exempt

---

[3] Telecommunications services account for all the projected revenue shown in Exhibit 12-3 prior to 1998.

[4] In France, for example, the TGV operated initially at 168 miles per hour between Paris and Lyon. In 1989, a new generation of trains began routine operations at 186 mph. In 1990, one such train set a world rail speed record of 320 mph using daily passenger-train trackage. In 1993, French trains would begin operating regularly at 200 mph.

financing, would be assembled in Texas by Bombardier and leased or purchased by THSRC for $1.1 billion.

To protect itself against cost overruns and delays, THSRC had estimated costs and construction schedules conservatively. It also planned to spread construction contracts among 20 to 30 different companies, each strong enough to submit a guaranteed maximum price bid, backed by performance bonds. The companies awarded contracts in this way could then subcontract as they saw fit. To cover operating losses during start-up and initial investments in working capital THSRC had to arrange substantial additional financing. Depending partly on how it was financed, THSRC could register losses in early years in the range of $0.5 to $1.0 billion. This brought the estimated total cost of the system to $6.3 to $6.8 billion.[5]

Exhibit 12-3 summarizes THSRC's estimated cash flows, *excluding financing cash flows*, for the period 1992 to 2018. Exhibit 12-4 shows the net present value of these project cash flows over a range of discount rates, assuming the project may be viewed as a perpetuity with a constant growth rate over all the years following 2018.

EVOLUTION OF THE FINANCING PLAN

THSRC expected to pass through five phases, each characterized by a different set of activities, uncertainties, and funds needs. A preliminary phase of relatively low expenditures would last until sometime in 1993. A two-year development phase would mark the beginning of large expenditures and involve some irreversible investments. The construction phase would last five years and involve heavy expenditures in many locations. A start-up phase would begin in 1998 and last about two or three years as the system swung into full operation and THSRC made adjustments in operating policies and systems. Finally, the high-speed rail system would arrive at a steady state characterized by stable operations and a new equilibrium in the Texas intercity transportation market. These phases are shown schematically in Exhibit 12-5.

Consortium members had always known that their financing program would be subject to certain constraints. It could rely on no financial aid from the State of Texas, which meant, broadly, no state grants, subsidies, tax breaks, or credit support. It had to meet a strict timetable, ensuring timely access to funds early in the project for heavy development and construction expenditures. It had to provide THSRC flexibility to survive setbacks either in the field or in the capital markets. And it had to provide a fair expected return for later, outside investors without giving up the profit opportunities that had attracted the Consortium members in the first place.

Early Ideas

There were few good models on which to base the financing plan. MK executives, William Gerber, and their advisors studied various approaches and identified specific advantages and disadvantages associated with each. Then they considered ways to enhance the benefits and/or mitigate the costs associated with a given program. Several approaches were studied and modified or discarded before the Consortium arrived at the plan submitted with its franchise application.

---

[5] All expenditures are expressed in nominal dollars for the year in which they occur (see Exhibit 12-3). These figures were based on constant-dollar estimates for each item. Then, different price indices were applied to each item to inflate constant-dollar estimates to nominal dollars in the appropriate year.

EXHIBIT 12-3

PROJECT CASH FLOWS (IN MILLIONS OF DOLLARS)

Year	1992	1993	1994	1995	1996	1997	1998	1999	2000	2001	2002	2003	2004	2005
Constant dollars														
Revenue				8.9	26.8	26.8	94.9	331.0	603.0	681.8	711.9	743.4	776.3	810.6
Excise tax				0.9	2.7	2.7	9.5	33.1	60.3	68.2	71.2	74.3	77.6	81.1
Operating costs						22.5	90.0	180.0	180.0	180.0	180.0	180.0	180.0	180.0
Property taxes							36.0	36.0	36.0	36.0	36.0	36.0	36.0	36.0
Total (cash) costs				0.9		25.2	135.5	249.1	276.3	284.2	287.2	290.3	293.6	297.1
EBITD (constant $)				8.0	24.1	1.6	(40.6)	81.9	326.7	397.6	424.7	453.1	482.7	513.5
Nominal dollars														
EBITD (nominal $)				9.1	28.7	2.0	(52.9)	111.5	464.6	590.9	659.5	735.3	818.6	910.0
Depreciation							79.2	79.2	79.2	79.2	88.6	88.6	88.6	88.6
EBIT				9.1	28.7	2.0	(132.1)	32.3	385.4	511.7	570.9	646.7	730.0	821.4
Tax @ 38%				3.5	10.9	0.8	(15.1)	0.0	123.7	194.4	217.0	245.8	277.4	312.1
EBIAT				5.7	17.8	1.2	(116.9)	32.3	261.7	317.2	354.0	401.0	452.6	509.3
Depreciation							79.2	79.2	79.2	79.2	88.6	88.6	88.6	88.6
Operating cash flow				5.7	17.8	1.2	(37.7)	111.5	340.9	396.4	442.6	489.6	541.2	597.9
Expenditures (nominal $)														
Preliminary	20.0	20.0												
Development		56.0	140.0	84.0										
Right of way		13.5	32.1	184.4										
Infrastructure (private)				410.6	657.0	574.8								
Infrastructure (public)				615.9	985.4	862.3								
Rolling stock				226.4	283.0	339.6								
Net working capital additions							283.0							
Additional trainsets, overhauls							9.9	26.3	32.7	12.5	7.4	8.1	8.8	9.6
Infrastructure renewal											187.9			
Total expenditures	20.0	89.5	172.1	1521.3	1925.4	1776.7	292.9	26.3	32.7	12.5	195.3	8.1	8.8	9.6
Project free cash flow (FCF)	(20.0)	(89.5)	(172.1)	(1,515.7)	(1,907.6)	(1,775.5)	(330.7)	85.2	308.2	383.9	247.3	481.5	532.4	588.2

(Continued)

EXHIBIT 12-3 *(Continued)*

Year	2006	2007	2008	2009	2010	2011	2012	2013	2014	2015	2016	2017	2018
Constant dollars													
Revenue	846.6	884.2	923.5	964.6	1,007.7	1,039.2	1,071.7	1,105.3	1,139.9	1,175.7	1,212.5	1,250.5	1,289.7
Excise tax	9.9												
Operating costs	180.0	180.0	180.0	180.0	180.0	180.0	180.0	180.0	180.0	180.0	180.0	180.0	180.0
Property taxes	36.0	36.0	36.0	36.0	36.0	36.0	36.0	36.0	36.0	36.0	36.0	36.0	36.0
Total (cash) costs	225.9	216.0	216.0	216.0	216.0	216.0	216.0	216.0	216.0	216.0	216.0	216.0	216.0
EBITD (constant $)	620.7	668.2	707.5	748.6	791.7	823.2	855.7	889.3	923.9	959.7	996.5	1,034.5	1,073.7
Nominal dollars													
EBITD (nominal $)	1,149.5	1,293.2	1,430.8	1,582.1	1,748.5	1,899.8	2,063.7	2,241.3	2,433.2	2,641.3	2,865.9	3,109.1	3,372.1
Depreciation	103.3	106.9	122.9	123.2	123.7	128.2	132.9	138.1	143.5	149.1	155.3	156.7	78.9
EBIT	1,046.2	1,186.3	1,307.9	1,458.9	1,624.8	1,771.6	1,930.8	2,103.2	2,289.7	2,492.2	2,710.6	2,952.4	3,293.2
Tax @ 38%	397.6	450.8	497.0	554.4	617.4	673.2	733.7	799.2	870.1	947.0	1,030.0	1,121.9	1,251.4
EBIAT	648.6	735.5	810.9	904.5	1,007.3	1,098.4	1,197.1	1,304.0	1,419.6	1,545.1	1,680.6	1,830.5	2,041.8
Depreciation	103.3	106.9	122.9	123.2	123.7	128.2	132.9	138.1	143.5	149.1	155.3	156.7	78.9
Operating cash flow	751.9	842.4	933.8	1,027.7	1,131.0	1,226.6	1,330.0	1,442.1	1,563.1	1,694.2	1,835.9	1,987.2	2,120.7
Expenditures (nominal $)													
Preliminary													
Development													
Right of way													
Infrastructure (private)													
Infrastructure (public)													
Rolling stock													
Net working capital additions	10.6	11.5	12.6	13.7	15.0	13.9	15.0	16.2	17.4	18.8	20.2	21.8	23.5
Additional trainsets, overhauls	287.8	66.6	314.3			79.5	83.0	86.8	90.7	94.8	99.0		
Infrastructure renewal	5.6	5.8	6.1	6.4	10.0	10.4	10.9	16.3	17.0	17.8	26.0	27.1	28.4
Total expenditures	304.0	83.9	333.0	20.1	25.0	103.8	108.9	119.3	125.1	131.4	145.2	48.9	51.9
Project free cash flow (FCF)	448.0	758.5	600.8	1,007.6	1,106.0	1,122.8	1,221.1	1,322.8	1,438.0	1,562.9	1,690.7	1,938.3	2,068.8

Source: Company documents.

EXHIBIT 12-4

NET PRESENT VALUE OF PROJECT FREE CASH FLOWS (FCF)

Discount Rate	NPV of Project FCF
7.0%	$14,653
7.5	10,643
8.0	7,868
8.5	5,858
9.0	4,354
9.5	3,199
10.0	2,296
10.5	1,579
11.0	1,002
11.5	534
12.0	150
12.5	(166)
13.0	(427)
13.5	(644)
14.0	(825)
14.5	(975)
15.0	(1,101)
15.5	(1,205)
16.0	(1,292)
16.5	(1,364)
17.0	(1,423)
17.5	(1,471)
18.0	(1,510)

Note: Net present values are computed as the present value, at each discount rate, of the project free cash flows presented in Exhibit 12-3 together with a terminal value. The terminal value in each case is the discounted value (at each rate) in 2018 of a growing perpetuity. The first (year 2019) cash flow of the perpetuity equals $2,068.8 × 1.045 and it is assumed to grow at 4.50% per year.

Source: Casewriter.

The first idea was simply to break the financing into two stages, much like a real estate development project. In essence, a massive construction loan would be taken down as needed and then completely refinanced with a combination of debt and equity when the project was complete. This approach had the compelling virtues of simplicity and the avoidance of early dilution of the founders' equity interests. However, it offered little security to construction lenders, who would be stuck with partially completed rail infrastructure spread over hundreds of square miles in the event that the project was abandoned by its sponsors or halted by opponents. Such a plan also created huge tax shields well before the project itself could use them.

A plan dubbed "late equity" was considered next. Under this approach, a combination of construction loans and tax-exempt debt would finance development expenditures and infrastructure. A substantial equity issue would follow, to finance rolling stock and start-up reserves. When the project was complete, construction loans would be refinanced. Tax-exempt debt could be refinanced and/or retired out of operating cash flow. However, when shown this plan, several banks felt that early lenders still had inadequate protection. Early on, they argued, either loan guarantees or more equity would be required to support borrowing for infrastructure.

EXHIBIT 12-5

PROJECT PHASES AND SCHEDULE OF ACTIVITIES

1990	1992	1994	1996	1998	2000	2002	2004	2006

Preliminary

    Development

        Construction   Start-up Operations   Steady-State Operations

> Project Phases

Preliminary Studies

    Franchise Awarded

        Engineering   Dallas–Houston Start-up

        EIS Prepared

        Permitting   Dallas–San Antonio Start-up

        Right-of-Way Acquired   Rapid Growth in Ridership

        Fixed Facilities Construction   New Market Equilibrium Established

        Rolling Stock Acquired   Stable, Predictable Cash Flows

> Real Activities

Founders Equity

    Venture Equity

        Construction Equity

        Tax-Exempt Debt   Old Debt Retirement

        Taxable Debt   New Debt Issued

        Common Dividends Initiated

        Stable Capital Structure Established

> Financing Activities

Source: Casewriter.

A plan to issue debt and equity as needed, in roughly constant proportion, would provide earlier protection for construction lenders, assuming the proportion of equity was high enough. But this raised other concerns. Raising equity repeatedly would be time-consuming and expensive at best, and poor market conditions or unsatisfactory progress could make it difficult or impossible to raise equity for an unfinished project. That in turn might delay or prevent other financing, which almost certainly would delay construction.

A classic project financing approach would bring equity in first and out last, thereby providing maximum protection for lenders. However, raising all the equity up front was expensive. It would leave the company with excess cash until the heavy expenditures started in 1995. In the meantime, excess funds would earn little more than Treasury-bill returns, far less than the return equity investors expected for a risky project.[6] On the other hand, unlike oil-field and mine development projects in which project financing was common, a high-speed rail network was not a depleting asset. It seemed unnecessary to pay off *all* the debt before equity investors began receiving returns. Indeed, once it reached a steady state, the project would have substantial debt capacity that could be used to reduce its tax liability.

[6] In mid-July 1991, the yield on 90-day Treasury bills was 5.6%. For 10- and 30-year Treasury bonds, yields were 8.0% and 8.6%, respectively.

The Financing Program Under Study

The financing plan that had evolved by the summer of 1991 employed a project financing approach with a few important modifications. To minimize expensive overfunding, equity would be raised at the outset in two successive offerings. The first would be an issue of *founders equity*, totaling $60 to $90 million and substantially subscribed by Consortium members and a few selected financial institutions. Subscribers would contribute a total of $30 million initially, with the balance payable as the project progressed. A second issue of common stock, termed *venture equity*, also would be placed privately, sometime in mid-1993. Commitments of between $90 and $120 million would be sought, to be drawn down on a predetermined quarterly schedule through 1993–1994. Gerber and THSRC's advisors believed that venture equity investors would expect compounded returns of 20 to 25% per year. Potential investors included the founders, the venture pools of pension funds, endowments, and insurance companies, and large private investors from Texas and elsewhere. These funds would see the project through most of the major expenditures of the development phase.

To fund construction, $1.5 billion of *construction equity* would be issued at year-end 1994. Unlike prior issues, this one would be fully paid at closing. Conditions permitting, it might be sold as public, 9% pay-in-kind convertible preferred stock that would become cash-pay in 2003. Holders would be expected to convert to common stock once operating cash flow permitted common dividends to rise above the 9% preferred dividend. Construction equity would be priced to give expected returns of 16 to 20% per year, including dividends. If the issue had to be privately placed, it would be sold to pension funds and other large institutions in the United States and abroad. If sold publicly, many mutual funds and smaller investors could be targeted.

The rest of the construction financing would come from a combination of tax-exempt bonds and taxable bank debt. Tax-exempt issues would total $1.5 to $2.0 billion and be used as needed to finance urban and electrical infrastructure. Because they would not be backed by the taxing authority of any government entity, THSRC planned to back them with a nine-year letter-of-credit (LOC) facility, renewable each year for a new nine-year term. This "evergreen" LOC facility would be syndicated among AAA- and AA-rated banks at an expected cost of 1.75%. Each series of tax-exempt bonds would be retired in level payments by the time the LOC facility finally terminated after 18 years. The cost of the bonds, including the LOC, was expected to be 8.75%. Targeted investors included mutual funds, some institutions, and individuals. Although current Texas law capped the number and amounts of tax-exempt financings any one project could undertake in the state, THSRC expected that its request for an exemption from this restriction would be granted.

The taxable bank debt also would be syndicated, as a fixed-rate 18-year term loan with an expected interest rate of 10.5%. The facility would be set up at the end of 1994, to be drawn upon as needed through 1999. In the first two years (1995 to 1996), interest would be capitalized; in the second two, interest only would be paid in cash. Then repayment would follow a 14-year amortization schedule. By funding certain assets with taxable debt, THSRC retained substantial depreciation tax shields that would be forfeited if tax-exempt debt was issued instead.

Debt retirement would accelerate as THSRC swung into full operations at the turn of the century. Debt would be retired rather than refinanced until net operating loss (NOL) carryforwards from early years were used up. By 2005, NOLs would be gone and THSRC was expected to have interest coverage of more than 8x. It could then re-lever itself to a utility-like debt ratio. At that point, if not earlier, it could begin paying common dividends and/or repurchasing stock. The main features of this financing program are summarized in Exhibit 12-6.

EXHIBIT 12-6

SUMMARY OF FINANCING PLAN, JULY 1991 (IN MILLIONS OF DOLLARS)

Year	1992	1993	1994	1995	1996	1997	1998	1999	2000	2001	2002	2003	2004	2005
Equity issues														
Founders equity	30.0	30.0												
Venture equity		55.0	50.0											
Construction equity[a]			1,500.0											
Debt issues														
Tax exempt[b]				350.0	620.0	650.0	280.0	390.0						
Taxable					360.0	1,630.0	1,020.0							
Debt repayments														
Tax exempt[b]				(8.7)	(26.6)	(49.0)	(63.1)	(68.6)	(74.6)	(81.1)	(88.2)	(95.9)	(104.3)	(113.4)
Taxable[c]								(248.3)	(248.3)	(248.3)	(248.3)	(248.3)	(248.3)	(248.3)
Net debt issued				341.3	953.4	2,231.0	1,236.9	73.1	(322.9)	(329.4)	(336.5)	(344.2)	(352.6)	(361.7)
Annual net financing	30.0	85.0	1,550.0	341.3	953.4	2,231.0	1,236.9	73.1						
Cumulative financing	30.0	115.0	1,665.0	2,006.3	2,959.7	5,190.7	6,427.6	6,500.7						

Year	2006	2007	2008	2009	2010	2011	2012	2013	2014	2015	2016	2017	2018
Debt issues													
Taxable[c,d]	1,911.4	456.0	437.1	480.1	528.2	480.6	520.2	563.6	609.5	660.4	713.3	772.0	835.0
Debt repayments													
Tax exempt[b]	(123.4)	(134.2)	(145.9)	(158.7)	(172.6)	(187.7)	(204.1)						
Net debt issued	1,788.0	321.8	291.2	321.4	355.6	292.9	316.1	563.6	609.5	660.4	713.3	772.0	835.0

[a] Construction equity would be issued at the end of 1994 or the beginning of 1995.

[b] Tax-exempt debt is assumed to be issued at the beginning of 1995; the first principal repayment is due during the same year. All tax-exempt issues are serviced with level payments of principal and interest through 2012, when the supporting letter of credit will expire.

[c] Taxable debt *excludes* $37.8 million of capitalized interest during 1996.

[d] Taxable debt is assumed to be entirely refinanced in 2006 and additional, new debt of $1.9 billion issued, bringing total taxable debt outstanding in 2006 to $3.65 billion. Subsequently, taxable debt is issued in amounts required to maintain annual interest coverage (EBITD/interest) of 3×.

Source: Company documents.

EXHIBIT 12-7

PROJECT AND FINANCING CASH FLOWS WITH HYPOTHETICAL MODIFIED FINANCING PROGRAM (IN MILLIONS OF DOLLARS)

Year	1992	1993	1994	1995	1996	1997	1998	1999	2000	2001	2002	2003	2004	2005
1. EBITD (Nominal $)	0.0	0.0	0.0	9.1	28.7	2.0	(52.9)	111.5	464.6	590.9	659.5	735.3	818.6	910.0
2. Tax exempt interest				30.6	84.1	138.7	158.9	153.4	147.4	140.8	133.7	126.0	117.6	108.5
3. Taxable interest						154.6	191.3	191.3	177.6	164.0	150.3	136.7	123.0	109.3
4. Depreciation							79.2	79.2	79.2	79.2	88.6	88.6	88.6	88.6
5. Income (loss) before tax				(21.5)	(55.4)	(291.2)	(482.3)	(312.4)	60.4	206.9	286.9	384.1	489.4	603.6
6. Tax @ 38%													100.6	229.4
7. Net income/(loss)				(21.5)	(55.4)	(291.2)	(482.3)	(312.4)	60.4	206.9	286.9	384.1	388.8	374.2
8. Depreciation							79.2	79.2	79.2	79.2	88.6	88.6	88.6	88.6
9. *Levered operating cash flow*	0.0	0.0	0.0	(21.5)	(55.4)	(291.2)	(403.1)	(233.2)	139.6	286.1	375.5	472.7	477.4	462.8
Expenditures														
10. Preliminary	20.0	20.0												
11. Development		56.0	140.0	84.0										
12. Right of way		13.5	32.1	184.4										
13. Infrastructure (private)				410.6	657.0	574.8								
14. Infrastructure (public)				615.9	985.4	862.3								
15. Rolling stock				226.4	283.0	339.6	283.0							
16. Net working capital additions							9.9	26.3	32.7	12.5	7.4	8.1	8.8	9.6
17. Additional trainsets, overhauls											187.9			
18. Infrastructure renewal														
19. *Total expenditures*	20.0	89.5	172.1	1,521.3	1,925.4	1,776.7	292.9	26.3	32.7	12.5	195.3	8.1	8.8	9.6
Debt Financing														
20. Tax-exempt debt issued				350.0	620.0	650.0	280.0							
21. Taxable debt issued					400.0	1,030.0	350.0							
22. Federal trust funds in/(out)				80.0	750.0	1,200.0	670.0							
23. Tax-exempt debt repaid				(8.7)	(26.6)	(49.0)	(63.1)	(68.6)	(74.6)	(81.1)	(88.2)	(95.9)	(104.3)	(113.4)
24. Taxable debt repaid								(130.1)	(130.1)	(130.1)	(130.1)	(130.1)	(130.1)	(130.1)
25. *Net New Debt*	0.0	0.0	0.0	421.3	1,743.4	2,831.0	1,236.9	(198.7)	(204.7)	(211.3)	(218.3)	(226.1)	(234.5)	(243.6)
26. Total private debt outstanding				341.3	1,334.7	2,965.7	3,532.6	3,333.9	3,129.2	2,918.0	2,699.7	2,473.7	2,239.3	1,995.8
27. Federal financing outstanding				80.0	830.0	2,030.0	2,700.0	2,700.0	2,700.0	2,700.0	2,700.0	2,700.0	2,700.0	2,700.0
28. Total debt outstanding				421.3	2,164.7	4,995.7	6,232.6	6,033.9	5,829.3	5,618.0	5,399.7	5,173.7	4,939.3	4,695.8
29. *Total Funding Need (cash flow)*	(20.0)	(89.5)	(172.1)	(1,121.5)	(237.4)	763.1	540.9	(458.2)	(97.8)	62.3	(38.1)	238.5	234.1	209.6
30. Use of cash savings from prior year	0.0	10.0	5.5	883.4	1.9	0.0	0.0	0.0	0.0	0.0	0.0	0.0	0.0	0.0
31. Increase in cash savings (cash use)	(10.0)	(5.5)	(883.4)	(1.9)	0.0	0.0	0.0	0.0	0.0	0.0	0.0	0.0	0.0	0.0
32. *Equity Cash Flow*	(30.0)	(85.0)	(1,050.0)	(240.0)	(235.5)	763.1	540.9	(458.2)	(97.8)	62.3	(38.1)	238.5	234.1	209.6

(*Continued*)

EXHIBIT 12-7 (Continued)

Year	1992	1993	1994	1995	1996	1997	1998	1999	2000	2001	2002	2003	2004	2005
Equity Financing														
33. Founders equity issued	30.0	30.0												
34. Venture equity issued		55.0	50.0											
35. Construction equity issued			1,000.0											
36. Other equity issued				240.0	235.5									
37. *Total Equity Issued*	30.0	85.0	1,050.0	240.0	235.5	0.0	0.0	0.0	0.0	0.0	0.0	0.0	0.0	0.0

Year	2006	2007	2008	2009	2010	2011	2012	2013	2014	2015	2016	2017	2018
1. EBITD (Nominal $)	1,149.5	1,293.2	1,430.8	1,582.1	1,748.5	1,899.8	2,063.7	2,241.3	2,433.2	2,641.3	2,865.9	3,109.1	3,372.1
2. Tax exempt interest	98.6	87.8	76.0	63.3	49.4	34.3	17.9						
3. Taxable interest	383.2	431.1	476.9	527.4	582.8	633.3	687.9	747.1	811.1	880.4	955.3	1,036.4	1,124.0
4. Depreciation	103.3	106.9	122.9	123.2	123.7	128.2	132.9	138.1	143.5	149.1	155.3	156.7	78.9
5. Income (loss) before tax	564.5	667.4	755.0	868.3	992.6	1,104.1	1,225.0	1,356.1	1,478.7	1,611.7	1,755.3	1,916.0	2,169.2
6. Tax @ 38%	214.5	253.6	286.9	329.9	377.2	419.5	465.5	515.3	561.9	612.5	667.0	728.1	824.3
7. Net income/(loss)	350.0	413.8	468.1	538.3	615.4	684.5	759.5	840.8	916.8	999.3	1,088.3	1,187.9	1,344.9
8. Depreciation	103.3	106.9	122.9	123.2	123.7	128.2	132.9	138.1	143.5	149.1	155.3	156.7	78.9
9. *Levered operating cash flow*	453.3	520.7	591.0	661.5	739.1	812.7	892.4	978.9	1,060.3	1,148.4	1,243.6	1,344.6	1,423.8
Expenditures													
10. Preliminary													
11. Development													
12. Right of way													
13. Infrastructure (private)													
14. Infrastructure (public)													
15. Rolling stock													
16. Net working capital additions	10.6	11.5	12.6	13.7	15.0	13.9	15.0	16.2	17.4	18.8	20.2	21.8	23.5
17. Additional trainsets, overhauls	287.8	66.6	314.3			79.5	83.0	86.8	90.7	94.8	99.0		
18. Infrastructure renewal	5.6	5.8	6.1	6.4	10.0	10.4	10.9	16.3	17.0	17.8	26.0	27.1	28.4
19. *Total expenditures*	304.0	83.9	333.0	20.1	25.0	103.8	108.9	119.3	125.1	131.4	145.2	48.9	51.9

(Continued)

EXHIBIT 12-7 (Continued)

Year	2006	2007	2008	2009	2010	2011	2012	2013	2014	2015	2016	2017	2018
Debt Financing													
20. Tax-exempt debt issued													
21. Taxable debt issued	2,738.2	456.0	437.1	480.1	528.2	480.6	520.2	563.6	609.5	660.4	713.3	772.0	835.0
22. Federal trust funds in/(out)	(2,700.0)												
23. Tax-exempt debt repaid	(123.4)	(134.2)	(145.9)	(158.7)	(172.6)	(187.7)	(204.1)						
24. Taxable debt repaid													
25. *Net New Debt*	(85.2)	321.9	291.1	321.5	355.6	292.9	316.2	563.6	609.5	660.4	713.3	772.0	835.0
26. Total private debt outstanding	4,610.6	4,932.4	5,223.6	5,545.0	5,900.6	6,193.5	6,509.6	7,073.2	7,682.7	8,343.1	9,056.4	9,828.4	10,663.4
27. Federal financing outstanding	0.0	0.0	0.0	0.0	0.0	0.0	0.0	0.0	0.0	0.0	0.0	0.0	0.0
28. Total debt outstanding	4,610.6	4,932.4	5,223.6	5,545.0	5,900.6	6,193.5	6,509.6	7,073.2	7,682.7	8,343.1	9,056.4	9,828.4	10,663.4
29. *Total Funding Need (cash flow)*	64.1	758.7	549.1	962.9	1,069.7	1,001.8	1,099.7	1,423.2	1,544.7	1,677.4	1,811.7	2,067.7	2,206.9
30. Use of cash savings from prior year	0.0	0.0	0.0	0.0	0.0	0.0	0.0	0.0	0.0	0.0	0.0	0.0	0.0
31. Increase in cash savings (cash use)	0.0	0.0	0.0	0.0	0.0	0.0	0.0	0.0	0.0	0.0	0.0	0.0	0.0
32. *Equity Cash Flow*	64.1	758.7	549.1	962.9	1,069.7	1,001.8	1,099.7	1,423.2	1,544.7	1,677.4	1,811.7	2,067.7	2,206.9
Equity Financing													
33. Founders equity issued													
34. Venture equity issued													
35. Construction equity issued													
36. Other equity issued													
37. *Total Equity Issued*	0.0	0.0	0.0	0.0	0.0	0.0	0.0	0.0	0.0	0.0	0.0	0.0	0.0

Notes:

Line 1   From Exhibit 12-3.

Line 2   Assumes each new series of tax-tax-exempt debt costs 8.75% and is retired in level yearly payments from the date of issue through 2012.

Line 3   Assumes outstanding taxable debt pays interest at 10.5%.

Line 4   From Exhibit 12-3.

Line 5   Line 1 minus the sum of lines 2–4; ignores the interest income on the cash savings account (line 31).

Line 6   Assumes net operating losses are carried forward and used to offset future taxable income through 2004. Assumes no investment or other tax credits.

Line 7   Line 5 minus line 6.

Line 8   Equals line 4.

Line 9   Line 7 plus line 8.

Line 10–19   From Exhibit 12-3.

Line 20–23   Assumed, under hypothetical revisions to the current financing plan, shown in Exhibit 12-6. Taxable debt is issued in 2006 to refinance federal trust fund balance, and to bring total debt to a level such that EBITD/Total Taxable Interest = 3.0.

Line 23   Aggregate repayments of all outstanding tax-exempt series.

Line 24   Taxable debt is retired on a straight-line, 14-year amortization schedule with payments beginning in 1999. This schedule is effectively discontinued in 2006, following the refinancing.

Line 25   Sum of lines 20–24.

Line 26   Cumulative debt issues (lines 20, 21, and 22) net cumulative repayments (lines 23 and 24).

Line 27   Cumulative federal trust funds received and repaid (line 22).

Line 28   Line 26 plus line 27.

Line 29   Line 9 minus line 19 plus line 25. Does not include terminal value in year 2018.

Line 30   The amount of cash available to meet current-year funding need (line 31 from the prior year)

Line 31   A plug number equal to the difference between equity invested (line 37) less the funding need (line 29) plus cash balances (line 30). Does not include terminal value.

Line 32   Sum of line 29 to 31. Does not include terminal value.

Line 33–36   Assumed, under hypothetical revisions to the current financing plan, shown in Exhibit 12-6.

Line 37   Sum of lines 33 to 36.

Source: Casewriter.

EXHIBIT 12-8

NET PRESENT VALUE OF EQUITY CASH FLOWS

Discount Rate	NPV of Equity Cash Flows	Discount Rate	NPV of Equity Cash Flows	Discount Rate	NPV of Equity Cash Flows
10.0%	$4,626	15.5	561	20.5	(168)
10.5	3,834	16.0	437	21.0	(202)
11.0	3,190	16.5	330	21.5	(232)
11.5	2,662	17.0	236	22.0	(258)
12.0	2,223	17.5	153	22.5	(281)
12.5	1,856	18.0	81	23.0	(302)
13.0	1,547	18.5	18	23.5	(320)
13.5	1,285	19.0	(38)	24.0	(336)
14.0	1,061	19.5	(87)	24.5	(350)
14.5	869	20.0	(130)	25.0	(362)
15.0	704				

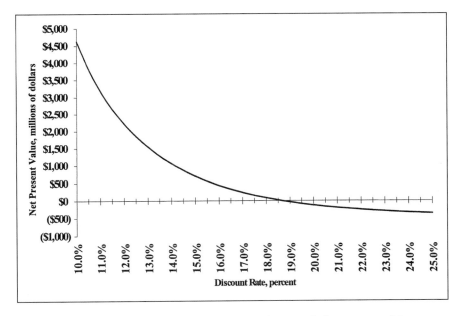

Note: Net present values are computed as the present value, at each discount rate, of the equity cash flows presented in Exhibit 12-7 together with a terminal value. The terminal value in each case is the discounted value (at each rate) in 2018 of a growing perpetuity. The first (year 2019) cash flow of the perpetuity equals $2,206.9 × 1.045, and it is assumed to grow at 4.50% per year.

Source: Casewriter.

Possible Modifications

Gerber was pursuing ideas to address several remaining problems. One problem was that raising $1.5 billion in equity in late 1994 or early 1995 left the company expensively overfunded for a while. Another was that interest charges on the debt issued to fund construction created huge NOLs that might expire before taxable income in later years offset them. Both these problems reduced expected returns to the Consortium investors and distorted the company's capital structure and payout policies. Other problems might or might not prove significant. For example, it was unclear in 1991 how much AAA- and AA-rated banking capacity actually would be available for underwriting nine-year LOCs. Similarly, THSRC's ability to syndicate the bank debt and place the $1.5 billion equity issue might be affected by investors' perceptions of the (mis)fortunes of the Eurotunnel, which employed a similar, though more primitive, financing approach. Because of early flaws in its development plan, Eurotunnel had recently encountered significant cost overruns that forced lenders and equity investors to supply more capital or have their ownership diluted.

As one potential adjustment to the financing program, Gerber was monitoring the availability of financing assistance from the U.S. government, which in previous decades had actively assisted the development of the nation's highway and airport systems. Such assistance was not currently available to THSRC, but the political prospects for treating new high-speed rail projects the same as other major transportation infrastructure projects seemed quite favorable. In 1991, the U.S. Interstate Highway system was finally completed, which might leave budgetary room for other new transportation initiatives. More generally, there seemed to be a consensus among citizens that the government had lately neglected transportation infrastructure, which had deteriorated as a result. Many would-be lawmakers were planning election campaigns that stressed the need for increased federal spending in this area, both to improve the nation's infrastructure and to create construction jobs. Moreover, a growing number of voters and politicians felt that "partnerships" between the government and profit-seeking private companies could perform many tasks more efficiently than could the government alone.

Exhibit 12-7 shows how THSRC's financing program might be modified if federal assistance became available. It incorporates $2.7 billion in federal financing over the four years 1995–1998 in lieu of private taxable debt. These "trust" funds are then repaid to the government for use in other projects as cash flow permits, but in any case by 2006, when THSRC would be able to refinance the federal contribution in the capital markets. As a consequence, the required equity issue in 1994–1995 drops from $1.5 to $1.0 billion, which mitigates the overfunding problem. Less taxable debt is issued in 1996–1998, and none at all in 1999. Because interest charges would be lower, NOLs would be lower and THSRC would return to tax-paying status earlier. The resulting cash flows for equity investors are shown at the bottom of Exhibit 12-7. The net present values of these equity cash flows, over a range of discount rates, are presented in Exhibit 12-8.

If there were no objectionable preconditions attached, it clearly would be attractive to use whatever federal resources were available. However, the best way to modify the rest of the financing program, given the availability of some federal assistance, was much less clear. There were many possible alternatives to the scheme presented in Exhibit 12-7. Furthermore, before Gerber and his team proceeded with implementation, they needed to ensure that THSRC was prepared for obvious contingencies. The financing program had to remain viable in the event that federal assistance was not available, or became available later than THSRC might wish.

13

Contractual Innovation in the U.K. Energy Markets: Enron Europe, The Eastern Group, and the Sutton Bridge Project

Co-written with Peter Tufano

On December 4, 1996, Stewart Seeligson of Enron Europe and Paul Danielsen of The Eastern Group shook hands and said goodbye as they left yet another late night negotiating session. These two men and their colleagues had met at least three times weekly over the past two months as they attempted to reach an agreement on an innovative business relationship. Seeligson, who had been transferred recently from the risk management department of Enron's global headquarters in Houston, was a member of Enron's asset development team in London. Danielsen was the Head of Contract Trading at Eastern Electricity, the fourth-largest power generator and one of the largest marketers of natural gas in the United Kingdom. The deal that had occupied their attention would deliver to Eastern much of the economics of building a new combined cycle gas turbine (CCGT) power station.

The innovative deal would give Eastern the right to run a "virtual" power plant at will. Enron would sell to Eastern a long-term option to convert natural gas into electricity. Enron planned to hedge its exposure by constructing an actual CCGT plant and by trading in the gas and electric markets. While Eastern's right to receive power proceeds and Enron's right to operate the plant were similar in character, there was no legal or physical connection between Enron's physical plant and Eastern's virtual plant.

Professors Benjamin C. Esty and Peter Tufano, assisted by Research Associate Matthew Bailey, prepared this case. HBS cases are developed solely as the basis for class discussion. Cases are not intended to serve as endorsements, sources of primary data, or illustrations of effective or ineffective management.

Seeligson and Danielsen had agreed on a 13-page, single-spaced term sheet describing the proposed deal, but still had to resolve many issues before they could draft a more definitive agreement. This structure was vastly different from the traditional independent power plant (IPP) structure, and both men would have to convince their superiors of its wisdom—once they had explained how it worked.

THE U.K. ENERGY MARKETS

Based on the principle that energy was "the lifeblood of economic activity and social welfare," the European Commission (EC) favored an integrated energy market with full and open competition in both gas and electricity. In fact, the Commission was drafting a Directive in late 1996 that required energy deregulation for all member countries. The United Kingdom, which began the process of deregulation with the passage of the Electricity Act of 1983 and, more recently, the Electricity Act of 1989, was ahead of the EC in terms of deregulation. The 1989 Act mandated privatization of the U.K. power market and restructuring along functional lines according to a phased-in schedule. Similarly, the Natural Gas Acts of 1986 and of 1995 created the structure for a deregulated gas market. Given this rapidly changing business environment, both Enron and Eastern saw integration of energy markets as offering enormous commercial opportunities.

THE POWER MARKET

Deregulation in the power market introduced competition at almost every stage in the industry: generation, transmission, distribution, and supply. Generation involved the production of electricity. Although the United Kingdom had over 40 licensed generators of power, three firms (National Power plc, PowerGen plc, and British Energy plc) accounted for 77% of power generation in 1995.[1] Coal and oil were burned to produce 40% of generation capacity, nuclear combustion accounted for 25%, gas accounted for 25%, and the remainder was obtained through imports or other nonfossil fuels. To permit economies of scale, regulators mandated that transmission—the transfer of electricity across high-voltage wires known as the "grid"—be carried out by a single firm, the National Grid Company. Distribution, the delivery of electricity via low-voltage wires to end users, and supply, the sale of electricity to consumers, were done by Regional Electric Companies (RECs). The Electricity Act of 1989 created 12 RECs and made them responsible for supplying electricity to customers who had not yet been phased into the new competitive market. Eastern was the largest of the 12 RECs.

Total U.K. electricity sales were 280,000 gigawatt hours (GWh) in 1995 and were growing about 1% per year. The price of electricity was determined by the "pool," an auction mechanism in which all generators participated. Each day by 10:00 A.M., generators submitted schedules detailing how much power they were willing to deliver for each half-hour time slot for the next day and at what price.[2] Arranged in ascending order based on price (in "merit order"), these bids formed the supply schedule for power for each half-hour period.

The National Grid Company forecasted daily demand based on historical models of actual demand. Each day at 4:00 P.M., it announced the next day's "pool" price for

---

[1] Electricity Association, *Electricity Industry Review* (January 1999).

[2] Given the concentration of generating capacity in the United Kingdom, there was some political debate over whether electric prices represented "fair" market prices.

each half-hour period, which was equal to the bid price from the most expensive generating unit dispatched (instructed to generate electricity during that time slot) in order to meet system demand. The cost of this marginal generator was known as the System Marginal Price (SMP). All generators selected to provide power during a given half-hour period received the same Pool Purchase Price (PPP), an amount equal to the sum of SMP plus a capacity payment that reflected the projected tightness of supply. From the demand side, consumers paid the Pool Selling Price (PSP), an amount equal to the sum of the PPP plus an "uplift" component that reflected the cost of maintaining the system; uplift added a fairly constant 8% to the PPP. In 1995 and 1996, the average SMP was £19.40 per megawatt hour (MWh), PPP was £23.86 per MWh, and PSP was £25.90 per MWh. The Appendix presents data on electric and gas markets, and in particular Appendix Exhibit 13-A1 provides a plot of the average daily PPP over the period from 1994 to 1996.

Given the pool mechanism, electricity prices varied every half-hour during the day. Appendix Exhibit 13-A2 reports the mean and median half-hourly prices over the previous two years, for both weekdays and weekends. Prices fluctuated in response to a variety of short-term, seasonal, and long-run factors, including variations in the cost of fuel (e.g., gas vs. oil), weather, plant failures, plant utilization rates, holidays, changes in generation technology, and the economy's rate of long-run growth. During the 1990s, the monthly average PPP had ranged from as low as £12/MWh in early 1995, to as high as £50/MWh when the system was stressed by strikes and failures of certain peak load generators. This variation in monthly average prices masked extraordinary variation in the daily and half-hourly intraday prices, as measured by the volatility of energy prices (see Appendix Exhibit 13-A3).

RECs bought power from the pool at the volatile PPP, and sold power to consumers at less volatile prices. They were therefore exposed to fluctuations in power prices. To hedge out PPP fluctuations, participants in the power market had begun to create risk management contracts. Power traders, like those at Enron and Eastern, bought and sold spot electricity along with forward and option contracts. Power traders were faced with the challenge—and the opportunity—of dealing in rapidly changing and volatile markets. There was some liquidity in forward contracts for maturities of four to five years, but longer dated forward contracts were infrequent, with only perhaps 10 to 20 transactions maturing beyond five years. Because it was not possible to store electricity, even rudimentary forward curves for power were highly volatile. For very long-term forward contracts, the forward price was often thought to be related to the operating costs that would be incurred by newly built efficient power plants. Given the large uncertainty in longer-term forward curves, the bid-ask spreads for these contracts were substantially larger than for shorter-dated contracts. Appendix Exhibit 13-A4 reflects one set of estimates for forward prices as of late 1996, which show a slight long-run reduction in the forward prices over time.

Without information on actively traded option prices, it was not possible to extract implied volatilities of electric prices. However one could estimate the historical volatility of power. Naïve calculations of historical volatilities showed extraordinary levels of volatility, peaking above 1,000% per annum for intraday prices (one half-hour period to the same period the next day), 600% for volatility of average daily prices, and 200% for volatilities of average weekly prices. However, these calculations failed to take into account the extreme regularities in electric prices (due to predictable intraday or seasonal patterns) and the strong mean reversion in prices. For example, in Appendix Exhibit 13-A1, there are large spikes in the price of power in late 1995 and early 1996. The price rapidly subsided after these spikes, consistent with strong mean reversion of prices.

After controlling for these factors, the volatilities acknowledged by traders were considerably lower—under 50% per annum for short dated options as shown in Appendix Exhibit 13-A4. By this one set of estimates, volatilities for very long dated power options could be under 10% to 15%, considerably below the levels of volatility currently being experienced. This reduction in volatility over time was, however, by no means certain.

Despite the ongoing regulatory and political discussions about how to set pool prices, both Enron and Eastern believed that the informational and strategic benefits of early involvement in power (and gas) markets were substantial. For this reason, they were committed to the markets and staffed their trading operations accordingly.

THE NATURAL GAS MARKET

Just as deregulation created a legal separation between the segments of the power industry, it separated the transportation (pipelines) from the supply of gas. Transco managed the National Transmission System (NTS) and was responsible for setting prices for gas transportation. There were approximately 50 gas suppliers, or marketers, in the United Kingdom in a market that had annual sales of £10 billion.

In the short run, gas prices, like electricity prices, fluctuated in response to temporary supply and demand imbalances. Unlike electricity, however, gas could be stored. As a result, gas prices were much less volatile than power prices, especially on an intraday basis. A second difference between the two markets was that gas indices were set daily instead of half hourly. Appendix Exhibits 13-A5 and 13-A6 show the price and historical volatility of U.K. gas, respectively. During 1995 and 1996, the average price of gas per MMBtu was £1.15 and £1.28, respectively. In the longer term, there were different scenarios about how tight gas supplies might be relative to demand, as a function of economic growth, adoption of gas technology for power generation, and new supplies of natural gas.

Traders created a variety of contracts that allowed gas suppliers and consumers to adjust their exposures to price fluctuations.[3] As of late 1996, there were no exchange-traded contracts on gas delivered in the United Kingdom. However, private gas traders and marketers offered over-the-counter (OTC) contracts including natural gas swaps, forward contracts, and options. Public quotations of these forward contracts were reported on maturities of one year or less. The market for longer-dated forwards and options was relatively thin. Appendix Exhibit 13-A7 reports a set of representative forward prices and option volatilities as of late 1996.

The relationship between gas and electricity prices was complex and changing. Gas was used for purposes other than electricity generation, and electric power prices were set by the cost of the marginal power producer, which in many cases did not use natural gas as a fuel. As a result, short-run correlations between gas and electricity prices were under 10% at the daily level and approximately 0% at the monthly level. Nevertheless, industry analysts expected the correlation to be much higher, possibility as high as 20% to 40% in the longer term as a greater fraction of electricity was generated from gas.

THE EASTERN GROUP

The Hanson Group PLC, a diversified U.K. holding company, purchased The Eastern Group in August 1995 for £2.5 billion. The Eastern Group, the holding company for

---

[3] See the Harvard Business School case study entitled "Enron Gas Services" (No. 294-076) for a description of contracting in the natural gas industry in the United States.

EXHIBIT 13-1A

FINANCIAL SUMMARIES FOR THE EASTERN GROUP
(ALL FIGURES IN £ MILLIONS)

	1995/1996[a]	1994/1995	1993/1994
Revenue	£2,119	£2,061	£1,846
Cost of Sales	1,709	1,507	1,336
Gross Profit	410	554	511
Operating Costs	367	302	316
Operating Profit	43	252	195
Profit Before Tax	258	204	177
Profit After Tax	220	141	123
Total Assets	2,364	2,053	1,545
Long-term Liabilities	682	487	—
Shareholders' Equity (Book Value)	1,189	832	870
Shareholders' Equity (Market Value)[b]	N/A	1,424	1,783
Operating Cash Flow	53	199	431
Debt-to-Equity (Book Value)	57%	58%	0%
Debt-to-Total Capital (Book Value)	36%	31%	0%
Interest Coverage[c]	6.62	7.58	11.12
Bond Credit Rating	Aa3	Aa1	Aa1

[a] Fiscal year ending March 31.

[b] The value of Eastern is not available for March 1996 due to its acquisition by Hanson plc.

[c] As measured by the ratio of earnings before interest, tax, depreciation and amortization (EBITDA) to total interest.

Source: Adapted from Global Access and Bloomberg.

Eastern Electricity and Eastern Natural Gas, served more than 3 million customers in northern London and eastern England. Exhibit 13-1a provides summary financial data on The Eastern Group.

Eastern's business model was more extensive than merely distributing electricity to consumers, its formal role as a REC. When Eastern was privatized in 1990, James Smith, Eastern Group's chief executive officer at the time, announced his intention to create a diversified energy company with new generating capacity and natural gas resources. The logic behind the firm's diversification strategy was to combine gas supply with gas-fired electricity generation to "arbitrage between the two (markets) depending on price."[4] While over 80% of its profits in 1994 had come from its traditional regulated electric distribution businesses, the firm's goal was to have more than half of its profits come from deregulated businesses by 2000. Senior Eastern executives defined the scope of the firm's activity as including "the entire value chain for electricity—from fuel source via the electricity pool to customers' meters."

To accomplish this goal, the firm expanded its operations into both power generation and gas upstream trading and supply. In 1996, Eastern expanded its generating

[4] David Wighton, "Hanson's Bid for Eastern Group," *Financial Times*, August 1, 1995.

capacity by acquiring 6,000 MW of coal-fired generating capacity from National Power and PowerGen after they were required to divest the plants by the Office of Electricity Regulation (OFFER), the U.K. power regulator. The forced divestiture of coal-fired plants, plants that were higher in merit order and were more likely to set pool prices, was done to prevent manipulation by the largest generators who controlled more than 90% of the generating capacity that typically set pool prices. According to Eastern executives, these acquisitions were "a major step towards enhancing competition in generation. This mid-merit and peak capacity complements the successful baseload generation of our Peterborough plant, giving us the ability to compete vigorously across all sections of the generation market."[5] With this capacity, Eastern became the United Kingdom's third largest fossil-fuel generator and its fourth largest power generator.

To permit this acquisition, OFFER relaxed Eastern's "own generation" limit of 1,000 MW, a regulatory restriction on the amount of generating capacity Eastern could own. Collectively, the 12 RECs were allowed to own 8,200 MW of generating capacity, with individual limits ranging from 400 MW to 1,000 MW. The regulators imposed these limits to prevent vertical integration from electricity generation to supply. Eastern already had stations under operation or in construction totaling over 850 MW, so its acquisition of 6,000 MW was unlikely to be repeated in the near future.[6] Like Eastern, other RECs were near their "own generation" limits and were asking the regulators for additional generating capacity.

Eastern also expanded into natural gas during the early 1990s. In what the popular press termed the "dash for gas," Eastern, Enron, and many other firms, sensing opportunities in the rapidly changing gas market, began negotiating for gas supplies. Eastern executives explained their decision:

> Gas is an important part of our strategy . . . all our businesses slot together in a supply chain of electricity. While competition in gas trading may be fierce, we believe our strategy of taking positions in each step of the gas trading chain, from production to retailing, has been, and will continue to be, justified by our results.[7]

As part of this strategy, Eastern signed several large "take-or-pay" contracts and took equity positions in a number of other North Sea fields.[8] With this gas, Eastern then launched a major marketing campaign in March 1996. The strategy paid off in terms of market share as Eastern moved from being the sixth-largest U.K. gas supplier in 1995 to the second largest in late 1996. Eastern's activities in the gas and electric businesses were seen as being strategically related in that it could provide gas and bid for electricity. One Eastern executive noted, "Our emphasis is to create a lot of options, and call the right options at the right time."[9]

---

[5] Universal News Services, "PowerGen and Eastern Sign Heads of Agreement on Disposal of 2000 MW of Plant," September 18, 1995. A "baseload" plant is a plant with low variable costs that is operated almost all of the time; a "peaking" plant typically has high variable costs and is operated only when the price of electricity is high.

[6] "U.K. Okays Eastern Group purchase of 4,000 MW from National Power," *Electric Utility Week*, June 10, 1994, p. 15. Some observers thought it curious that the Department of Trade and Industry permitted Eastern's vertical integration into generation at a time when it was blocking National Power's and PowerGen's attempts to vertically integrate into distribution through acquisitions of other RECs.

[7] Noni Stacey, "Eastern Eyes Gas Opportunity," *The Scotsman*, June 27, 1995, quoting Eric Anstee, Eastern Group finance director.

[8] In a "take-or-pay" contract, a firm enters into the obligation to pay for a certain fixed quantity of gas at fixed prices. A take-or-pay contract is similar to a forward contract. Enron had also entered into similar contracts for North Sea gas at roughly this same time.

[9] David Knott, "New Players Cut a Swath in U.K.'s Liberalized Gas Market," *Oil and Gas Journal*, October 14, 1996, p. 23.

One potential complication at this time was the fact that the Hanson Group was restructuring its businesses in anticipation of divesting several of them. According to the plan, Hanson was going to spin-off Eastern and Peabody Coal, the world's largest private coal producer, into a separate energy company sometime in early to mid 1997. In preparation for a possible divestiture, Eastern was reorganizing its internal operations.

ENRON CORPORATION[10]

Enron Corporation was one of the world's largest integrated natural gas and electricity companies. Led by Ken Lay, its chairman and chief executive officer, and Jeff Skilling, its newly appointed president and chief operating officer, Enron engaged in exploration and production, gas transportation and distribution, and wholesale energy operations and services. Exhibit 13-1b provides summary financial data on Enron Corporation.

In late 1996, Enron was organized into six units: Enron Oil and Gas, which was one of the largest independent oil and gas companies in the United States; Enron Gas Pipeline Group, which operated the firm's U.S. interstate pipelines; Enron Ventures, which provided engineering and construction services; Enron International, which provided merchant and finance services for international integrated energy projects; Enron Renewable Energy Corporation, a supplier of renewable energy; and Enron Capital and Trade Resources (ECT).[11] ECT itself was a firm with many different operating activities, including the following:

- Largest buyer and seller of natural gas in North America
- Largest nonregulated merchant of power in the United States
- Owner and operator of intrastate pipelines
- Manager of the world's largest portfolio of natural gas risk management contracts
- Significant supplier of energy financial services
- Owner and operator of the world's largest natural gas-fired plant in Teesside, United Kingdom
- Largest nonregulated merchant of natural gas in the United Kingdom
- Largest nonregulated merchant of power in the United Kingdom and Nordic region

Enron's scope of business activity ranged from long-term projects to construct and operate power plants to minute-by-minute trading of gas and power. The firm was known for its creativity in solving customer needs and its extreme aggressiveness in attacking new business opportunities. For example, the Wholesale Energy Operations and Services group was one of the leading innovators of a wide variety of risk management and financing contracts in the energy sector. The firm's asset development group tackled some of the most complex power projects around the world including the 1,875 MW power plant in Teesside, England and the 2,450 MW plant in Dabhol, India.[12] Enron strove to link different, and sometimes distant, parts of the firm. In the United States, traders and pipeline experts collaborated to exploit price differentials between gas and

[10] See the Harvard Business School case study entitled "Enron Gas Services" (No. 294-076) for a description of Enron's activities in the U.S. gas markets in the early 1990s.

[11] Skilling had founded the group within the firm that became ECT and was its chairman and CEO before being promoted to president and COO of Enron Corp. in late 1996.

[12] The Harvard Business School cases "Enron Development Corporation: The Dabhol Power Project in Maharashtra, India A & B" (No. 797-085 and No. 797-086) describe the Dabhol project.

EXHIBIT 13-1B

FINANCIAL SUMMARIES FOR ENRON CORPORATION (ALL FIGURES IN $ MILLIONS)[a]

	1995/1996	1994/1995	1993/1994
Revenue	$13,289	$9,189	$8,984
Cost of Sales	10,478	6,733	6,517
Gross Profit	2,811	2,456	2,467
Operating Costs	2,121	1,838	1,751
Operating Profit	690	618	716
Profit Before Tax	855	805	620
Profit After Tax	584	520	453
Total Assets	16,137	13,239	11,966
Long-term Liabilities	7,359	6,716	6,121
Shareholders' Equity (Book Value)	5,070	4,091	3,547
Shareholders' Equity (Market Value)	11,038	9,587	8,326
Operating Cash Flow	1,040	−15	504
Debt-to-Equity (Book Value)	145%	164%	172%
Debt-to-Total Capital (Book Value)	40%	43%	44%
Interest Coverage	4.07	3.48	4.10
Bond Credit Rating	Baa2	Baa2	Baa2

[a] On November 29, 1996, the sterling/dollar exchange rate was $1.6820 per pound sterling.

Source: Adapted from Global Access and Bloomberg.

power prices in distant locations. Looking forward, as the oil, gas, and power sectors converged, the organization would need to find ways to ensure that its various groups worked together to capitalize on new business opportunities.

The proposed transaction with Eastern was attractive from this perspective because it linked the firm's asset development group with its trading operations in a novel fashion. Enron Development Corporation (EDC), Enron's asset development group, had been very successful developing energy infrastructure projects around the world. Historically, this group had very little integration with ECT, Enron's risk management division, which had operated in North America until 1994. But as it became clear that Europe was deregulating its gas and electricity markets, ECT assumed responsibility for the United Kingdom in 1994 and then all of Europe in late 1996.

Prior to 1996, ECT had acted as only a provider of risk management services to the energy markets. Members of the group viewed energy assets, such as power stations and the companies that owned them, as potential counterparties only. Yet this kind of thinking was beginning to change as the traders began to think of assets as potential tools for risk management. Based on this premise, ECT created its own asset development team in Europe comprised of people from EDC with traditional asset development experience and people, like Seeligson, transferred from ECT with energy risk management expertise.

SUTTON BRIDGE AS A TRADITIONAL IPP

In 1995, Enron Europe's asset development team paid $20 million to a consortium of investors for the option to build a 700 MW power plant near Sutton Bridge, Lincolnshire, a town 140 kilometers north of London. The consortium had obtained all of the necessary permits and licenses to develop a CCGT plant but decided to sell the option after it was unable to hedge the electric price risk.

Initially, Enron envisioned structuring the project as an independent power plant (IPP) similar to the structures EDC had successfully used in other regulated markets. Typically, IPP developers created a separate project company and financed it on a non-recourse basis, which kept the asset off of their balance sheet. The developer's job was to assemble a "contractual bundle" to manage the project's key risks. Richard DiMichele, head of Enron's asset development group, was in charge of negotiating these contracts for Sutton Bridge. An *engineering, procurement, and construction (EPC) contract* would ensure that the plant was built as specified for a set price and by a certain date. An *operating and maintenance contract* would provide for the physical operations of the plant, typically at a fixed fee. A *gas supply agreement* would ensure the plant had access to gas at predetermined prices and quantities. And finally, an offtake or *power purchase agreement (PPA)*, whereby a customer would agree to buy a given quantity of electricity at a given price, would eliminate electric price risk. In regulated and developing markets, the government is typically the counterparty to the PPA; in deregulated markets, private companies—other generators, a distributor, or a large end user—were likely counterparties.[13]

These four contracts were designed to transfer various project risks to parties that were better suited than the development company to handle them. For example, the EPC contract would transfer construction risk to an experienced builder while the PPA would transfer electricity price risk to one of the major electric utilities. From the project's perspective, the goal was to eliminate market risk through long-term, fixed-price contracts. Once the contracts were in place, the IPP would generate an annuity income stream equal to the difference between electricity revenues and gas supply, operating, and financing expenses. Their steady income stream meant IPPs could support highly leveraged capital structures; they often had debt-to-total capitalization ratios of 70% to 90%. In contrast, merchant power plants (MPPs) retained gas and/or electric price exposure. Enron's asset development team initially began negotiating power purchase agreements with representatives from three utilities—Scottish Power, Nuclear Energy, and The Eastern Group—with the intent of constructing an IPP. Because many utilities had lost money on previous PPAs when technological changes lowered generating costs well below the contracted price, they were reluctant to sign long-term, fixed-price contracts. To even consider signing a PPA, they would generally demand equity ownership (if allowed by the regulators). The downside of shared ownership was that it complicated up-front negotiations as well as ongoing operating decisions.

The IPP structure had other drawbacks from Enron's perspective. Given the extensive risk mitigation, the plant could easily turn out to be a low-risk/low-return investment. The combination of a development fee, which might equal 4% of the total investment, and an annuity spread from on-going operations produced acceptable, though not exceptional, returns. More importantly, the structure did not capitalize on Enron's strengths in trading and risk management. For these reasons, the Enron and

---

[13] The Harvard Business School case, "Tennessee Valley Authority: Option Purchase Agreements" (No. 296-038), details a form of power purchase contract in which a large generator sought to buy options on power. Enron was one of its counterparties in this transaction.

Eastern teams began to contemplate a different structure in September 1996 that would better meet their respective needs and better capitalize on their respective strengths.

SUTTON BRIDGE: THE ALTERNATIVE PROPOSAL

Under the alternative proposal, Eastern would have a contractual interest in a synthetic or "virtual" plant, but no direct or indirect legal ownership whatsoever in a physical plant, nor any obligation to buy power at fixed prices. Instead, Eastern would have the right, but not the obligation, to deliver natural gas and receive cash payments equal to the market value of a certain amount of electricity. Unlike an IPP where Eastern was committed to buy a fixed quantity of electricity, this contract would allow Eastern to receive electricity proceeds only when it was economic to do so. If gas prices were low relative to electric prices, Eastern would exercise its contractual right to receive electricity proceeds. However, if gas prices were high relative to electric prices, Eastern could sell the gas in the market rather than convert it into electricity.

The alternative proposal involved two independent, though economically linked, Capacity and Tolling Agreements (CTAs), agreements that gave parties the right to exchange one commodity for the value of another. Exhibit 13-2 illustrates the fundamental

---

EXHIBIT 13-2

SCHEMATIC OF EASTERN–ENRON–SUTTON BRIDGE CTAs

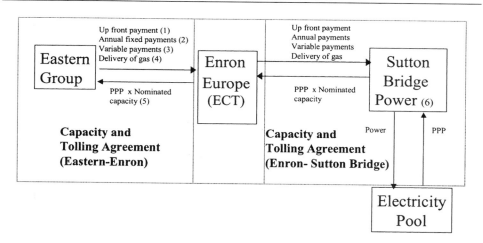

(1) Eastern would pay Enron approximately £9 million up front.

(2) Eastern would make fixed annual capacity payments of £68.8 million per year.

(3) Eastern would make variable payments of £357.5 for every half hour the plant was operational.

(4) For each kWh that Eastern wished to receive PPP, it would deliver natural gas in the amount dictated by the contractual heat rate. Under a separate agreement with Enron, Eastern would buy this gas from Enron at the index price plus 2%.

(5) Eastern could nominate up to 700 MW in the summer and 735 MW in the winter. There would be pre-specified numbers of maintenance days during which the Eastern-Enron CTA would be suspended. The CTA would last 15 years.

(6) Enron would initially own Sutton Bridge, but was likely to sell part of its holdings to investors over time. Enron was contracted to build and operate the plant, but anticipated it would sign a contract with General Electric to perform these tasks.

Source: Sutton Bridge Term Sheets (Enron and Eastern).

contracts under the alternative proposal. The first CTA, between Eastern and Enron, would allow Eastern to exchange physical gas for power pool proceeds—this contract governed the virtual plant. Exhibit 13-3 summarizes the key aspects of the CTA between Eastern and Enron. To offset the risk from the Eastern CTA, Enron's traders could enter into an offsetting CTA with another party or they could construct a "hedge" using the physical plant at Sutton Bridge. By creating a second CTA between Enron and Sutton Bridge Power, the special purpose vehicle that would own the physical power plant, Enron would also have the right to exchange gas for power pool proceeds.

The Eastern-Enron Capacity and Tolling Agreement

Each day, Eastern could decide whether to exercise its option to exchange gas for pool proceeds over 48 half-hour periods for the following day.[14] The amount of gas required for delivery was based on the number of megawatts (MWs) nominated by Eastern—up to a maximum of 700 MW in the summer (April to September) and 735 MW in the winter (October to March). The amount of gas required would also be a function of a contractual "heat rate," the rate at which gas could be converted into electricity. Although the two parties had not yet agreed on a specific number, it would likely be somewhere between the heat rates for old and new CCGT technologies: 6,800 to 7,600 Btu per kWh (or 6.8 to 7.6 MMBtu/MWh; Exhibit 13-4 shows efficiencies, or heat rates, for various generating technologies). For example, if they agreed to a heat rate of 7,200 Btu/kWh and Eastern wanted to receive power pool proceeds for an hour on its full summer capacity of 700 MW, then it would deliver 5,040 MMBtus of gas (= 700 MWh × 1000 kWh/MWh × 7,200 Btu/kWh × 1 MMBtu/1,000,000 Btu) and would receive a payment equal to the market value of 700 MW for one hour at PPP.

According to the current term sheet, though subject to final revision, Eastern would pay a fixed charge, a variable charge, and other operating and maintenance expenses. The fixed charge or capacity payment of £68.8 million per year would cover all fixed costs and debt service requirements as well as provide a minimum return on equity capital for the actual plant. Thus, even if Eastern never asked for power proceeds and the actual plant was never actually used, the capacity payments alone would pay for the physical plant. The variable charge of £357.5 per half hour of plant operation would cover expected operating and maintenance expenses in the event Eastern did exercise its option to receive pool proceeds. Eastern would have to pay these variable costs on a minimum of 15,000 half-hourly periods each year. Finally, Eastern also agreed to cover all charges for transporting gas as well as start-up/shut-down expenses that were essentially similar to those incurred by the physical plant. Eastern agreed to pay gas transportation charges based on Transco's published rates for delivery to the physical plant. These costs averaged 10% to 15% of the total delivered gas cost.

The Enron-Sutton Bridge Capacity and Tolling Agreement

Under the second CTA, between Enron and Sutton Bridge Power, Enron would supply natural gas and pay fixed and variable costs in exchange for power pool proceeds. To the extent possible, the second CTA would mirror the first CTA between Eastern and ECT. However, key contractual features of the Enron-Sutton Bridge CTA would

---

[14] Rather than physically deliver gas to Enron, Eastern could obtain the gas from ECT. Eastern and Enron planned to sign an independent Gas Supply Agreement under which Eastern would pay Enron 102% of the monthly gas index whenever gas actually flowed, that is, whenever it was economic to operate the plant.

EXHIBIT 13-3

SUMMARY OF THE EASTERN/ENRON CAPACITY TOLLING AGREEMENT TERM SHEET

Definitions:

Owner	Enron or Affiliate
Offtaker	Eastern Electricity or Affiliate

Principles of Agreement:

The purpose of the Capacity and Tolling Agreement (CTA) is to establish the rights and obligations of the Parties in respect to the Offtaker's option. The Offtaker will pay the Owner Fixed Payments, Variable Payments, and other payments as specified in this agreement for the option ("CTA Option") to exchange natural gas for Pool proceeds.

Term: 15 years beginning May 1, 1999

Fixed Payments:

One-time up-front	£9 million
Annual	£68.8 million, payable on a daily basis

Variable Payments:

Rate	£357.50 per half-hour period of operation
Start-up/Shutdown	Each event will accrue two half-hour periods
Minimum	Offtaker will pay for at least 15,000 half-hour periods per year

Start-up Charge:

Offtaker will reimburse the Owner the cost of importing electricity for Start-Up.

Maximum Contractual Volume:

Summer	700 MW (April to September)
Winter	735 MW (October to May)

Offtake Instructions:

By 8:00 A.M. on the day prior to each Operating Day, the Offtaker will state:
(1) the number of half-hour periods and contractual volume for each period
—if the contractual volume is zero for any period, it will be considered a Shut Down
—each Shutdown will last for a minimum of four consecutive Half-Hour Periods
—each Shutdown will incur a shut-down charge
—the Offtaker is limited to 600 Start Ups in any three-year period
(2) an estimate of the volume of gas to be delivered

Planned Maintenance:

There will be 12 to 30 days of planned maintenance per year during which the CTA will be suspended.

Transportation Charge:

Offtaker will pay the Owner a transportation charge as follows:
Fixed: payable whether or not the CTA Option is exercised
Variable: payable only when the Off-taker elects to convert gas to electricity

Force Majeure:

The occurrence of a *Force Majeure* event will relieve both Parties from their obligations under the CTA, but only to the extent that the affected Party is prevented from complying with its obligations by the relevant Force Majeure event.

Credit Terms:

Each Party will provide reasonable credit support including a parent company guarantee. In addition, third-party credit support will be required if a party undergoes a material adverse change.

Source: Sutton Bridge Term Sheets (Enron and Eastern).

EXHIBIT 13-4

COMPARISON OF ALTERNATIVE GENERATION TECHNOLOGIES

Generating Technology[a]	Efficiency[b]		Heat Rate (MMBtus per MWh)[c]	Cost to build (per KW)[d]
	Best Case (LHV)	Typical (HHV)		
OCGT—Old construction	30%	27%	12.6	n/a
OCGT—New construction	40%	36%	9.5	$250–$400
CCGT—Old construction	50%	45%	7.6	n/a
CCGT—New construction	56%	50%	6.8	$500
Rankine Cycle Steam—Old construction	37%	33%	10.2	n/a
Rankine Cycle Steam—Sub-critical	40%	36%	9.5	$550
Rankine Cycle Steam—Super-critical	45%	41%	8.4	$600
Diesel	42%	38%	9.0	$270

[a] Technologies: OCGT = open cycle gas turbine; CCGT = combined cycle gas turbin. The Sutton Bridge plant would use newer CCGT technology.

[b] Best case efficiency assumes that all possible energy in a fuel can be used in producing electricity (i.e., there are no losses). Typical efficiency reflects some expected loss of energy in converting fuels to electricity.

[c] The Heat Rate is the number of MMBtu's needed to produce 1 megawatt-hour (MWh). Lower numbers represent more efficient technologies.

[d] Cost to build excludes financing costs and reflects estimates of EPC contracts available in late 1996.

Source: Enron Corporation

reflect the plant's *actual* physical properties (capacity, heat rate, and maintenance costs) whereas the Eastern-Enron CTA would reflect *contractual* levels of these aspects of plant operation. This structure would leave Enron exposed to the differences between actual and contracted levels of plant performance. Both agreements would begin in late spring of 1999 and last 15 years, even though the plant would have a useful life of perhaps 30 years. Exhibit 13-5 provides current capital market data; Exhibit 13-6 provides financial projections for the two CTA agreements.

The Physical Plant at Sutton Bridge

As of December 1996, Enron had received regulatory permission to build a 700 MW power plant. Enron engineers estimated it would take approximately two years to construct the power island (the generator itself), the 2.2 km gas pipeline from the national transmission system to the plant, and the 3.5 km overhead transmission line from the plant to the national electricity grid. Once complete, the plant would operate in two distinct phases: a 15-year CTA phase during which Enron claimed the plant's output followed by an indefinite merchant phase.[15] Enron managers expected to fund construction and repay debt prior to the merchant phase even though the exact details of the financial plan had not yet been worked out. Exhibit 13-7 provides a breakdown of sources and uses of funds for the construction of the physical plant.

[15] Enron would have the right to extend its CTA on an annual basis at the end of the initial 15-year term.

EXHIBIT 13-5

US AND UK INTEREST RATES AS OF NOVEMBER 29, 1996

	Maturity					
	1 Year	2 Year	3 Year	5 Year	10 Year	15 Year
Rates in £ (UK pounds):						
Government bonds	6.61%	6.74%	6.76%	7.04%	7.35%	7.57%
A-rated corporate bonds	6.57%	6.98%	7.11%	7.47%	7.98%	8.26%
BBB-rated corporate bonds	6.79%	7.12%	7.33%	7.73%	8.20%	8.68%
Rates in $ (US dollars):						
Government bonds	5.36%	5.60%	5.71%	5.83%	6.05%	6.11%
A-rated corporate bonds	5.77%	5.95%	6.08%	6.24%	6.61%	6.83%
BBB-rated corporate bonds	5.96%	6.10%	6.22%	6.45%	6.79%	7.05%

Source: Adapted from Bloomberg. All rates quoted on a semiannual basis.

Enron, as the general contractor for the project, agreed to sign a fixed-price, date-certain, turnkey contract for construction, and to pay liquidated damages for either completion delays or substandard performance. The plant would contain two 260 MW gas turbines and a linked 270 MW steam turbine giving it a potential output of 790 MW, and the ability to produce 760 MW of power in the winter and 743 MW in the summer. Because Enron had regulatory approval to produce only 700 MW of power, it had applied for, and expected to get, approval for the additional 90 MW of generating capacity.

Enron planned to subcontract the manufacture and installation of the turbines to General Electric (GE), a AAA-rated company with extensive experience in constructing and operating power generating equipment. GE proposed to use its newest turbines, the 9FA+, even though early versions of the turbines had experienced high failure rates. GE had analyzed the problems, corrected the design flaws, and was seeking commercial applications for the redesigned turbines. If the new design worked as expected, Sutton Bridge would be among the most efficient gas plants in the industry (see Exhibit 13-4). GE indicated a willingness to provide a "new product" guarantee against completion delays and performance problems. Specifically, GE was willing to guarantee a minimum heat rate of 6,950 Btu/kWh. While such completion guarantees subject to performance targets were standard practice in the industry, GE was willing to go one step further by guaranteeing minimum performance levels for the life of the project. If the turbines failed to achieve minimum performance levels, GE would pay liquidated damages to cover the difference. At the same time, any contract would likely include bonuses for availability and efficiency above the contracted rates.

Once the plant passed a series of completion tests, which would be verified by an independent consultant, it would enter the CTA phase. During this phase, the plant would be exposed to neither fuel nor pool price risk regardless of use, because Enron's payments would cover all fixed and operating costs. Enron expected that GE would operate the plant subject to a fixed-price management fee. This arrangement was unique because Enron engineers were usually responsible for daily operations at Enron plants. Yet the arrangement fit with GE's desire to expand its service operations. Jack Welch,

EXHIBIT 13-6

FINANCIAL PROJECTIONS UNDER THE TWO CTA AGREEMENTS

Year	Eastern Payments (Eastern/Enron CTA)		Sutton Bridge Power Operating & Maintenance Expenses (Enron/Sutton Bridge CTA)		
	Fixed	Variable	Fixed	Variable	Other
1999	£57.6	£3.7	£5.2	£3.7	£ 7.2
2000	68.8	4.5	6.3	4.5	9.0
2001	68.8	4.5	6.5	4.5	9.1
2002	68.8	4.6	6.7	4.6	9.4
2003	68.8	4.5	6.9	4.5	9.7
2004	68.8	4.2	7.1	4.2	10.0
2005	68.8	4.7	7.4	4.7	10.2
2006	68.8	4.8	7.6	4.8	10.4
2007	68.8	4.9	7.8	4.9	10.8
2008	68.8	5.1	8.0	5.1	11.2
2009	68.8	5.1	8.3	5.1	11.4
2010	68.8	4.6	8.5	4.6	11.8
2011	68.8	5.3	8.8	5.3	12.1
2012	68.8	5.2	9.0	5.2	12.5
2013	68.8	5.3	9.3	5.3	12.8
2014	68.8	1.8	9.6	1.8	13.2

Notes: Assumes the Enron/Sutton Bridge CTA begins on March 1, 1999. The columns "Eastern payments" represent planned payments from Eastern to Enron under their CTA agreement, assuming the CTA is fully exercised. These exclude gas transportation charges, which Eastern would pay to Enron. The "Sutton Bridge Operating and Maintenance Expenses" include the costs to operate the plant but do not include financing charges.

Sutton Bridge Power would pay taxes at the rate of 33%. It would enjoy depreciation tax shields from tangible assets assuming straight-line depreciation over 40 years (the plant's useful life), and interest tax shields from debt payments assuming 15-year amortization and a debt rate of 8.75%.

Asset betas for utilities in the United States and the United Kingdom with gas-fired capacity ranged from 0.26 to 0.45 during 1996. The historical equity risk premium in the U.K. market (i.e., the arithmetic average of the spread between equity returns and long-term U.K. Gilts) was 7.94% from 1919 to 1993 (*Source:* Barclays de Zoete Wedd Securities Ltd., *The BXW Equity-Gilt Study*, 39th ed., January 1994).

Source: Enron, casewriters' estimates.

GE's CEO, commented: "Our job is to sell more than just the box. . . . We're in the services business to expand our pie."[16]

Another novel feature of this structure was that Enron traders would play a central role in determining operating or dispatch decisions. As a result, the plant would become part of their risk books containing the firm's long and short positions in gas and power. This organizational structure ensured that the plant would run only when it was

---

[16] Tim Smart, "Jack Welch's Encore," *Business Week*, October 28, 1996, p. 154.

EXHIBIT 13-7

SUTTON BRIDGE CONSTRUCTION SOURCES AND USES OF FUNDS

	£ (in millions)
Sources of Funds	
Debt Proceeds	£286
Capital Contributions from Shareholders	42
Operating Cash Flow Post-Completion Date	9
Total Sources of Funds	**337**
Uses of Funds	
Construction Costs	£240
Financing, Legal and Consultants Fees	16
Construction Insurance	6
Development Costs and Fees	26
Interest During Construction (net)	31
Other Fees & Expenses	18
Total Uses of Funds	**337**

Source: Enron.

---

optimal to do so, that is, when the gas input price plus operating expenses were less than pool prices. (Exhibit 13-8 shows the historical price differential between the gas cost needed to produce one megawatt-hour of power and the actual price per megawatt hour of power produced assuming highly efficient gas production technology.) In contrast, a power plant operating under an IPP structure would run continuously regardless of current market conditions.

After CTA phase ended, the plant would enter a merchant phase in which it would be exposed to both fuel and pool price risks. At that time, the plant's ability to service its debt and provide equity returns would be a function of its ability to burn gas to generate competitively-priced power. According to independent gas experts, Sutton Bridge would "have a wide choice of gas suppliers and a range of flexible contract terms beginning in 2014 and extending through 2022."

Because of the risk during the merchant phase, the Enron team figured that most, if not all, the project debt would have to be repaid during the CTA phase. The current plan called for 15-year commercial bank loans to finance construction, though Enron would, if possible, issue longer-term project bonds. Enron's treasury group assured the deal team that they could finance the deal as long as Enron Corporation guaranteed the Enron/Sutton Bridge Power CTA. With these assurances, the team concentrated on working out the commercial and physical details, leaving the financing details to be resolved at a later date.

DECISIONS

The alternative proposal, though novel in many respects and risky in untraditional ways, held great appeal for both Eastern and Enron. For Eastern, this deal would cement its transformation into an integrated energy company competing in a deregulated environment. Under the alternative structure, Eastern would have an outlet for its gas re-

EXHIBIT 13-8

PRICE/COST DIFFERENTIAL FOR THE PRODUCTION OF ONE MWH USING CCGT TECHNOLOGY (1/94 TO 11/96)

Price/Cost Differential From 1/94 to 11/96

Note: This graph shows the difference between the average daily price of one MWh of electricity and the cost of the gas needed to produce one MWh of electricity using efficient CCGT technology. It is calculated using the formula: Differential = market price of one MWh − (7.400 * cost of one MMBtu), where the implied heat rate is 7.400 MMBtus per MWh. The calculation does not include transportation, variable tolling, or fixed costs. The calculation uses weekly data prior to June 1996 and daily data thereafter.

Source: Casewriters' calculations.

serves as well as additional capacity for its trading operations. The virtual plant would therefore be consistent with its desire to arbitrage between the gas and electricity markets on a daily basis. Like Eastern, Enron saw the deal as a way to further develop its European trading operations and strengthen its reputation as an innovator in the rapidly changing European energy markets.

While Seeligson and Danielsen had kept their respective managers informed about the status of the deal over the course of the past six months, they now had to agree on a contractual heat rate and get formal approval for the deal. Each set of executives had to make sure that the proposal made strategic and financial sense, that it would deliver an appropriate financial return, and that the risks were commensurate with the returns. From Enron's perspective, it still had to structure the special purpose company known as Sutton Bridge Power, agree on a financial structure for the actual plant, draft the legal documents, and figure out how to value and "book" the transactions. Because Enron was the only nonfinancial firm to adopt "mark-to-market" accounting rules, this final step was likely to be complex.

GLOSSARY

Btu: British thermal unit, the amount of heat needed to raise the temperature of one pound of water by one degree Fahrenheit
  —**MBtu** = 1,000 Btu's
  —**MMBtu** = 1 million Btu's

CCGT: combined cycle gas turbine

CFD: contract for differences

CTA: capacity tolling agreement

De-loading: the process of shutting down a power plant

ECT: Enron Capital & Trade Resources Corporation, a Delaware corporation

EFA: electricity forward agreement

EPC Contract: engineering, procurement, and construction contract

Half-hour period: one of 48 time slots in which power is sold in the U.K. market

Heat rate: a measure of fuel conversion efficiency. A heat rate of 8,150 requires 81.50 therms to produce each MWh of power

IPP: Independent power plant

MPP: merchant power plant, a plant with uncertain electricity output prices and quantities

National Grid: the high-voltage national electricity transmission system operating primarily in England and Wales which offers connections to and use of the system to generators and suppliers of electricity

National Transmission System (NTS):   the main pipeline system operated by Transco for the conveyance of gas in Great Britain

OFFER: the Office of Electricity Regulation (U.K. power regulator)

Power island: the power plant's generating and other associated equipment

PPA: power purchase agreement, an agreement to buy a given amount of power at a given price

PPP: pool purchase price consisting of the system marginal price (SMP) plus a capacity payment

REC: the 12 regional electric companies that came into existence in 1990 as a result of the restructuring and privatization of the electricity supply industry in England and Wales

SBP: Sutton Bridge Power, a company incorporated in England and Wales with unlimited liability

SMP: system marginal price

Take-or-pay contract: a contract obligating a firm to buy a fixed quantity of gas at fixed prices, similar to a forward contract

Therm: a measure of heat content of a fuel—10 therms equals 1 MMBtu equals 2.927 kilowatt hours

Transco: the manager of the National Transmission System (NTS)

Uplift: includes all additional costs incurred by the Pool

Watt: a unit of electric power equal to the power in a circuit in which a current of one ampere flows across a potential difference of one volt
  —**kW:** kilowatt is 1,000 watts
  —**kWh:** kilowatt-hour is 1,000 watts for one hour
  —**MW:** megawatt is 1 million watts
  —**MWh:** megawatt-hour is 1 million watts for one hour
  —**GWh:** gigawatt-hour is 1 billion watts for one hour

U.K. GAS AND ELECTRICITY MARKETS

EXHIBIT 13-A1

U.K. ELECTRICITY POOL PRICES, JANUARY 1994 TO NOVEMBER 1996

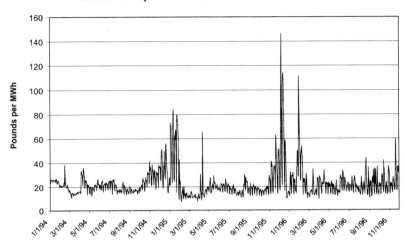

UK Electricity Pool Prices Jan. 1994 to Nov. 1996

Note: The prices shown were the arithmetic averages of the 48 half-hourly pool prices posted each day, but do not take into account the volume of power delivered in each half-hour period. The price was reported in pounds per megawatt hour (£/MWh). The average price of electricity on November 29, 1996, it was £33.62/MWh; during the month of November 1996, it was £26.57/MWh; and throughout the previous 12 months, it was £25.26/MWh.

Source: Enron Corporation.

EXHIBIT 13-A2

POOL PRICES BY HALF-HOUR PERIOD

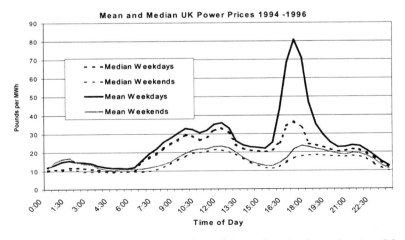

Mean and Median UK Power Prices 1994 -1996

Note: This figure plots the mean and median PPP for weekdays and weekends as a function of the time of day over the prior two years.

Source: Casewriters' calculations.

(Continued)

EXHIBIT 13-A3

VOLATILITY OF THE AVERAGE POWER POOL PRICE

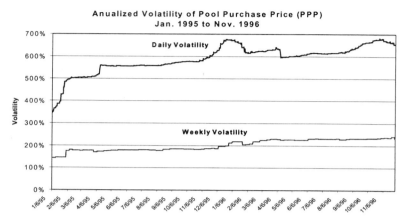

Note: Historical volatility is measured by the standard deviation of the natural log of daily (and weekly) electricity price changes over the previous 365 days. (The price change is defined as the ratio of the price on a given day (week) over the price on the prior day (week).) The historical volatility of the daily and weekly average electricity prices was 654% and 232%, respectively, as of 11/29/96.

Source: Casewriter calculations.

EXHIBIT 13-A4

PROJECTIONS OF FORWARD PRICES AND VOLATILITIES IN THE U.K. POWER MARKET

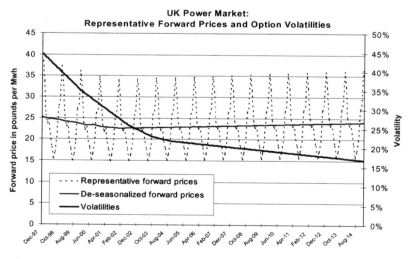

Note: This figure shows "representative" forward prices and volatilities for contracts with maturities of one year and longer. They do not represent Enron's positions or beliefs. The "saw tooth" pattern of the forward prices represents anticipated seasonality of prices. Short-term (one month) implied volatilities were about 50% annually. The implied convenience yields for maturities of one to five years ranged from 7% to 10%.

Source: Enron Corporation.

EXHIBIT 13-A5

U.K. NATURAL GAS PRICE DATA

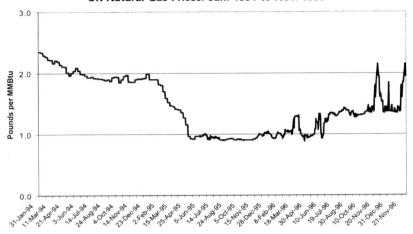

UK Natural Gas Prices: Jan. 1994 to Nov. 1996

Note: These prices were the day-ahead prices expressed in pounds per MMBtu. Weekly data were available through June 2, 1995, daily prices were available thereafter. The average price of gas on November 29, 1996, was £1.95/MMBtu; during November 1996, it was £1.59/MMBtu; and during year-to-date (YTD) 1996, it was £1.28/MMBtu.

Source: PH Energy Analysts Ltd.

EXHIBIT 13-A6

HISTORICAL VOLATILITY OF U.K. NATURAL GAS PRICES

Annualized Volatility of Gas Prices: Jan. 1995 to Nov. 1996

Daily Volatility

Weekly Volatility

Note: Historical volatility was measured by the annualized standard deviation of the natural log of gas price changes over the prior year. The volatility for the daily data starts in June 1996, a year after the daily data became available. The historical volatility based on the price of natural gas on November 29, 1996, was 64% using weekly data, and 55% using daily data. Short term (one month) implied volatilities were approximately 45% annually.

Source: PH Energy Analysts Ltd.

EXHIBIT 13-A7

PROJECTED FORWARD PRICES AND VOLATILITIES
IN THE U.K. NATURAL GAS MARKET

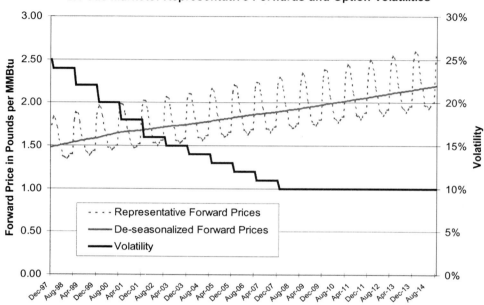

UK Gas Markets: Representative Forwards and Option Volatilities

Note: These estimates were "representative" forward prices and volatilities for contracts with maturities of one year or longer. They do not represent Enron's positions or beliefs. The "sawtooth" pattern of the forward prices represents anticipated seasonality of prices. The implied convenience yields on a one-year forward contract were approximately 31%.

Source: Enron Corporation.

14

Bidding for Antamina

In late June 1996, the team charged with business development at RTZ-CRA Limited had to make a recommendation to the senior executives of the London-based natural resources firm regarding a bid the firm might choose to make to acquire a rich copper mine in Peru. The Antamina project was being offered for sale by auction as part of the privatization of Peru's state mining company, Centromin. The business development team had to determine what Antamina was worth and to recommend how RTZ-CRA should bid in the upcoming auction.

CENTROMIN AND ANTAMINA

In the mid-1990s, across the globe, governments were seeking to return public enterprises to private hands, with privatization programs underway in Western and Eastern Europe, the former Soviet Union, and Latin America. In Peru, the government sought to return many of its state-owned firms to private ownership. In June 1996, it sold off a 60% stake in Petroperu's largest refinery, La Pampilla, for $323 million, and earlier in the year, had attempted to auction five gold prospects, but received only one bid.

The country's Energy and Mines Minister, Daniel Hokama, explained the privatization program as a move to stimulate a free-market economy. "At the moment the treasury is not in particular need of money, but what's imperative is that we allow private companies to carry out what state entities have been doing."[1]

The government planned further privatization that would bring in $5.75 billion in cash and investment commitments in 1996–1999 (in comparison to the $9.6 billion raised from 1992 to 1996). One of the larger entities that would be sold would be Centromin, Peru's largest state-owned mining company. With 10,000 employees, the firm owned seven mines, a metallurgical complex, four hydroelectric plants, a railway system, port facilities, and numerous undeveloped natural resource deposits. Prior to 1974, the firm had been owned by U.S.-based Cerro de Pasco Corporation. In that year it was

---

Professor Peter Tufano and Lecturer Alberto Moel prepared this case as the basis for class discussion rather than to illustrate either effective or ineffective handling of an administrative situation. This case can be used in conjunction with the note "Copper and Zinc Markets 1996," HBS Case No. 297-055.

[1] Saul Hudson, "Interview: Peru Upbeat on Energy and Mining," *Reuters Financial Service*, June 14, 1996.

nationalized by the Peruvian government.[2] The government had attempted to sell the entire company in 1994 and 1995, but these efforts apparently were unsuccessful. Under the government's current plan, Centromin's 11 properties would be sold off piecemeal over 1996 and 1997. The two first parcels to be sold off were a gold mine and the Antamina parcel. Most industry observers felt that the government would be selling off a number of interesting parcels over the coming few years.

The Antamina mine, located 482 kilometers north of Lima, Peru, was a rich polymetallic deposit, with especially valuable copper ore. Based on engineering reports made public by the government as part of the auction, the property had proven and probable ore reserves estimated at 126.8 million metric tons of ore[3] containing 1.61% copper and 1.33% zinc. Centromin management had publicly stated that these figures vastly underestimated the likely reserves of the property. They suggested that the potential ore body could be up to 913 m tons, although most industry observers were highly skeptical of this estimate. While part of the ore body had been well-studied by geologists, there had been virtually no geologic study of a large portion of the deposit. As a result, there was large uncertainty about the size of the reserves.

From a practical perspective, none of the potential bidders could carry out anything but limited geologic work on the properties before the bids were due, and therefore all of the bidders had to rely on their analysis of the 20-year-old surveys produced by Cerro de Pasco. In addition, the government was not willing to represent or guarantee the amount of reserves.

A feasibility study, which would largely constitute additional geological exploration through drilling, would more precisely establish the amount and quality of ore in the Antamina property. This exploration, which would cost approximately $24 million, was expected to take about 2 years, and would be completed before mine construction began. Once that additional geological work had been completed, the developer of the property would be "more confident" of the *expected* resources, typically knowing them within a band of ±20%. However, as a result of the additional exploration, one could ascertain the *minimum* quantity of ore with even greater certainty.

Were the subsequent geological work to suggest the mine was economically feasible, the property would have to be developed in order to be able to extract the copper and other metals. Antamina was located in a remote region in the mountains of Peru at 4,000 meters above sea level and 200 km from the ocean. Developing this site would include the construction of roads, mining rigs, crushing plants and other ancillary facilities, and the purchase and transport of heavy mining equipment, and was expected to last three years. The output of the mine would be a copper sulphide slurry containing 26% copper and a zinc sulfide slurry containing 50% zinc. The capital expenditures to develop the mine (not including the feasibility study) ranged from $581 million to $622 million (in 1996 U.S. dollars) and were a function of the amount of ore found. Much of this capital expenditure, virtually all of the project's revenues, and over half of the project's operating costs would be in U.S. dollars, with the remainder being primarily in the Peruvian Sol.

Estimates of operating and capital costs can be made by comparison with similar existing mines. Exhibit 14-1 shows estimates (from a feasibility study), of mine life,

---

[2] The pro-foreign investment climate in Peru in 1996 was not only very different from that of a few years ago but very different from that of other countries. There was no guarantee that the business-friendly climate in Peru would continue in the future.

[3] A metric ton is 1,000 kilograms, or 2,204.6 pounds.

EXHIBIT 14-1

HBS CASEWRITER ESTIMATES OF
ANTAMINA COPPER MINE CHARACTERISTICS

Scenario		Low Case	Expected	High Case
Mine life	(Years)	12	14	18
Copper production	(million lbs/year)	313	339	365
Zinc production	(million lbs/year)	155	168	181
Operating costs[a]	(millions of 1996 U.S. $)	131	138	145
Copper treatment charge[b]	(1996 U.S. dollars/lb)	0.28	0.28	0.28
Zinc treatment charge[b]	(1996 U.S. dollars/lb)	0.22	0.22	0.22
Feasibility study[c]				
1996	(millions of 1996 U.S. $)	6	6	6
1997	(millions of 1996 U.S. $)	18	18	18
Capital expenditures[c]				
1998	(millions of 1996 U.S. $)	54	55	55
1999	(millions of 1996 U.S. $)	246	255	264
2000	(millions of 1996 U.S. $)	281	292	303
Per year after 2000[c]	(millions of 1996 U.S. $)	8.7	9.0	9.3
Closure costs[c]	(millions of 1996 U.S. $)	45	45	45

Other assumptions

(1) Working capital is 25% of net revenue (gross revenue less treatment charges).

(2) Tax rate is 30%.

(3) Depreciation is 5-year straight line starting in 2001.

(4) In mid-1996, the 10-year forecast for annual inflation (the GDP price index) in U.S. dollars ranged from 2.0% to 3.2%, with a consensus forecast of 2.6%. Inflation estimates are taken from Blue Chip Economic Indicators (Capitol Publications, Inc. Alexandria, VA, March and October 1996). The inflation rates for the project's operating costs, feasibility study, capital expenditures, and closure costs could differ from the economy wide inflation rates, and some experts estimated them to be at least 3.5% per annum.

[a] While the operating costs are expressed in U.S. dollars, less than half would be in set in Peruvian Sols. These costs are expressed in real (1996) amounts and exclude the treatment charges paid to a smelter.

[b] The treatment charges were paid by the mining company to smelters (typically in Japan) and would be set and paid in U.S. dollars. These treatment charges are set by contract with the smelter and tend to adjust with the relative demand for smelting capacity, which tends to increase with the price of copper. From the smelter, the mining company received revenue equal to the amount of metal produced times the U.S. dollar market price of copper (or zinc) minus the treatment charge.

[c] The feasibility study, the initial and continuing capital expenditures, and the closure costs are expressed in real (1996) amounts. These expenses would primarily be set and paid in U.S. dollars.

Sources: Harvard Business School casewriter estimates based on industry standards, conversations with consultants, and trade press sources.

yearly production, capital expenditures, and operating costs for three development scenarios corresponding to three different outcomes of the quantity of ore in the deposit. The expected scenario can be thought to represent the mean or the median of the distribution of the possible ore content of the deposit, the low scenario to represent 1 to 1.5 standard deviations below the mean, and the high scenario to represent

1 to 1.5 standard deviations above the mean.[4] Exhibit 14-2 gives additional capital markets and exchange rate data.[5]

THE BIDDING PROCESS FOR ANTAMINA

The Peruvian government had established an unusual procedure by which it would auction off the Antamina property. The property would be offered in a public, sealed-bid auction. Each bidder was required to specify an initial payment to be made at the closing of the sale, plus an investment commitment for the project, to be completed within five years. The bids would be evaluated on the basis of the sum of the initial payment plus 30% of the investment commitment. According to auction procedure, the minimum initial payment was $17.5 million, and the minimum investment commitment was $135 million. The highest bid that exceeded these minimums would be awarded the project.

The winner of the bidding could decide at the end of two years after the closing to return the property to Centromin, provided that they had spent a minimum of $13.5 million on the exploration and development of the property over the first two years, in addition to the initial payment amount. Were they not to return the property to Centromin at the end of two years, they would be obligated to develop the property. Were their actual investment in developing Antamina to fall short of their investment commitment (which was stated at the time of their initial bid), they would have to pay a penalty to Centromin. This penalty, paid at the end of five years, would equal 30% of the difference between their investment commitment less the actual investment made, if that difference was positive. (If the winning bidder spent more than their prestated investment commitment, there would be no penalty to be paid nor any rebate received from Centromin.) For example, if the new owner had committed to an investment of $500 million, but only invested $400 million after five years, the new owner would have to pay $30 million (30 percent of $500 million minus $400 million) to Centromin as a penalty.

Although the government's interest in selling the Antamina property was in part to raise funds, it was also interested in ensuring the development of the property and its long-term ability to affect the countries balance of trade. According to one Centromin official, "We obviously want to sell at an interesting price, but the principal objective is to maintain and develop the sector by attracting quality companies."[6] In discussing its goals, another company spokesman noted that "more than the amounts paid for the transfer of each production unit, our main concern is for the amounts that the new owners will invest to improve, modernize or expand those units."

---

[4] The standard deviation measures the absolute dispersion or variability of a distribution. The greater the standard deviation, the greater the magnitude of the deviation of the points in the distribution from their mean. Analytically, the standard deviation σ of a distribution with N points is given by

$$\sigma = \sqrt{\frac{1}{N} \sum_i (x_i - \bar{x})}$$

where x_i is the ith sample point and $\bar{x}$ is the mean of the distribution. 65% of the distribution lies within ± 1 standard deviations from the mean; 95% of the distribution lies within ± 2 standard deviations from the mean.

[5] On June 25, 1996, the spot price of copper was $0.95/lb, and the spot price of zinc was $0.46/lb. For information on copper and zinc markets and prices, see "Copper and Zinc Markets 1996," HBS Case No. 297-055.

[6] Saul Hudson, "Forty firms qualify for Peru copper prospect sale," *Reuters Financial Service*, June 21, 1996.

EXHIBIT 14-2

CAPITAL MARKETS AND EXCHANGE RATE DATA FOR JUNE 25, 1996

Bond Yields (U.S. corporate industrial bonds in %)

Maturity (years)	Treasury	AAA	AA	A	BBB	BB+	BB/BB−	B
1	5.76	5.91	6.00	6.01	6.27	6.51	7.28	8.21
5	6.69	7.06	7.16	7.27	7.59	8.02	9.63	10.67
10	6.90	7.37	7.17	7.63	7.96	8.48	10.46	N/A
15	7.02	7.54	7.65	7.83	8.18	8.75	N/A	N/A
20	7.20	7.76	7.87	8.07	8.43	N/A	N/A	N/A
25	7.22	7.81	7.92	8.13	N/A	N/A	N/A	N/A

Source: Compiled from *Standard and Poor's Weekly Bond Indexes*, August 1996.

Peruvian Sol/U.S. Dollar Exchange Rates

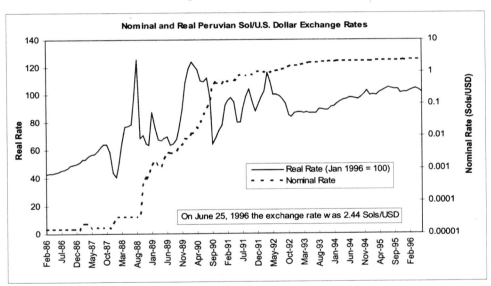

Source: Datastream and J.P. Morgan.

The sealed bids were due on July 12, 1996. Initially, over 40 potential firms had shown interest in the property and had been prequalified to bid. All qualified bidders had to have a net worth of at least 100 million U.S. dollars and experience in operating substantial mines (of at least 10,000 tons of treated ore per day). However, the recent unrest in the copper market was held to explain why only a handful of these 40 firms had serious interest in the bidding. According to press reports, 12 firms from Canada, South Africa, England, and Japan had expressed a serious interest in the property and had visited the "data room" made available by Centromin. Of these, by early

June only three—RTZ-CRA, Noranda, and a joint venture of Inmet Mining and Rio Algom—were believed to submit bids.

Noranda Inc. was an integrated mining concern based in Toronto, Canada, employing 31,000 people. It mined, smelted, refined, and marketed copper, zinc, nickel, lead, silver, and gold. It also fabricated and marketed aluminum products, are produced and marketed oil and gas, lumber, pulp, and paper. In 1995, Noranda produced 483,000 tons of copper, 364,000 tons of zinc, 106,000 tons of lead, and 84,000 tons of nickel. Noranda, with a market capitalization of over $4 billion, was among the 10 largest mining concerns in the world.

Inmet Mining Corporation, based in Toronto, Canada, had interests in mining properties in North America, Europe, North Africa, Turkey, and Australia. In 1995, Inmet produced 90,000 tons of copper, 66,100 tons of zinc, 133,900 ounces of gold, 2.5 million ounces of silver, tungsten, and other industrial minerals. 1995 was the first year that Inmet operated as an independent company, following its sale by parent company Metallgesellschaft AG, a large German diversified metals and heavy industry conglomerate. Inmet was spun off by Metallgesellschaft as part of the restructuring program after the firm suffered heavy losses resulting from adverse oil hedging and trading transactions in 1995.

Inmet's partner in bidding for Antamina was Rio Algom Limited, a Canadian mining and metals distribution company with headquarters in Toronto. The company produced 197,000 tons of copper from mines in Chile and British Columbia. Other mining interests include uranium in Northern Ontario and New Mexico, and coal in British Columbia. Rio Algom also owned and operated a large metals distribution business, with 62 offices serving more than 50,000 customers.

See Exhibit 14-3 for additional information on Noranda, Inmet Mining, and Rio Algom. The Business Development group at RTZ-CRA felt that none of the bidders would have any special expertise in running the Antamina property nor any differential ability to finance the project.

RTZ-CRA LIMITED

RTZ-CRA, the world's largest mining group, concentrated on the development of large, long-life mines capable of sustaining competitive advantage and of delivering superior returns to shareholders over many years. With revenues of over $8 billion, a market value of over $10 billion, an operating cash flow of $2.5 billion, a debt to total capital ratio of 15%, and 51,000 employees, RTZ-CRA was unrivaled in size and financial strength. It was one of two worldwide mining companies with an AA rating by Moody's and Standard & Poor's. See Exhibit 14-4 for financial and operating data on RTZ-CRA.

Well-balanced both by product and geographically, RTZ-CRA was strongly represented in North America and Australia with additional assets in South America, Asia, Europe, and Southern Africa. Principal products were copper, aluminum, coal, iron ore, and gold. RTZ-CRA's main competitors were BHP/Magma and Western Mining from Australia, Phelps Dodge and Newmont from the United States, Noranda, Barrick Gold, and Placer Dome from Canada, and the government-owned mining concerns in Chile, India, Brazil, and Malaysia.

RTZ-CRA was one of the world's largest copper producers. With significant interests in the United States, South Africa, Chile, and Indonesia, RTZ-CRA's copper production reached 640,000 tons in 1995 (about 7% of world production), a 5% increase

EXHIBIT 14-3

INFORMATION ON LIKELY BIDDERS FOR ANTAMINA

Noranda Inc.

Product Segment Data (U.S. dollar millions) 1995

	Sales	Operating Income	Assets
Mining/Metals	5,800	442	7,090
Forest Products	2,413	173	2,483
Oil/Gas	182	8	1,793

Geographic Segment Data (U.S. dollar millions) 1995

	Sales	Operating Income	Assets
Canada	5,146	394	7,733
United States	3,136	132	2,353
Other	1,200	84	1,540

Key Financial Items (U.S. dollar millions, except as noted)

Fiscal Year Ending:	12/31/93	12/31/94	12/31/95
Market Cap.	4,063	4,219	4,866
Common Equity	2,648	2,816	3,285
Total Assets	7,369	8,436	9,449
Long Term Debt		2,941	3,292
Sales	3,969	4,728	6,144
Net Income	−28	235	382
Market Price—Close (Can$)	25.87	26.50	28.12
Bond Rating	BB	BB	BB
Market Beta vs. S&P 500[a]	------------------------- 0.82 -------------------------		
P/E Ratio—Close	nm	18	12

Note: Market Cap (in U.S. dollars) on June 25, 1996 was $ 6,843 million.

[a] Calculated from weekly data for the period January 1, 1993 to December 31, 1995.

Source: Worldscope, Bloomberg and Annual Reports.

(Continued)

from 1994. RTZ-CRA's copper mining operations were geographically dispersed and thus were not configured to benefit from synergies resulting from geographic proximity. In this context, while the Peruvian Antamina property was potentially interesting to RTZ-CRA, if it could be acquired at an economic price, it was not seen as having any unique strategic value to the firm. Thus, the primary rationale for purchasing the property was its feasibility as a standalone project which generated positive value for the firm.

RTZ-CRA was a true multinational firm, with its assets, earnings and cash flows linked to a wide variety of currencies, but primarily the U.S. dollar. RTZ-CRA was managed as a predominantly U.S. dollar business. For example, it borrowed in U.S. dollars.

EXHIBIT 14-3   (*Continued*)

INFORMATION ON LIKELY BIDDERS FOR ANTAMINA

Inmet Mining Corporation

Product Segment Data (U.S. dollar millions) 1995

	Sales	Operating Income	Assets
Mining	1,065	9.2	1,612

Geographic Segment Data (U.S. dollar millions) 1995

	Sales	Operating Income	Assets
Canada	28	−1.4	721.8
United States	124	−243.2	NA
Europe	876	12.6	457.8
Developing Countries	37	36.5	352.1

Key Financial Items (U.S. dollar millions, except as noted)

Fiscal Year Ending:	12/31/93	12/31/94	12/31/95
Market Cap.	744	695	595
Common Equity	764	767	642
Total Assets	1,212	1,203	1,181
Long Term Debt		213	118
Sales	218	592	781
Net Income	1	22	−323
Market Price—Close (Can$)	11.37	12.00	10.00
Bond Rating	N/R	N/R	N/R
Market Beta vs. S&P 500[a]	---------- 0.84 ----------		
P/E Ratio—Close	569	32	nm

Note: Market Cap (in U.S. dollar) on June 25, 1996 was $771 million.

[a] Calculated from weekly data for the period January 1, 1993 to December 31, 1995.

Source: Worldscope, Bloomberg, and Annual Reports.

(*Continued*)

EXHIBIT 14-3 *(Continued)*

INFORMATION ON LIKELY BIDDERS FOR ANTAMINA

Rio Algom Limited

Product Segment Data (U.S. dollar millions) 1995

	Sales	Operating Income	Assets
Metals Distribution	1,597	93	525
Mining	385	157	1,183

Geographic Segment Data (U.S. dollar millions) 1995

	Sales	Operating Income	Assets
Canada	486	123	671
United States	1,112	48	575
Australia/New Zealand	249	22	NA
Chile	136	57	479
Argentina	NA	NA	257

Key Financial Items (U.S. dollar millions, except as noted)

Fiscal Year Ending:	12/31/93	12/31/94	12/31/95
Market Cap.	739	991	969
Common Equity	491	643	721
Total Assets	1,280	1,413	1,657
Long Term Debt		802	910
Sales	722	864	1,453
Net Income	26	54	97
Market Price—Close (Can$)	22.37	26.75	25.37
Bond Rating	N/R	N/R	BBB
Market Beta vs. S&P 500[a]		0.64	
P/E Ratio—Close	23	18	10

Note: Market Cap (in U.S. dollar) on June 25, 1996 was $1,442 million

[a] Calculated from weekly data for the period January 1, 1993 to December 31, 1995.

Source: Worldscope, Bloomberg, and Annual Reports.

EXHIBIT 14-4

RTZ-CRA LIMITED FINANCIAL AND OPERATING DATA

Product Segment Data (U.S. dollar millions) 1995

	Sales	Operating Income	Assets
Copper	1,326	738	3,185
Industrial Minerals	1,075	301	1,210
Aluminum	991	280	1,178
Coal	902	194	909
Iron Ore	610	229	872
Gold	425	NA	NA
Other Products	308	63	540

Geographic Segment Data (U.S. dollar millions) 1995

	Sales	Operating Income	Assets
Europe	509	55	386
Australia/New Zealand	2,175	463	3,057
Africa	557	242	428
South America	298	146	487
North America	1,784	574	2,987
Other Countries	314	111	549

Key Financial Items (U.S. dollar millions, except as noted)

Fiscal Year Ending:	12/31/93	12/31/94	12/31/95
Market Cap.	12,784	13,812	15,535
Common Equity	4,703	5,379	6,986
Total Assets	8,825	10,095	15,776
Long Term Debt		2,127	2,205
Sales	2,991	3,581	7,579
Net Income	425	958	1,266
Market Price—Close (UK Pounds)	8.12	8.27	9.36
Bond Rating	AA	AA	AA
Market Beta vs. S&P 500[a]	------------------------- 0.53 -------------------------		
P/E Ratio—Close	30.07	14.41	16.03

Note: Market Cap (in U.S. dollars) on 06/25/96 was $10,175 million

[a] Calculated from weekly data for the period January 1, 1993 to December 31, 1995.

Sources: Annual Reports, compiled from Worldscope.

In its stated policies, RTZ-CRA reported that its natural diversity of exposure to currencies provided a substantial degree of protection against currency fluctuations, and thus the firm did not engage in any short-term currency hedging. It also had a policy against hedging commodity price fluctuations. RTZ-CRA's normal policy was to sell its products at prevailing market prices. RTZ-CRA believed that its exposure to commodity prices was naturally diversified by virtue of its broad product line and did not believe an active short-term commodity price hedging program would add value to the firm, nor did it engage in an active commodity trading operation.

THE DECISION

It was now June 25, 1996, and the business development team at RTZ-CRA had a little over two weeks to value the mine, develop a bidding strategy against the likely competitors, and make their recommendation to senior management.

MANAGING RISKY PROJECTS

15

Petrolera Zuata, Petrozuata C.A.

The first three weeks of January 1997 had been especially hectic for José Sifontes, Ted Helms, and Francisco Bustillos from the Corporate Finance Department at Petróleos de Venezuela S.A. (PDVSA), and Miguel Espinosa, Bob Heinrich, and Tom Casbeer from the Treasury Department at Conoco Inc. They had been working around the clock with their financial advisors, Chris Hasty and John Laxmi from Citicorp's Global Project Finance Group, developing the financing strategy for Petrolera Zuata, Petrozuata C.A (Petrozuata), a proposed crude oil development project in Venezuela.

In less than a week, Petrozuata's planning team would conduct a series of meetings regarding how to finance the $2.4 billion project. According to the plan, they would simultaneously pursue funding from development agencies, banks, and the capital markets. Depending on each source's interest and availability, they would choose an optimal mix from among the various options. In Washington, D.C., the team would meet with several multilateral and bilateral agencies, including the U.S. Export-Import Bank, (U.S. Exim) the Overseas Private Investment Corporation (OPIC), and the International Finance Corporation (IFC) to gauge their interest in participating in the deal. Following these meetings, they would fly to New York to meet with Standard and Poor's (S&P), Moody's, and Duff & Phelps to discuss how the capital markets might view the project and whether project bonds might receive an investment-grade rating. To assist with the ratings process and a possible bond offering, the sponsors (PDVSA and Conoco) had just selected Credit Suisse-First Boston (CSFB) and Citicorp as lead underwriters, and bankers from each firm would also attend the meetings. Even though the team believed that the proposed deal structure merited an investment-grade rating, they were interested in the rating agencies' perspectives and would consider specific adjustments to the deal structure as long as the changes did not significantly diminish the sponsors' financial or operating flexibility.

Research Associate Matthew Mateo Millett prepared this case under the supervision of Professor Benjamin C. Esty. HBS cases are developed solely as the basis for class discussion. Cases are not intended to serve as endorsements, sources of primary data, or illustrations of effective or ineffective management.

THE REPUBLIC OF VENEZUELA

Although Venezuela enjoyed a thriving democracy following the overthrow of its last military dictatorship in 1958, its economy grew by fits and starts largely due to dependence on the petroleum industry. Although petrodollars fueled growth in public expenditures during periods of high oil prices, the government's inability to curtail spending during periods of depressed oil prices led to inflation, currency devaluations, and macroeconomic instability. For example, a 20% decline in oil prices in 1988 precipitated a debt crisis, a situation remedied after the Pérez government restructured the country's bilateral debt as part of a comprehensive fiscal reform program backed by the International Monetary Fund and other international lending agencies. See Exhibit 15-1.

Although the Venezuelan economy improved in the early 1990s, political instability, including two failed military coups and the impeachment of President Pérez, soon undermined the recovery. The country's second largest bank collapsed in late 1993 triggering a financial sector crisis of unprecedented severity. In response, the newly elected Caldera administration suspended a number of constitutional rights, imposed price controls on basic goods and services, and took direct control over most of the banking system. It also closed the foreign exchange markets and began rationing foreign currency to the private sector, a policy that had been used previously during the 1980s' debt crisis. Due to a lack of administrative procedures for converting bolivars (Venezuela's national currency) into foreign currency, several private firms temporarily defaulted on their foreign currency debt, even though some had sufficient funds to service their debt. The government also fell into arrears on its own foreign currency debt and even defaulted on some local currency bonds.

After three years of economic turmoil, President Caldera announced an economic and social reform program called *Agenda Venezuela* in April 1996. The program eliminated price and exchange-rate controls, deregulated interest rates, reinforced a restrictive monetary policy, increased taxes, privatized a number of state-owned enterprises and financial institutions, and again restructured Venezuela's bilateral debt. *Agenda Venezuela* met with opposition from various sectors including Venezuelan labor unions, which had historically opposed wage cuts and price increases. But by late 1996, the program was on track and the economy had begun to recover. However, with the 1998 presidential elections on the horizon, public pressure to relax the unpopular austerity measures was growing.

Petróleos de Venezuela S.A. (PDVSA)

The Venezuelan government nationalized the domestic oil industry effective January 1, 1976, paying Royal Dutch Shell, Exxon, Conoco, Gulf, and Mobil, among others, a total of $1 billion in bonds and cash for their Venezuelan assets.[1] The government established PDVSA as a state-owned enterprise vested with commercial and financial autonomy to "efficiently develop and manage the country's hydrocarbon resources and promote economic development." Organizationally, PDVSA had three vertically integrated subsidiaries: Maraven, Lagoven, and Corpoven. Because Venezuela was a member of the Organization of the Petroleum Exporting Countries (OPEC), PDVSA was subject to OPEC policies and production quotas.

---

[1] The compensation package was approximately 20% of market value according to the foreign oil companies. David Gordon, "Too Much at Stake," *The Economist*, December 27, 1975, p. 12.

EXHIBIT 15-1

VENEZUELAN MACROECONOMIC DATA, 1970–1996

Year	Real GDP Growth	Per Capita GDP Growth[a]	Government Surplus/GDP[a]	Total Debt Stock/GDP	Oil Exports/Total Exports	Oil Exports/GDP	Unemployment Rate	Inflation Rate	Interest Rates[b]	Exchange Rate[c]
1970	7.3%	3.7%	(0.9%)	6.9%	89.0%	17.2%	7.8%	2.5%	...	4.450
1971	2.4	(1.0)	0.5	12.7	92.2	19.0	...	3.2	...	4.350
1972	2.5	(1.0)	(0.2)	15.2	91.4	17.3	...	2.8	...	4.350
1973	6.1	2.5	1.6	14.0	88.6	21.6	...	4.1	...	4.285
1974	5.2	1.7	2.4	8.6	95.2	33.4	7.6	8.3	...	4.285
1975	5.1	1.5	0.6	6.8	94.6	25.6	8.3	10.3	...	4.285
1976	8.3	4.6	0.5	13.3	94.2	23.6	6.8	7.6	...	4.293
1977	6.2	2.5	(4.4)	25.1	95.4	21.3	5.5	7.8	...	4.293
1978	2.2	(1.3)	(3.6)	35.7	95.1	18.8	5.1	7.1	...	4.293
1979	1.3	(2.0)	2.1	42.2	95.2	23.9	5.8	12.4	...	4.293
1980	(2.5)	(5.5)	0.0	42.0	94.9	26.2	6.6	21.5	...	4.293
1981	(0.2)	(3.0)	2.2	41.0	94.6	24.3	6.8	16.2	...	4.293
1982	0.8	(1.8)	(2.1)	40.2	94.7	19.5	7.8	9.6	...	4.293
1983	(5.2)	(7.5)	(0.6)	48.1	91.3	17.4	11.2	6.3	...	4.300
1984	(0.5)	(2.9)	2.8	63.8	87.7	21.0	14.3	12.2	13.15%	7.500
1985	1.1	(1.4)	2.0	59.0	82.6	17.3	14.3	11.4	12.55	7.500
1986	6.2	3.5	(0.4)	56.4	69.2	10.9	12.1	11.5	12.07	14.500
1987	4.5	1.7	(1.7)	73.8	81.8	14.9	9.9	28.1	13.49	14.500
1988	6.2	3.4	(6.1)	57.5	76.4	13.5	7.9	29.3	14.86	14.500
1989	(8.5)	(10.8)	(1.1)	75.6	74.9	23.4	9.7	84.7	17.32	43.079
1990	7.5	4.9	(2.1)	68.3	80.0	29.2	11.0	40.6	20.06	50.380
1991	10.1	7.5	(1.4)	63.8	81.1	23.1	10.1	34.2	27.14	61.554
1992	7.4	4.9	(3.8)	62.4	79.0	18.7	8.1	31.4	31.66	79.450
1993	(0.6)	(2.8)	(2.5)	62.2	74.7	18.0	6.8	38.1	41.03	105.640
1994	(2.5)	(4.6)	(6.8)	62.6	72.7	20.2	8.9	60.8	54.73	170.000
1995	3.7	1.5	(4.6)	46.0	74.4	17.9	10.9	59.9	53.38	290.000
1996	(0.4)	(2.5)	0.2	49.9	80.4	26.7	12.3	99.9	49.09	476.500

[a] Negative values signify Government Deficit/GDP.

[b] The interest rates provided are yields to maturity on long-term Venezuelan government bonds.

[c] The exchange rates provided are the official bolivar/U.S. dollar exchange rates determined by the Venezuelan government. Prior to 1989 and between 1994 and early 1996, the government fixed the exchange rate. Between 1989 and 1994 and after early 1996, the government allowed the bolivar to float freely against the U.S. dollar.

Sources: Inter-American Development Bank; and *International Financial Statistics*, International Monetary Fund.

As of 1996, PDVSA's oil and gas reserves were located exclusively in Venezuela, while its refining operations were located in the United States, Europe, and the Caribbean, as well as Venezuela. Through its wholly-owned U.S. subsidiaries, CITGO Petroleum Corporation and the Lemont Refinery, PDVSA had the third largest refinery capacity and the largest retail gasoline network in the United States. It was the world's second largest oil and gas company,[2] ranking behind Saudi Aramco and ahead of Royal Dutch Shell, the tenth most profitable corporation in the world, and generally viewed as one of the best managed national oil companies.[3] Domestically, PDVSA provided 78% of Venezuela's export revenues, 59% of the government's fiscal revenues, and 26% of the nation's GDP. See Exhibits 15-1, 15-2, and 15-3.

[2] According to a *Petroleum Intelligence Weekly* study cited in *The Oil Daily*, December 17, 1996, p. 2.

[3] See *The Petroleum Economist*, June 1993, p. 47, and June 1995, p. 12.

EXHIBIT 15-2

DU PONT AND PDVSA BALANCE SHEETS (U.S. DOLLARS IN MILLIONS), 1995–1996

	Du Pont		PDVSA	
	1996	1995	1996	1995
Assets				
Cash	$ 1,319	$ 1,455	$ 2,745	$ 464
Accounts and notes receivable	5,193	4,912	3,429	3,226
Inventory	3,706	3,737	1,740	1,551
Prepaid expenses	297	276	1,124	729
Deferred income taxes	588	575	508	429
Total current assets	$11,103	$10,955	$ 9,546	$ 6,399
Property, plant, and equipment	$21,213	$21,341	$32,957	$30,774
Investment in affiliates	2,278	1,846	1,863	1,899
Other assets	3,393	3,170	1,036	853
Total assets	**$37,987**	**$37,312**	**$45,402**	**$39,925**
Liabilities and equity				
Accounts payable	$2,757	$ 2,636	$ 2,033	$ 1,672
Current portion of long-term debt	300	551	1,137	1,074
Short-term debt and lease obligations	3,610	5,606	—	—
Income taxes	526	470	2,616	351
Other accrued liabilities	3,794	3,468	1,156	952
Total current liabilities	$10,987	$12,731	$ 6,942	$ 4,049
Long-term debt	$ 4,983	$ 5,572	$ 4,668	$ 4,933
Capital lease obligations	104	106	455	531
Deferred income taxes	2,133	1,783	19	313
Other liabilities	8,451	8,454	1,166	1,168
Total liabilities	$26,658	$28,646	$13,250	$10,994
Minority interests	$ 620	$ 230	$ 354	$ 271
Total stockholders' equity	10,709	8,436	31,798	28,660
Total liabilities and equity	**$37,987**	**$37,312**	**$45,402**	**$39,925**

Sources: Du Pont 1996 Annual Report; and PDVSA 1996 Form 20-F.

EXHIBIT 15-3

DU PONT AND PDVSA INCOME STATEMENTS (U.S. DOLLARS IN MILLIONS), 1995–1996

	Du Pont		PDVSA	
	1996	**1995**	**1996**	**1995**
Sales	$43,810	$42,163	$32,786	$25,050
Other income	1,340	1,059	1,069	991
Total income	$45,150	$43,222	$33,855	$26,041
Cost of goods sold	$25,144	$23,363	$15,720	$14,061
Selling, general, and administrative expenses	2,856	2,995	967	1,163
Depreciation, depletion, and amortization	2,621	2,722	2,749	2,400
Exploration expenses	1,436	1,398	142	118
Interest and debt expense	713	758	343	421
Taxes other than on income	6,399	6,596	3,203	2,513
Other expense (income), net	—	—	79	(354)
Equity earnings of affiliates	—	—	(89)	(132)
Minority interests	—	—	19	23
Total costs and expenses	$39,169	$37,832	$23,133	$20,213
Earnings before income taxes	$ 5,981	$ 5,390	$10,722	$ 5,828
Provision for income taxes	(2,345)	(2,097)	(6,227)	(2,455)
Net income	**$ 3,636**	**$ 3,293**	**$ 4,495**	**$ 3,373**
Earnings per share of common stock	$6.47	$5.61		
Average number of common shares (millions)	560.7	585.1		
Year-end stock price	$34.94	$47.06		

Sources: Du Pont 1996 Annual Report; and PDVSA 1996 Form 20-F.

As a state-owned enterprise, PDVSA paid the standard 34% corporate income tax rate; its operating subsidiaries paid royalties at the rate of 16.67% (times the value of crude oil produced) and income taxes at the rate of 67.7%. However, neither state nor municipal governments could tax PDVSA or its subsidiaries. Venezuelan law required the Central Bank to sell PDVSA foreign currency on a priority basis to meet its foreign exchange requirements, making it the only domestic company granted such a priority. The government also allowed PDVSA to maintain an offshore liquidity account of up to $600 million. Consequently, it had never rescheduled any of its debt or experienced debt payment delays. The law also required PDVSA to sell its foreign currency to the Central Bank after settling all foreign currency operating expenses, meeting external debt service obligations, and funding the liquidity account.

La Apertura ("The Opening")

In 1990, PDVSA began a long-term expansion initiative with the goals of doubling its domestic oil and gas production, increasing its refining capacity, and augmenting its international marketing operations. One of the company's major challenges was raising

$65 billion to fund this initiative. According to PDVSA, "The most limited resource that our petroleum industry has today is money."[4] To fund the expansion, PDVSA established a key strategy called *La Apertura* which opened the Venezuelan oil sector to foreign oil companies through profit-sharing agreements, operating service agreements, and strategic joint-venture associations. This strategy required a delicate balance between convincing the government that foreign investment would improve the domestic economy while at the same time making the business environment attractive to potential investors.

As part of this strategy, PDVSA targeted the Orinoco Belt in central Venezuela, the largest known heavy/extra heavy oil accumulation in the world, for development through strategic associations. It put forth specific criteria for identifying and selecting foreign partners, the most important of which were technological know-how, crude oil marketing capacity, and creditworthiness. In terms of ownership, PDVSA, or its subsidiaries, would contribute less than 50% of the associations' equity, but would retain voting control through the use of dual classes of stocks (PDVSA would get "priority" shares, while the foreign entities would get "partner" shares.) Because PDVSA would be a minority owner, the associations would be classified as private companies, which meant that they would not be consolidated into PDVSA's balance sheet. More importantly, they would not be bound by the numerous regulations facing public companies on such things as contract bidding procedures. Finally, the government agreed to lower the royalty rate for strategic associations during the early operating years while the Congress agreed to lower the income tax rate to 34% to improve the economics for heavy crude projects. As part of the agreement, the strategic associations would maximize Venezuelan content subject to price, quality, and deliverability.

In 1993, the Venezuelan Congress approved the first two in a series of planned strategic associations between PDVSA, its subsidiaries, and foreign oil companies. The first joint venture, Petrozuata, was between Maraven and Conoco Inc.; the second, Sincor, was between Maraven and three other international oil companies—TOTAL, Statoil, and Norsk Hydro.

Maraven, the PDVSA subsidiary involved in both deals, produced 30% of the Venezuela's crude oil, 14.5% of its natural gas, and 18.4% of its gas liquids in 1996. It also controlled 34% of all proven Venezuelan reserves, owned and operated two refineries in Venezuela, and had recently completed a $2.7 billion expansion of its Cardón refinery. See Exhibit 15-4.

CONOCO INC.

Petrozuata's other sponsor, Conoco, was the petroleum subsidiary of E. I. du Pont de Nemours and Company (Du Pont). Du Pont, one of the largest chemical producers in the world, operated some 200 manufacturing and processing facilities in 70 countries around the world and employed nearly 97,000 people in 1996. See Exhibits 15-2 and 15-3.

Conoco was an integrated global petroleum company with some 15,000 employees in over 40 countries. It produced 445,000 barrels per calendar day (BPCD) of crude oil and refined 720,000 BPCD in 1996.[5] Its marketing activities included selling gaso-

---

[4] Joseph Mann, "Survey of Venezuela," *The Financial Times*, December 4, 1992, p. 14.

[5] 1 barrel = 42 U.S. gallons.

EXHIBIT 15-4

CONOCO AND MARAVEN FINANCIAL INFORMATION (U.S. DOLLARS IN MILLIONS), 1995–1996

	Conoco		Maraven	
	1996	1995	1996	1995
Sales	$20,579	$17,958	$ 5,503	$ 4,073
Operating profit	1,818	1,257	3,574	1,924
Provision for income taxes	(933)	(660)	na	na
Equity in earnings of affiliates	(25)	22	—	—
After-tax operating income	$ 860	$ 619	$ 1,070	($16)
Identifiable assets	$13,018	$12,634	$10,814	$10,093
Depreciation, depletion, and amortization	1,128	1,111	940	770
Capital expenditures	1,616	1,714	612	1,871

Sources: Du Pont 1996 Annual Report; and PDVSA.

line, diesel, and motor oils through some 4,000 retail outlets in the United States, Europe, and Asia, while its transportation operations included ownership of seven oil tankers and interests in 8,000 miles of pipelines. See Exhibit 15-4.

Conoco was a recognized world leader in both refining technology and project development. It recently completed the $750 million Excel Paralubes hydrocracker project at its Lake Charles refinery in Louisiana, the $440 million Ardalin oil-field development project in Arctic Russia, and the $3.5 billion Heidrun offshore oil-field development project in Norway, for which it earned the 1996 Distinguished Achievement Award from the Offshore Technology Conference.

PETROLERA ZUATA, PETROZUATA C.A. (PETROZUATA)

PDVSA and Conoco began early feasibility studies for a joint project in 1992. Initial conversations concerned the development of a refinery project in Venezuela using Conoco's technology, but soon the parties were considering a fully integrated production, transportation, and refining project. Miguel Espinosa of Conoco described the decision to participate this way:

> In spite of our previous experience in Venezuela, we were eager to participate in the Venezuelan oil sector once again. We had long-standing commercial relationships with PDVSA—buying their crude to supply our refineries—and strong personal relationships. When the door opened, we took the opportunity.

Conoco was enthusiastic about a project in the Orinoco Belt for several reasons. First, the joint venture would be a development and not an exploration project. Second, it would provide Conoco with a low-cost source of reserves and a long-term supply of crude for its Lake Charles refinery. Finally, Conoco had the project experience and technological know-how to get the job done.

On the other side of the deal, PDVSA was excited to have Conoco as its first joint-venture partner. José Sifontes said:

> Because this was our first project, it would set the standard for future deals. Maraven had the heavy crude oil reserves and production technology, while Conoco had proven production and refining technology. The project could draw on Conoco's and Maraven's recent project experience to assemble a world-class management team and Du Pont's creditworthiness in financing. If done correctly, this deal would establish the benchmark for similar projects as Venezuela reopened its oil sector to foreign investment.

After four years of planning, Maraven and Conoco Orinoco, a Conoco affiliate established to hold equity in the project, formed Petrolera Zuata, Petrozuata C.A. (Petrozuata), the company responsible for constructing, financing, and managing the Petrozuata project. The association agreement, under which Maraven and Conoco Orinoco owned 49.9% and 50.1% of Petrozuata, respectively, had a term of 35 years beginning once production commenced in 2001. At the end of the agreement, Conoco would transfer its shares to Maraven at no cost.

The Petrozuata Project

The Petrozuata project had three main components: a series of inland wells to produce the extra heavy crude, a pipeline system to transport the crude to the coast, and an upgrader facility to partially refine the extra heavy crude. While it was somewhat unusual to finance a project with multiple components on a standalone basis, PDVSA and Conoco believed that Petrozuata was a truly integrated facility. Exhibit 15-5 provides an overview of the project, and Exhibit 15-6 provides a diagram of the project's contracts and commitments.

Petrozuata's upstream oil-field development consisted of drilling oil wells and constructing other related infrastructure. The company hired DeGolyer & MacNaughton, a U.S.-based oil and gas consulting firm with 60 years of experience in over 100 countries, to independently evaluate the project's reserves. They estimated that Petrozuata's assigned area contained 21.5 billion barrels of extra heavy crude oil, more than enough to sustain the planned production level of 120,000 BPCD. To produce the oil, Petrozuata planned to drill horizontal wells, an established drilling technique used in the Orinoco Belt and around the world. The crude would then be mixed with naphtha (a diluent) to reduce its viscosity and facilitate transportation from the oil fields to the coast.

Petrozuata planned to build two 125-mile steel pipelines to transport the mixture from the Orinoco Belt to the northeastern coastal city of José. A 36-inch pipeline would transport diluted crude to José, while a 20-inch pipeline would transport the diluent back to the oil fields for reuse. The pipeline would have the capacity to transport approximately 510,000 BPCD of diluted crude, an amount greater than the 160,000 BPCD capacity required for the project (120,000 BPCD of extra heavy crude oil and 40,000 BPCD of diluent). Petrozuata planned to sell the excess capacity to future projects in the area. The terrain between the oil fields and José was relatively flat and sparsely populated, and Petrozuata planned to lay most of the pipeline underground once it purchased the necessary land rights under the legal principle of eminent domain.

The pipeline would lead to downstream facilities consisting of an upgrader and loading facilities that represented 60% of the project's total construction cost. The upgrader would refine the extra heavy crude into higher-grade syncrude. Although variability in the crude's quality would diminish refining efficiency, the engineers did not

EXHIBIT 15-5

PETROZUATA PROJECT OVERVIEW

Project Schedule

	Date
• Begin Detailed Engineering for the Project	May 1996
• Start Oil-Field Construction	March 1997
• Award Contracts for Upgrader	June 1997
• Complete Oil-Field Development and Pipeline Construction	August 1998
• Begin Early Oil Production	August 1998
• Mechanical Completion of Project	July 2000
• Begin Completion Test	April 2001
• Final Completion Date	December 2001
• Final Completion Date in Case of *Force Majeure* Extension	September 2002

287

EXHIBIT 15-6

PETROZUATA CONTRACTS AND COMMITMENTS

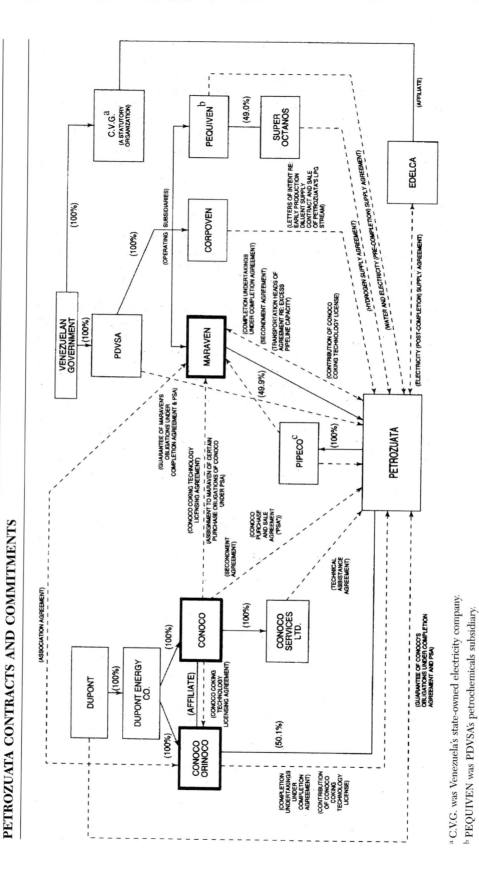

[a] C.V.G. was Venezuela's state-owned electricity company.

[b] PEQUIVEN was PDVSA's petrochemicals subsidiary.

[c] PIPECO was Petrozuata's pipeline subsidiary.

Source: Petrozuata Planning Documents.

expect this to be a major problem. The upgrader was designed to produce 102,000 BPCD of syncrude and several byproducts using proven Conoco refining technology. Once produced, the syncrude would be transferred via undersea loading lines into ocean-going tankers.

Petrozuata would act as the general contractor for the project. Although the project would be nearly self-sufficient in terms of electricity, water, and gas after completion, Petrozuata would contract with Venezuelan firms to provide these inputs during construction. The company anticipated awarding upstream construction contracts to Venezuelan engineering and construction companies that appeared in PDVSA's Registry of Authorized Contractors. The company put the engineering, procurement, and construction (EPC) contracts for the pipelines and downstream facilities out to bid to consortia of experienced contractors, including Mitsubishi Heavy Industries and Bechtel, two of the world's leading engineering and construction companies.

Stone & Webster Overseas Consultants, Inc., a U.S.-based consulting and engineering firm with over 100 years of petroleum project engineering experience, independently evaluated the project design, reviewed the performance and cost projections, and assessed the construction schedule. They concluded that the project's design was in accordance with good industry practice, its projected performance and costs were reasonable, and its construction schedule was aggressive but achievable. Moreover, it would comply with Venezuelan environmental laws and regulations as well as World Bank environmental standards.

Petrozuata's sponsors made a number of commitments to ensure successful completion of the project. First, Conoco and Maraven agreed to *severally*[6] provide funds to Petrozuata to pay project expenses, including any unexpected cost overruns, prior to completion. The parent corporations, Du Pont and PDVSA, guaranteed these obligations. Given the difference in ratings between the companies—Du Pont (AA−) and PDVSA (B)—this guarantee structure was somewhat unique. More typical completion guarantees involved either a letter of credit covering the lower-rated party's obligations or a *joint* guarantee with a fee paid by the lower-rated to the higher-rated sponsor. The completion guarantee also included severe penalties for failing to meet these obligations, and incentives to cover the other party's shortfalls. Second, the construction budget contained a $38 million contingency for upstream facilities, a $139 million contingency for downstream facilities, and sufficient funds to pay premiums on a construction all-risk insurance policy covering up to $1.5 billion of physical loss or damage.

Once Petrozuata completed construction, the sponsor guarantees would end, and project debt would become nonrecourse to the sponsors. In order to declare completion, however, Petrozuata would have to meet a number of criteria, including a 90-day operations test during which the production, pipeline, and upgrader would have to meet prescribed production levels and quality specifications. If Petrozuata did not complete the project by December 2001, a date it could extend for a defined period in the case of *force majeure*,[7] all debt would immediately become due and payable. Engineering consultants described the criteria as comprehensive and sufficient to ensure lender protection.

---

[6] A *several* guarantee means that each party is liable for its own share of the total but is not liable for its partner's share. In contrast, a *joint* guarantee means that each party is liable for the total amount.

[7] *Black's Law Dictionary* (5th ed.) (1979) defines *force majeure* as "causes which are outside the control of the parties and could not be avoided by exercise of due care." For Petrozuata, *force majeure* included government actions, acts of war or insurrection, acts of God, labor strikes or lockouts, or any other event beyond the control of the participants except a change in the price of crude oil on the international markets.

The Off-take Agreement

Conoco and Petrozuata signed a purchase agreement under which Conoco, with a guarantee from Du Pont, agreed to purchase the first 104,000 BPCD of Petrozuata's syncrude for the 35-year life of the project at a price based on the market price of Maya crude. Conoco planned to refine 62% of the syncrude at its Lake Charles refinery, while Maraven would purchase the balance from Conoco and refine it at its Cardón refinery in Venezuela (see Exhibits 15-5 and 15-6). Conoco was not required to purchase the syncrude during scheduled refinery downtime or in the case of *force majeure*. Because Petrozuata anticipated the development of a broader market for syncrude, it retained the right to sell the syncrude to third parties if it could get a higher price. The most likely customers were refineries that could efficiently process syncrude, the majority of which were located along the U.S. Gulf Coast.

Petrozuata hired Chem Systems Inc., a U.S.-based consulting firm specializing in petroleum marketing, to independently evaluate the project's marketing strategy and pricing formula. Chem Systems concluded that all of the byproducts would be readily salable and that the syncrude pricing formula was reasonable and consistent with expected market developments. It also estimated that a third-party market for Petrozuata's syncrude would develop within three to five years, and that third-party sales might realize approximately $1.00 per barrel (in 1996 dollars) more on average than the prices payable under the Conoco purchase agreement.

Payment Priority: The Cash Waterfall

The "cash waterfall," or prioritization of cash flows, was a key element of the contractual agreements. Petrozuata's customers would deposit their dollar-denominated funds from the purchase of syncrude and byproducts into an offshore proceeds account maintained by Bankers Trust, an arrangement authorized by the Venezuelan government and governed by the laws of New York. The Trustee would then disburse cash according to a payment hierarchy. First, the Trustee would fund a 90-day operating expense account; second, service the project's debt obligations; and, third, make deposits to a Debt Service Reserve Account (DSRA) as needed to maintain six months of principal and interest. Finally, the Trustee would transfer any remaining funds to Petrozuata for distribution to its equityholders, subject to the restriction that the project maintain a one-year historical and one-year projected Debt Service Coverage Ratio (DSCR) of 1.35X.[8]

FUNDING THE PETROZUATA PROJECT

When PDVSA first embarked on *La Apertura*, it was unclear how the strategic associations would be funded. Francisco Bustillos described PDVSA's decision to use a project finance structure for the Petrozuata deal this way:

> We had a great project, but we didn't know if project finance was the best alternative. Given the strength of PDVSA's balance sheet, we would have had no trouble financing the deal through a corporate issue. But because this was the first in a series of planned projects, and because our financial flexibility is absolutely critical to our success, we decided to use the project finance structure to preserve our debt capacity.

---

[8] DSCR = (Cash Available for Debt Service or CADS)/(Principal + Interest).

For these reasons, Petrozuata's planning team decided to proceed under the assumption that the project would be financed on a standalone, nonrecourse basis (at least after the construction phase). The team decided that 60% of the $2.425 billion expenditure would come from debt financing. Sifontes described the choice this way: "We could have gone higher, but we chose to invest more equity to show our commitment to the project." If the funding were successful, it would far exceed the $50 to $200 million deals that were more typical in Latin America. Having decided on a capital structure, they still had to decide on where to get the equity and what kind of debt to use.

Sources of Equity Funds

Under the proposed capital structure, Petrozuata would need $975 million of equity to finance construction between 1996 and 2000. To get the project started and cover expenses through 1996, Maraven and Conoco contributed $79 million of paid-in capital. Because Petrozuata projected completion of the oil fields and pipeline in August 1998, the sponsors planned to sell early production crude and use the proceeds to fund $530 million of the financing need. Sifontes acknowledged that "funding the construction with early production cash flows would be risky, but we had a good execution plan, strong sponsor guarantees, and experience marketing heavy crude." The sponsors planned to fund the difference between early production cash flows and remaining project costs with additional equity contributions. Exhibit 15-7 provides sources and uses of funds for 1996 to 2000.

Sources of Debt Financing

Given Venezuela's political and economic instability in early 1996 and the unprecedented size of the financing, Petrozuata's planning team initially envisioned raising debt from commercial banks with loan guarantees from bilateral and multilateral agencies.[9] According to the initial financing plan, Petrozuata would approach a number of agencies, including the U.S. ExIm Bank, Export Development Corporation of Canada (EDC), OPIC, and IFC to gauge their interest in providing political risk insurance (PRI) or, in some cases, investing directly in the project. While the team initially thought they could get up to $200 million of uncovered bank loans (loans without PRI), the majority of the debt would probably require PRI.

The major advantage of using bank debt was that Petrozuata could draw on its credit line as needed, thereby allowing it to match its cash inflows and outflows. In the current interest rate environment, they expected to pay six-month LIBOR plus 75 to 200 basis points for the bank debt (a rate of 7.50% to 8.75%). Bank loans, however, had a number of disadvantages: short maturities, restrictive covenants, variable interest rates, and limited size. The problem with a short maturity was that payments during Petrozuata's early years of operation would increase the financial risk posed by oil price volatility and construction delays. Bank debt would also be expensive if lenders required PRI to cover Venezuelan country risk. While the inclusion of PRI might add an additional 300 basis points on top of the borrowing rate, the main problem with covered bank debt was that it could take 12 to 18 months to arrange.

---

[9] Bilateral agencies provide loans and loan guarantees to purchase equipment manufactured in the exporting country. Multilateral agencies provide loans and loan guarantees to foster economic growth in developing nations. Loan guarantees, or political risk insurance (PRI), protect creditors against political and sovereign risks such as currency nonconvertibility, expropriation, political violence, and war.

EXHIBIT 15-7

SOURCES AND USES OF FUNDS (U.S. DOLLARS IN THOUSANDS), 1996–2000

	1996	1997	1998	1999	2000	Total
Uses						
Capital Expenditures						
Crude Oil Production	$11,995	$ 191,849	$151,141	$ 77,092	$ 16,702	$ 448,780
Crude Oil Pipeline	655	170,512	45,121	0	0	216,288
Upgrader & Loading Facility[a]	14,345	243,305	510,987	230,306	67,912	1,066,854
Upstream Contingency	0	0	0	0	37,925	37,925
Total Capex	$26,994	$ 605,666	$707,249	$307,399	$122,539	$1,769,847
Other Costs						
Deferred Development Costs and Operating Expenditures	$52,040	$ 23,328	$ 71,724	$ 0	$ 0	$ 147,093
Initial Cash Balance	0	0	10,000	0	0	10,000
Financing Costs	0	61,134	86,816	94,955	111,556	354,461
Legal & Advisory Fees	0	15,000	0	0	0	15,000
Debt Service Reserve	0	0	0	0	80,865	80,865
Excess Cash Balance	0	47,213	0	0	195	47,408
Total Uses	**$79,035**	**$ 752,341**	**$875,789**	**$402,353**	**$315,155**	**$2,424,673**
Sources						
Total Project Debt	$ 0	$1,000,000	$ 24,299	$242,981	$182,720	$1,450,000
Shareholder Funds						
Initial Paid in Capital	$79,035	$ 0	$ 0	$ 0	$ 0	$ 79,035
Additional Paid-in Capital	0	1,986	550,148	(1,576)	(185,047)	365,511
Operating Cash Flow[b]	0	47,213	4,484	160,948	317,481	530,126
Total Shareholder Funds	$79,035	$ 49,199	$554,632	$159,373	$132,434	$ 974,673
Total Sources	**$79,035**	**$1,049,199**	**$578,931**	**$402,353**	**$315,155**	**$2,424,673**

[a] Includes a $139 million contingency.

[b] Includes interest income.

Source: Petrozuata Planning Documents.

Because of the time and cost of arranging "covered" bank debt, the team began to consider other options including the public bond market. Generally, public bonds had long maturities (often greater than 10 years), fixed interest rates, and fewer, more flexible covenants. They were also available in larger amounts (often greater than $100 million). The major disadvantage of bond financing was that the funds had to be raised in a lump sum. To the extent that there were unused proceeds, the excess funds would create a drag on earnings (known as negative carry) because the investment rate on those funds would be less than the borrowing rate on the debt. In any case, it was highly unlikely that an emerging market project could tap the public debt markets.

Instead, a more feasible alternative was the private placement market and, in particular, the Rule 144A market. Privately placed bonds not only shared the advantages of public bonds, but also had the additional advantage of speed: 144A bonds could be underwritten within six months because they did not require initial disclosure to the

Securities and Exchange Commission (SEC). In exchange for less onerous initial and ongoing disclosure requirements (although no less complete), only qualified institutional investors could buy 144A bonds (similar rules applied to re-sales).

The bankers felt that a window of opportunity was opening in late 1996 as Venezuela's financial condition was improving and the U.S. bond market was heating up. As a result, the bankers thought they might be able to issue up to $650 million in project bonds at rates of 8.0% to 9.0% as long as the markets remained hot and Petrozuata could get an investment-grade rating. If the markets cooled down a little, then they would decrease the size of the offering; if the markets cooled down significantly or if Petrozuata could not get an investment-grade rating, then they would drop the offering completely. In any case, they would continue discussions with the development agencies and banks as alternative sources of funds. Toward that end, the team sent Requests for Proposals (RFP) to several banks to gauge their interest in the deal and to see whether they would require PRI coverage.

The fact that both Venezuela and PDVSA had subinvestment-grade ratings remained a potential stumbling block because it would not be economical to issue non-investment-grade bonds. One note of cautious optimism came when Ras Laffan, a $3.7 billion natural gas project in Qatar, issued $1.2 billion of 144A project bonds in mid-December 1996.[10] The bonds not only received an investment-grade rating, but also set a record as the largest emerging market project financing to date. Given PDVSA's substantial capital needs, opening the capital markets as a new source of funds was important both to this deal and to future deals.

Rating Petrozuata's Project Bonds

In addition to the financial advisors from Citicorp, the newly hired bankers from CS First Boston, Wallace Henderson, Jonathan Bram, and Andy Brooks, would play an important role in shepherding the project through the ratings process. They knew that the rating agencies' credit risk assignment process centered on identifying a project's weakest links in operations, financing, or between the two. In Petrozuata's case, the rating agencies would assess three main factors: the sponsors' creditworthiness, project economics, and Venezuela's sovereign risk.

Because Conoco and Maraven were subsidiaries without publicly traded debt, the rating agencies would primarily consider the creditworthiness of their respective parent companies. S&P and Moody's rated Du Pont's long-term senior unsecured debt Aa3 and AA−, respectively. Conoco's standalone creditworthiness was also relevant because Du Pont could spin off or sell its petroleum subsidiary. As for PDVSA, its long-term senior unsecured debt had the same credit rating as the Republic of Venezuela, B from S&P and Ba2 from Moody's. According to Bustillos, "PDVSA would have a AAA rating if it were located in the United States—but because it was in Venezuela and its lone shareholder was the Venezuelan government, its rating was capped by the sovereign rating."

To assess Petrozuata's economics, the rating agencies would analyze the project's technical, reserve, and construction risks, and examine its financial projections. Then, to assess the inherent business risk, they would analyze companies in similar lines of business or similar projects. See Exhibit 15-8. Because Petrozuata would have to meet its debt obligations even if oil prices decreased, Petrozuata's planning team would

---

[10] Ras Laffan's offering received a BBB+ rating from S&P. The project's participants were the Qatari government (BBB), Mobil (AA), Qatar General Petroleum (BBB), and Korea Gas (AA−).

EXHIBIT 15-8

OIL AND GAS INDUSTRY COMPARABLES, 1996 (UNLESS OTHERWISE INDICATED)

	S&P Rating	Country	Country Rating	Debt to Value (%)	Pretax Interest Coverage (X)	EBITDA/ Interest (X)	Operating Income as a % of Revenue	Revenues ($ millions)
Oil & Gas Projects								
Athabasca Oil Sands	BBB	Canada	AA+	26.8%	8.15X	11.09X	32.3%	$ 251.5
Canadian Oil Sands	BBB+	Canada	AA+	22.9	8.62	13.49	30.7	118.3
YPF Sociedad Anonima	BBB	Argentina	BBB–	34.8	4.77	8.20	44.0	5,937.0
Ras Laffan (2001)	BBB+	Qatar	BBB	62.7	4.51	na	51.1	851.6
Petrozuata (2001)	**???**	**Venezuela**	**B**	**60.0**	**4.70**	**3.65**	**79.4**	**569.2**
Independent Oil Companies								
Apache	BBB	US	AAA	45.8X	2.68X	5.85X	60.1%	$ 976.0
Burlington Resources	A–	US	AAA	37.9	3.70	6.56	62.6	1,293.0
Husky Oil	BBB	Canada	AA+	41.9	2.66	5.02	39.7	1,272.9
Noble Affiliates	BBB	US	AAA	54.1	4.49	10.72	46.0	878.3
Norcen Energy Resources	BBB	Canada	AA+	49.6	1.49	4.99	42.2	1,257.3
Talisman Energy	BBB+	Canada	AA+	30.0	4.54	10.24	59.0	1,182.9
Integrated Oil Companies								
Amoco	AAA	US	AAA	26.6X	13.08X	21.22X	18.9%	$ 32,150.0
Chevron	AA	US	AAA	32.0	9.85	14.20	16.9	37,580.0
Exxon	AAA	US	AAA	21.0	10.25	15.06	13.8	116,728.0
Mobil	AA	US	AAA	32.7	11.73	16.69	11.9	71,129.0
Texaco	A+	US	AAA	39.3	5.68	8.83	10.1	44,561.0
Shell Canada	AA	Canada	AA+	20.6	6.57	10.47	19.7	5,140.0
PDVSA	**B**	**Venezuela**	**B**	**15.4**	**32.26**	**40.27**	**48.7**	**33,855.0**

Sources: S&P Global Sector Review; Bloomberg; and casewriter estimates.

present a scenario analysis using historical crude prices to illustrate the project's vulnerability to oil price declines.

On the issue of sovereign risk, the rating agencies would consider three principal risks: possible government action, currency market volatility, and Venezuelan business conditions. The government could impose foreign exchange controls once again; it could ask Conoco to divert its payments for syncrude outside of the structure of the revenue waterfall; or it could order Petrozuata to sell syncrude to an entity other than Conoco. Beyond outright seizure of assets, the government could affect the project's economics by changing the tax or royalty rates. The second sovereign risk centered on exchange rates. An appreciation of the bolivar would increase Petrozuata's operating expenses and tax liability relative to its dollar-denominated revenues. Finally, Petrozuata would be exposed to Venezuelan business risks such as the creditworthiness of local suppliers and contractors, the fragility of the Venezuelan financial sector, and the volatility of the labor market. Exhibit 15-9 provides sovereign credit ratings for Venezuela and other countries.

Financial Projections and Analysis

In preparation for the meetings, the planning team put the finishing touches on their financial projections and sensitivity analysis. They used their financial model to assess the project's revenue assumptions, operating costs, sponsor returns, and debt coverage ratios. First, along with Chem Systems, the team finalized the syncrude price projections used in the model. For 1998, the base case assumed a syncrude price of $12.87 per barrel, well below the current Maya price of $18.62 per barrel. As the meetings approached, however, petroleum analysts were predicting a decrease in the price of Maya to about $16.00 per barrel within the next few months.

In terms of operating costs, the project's major post-completion costs included labor and overhead (38%), well servicing (15%), utilities (13%), and maintenance materials (8%). Its projected finding and development (F&D) costs were very low, approximately $0.25 per barrel. In comparison, Athabasca, a Canadian project with a cost structure more typical of oil and gas projects, had F&D costs of $1.13 per barrel, while the petroleum industry's median F&D cost was $4.96 per barrel.[11] Furthermore, Petrozuata's 2001 cash operating cost of $3.19 per barrel was well below both and the industry median and Athabasca's cash operating costs of $8.55 and $9.36, respectively.[12]

The team then analyzed sponsor returns. Exhibit 15-10a presents cash flow projections assuming reduced income tax rates for the project's 35-year life, a reduced royalty rate through 2008, and a mixture of bank, agency, and bond financing. In particular, the projections assumed that the sponsors could issue at least $650 million in project bonds and that the rest of the debt would come from banks and various agencies. Exhibit 15-10b provides capital markets data, while Exhibit 15-11 shows the calculation of the project's cost of capital.

Finally, the team assessed the project's debt capacity, minimum debt service coverage ratio (DSCR), and breakeven oil price. To get an investment-grade rating, the project's base case DSCR would probably have to exceed 1.80X (if not 2.0X); its DSCR under various stress cases would probably have to exceed 1.50X; and its breakeven price would have to be low enough so that the project could cover all operating and

[11] Standard & Poor's estimate.
[12] Ibid.

EXHIBIT 15-9

CREDIT RATINGS FOR SELECTED SOVEREIGN FOREIGN CURRENCY LONG-TERM DEBT[a]

Sovereign	S&P[b]		Moody's[b]		Institutional Investor[c]	
	Dec. 1994	Dec. 1996	Dec. 1994	Dec. 1996	Sept. 1994	Sept. 1996
North America						
Canada	AA+	AA+	Aa1	Aa2	81.3	79.4
Mexico	BB	BB	Baa1	Ba2	46.1	41.6
United States	AAA	AAA	Aaa	Aaa	90.8	90.7
Central America						
Costa Rica	n/r	n/r	n/r	n/r	30.3	33.9
Panama	n/r	n/r	n/r	n/r	24.4	28.5
South America						
Argentina	BB−	BB−	B2	B1	37.3	38.9
Bolivia	n/r	n/r	n/r	n/r	21.4	25.4
Brazil	B+	B+	B1	B1	30.3	38.3
Chile	BBB+	A−	Baa2	Baa1	54.9	61.2
Colombia	n/r	BBB−	n/r	Baa3	44.4	46.7
Ecuador	n/r	n/r	n/r	n/r	24.5	26.4
Peru	n/r	n/r	n/r	B3	21.0	30.0
Venezuela	B+	B	Ba2	Ba2	36.0	32.0

[a] A foreign currency long-term debt rating is the rating agency's assessment of each government's capacity and willingness to repay its foreign currency denominated long-term debt according to the debt's terms. n/r = not rated.

[b] The following table provides a guide to S&P's and Moody's ratings. Note that between ratings categories, there are modifiers: S&P uses two (+ and −); and Moody's uses three (1, 2, and 3), where 1 is the highest rank.

S&P	Moody's
Investment Grade	
AAA	Aaa
AA	Aa
A	A
BBB	Baa
Non-investment Grade	
BB	Ba
B	B
CCC	Caa
CC	Ca
C	C

[c] Institutional Investor's "Country Credit Ratings" were based on a survey of 75 to 100 international banks. Bankers were asked to grade each country on a scale of 0 to 100, with 100 representing the least chance of default.

Source: Bloomberg; and "Country Credit Ratings," *Institutional Investor*, March 1995 and September 1996.

EXHIBIT 15-10A

PETROZUATA EQUITY CASH FLOW PROJECTIONS (U.S. DOLLARS IN THOUSANDS)

Year	Forecast Price of Syncrude	Total Revenue	Cash Available for Debt Service (CADS)	Total Debt Service	Cash Used for Debt Service Reserve Account	Equity Cash Flows		Total Debt
						Dividends	Investment	
1996	$12.25	$ 0					($79,035)	$ 0
1997	12.56	0		($61,134)			(1,986)	1,000,000
1998	12.87	78,524		(86,816)			(550,148)	1,024,299
1999	13.19	429,059		(94,955)		$ 1,576		1,267,280
2000	13.52	804,108	$317,481	(111,556)	($80,865)	185,047		1,450,000
2001	13.86	569,156	384,765	(160,922)	1,614	225,457		1,411,111
2002	14.21	583,597	389,154	(157,694)	1,614	233,074		1,372,222
2003	14.56	598,398	366,575	(154,466)	(11,509)	200,600		1,333,333
2004	14.93	613,568	401,552	(176,949)	(5,700)	218,903		1,268,856
2005	15.30	629,117	398,211	(188,009)	(6,345)	203,857		1,187,614
2006	15.68	645,052	433,477	(200,307)	(550)	232,620		1,086,961
2007	16.07	661,386	435,267	(201,204)	(4,671)	229,393		977,484
2008	16.47	678,126	438,118	(210,153)	10,623	238,588		849,556
2009	16.89	695,283	373,182	(166,148)	19,595	226,629		755,137
2010	17.31	712,869	371,469	(150,455)	(4,135)	216,878		669,137
2011	17.74	730,892	378,471	(158,377)	(3,438)	216,655		567,137
2012	18.19	749,365	387,428	(164,964)	40,417	262,881		449,137
2013	18.64	768,299	328,978	(85,668)	(933)	242,378		401,689
2014	18.64	768,798	358,441	(87,403)	(19,051)	251,988		348,241
2015	18.64	769,309	391,545	(124,573)	(6,498)	260,474		252,034
2016	18.64	769,831	383,528	(137,103)	4,468	250,893		134,448
2017	18.64	770,365	382,868	(68,691)	62,038	376,215		75,000
2018	18.64	770,911	327,531	(6,653)	0	320,878		75,000
2019	18.64	771,468	308,024	(6,653)	0	301,370		75,000
2020	18.64	781,859	283,051	(6,653)	0	276,398		75,000
2021	18.64	782,441	299,464	(6,653)	0	292,810		75,000
2022	18.64	783,036	295,554	(81,653)	3,327	217,227		0
2023	18.64	783,644	294,578	0	0	294,578		
2024	18.64	784,266	289,656			289,656		
2025	18.64	784,901	289,705			289,705		
2026	18.64	785,550	278,074			278,074		
2027	18.64	786,214	276,806			276,806		
2028	18.64	786,891	274,449			274,449		
2029	18.64	787,584	263,604			263,604		
2030	18.64	788,291	247,540			247,540		
2031	18.64	789,014	250,329			250,329		
2032	18.64	789,753	242,937			242,937		
2033	18.64	790,508	240,644			240,644		
2034	18.64	791,279	226,196			226,196		

EXHIBIT 15-10B

CAPITAL MARKETS DATA (AS OF JANUARY 1997)

Government or Interbank Debt	Yields	Corporate Bond Ratings (U.S. Industrials)	Yields
Federal Funds Rate	5.19%	AAA	7.13%
3-month Treasury Bill	5.03	AA	7.21
3-month LIBOR	5.78	A	7.39
10-year Treasury Bond	6.56	BBB	7.70
30-year Treasury Bond	6.81	BB	8.69

Sources: Petrozuata Planning Documents; Federal Reserve Bulletin; S&P Bond Guide, and casewriter estimates.

---

financing costs if oil prices fell substantially. The team estimated the project's nominal breakeven price (i.e., where DSCR = 1.0X) to be $8.63 per barrel in 2008, the year of highest forecasted debt service. Exhibit 15-12 provides information on historical crude prices.

CONCLUSION

The upcoming meetings in Washington and New York were indicative of the planning team's financing strategy. In Washington, the team would advance the agency financing option; in New York, they would advance the capital markets and bank financing options. The plan, at least with the rating agencies, was to tell them "we consider Petrozuata an investment-grade project." According to Sifontes:

> We could not leave any gaps in the documentation. We needed to convince the rating agencies that the project was an excellent opportunity for the sponsors and for potential lenders. While we would admit there were risks, we would show how the deal structure effectively mitigated those risks where possible.

In fact, the theme for the meeting was: "Petrozuata: sterling sponsorship, sound project fundamentals, and strong financial structure." If the rating agencies agreed, then the sponsors might get the investment-grade rating they were after. On the other hand, if the rating agencies disagreed, then the sponsors would have to pursue the original plan of agency and bank financing.

EXHIBIT 15-11

COST OF CAPITAL CALCULATION

The appropriate discount rate for discounting free cash flows (FCF) is the weighted average cost of capital, which is defined as:

$$\text{WACC} = (K_D)\,(1 - \tau)\,(D/(D + E)) + (K_E)\,(E/(D + E))$$

where
K_D = expected cost of debt for the project
K_E = expected cost of equity for the project
τ = expected effective tax rate
D = expected market value of the debt level of the project
E = expected market value of the equity level of the project

Although the NPV formula calls for a different WACC in each year, generally one WACC is used for the term of the project. The most difficult input to calculate is the project's cost of equity (K_E), which takes into account the risk related to the business. Business risk is calculated through observed costs of equity of publicly listed comparable companies, as reflected in their observed equity betas. Because companies in their developing stages have a greater amount of business risk than companies in more mature stages, a start-up premium (SP) adjustment is made. A premium for country risk (CP) is determined separately and then added to the cost of equity.

$$K_E = R_f + \beta_E\,(R_M - R_f) + SP + CP$$

- Petrozuata's equity beta (β_E) is 0.94, which is estimated by relevering the average asset beta ($\beta_A = 0.38$) from a sample of four U.S. oil refineries (Ashland, Tosco, Ultramar, and Valero Energy), assuming a capital structure with 60% debt.
- Based on average data from 1926 to 1994:
  a) The current 7.00% yield on long-term U.S. Treasury bonds less a 1.4% liquidity premium is a proxy for the risk-free rate (5.60% = 7.00% − 1.40%). The 1.4% represents the average premium of long-term Treasury bonds over short-term Treasury bills.
  b) A **7.0% risk premium** is generally used. The premium is based on the average returns of large company stocks less the returns of long-term Treasury bonds.
  c) The equity market risk premium for start-up companies has averaged 2.1%.
- The approximate spread of Venezuelan Eurobonds over U.S. Treasury bonds (1000 basis points) would generally be used to determine the country risk premium. Actually, this spread should be considered the upper bound for political risk because the probability of expropriation of a local project is lower than the default risk of a developing country's government bond. The premium can be scaled down under circumstances specific to a particular operating situation. In this case, an appropriate country risk premium for Petrozuata is two-thirds of that, or 667 basis points, especially given the export nature of the project and its U.S. dollar revenues.
- The assumed 10% cost of debt is a conservative estimate of what Petrozuata might have to pay for uncovered bank debt.

Using these inputs and the assumption that the project will be funded with 60% debt and face an income tax rate of 35%, Petrozuata's cost of equity (K_E) and WACC are:

$$K_E = 5.60\% + (0.94)\,(7.00\%) + 2.1\% + 6.67\% = \mathbf{20.97\%}$$

$$\text{WACC} = (60\%)\,(1 - 0.35)\,(10\%) + (40\%)\,(20.97\%) = \mathbf{12.29\%}$$

Source: Petrozuata Planning Documents.

EXHIBIT 15-12

HISTORICAL MONTHLY CRUDE PRICES (U.S. DOLLARS PER BARREL), 1974–1996

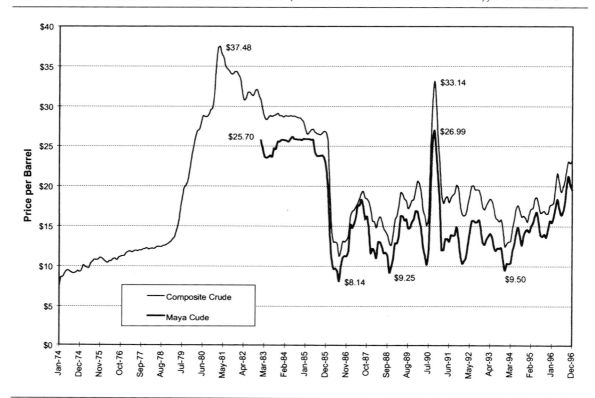

	Full Data Sample 1982–1996	10 Years 1986–1996	5 Years 1991–1996
Average Maya Price ($/barrel)	$16.57	$14.27	$14.25
Average Monthly Change in Maya Price (%)	0.29%	0.47%	0.22%
Standard Deviation of Monthly Price Changes (%)	9.74	10.91	7.95
Standard Deviation of Annual Price Changes (%)	33.73	37.79	27.54

Sources: The composite crude prices are from *Monthly Energy Review*; 1974–1996; Charles Riner of the Energy Information Administration provided the Maya Crude prices.

16

Poland's A2 Motorway

Unlike other infrastructure sectors, where the provision of services is monopolistic in nature or the demand risks are mitigated by contracts with a known, credit-worthy off-taker, toll roads and their operators increasingly will be exposed to users that are sensitive to time-value tradeoffs and underlying economic variables.

—Standard & Poor's[1]

Wojciech Gebicki (pronounced Voy'-check Geh-beet'-ski), vice president—finance, and chief financial officer of Autostrada Wielkopolska, S.A. (AWSA), sat in his Warsaw office preparing for a meeting he had scheduled for the following day with bankers from Credit Lyonnais and Commerzbank. AWSA, a consortium of Polish and Western European firms, had won an exclusive concession to build and operate a major segment of the proposed A2 Motorway, the first private toll road in Poland. Gebicki had been hired by AWSA in October 1999, to secure a €242 million commercial bank loan as part of the project's €934 million total cost. The financing plan, which had undergone numerous changes since AWSA won the concession in 1997, reflected input from AWSA, its legal advisors Mike Webster and Piotr Swiecicki (Pio'-ter Shven-cheet'-ski) from Baker & McKenzie, the shareholder Finance Committee led by Anfrid Lenned of NCC (a large Swedish construction company), and the company's financial advisor Stephen Uhlig from Deutsche Bank, as well as representatives from the Polish Ministries of Transport and Finance.

Four months earlier, in February 2000, AWSA had chosen Credit Lyonnais and Commerzbank as joint lead arrangers for the bank financing. Although the banks had submitted a firm underwriting proposal, their commitment was subject to due diligence, including a review of the underlying traffic forecasts and financial projections. In requesting this meeting, the bankers had expressed concerns with the traffic forecasts, and indicated the deal might require an additional €60 million to €90 million of equity to cover shortfalls in certain downside scenarios. Gebicki worried that any change

Dean's Research Fellow Michael Kane and Professor Benjamin C. Esty prepared this case. HBS cases are developed solely as the basis for class discussion. Cases are not intended to serve as endorsements, sources of primary data, or illustrations of effective or ineffective management.

[1] Forsgren, K., et al., "The Toll Road Sector: Smooth Conditions Overall But Watch for Caution Flags," *Standard & Poor's Infrastructure Finance*, October 1999, p. 149.

at this point would, at a minimum, entail difficult negotiations with the shareholders and could, in the extreme, derail the entire concession. If the financing were not closed by July 29, less than six weeks away, the concession would expire. Before his recent conversation with the bankers, he had been convinced that the project structure was solid and that the deal team had effectively assessed, mitigated, and allocated all of the major risks. But now, he knew they would have to revisit many of the key assumptions, particularly those with regard to the revenue and traffic forecasts.

POLAND AND THE TOLL MOTORWAYS ACT

Poland provided a natural land bridge between Eastern and Western Europe. With a land area of 128,000 square miles and a population of some 39 million people, it was the largest of the former Soviet Union satellite countries in Central Europe (see Exhibit 16-1). Under the Polish Communist Party, there had been state ownership of most businesses, centralized planning, price controls and subsidies, and a welfare state. Although Poland achieved some economic growth during the 1980s, it experienced recurring shortages of consumer goods, labor unrest, hyperinflation, and government deficits.

With Gorbachev's *glasnost* came the collapse of the Communist Party's control of Poland. The Solidarity movement won the elections of June 1989 and ushered in an era of economic and political reform. Finance Minister Leszek Balcerowicz implemented a liberalization program known as the "Big Bang."[2] Despite the harsh impact this "shock therapy" had on the country, Poland maintained political stability. In the subsequent years, GDP grew, inflation subsided, and the currency (the zloty[3] or PLN) stabilized (see Exhibits 16-2, 16-3a, and 16-3b). By early 2000, it appeared that Poland had succeeded in building political democracy and a free market economy, though it still had a long way to go to achieve economic parity with most Western European countries. Its GDP per capita of $7,270 still lagged behind that of other Central European countries like Hungary ($9,020) and the Czech Republic ($11,300), and remained far behind that of European Union (EU) members such as Greece ($16,800), Spain ($19,300), and Germany ($24,800). As further links to Western Europe, Poland joined NATO in 1999 and was a leading candidate to join the EU in the first expansion wave planned for 2004. Admission to the EU was a high priority for the Polish government and all of the major political parties.

Besides reforming the economy, the government also recognized the need to upgrade and expand the country's transportation infrastructure. Toward that end, the government approved the construction of a 2,600-km[4] tolled motorway system in September 1993, which consisted of four main routes, two running east-west (the A2 and A4 motorways in Exhibit 16-1) and two running north-south (A1 and A3 in Exhibit 16-1). Compared to Poland's 264 km of existing motorways, 130 km of which was built before World War II, the program represented an ambitious target.[5] The government hoped

[2] Kennedy and Sandler, "Shock Therapy in Eastern Europe: The Polish and Czechoslovak Economic Reforms," Harvard Business School Case No. 797-068 (Boston: Harvard Business School Publishing, 1997, Rev. 3/13/99), p. 7.

[3] Since January 1, 1999, the zloty had been pegged to the U.S. dollar (45%) and the Euro (55%). Since March 25, 1999, the rate of monthly devaluation had been 0.3%, and the zloty had been allowed to float within a band of ± 15% around the central parties. (*Source:* International Monetary Fund Website: http://dsbb.imf.org/country/pol)

[4] 100 kilometers or km equals 62.2 miles.

[5] International Road Federation, *World Road Statistics 1999 Edition*, p. 26.

EXHIBIT 16-1

THE POLISH MOTORWAY PROGRAM

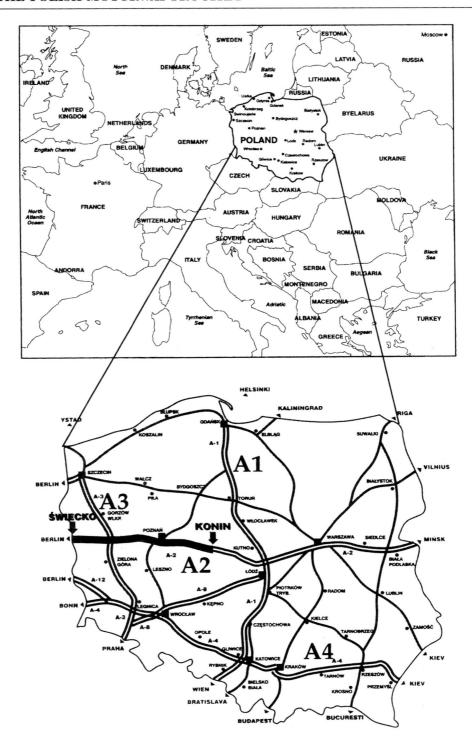

Source: Casewriter, Deutsche Bank AG, *A2 Motorway—POLAND, Information Memorandum,* November 1999.

EXHIBIT 16-2

POLISH ECONOMIC DATA 1991–1999

	Units	1991	1992	1993	1994	1995	1996	1997	1998	1999
Population	million	38.2	38.4	38.5	38.5	38.6	38.6	38.6	38.7	38.7
Macroeconomic Data										
Gross domestic product (real)	million PLN	52,121	53,490	55,422	58,409	62,477	66,245	70,778	74,200	77,250
Change in real GDP	% change	−7.0	2.6	3.8	5.2	7.0	6.0	6.8	4.8	4.1
Nominal GDP per capita	$US	$4,240	$4,450	$4,715	$5,050	$5,520	$5,960	$6,480	$6,880	$7,270
Unemployment rate	percent	n/a	13.6	15.0	16.5	15.2	14.3	11.5	10.0	12.3
Total exports (fob)	million $US	14,913	13,187	14,219	17,272	22,893	24,440	25,751	28,229	27,407
Total imports (cif)	million $US	15,766	16,142	18,779	21,596	29,073	37,137	42,308	47,054	45,911
Foreign direct investment	million $US	291	678	1,715	1,875	3,659	4,498	4,908	6,365	n/a
Government fiscal balance	million zloty	n/a	n/a	n/a	(4,812)	(5,762)	(7,826)	(6,162)	(5,561)	n/a
Rates and Inflation										
Exchange rate (average)	zloty/$US	1.06	1.36	1.81	2.27	2.43	2.70	3.28	3.48	3.97
Bank lending rate	% p.a.	54.6	39.0	35.3	32.8	33.5	26.1	25.0	24.5	17.0
Consumer prices	% change	60.4	44.3	37.6	29.5	21.6	18.5	13.2	8.6	9.8
Country Credit Ratings										
S&P Long-term Foreign Currency Debt Rating		Not rated	Not rated	Not rated	Not rated	BB	BBB−	BBB−	BBB−	BBB
Institutional Investor Country Credit Rating[a]		24.4	24.7	28.6	33.1	37.6	44.0	50.2	56.7	57.5
ICRG Composite Risk Rating[b]		61.0	70.5	73.5	76.0	78.0	80.0	79.3	82.0	74.8

[a] The *Institutional Investor* country credit rating is based on a semiannual survey of 75 to 100 international bankers who were asked to grade each country on a scale of 1 (very high chance of default) to 100 (least chance of default), and is available at www.iimagazine.com.

[b] The International Country Risk Guide (ICRG) provides a rating composed of 22 variables in three risk categories: political (100 points), financial (50 points), and economic (50 points). ICRG provides ratings for 140 countries on a monthly basis where higher numbers indicate lower risk. The composite risk rating equals the sum of the individual ratings divided by two: 0 to 49.5 is considered very high risk; 80 to 100 is considered very low risk.

Sources: The Economist Intelligence Unit, *EIU Country Profile and EIU Country Report*, May 2001, p. 7; International Monetary Fund, *International Financial Statistics Yearbook 2000*, pp. 806–809; *Standard & Poor's Credit Week*, June 11, 1997, p. 25.

EXHIBIT 16-3A

CURRENCY EXCHANGE RATES

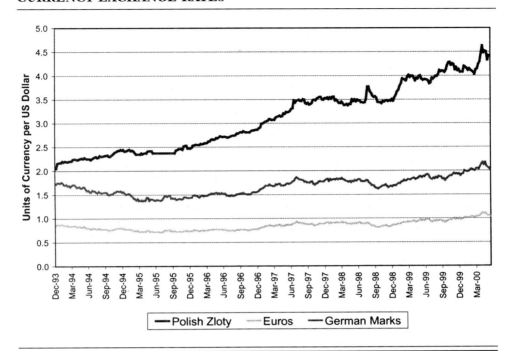

EXHIBIT 16-3B

INTEREST RATES

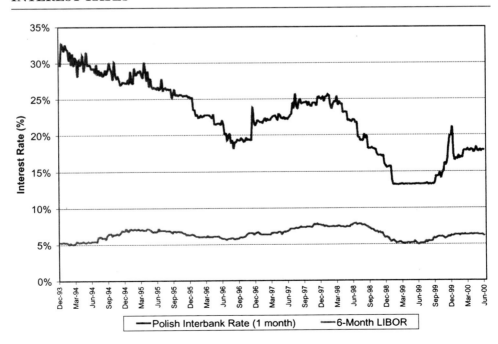

Source: Created from Datastream data.

that private enterprise would provide a substantial fraction of the estimated U.S. $10 billion cost under the "build-operate-transfer" (BOT) model used for infrastructure projects around the world.[6] Under the BOT model, the government retained ownership of the motorway while the private companies that financed construction, known as concessionaires, had the right to operate the motorway and receive profits for a defined period of time. When a concession ended, the concessionaire would transfer operations and control back to the government.

The Toll Motorways Act of 1994 and followup legislation provided the legal framework for the program. It authorized the government to grant concessions on a competitive tender basis for the construction and operation of tolled motorways. In addition, the Act authorized the government to guarantee financing for up to 50% of the total cost of construction, create a new government agency to oversee the program, and take land for the motorways by eminent domain.

THE A2 MOTORWAY PROJECT

The government selected the A2 Motorway as the first concession. When complete, it would be part of the Paris–Berlin–Warsaw–Moscow transit corridor and would eventually become part of the €30 billion Trans-European Network (TENs), a modern transportation system linking EU member countries.[7] The motorway would run from the German border at Swiecko, though the cities of Poznan and Warsaw, to Belarus. Like much of Poland, the route was predominantly farmland with rolling hills and plains, terrain that presented few obstacles to highway construction.

Selection of the A2 to lead off the motorway program was consistent with the fact that Germany and Russia were two of Poland's largest trading partners. Germany alone accounted for almost one-third of Poland's exports and 25% of its imports. A vice president of the European Investment Bank (EIB), a multilateral lending agency with a strong interest in backing Central European infrastructure development, said: "Today, trucks moving between Berlin and Warsaw have an average speed of 20 km per hour; it is not possible to really integrate Poland with the EU in such a situation."[8]

AWSA decided that the A2 would be an "open" toll road, which meant that tollbooths would be located along the main route. While they could have chosen other structures, notably a "closed" toll system with tollbooths at entrance and exit ramps or a "shadow" toll system with periodic toll payments from the government rather than drivers, they chose to use an open system because it was cheaper to build and operate, and minimized government involvement.

THE CONCESSION AGREEMENT

In 1995, the government began a competitive tender process for the western portion of the A2. It awarded a 30-year BOT concession to AWSA in September 1997, for a fee of €10 million—later, the government extended the concession to 40 years to compensate AWSA for taking away a 100-km segment at the eastern end of the concession. Over the next two years, AWSA and the government negotiated several versions of the concession agreement. Gebicki commented:

---

[6] Baker & McKenzie, *The Polish Toll Motorway Project*, 2d ed. (Warsaw, 1998), p. 5.

[7] European Investment Bank, "Development of the Trans-European Transport Networks: the Way Forward," February 2001.

[8] "A2 Motorway Finally Approved," *Polish News Bulletin of the British and American Embassies*, February 4, 2000.

The challenge of this project was its size, setting (Poland), and lack of precedents. None of the principal parties, including the government, had any significant experience in structuring projects of this size. It was a complicated learning process on all fronts as we struggled to structure a deal that met international standards for financing and construction.

After two years of negotiations, they signed Annex No. 2 to the concession agreement on October 28, 1999. On the occasion, Poland's prime minister Jerzy Buzek said, "We shall drive to the European Union down this road."[9]

AWSA itself was a special-purpose consortium incorporated to bid on the A2 concession.[10] Polish firms with diversified commercial interests, such as hotels and tourism (Orbis), finance (Wielkopolski Bank Kredytowy), power transmission (PSE—owned by the Polish government), insurance (Warta), and private equity investors (Kulczyk Holding), owned 77% of the company. Western European firms, engaged primarily in heavy construction, owned the other 23% (Exhibits 16-4 and 16-5 detail the project structure and ownership, respectively.)

EXHIBIT 16-4

ORIGINAL PROJECT STRUCTURE AS PROPOSED BY AWSA

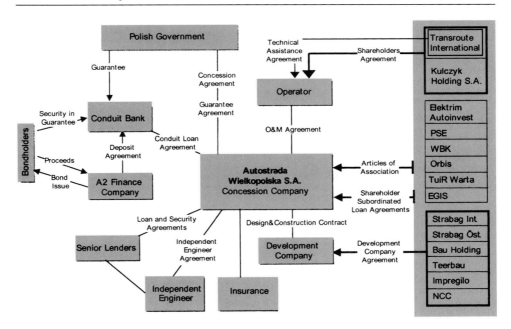

Source: Deutsche Bank AG, *A2 Motorway—POLAND, Information Memorandum*, November 1999.

---

[9] "Long and Winding Road to Europe," Polish News Bulletin of the British and American Embassies, November 2, 2000, reporting on articles in the November 2, 2000 issues of Gazeta Wyborcza, p. 16, and Prawo i Gospodarka, p. 1.

[10] The name *Autostrada Wielkopolska* meant "Greater Poland Motorway" and referred to the province containing Poznan, the provincial capital. The rest of the acronym, SA, referred to the fact that AWSA was a joint stock company.

EXHIBIT 16-5

OWNERSHIP OF AUTOSTRADA WIELKOPOLSKA S.A. AS OF NOVEMBER 1999

	Ownership (percent)	1998 (million Euros, consolidated)			
		Country	Assets	Revenues	NPAT[d]
Polish Shareholders					
PSE S.A. (Polish Power Co.)	19.77%		€1,490.0	€3,304.7	€8.3
Kulczyk Holding S.A.	18.83		84.6	22.3	21.5
Elektrim Autoinvest S.A.[a,b]	10.27		1,054.9	750.0	12.9
Wielkopolski Bank Kredytowy	9.98		2,047.8	386.8	45.3
ORBIS S.A.	9.22		276.1	176.5	17.2
TUiR Warta S.A. Insurance	4.75		478.6	251.2	10.8
Others (5 companies)	4.18				
Total	**76.99%**				
International Shareholders					
Strabag International	5.52%	Germany	1,263.4	2,198.6	(28.8)
Impregilo SpA[b]	4.75	Italy	2,780.3	973.0	18.6
NCC AB	4.75	Sweden	n/a	3,597.0	57.2
Teerbau GmbH[b]	4.75	Germany	319.2	701.5	2.2
Strabag Oesterreich[c]	2.00	Austria	133.0	1,030.0	19.8
Bau Holding AG	1.00	Austria	1,071.3	1,246.1	12.0
EGIS	0.24	France	430.6	412.4	(8.2)
Total	**23.01%**				

[a] Data are for the Elektrim Group consolidated including Elektrim Autoinvest S.A. and Elektrim S.A.

[b] Later sold shares and left the project company.

[c] Data is for 1997. Bau Holding acquired a controlling majority interest in the Strabag Group companies in 1998.

[d] NPAT = net profit after tax.

Source: Deutsche Bank AG, *A2 Motorway—POLAND, Information Memorandum*, November 1999.

The concession authorized AWSA to design, finance, build, and operate the western third of the A2 Motorway, a distance of 254 km. The concession application specified a phased plan of construction beginning at Konin and proceeding westward to Swiecko. Phase 1 (Konin to Nowy Tomysl) contained three roughly equal sections with sequential completion deadlines (see Exhibit 16-6). AWSA was obligated to finish Phase 1 within 6.25 years after financial close and had until December 2007 to finalize financing for Phase 2 (Nowy Tomysl to Swiecko) or the government could reassign that concession to another firm. The government was responsible for acquiring title to the land, by eminent domain if necessary, and transferring it to AWSA under a long-term lease within six weeks of financial close. Delivery of the lease, which carried an annual fee of PLN 5.5 million, was a condition precedent for release of construction funds. Although the government needed rights to more than 5,000 properties, it was confident it could deliver on time. It was AWSA's responsibility (via the General Contractor) to

EXHIBIT 16-6

THE A2 CONCESSION

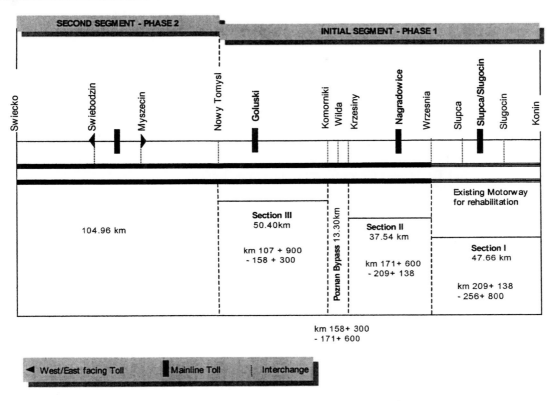

Source: Deutsche Bank AG, *A2 Motorway—POLAND, Information Memorandum*, November 1999.

get the local permits required for construction and operation, but the government agreed to support these efforts and to compensate AWSA in the event there were delays due to government authorities.

The government had the right to terminate the concession for "cause" or for defined forms of nonperformance, such as failure to commence or complete work by certain deadlines, or failure to make required payments to the government. If the government did terminate for cause, it would assume ownership and operation of the concession. All the financing would remain in place, and toll revenues would remain dedicated to debt service. The government also had the right to terminate in the public interest, without cause. In this case, it was obligated to compensate AWSA for the cost of fully retiring AWSA's debt obligations and for the net present value of the cash flow distributions that would have been made to shareholders had the concession not been canceled.[11]

The A2 concession provided several benefits to the government in addition to the annual lease payment. The most important benefits were employment during con-

[11] Deutsche Bank AG, *A2 Motorway—POLAND, Information Memorandum*, November 1999, p. 32.

struction, higher levels of commerce both within Poland and with its neighbors, value added taxes (VAT) applicable to the commercial tolls, and, possibly, a share in project cash flows. The government was entitled to receive 20% of distributable cash flow once the shareholders had received a cumulative real return of 10% or more on their invested capital, and 50% once they had received a return of 15% or more.

PHASE 1: DESIGN, CONSTRUCTION, AND FINANCING

AWSA expected to sign a fixed-price design and construction contract for Phase 1 with a new special-purpose joint-venture company (the Development Company or DC) owned by several AWSA shareholders with extensive construction experience. The owners, who jointly and severally guaranteed the DC's performance under the contract, included Strabag—one of the largest construction companies in Germany and Austria; NCC—a Swedish construction company; Impregilo—an Italian construction company; and Teerbau—a German civil engineering firm.

The design and construction costs for Phase 1 had been fixed at €16 million and €622 million, respectively. (Exhibit 16-7 shows Sources and Uses of Funds.) The euro-denominated contracts were "turnkey," meaning that the contractor was responsible for ensuring that AWSA could begin commercial operation on a specified date. Only in the event AWSA ordered changes to the design could the DC require additional compensation above the fixed price. The contracts provided for a 15% advance payment, with the remainder to be paid in monthly installments. An independent engineer retained

---

EXHIBIT 16-7

SOURCES AND USES OF FUNDS

Funding Requirement	Euro (mils)	PLN (mils)	Percent of Total	Funding Sources	Euro (mils)	PLN (mils)	Percent of Total
Construction costs	€622	2,804	66.5%	Equity	€108	461	10.9%
Design costs	16	69	1.6	Shareholder loan A	73	327	7.8
Owners' and other costs	63	269	6.4	Shareholder loan B	53	239	5.7
Pre-operating costs	3	13	0.3	**Shareholder funds**	235	1,027	24.4
Concession costs	10	37	0.9				
Project Costs	713	3,192	75.7	Senior debt	242	1,100	26.1
				Bonds (3 tranches)	266	1,196	28.4
Loan fees	9	38	0.9	Bond interest, F/X losses	135	630	14.9
Interest rolled-up	182	852	20.2	**Debt funds**	643	2,926	69.4
Capital reserve account	11	52	1.2				
O&M during construction	15	73	1.7	**Total Capital**	878	3,953	93.8
Taxes	2	8	0.2				
Working capital	(2)	(4)	(0.1)	Early toll revenues	34	164	3.9
Cash	4	5	0.1	Interest on cash balance	22	100	2.4
Total Requirement	**934**	**4,217**	**100.0**	**Total Sources**	**934**	**4,217**	**100.0**

Source: Deutsche Bank AG, *A2 Motorway—POLAND, Information Memorandum*, November 1999.

by AWSA, but reporting to the government and the senior lenders, would monitor construction and certify completion prior to each monthly disbursement.

Phase 1 construction would begin in Konin with the reconstruction of the old national Route 2 and had a scheduled opening date of July 2002. The second section involved new construction of a road running parallel to national Route 2 and extending to a bypass around the city of Poznan. It was scheduled to open in the middle of 2003. Construction of the Poznan Bypass, a toll-free road, was the government's responsibility. The third and final section, also new construction running parallel to national Route 2, would continue westward from the Poznan Bypass to Nowy Tomysl and would open in late 2005. Gebicki explained the construction plan this way:

> Although the staged approach extended the construction period, it was critical to the design. By staging construction, we maximized early revenue capture, which reduced the amount of external finance we needed. In addition, we expected that early road usage would produce hard data that would demonstrate the credibility of our traffic projections. With hard numbers on actual usage under tolled conditions, we would be in a much better position to negotiate the financing for Phase 2.

Besides the guarantee from its shareholders, the DC's performance was backed by usual performance bonds in favor of AWSA covering the 15% advance payment, performance under the contract up to €31 million, and work defects. A latent defects bond covered 5% of the contract price during construction, which was then reduced to 2.5% at completion of each section for the next for three years. The DC also agreed to pay AWSA liquidated damages for each day of delay beyond the specified completion date. Maximum damages were set at 5% of the contract price for each segment, an amount equal to roughly one year's projected toll revenues. If AWSA reached the maximum damages, it had the right to terminate the contract and replace the Development Company.

If, on the other hand, a *force majeure* event or government action caused a delay, then an insurance policy or the government (acting as an insurer of last resort for risks that could not be insured commercially), respectively, would compensate AWSA subject to a maximum annual loss of €650,000. The government also agreed to compensate AWSA for delays or increased costs caused by the discovery of archaeological or hazardous materials. Two independent consulting firms had already assessed the A2's environmental impact and concluded that it would meet Polish environmental standards, standards that some argued were stricter than World Bank standards.[12]

Phase 1 Operations

A new company, the Operating Company (OC), would operate and maintain the motorway under a 10-year renewable contract. Owned by three AWSA shareholders, the OC agreed to manage and maintain the motorway in exchange for a fixed annual fee paid in Polish zloty. The fee could be adjusted to reflect traffic growth and Polish inflation. Although this contract covered routine maintenance, AWSA remained responsible for heavy maintenance such as resurfacings.[13] The first resurfacing, scheduled for sometime between 2011 and 2015 depending on use, would cost approximately €43 million. One of the largest shareholders, Transroute, was part of the EGIS Group, a firm that managed toll roads in France, Australia, Hungary, the United Kingdom, and the United States.

[12] Ibid., p. 61.
[13] Ibid., p. 38.

Motorway revenue would come primarily from tolls, though AWSA would also receive a small amount of revenue from selling subconcessions to operate service areas (e.g., petrol stations, roadside restaurants, and eventually hotels). Toll revenue would depend on many factors, including the strength of the regional economies, international and local trade patterns, and alternative transportation routes. Over the past six years, independent consultants had produced three traffic studies: one for the government in 1994 prior to the concession tender process, one for AWSA in 1996 as it prepared to bid for the concession, and a third done by Wilbur Smith & Associates (WSA) in 1997, as part of AWSA's effort to finance Phase 1. The WSA study, which was updated in 1999, contained both traffic and revenue forecasts, and formed the basis for AWSA's financial projections.

Because the A2 Motorway was the first toll road in Poland, WSA had to rely on surveys of more than 50,000 motorists in 14 locations for data. Based on the surveys, WSA generated assumptions regarding types of vehicles, travel destinations, motorists' value of time, vehicle operating costs, capacity of alternative routes, growth in vehicle ownership, and other macroeconomic variables, and used them as inputs to a computer model that simulated driver behavior. Like the previous traffic consultants, WSA assumed that value of time, which was a function of Polish gross domestic project (GDP), would be the primary determinant of road use and drivers' willingness to pay tolls. WSA assumed that real per capita GDP would grow at 5% p.a. through 2002, decline to 4% p.a. through 2010, and then remain at 3% p.a. for the rest of the concession. Gebicki believed these assumptions were defendable given the high average growth rate recorded in Poland over the previous 10 years. Moreover, traffic growth on the existing Route 2 had grown at 6% annually over the last five years.

Using the model, WSA forecast that daily traffic would increase from 7,600 vehicles per day when the first section of Phase 1 opened in 2002 (approximately 50% of the 12,000 to 18,000 vehicles per day currently using national Route 2) to an average of 20,000 vehicles per day on each of the three sections by 2022 (see Exhibits 16-6 and 16-8). Whereas WSA assumed that the A2 would capture approximately 50% of the traffic, a ratings agency analyst noted that "Experience from successful toll roads that compete for traffic with toll-free roads suggests that viable market share ranges from 10% to 20% of a service area's total traffic volume.[14] An analyst from Standard & Poor's reiterated the concern: "newly tolled facilities . . . often face traffic levels as much as 50% below initial forecasts."[15] Fully aware of these concerns, Gebicki responded:

> In our view, the original government study was a little too optimistic; our 1996 study was more or less correct; and we think the recent Wilbur Smith analysis is probably too conservative. The reason why I think the Wilbur Smith study is too conservative is because they, like the consultants before them, cut the revenue projections contained in the previous studies by as much as 50%. In fact, Wilbur Smith assumed a lower value of driver time, lower perceived vehicle operating costs, and higher speeds on alternative routes. The result was a 16% decline in revenue in 2002 and a 50% decline in 2022.[16]

The concession agreement contained commitments by the government designed to generate satisfactory traffic volume. For example, the government agreed to complete the Poznan bypass and compensate AWSA for completion delays. The government also

---

[14] Fitch IBCA, Duff & Phelps, *Public Finance: Challenges of Start-Up Toll Roads*, June 9, 1999, p. 3.
[15] Forsgren, "The Toll Road Sector," pp. 148–9.
[16] The last part of this quotation comes from: "A2: Take two," *Project Finance*, December 2000, p. 21.

EXHIBIT 16-8

PROJECTED DAILY TRAFFIC AND TOLL RATES (NOMINAL CASH FLOWS IN POLISH ZLOTY)

	July–December, 2002			July–December, 2005			July–December, 2007			July–December, 2012		
	Average Daily Traffic	Toll per Vehicle	Semi-Annual Cash Flow (millions)	Average Daily Traffic	Toll per Vehicle	Semi-Annual Cash Flow (millions)	Average Daily Traffic	Toll per Vehicle	Semi-Annual Cash Flow (millions)	Average Daily Traffic	Toll per Vehicle	Semi-Annual Cash Flow (millions)
Type of Vehicle												
Passenger	3,400	9.48	3,539	14,200	12.53	32,560	15,800	15.04	43,487	20,600	20.80	78,412
Commercial 1	1,680	14.22	2,623	6,080	20.14	22,406	6,730	23.97	29,521	8,540	34.32	53,636
Commercial 2	710	21.33	1,663	2,590	30.25	14,338	2,660	35.91	17,479	3,090	51.48	29,110
Commercial 3	1,810	33.18	6,594	6,530	46.99	56,150	7,210	55.93	73,796	8,970	80.08	131,452
Total	7,600		14,419	29,400		125,454	32,400		164,283	41,200		292,610
Operating, Maintenance, and Other Costs			8,000			29,000			34,000			42,000
Operating Profit			6,419			96,454			130,283			250,610
Decrease/(Increase) in Net Working Capital			0			22,000			0			0
Taxes			0			0			0			0
Cash Flow Available for Debt Service			6,419			118,454			130,283			250,610
Senior Debt Payments												
Interest			0			40,000			36,000			6,000
Principal			0			39,000			42,000			149,000
Total			0			79,000			78,000			155,000

Source: Casewriter estimates based on Deutsche Bank Information Memorandum (November 1999) and Wilbur Smith Associates analysis.

agreed not to build or improve any competing road, not to impose tolls on any feeder roads, and to maintain the feeder roads. These commitments were backed by specific compensation provisions for losses suffered by AWSA.

With regard to toll levels, the concession agreement gave AWSA the right to set tolls in zloty, but limited both the initial and life-of-concession maximum tolls by class of vehicle. AWSA had the right to reset the actual tolls every six months, and there was a provision to adjust the maximum tolls to account for changes in Polish inflation and exchange rates. AWSA followed WSA's advice in setting the initial tolls at about 85% of the theoretical revenue-maximizing levels for each modeled period.

Although the forecasted toll revenues reflected a great deal of data and sophisticated computer analysis by experienced professionals, some level of traffic risk was unavoidable. In fact, there were examples, such as Hungary's M1/M15 toll road, where the projections were off considerably. M1 was a 42-km motorway extending from Budapest to the Austrian border on the route to Vienna. Completed in January 1996 at a cost of $265 million,[17] the motorway never generated the forecasted traffic volumes, in part because the operator set the initial toll rate at 1,000 Hungarian *forint* or U.S.$5.88 (a rate that would be equivalent on a per mile basis to a $50 toll for the 220-mile Massachusetts Turnpike in 1999).[18] Reported one correspondent: "Hungarians, socked in the wallet by a sinking economy, stayed away in droves. In its first year of operation, traffic on the M1 ran about 35% below original projections."[19] Among the other causes were Hungarian economic and currency weakness, customs delays at the Austrian border, and a good secondary road parallel to the M1.[20] Consequences included near bankruptcy of the operator, debt rescheduling, possible nationalization of the motorway by the government, and a lawsuit that led to a reduction in tolls.[21] Learning from this experience, AWSA set the initial tolls at approximately 10 zloty (US$2.50) per 50 km.

Insurance Arrangements

Acting with the advice of its insurance advisor Willis (formerly Willis Corroon), AWSA arranged for commercial insurance coverage as required by the concession agreement. During construction, there was all-risk coverage for property damage up to the full design and construction cost (€667 million), declining to U.S.$100 million per event post-completion. Covered risks included broadly defined *force majeure* events such as explosions, epidemics, contamination, floods, war, revolution, and riots. Insurance for lost profits due to delay in completion was set at 30 days' projected gross revenues. After completion, business interruption insurance would cover revenue losses for up to 12 months. Finally, third-party liability insurance was U.S. $50 million throughout the concession.

---

[17] "Hungarian Toll Road to Austrian Border Opens," *The Wall Street Journal*, January 5, 1996, p. B9B.

[18] *The Wall Street Journal Europe*, February 24, 1997, p. B9B.

[19] D. Michaels, "Rough Driving Ahead: Hungary's Setback Bodes Ill for Toll Roads," *The Wall Street Journal Europe*, February 24, 1997, p. 18.

[20] "Global Toll-Roads, For Whom the Tolls Fall," *Project & Trade Finance*, June 10, 1999, p. 17.

[21] "Reaction of the State to High Fees," (*Ohlas statu na vysoke poplatky*), Hospodarske Noviny, December 4, 1998, p. 8 (abstracted from the Czech publication by World Reporter™ and appearing in Dow Jones News Retrieval).

Financing Plan for Phase 1

The total estimated cost for Phase 1 was €934 million (see Exhibit 16-7). AWSA's financing plan was based on a model created by Deutsche Bank. The principal inputs to the model were the traffic and revenue forecasts; the construction and operating costs were less critical because they would be fixed contractually. Other key assumptions were that purchasing power parity would hold, Polish inflation would decrease from 6% in 2000 to 2% by 2008, and Polish corporate taxes would decrease from the current rate of 34% to 22% by 2004, in line with official government estimates. The theory underlying the financing plan was to maximize the use of senior debt, subject to maintaining a minimum debt service coverage ratio (DSCR) of 1.5 times under the Base Case revenue forecast (see Exhibits 16-9 and 16-10). As Deutsche Bank managing director Stephen Uhlig noted:

> The shape of the revenue curve is the key to the project's debt capacity. We sculpted the debt service to match the cash flows available. However, when the revenue projections changed, the principal repayment schedule had to change, as well. For example, when the downside scenarios became worse, we lost debt capacity. Because the total funding need remained constant, increasingly conservative forecasts created a funding gap that needed to be filled with other funds.

According to the plan, funding would come from three major sources: €242 million from commercial banks in the form of a senior secured project loan; three tranches of zero coupon bonds yielding proceeds of €266 million (with a face amount at €800 million); and €235 in subordinated debt and equity from AWSA shareholders (the second largest amount of equity financing ever raised by a Polish company). The senior debt would have a drawdown period of 5.5 years, followed by a six-month grace period and semiannual principal and interest payments thereafter. Because the loan rate was based on a spread over six-month LIBOR—the spread increased from 180 bp to 235 bp over time—the bankers wanted AWSA to use interest rate swaps to fix the rate. AWSA considered a similar arrangement to address the mismatch between zloty revenues and euro-denominated debt service, but decided against entering into a hedging agreement. Gebicki explained:

> We thought about trying to hedge the exchange rate risk, but couldn't do it. First, the instruments don't exist—you really can't go out more than a year without incurring major expense. Second, it's hard to synchronize the hedge given the variability of toll road revenue. And third, there was counterparty risk to cover for the hedging bank and AWSA didn't have any excess cash to post as collateral.

Senior debt principal payments varied depending on operating cash flow and created a final maturity that ranged from 13 years to 15 years. The minimum principal payments were set to be consistent with a 1.15X debt service coverage ratio under a downside scenario where traffic volume was 30% below Deutsche Bank's Base Case scenario. The documents also specified a target repayment schedule with an innovative "cash sweep" mechanism to ensure that extra cash flow was used to pay down senior debt or to create a sinking fund account for repayment of the zero coupon bonds.

The mezzanine debt, the zero coupon bonds, accrued interest based on an effective interest rate of between 7% and 9% p.a.—the exact rate would depend on the specific maturity, currency (U.S. dollars or Euros), and current market conditions at the

EXHIBIT 16-9

POLAND'S A2 MOTORWAY: SUMMARY OF FINANCIAL PROJECTIONS 2000 TO 2025 (IN MILLIONS OF POLISH ZLOTY)

Project Year	Calendar Year	Construction and Other Costs[a]	Toll Revenues[b]	Operating Costs	Taxes	Senior Debt[c] Principal	Interest	Bonds[c] (Mezzanine Debt) Principal	Interest	Refinancing[c] Principal	Interest	Shareholder Payouts on Subordinated Debt and Equity
1	2000	PLN (852)	PLN 0	PLN 0	PLN 0	PLN 243	PLN 6	PLN 1,147	PLN 63			PLN 372
2	2001	(746)	0	0	0	226	23		104			232
3	2002	(583)	21	(12)	0	203	40		116			175
4	2003	(433)	36	(18)	0	183	51		128			126
5	2004	(297)	57	(26)	0	159	65		142			83
6	2005	(98)	175	(42)	0	47	(3)		157			41
7	2006		278	(55)	0	(64)	(78)		171			0
8	2007		318	(74)	0	(78)	(73)		187			0
9	2008		358	(65)	0	(115)	(68)		203			0
10	2009		402	(82)	0	(143)	(60)		219			0
11	2010		451	(72)	0	(200)	(49)		237			0
12	2011		506	(186)[d]	0	(240)	(35)		257			0
13	2012		562	(81)	0	(301)	(17)	(1,300)	232	734	(19)	0
14	2013		605	(89)	0	(39)	(1)	(1,210)	148	842	(60)	0
15	2014		652	(199)	0			(1,191)	51	542	(102)	0
16	2015		705	(210)	0					(500)	(106)	0
17	2016		761	(107)	0					(588)	(77)	0
18	2017		821	(97)	0					(688)	(45)	0
19	2018		890	(96)	0					(342)	(9)	(451)
20	2019		964	(92)	0							(880)
21	2020		1,045	(89)	(13)							(952)
22	2021		1,132	(177)	(49)							(908)
23	2022		1,218	(87)	(61)							(1,086)
24	2023		1,282	(88)	(113)							(1,090)
25	2024		1,350	(187)	(144)							(1,018)
26	2025		1,421	(211)	(156)							(1,061)

[a] Construction and Other Costs includes design costs, fees, and working capital.

[b] Total Revenues includes other revenues.

[c] For interest amounts, positive numbers indicate accretion, and negative numbers indicate cash payments; for principal amounts, positive numbers indicate drawdowns, and negative numbers indicate cash repayments.

[d] For 2011, operating expenses include PLN104 million of extraordinary expense for resurfacing and maintenance.

Source: Deutsche Bank AG, Information Memorandum, November 1999.

316

EXHIBIT 16-10

POLAND'S A2 MOTORWAY: SUMMARY OF SENIOR DEBT SENSITIVITIES AND RATES OF RETURN

	Annual Debt Service Cover Ratio (ADSCR) for Senior Debt[a]		Minimum Annual Interest Cover Ratio (AICR)[b]	Net Present Value Loan Life Cover Ratio[c]	Senior Debt Maturity (Years)	Internal Rate of Return (Real % p.a.)
	Minimum	Average				
Base case	**1.50**×	**1.99**×	**2.57**×	**2.45**×	**13.0**	**9.24%**
30% traffic downsided	1.15	1.44	1.43	2.08	15.0	6.60
Macroeconomic sensitivities						
Traffic volume grows at 0%	1.14	1.78	2.39	2.45	14.5	5.24
Toll rates grow at 0%	1.09	1.48	2.32	2.36	14.5	5.83
Traffic ramp-up (slower than expected)	1.15	2.59	1.48	2.43	13.5	9.06
Higher Polish inflation (5% not 2%)	1.50	1.75	2.56	2.45	13.0	9.26
Higher long-term interest rates (by 50 bp)	1.50	1.73	2.39	2.41	13.0	9.26
Higher interest rates throughout concession	1.50	2.29	1.74	2.44	14.0	9.24
Higher interest and inflation rates	1.50	1.62	2.10	2.20	12.0	9.58
Exchange rates (10% zloty depreciation)	1.50	1.67	2.30	2.53	13.5	9.22
Higher corporate income tax (34%, not 22%)	1.50	1.97	2.56	2.45	13.0	9.24
Breakeven analysis						
Traffic downside of 35%	1.00	1.06	1.24	0.56	15.0	6.09
Toll rates grow at negative 0.4%	1.00	1.36	2.29	1.89	14.5	5.15
Traffic growth at negative 0.55%	1.00	1.43	2.34	2.10	14.5	4.22
Cost overrun sensitivities						
Renewal costs plus 100%	1.50	1.61	2.35	2.39	13.0	9.08
First heavy maintenance plus 100%	1.50	1.82	2.57	2.44	13.0	9.08

[a] ADSCR equals cash flow available for senior debt service plus transfers from the debt service reserve account divided by total senior debt service (interest and principal).

[b] AICR equals cash flow available for senior debt service divided by total interest on senior debt.

[c] Net Present Value (NPV) Loan Life Cover Ratio equals the NPV of future cash flows for senior debt divided by the outstanding loan balance at the beginning of the period.

Source: Deutsche Bank AG, Information Memorandum, November 1999.

time of launch. The bonds would mature by 2014, the longest possible maturity available in the zero coupon market according to the investment bankers. In addition, the bonds would be backed by a guarantee from the Polish government for up to €800 million in maximum future value terms. Under the Base Case projections, AWSA would be able to repay only a fraction of total amount outstanding at maturity, leaving the remainder to be refinanced. Because the bonds would be issued under a special legal structure that preserved the government's guarantee for the life of the concession, Gebicki believed AWSA would able to refinance the bonds, a bet on the future value of the government's guarantee. Although being able to extend the guarantee for the life of the concession was very beneficial, the €800 million ceiling presented a problem. The limit had been tentatively approved by the legislature as part of an authorization for all government guarantees. Yet some people criticized the A2 for absorbing more than its fair share of the total PLN 5.5 billion authorized for guarantees of all kinds. Given the trouble AWSA had securing the €800 million guarantee, Gebicki doubted AWSA could increase the limit.

Finally, shareholder capital came in the form of equity and deeply subordinated debt. Like the mezzanine debt, the subordinated debt did not pay cash interest. In fact, cash interest payments to shareholders were prohibited prior to repayment, defeasance, or cash collateralization of the bonds. This restriction meant that under the Base Case financial projections, the earliest interest payments to shareholders would not occur until 2018, and the shareholder loans would not be paid off until 2026.[22] The shareholders' debt had a margin of 9% over the short-term interbank lending rate for euros.

The financing documents required AWSA to have cash reserves in lender-controlled accounts for capital expenditures, heavy maintenance, and debt service. The capital expenditure reserve was prefunded from the construction financing and would cover the cost of upgrading access ramps. AWSA had to accumulate €43 million from operating cash flow in the maintenance reserve account to pay for the first major resurfacing, but no requirements for the two subsequent resurfacings. AWSA also had to build up a debt service equal to six months' accrued interest and the next scheduled principal payment for the senior debt. Finally, it had to maintain a sinking fund account for the partial retirement of the zero coupon bonds beginning in 2012, assuming cash flow was available.

A cash "waterfall" mechanism in the concession agreement spelled out how toll revenues would be allocated. The funds would be disbursed to pay the following obligations in order of priority: (a) current operating expenses, including land lease fees payable to the government under the concession; (b) capital expenditure and maintenance reserve accounts; (c) current interest and principal payments on senior debt; (d) senior debt service reserve account; and (e) all remaining cash to the zero coupon bond sinking fund. Supplementing the waterfall was a detailed intercreditor agreement among the lenders documenting their consent to the relative preferences and rankings spelled out by the financial documents. The financing plan received government approval and was incorporated in the final concession agreement, which was signed in October 1999.

The legal framework for the financing plan and loan documents had been developed by Baker & McKenzie and was designed to meet the prevailing expectations of the prospective Western European project finance lenders and eurobond purchasers. Because this was the first major project financing in Poland, there were few precedents to guide the lawyers. They decided the senior debt contracts would be governed by

---

[22] Deutsche Bank AG, *A2 Motorway—POLAND, Information Memorandum,* November 1999, pp. 51, 75, and 76.

U.K. common law. However, because the lenders' collateral and AWSA's principal assets were in Poland, enforcement of the lenders' rights would have to run through Polish courts and would be subject to Poland's civil law system. Joining disparate legal systems created discrepancies that had to be resolved. For example, Polish law did not allow interest on interest in default situations. Despite some uncertainties in the Polish legal system and the presence of potential conflicts between the systems, Baker & McKenzie would be expected to provide the lenders with satisfactory legal opinions as to the enforceability of their claims.

CONCLUSION

As Gebicki finished his review of the construction, operating, and financial plans for the concession, he found it difficult to imagine why the bankers would have concerns about the project. The fact that the banks had engaged their own transportation consultant forced Gebicki to consider the possibility that they had adopted an even more pessimistic "downside" financial case. New, more pessimistic scenarios would not only represent a deviation from the scenarios agreed to by the bankers in the original mandate letter, but they would also create a funding gap that would explain the bankers' request for additional equity. Gebicki was not sure how AWSA's shareholders would respond to such a request. Facing the July 29 deadline for financial close, the process of negotiating further commitments from 18 shareholders seemed an almost insurmountable challenge. Because the zero coupon bonds offered almost the same comfort to the senior lenders as equity, Gebicki briefly considered the possibility of issuing additional bonds, but he quickly abandoned the idea owing to the strict limit on the size of the government's guarantee.

Gebicki decided that his best option was to convince the bankers that their analysis was too pessimistic. As evidence, he could point to the early results from the A4 Toll Motorway. Although the A4 was launched after the A2, it had opened for traffic in April 2000 and was reportedly capturing some 80% of available traffic, well above Wilbur Smith's assumed 50% capture rate for the A2. Because the A4 was only 60 km long and connected two large cities, the bankers might reject the comparison. In any case, Gebicki had to marshal the strongest possible defense of AWSA's financial projections. If he failed to convince the bankers, then it would be up to the lead shareholders to make additional financial commitments or the financing would not close on time. Yet, only NCC, PSE, Kulczyk, and Strabag had expressed any willingness to provide additional funds.

Although this option seemed like a long shot, another potentially attractive option had recently emerged. A few days earlier, Gebicki had received a letter from the European Investment Bank (EIB) that expressed renewed interest in financing part of the A2 Motorway. Whereas EIB had previously expressed only limited interest in financing the A2, now it was entertaining the idea of a term loan in an amount roughly equal to the bond proceeds in the current financial plan. One problem with using EIB funds for Phase 1 was that Base Case cash flows could not service both the senior debt and an EIB loan. As a result, the EIB loan would have to accrue interest, yet Gebicki knew that the EIB traditionally allowed interest to accrue only during construction not during operations. Moreover, the EIB required *pari passu* treatment with other senior lenders. The proposed financing plan with its sequential repayment of debt obligations might, therefore, be another stumbling block. Finally, if the bankers insisted on a more pessimistic downside scenario, there would still be a large financing gap. With less than six weeks to go before the financing had to be closed, Gebicki doubted whether he could pull together a new financing plan before the deadline. Given the fact that there had been four different finance ministers since AWSA won the concession in 1997, the risk always existed that delays could result in a change of heart by any number of government officials.

Following his meeting with the bankers, Gebicki had to prepare a final recommendation on financing for AWSA's supervisory board. Depending on how his meeting with the bankers turned out, getting this approval might be his biggest challenge yet.

17

Restructuring Bulong's Project Debt

Project finance lenders are the quintessential optimists of the banking world. Where traditional commercial bankers can see only negatives and risks, project financiers look to see what's do-able and how to manage or isolate risks.[1]

—Ivor Ries, as quoted in the *Australian Financial Review*

Preston Resources submitted its scheme of arrangement to the Supreme Court of Western Australia on April 21, 2002. The scheme contained a restructuring plan for the secured debt of the company's principal subsidiary, Bulong Operations Pty. Ltd. (BOP). BOP's indebtedness consisted primarily of U.S. $185 million in senior secured notes, plus working capital loans and hedging contracts owed to Barclays Bank. For the restructuring plan to become effective, at least three entities had to approve it. Once Preston had received the court's approval, it could present the plan to the noteholders for approval. If a majority of the noteholders by number and 75% by value approved it, then Preston could present the plan to its shareholders. In exchange for being released from BOP's debt obligations, Preston would have to transfer 95% of BOP's equity to the noteholders. Whether the court, the noteholders, and the shareholders would approve this plan remained to be seen. If they did approve it, BOP and Preston would continue as operating companies; if they did not approve it, the alternative was almost certainly some kind of liquidation.

Research Associate Michael Kane and Professor Benjamin C. Esty prepared this case. This case was developed from published sources. HBS cases are developed solely as the basis for class discussion. Cases are not intended to serve as endorsements, sources of primary data, or illustrations of effective or ineffective management.

[1] Ivor Ries, "Banks Miss Out on Nickel Coup," *Australian Financial Review*, July 24, 1998, p. 76.

THE BULONG NICKEL PROJECT

The Nickel and Cobalt Industries

Nickel was used primarily in the production of stainless steel and other alloys. Industry experts estimated that the total global demand for primary nickel was slightly greater than one million tons and would grow at an annual rate of 3.6% through 2010.[2] Nickel reserves of 150 million tons were located in many different countries, though the largest suppliers were Russia, Canada, and Australia.[3] Six producers accounted for 66% of world production, while 30 smaller producers accounted for the rest.[4]

Cobalt, an extremely hard metal, was used in the production of super alloys and various specialty chemicals. Reflecting these limited applications, world cobalt demand was about 31,000 tons annually.[5] Most cobalt was found in nickel and copper ores and was produced as a byproduct of these metals. In fact, nickel producers typically netted cobalt revenues in calculating their nickel production cost.

Nickel and cobalt prices showed considerable volatility (see Exhibits 17-1 and 17-2). Despite increasing demand for nickel, nickel prices had trended downward in the 1990s to just over U.S. $2.00 per pound in late 1998. Experts attributed this decline to advances in processing technology and entry by new, low-cost producers. Almost all physical sales of nickel took place under negotiated bilateral contracts between producers, traders, and consumers using London Metal Exchange (LME) prices adjusted for quality, quantity, and delivery terms. Firms also traded nickel contracts on the LME for hedging purposes.

The Bulong Nickel Project

The Bulong nickel project grew out of a discovery in the 1970s of large deposits of high-grade nickel ore near Kalgoorlie in Western Australia (see Exhibit 17-3).[6] Resolute Limited, an Australian gold mining firm, acquired the mining rights to the property in 1987 and conducted various exploratory tests subsequently. In 1995, Resolute hired Bateman Kinhill Kilborn (Bateman), a multinational engineering and construction firm, to assess a proposed nickel mining project. The feasibility study encompassed all aspects of the project, with specialist consulting firms contributing sections on ore reserves, mining procedures, and processing design. It confirmed a shallow ore deposit containing approximately 440,000 tons of nickel and 36,000 tons of cobalt.[7] The initial plan called for processing 600,000 tons of ore annually to produce 8,000 tons of nickel and 670 tons of cobalt, though Resolute envisioned the potential to process over 2.5 million tons of ore annually.[8]

---

[2] Barclays Capital, *Bulong Operations Pty. Ltd. 12½% Senior Secured Notes due 2008, dated December 17, 1998.* The offering documents are referred to as the Prospectus, Annex A, and Annex B, p. B-3.

[3] U.S. Geological Survey, *Mineral Commodities Survey, 2002,* at ⟨http://minerals.usgs.gov/minerals/⟩.

[4] U.S. Geological Survey, *Minerals Yearbook—2000,* Nickel—World Review, at ⟨http://minerals.usgs.gov/minerals/⟩.

[5] Annex B, p. B-15.

[6] Annex B.

[7] Consistent with industry conventions, all weights are in metric tons (tonnes): one metric ton = 2,204.6 pounds.

[8] Annex A, p. A-12.

EXHIBIT 17-1

HISTORICAL METAL PRICES (U.S.$ PER POUND)

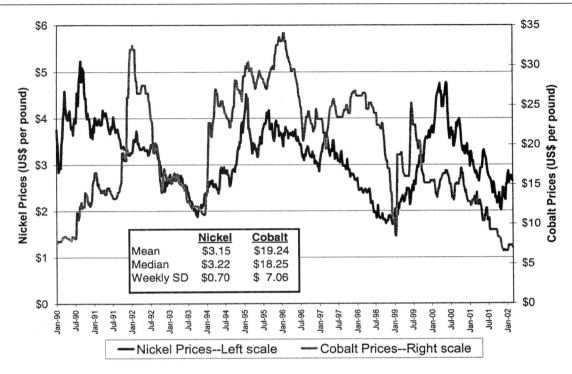

	Nickel	**Cobalt**
Mean	$3.15	$19.24
Median	$3.22	$18.25
Weekly SD	$0.70	$ 7.06

——Nickel Prices--Left scale　——Cobalt Prices--Right scale

Source: Adapted from Datastream.

After reviewing the study, Resolute's board approved the construction of several open-pit mines and a central processing plant.[9] According to Bateman's design, the processing plant would use a high-pressure acid leaching (PAL) technology tailored to extract the nickel and cobalt from the laterite ore. Most of the world's nickel was produced from sulfide ores using a smelting technology that was not appropriate for laterite ores. Bateman and others believed that PAL technology held great promise for tapping the world's extensive laterite reserves. In fact, two other companies—Murrin Murrin (projected nickel production of 45,000 tons annually) and Cawse (9,000 tons annually)—were building laterite nickel projects in Western Australia using PAL technology.[10] As shown in Exhibit 17-4, the Bulong process would treat batches of ore in a three-step process:

- **Ore Preparation:** Grinding, screening, and thickening transformed the ore into a slurry.
- **Leaching:** Pumping systems moved the slurry through heating vessels into an autoclave. The slurry was mixed with sulphuric acid and pressurized for 75 minutes at

[9] Annex A, p. A-12.
[10] M. Weir, "Laterites Fall Well Short of Launch Targets," *The West Australian*, May 1, 2001, p. 33.

EXHIBIT 17-2

LONDON METALS EXCHANGE (LME) NICKEL PRICES

Date	Spot and Forward Prices for Nickel (U.S.$ per pound)			
	Cash Settlement	3-Month	15-Month	27-Month
1/5/98	$2.71	$2.75	$2.86	$2.90
6/30/98	1.94	1.98	2.06	2.11
12/31/98	1.86	1.89	2.00	2.09
6/30/99	2.45	2.49	2.55	2.59
12/30/99	3.83	3.86	3.53	3.21
6/30/00	3.74	3.63	3.12	2.79
12/29/00	3.26	3.10	2.97	2.92
6/29/01	2.75	2.73	2.66	2.61
12/28/01	2.58	2.48	2.51	2.54
4/30/02	3.20	3.21	3.17	3.15

Source: Adapted from London Metals Exchange Web site ⟨http://www.lme.co.uk/⟩.

EXHIBIT 17-3

MAP OF AUSTRALIA AND MINE LOCATIONS

Source: Adapted by casewriter.

EXHIBIT 17-4

ORE PROCESSING

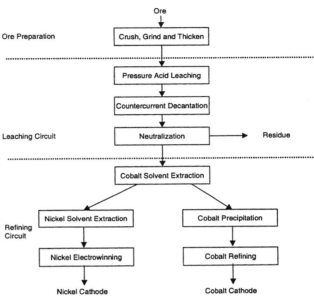

Simplified Process Flowsheet

Source: Adapted from Bulong Prospectus.

250°C. This process removed the nickel and cobalt from the ore, leaving them in separate solutions.

- **Refining:** The cobalt and nickel solutions separately underwent further refining prior to a final phase in which electricity was used to extract the metals from the solutions.

Behre Dolbear & Company, a mining consulting firm, reviewed the project as independent engineers for the banks that were financing construction. Although it identified a variety of processing risks, it was generally positive about the project and endorsed the reserve estimates, mining plan, and plant design. The firm's final report concluded:

The plant involves a mixture of new and established technologies that have been tested successfully at pilot scale. While the project is complex and involves an element of moderate technical risk, the flowsheet and proposed plant and equipment are considered appropriate to the project and offer the production of saleable metal without smelting. The projected performances and mineral recoveries are considered reasonable and have been derived through extensive testwork and investigation.[11]

[11] Annex A, p. A-5. Technically, this assessment came from their final report as independent engineers for the bond issue, not for the construction financing.

In 1997, Resolute awarded Bateman an engineering, procurement, and construction management (EPCM) contract to develop the Bulong project.[12] By September 1998, the mines were operating and Bateman had substantially completed the processing plant at a total cost of A$265 million.[13] Resolute had financed approximately half the construction cost through a project loan from Citibank and a leveraged lease on plant equipment, and had signed long-term contracts with local suppliers for all the key process inputs, such as sulphuric acid, electricity, and water. Resolute had arranged construction-risk and third-party liability insurance policies that expired upon completion and planned to replace them with a comprehensive insurance package following completion.

Resolute appointed Barclays Physical Trading Limited (BPTL), a wholly-owned subsidiary of Barclays Bank, as the exclusive marketing agent for all of the project's output. BPTL arranged a three-year offtake contract for 100% of the output with the German metals trading firm of Frank & Schulte, a unit of AA-rated VEBA A.G.. Bulong expected to transport the metal to the coast over existing roads and then ship it primarily to Europe and Japan. To supplement this plan for physical distribution, BOP entered into forward nickel contracts covering 100% of projected production for 1999 and 2000, as well as multiyear forward foreign exchange contracts (the "hedging facilities"). The nickel contracts locked in a sales price of U.S. $3.30 per pound while the foreign exchange contracts required Bulong to sell U.S. dollars and buy Australian dollars at an average price of U.S. $0.73 = A$1.00.[14] Foreign exchange risk was inherent in the project because nickel and cobalt sales would be in U.S. dollars while operating expenses would be in Australian dollars.

PRESTON RESOURCES LIMITED

Founded in 1986 and based in Perth, Preston explored for gold in Western Australia. In 1997, management bought the rights to undeveloped nickel reserves in the state of Queensland (see Exhibit 17-1). Preston hired Bateman to conduct a feasibility study for the construction of a large-scale mining and processing project at the Marlborough site. Bateman's work confirmed the presence of enough high-quality laterite ore to produce 25,000 tons of nickel and 2,000 tons of cobalt annually for 20 years. In May 1998, Barclays Capital, an investment banking affiliate of Barclays Bank, offered to provide A$700 million (U.S. $441 million) in development financing. For a company with virtually no revenue and consolidated assets of A$29 million (see Exhibits 17-5 and 17-6), the Marlborough project represented a major undertaking.[15]

Preston Acquires the Bulong Nickel Project

While undertaking the first steps for the Marlborough project, Preston got the opportunity to buy the Bulong mine. After some negotiation, Preston agreed to buy Bulong from Resolute in July 1998. Resolute's chief executive, Michael Carrick, said the sale left Resolute with a very strong balance sheet and the freedom to focus on its gold businesses in Australia and Africa.[16] Resolute, in addition to making the usual seller war-

---

[12] Prospectus, p. 51.

[13] Annex A, p. A-14.

[14] Preston Annual Report 1999, p. 43.

[15] Preston Annual Report 1998, pp. 2, 8, 10, and 20; Preston press release, July 1998.

[16] "Resolute Says Settles on Bulong Sale," *AAP News*, November 5, 1998; Source: *World Reporter*.

EXHIBIT 17-5

PRESTON RESOURCES LIMITED—PROFIT AND LOSS STATEMENT (CONSOLIDATED)[a]

	June 30 Year End (A$ 000)			
	1998	**1999**	**2000**	**2001**
Operating revenue	$ 231	$ 4,023	$ 62,259	$ 90,215
Payments to employees and suppliers	1,284	18,814	72,701	118,489
Depreciation and amortization	63	3,065	23,071	9,754
Interest expense	177	20,893	40,579	54,745
Other income (expense), net	(174)	(20,273)	(23,485)	37,859
Operating loss before abnormal items	(1,467)	(18,476)	(97,577)	(54,914)
Abnormal items before income tax[b]	(333)	(5,037)	(386,773)	(192,479)
Operating loss before income tax	(1,800)	(23,512)	(484,350)	(247,393)
Income tax attributable to operating loss (tax rate = 36%)	—	217	(12,869)	—
Operating loss after income tax	$(1,800)	$(23,295)	$(497,219)	$(247,393)
Accumulated losses:				
At the beginning of the financial year	(10,194)	(11,994)	(35,289)	(532,508)
At the end of the financial year	(11,994)	(35,289)	(532,508)	(779,901)
Stock price information:				
Closing price on June 30	$2.71	$0.82	n/a	n/a
Number of shares outstanding (millions)	43.2	64.7[c]	67.3[d]	67.3[d]

[a] Consolidating the principal subsidiaries of Preston Resources Limited, of which only Bulong Operations Pty. Ltd. and Bulong Nickel Pty. Ltd. had material assets and operations during the years shown.

[b] In FY00 and FY01, the write-offs were primarily due to Bulong (A$218 million), Marlborough (A$6 million), exploration costs (A$36 million), and deferred Bulong financing costs (A$15 million); also unrealized foreign exchange losses on the hedging facilities (A$303 million).

[c] Does not include 27.8 million shares issued to Resolute Limited at A$1.50 as part of the Bulong acquisition. In addition, there were 5.35 million shares under option agreements with exercise prices ranging from A$2.50 to A$2.74 at June 30, 1999.

[d] There were 8.37 million shares under option agreements with exercise prices ranging from A$1.50 to A$2.74 at June 30, 2000 and June 30, 2001. Preston was delisted in October 1999, with a last trading price of A$0.27.

Source: Preston Resources Limited Annual Report 1999, 2000, and 2001 (unaudited).

ranties for up to A$300 million in damages, agreed to provide interest-free, subordinated loans to Preston to cover construction cost overruns and working capital needs through February 28, 1999.[17] Preston's management described the transaction this way: "Bulong is a rare opportunity to acquire a high-quality project almost at the point where it commences production. It will provide substantial cash flows in the near term, and the experience of its skilled workforce will greatly assist in the development of our U.S. $450 million Marlborough project."[18] Despite management's optimism, Preston's stock price fell by 12% on the day of the announcement.

[17] Prospectus, p. 32.
[18] Preston Market Release, July 22, 1998, from Website, New Mine, March 28, 1999.

EXHIBIT 17-6

PRESTON RESOURCES LIMITED—BALANCE SHEET (CONSOLIDATED)

	June 30 Year End (A$ 000)			
	1998	**1999**	**2000**	**2001**
Current Assets				
Cash	$ 2,233	$ 21,442	$ 824	$ 301
Receivables	36	5,237	1,113	17,104
Inventories	—	10,741	8,942	8,669
Other	—	6,608	2,886	2,457
Total Current Assets	2,268	44,028	13,765	28,531
Non-Current Assets				
Receivables	—	—	—	—
Investments	110	269	1	1
Prop., plant, and equipment	257	367,839	115,100	109,481
Exploration expenditure	26,634	33,729	—	—
Other	60	46,865	2,414	1,023
Total Non-Current Assets	27,061	448,702	117,515	110,504
Total Assets	**29,329**	**492,730**	**131,280**	**139,035**
Current Liabilities				
Accounts payable	2,397	16,738	57,031	59,059
Borrowings	10,000	53,643	375,296	508,493
Provisions	14	2,881	603	932
Other (hedging liabilities)	—	—	123,992	243,616
Total Current Liabilities	12,411	73,262	556,922	812,100
Non-Current Liabilities				
Accounts payable	—	3,143	2,098	1,157
Borrowings	—	279,964	—	—
Provisions	—	69,514	2,631	3,542
Total Non-Current Liabilities	—	352,621	4,729	4,699
Total Liabilities	12,411	425,882	561,651	816,799
Net Assets	**16,918**	**66,848**	**(430,371)**	**(677,764)**
Equity				
Share capital	26,825	100,575	102,137	102,137
Reserves	2,087	1,562	—	—
Accumulated losses	(11,994)	(35,289)	(532,508)	(779,901)
Total Equity	**16,918**	**66,848**	**(430,371)**	**(677,764)**

Source: Adapted from Preston Resources Limited Annual Reports from 1999, 2000, and 2001 (unaudited).

Preston acquired 100% of BOP and its wholly-owned subsidiary Bulong Nickel Pty. Ltd. (BNP) in November 1998 (see Exhibit 17-7). Assuming the Bulong and Marlborough mines produced at expected levels following the acquisition, Preston would become the world's sixth-largest nickel producer and fourth-largest cobalt producer by 2003.[19] Based on the nature of the mines and the PAL technology, Preston would also be one of the world's low-cost producers (see Exhibit 17-8). In fact, Preston claimed

[19] Preston Annual Report 1999, p. 6.

EXHIBIT 17-7

CORPORATE STRUCTURE

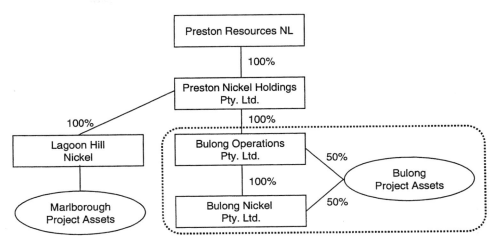

Source: Adapted from Bulong Prospectus, p. 16.

EXHIBIT 17-8

BULONG COST POSITION

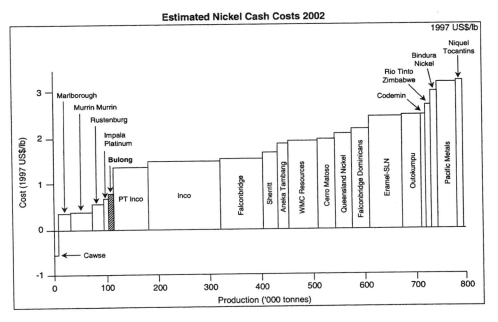

Note: Assumes cobalt (a byproduct) is sold at $15.00 per pound.

Source: Adapted from Bulong Prospectus, Annex B, p. B-10.

that Bulong would have an average cash production cost of U.S. $1.04 per pound over the first five years versus U.S. $2.10 per pound for other major producers in the Western world.[20]

Preston funded the $319 million acquisition price by borrowing A$260.5 million from Barclays in the form of a bridge loan, issuing A$39.9 million of new equity to Resolute, assuming A$11.1 million in liabilities, and paying A$7.5 million of cash on a deferred basis.[21] As part of the transaction, Barclays became the counterparty for Bulong's foreign exchange contracts. At the time, the contracts had a negative net value on a mark-to-market basis of A$33 million, a liability that Preston assumed from Resolute.[22] In addition to assuming the foreign exchange liabilities, Preston guaranteed the Barclays bridge loan and contributed A$30 million of new equity—A$10 million from institutional investors and A$20 million from Resolute—priced at A$1.50 per share. Through this transaction, Resolute became Preston's largest shareholder with a 19.9% ownership interest.

The deal attracted much attention from the local press. One commentator wrote: "Barclays . . . has taken the view that it wants exposure to the nickel business and has chosen Preston to be its vehicle."[23] Another commented:

> Former Perth stockbroker Colin Ikin achieved a minor miracle this week. Using a company with little track record and just $9 million in the bank, he edged closer to lining up more than $1 billion in project finance for nickel mines in Western Australia and Queensland. Within three years [his company] . . . will be one of the country's largest nickel and cobalt producers.[24]

According to Preston's financial projections (see Exhibit 17-9), Bulong would have an unleveraged, after-tax internal rate of return of 18% (nominal).[25] The projections assumed average annual nickel and cobalt prices of U.S. $3.25 and U.S. $15.00 per pound, respectively; production of LME-grade nickel at design levels beginning in mid-2000; and an average exchange rate of approximately U.S. $0.68 = A$1.00. Exhibit 17-10 provides management's production and pricing assumptions. It also shows pricing assumptions from CRU International, a minerals consulting firm hired to provide independent pricing forecasts.

The Senior Secured Note Financing

Because Preston financed the acquisition with a bridge loan that matured on March 31, 1999, it needed to arrange permanent financing for the project. The two most realistic options were a term loan from banks or a project bond placed with institutional investors. Whereas banks had traditionally dominated project financings in Australia, the Murrin Murrin and Cawse projects had recently tapped the U.S. institutional debt market, raising U.S. $420 million and U.S. $225 million, respectively, in 10-year project bonds.[26] Market conditions, however, were less favorable in the fall of 1998 because

---

[20] Prospectus, p. 42.

[21] Preston Annual Report 1998, p. 18; includes casewriter estimates to simplify the transaction consideration.

[22] Prospectus, p. 11.

[23] B. Hextall, "Preston Enters Premier Nickel League," *Australian Financial Review*, July 23, 1998, p. 21.

[24] I. Ries, " Banks Miss Out on Nickel Coup," *Australian Financial Review*, July 24, 1998.

[25] Preston Market Release, February 1, 2001, p. 1 ⟨http://www.prestonres.com.au⟩.

[26] R. Hogan, "US Financing Deal Alarms Banks," *Australian Financial Review*, August 26, 1997, p. 36; "Australia/Centaur/Note Issue—Funding for Cawse Project," *Dow Jones International News*, November 24, 1997.

EXHIBIT 17-9

BULONG OPERATIONS PTY. LTD.—SUMMARY FINANCIAL PROJECTION (A$ IN THOUSANDS, EXCEPT OTHERWISE INDICATED, IN CONSTANT/REAL 1998 DOLLARS)

Projected Fiscal Years Ending June 30

	1999 (partial year)	2000	2001	2002	2003	2004	2005	2006	2007	2008	2009
Financial Projections											
Revenues											
Nickel	$ 15,777	$ 99,241	$ 89,392	$ 82,401	$ 82,867	$ 77,635	$ 89,099	$ 83,706	$ 86,384	$ 80,560	$ 92,767
Cobalt	10,658	64,445	54,492	47,604	33,382	25,053	31,841	33,174	30,211	26,446	35,902
Selling & marketing exp.	(813)	(4,664)	(4,831)	—	—	—	—	—	—	—	—
Net oper. revenue	25,622	159,022	139,053	130,005	116,249	102,689	120,940	116,880	116,596	107,007	128,669
EBITDA	14,834	91,982	69,662	60,058	49,024	38,741	56,176	51,913	52,133	42,912	58,148
Interest expense	18,353	36,706	36,706	36,706	36,706	36,706	19,412	14,486	10,036	4,896	284
Interest income	601	875	866	3,420	4,645	5,521	5,936	339	245	149	52
Tax expense (credit)	3,166	(18,910)	(5,854)	(3,251)	348	6,920	(8,176)	(6,640)	(8,464)	(6,881)	(13,862)
Net Income	(8,015)	18,775	9,334	4,708	(1,691)	(13,374)	13,483	10,733	13,975	11,126	23,572
Cash Flow Items											
Capital expenditures	3,000	3,025	3,025	3,025	3,025	3,025	3,025	3,025	3,025	3,025	3,025
Depreciation	6,737	13,987	14,155	14,333	14,522	14,724	14,940	15,173	15,425	15,700	16,002
Amortization	1,525	4,479	4,479	4,479	4,479	4,479	4,479	4,479	4,479	4,479	4,479
Incr/(Decr) in Net WC	25,167	5,457	157	1,848	(770)	558	1,085	625	771	546	(998)
Balance Sheet Data											
Adjusted cash	16,001	30,297	37,957	43,431	47,108	1,513	1,513	1,513	1,513	1,513	55,273
Total debt	293,651	293,651	293,651	293,651	293,651	155,298	155,887	80,288	39,171	2,270	—
DSR account	18,363	18,353	18,353	18,353	18,353	9,706	7,243	5,018	2,448	142	—
Cash sweep account	—	38,350	61,330	77,753	88,784	—	—	—	—	—	—
Net debt	275,298	236,948	213,968	197,545	186,514	145,592	108,644	75,270	36,723	2,128	
Shareholders' equity	113,788	132,562	141,897	146,604	144,914	131,540	145,003	155,736	169,711	180,837	204,409
Key Credit Statistics											
EBITDA/Net interest exp.	NM	2.6×	1.9×	1.8×	1.5×	1.2×	4.2×	3.7×	5.3×	9.0×	NM
Net deb /EBITDA	NM	2.6×	3.1×	3.3×	3.8×	3.8×	1.9×	1.4×	0.7×	0.0×	NM

Source: Adapted from Bulong Prospectus.

EXHIBIT 17-10

SUMMARY OF SIGNIFICANT ASSUMPTIONS FOR THE FINANCIAL PROJECTIONS

	1999[a] (partial year)	2000	2001	2002	2003	2004	2005	2006	2007	2008	2009
						Projected Fiscal Years Ending June 30					
Production Assumptions											
Ore mined (000 tons)	1,066	1,203	760	1,134	492	695	760	671	649	858	266
Mined grade											
Nickel (%)	1.25	1.38	1.36	1.31	1.23	1.18	1.21	1.30	1.28	1.30	1.13
Cobalt (%)	0.09	0.13	0.11	0.12	0.12	0.09	0.10	0.13	0.08	0.09	0.09
Ore processed (000 tons)	144	537	600	600	600	600	600	600	600	600	600
Processed grade											
Nickel (%)	1.64	1.74	1.62	1.43	1.39	1.31	1.50	1.41	1.45	1.34	1.55
Cobalt (%)	0.16	0.15	0.14	0.15	0.11	0.09	0.12	0.12	0.11	0.10	0.13
Recovery Rates											
Nickel (%)	85.3	92.1	93.1	92.3	93.7	93.7	93.7	93.7	93.7	93.7	92.9
Cobalt (%)	85.3	90.7	91.4	90.5	92.0	91.8	91.8	91.8	91.8	91.8	91.8
Production—output sold[b]											
Nickel (tons)	1,367	8,604	9,033	7,925	7,820	7,337	8,405	7,899	8,152	7,522	8,662
Cobalt (tons)	141	737	758	794	630	513	651	678	618	535	726
Nickel cash production cost w/cobalt credit (US$/lb)	$2.58	0.18	0.28	0.55	0.95	1.32	0.91	0.93	0.99	1.24	0.87
Financial Assumptions (in constant 1998 dollars)											
Pricing—Bulong Management Assumptions											
Nickel (US$/lb)[c]	$3.30	3.30	3.10	3.25	3.25	3.25	3.25	3.25	3.25	3.25	3.25
Cobalt (US$/lb)[d]	$21.60	25.00	22.50	18.75	16.25	15.00	15.00	15.00	15.00	15.00	15.00
Pricing—CRU Assumptions											
Nickel (US$/lb)	$2.03	2.07	2.25	2.30	2.54	2.91	3.03	3.03	3.03	3.03	3.03
Cobalt (US$/lb)	$22.56	19.95	16.31	13.39	11.90	11.31	10.74	10.20	9.69	9.21	8.74
Exchange Rate: US$/A$	0.63	0.63	0.69	0.69	0.68	0.68	0.68	0.68	0.68	0.67	0.67

[a] Represents the six-month period beginning with the commencement of commercial production in January 1999.

[b] Production has been adjusted in 1999 to take account of work-in-progress.

[c] Reflects existing nickel hedges for 100% of production in fiscal years 1999 and 2000.

[d] Reflects the weighted average price for cobalt based on the hedged cobalt price for 80 tons of cobalt at US$19 and a forecast spot cobalt price of US$25 in fiscal year 1999.

Source: Adapted from Bulong Prospectus.

of the Asian and Russian crises and the recent collapse of Long Term Capital, a U.S. hedge fund.

Before being able to issue a bond, however, Bulong would have to get a rating from Moody's or Standard & Poor's. Given the nature of mining projects in general and Bulong in particular, a project bond would probably not garner an investment-grade rating. In addition, it would require additional fees, some delay, and, possibly, structural changes to the deal at the behest of the rating agencies. In terms of pricing, institutional lenders would expect up-front fees of around 3% and fixed interest rates of approximately 12%. A bank loan, by way of contrast, would have a shorter maturity, lower up-front fees, and a floating interest rate based on a spread over LIBOR—the rate would probably be slightly lower than the fixed rates available in the high-yield bond market. The banks would, however, require Bulong to enter some kind of fixed-for-floating swap contract to eliminate interest rate risk. The combination of the loan rate plus the swap fees would likely be close to the bond rate.

The major drawbacks of a bank financing were likely to be a tighter covenant package with financial performance default triggers, mechanisms for lender control of the project's cash flow, more frequent performance reporting, and required repayment of principal in installments commencing soon after closing. The institutional lenders, on the other hand, typically required less onerous covenant and reporting packages, did not impose tight cash-control measures, and at times *preferred* principal payments to be back-ended. In some cases, they even accepted a "bullet" form of repayment with the full loan amount due in one final payment. The ability to defer principal payments appealed to sponsors because it meant that early cash flows could be applied to project costs, debt service, and equity distributions.

One of the major differences between the two types of financings was that institutional lenders rarely provided additional borrowings. Having closed and funded, they expected to hold their notes with little further interaction with the borrower other than to receive scheduled interest and principal payments. The financing documentation for a bond issue, called an indenture, usually permitted the borrower to incur limited amounts of additional indebtedness, such as subordinated debt and working capital loans. Such loans typically came from other sources because institutional lenders rarely made short-term loans. Bank deals, on the other hand, frequently provided for the same group of banks to make further loans for specific purposes such as funding working capital requirements.

Another disadvantage of the institutional market was that after a deal had closed and funding had begun it was usually more difficult for the borrower to communicate with the lenders and, therefore, harder to get timely action on requests for waivers and amendments. Because most institutional deals did not require changes, institutional lenders were unaccustomed to requests for amendments. Another reason it was difficult to get approvals for waivers was that institutional deals lacked a lead financial institution through which the borrower could access the lender group. The investment bank that structured and distributed the deal usually did not participate as a lender. Instead, a trustee administered the indenture agreement and processed debt repayments. The trustee, typically a commercial bank, had no stake in the deal and no relationship with the borrower. In contrast, the lead bank in a syndicated term loan was typically a lender and had a relationship with the borrower. For this reason, it took an active role in getting other banks to approve waivers and amendments.

After considering the options, Preston and Barclays decided to issue a project bond in the U.S. Regulation 144A market. On December 15, 1998, Barclays closed a U.S. $185 million private placement of 12.5% fixed rate senior secured notes for BOP. The notes were secured by substantially all of Bulong's assets and were nonrecourse to Preston. They had a 10-year final maturity with semiannual interest payments of U.S. $11.6 million (A$18.3 million) commencing on June 15, 1999. There was a mandatory sinking fund of U.S. $50 million by December 2006, increasing to U.S. $75 million by December 2007, and no covenants relating to the project's operating performance.[27]

The Bulong note indenture was structured somewhat tighter than most institutional deals, with some terms more typical of bank financing. The deal included a "cash waterfall" structure of collateral accounts at Barclays that controlled project cash flow, a "cash trap" that held 75% of operating cash flow for sinking fund obligations and repayment at final maturity, and a debt service reserve account (DSRA). After each interest payment, Bulong had 30 days to replenish the DSRA with the next semiannual interest payment. Also, there were covenants restricting other indebtedness (to approximately U.S. $13 million), liens, shareholder distributions, and affiliate transactions. Waivers and amendments of indenture provisions required the approval of a majority of the noteholders, by value, except for interest rate changes, which required unanimous approval.

The notes received subinvestment-grade ratings from both Moody's Investors Service (B2) and Standard & Poor's (B+). Moody's commented:

> The rating acknowledges Bulong's projected low cost position, short-term hedging program, strong offtake agreement, and very strong project structure as supporting factors for the rating. However, the rating also considers weak current and future potential nickel pricing, downward trends in cobalt pricing, technological and commissioning risks, the absence of other ongoing operations to help support the project during ramp-up, as well as the lack of any meaningful ownership or support from highly creditworthy third parties.[28]

Proceeds to Bulong, after an underwriting fee of U.S. $5.5 million and offering expenses of U.S .$2.4 million, were U.S. $177 million. The proceeds were used to repay Barclay's bridge financing (U.S. $165 million including accrued interest) and to prefund the debt service reserve account (U.S. $11.6 million to cover the June 1999 interest payment). The note issue left BOP with a pro forma debt-to-total capitalization ratio of 72% and cash reserves of A$66 million.[29]

BULONG PERFORMANCE FROM 1998 TO 2000

Start-Up Operations

Project start-up consisted of two sequential phases. *Commissioning* involved testing the plant's major systems, while *ramp-up* involved processing progressively larger volumes of ore until the plant reached the designated output and quality levels. Bateman's responsibilities under the EPCM contract ended with "practical completion," defined as the completion of commissioning. While not responsible for ramp-up, Bateman had agreed to make key personnel available as needed. The EPCM contract provided that Bateman would be responsible for construction cost overruns up to A$5 million and for

---

[27] Adapted from the Bulong Prospectus, December 17, 1998, cover sheet plus pp. 1–5.

[28] "Moody's Assigns B2 to Sen. Sec. Project Notes of Bulong Operations PTY LTD, Pre-Sale Report," Moody's Investors Service, December 1998, p. 1.

[29] Adapted from the Bulong Prospectus, December 17, 1998, cover sheet plus pp. 6, 14, and 15.

liquidated damages up to A\$2 million if the plant did not meet certain operating benchmarks during ramp-up.[30] Bulong management assumed that commissioning would be completed in December 1998 and ramp-up would be completed 18 months later in June 2000.[31] Behre Dolbear, which conducted an independent technical review in connection with the note offering, estimated it would take at least two years to reach full capacity.[32]

Contrary to expectations, Bulong did not complete commissioning by December 1998.[33] When the company fed ore into the autoclave, key parts failed almost immediately, causing a two-month delay. Operations resumed in March 1999 but stopped in August because certain critical valves were limiting throughput. After installing larger valves, the plant soon achieved its designed capacity. In October, Preston CEO Ikin commented:

> Any company dealing with the latest processes anticipates technical issues in the commissioning and ramp up stages of a new plant and I am pleased to report that at Bulong we continue to make significant progress. Commercial metal production commenced at Bulong in April 1999 and target quality was achieved by May. At the date of this report some 1,000 tonnes of nickel and 16 tonnes of cobalt have been shipped and sold.[34]

Yet, two months later, gypsum precipitation began to clog the pipes, pumps, and valves.[35] Although Bulong managed to solve this problem by May 2000, a number of valves and seals failed shortly thereafter, causing six weeks of lost production.[36] Operations resumed in July, only to encounter further problems involving fluid contamination. After resolving this problem, Bulong achieved record output in August, September, and October 2000. Management commented, "Since June plant performance has improved dramatically, and the operation is now covering cash operating costs but is not generating sufficient funds to clear all past financial obligations."[37] Except for scheduled maintenance interruptions and problems caused by a power outage in the region, Bulong operated continuously during 2001. However, processing rates reached design levels for only short periods, resulting in substantial shortfalls in production volumes (see Exhibit 17-11).

Ikin summarized the history of Bulong by saying it "has not worked as we expected at all, it has not worked as the experts expected and the end result is not pretty, I'm afraid."[38] Bulong was not alone in its difficulties. According to a local paper, Western Australia's three laterite nickel projects (Bulong, Murrin Murrin, and Cawse), which cost \$1.6 billion to develop, were operating at 50% capacity and had cash costs well above the expected U.S. \$1.00 per pound.[39] By 2001, all three projects were in default.

---

[30] Ibid., p. 51.

[31] Ibid., p. 50.

[32] Annex A, p. A-10.

[33] Prospectus, p. 50.

[34] Preston Annual Report 1999, p. 4.

[35] Preston Market Release—Bulong Finance Update, November 30, 2000, ⟨http://www.prestonres.com.au/news⟩.

[36] Ibid.

[37] Ibid.

[38] S. Kemp, "\$500m Loss Puts Heat on Preston," *The West Australian*, February 3, 2001, p. 63.

[39] M. Weir, "Laterites Fall Well Short of Launch Targets," *The West Australian*, May 1, 2000, p. 33.

EXHIBIT 17-11

ACTUAL VS. TARGET PERFORMANCE FOR THE BULONG PROJECT (ALL AMOUNT IN A$000 UNLESS NOTED)[a]

	11 months to May 2000			12 months to June 2001			9 months to March 2002		
	Actual	Target	Variance	Actual	Target	Variance	Actual	Target	Variance
Production									
Inputs									
Leach Feed	276,607	334,145	(57,538)	437,493	459,350	(21,857)	335,785	399,204	(63,419)
NI Grade (%)	1.91%	1.80%	0.11%	1.82%	1.83%	-0.01%	1.78%	1.74%	0.04%
CO Grade (%)	0.14%	0.15%	-0.01%	0.14%	0.14%	0.00%	0.13%	0.12%	0.01%
Output (b)									
Ni (tons)	4,006.4	4,908.0	(901.6)	6,352.5	7,579.0	(1,226.5)	4,894.6	6,012.4	(1,117.8)
Co (tons)	213.6	335.0	(121.4)	407.6	554.0	(146.4)	293.5	403.7	(110.2)
Metallurgical Performance									
Plant Recovery Rate									
Nickel	70.5%	92.0%	-21.5%	77.5%	92.9%	-15.4%	82.6%	86.6%	-4.0%
Cobalt	56.5%	91.6%	-35.1%	70.2%	91.6%	-21.4%	67.7%	82.0%	-14.3%
Plant Utilization	32.0%	93.8%	-61.8%	87.8%	88.2%	-0.4%	na	na	na
Cash Operating Costs									
Commercial Operations	$ 5,892.3	$ 5,478.3	($414.0)	$ 6,995.8	$ 6,870.0	($ 125.8)	$ 6,016.1	$ 5,226.7	($ 789.4)
Mining	$ 5,888.4	$ 7,208.6	$ 1,320.2	$ 6,455.6	$ 8,244.4	$ 1,788.8	$ 6,749.8	$ 5,759.9	($ 989.9)
Leaching	$24,335.4	$23,825.7	($ 509.7)	$27,920.9	$32,613.5	$ 4,692.6	$20,167.0	$21,209.9	($ 1,042.9)
Refining	$19,178.2	$17,927.6	($1,250.6)	$33,712.3	$27,030.5	($6,681.8)	$22,685.9	$24,037.5	($ 1,351.6)
Health & Safety	$ 0.0	0.0	0.0	$ 983.5	$ 971.2	($ 12.3)	$ 769.1	$ 800.7	$ 31.6
Maintenance	$ 2,025.7	$ 1,966.3	($ 59.4)	$12,914.2	$12,385.4	($ 528.8)	$10,246.0	$ 8,653.3	($1,592.7)
Production Services	$20,223.4	$12,407.9	($7,815.5)	$ 3,211.6	$ 4,985.6	$ 1,774.0	$ 1,588.9	$ 2,119.3	$ 530.4
Total	$77,543.4	$68,814.4	($8,729.0)	$92,193.9	$93,100.6	$ 906.7	$68,222.8	$67,807.3	($ 415.5)
$ Cost per ton of metal	$ 18,353	$ 13,196	($5,157.0)	$ 13,647	$ 11,270	($2,376.2)	$ 14,144	$ 10,946	($3,198.0)
Revenue[b]									
Nickel sales							$50,712.3		
Cobalt sales							$ 5,505.6		
Total							$56,217.9		
Labor									
Number of FTE							219.1	225.0	5.9
$ Cost per ton of metal							$ 3,765	$ 2,853	($912)

[a] Financial statements are for the project only. They do not include certain head office revenue, executive compensation, and certain administrative expenses.

[b] Metal output may exceed or be less than metal sales depending on net inventory change. In the FY02 period above, sales exceeded output.

Source: Company documents, casewriter analysis.

Start-Up Financing

Although the original projections showed positive operating cash flow beginning in 1999 (see Exhibit 17-9), the operating problems created a downward cash flow spiral: delayed cash flows limited Bulong's ability to pay for needed repairs, which, in turn, further delayed revenue generation. In an attempt to raise cash, Preston initially tapped Resolute's obligation to make interest-free subordinated loans. Borrowings from Resolute reached A$44 million by June 1999 and A$47 million by June 2000.[40] Preston then turned to Barclays for an A$5 million working capital loan in October 1999—this loan would later grow to A$30 million by year-end 2000. At the time, Preston considered two other options to raise additional funds. First, it considered issuing A$75 million of new equity, an option that was limited by the fact that Preston had been delisted from the Australian Stock Exchange (ASX) in October 1999, with a final trading price of A$0.27 per share (see Exhibit 17-12). Preston also considered a joint venture with the Australian firm Anaconda Nickel Ltd. In the end, management did not complete either option.[41]

Although Bulong made both required interest payments in 1999, it failed to replenish the DSRA within 30 days after the December payment. Under the note in-

[40] Preston Annual Report 1999, p. 37.

[41] "Nickel Miner Preston Struggles to Escape Financial Difficulties," *The Asian Wall Street Journal*, November 26, 1999, p. 19.

EXHIBIT 17-12

PRESTON RESOURCES STOCK PRICE HISTORY (IN A$)

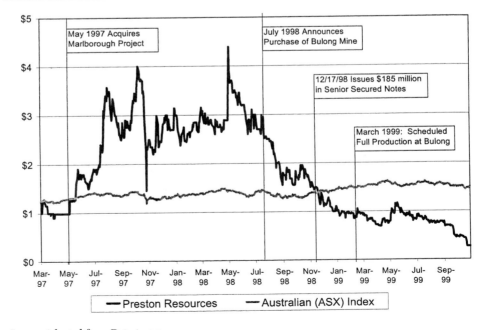

Source: Adapted from Datastream.

denture, failure to replenish the account constituted an event of default, which could have triggered an acceleration of the notes. Instead, Preston, Barclays, and the noteholders executed a 90-day "standstill agreement" in January 2000 by which they agreed not to take any enforcement actions and to work toward a restructuring of the notes. They subsequently renewed the agreement when it expired in April.[42]

Bulong failed to make the June 2000 interest payment as well, creating a second event of default. When Preston closed its books for the 2000 fiscal year (see Exhibits 17-5 and 17-6), it reported an abnormal pretax charge of A$387 million, including an A$218 million write-down of the Bulong project to a carrying value of A$115 million; the value was determined by discounting 10 years of projected cash flows. Preston also disclosed that it was suing Bateman for A$5.75 million under the EPCM contract and for "substantial" damages resulting from the original feasibility study. Finally, Preston reported its unrealized exposure under the hedging facilities had become an A$124 million liability.[43] Whereas Preston wrote off part of its investment in the Bulong project, Resolute wrote off its investment entirely (A$48 million of Preston stock and A$49 million of subordinated loans).

By early 2002 Bulong's working capital borrowings from Barclays had increased to A$43.5 million, and its unrealized losses on the hedging facilities had increased to A$240 million, largely due to the foreign currency contracts, as the Australian dollar had depreciated from U.S. $0.63 in November 1998 to U.S. $0.51 in December 2001.[44] In addition to the Bulong loans, Barclays had also been making working capital loans for the development of the Marlborough project. Preston pledged all the Marlborough assets to Barclays as collateral for these loans.[45] As a result, Barclays joined the noteholders as secured creditors. In total, Bulong and Preston owed the secured creditors more than A$700 million.[46]

THE FIRST AND SECOND RESTRUCTURING PLANS

In April 2000 Preston announced an agreement in principle with the bondholders on a plan to restructure the senior secured notes.[47] The main points were eliminating the DSRA requirement, capitalizing the June and December 2000 interest payments in the form of new bonds, and transferring a 50% equity interest in Preston Nickel Holdings Pty. Ltd. to the noteholders and Barclays. Preston expected the restructuring would be completed by the middle of the year, following approvals by the Australian courts, the noteholders, and Preston's shareholders.[48]

During 2000, Preston continued to discuss the restructuring with Barclays and the noteholders but could not reach an agreement until December, when it announced a *second* restructuring plan. Like the first plan, the second plan dropped the DSRA requirement, maintained a 12.5% annual interest rate, and capitalized the June and December 2000 interest payments. However, it replaced all scheduled future interest and

---

[42] Preston Annual Report 2000, p. 4; Prospectus, p. 23.

[43] Preston Annual Report 2000, pp. 21, 31, and 34.

[44] Preston Annual Report 2001, p. 39.

[45] Ibid., p. 48.

[46] "Australia: Preston Urges Revamp to Avoid Liquidation," *Reuters English News Service*, June 21, 2002.

[47] Preston Market Release, Bulong Debt Restructuring, April 13, 2000, ⟨http://www.prestonres.com.au/news⟩.

[48] Preston Market Release, April 13, 2000 ⟨www.prestonres.com.au/news⟩.

principal payments with a mechanism that effectively converted the notes into equity. A new sweep account would be set up to accumulate cash flow after operating expenses. At the end of each quarter, any balance in the account in excess of A$15 million would be distributed as debt service to the noteholders and Barclays. The notes and working capital loans would mature only as payments under this mechanism were sufficient to repay the outstanding principal amounts plus accrued interest. Similarly, the obligations under the hedging facilities would be payable from operating cash flow, as available, ratably with payments on the notes and working capital loans. Barclays would agree to release Preston from its guarantees of the hedging facilities and the working capital loans. In consideration of these changes, Preston would transfer 95% of its equity interest in the Bulong companies to the noteholders and Barclays. Preston would retain the other 5% of Bulong, own 100% of the Marlborough project, and be essentially debt free. Referring to the second plan, CEO Ikin concluded, "If we go ahead [with the second restructuring plan], we will live to face another day. We will have 5% of the company and no debt."[49]

The second plan also included a side agreement between Preston and Resolute under which Resolute agreed to forgive subordinated loans and accrued interest totaling A$49 million and to surrender its ownership interests. In return, Preston agreed to release Resolute from all obligations under the original sale agreement.[50]

Management originally predicted that the second plan would go into effect during the first half of 2001.[51] Yet the summer came and went with no agreement. In December 2001, almost two years after Bulong's initial default, Preston announced that the noteholders had approved the second plan together with a new standstill agreement. Preston estimated that the restructuring would take effect by the end of March 2002. Preston's CEO Adrian Griffin said:

> These arrangements will provide a positive environment for the continuation of operations at Bulong and will . . . permit the project debt to be restructured, relieving the operation from the financial burden of making further interest and principal repayments . . . there will be no adverse impact on unsecured creditors, who will be advantaged by the improved financial position.[52]

CONCLUSION

On April 21, 2002, Preston announced that it had submitted the two schemes of arrangement (one for BOP and one for its subsidiary BNP) to the Supreme Court of Western Australia. To be approved, Australian law required the court to determine that the restructuring plan tangibly benefited the debtor and that the debtor would be legally solvent under the plan. In addition to court approval, Australian law required that 75% of the noteholders by value and a majority by number also approve the schemes. Separately, pursuant to rules of the Australian Stock Exchange, Preston's shareholders had to approve the transfer of 95% of the Bulong companies to the noteholders and other secured creditors. Court hearings on the schemes began on April 26 and concluded on May 17 with a determination that the schemes qualified for submission to the secured

[49] J. Counsel, "Preston Digs Itself out of Debt Hole," *Sydney Morning Herald Home Page*, June 18, 2001.
[50] Preston Annual Report for the Year Ended 30 June 2001, p. 48.
[51] Preston Annual Report 2000, dated December 22, 2000, pp. 5–6, p. 39; Preston Market Release—Bulong Financial Update, November 30, 2000.
[52] Preston Market Release, December 21, 2001 ⟨http://www.prestonres.com.au/news⟩.

creditors. Management planned to present the schemes to the secured creditors at a special meeting on June 20. Assuming the secured creditors and the Supreme Court approved the schemes, management would then present the restructuring plan to shareholders at the company's annual general meeting on July 15.

If the secured creditors did not approve the schemes of arrangement, some form of liquidation was likely to occur. As secured creditors, Barclays or any of the noteholders could place both Preston and Bulong in receivership. The receiver would have the power to seize and sell collateral for the secured creditors' benefit. As a point of reference, the Cawse nickel project and its parent corporation, Centaur Mining, had gone into receivership in 2001. The combined entity had total debts of A\$654 million, including a U.S. \$225 million bond issued to finance the Cawse project. Through an auction, the receiver sold the Cawse project for an estimated U.S. \$22.1 million (A\$35 million).[53] Another possibility, leading to a similar outcome, would be that one or more unsecured creditors would file for the appointment of a liquidator. Although no assets would be available to a liquidator for the unsecured creditors, initiating the process would, as a practical matter, terminate project operations and force Barclays and the noteholders to pursue a receivership to protect their interests. Yet a third possibility was that Preston could cause Bulong to file for protection from creditors and seek reorganization under the Australian equivalent of Chapter 11 of the U.S. Bankruptcy Act. However, Australian law gave secured creditors a 10-day period in which they could block a debtor's reorganization proceeding and pursue their rights in receivership.

None of these options seemed as attractive as restructuring the project's debt obligations, but Preston had a long way to go before the restructuring plan could take effect. That said, Griffin and Preston's other senior managers had to be sure they had structured the best deal possible and that the noteholders and shareholders would approve it.

---

[53] B. Fitzgerald, "Centaur Burns in Fire Sale," *The Age*, December 29, 2001, p. 18.

18

Mobile Energy
Services Company

When Al Dunlap became the CEO of Scott Paper Company in April 1994, he had already acquired the nickname "Chainsaw Al" for his aggressive approach to corporate restructuring. Dunlap, who publicly likened Scott Paper (Scott) to a "beached whale," wanted to refocus the company on consumer products by divesting its noncore businesses.[1] Scott was, at the time, a leading manufacturer of tissue products and a vertically integrated company. In Mobile, Alabama, for example, the company owned and operated 525,000 acres of timberland, three mills (pulp, paper, and tissue), and an energy complex that produced all of the facility's energy needs.

In 1994, Scott sold the Mobile paper mill to a group of investors and the Mobile energy complex, a cogeneration plant, to the Southern Company (Southern).[2] Southern financed the $350 million acquisition with a bridge loan and created a new company, Mobile Energy Services Company L.L.C. (MESC, pronounced "mesk"), to own and manage the energy complex. As of August 1995, MESC hoped to raise $340 million, $255 million in nonrecourse project bonds and $85 million in municipal bonds, to repay the bridge loan.

THE MOBILE FACILITY

The Mobile facility was located on 730 contiguous acres in Alabama (see Exhibit 18-1). The nearby timberlands supplied wood to the pulp mill, which debarked the logs,

Professor Benjamin C. Esty and Research Associate Aldo Sesia Jr. prepared this case. This case was developed from published sources. HBS cases are developed solely as the basis for class discussion. Cases are not intended to serve as endorsements, sources of primary data, or illustrations of effective or ineffective management.

[1] "The Shredder: Did CEO Dunlap Save Scott Paper—or Just Pretty It Up?" *BusinessWeek*, January 15, 1996, p. 57.

[2] A cogeneration energy plant uses a single fuel source to produce steam and thermal energy, which are then used to produce electricity.

EXHIBIT 18-1

MOBILE FACILITY PRODUCTION AND ENERGY FLOW

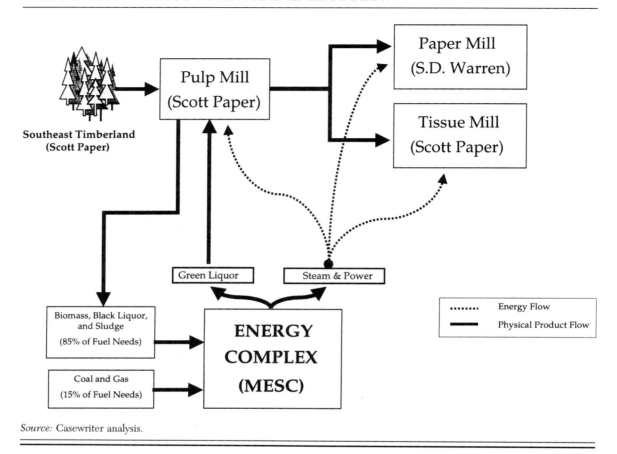

Source: Casewriter analysis.

chipped them, and turned the wood chips into virgin pulp using a chemical process.[3] It then sold pulp to the Mobile paper and tissue mills, providing them with all of their pulp needs. The tissue mill produced toilet paper, tissue paper, and paper napkins, while the paper mill produced publication-quality paper, printer paper, and self-adhesive labels.

During the pulp manufacturing process, the pulp mill created several byproducts: biomass (a wood waste such as bark), sludge, and black liquor.[4] These byproducts supplied 85% of the energy complex's fuel needs; coal and natural gas bought from outside vendors provided the remaining 15%. With these fuels, the energy complex pro-

---

[3] Virgin pulp is made from new wood fibers (i.e., wood chips) rather than from recycled materials.

[4] Cooking wood chips in a chemical solution separates the wood fibers from lignin, an organic glue. A by-product of this process is a liquid residue known as black liquor. Black liquor can be concentrated and burned to produce thermal energy and a liquid known as green liquor, which is then used in the pulping process.

duced steam and power (electricity), which it sold to the mills, and produced green liquor used in the pulping process. The energy complex supplied the three mills with 100% of their steam and 98% of their power needs. It provided the pulp mill with virtually all of its green liquor requirements.[5]

As soon as Dunlap arrived, he began to sell Scott's noncore assets. First, he sold S. D. Warren (Warren). the company's largest subsidiary and owner of the Mobile paper mill, to a group headed by Sappi Ltd., the largest forest products company in Africa. Then he sold the Mobile energy complex to Southern, a large U.S. energy holding company. (See Exhibits 18-2a and 18-2b for company financial statements.) Dunlap also said he wanted to sell the timberlands and the pulp mill at some point in the future. Commenting on the sale of the energy complex, Dunlap said:

> This marks the completion of another key phase of my plans for Scott. We have now looked at all of our assets to determine what fits with our future. The Mobile energy complex is one of a number of assets where we can free up capital to invest in our core business. . . . The sale of these assets will reduce our capital intensity, allow us to redeploy the proceeds to strengthen our balance sheet by reducing debt and help build the foundation to transition Scott to a global consumer products company.[6]

As part of the transition to independent ownership, Warren signed a 25-year pulp supply agreement with Scott to ensure the mills continued to operate in an integrated fashion.

EXHIBIT 18-2A

COMPANY INCOME STATEMENTS, FISCAL YEAR 1994 (MILLIONS)

	Southern Company	S.D. Warren Company	Scott Paper Company	Kimberly-Clark Corporation
Revenues	$8,297	$315	$3,581	$7,364
Costs and other deductions	4,975	287	3,080	6,545
Depreciation, deletion, and amortization	896	NA	NA	NA
Interest and debt expenses	726	2	121	129
Total costs	6,597	289	3,201	6,678
Income before income taxes	1,700	26	380	741
Income taxes	711	10	140	276
Other (loss)	—	—	(30)	70
Net income	**989**	**15**	**210**	**535**

Source: Global Access and casewriter estimates.

---

[5] Mobile Energy Services Company L.L.C., First Mortgage Bond Prospectus, August 15, 1996, p. 2.

[6] "Scott Paper Signs Letter of Intent for US$ 350 Million Energy Facility Sale, Plans to Divest Additional Nonstrategic Assets for US$ 1 Billion," *Canadian Corporate News*, October 24, 1994, Article 24.

EXHIBIT 18-2B

COMPANY BALANCE SHEETS, AS OF DECEMBER 31, 1994 (MILLIONS)

	Southern Company	S.D. Warren[a] Company	Scott Paper Company	Kimberly-Clark Corporation
Assets				
Current assets	$ 2,368	$ 344	$2,309	$1,810
Fixed assets less depreciation and depletion	21,117	1,346	2,482	4,199
Other assets	3,557	170	835	707
Total assets	**27,042**	**1,860**	**5,626**	**6,716**
Liabilities				
Current liabilities	2,549	146	1,174	1,287
Total debt	7,822	1,215	1,858	1,701
Other liabilities	7,053	104	842	1,132
Total liabilities	17,424	1,466	3,874	4,120
Shareholders' equity	9,618	394	1,750	2,596
Total liabilities and shareholders' equity	**27,042**	**1,860**	**5,626**	**6,716**
Moody's Bond Rating (as of July 1995)	A1[b]	B1	A2	Aa2
Debt-to-Total Capital (book value)	44.9%	75.5%	51.5%	39.6%
Stock price (as of December 31, 1994)	$12.22	na	$34.56	$25.19

[a] S.D. Warren's balance sheet is as of December 20, 1994.

[b] The Southern Company bond rating represents the average rating of its five power utilities.

Source: Complied from Global Access; Compustat; Bloomberg Financial Markets; *Moody's Investors Services Bond Record*, Vol. 62, No. 7 (July 1995); and casewriter estimates.

THE ENERGY COMPLEX

Southern paid $265 million in cash for the Mobile energy complex and assumed Scott's $85 million tax-exempt bond for a total purchase price of $350 million. (According to industry participants, other bids for the complex ranged from $200 million to $250 million.) Although this acquisition was Southern's first foray into the pulp and paper industry, Newton Houston, a manager at Southern, explained the rationale:

> Historically, the paper industry has been highly vertically integrated. Paper producers have tried to own everything from the dirt that their trees grow in to the trucks that deliver their products. . . . It is very difficult to manage such diverse businesses. Partnerships like this [Southern's venture at Mobile] are going to become more prevalent. And as focused specialists—transportation specialists, energy specialists, information specialists—come into the [paper] industry, competitive pressures will continue to rise. The specialists bring expertise and economies of scale in their areas of specialization that traditionally integrated paper companies will have difficulty matching.[7]

Two of Southern's wholly-owned subsidiaries, Mobile Energy Services Holding Incorporated and Southern Electric International, owned 99% and 1% of the energy

[7] Kirck J. Finchem, "Energy Partnership Serves Well at Mobile Pulp, Paper Complex. (Southern Co. operates electric power facility at Alabama site)," *Pulp & Paper*, August 1, 1997, p. 55.

complex, respectively. Renamed the Mobile Energy Services Company L.L.C., the energy complex was established as a limited liability company (LLC). Rather than paying taxes, MESC would flow income through to its parent corporations and be taxed at their marginal rates.

The Contracts

Before MESC took control of the energy complex, it signed 25-year operating contracts with Scott, as the owner of the pulp and tissue mills, and with Warren, as the owner of the paper mill. Twelve major contracts governed their business relationships. The two most important contracts were the Master Operating Agreement (MOA) and the Energy Services Agreement (ESA). (Exhibit 18-3 describes key contractual details.) The MOA and ESA stipulated the input/output quantities and prices for transactions between MESC and the mills.

EXHIBIT 18-3

SUMMARY OF PRINCIPAL CONTRACTUAL TERMS

ENERGY SERVICES AGREEMENTS AND MASTER OPERATING AGREEMENT

MESC is party to a Pulp Mill Energy Services Agreement with the Pulp Mill Owner, a Tissue Mill Energy Services Agreement with the Tissue Mill Owner, a Paper Mill Energy Services Agreement with the Paper Mill Owner and a Master Operating Agreement with each of Scott, the Pulp Mill Owner, the Tissue Mill Owner and the Paper Mill Owner. These agreements set forth the obligations of MESC, Scott and the Mill Owners to sell and purchase Liquor Processing Services, Steam Processing Services and Power Processing Services, to deliver or dispose of certain waste products or by-products produced by the Energy Complex and the Pulp Mill, and to manage the operations of the Energy Complex and the Mills.

Term

The Energy Services Agreements (ESAs) and the Master Operating Agreement (MOA) each have an initial term of 25 years.

Processing Services

Each Mill Owner is obligated to purchase its entire requirements for the Processing Services, up to the Maximum Capacities, from MESC unless MESC fails to satisfy such requirements due to capacity constraints or any other reason. MESC is obligated to supply the Mills' requirements for the Processing Services, up to the Aggregate Demand for each Processing Service.

The Aggregate Demand levels are fixed by the MOA until December 1999 and, thereafter, are reset periodically in accordance with the MOA to reflect the Mills' actual aggregate usage of Processing Services.

On the last day of the first five-contract year period (the "Initial Demand Period") and on the last day of each subsequent two-contract year period (each such period a "Demand Period" and each such date a "Demand Anniversary Date"), any Mill Owner whose peak usage of a particular Processing Service was below the low end of a range established for such Mill under the MOA with respect to such Processing Service (each such range a "Demand Band") has the option to reset its Demand for such Processing Service to a level not less than its peak usage during the Demand Period then ended. If a Mill's peak usage of a Processing Service was within the applicable Demand Band, the Mill's Demand cannot be reset to a lower level on the Demand Anniversary Date.

Sales to Third Parties

The Energy Services Agreements permit MESC to sell to any person, on an as-available fully interruptible basis, any of the services or products that the Energy Complex is capable of producing in excess of the Mills' requirements for such services or products at any given time.

(Continued)

EXHIBIT 18-3 *(Continued)*

Charges

The ESAs and the MOA obligate each Mill Owner to pay MESC a Demand Charge for each of the Processing Services that such Mill Owner is entitled to receive under its ESA and a Processing Charge for the Processing Services the Mill Owner actually receives. All such charges are invoiced, and are required to be paid on a monthly basis.

The Demand Charges are based upon the Demand levels in effect from time to time as determined pursuant to the procedures described above.

The Processing Charges are based upon each Mill's actual monthly usage of Processing Services. The Processing Charges were designed generally to cover the balance of the Company's costs that are not projected to be covered by the Demand Charges, including variable costs such as fuel related expenses, and to credit the appropriate Mills for certain energy value attributable to condensate flow that is provided by the Mills to the Energy Complex. There can be no assurance, however, that the Processing Charges will at all times cover such costs, including variable costs such as fuel related expenses.

Financial Adjustments

The MOA entitles MESC to request an increase in the amounts payable to the Company (a "Financial Adjustment") if, subject to certain conditions set forth in the MOA, (A) a federal energy tax on fuels used in the generation of electricity or steam (B) MESC must incur capital or operational expenditures at the Energy Complex because (i) of a modification of or charge in operations at a Mill (ii) any Mill Product becomes characterized as a Hazardous Material for any reason (iii) the Cluster Rules (and certain related regulations) become effective.

MESC will not be entitled to a Financial Adjustment unless MESC incurs, as a result of Adverse Financial Effects of Financial Adjustment Events, (A) capital expenditures in excess of $500,000 or (B) operational expenditures in excess of $100,000.

Force Majeure

Each party is excused from failure to perform its obligations under the Project Agreement if, and to the extent that, such failure is due to a Force Majeure Event, whether such Force Majeure Event is suffered directly by such party's Mill or Energy Complex or otherwise causes an interruption of operations at the Site. The affected party is obligated to provide prompt notice to the other parties upon becoming aware of the Force Majeure Event, and is obligated to make all reasonable efforts to remedy the Force Majeure Event, if practica-

ble, and to mitigate the adverse effects of the Force Majeure Event.

If a Force Majeure Event were to affect only the Mills or the Mill Owners, each affected Mill Owner would be required to continue to pay Demand Charges (at a level consistent with its Demand for each applicable Processing Service immediately prior to such Force Majeure Event) for six months after the occurrence of the Force Majeure Event; thereafter, each affected Mill Owner would be required to pay Demand Charges at a level consistent with such Mill Owner's capability, if any, to use all or a portion of the Actual Energy Complex Capacity available.

Insurance

MESC is required to maintain (a) property damage insurance in a minimum aggregate amount of $350,000,000 or the Company's outstanding obligations with respect to the financing or refinancing of the Energy Complex, whichever is greater.

Mill Closure and Termination of Agreements by Mill Owners

Each Mill Owner has the right to terminate its ESA upon a Mill Closure with respect to such Mill Owner's Mill. A terminating Mill Owner is obligated to provide MESC and the other Mill Owners six months prior written notice of its intention to terminate its ESA; termination is deemed to occur upon the expiration of such six-month period. The terminating Mill Owner is obligated to pay MESC such Mill's Demand Charges (at the levels in effect immediately prior to the giving of notice) for the greater of (i) six months from the date of termination or (ii) the end of the then current Demand Period. All obligations incurred by the terminating Mill Owner prior to the termination of its ESA (and all obligations to pay Demand Charges pursuant to the preceding sentence) survive the termination, and must be timely performed or paid by the terminating Mill Owner. In addition, the terminating Mill Owner must give reasonable assistance to MESC in the Company's endeavors to create new business opportunities for the Energy Complex; however, the terminating Mill Owner will have no liability or other monetary obligation to the MESC if such business opportunities are not available or are not created. Notwithstanding the termination of a Mill Owner's ESA, if a Closing Mill Owner or any of its successors or assigns recommences operations on its Mill site that require steam, electricity, or green liquor, they must request that MESC reinstate the ESA on identical terms. MESC will have the right, but not obligation, to reinstate the ESA.

Source: Adapted from Mobile Energy Services Company L.L.C. Bond Prospectus, August 15, 1995, pp. 92–115.

MESC Inputs

The contracts obligated the pulp mill to supply MESC with byproducts, its chief input, at no cost. When needed, MESC would purchase coal and gas to supplement its fuel needs.

MESC Outputs

The contracts stipulated the quantities and prices for steam, power, and liquor produced by the energy complex. One contract set demand levels—the amount of capacity the energy complex would reserve for each mill. (See Exhibit 18-4 for current demand levels.) The energy complex charged the mills fees based on the demand levels and actual service use. Accordingly, the contracts broke the charges into two categories: *demand charges* and *processing charges*. Demand charges equaled a mill's demand level multiplied by a demand rate that was fixed for the term of the contracts, subject to inflation adjustments. Revenues from demand charges, payable regardless of actual service use, included a return on capital and covered fixed costs such as capital expenditures and debt service. Processing charges covered the energy complex's purchased fuel (coal and gas) and variable operating costs. The contracts permitted MESC to pass all of its fuel cost directly to the mills as long as it operated within specific efficiency levels outlined in the contracts. Processing charges for variable operating costs equaled actual mill service use multiplied by a rate that was fixed for the term of the contracts, subject to inflation adjustments. Because MESC sold its power to the mills rather than into the local power grid, it was considered an "inside the fence" generating plant. Consequently, neither the Federal Energy Regulatory Commission (FERC) nor the Alabama Public Service Commission regulated the rates it charged.

There were three other agreements involving all of the parties. One, the Common Services Agreement, required the mills and the energy complex to share the responsibility and cost for common areas and shared services, such as parking and security. A second agreement, the Mill Environmental Indemnity Agreement, obligated each party to protect against environmental violations that could affect the other parties. A third agreement, the Water Procurement and Effluent Services Agreement, outlined the rights, obligations, and allocation of water usage and procurement as well as the provision of water treatment utilities and services, including wastewater.

EXHIBIT 18-4

DEMAND LEVELS AS OF AUGUST 15, 1995

	Power Processing Services	Steam Processing Services	Liquor Processing Services
Pulp Mill	34%	42%	100%
Tissue Mill	42	23	N/A
Paper Mill	24	35	N/A
Total	100%	100%	100%

Source: Mobile Energy Services Company L.L.C. Bond Prospectus, August 15, 1995, p. 7.

EXHIBIT 18-5

MESC ACQUISITION SOURCES AND USES OF CASH (IN THOUSANDS)

Sources of Cash		Uses of Cash	
Senior Taxable Debt	$ 255,21	Purchase Price	$350,000
Tax Exempt Bonds	85,000	Financing Costs	47,088
Total Debt	340,210	Development and Start-up Costs	5,787
Cash Equity	75,562	Capital Expenditures	12,897
Southern Co. Guarantees	40,844	Reserves (Guarantees)	
Total Equity	116,406	Senior Taxable Debt	21,936
		Tax Exempt Debt	5,908
Total Sources of Funds	**$456,616**	Maintenance	13,000
Total Sources of Cash	**$415,772**	Total Reserves	40,844
		Total Uses of Funds	**$456,616**
		Total Uses of Cash	**$415,772**

Source: Adapted from Stone & Webster's "Independent Engineering Report Mobile, Alabama Energy and Black Liquor Recovery Complex," August 15, 1995, Attachment 3.

In addition, MESC had a 25-year maintenance agreement with Southern Electric whereby Southern Electric would operate and maintain the energy complex. MESC also had a long-term lease with Scott for the land under the energy complex. And finally, MESC had an agreement with the pulp mill to dispose of the energy complex's boiler ash.

Financing

MESC planned to refinance the acquisition bridge loan by issuing $255 million in mortgage bonds and $85 million in tax-exempt bonds (see Exhibit 18-5). The mortgage bonds had an 8.665% coupon and a 22-year maturity (due January 2017). The bonds would rank *pari passu* in right of payment with all future senior debt and senior to all future subordinated debt and were nonrecourse to the shareholders of the Southern Company, Mobile Energy Services Holding, and Southern Electric International.[8]

REPORTS BY INDEPENDENT EXPERTS

To support the bond offerings, MESC and its lenders hired two independent experts, Jaakko Pöyry Consulting Incorporated and Stone & Webster Engineering Corporation, to review the three mills and the energy complex, respectively.

Jaakko Pöyry[9]

Jaakko Pöyry (pronounced "ya-koh poor-ee") was part of the Jaakko Pöyry Group, a Finnish company founded in 1958 to provide engineering services to the Scandinavian

[8] Mobile Energy Services Company L.L.C., First Mortgage Bond Prospectus, August 15, 1996, p. 1.
[9] Conclusions taken from Mobile Facility Mill Risk Assessment, Jaakko Pöyry Consulting Inc., July 12, 1995 and Supplement dated July 20, 1995, pp. E/2, E/13, E/18, 3, 6, 12, 13, 15, 16, 19, 21, 24, 29, 58, and 59.

paper and pulp industry. The firm provided consulting services to forest product companies, financial institutions, and governments around the world. Hired to evaluate the long-term business viability of the mills, Jaakko Pöyry consultants visited each plant and conducted interviews with managers. The consultants also reviewed each facility's production history, analyzed the pulp agreement between Scott and Warren, and forecast the market demand for tissue and paper products (see Exhibit 18-6 for historical production levels). The final report dedicated 17, 24, and 8 pages to the tissue mill, paper mill, and pulp mill, respectively.

Tissue Mill

Jaakko Pöyry identified the Mobile mill as the "centerpiece" of Scott's North American network. The consultants reported that the production machines used current technology, and the efficiency levels were as high as any tissue mill in the world.[10] Furthermore, they concluded that the Mobile tissue mill appeared to be the low-cost producer among Scott's six tissue plants and held a cost advantage over standalone, nonintegrated tissue mills. The mill's pulp costs were approximately half those of nonintegrated mills. However, Jaakko Pöyry pointed out that the Mobile tissue mill was an average-cost producer when compared to integrated mills. The consultants attributed this loss in competitive position to the demand charges the pulp mill paid to MESC and passed through to the tissue mill. The tissue mill's scale, however, offset some of

---

EXHIBIT 18-6

HISTORICAL PRODUCTION LEVELS AT THE MOBILE FACILITY, 1984–1994

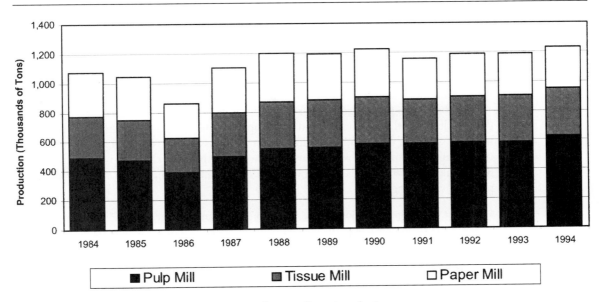

Note: A strike occurred in 1986; 1994 data represent a forecast of actual production.

Source: Adapted from Mobile Energy Services Company L.L.C. Bond Prospectus, August 15, 1995, p. 55.

---

[10] Mobile Facility Mill Risk Assessment, Jaakko Pöyry Consulting Inc., July 12, 1995 and Supplement dated July 20, 1995, p. 13.

the effect of having higher pulp costs. Jaakko Pöyry forecast that total tissue demand would grow annually about 2.2% through 2015.

Paper Mill

According to Jaako Pöyry, the mill's production efficiencies were industry standard but were trending downward and needed to be refurbished at some point in the future. Although the mill held a cost advantage over nonintegrated paper mills, it could be at a slight cost disadvantage vis-à-vis integrated paper mills under certain market scenarios. Part of the cost disadvantage was due to the pulp ESA, which required the paper mill to purchase 85% of its pulp from the Mobile pulp mill. Also, according to Jaakko Pöyry, management planned to relocate one of the mill's product lines to another Warren plant. As for the market, the firm forecast that U.S. paper product demand would grow about 3% annually through 2015.

In summarizing its analysis of the tissue and paper mills, Jaakko Pöyry stated:

> Permanent, substantial curtailment of tissue production at the Tissue Mill is not likely in our opinion. . . . The less central role of the Paper Mill in the S.D. Warren system and the less secure market position of Paper Mill's products make curtailments more possible over the long term. The Pulp Agreement reduces the likelihood of permanent curtailment in the Paper Mill.[11]

Pulp Mill

One of the largest pulp facilities in the industry, the Mobile mill produced nearly 60% of Scott's virgin pulp in North America.[12] To determine the mill's cost position, Jaakko Pöyry compared the mill's production operating costs, efficiencies, and scale against competing pulp mills. When analyzing the mill's operating costs, it excluded the demand charges paid for steam, power, and liquor under the assumption these costs were competitively priced and, therefore, similar to what other integrated mills paid.[13] Although Jaakko Pöyry did have market price data for steam and power, it did not have readily observable prices for the liquor processing services because an open and active market did not exist. Instead, liquor processing services tended to be negotiated in private transactions inside integrated facilities.

According to the consultants' report, the pulp mill was a low- to average-cost producer. Although the mill had adequate equipment and average efficiencies, it benefited from its scale. In addition, the mill's timber and labor costs were at or near the industry averages. Despite the recent emergence of cheaper recycled pulp for certain products, Jaakko Pöyry expected the pulp mill to remain a competitive supplier of virgin pulp over the long term:

> Absent unanticipated major environmental problems and subject to continuing stable supply of wood, shutdown or permanent curtailment of the Pulp Mill is in our opinion unlikely. We estimate the Pulp Mill to be a competitive supplier of virgin pulp and it should continue to be so in the future. . . . Even in the event of permanent curtailment in the Tissue or Paper Mill, it is likely that the Pulp Mill would pursue ways to sell pulp to the market due to the importance of high capacity utilization to the Pulp Mill's economic viability.[14]

[11] Ibid., pp. 71, 76, and 77.

[12] Mobile Energy Services Company L.L.C., First Mortgage Bond Prospectus, August 15, 1996, p. 9.

[13] Mobile Facility Mill Risk Assessment, Jaakko Pöyry Consulting Inc., July 12, 1995 and Supplement dated July 20, 1995, p. 57.

[14] Ibid., p. E/15.

One concern, however, was impending environmental regulations. The U.S. Environmental Protection Agency (EPA) had proposed new regulations on the wastewater and air pollutants produced by pulp and paper manufacturers. The regulations, known as the "Cluster Rules," would affect each of the Mobile mills to varying degrees. The mills were not contractually obligated to comply with the new regulations and could, therefore, shut down rather than incur the expense to comply with the new regulations. Jaakko Pöyry, in conjunction with management, estimated the pulp mill would need to spend $150 million to $200 million on modifications. The firm did not have enough information to estimate capital expenditures related to the Cluster Rules for the paper or tissue mill. The pulp and paper industry expected the EPA to present a revised version of the Cluster Rules by September 1995. Jaakko Pöyry concluded:

> We believe the pulp mill to be competitively positioned . . . in a way that would justify it undertaking these substantial capital expenditures and, therefore, based on our view concerning the likely form of the Cluster Rules, we believe that the Pulp Mill will undertake the appropriate capital expenditures.[15]

In making its final conclusion, Jaakko Pöyry reviewed the history of integrated facilities in North America. Only two out of approximately 40 facilities of the same size as the Mobile facility had closed in the previous 25 years, and only 3% of total pulp, paper, tissue, and board capacity had shut down permanently.[16] Furthermore, Jaakko Pöyry concluded that new greenfield projects were less feasible because of the costs associated with environmental regulations. Consequently, companies like Scott were more likely to invest in ongoing projects rather than build new ones.

Stone & Webster[17]

With nearly 90 years of experience in energy process engineering and consulting, Stone & Webster provided management services to utility companies and had worked on hundreds of energy projects worldwide. The firm performed due diligence on project finance transactions and evaluated power plants as part of the capital-raising process. MESC and its lenders hired Stone & Webster to evaluate the Mobile energy complex's efficiency, capacity, contracts, and budgets.

Stone & Webster reached two conclusions. First, the energy complex was capable of meeting the requirements of the ESA. The assets were industry standard, reliable, and, with regular maintenance, had a useful life of 25 or more years. Moreover, the energy complex's historical performance levels, including its annual downtime rate of 6%, were acceptable and good indicators of future performance. Second, Stone & Webster developed a financial model to evaluate the energy complex's projected revenues and costs. To build revenue projections, the firm utilized Jaakko Pöyry's estimates of mill demand in conjunction with the prices and quantities outlined in the ESA (see Exhibit 18-7). MESC provided the cost projections, and Stone & Webster verified them for reasonableness. The firm produced a baseline set of financial projections (see Exhibits 18-8a and 18-8b) and ran sensitivity analyses based on various "stress" cases (see Exhibit 18-9). From these analyses, Stone & Webster concluded:

---

[15] Ibid., p. E/13.

[16] Ibid., p. 68.

[17] Conclusions taken from Stone & Webster's Independent Engineering Report Mobile, Alabama Energy and Black Liquor Recovery Complex, August 15, 1995, pp. 21, 58, and 59.

EXHIBIT 18-7

**PROJECTED ENERGY COMPLEX REVENUES
BY MILL OVER LIFE OF THE BOND**

	Percent of Total Projected Revenue (Range)	
Pulp Mill	50.1%	39.3%
Tissue Mill	25.3	31.2
Paper Mill	24.6	29.5
	100.0%	100.0%

Source: Adapted from Stone & Webster Engineering Corporation,
"Independent Engineer's Report Mobile, Alabama Energy and Black
Liquor Recovery Complex," August 15, 1995, p. 49.

The [baseline] projection indicates the Energy Complex revenues . . . are adequate to pay all annual operating and maintenance expenses (including provisions for major maintenance), fuel costs, and other operating expenses and provide an average debt service coverage ratio of . . . 1.51× for the First Mortgage Bonds. . . . A number of sensitivity analyses have been performed to determine the susceptibility of the project economics to changes in steam, electricity, and liquor usage; net capacity factor; operating expenses; inflation; and interest rates. These analyses demonstrate that the debt service coverage ratios remain adequate.[18]

RATING AGENCY AND ANALYST PERSPECTIVES ON THE MORTGAGE BONDS

Credit-rating agencies and investment firms utilized the independent experts' studies as well as their own internal analyses to rate the MESC bond offer. Each of the three leading credit rating agencies—Moody's Investor Services, Fitch Investor Services, and Standard & Poor's—gave the bonds an investment grade rating, while Merrill Lynch & Company recommended the bonds for investment purposes.

Moody's assigned a Baa3 rating to the bonds, citing the energy complex's operational importance to the mills, low fuel costs, and use of proven technology. The analyst noted:

> Project agreements preserve a high degree of flexibility for the mill owners in terms of their contractual obligations, allowing them to shut down their mills or reduce demand charges payable to the energy complex based upon historic production levels. However, the risks of a mill shutdown or a significant curtailment of production capacity are mitigated by the long operating history of the mills. . . . [W]hile base coverages are somewhat low in relation to other project financing transactions, coverage levels remain adequate under a number of downside scenarios, including closure of the S.D. Warren paper mill. . . . The rating also reflects the involvement of Southern . . . which has committed to retain at least 50% ownership in MESC and will operate the energy complex.[19]

---

[18] Stone & Webster's Independent Engineering Report Mobile Alabama Energy and Black Liquor Recovery Complex, August 15, 1995, p. 60.

[19] "Moody's Assigns Baa3 Rating to First Mortgage Bonds of Mobile Energy Services Company, L.L.C.," Moody's Investors Services, August 14, 1995.

EXHIBIT 18-8A

MESC BASE CASE FINANCIAL PROJECTIONS, 1995–2019 (IN THOUSANDS)

Year	Revenue				Cash Expenses					Cash Operating Income
	Demand Charges	Processing Charges	Operations & Maintenance	Total	Fuel	Operations & Maintenance	Capital Expenditures	Other	Total	
1995	$56,284	$19,352	$ 7,792	$ 83,428	$ 8,211	$18,633	$ 5,611	$3,378	$35,833	$47,595
1996	56,610	20,029	8,065	84,704	8,496	19,285	5,807	3,489	37,077	47,627
1997	56,947	20,730	8,347	86,024	8,796	19,960	6,010	3,605	38,371	47,653
1998	57,298	21,456	8,839	87,593	9,104	20,659	6,221	3,724	39,708	47,885
1999	57,657	22,207	8,942	88,806	9,422	21,380	6,438	3,849	41,089	47,717
2000	58,030	22,984	9,254	90,268	9,752	22,129	6,664	3,977	42,522	47,746
2001	58,417	23,789	9,578	91,784	10,093	22,905	6,897	4,109	44,004	47,780
2002	58,817	24,621	9,914	93,352	10,446	23,707	7,138	4,196	45,487	47,865
2003	59,231	25,483	10,261	94,975	10,812	24,535	7,388	4,388	47,123	47,852
2004	59,680	26,375	10,820	96,875	11,191	25,394	7,647	4,534	48,766	48,109
2005	60,104	27,298	10,991	98,393	11,582	26,282	7,914	4,706	50,484	47,909
2006	60,563	28,253	11,376	100,192	11,988	27,203	8,192	4,841	52,224	47,968
2007	61,038	29,242	11,774	102,054	12,407	28,155	8,478	5,003	54,043	48,011
2008	61,530	30,265	12,186	103,981	12,841	29,140	8,775	5,172	55,928	48,053
2009	62,039	31,325	12,613	105,977	13,291	30,160	9,082	5,344	57,877	48,100
2010	62,566	32,242	13,054	107,862	13,758	31,216	9,400	5,524	59,898	47,964
2011	63,112	33,556	13,511	110,179	14,237	32,307	9,729	5,708	61,981	48,198
2012	63,676	34,731	13,984	112,391	14,736	33,439	10,069	5,900	64,144	48,247
2013	64,261	35,945	14,474	114,680	15,252	34,610	10,422	6,198	66,482	48,198
2014	65,066	37,004	14,980	117,050	15,785	35,821	10,787	6,303	68,696	48,354
2015	65,983	38,015	15,504	119,502	16,338	37,075	11,164	6,515	71,092	48,410
2016	66,933	39,060	16,047	122,040	16,910	38,372	11,555	6,734	73,571	48,469
2017	67,916	40,143	16,609	124,668	17,502	39,716	11,959	6,961	76,138	48,530
2018	68,933	41,263	17,190	127,386	18,114	41,106	12,378	7,194	78,792	48,594
2019	69,986	42,423	17,792	130,201	18,748	42,545	12,811	7,436	81,540	48,661

Source: Adapted from Stone & Webster Engineering Corporation, "Independent Engineer's Report Mobile, Alabama Energy and Black Liquor Recovery," Attachment 3.

EXHIBIT 18-8B

MOBILE ENERGY SERVICES BASE CASE FINANCIAL PROJECTIONS, 1995–2019 (IN THOUSANDS)

Year	Cash Operating Income	First Mortgage Bond		Tax Exempt Bond		Fees	Total Debt Service	Cash Available After Debt Service
		Interest	Principal	Interest	Principal			
1995	$47,595	$7,801	$2,380	$2,084	$ 0	$128	$12,393	$35,202
1996	47,627	21,755	7,030	5,908	0	386	35,079	12,548
1997	47,653	21,132	7,670	5,908	0	389	35,099	12,554
1998	47,885	20,458	8,100	5,908	0	392	34,858	13,027
1999	47,717	19,476	8,580	5,908	0	395	34,629	13,088
2000	47,746	18,992	9,100	5,908	0	399	34,399	13,347
2001	47,780	18,193	9,570	5,908	0	402	34,073	13,707
2002	47,865	17,358	9,820	5,908	0	406	33,492	14,373
2003	47,852	16,498	10,240	5,908	0	409	33,055	14,797
2004	48,109	15,606	10,480	5,908	0	413	32,407	15,702
2005	47,909	14,667	10,990	5,908	0	417	31,982	15,927
2006	47,968	13,722	11,560	5,908	0	421	31,611	16,357
2007	48,011	12,707	12,180	5,908	0	426	31,221	16,790
2008	48,053	11,635	12,880	5,908	0	430	30,853	17,200
2009	48,100	10,504	13,540	5,908	0	435	30,387	17,713
2010	47,964	9,303	14,490	5,908	0	439	30,140	17,824
2011	48,198	8,028	15,420	5,908	0	444	29,800	18,398
2012	48,247	6,689	16,440	5,908	0	449	29,486	18,761
2013	48,198	5,221	17,560	5,908	0	454	29,143	19,055
2014	48,354	3,689	18,960	5,908	0	460	29,017	19,337
2015	48,410	1,996	20,320	5,908	0	465	28,689	19,721
2016	48,469	507	7,800	5,908	13,700	471	28,386	20,083
2017	48,530	0	0	4,955	22,400	477	27,832	20,698
2018	48,594	0	0	3,399	23,750	483	27,632	20,962
2019	48,661	0	0	1,748	25,150	490	27,388	21,273

Source: Adapted from Stone & Webster Engineering Corporation, "Independent Engineer's Report Mobile, Alabama Energy and Black Liquor Recovery," Attachment 3.

EXHIBIT 18-9

MOBILE ENERGY SERVICES COMPANY L.L.C., PRO FORMA SENSITIVITY ANALYSIS (IN THOUSANDS)

	Base Case	Paper Mill Shutdown[a]	Coal Price 6% Greater Than Base Case	Operating & Maintenance Expense 10% Greater Than Base Case	Inflation Rate of 2.0% vs. Base Case of 3.5%	Processing Service Usage 11% Less Than Base Case[b]
Total Revenue						
1995	$83,428	$83,428	$83,428	$83,428	$82,900	$78,196
2000	90,268	80,851	90,269	90,269	86,638	84,064
2005	98,393	75,799	98,393	96,393	90,766	86,770
Cash Operating Income						
1995	$47,595	$47,597	$47,280	$45,173	$47,582	$45,568
2000	47,746	47,085	47,369	44,867	47,645	45,337
2005	47,909	36,740	47,479	44,508	47,714	40,824
Debt Service Coverage Ratio						
Minimum	1.36X	1.11X	1.35X	1.28X	1.36X	1.23X
Weighted Avg. (22 yrs)	1.51X	1.24X	1.49X	1.39X	1.50X	1.31X

[a] Paper mill shuts down indefinitely in 2000; demand charges reset for January 2002.

[b] Power and steam processing usage down 11% effective for January 2002.

Source: Adapted from Stone & Webster Engineering Corporation, "Independent Engineers Report Mobile, Alabama Energy and Black Liquor Recovery Complex," Attachments 3 and 4.

Fitch, too, gave the bonds an investment grade rating (BBB−), citing the positive history of large-scale integrated projects and the absence of completion risk. Besides the risks associated with mill closure or reductions in processing service demand levels, Fitch pointed to several other risks: the fact a mill owner could sell a mill without consent from the other mill owners or MESC, the potential costs of environmental regulation, and Warren's high leverage ratio. The Fitch analysts wrote:

> The tissue mill and pulp mill, representing 76% of MESC's 1995 revenue, are highly competitive and strategically situated facilities. . . . Integrated facilities like [these mills] enjoy a significant cost advantage versus stand-alone mills. . . . [T]he services provided by MESC are essential to the mills' operation and difficult for the mills to obtain in comparable amounts and quality at lower aggregate cost from other sources. . . . MESC's financial structure and security provisions provide adequate stability for the project.[20]

Like the other rating agencies, Standard & Poor's gave the bond an investment-grade rating (BBB−). The firm asked Stone & Webster to run additional sensitivity analyses on the energy complex, from which the rating agency concluded MESC would

[20] "Mobile Energy Services Co., L.L.C., Global Power Electric Special Report," Fitch Investor's Services, September 18, 1995.

be able to adequately service its debt at the BBB− level under all scenarios (see Exhibit 18-9).[21] Among the project's strengths, S&P listed Southern's involvement. As project sponsor, Southern had expertise in running energy plants, and the company had invested $117 million in the project ($76 million in cash and $41 million in guarantees) including a debt service reserve fund that covered 12 months of interest (see Exhibit 18-5). According to the Standard & Poor's analyst:

> The project documents, for the most part, are structured tightly and clearly outline the major issues that could arise, including an arbitration process. . . . The mills currently pay MESC an all-in rate of 3.3 cents per kWh, which is equivalent to the lowest rate available in the state. . . . The current steam processing charges to the mills is $4.48 per million btu, and according to the independent engineers, should a mill owner want to provide their own steam with a boiler, the cost would be approximately $5.76 per million btu.[22]

Investment firms also evaluated the bond offering as a possible investment. Among them, Merrill Lynch & Company compared the MESC bond with the bond offerings of other cogeneration energy plants. (Exhibit 18-10 provides bond prices for similar bonds, and Exhibits 18-11a and 18-11b provide current information on the capital markets as of August 15, 1995.) When comparing the MESC bonds with other cogeneration bonds, the Merrill Lynch analyst wrote:

> [T]he Mobile Energy Bonds give good value versus [other cogeneration bonds]. Some spread off the other names is justified because, unlike the other projects, the Mobile Energy contracts can be terminated by the buyers if they choose to close the mills taking the power and services. We think the risk of any such closure is very low over the next 10 years, and fairly low to the Bonds' maturity in 2017. . . . As an inside the fence project with strong

EXHIBIT 18-10

MESC BOND PRICING VS. OTHER COGENERATION FACILITIES

Cogeneration Facility	Issue Date	Coupon	Proceeds (millions)	Maturity	Ratings		Callable	Spread over Comparable Treasury
					S&P	Moody's		
Mobile Energy Services Co. L.L.C.	8/15/95	8.655%	$255.2	1/1/17	BBB−	Baa3	No	1.715%
Midland Cogeneration Venture	11/1/91	10.330	310.6	7/23/02	BB+	Ba1	No	2.810
Sithe/Independence Funding	1/19/93	8.500	150.6	12/30/07	BBB−	Baa3	No	1.310
Selkirk Cogeneration	5/6/94	8.650	165.0	5/6/07	BBB−	Baa3	No	1.140
Indiantown Cogeneration	11/9/94	9.260	505.0	11/9/10	BBB−	Baa3	No	1.260

Source: Adapted from Thompson Financial Securities Data Corporation and casewriter estimates.

[21] Standard & Poor's Global Project Finance, July 1996, p. 226.
[22] Ibid., pp. 222 and 225.

EXHIBIT 18-11A

TREASURY BOND SPREADS VS. 3-MONTH TREASURY BILL AS OF AUGUST 15, 1995

Treasury Security	Yield	Spread vs. 3-Month Treasury Bill
3-Month Treasury Bill	5.57%	—
1-Year Note	5.75	0.18%
5-Year Note	6.24	0.67
10-Year Bond	6.49	0.92
30-Year Bond	6.86	1.29
Prime Rate	8.75%	3.18%

Source: Adapted from Datastream.

EXHIBIT 18-11B

CORPORATE BOND SPREADS VS. 10-YEAR TREASURY BOND AS OF AUGUST 15, 1995

Corporate Credit Rating	Yield	Spread vs. 10-Year Treasury Bond
AAA	6.70%	0.21%
AA	6.76	0.27
A	6.93	0.44
BBB	7.05	0.56
BB	8.52	2.03
B	10.04	3.55

Source: Adapted from Datastream.

offtake contracts, Mobile Energy is insulated from any pressures of competition. . . . As long as the mills are functioning, the complex should be viable and profitable.[23]

CONCLUSION

MESC filed a Form S-1 Registration Statement with the U.S. Securities and Exchange Commission (SEC) for the mortgage bond offering in May 1995. Two months later, on July 17, Scott announced its intent to merge with Kimberly-Clark Corporation, a maker of tissue and paper products for consumers and commercial users. The deal, pending SEC and shareholder approval, was expected to close by the end of 1995. Scott also

[23] "Mobile Energy Power Inside the Fence in Alabama," Merrill Lynch Company, April 28, 1998, pp. 1 and 4.

announced that it was suspending its efforts to sell its pulp and timberland operations due to the merger. Three days after the merger announcement, Jaakko Pöyry stated that the operating benefits of the Mobile facility were likely to be preserved under the merged company.[24] Later, Fitch analysts wrote that they determined the pulp and paper mill would be a strategic resource for the merged company.[25] And the Moody's analyst commented:

> The credit quality of the Kimberly/Scott combination is high and therefore important to Moody's rating assignment. If a new owner of the tissue or pulp mills were to be of materially lower credit quality, or in Moody's judgment was less capable or experienced in mill operation, this could have a significant negative implication for the credit rating of MESC.[26]

Despite the merger, MESC planned to proceed with the bond offering. On August 15, 1995, MESC published the mortgage bond prospectus, including reports from the independent experts. With this information, investors had to decide whether to purchase the mortgage bonds.

[24] Mobile Facility Mill Risk Assessment, Jaakko Pöyry Consulting Inc., July 12, 1995 and Supplement dated July 20, 1995, p. S/2.

[25] "Mobile Energy Services Co., L.L.C., Global Power Electric Special Report," Fitch Investor's Services, September 18, 1995.

[26] "Moody's Assigns Baa3 Rating to First Mortgage Bonds of Mobile Energy Services Company, L.L.C.," Moody's Investors Services, August 14, 1995.

19

Financing the Mozal Project

Mozal represents a leap of faith in the economy of a poor African country that is still recovering from a long civil war and years of central planning.[1]

Mozal is a wonderful example of the African renaissance being alive. . . . We know they (the sponsors) are going to make money.[2]

Takuro Kimura and Akbar Husain of the International Finance Corporation's (IFC) Sub-Saharan Africa Department were adding the finishing touches to a report for the IFC's board of directors. In the report, they were recommending a $120 million investment in the Mozal project, a $1.4 billion aluminum smelter in Mozambique. While board approval at the June 1997 meeting was not a binding commitment to lend, it would be their last signoff on the deal and a signal of IFC's commitment to the project. More importantly, their approval would allow the project team to proceed with structuring the deal, even though it could take up to 18 months to finalize all the details.

What made this recommendation difficult was the fact that it would be the IFC's largest investment ever and by far its largest investment in Africa. At $1.4 billion, it would also be large relative to Mozambique's gross domestic product (GDP) of $1.7 billion. Perhaps more important than its size, however, was its location. Mozambique was one of the poorest countries in the world and had only recently emerged from a 17-year civil war that had destroyed most of the country's infrastructure. Despite the size and location, Kimura and Husain were recommending approval based on the project's significant economic and developmental benefits. The project was, after all, consistent with the IFC's mission of promoting private sector investment in developing countries as a way to reduce poverty and improve people's lives.

Research Associate Fuaad A. Qureshi prepared this case under the supervision of Professor Benjamin C. Esty. HBS cases are developed solely as the basis for class discussion. Cases are not intended to serve as endorsements, sources of primary data, or illustrations of effective or ineffective management.

[1] N. Shaxson, "Mozal: $1.34bn Put into the Melting Pot," *The Financial Times*, June 29, 1998, p. 3.

[2] Cheryl Carolus, South African High Commission, as quoted in "Southern Africa Deal Lifts Project Hopes," *Corporate Finance*, June 1998, p. 8.

THE INVESTMENT OPPORTUNITY

The Mozal project was a joint venture between Alusaf and the Industrial Development Corporation (IDC) of South Africa. Alusaf was the aluminum subsidiary of the Gencor Group, a South African natural resource company. (Exhibits 19-1a and 19-1b provide financial data for both Gencor and Alusaf.) Gencor became the world's fourth largest aluminum producer after acquiring Billiton from Royal Dutch Shell in 1994 and finishing the $1.8 billion Hillside Smelter in Richards Bay, South Africa, in 1996. Hillside was, at the time, the world's largest greenfield aluminum smelter. As of June 1997, Gencor had two divisions, one for precious metals (gold and platinum) and the other for base metals (aluminum, nickel, steel, etc.), and was in the process of spinning off the base metals division into a publicly traded company under the Billiton name. Paul Snyman and Louis Irvine, Alusaf's Financial director and treasurer, respectively, were leading the Mozal negotiations.

The project's other sponsor was IDC, a $3.6 billion government-owned development bank located in South Africa with a longstanding business relationship with Alusaf. IDC's mission was to contribute to sustainable growth in South Africa by promoting entrepreneurship and financing private sector enterprises. In fact, IDC was instrumental in financing the Hillside smelter. It regularly took both debt and equity positions in new ventures, though it did not seek control or day-to-day management involvement. As of 1996, IDC's five-year plan called for $5 billion of industrial investment, including a number of investments outside of South Africa. Jaco Kriek, IDC's head of Project and Structured Finance and its lead negotiator on the Mozal deal, described IDC's involvement this way, "As part of our mandate, we actively seek investment opportunities in Southern Africa as a way to ensure economic stability in the region."

According to the feasibility study, Alusaf and IDC would each own 25% of Mozal; ownership of the remaining 50% had yet to be determined. While it was possible that one or both of the original sponsors would increase its investment, they were more interested in finding an industry participant to join the deal and share the output. Mitsubishi Corporation, the $78 billion Japanese industrial conglomerate with a large

---

EXHIBIT 19-1A

GENCOR AND ALUSAF INCOME STATEMENTS ON JUNE 30, 1996 ($US MILLIONS)

	Gencor Group	Alusaf Group
Turnover	$3,342.3	$657.3
Subsidiary turnover	(1,182.1)	0.0
Cost of sales	(1,653.8)	(551.3)
Other operating cost	(53.0)	0.0
Operating Income	453.3	106.0
Investment income	217.6	5.8
Net finance cost	(26.5)	(47.1)
Other costs/income	41.9	0.0
Profit before taxation	686.3	64.7
Taxation	(121.4)	(23.0)
Profit after taxation	564.9	41.7

EXHIBIT 19-1B

GENCOR AND ALUSAF BALANCE SHEETS ON
JUNE 30, 1996 ($U.S. MILLIONS)

	Gencor Group	Alusaf Group
Capital Employed		
Shareholders' interest	$2,752.6	$ 872.9
Outside interests	610.3	0.0
Long-term loans	679.5	563.7
Long-term provisions	293.1	0.0
Deferred taxation	130.5	187.0
Total capital	**4,466.0**	**1,623.6**
Employment of Capital		
Fixed assets	1,820.2	1,455.1
Investments	1,834.8	52.6
Other non-current assets	300.1	0.0
Current assets		
Trading stock	433.2	184.1
Amounts receivable	578.8	145.1
Other	0.0	63.7
Cash resources	852.4	0.0
Total current assets	1,864.4	392.9
Total assets	5,819.5	1,900.7
Current liabilities		
Loans and payables	1,287.6	262.6
Dividends payable	65.9	14.4
Total current liabilities	1,353.5	277.1
Total employment	**4,466.0**	**1,623.6**

Note: Assumes 3.996 South African Rand equal $1.00 U.S.

Source: Company Annual Reports.

metals group, was the leading candidate at the time. Seiei Ono, a senior manager in the Metals Department, had been negotiating a possible deal with IDC and Alusaf.

Aluminum Production

Because aluminum does not occur naturally in its pure form, it must be processed from compounds containing aluminum. The primary raw material for producing aluminum is bauxite, which comes mainly from mines in Australia, Guinea, Brazil, and Jamaica. Once mined, bauxite is refined into an intermediate product called alumina and then transformed into aluminum in a smelter. This energy-intensive process yielded one ton of aluminum for every two tons of alumina.

Aluminum was used primarily in the transportation, construction, packaging, machinery, and electrical industries. Industry demand stood at 20 million tons per year and was expected to grow at 2% to 3% per year. In terms of supply, even though secondary production in the form of recycling and scrap was growing, analysts projected a need for five million tons of new primary capacity over the next ten years.

The interaction of supply and demand was the major determinant of aluminum prices. Investment funds, however, also affected market prices and volatility through speculation, particularly during 1995. Exhibit 19-2 shows aluminum prices from the London Metal Exchange (LME) over the past ten years. During this time, prices fluctuated between a low of $1,040 per ton in November 1993 and a high of $3,645 per ton in June 1988.

The Mozal Project

The Mozal project began as the confluence of interests among three entities: Eskom, Alusaf, and the Mozambican government. Eskom, the South African power utility that provided 95% of the country's and 50% of the continent's power, wanted to expand its operations outside of South Africa and utilize some of its excess capacity. In Mozambique, it saw an opportunity to rebuild some of the country's damaged electricity infrastructure and to develop inexpensive hydroelectric-generating capacity on the Zambezi River. Alusaf, too, saw an opportunity in Mozambique. It wanted to build another aluminum smelter making use of the potential availability of hydroelectric power in Mozambique. Such a plant would also benefit from access to Maputo's harbor and proximity to the Hillside smelter in Richards Bay. Given their shared interests, they met with officials from the Mozambican government to see if there were sufficient interest in supporting the construction of a smelter in Mozambique. From these discussions, the parties developed the Mozal project that provided Mozambique with new electri-

EXHIBIT 19-2

LONDON METAL EXCHANGE PRICES FOR PRIMARY ALUMINUM (1987–1997) (CASH SETTLEMENT PRICE $USD PER TON)

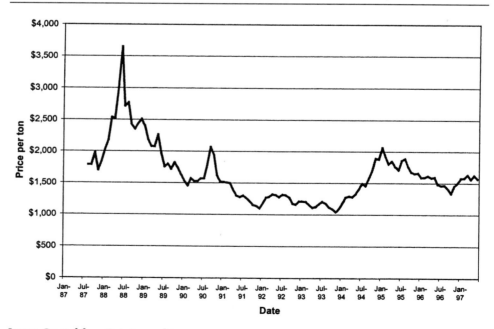

Source: Created from Datastream data.

EXHIBIT 19-3

ARTIST'S RENDITION OF THE MOZAL ALUMINUM SMELTER

Source: Company documents.

cal and industrial infrastructure, Eskom with an entrée into Mozambique and a customer for its excess power, and Alusaf with a new smelter and access to competitively-priced power.

Exhibit 19-3 provides an artist's rendition of the smelter as it would appear along the Maputo Corridor, a major trading route between Johannesburg, South Africa, and the Mozambican capital of Maputo. The team estimated it would take 34 months to complete the project and another six months to reach full capacity. Although Mozal, a single-potline smelter with annual capacity of 250,000 tons, was half the size of the Hillside smelter, a double-potline smelter with annual capacity of 500,000 tons, it would be constructed with all of the necessary infrastructure to double capacity at some point in the future. For example, the sponsors would have to build a dedicated berth in Maputo harbor to handle the import of raw materials and the export of aluminum, but this berth could handle the plant expansion without additional expense. Like Hillside, Mozal would use proven, state-of-the-art smelting technology from Pechiney of France. And since construction was winding down at the Hillside project, they could use essentially the same project construction team and the same contractors under similar lump-sum, turnkey contracts. Exhibit 19-4 shows the project's sources and uses of cash. Based on these projections, Mozal would have an overall capital cost of $4,750 per ton compared to an average capital cost of $4,850 per ton for other recently constructed smelters.

EXHIBIT 19-4

SOURCES AND USES OF CASH ($ MILLIONS)

Uses of Cash			Sources of Cash			
Total direct costs		$ 772	Equity			
			Gencor/Alusaf	$125		
Total indirect costs		226	IDC	125		
			Others	250		
Capital costs			Total		500	37%
Contingency	75					
Price escalation	90		Quasi-equity (subordinated debt)			
Total		165	Int'l Finance Corp. (IFC)	65		
			Other development			
Start-up costs			financial institutions	85		
Initial working capital	49		Total		150	11
Pre-completion interest	153					
Total		202	Cash generation	35	35	2
Total Uses		**1,365**	Export credit			
			IDC—arranged	400		
			Coface insured	140		
			Loans			
			Int'l Finance Corp. (IFC)	55		
			Other development			
			financial institutions	85		
			Total Senior Debt		680	50
			Total Sources		**1,365**	**100**

Source: Company documents.

In terms of operations, the major inputs needed to produce aluminum were alumina, electricity, labor, and other raw materials. Alumina accounted for approximately one-third of production costs and would be imported from Billiton's Australian operations under a 25-year supply agreement. The sponsors agreed to set the price for alumina as a function of the LME aluminum prices, thereby creating a natural hedge for the project. When output prices were high, input prices would be high, and vice versa.

Eskom and Electricidade de Moçambique (EdM), the Mozambican electricity company, would supply electricity under a 25-year contract. They planned to build two 400 kilovolts (kV) transmission lines from South Africa to Maputo to supply the plant with 450 megawatts (MW) of power. Like alumina, the electricity price would be, at least in later years, a function of LME aluminum prices. Unlike alumina prices, which were set in competitive markets, albeit under long-term contracts, electricity prices were negotiated prices. The variation in negotiated prices combined with the fact electricity accounted for 25% of total production costs, meant that electricity was the most important determinant of a plant's competitive position.

Labor and other raw materials were less important determinants of a plant's competitive position. Initially, the skilled labor and management expertise would come from South Africa. Billiton/Alusaf, in particular, would provide plant management for which it would receive a management fee. The majority of the unskilled labor, both during construction and for operations, would come from Mozambique. The low cost of labor in Mozambique meant the plant's labor costs would be one-fifth that of a typical

Western-world smelter. Other raw materials, such as coke, petroleum, and liquid pitch, would be imported from the same suppliers that were currently supplying the Hillside smelter under similar long-term supply arrangements.

Finally, there were taxes and other fees. Because the plant was targeted for an Industrial Free Zone, it would be exempt from customs duties and income taxes, though it would be subject to a 1% sales tax. The sponsors planned to purchase all of the output subject to long-term purchase agreements at market prices. Currency exposure was not a problem since the major inputs and all of the output would be denominated in U.S. dollars. A trustee, such as Chase Manhattan Corporation, would be responsible for collecting sale proceeds, paying debtholders, remitting operating expenses, and distributing remaining cash flows to the sponsors in the form of dividends.

Based on this construction and operating plan, Mozal would be a low-cost producer—its production costs would be in the lowest 5% of industry capacity (see Exhibit 19-5). The average production cost *excluding* depreciation and financing charges for the world's 164 aluminum smelters was $1,510 per ton. In comparison, Mozal's projected breakeven price *including* depreciation and financing charges was $1,493 per ton in the fourth year (in constant 1997 dollars), declining to $1,070 in the eleventh year. These breakeven prices were relatively protected from aluminum price volatility because two-thirds of production costs were variable, of which almost 75% varied with LME prices.

Exhibit 19-6 shows Mozal's projected cash flows in constant 1997 dollars. The projections assumed an aluminum price of $1,750 per ton compared to a current market

---

EXHIBIT 19-5

THE WORLD COST CURVE OF ALUMINUM SMELTERS (JUNE 1997)

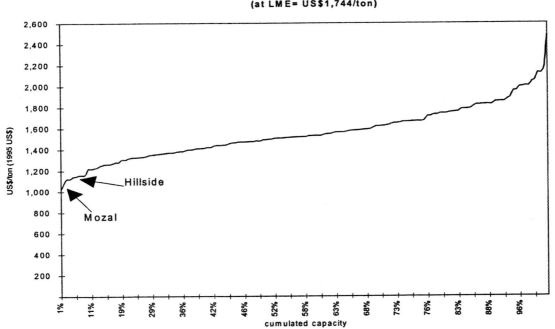

Graph 8: The World Cost Curve of Aluminum Smelters (1997)
(at LME= US$1,744/ton)

Sources: CRU International, IFC Analysis.

EXHIBIT 19-6

SUMMARY OF FINANCIAL PROJECTIONS IN CONSTANT 1997 DOLLARS ($ MILLIONS)

	1997	1998	1999	2000	2001	2002	2003	2004	2005	2006	2007	2008	2009	2010	2011	2012
Total assets	$163	$778	$1,252	$1,328	$1,272	$1,202	$1,132	$1,062	$991	$921	$851	$750	$687	$607	$570	$530
Short-term assets/Cash				96	126	142	157	172	188	203	219	204	226	226	226	226
Current senior debt			29	57	70	70	70	70	70	70	70	33	53	13	0	0
Net senior debt	63	366	595	592	522	451	381	311	240	170	100	67	13	0	0	0
Subordinated debt (quasi-equity)		85	144	150	150	150	150	150	150	150	150	120	90	60	30	0
Retained earnings				13	13	13	13	13	13	13	13	13	13	13	13	13
Share capital	100	327	484	500	500	500	500	500	500	500	500	500	500	500	500	500
Total capital	163	778	1,252	1,312	1,255	1,184	1,114	1,044	973	903	833	733	669	586	543	513
Senior debt/Total capital	39%	47%	50%	49%	47%	44%	40%	36%	32%	27%	20%	14%	10%	2%	0%	0%
Current ratio				1.3	1.4	1.6	1.8	2.0	2.1	2.3	2.5	4.0	3.2	7.1	12.8	16.1
DSCR (senior debt)[a]				5.2	1.7	1.6	1.7	1.8	1.9	2.0	2.0	2.1	4.3	3.0	12.1	na
DSCR (total debt)[a]				4.6	1.6	1.5	1.6	1.6	1.7	1.8	1.7	1.4	2.2	1.8	3.4	5.2
Sales				394	429	429	429	429	429	429	429	429	429	429	429	429
Cash flow before interest and principal repayment				170	189	190	190	186	187	187	171	170	171	170	170	170
Interest on senior debt				12	52	47	41	35	29	23	17	11	7	4	1	0
Senior debt principal repayment				29	57	70	70	70	70	70	70	70	33	53	13	0
Equity investment[b]	100	312	216	22												
Dividends and subordinated debt interest				63	51	57	63	66	72	79	68	73	79	106	125	140
Subordinated debt principal repayment												30	30	30	30	30

[a] DSCR = debt service coverage ratio = cash flow/(principal + interest).

[b] The equity investment includes both equity and subordinated debt (quasi-equity) investments.

Source: Company documents, IFC analysis, and casewriter estimates.

price of $1,560 in June 1997. Over the past 30 years, there were only two years—1992 and 1993—when the average real price of aluminum price fell below $1,500 in 1997 dollars. Louis Irvine commented:

> Obviously, we would like to see aluminum prices higher, but the project is able to sustain a low LME aluminum price. Hillside was built at a time of low aluminum prices, which rose after the project came to fruition.[3]

Mozambique: A Brief History

The Portuguese ruled Mozambique as a colony from the sixteenth century until the Marxist Frente de Libertação de Moçambique (Frelimo) declared independence in 1975. Shortly thereafter, a civil war broke out between Frelimo and a rural-based rebel group known as the Resistencia de Moçambique (Renamo). A U.S. official described this war as "one of the most brutal holocausts against ordinary human beings since World War II. Between 1975 and 1992, the war claimed the lives of over 700,000 people . . . most of these were victims of the Renamo."[4] Besides the human toll, the war destroyed most of the country's infrastructure.

The two sides signed a peace accord in 1992 that ushered in a period of transition from war to peace, from socialism to capitalism, and from one-party rule to democracy. In an effort to hasten the transition to a market economy, the Mozambican government initiated a series of economic reforms. They privatized more than 900 state-owned enterprises, including the Commercial Bank of Mozambique, and removed price controls from goods and services. The country held its first presidential elections in 1994. Frelimo won, but Renamo made a surprisingly strong showing.

Exhibit 19-7 provides macroeconomic data for Mozambique from 1980 through 1996 and clearly shows the devastating effect the war had on the country: real gross domestic product sank and did not recover until the early 1990s. Throughout the period, Mozambique ran enormous current account and government deficits causing it to sink deeper and deeper into debt. War, crime, corruption, and an inefficient Marxist bureaucracy hindered private sector investment and economic development.[5] According to a study done by the World Bank, starting a new enterprise entailed 12 procedures, 151 steps, and 70 government bodies. If done sequentially, this process could take up to five years.[6] Conditions were, however, improving, particularly since the end of the war: GDP and foreign direct investment were increasing while inflation was falling. One reflection of these changes was the improvement in the country's *Institutional Investor* and International Country Risk Guide (ICRG) risk ratings from 7.6 to 14.0.

Despite this improvement, Mozambique remained by almost any measure a very poor, underdeveloped country. Exhibit 19-8 compares Mozambique against to Sub-Saharan countries along several dimensions. Relative to other countries, Mozambique had a lower per capita income, higher indebtedness, and higher country risk. According to the World Economic Forum, out of 20 African countries surveyed, Mozambique ranked last in terms of road infrastructure, completion of secondary education, and

---

[3] Andi Spicer, 1999, "Mozal Brings Mozambique into World View," *Project Finance International Yearbook*, p. 144.

[4] Imani Countess, "Urge a Prompt, Peaceful Mozambique Vote," *Christian Science Monitor*, June 23, 1994, p. 19.

[5] Economist Intelligence Unit, Mozambique Country Profile, 1997–1998, p. 15.

[6] Ibid., 2nd Quarter, 1997, p. 11.

EXHIBIT 19-7

MOZAMBICAN MACROECONOMIC DATA, 1980–1996

Year	Real GDP (1987 $) ($ mil.)	Real GNP per Capita (dollars)	CPI Inflation (percent)	National Exports ($ mil.)	Current Account Balance (as % of GDP)	Net Foreign Direct Investment ($ mil.)	Total External Debt (as % of GDP)	Government Budget Balance (% GDP)	Human Development Index (HDI)[a]	Institutional Investor Country Risk Rating[b]	ICRG Risk Ratings[c]			
											Political	Financial	Economic	Composite
1980	$1,564	NA	NA	$399	−20.9%	$0	0.0%	−11.4%	NA	NA	NA	NA	NA	NA
1981	1,746	NA	NA	460	−17.8	0	0.0	NA	NA	NA	NA	NA	NA	NA
1982	1,686	$189	NA	400	−20.2	0	0.0	NA	NA	NA	NA	NA	NA	NA
1983	1,471	160	NA	298	−18.2	0	3.6	NA	NA	NA	NA	NA	NA	NA
1984	1,215	120	NA	214	−15.9	0	61.6	NA	NA	NA	NA	NA	NA	NA
1985	1,207	140	47.8%	184	−11.7	0	104.4	−18.4	NA	NA	42.0	23.0	6.0	35.5
1986	1,179	170	12.2	192	−13.6	2	115.0	−24.4	NA	NA	40.0	22.0	6.0	34.0
1987	1,353	140	175.8	176	−51.2	6	303.4	−22.9	NA	NA	43.0	25.0	4.5	36.3
1988	1,464	110	55.0	188	−61.1	5	344.8	−27.0	NA	NA	50.0	26.0	7.0	41.5
1989	1,559	90	42.1	200	−63.8	3	327.4	−24.8	NA	7.6	49.0	26.0	8.0	41.5
1990	1,574	90	49.2	229	−59.9	9	323.3	−29.2	0.239	7.3	46.0	26.0	13.5	42.8
1991	1,651	90	33.3	309	−51.1	23	327.4	−24.9	0.155	7.0	45.0	26.0	14.5	42.8
1992	1,638	80	45.1	304	−59.4	25	413.7	−26.3	0.246	7.0	38.0	24.0	15.5	38.8
1993	1,946	90	42.3	312	−58.5	32	369.4	−22.2	0.261	7.5	41.0	24.0	19.5	42.3
1994	2,033	90	63.1	355	−60.4	35	394.3	−29.7	0.281	11.9	52.0	24.0	17.5	46.8
1995	2,061	80	54.4	407	−46.3	45	395.4	−20.8	0.281	12.8	58.0	24.0	13.0	47.5
1996	2,193	90	44.6	479	−38.9	73	332.1	−17.0	NA	14.0	54.0	24.0	19.5	48.8
6/97											56.0	24.0	20.0	50.0

[a] The HDI is an index used by the United Nations Development Program (UNDP) to measure the overall achievements in a country in three basic dimensions of human development—longevity, knowledge, and a decent standard of living. The score ranges from 0 (low) to 1.00 (high).

[b] The Institutional Investor rating is based on a survey of 75–100 international bankers who were asked to grade each country on a scale of 1 (very high chance of default) to 100 (least chance of default).

[c] The International Country Risk Guide (ICRG) provides a rating composed of 22 variables in three subcategories or risk: political (100 points), financial (50 points), and economic (50 points). ICRG provides ratings for 140 countries on a monthly basis where higher numbers indicate lower risk.

The political risk rating measure a country's political stability.

The financial risk rating measures a country's ability to finance its official, commercial, and trade debt obligations.

The economic risk rating measures the country's current economic strengths and weaknesses.

The composite risk rating equals the sum of the individual ratings divided by two: 0.0 to 49.5 is considered very high risk; 80.0 to 100.0 is considered very low risk.

Sources: African Development Indicators (various years), World Bank, World Economic Outlook, International Monetary Fund (various years), Human Development Report, UNDP (various years), Institutional Investor International Edition, and International Country Risk Guide.

EXHIBIT 19-8

SUB-SAHARAN AFRICAN MACROECONOMIC DATA (1996 UNLESS OTHERWISE NOTED)

Country	Population (millions)	Life Expectancy (years)	United Nations HDI (1995)[a] Score	United Nations HDI (1995)[a] Rank	Nominal GDP ($ mil.)	GDP per Capita (dollars)	1990–96 Real GDP Growth (percent)	Total Debt (% GDP)	ICRG Ratings[b] Political Risk	ICRG Ratings[b] Composite Risk	Institutional Investor March 1997 Rank[c]	Institutional Investor March 1997 Rating[d]	Institutional Investor March 1990 Rating[d]
Mozambique	18.0	45	0.281	166	$ 1,715	$ 90	5.5%	355%	50.0	56.0	116	14.9	7.5
Angola	11.1	46	0.344	156	NA	340	−2.9	37	50.0	54.0	123	12.5	12.2
Botswana	1.5	51	0.678	97	NA	NA	4.8	15	80.5	72.0	45	49.5	NA
Burundi	6.4	47	0.241	170	899	140	−2.6	103	NA	NA	NA	NA	NA
Congo (Zaire)	45.2	53	0.383	143	19,437	NA	−7.0	142	37.0	36.0	131	8.1	8.3
Gabon	1.1	55	0.568	120	5,704	3,620	2.5	76	67.5	58.0	92	24.1	29.8
Kenya	27.4	58	0.463	137	9,272	330	1.9	58	69.0	68.0	81	27.9	29.7
Lesotho	2.0	58	0.469	134	NA	670	5.0	70	NA	NA	NA	NA	NA
Madagascar	13.7	58	0.348	153	4,156	240	0.3	113	58.5	60.0	101	19.8	15.2
Malawi	10.0	43	0.334	161	NA	180	3.0	134	63.0	66.0	NA	NA	NA
Namibia	1.6	56	0.644	107	3,026	2,080	4.3	NA	78.5	80.0	NA	NA	NA
Rwanda	6.7	41	NA	NA	1,330	190	−8.7	77	NA	NA	NA	NA	NA
South Africa	37.6	65	0.717	89	126,301	3,140	0.8	NA	75.5	75.0	51	46.0	34.0
Swaziland	0.9	57	0.597	115	1,069	NA	2.1	22	NA	NA	74	31.8	18.7
Tanzania	30.5	50	0.358	150	NA	130	3.4	136	63.0	62.0	105	18.1	10.1
Uganda	19.8	43	0.340	160	6,005	290	6.9	52	57.5	52.0	107	17.7	5.4
Zambia	9.2	44	0.378	146	4,168	430	0.0	120	61.5	66.0	113	16.1	9.0
Zimbabwe	11.6	56	0.507	130	7,509	620	1.0	42	61.0	65.0	71	32.3	27.8

[a] The United Nations Human Development Index (HDI) is a rating of human development across 174 countries. The score ranges from 0 (low) to 1.00 (high); the rank ranges from 1 (high) to 174 (low).

[b] The International Country Risk Guide (ICRG) provides a rating composed of 22 variables in three subcategories of risk: political (100 points), financial (50 points), and economic (50 points). ICRG provides ratings for 140 countries on a monthly basis.

The political risk rating measure a country's political stability.

The composite risk rating equals the sum of the individual ratings divided by two: 0.0 to 49.5 is very high risk; 80.0 to 100.0 is very low risk.

[c] The *Institutional Investor* rank is out of 135 rated countries (low numbers represent less risky countries).

[d] The *Institutional Investor* rating is based on a survey of 75 to 100 international bankers who were asked to grade each country on a scale of 1 to 100, with 100 representing the least chance of default.

Sources: African Development Indicators (various years), World Bank, United Nations, and Institutional Investor International Edition.

legal effectiveness (i.e., stability and certainty of the legal system). It ranked second to last in terms of openness to trade, and time and expense needed to obtain permits and licenses.[7]

What was most noticeable at this stage in the country's development was the speed with which things could and were changing. For example, the Economist Intelligence Unit (EIU) painted a somewhat pessimistic picture of the situation in early 1996:

> [T]he country is a long way from being truly calm or stable. . . . There may well be more violent confrontations . . . (because) the degree of bitterness between the two groups (Frelimo and Renamo) remains excessive. . . . The delicate peace and new democratic system have come under increasing strain in recent months and it is clear that, ultimately, an improvement in the political situation is dependant on an improvement in the economy.[8]

Yet only a year later in 1997, the EIU had become decidedly more optimistic:

> The economic outlook is bright, and will be underpinned by buoyant international investment, which has been responsive to the government's ongoing commitment to monetary reform and prudent monetary and fiscal management. . . . On the economic front, the government is hoping that its continued withdrawal from key spheres of formal economic activity, complemented by heavy investment in infrastructure and the simplification of the archaic regulatory environment will underpin real GDP growth and make in-roads in alleviating rural poverty.[9]

Recognizing these problems, the Mozambican government was actively trying to improve the macroeconomic situation and the climate for private sector investment. It had recently applied for entry into the Highly Indebted Poor Countries (HIPC) Debt Initiative, a debt forgiveness program established by the World Bank and the International Monetary Fund (IMF) in 1996 to help poor countries achieve overall debt sustainability. With regard to investment, it signed the Investment Protection and Promotion Agreement with the South African government in May 1997. In this agreement, the governments pledged to honor and protect cross-border investments. And finally, the government established a special liaison committee to shepherd the Mozal project through the country's Byzantine regulatory and administrative procedures.

When asked why Alusaf wanted to invest in Mozambique given its history and current state of affairs, Irvine replied, "In addition to the attractive power tariffs, attractive labor costs, and very favorable investment incentives, we have a well-structured deal. We have identified the risks and dealt with them appropriately." Alusaf's chairman, Rob Barbour, added:

> Our role as sponsors is to create an environment for success. This means empowering the Mozambican people with job training, AIDS awareness programs, and additional housing. It also means establishing commercial ties with local businesses to bolster the Mozambican economy.

FINANCING THE MOZAL PROJECT

The sponsors planned to finance the $1.4 billion project using a combination of equity (including $35 million of cash generated during start-up), subordinated debt, and

---

[7] World Economic Forum, 1998, The African Competitiveness Report—1998 (Geneva, Switzerland).

[8] Economist Intelligence Unit, Mozambique Country Report, 1st Quarter, 1996, pp. 4–5.

[9] Ibid., 2nd Quarter, 1997, pp. 7–8.

senior debt (see Exhibit 19-4). Alusaf and IDC each planned to invest $125 million, while one or more additional equity partners would invest another $250 million.

Next, the deal would contain $150 million of 15-year subordinated debt, with $65 million coming from the IFC and $85 million coming from other development institutions. The subordinated debt would have a fixed, base interest rate, a variable interest rate component linked to Mozal's total sales, and a repayment schedule beginning in year 11. In return for giving away some of the upside, the sponsors asked for, and expected to get some, concessions on the downside. During periods of low LME prices, the subordinated lenders would defer both base and variable interest payments.[10] Because the value of the subordinated debt was dependent on project performance, it was considered "quasi-equity."

Finally, senior debtholders would provide $680 million, or 50% of total capital. IDC and Coface (Compagnie Française d'Assurance pour le Commerce Extérieur), a French export credit agency (ECA) supporting the use of Pechiney technology, would arrange $540 million of ECA covered finance. ECAs were bilateral organizations that insured creditors in an effort to promote domestic exports. To encourage participation by South African banks, IDC was in advanced discussions with the Credit Guarantee and Insurance Corporation (CGIC), the South African ECA, about providing insurance for $400 million of senior debt. This type of insurance would protect creditors against losses resulting from commercial insolvency and political risks like war, expropriation, breach of contract, or currency inconvertibility. Coface, too, was expected to provide 85% cover for loans made by French banks. Development institutions, including the IFC, would provide the final $140 million.

At this stage, none of the lenders had committed any funds, even though the sponsors had held preliminary discussions with a series of banks, ECAs, and development agencies. The banks, however, seemed to be the real logjam and convincing them to participate had become a top priority. On the one hand, the sponsors had a proven track record. Irvine noted, "Fortunately, we had the Hillside smelter as an example to show potential lenders—we finished that project four months ahead of schedule and 21% under budget." On the other hand, this was Mozambique, not South Africa. IDC's Jaco Kriek knew it would be a challenge to get the banks on board:

> Initially, the banks had no interest in financing a Mozambican project, especially a limited-recourse deal. From their perspective, IFC involvement was absolutely necessary. They (the IFC) have lots of experience in emerging markets and know how to structure deals. But in the end, it has to be a team effort. We need everyone—banks, development agencies, ECAs, committed governments, quality sponsors, and an experienced international operator—to raise the funds.

Alusaf's Louis Irvine echoed these sentiments: "There is no doubting the IFC's importance. They bring credibility to a project and provide comfort to potential lenders." Rather than convincing the banks to participate in the deal, the challenge became one of convincing the IFC to participate.

THE INTERNATIONAL FINANCE CORPORATION (IFC)

The International Finance Corporation (IFC), a member of the World Bank Group, promoted private sector investment in developing countries as a way to reduce poverty and improve people's lives. Founded in 1956 and owned by its 172 member countries,

[10] Spicer, "Mozal Brings Mozambique into World View," p. 143.

the IFC was the world's largest multilateral source of debt and equity financing for private sector projects. The IFC differed from other multilateral development institutions such as the African Development Bank (AfDB) or the European Bank for Reconstruction and Development (EBRD) because its loans were not backed by sovereign guarantees and its capital was paid-in rather than callable on demand.

Since 1956, it had committed more than $21.2 billion in financing for its own account and arranged over $15 billion in syndications and underwriting in 129 developing countries.[11] To be eligible for IFC funds, projects must have private ownership, be commercially viable and environmentally sound, and provide significant development benefits to the local economy. Exhibit 19-9a provides a summary of IFC approvals and commitments since 1988. In the year ending June 1997, the IFC was expected to approve 275 projects, invest $3 billion for its own account, and make $400 million of net income. Exhibit 19-9b provides the regional breakdown of these investments—only 7% of total investments were in Sub-Saharan Africa. Exhibits 19-10a and 19-10b show the IFC's ten largest investments worldwide and in the Sub-Saharan African region, respectively.

Most of these investments, particularly the greenfield projects, were in risky country environments. In fact, in a survey of 233 recent greenfield projects financed by the IFC, 77% were in countries with an *Institutional Investor* rating of less than 45 at the time of approval and 27% were in high-risk countries with a rating of less than 25.[12] In contrast, approximately 10% of all project finance deals occurred in countries with a rating less than 25. As noted by a senior IFC official, the corporation was supposed to invest in high-risk countries: "Our goal in life is to disappear, to no longer be needed. But until then, our job is to go to the places no one else wants to go, and to finance the projects no one else wants to finance." Such a strategy, however, could easily jeopardize the IFC's AAA rating and its ability to attract low-cost funds for investment purposes.

IFC as a Development Lender

The IFC contributed to development lending by appraising prospective projects, structuring the legal and financial documents, providing long-term capital, and deterring sovereign interference. A multidisciplinary team including investment officers, economists, engineers, lawyers, and industrial experts did the initial review. The goal of the appraisal was to uncover information about the project, the sponsors, and the host government that might not be widely available or well understood by other lenders. In particular, the appraisal was meant to evaluate project risks and returns, sovereign risks, and overall consistency with a country's long-run growth strategy. The IFC was uniquely qualified to do this analysis given its extensive experience with development lending and its ties to local governments through its association with the World Bank.

For the Mozal project, the appraisal lasted from January to March 1997 and was paid for by the sponsors. It concluded that the project was viable and had acceptable financial and economic rates of return. The *financial* rate of return was the project's internal rate of return based on constant price projections of pre-interest, *after* income tax cash flows less project costs (free cash flow). The *economic* rate of return was the project's internal rate of return to the host country. It was based on constant price projections of pre-interest, *before* income tax cash flows adjusted for economic distortions and transfer payments, less project costs. If successful, Mozal would have a very

---

[11] IFC Annual Report, 1997, p. 1.

[12] International Finance Corporation, 1999, *Project Finance in Developing Countries*, Lessons of Experience #7, Washington, DC, p. 31.

EXHIBIT 19-9A

SUMMARY OF IFC FINANCIAL AND OPERATING STATISTICS, 1980–1997 EST.

Year	Number of Projects Approved	Total Approved Financing for Own Account	Total Committed Portfolio for Own Account	Number of Firms in Committed Portfolio	Non-Accrual Loans as % of Total[a]	Principal in Arrears as % of Total[b]	Net Income (millions)	Total Assets[c] (millions)	Total Assets less Derivatives[c] (millions)
1980	55	$ 681	$ 402	288	n/a	n/a	$ 20.7	$ 908	$ 908
1981	56	811	749	314	n/a	n/a	19.5	1,085	1,085
1982	65	612	1,049	333	n/a	n/a	21.6	1,233	1,233
1983	58	845	1,267	341	n/a	n/a	23.0	1,314	1,314
1984	62	696	1,622	349	n/a	n/a	26.3	1,390	1,390
1985	75	937	1,979	366	n/a	n/a	28.3	1,673	1,673
1986	85	1,156	2,518	377	18.0%	4.1%	25.4	2,236	2,236
1987	92	920	3,260	404	15.8	6.1	53.8	2,814	2,806
1988	95	1,039	3,374	454	11.1	5.0	100.6	3,427	3,425
1989	92	1,292	4,045	468	7.5	3.2	196.5	4,006	3,995
1990	122	1,505	4,752	495	5.2	2.5	157.0	5,606	5,580
1991	152	1,540	5,494	618	5.6	2.3	165.9	6,648	6,594
1992	167	1,773	6,423	703	6.7	3.7	180.2	8,133	7,908
1993	185	2,133	7,132	798	8.3	4.3	141.7	8,913	8,698
1994	231	2,463	7,893	868	7.2	4.0	258.2	14,723	10,122
1995	213	2,877	9,461	939	6.5	3.9	188.0	18,228	11,977
1996	264	3,248	9,844	985	5.6	3.3	345.8	22,640	14,502
1997 Est.	276	3,317	10,521	1,046	4.9	2.7	431.9	28,975	17,575

[a] Nonaccrual means the loans are not accruing interest in a timely fashion.

[b] Principal in arrears means the amount of principal not paid when it was due.

[c] The dollar value of derivatives represents receivables from currency swaps, interest rate swaps, and covered forwards not the *net* notional amount. Prior to 1994, derivative usage was reported as the difference between derivative receivables (an asset) and derivatives payables (a liability).

Source: International Finance Corporation, Annual Reports.

EXHIBIT 19-9B

IFC INVESTMENTS BY REGION AS OF JUNE 30, 1997 ($ MILLIONS)

Region	Investments Held for IFC ($ millions)			
	Loans	Equity at Cost	Total	Percent of Total
Latin America and the Caribbean	$3,278.2	$ 773.2	$ 4,051.4	38.4%
Asia	2,284.5	606.6	2,891.0	27.4
Europe	1,080.3	335.7	1,416.0	13.4
Central Asia, Middle East, and North Africa	1,003.2	246.3	1,249.5	11.8
Sub-Saharan Africa	594.4	188.1	782.5	7.4
Worldwide investments	82.0	87.3	169.3	1.6
Total	**8,322.5**	**2,237.7**	**10,559.7**	**100.0**

Source: International Finance Corporation: 1997 Investment Portfolio.

---

significant developmental impact and, therefore, an attractive economic rate of return. Exhibit 19-11 provides an analysis of IFC's historical investment performance in terms of *ex ante* (before investment) versus *ex post* (following investment) rates of return for investments made between 1978 and 1995.

According to the appraisal, the project would increase exports by $430 million, GDP by $157 million (by 9%), and net foreign exchange by $161 million per year. Mozal would also generate 5,000 construction jobs and 873 permanent jobs—90% of the permanent positions would be held by Mozambicans—as well as develop human capital among Mozambicans through managerial, health, and other skills training. Besides building human capital, the IFC hoped the project would provide critical infrastructure and spur investment along the Maputo Corridor. One of the IFC's most important contributions in the appraisal stage was its environmental and social impact assessment. The IFC worked with the sponsors and the Mozambican government to ensure these issues were discussed and handled properly. The IFC was known for the quality of its due diligence, especially in high-risk environments where such information was difficult to collect and interpret. In many deals, particularly syndicated deals, other creditors wanted, and often paid for, a copy of the IFC's information memorandum. Much of the information contained in the offering memoranda came from the IFC's detailed appraisal analysis.

In those instances where the appraisal yielded positive results, the IFC then took a leading role in structuring the legal and financial contracts. Through the years, it had acquired a reputation as an "honest broker" because it insisted that projects be fair to all parties including the sovereign entity involved. This focus on fairness stemmed from a deep-seated belief that "if it's not fair, it's not sustainable." If nothing else, the lesson from the large number of expropriations in the 1960s and 1970s was that greedy sponsors created their own demise by front-loading income and trying to extract maximum returns. The IFC's multilateral ownership structure, whereby it represented many varied interests, and its development objectives further enhanced its reputation for fairness.

A simple example shows how the IFC could create value for all parties by structuring fairer deals. Consider a project that cost $105 to build. Assuming no IFC in-

EXHIBIT 19-10A

TEN LARGEST IFC INVESTMENTS AS OF JUNE 30, 1997 ($ MILLIONS)

Project Name	Country	Sector	Year of Investment	Original Commitment		Investments Held for IFC		
				Total IFC	Total in Syndicate	Loans	Equity at Cost	Total
1) Star Petroleum	Thailand	Oil Refining	94	$100.0	$350.0	$100.0	$ 0.0	$100.0
2) Thai Petrochemicals	Thailand	Chemicals	97	100.0	400.0	100.0	0.0	100.0
3) Ispat Industries	India	Mining/Extraction	92,95,97	102.8	85.0	85.5	5.8	91.3
4) Aguas Argentinas	Argentina	Infrastructure	96	85.0	307.5	75.1	7.0	82.1
5) Ceval Alimentos	Brazil	Food/Agribusiness	93,96	90.0	130.0	68.6	10.0	78.6
6) Compañía Teléfonos	Venezuela	Infrastructure	96	75.0	185.6	75.0	0.0	75.0
7) Sadia Concórdia	Brazil	Food/Agribusiness	94,95,97	80.0	222.0	64.0	10.0	74.0
8) Hopewell Power	Philippines	Infrastructure	93	70.0	11.0	60.0	10.0	70.0
9) Mass Transit System	Thailand	Infrastructure	97	69.7	0.0	59.8	9.8	69.7
10) Bridas S.A.P.I.C.	Argentina	Mining/Extraction	93,96	80.0	100.0	42.1	25.0	67.1

EXHIBIT 19-10B

LARGEST IFC INVESTMENTS IN SUB-SAHARAN AFRICA AS OF JUNE 30, 1997 ($ MILLIONS)

Project Name	Country	Sector	Year of Investment	Original Commitment		Investments Held for IFC		
				Total IFC	Total in Syndicate	Loans	Equity at Cost	Total
1) Pecten Cameroon	Cameroon	Mining/Extraction	92,96,97	$74.5	$177.9	$ 49.3	$ 0.0	$ 49.3
2) Energy Haute Mer	Congo Rep.	Mining/Extraction	96	46.8	25.0	43.9	2.9	46.8
3) Mines d'Or	Mali	Mining/Extraction	95	39.8	25	35.0	4.8	39.8
4) Block CI-11	Côte d'Ivoire	Mining/Extraction	93,95	38.7	0.0	0.0	38.7	38.7
5) Panafrican Paper	Kenya	Timber/Paper	70,90,96	69.0	4.0	30.0	4.5	34.5
6) Minière de Syama	Mali	Mining/Extraction	94	28.1	0.0	26.7	1.4	28.1
7) Mobil/Nigeria	Nigeria	Mining/Extraction	91	75.0	95	22.5	0.0	22.5
8) SA Capital Growth	South Africa	Financial Services	96	20.0	0.0	0.0	20.0	20.0
9) Tourist Co.	Nigeria	Hotels/Tourism	94	17.5	0.0	15.0	2.5	17.5
10) Goldfields Ltd.	Ghana	Mining/Extraction	90,92,97	27.0	18.5	13.6	3.0	16.6
255 other investments	34 countries					236.0	77.8	313.8
					Total	594.4	188.1	782.5

Source: International Finance Corporation: 1997 Investment Portfolio.

EXHIBIT 19-11

IFC INVESTMENT RETURNS, 1978–1995

Region	Median Rates of Return (ROR) 347 IFC Projects Completed from 1978–1995			
	Financial ROR[a]		Economic ROR[b]	
	Ex Ante[c]	Ex Post[d]	Ex Ante[c]	Ex Post[d]
Africa	18.0%	9.0%	19.0%	10.0%
Asia	19.0	14.0	20.0	13.0
CAMENA[e]	20.5	11.4	24.0	13.6
Europe	19.4	12.0	19.9	15.0
Latin America[f]	20.0	13.0	20.0	12.0
Average	**19.0**	**12.0**	**20.0**	**12.0**

[a] Financial rate of return (ROR) is the project's internal rate of return based on constant price projections of pre-interest, after-tax cash flows, less project costs.

[b] Economic rate of return (ROR) is the project's internal rate of return based on constant price projections of pre-interest, pre-tax cash flows adjusted for economic distortions and transfer payments, less project costs.

[c] *Ex ante* estimates were made prior to project implementation.

[d] *Ex post* estimates were made during an Investment Assessment Report which is typically done several years after project implementation.

[e] CAMENA = Central Asia, Middle East, and North Africa.

[f] Includes the Caribbean.

Source: IFC Economics Department, cited in the Annex to *Private Sector and Development: Five Case Studies*, The World Bank, March 1, 1997.

volvement, the project would succeed with probability 66.7% and be worth $150 to the sponsor, or would be expropriated with 33.3% probability and be worth $0 to the sponsor. Thus the expected value is negative $5, equal to [(66.7% * $150 + 33.3% * $0) − $105], which means the sponsor would not invest. With IFC involvement, the project would be worth less to the sponsor, say $130, but more to the host government because of transferred benefits. As a result, the probability of expropriation might fall to 10%. In this case, the expected value becomes $12, equal to [(90% * $130 + 10% * $0) − $105], and the sponsor would be willing to invest. Both sides are better off compared to not building the plant.

Having structured thousands of deals in developing countries, the IFC had considerable experience in coordinating large, diverse groups and resolving complex legal issues. Azmat Taufique, the manager of the IFC's Mining Division, commented:

> We are in the business of making finance happen in difficult settings. The IFC brings cutting-edge tools and analysis to complex project finance problems, and it provides solutions that are acceptable to wide-ranging parties in all kinds of settings. One measure of our success is the fact that sponsors not only come to us to do the hard deals, but come back to us for other deals.

Two examples of where the IFC could play an advisory role in the Mozal transaction were the integration of diverse legal systems and the definition of the circumstances under which the sponsors would be released from their completion guarantees.

Mozambique had a civil law system based on statutes from the colonial era. In contrast, South Africa had a common law system based on judicial rulings and precedent. These two systems were fundamentally different, yet would have to be reconciled in a single set of legal documents. In the past, IFC had successfully resolved this kind of issue, though it was not always an easy thing to do. The benefit of having well-constructed legal documents was that they greatly simplified dispute resolution when and if there were disagreements.

A second potentially complicated legal issue, particularly given the setting, revolved around the sponsors' completion guarantees. As with any deal, the parties would have to agree on definitions of both technical and financial completion. The more contentious issue, however, was what kinds of political events would release the sponsors from this obligation. For example, if the Mozambican government increased taxes, causing a 5% reduction in the sponsors' equity value, would that constitute a sufficiently important political event to justify ending their contractual obligation to finish the project? What if the government expropriated 50% of equity value? While acts of total expropriation had become relatively rare in recent years, "creeping" expropriation was much more common. For example, the Indonesian government raised tariffs from 0% to 20% on the Chandra Asri project's primary input in 1996; the Indian state government of Maharashtra unilaterally canceled contracts with Enron on the Dabhol power project in 1995, and the Thai government refused to honor promises to increase and share tolls with the contractor of a newly constructed toll road in Bangkok in 1993.

Once the legal documentation was complete, the IFC provided long-term financing in a variety of forms: senior debt, subordinated debt (quasi-equity), and equity. The senior debt was further broken down into two types of loans: "A loans" for the IFC's own portfolio and "B loans" for syndication to other institutions, with the IFC as the lender of record. For the Mozal deal, in particular, the sponsors had requested an A loan only.

Three features distinguished IFC participation. First, it was willing to make loans with longer maturities (7 to 12 years on the senior debt and 8 to 15 years on the subordinated debt), which provided better matching for long-lived project assets. Next, it was willing to lend on a subordinated basis, thereby exposing itself to greater losses. And third, the IFC valued development benefits. Thus, compared to private lenders, the IFC could either accept a lower financial rate of return for the same risk, or it could accept more risk for the same financial rate of return. In both cases, the economic rate of return would make up the difference. But this approach, could get the IFC in trouble, as one government official observed:

> The IFC is on a mission impossible. If it acts like a development bank and the return on investment is too low, it gets criticized for being imprudent. If, on the other hand, it (acts like a merchant bank) and gets into a project that is attractive and steals business from, say, Citicorp, it gets rapped on the knuckles for competing with the private sector using public funds.[13]

When, and if, the IFC agreed to participate, it had a catalytic or "demonstration" effect on other lenders. It increased the likelihood that others would participate in the deal at hand and it was supposed to generate future investment in other private sector ventures. Exhibit 19-12, which shows how country risk ratings change following IFC investment in high-risk countries, provides some evidence on IFC's role as a catalyst for future investment.

[13] J. Friedland, "The IFC's Identity Crisis," *Institutional Investor*, September 1986, p. 139.

EXHIBIT 19-12

THE IMPACT OF IFC INVESTMENT ON COUNTRY RISK SCORES

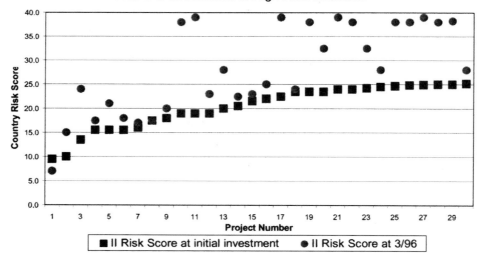

Changes in Institutional Investor Country Risk Scores
After IFC Investments in High Risk Countries

Legend: ■ II Risk Score at initial investment   ● II Risk Score at 3/96

Source: IFC Financing Private Infrastructure (Washington, DC, 1996), p. 23.

Finally, the IFC played a role in deterring adverse sovereign actions that could result in either default or reduction in equity value. As an "honest broker," the IFC made sure a project was consistent with a country's long-run development strategy in an effort to reduce the incentives for short-term opportunistic behavior. It structured deals accordingly and then led the annual project review to ensure the contracts were being upheld.

The fact that the IFC was part of the World Bank Group also helped reduce political risk. The historical record shows that governments gave higher priority to obligations from multilateral lending institutions such as the World Bank Group when they could not service all of their external debt. One of the main reasons why they have received preferential treatment was that they are often the only source of new lending to countries in financial distress. In fact, IFC debt repayments have never been included in a sovereign debt rescheduling or a general debt-servicing moratorium.

Because of this track record, rating agencies like Standard & Poor's (S&P) asserted that IFC involvement conferred an "umbrella" or "halo effect" on projects and a "preferred status" on creditors. Referring to this effect, an S&P analyst noted:

> [T]he halo effect does exist, and it comes primarily from two sources—deterrence value and indirect access to a multilateral's preferred creditor status. . . . (The IFC's) preferred creditor status is not a matter of law, but one of well-established conduct.[14]

[14] S. G. Smith, "Benefits and Limits of Official Sources of Infrastructure Credits, *Infrastructure Finance: Project Finance, Utilities, and Concession*, Standard and Poor's Corporation, September 1998, pp. 83–84.

CONCLUSION

Even though many aspects of the deal were still undetermined (e.g., who would provide the other 50% of the equity, who would buy 50% of the output, how were they going to structure the sponsors' completion guarantees, etc.), Kimura and Husain had been instructed by their superiors to prepare a recommendation for the IFC's Board on the grounds that

> Authorization at this time of IFC's proposed investment would enhance the IFC's leadership role, send a strong signal to prospective investors, and ultimately facilitate the timely completion of the negotiations.

While Kimura and Husain were arguing for approval, they were, nevertheless mindful of the risks created by such a large investment. Their colleague, Azmat Taufique, who agreed with the recommendation, raised the critical issue that the Board would have to decide:

> The real question here is not whether to do a deal in Mozambique—there is clearly a need—but rather whether this is the right time and the right deal to be making such a large investment, especially when several important features are still unresolved.

The project team believed in their recommendation but wondered whether the Board would agree that the potential financial and developmental benefits justified the risks. If the IFC's largest investment were to subsequently fail, the failure would call into question the IFC's ability to assess project risk and structure deals in emerging markets. Perhaps more important than the IFC's reputation would be the cost to Mozambique in terms of lost development opportunities. A highly visible failure, for whatever reason, might deter future investment for many years to come. With these thoughts running through their minds, Kimura and Husain began printing their report.

MODULE 4

FINANCING PROJECTS

20

Chase's Strategy for Syndicating the Hong Kong Disneyland Loan (A)

We are investment bankers, not commercial bankers, which means that we underwrite to distribute, not to put a loan on our balance sheet.

—Matt Harris, Managing Director, Chase Securities

In August 2000, Hongkong International Theme Parks Limited (HKTP), an entity jointly owned by The Walt Disney Company and the Hong Kong government, awarded Chase Manhattan Bank the mandate to lead a HK$3.3 billion bank financing for the construction of the HK$14 billion Hong Kong Disneyland theme park and resort complex. Disney chose Chase from among 17 major banks invited to bid on the deal because of its global leadership in syndicated finance and its firm commitment to underwrite the full loan amount. Given this commitment, Chase was responsible for raising the funds regardless of how the bank market reacted to the deal.

Although Chase's Global Syndicated Finance Group was headquartered in New York, its Hong Kong office was responsible for executing the deal. The deal team, including Managing Directors Matt Harris and Charles Pelham, Vice President Jose Cortes, Senior Associate Vivek Chandiramani, and Analyst Lynnette Yeo, had to deliver a syndication that met both the bank market's expectations for participation levels and credit quality, and the sponsors' desire for a rapid closing with a supportive bank group. Chase's ability to execute this transaction would have direct consequences for its reputation as a leader in syndicated finance, its returns as an underwriter, and its credit exposure as a lender. As the team evaluated alternative syndication strategies, they had to decide whether to proceed directly into a general syndication or whether to pursue a two-stage syndication with a subunderwriting prior to general syndication. In either

Dean's Research Fellow Michael Kane prepared this case under the supervision of Professor Benjamin C. Esty. HBS cases are developed solely as the basis for class discussion. Cases are not intended to serve as endorsements, sources of primary data, or illustrations of effective or ineffective management.

case, they had to decide which banks to invite, how to allocate fees and titles, and how much of the loan they wanted to retain on their balance sheet.

HONG KONG DISNEYLAND

Hong Kong

In 1997, after 150 years as a British Colony, Hong Kong became the Hong Kong Special Administrative Region (HKSAR) within the People's Republic of China. Under a transfer of sovereignty agreement, China assured the SAR a "high degree of autonomy" under a "one country, two systems" concept. Despite some concerns about political freedoms and civil rights, the transfer preserved the British legal system and a free market economy. The new government maintained a system of low taxes, unrestricted capital movement, a stable Hong Kong dollar (officially linked to the U.S. dollar since 1983 at HK$7.80 = US$1.00), and a duty-free port.

As one of the Asian "tigers," Hong Kong enjoyed a prosperity that ranked it with the largest countries in Western Europe. Its economy was based on services, tourism, and international trade, reflecting the fact that Hong Kong had few natural resources and relatively high labor costs. Like other countries in the region, Hong Kong fell into recession following the Thai currency crisis in 1997. The unemployment rate more than doubled, GDP fell for the first time in 20 years, and the stock market crashed (see Exhibits 20-1 and 20-2). While some saw a tentative recovery in progress by mid-1999, the decline in output remained a subject of public concern:

> So many people in Hong Kong are banking on a Disney theme park to create more jobs and end a slump in tourism that Mr. Rowse [commissioner of tourism and a top negotiator on the Disney project] laments he can no longer attend a dinner party without being pumped on the progress of his work.[1]

EXHIBIT 20-1

HONG KONG KEY ECONOMIC DATA, 1995–1999

	1995	1996	1997	1998	1999
Population (millions)	6.2	6.3	6.5	6.7	6.8
Real GDP (billions USD—1996 Prices)	$147.5	$154.1	$161.8	$153.4	$158.1
Exports (billions USD—1996 Prices)	$20.8	$21.9	$23.1	$22.0	$22.9
HK$/USD Exchange Rate	7.73	7.74	7.75	7.75	7.77
HK$ Prime Rate	8.50%	8.75%	8.50%	9.50%	9.00%
Consumer Price Index (Percent change)	6.4%	6.7%	4.8%	−1.4%	−2.9%
Commercial Bank Loans (millions USD)	$700	$1,034	$3,406	$1,800	$2,000
Foreign Exch. Reserves (billions USD)	$55.4	$63.8	$92.8	$89.6	$96.2
Unemployment Rate (%)	3.2%	2.8%	2.2%	4.7%	6.3%
Tourism (visitors in millions)	10,200	11,702	10,406	9,575	10,678

Sources: Economist Intelligence Unit; Hong Kong Government Web Site http//www.info.gov.hk.

[1] B. Orwall and C. Mungan, "Disney and Hong Kong to Extend Talks on Possible Construction of Theme Park," *The Wall Street Journal*, June 30, 1999, p. B9.

EXHIBIT 20-2

HONG KONG MARKET CONDITIONS, 1989 TO 2000

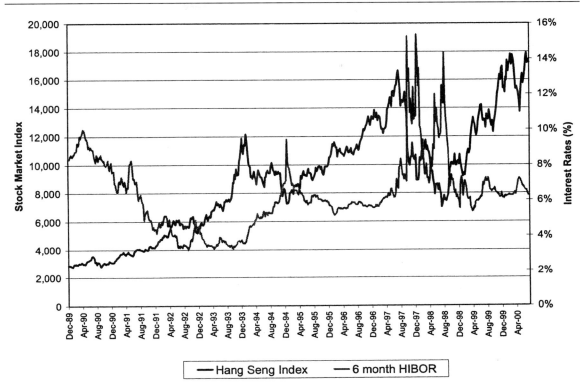

Source: Created from Datastream data.

The Walt Disney Company

From modest beginnings in 1923, Disney had become a multinational, multimedia entertainment giant with revenues in excess of $20 billion, an "A" debt rating, and more than $5 billion in annual operating cash flow. (Exhibits 20-3a and 20-3b present Disney's financial data.) Disney operated five business segments: Theme Parks and Resorts, Media Networks, Studio Entertainment, Consumer Products, and Internet/Direct Marketing. CEO Michael Eisner described the company this way:

> We now have seven theme parks (with four more in the works), 27 hotels with 36,888 rooms, two cruise ships, 728 Disney stores, one broadcast network, 10 TV stations, nine international Disney channels, 42 radio stations, an Internet portal, five major Internet web sites, interests in nine U.S. cable networks and . . . [a library containing thousands of animated and live films and TV episodes].[2]

In its Theme Parks and Resorts segment, the company owned and operated the original Disneyland in Anaheim, California, and the Walt Disney World resort complex in

---

[2] The Walt Disney Company 1999 Annual Report, p. 2.

EXHIBIT 20-3A

THE WALT DISNEY COMPANY FINANCIAL STATISTICS, 1995–1999 (U.S.$ BILLIONS)

	1995	1996[a]	1997	1998	1999
Income Statement					
Revenues	$12.2	$18.7	$22.5	$23.0	$23.4
Operating Income[b]	2.5	3.0	4.4	4.0	3.4
EBITDA	4.1	5.5	7.3	7.5	7.0
Interest expense(net)	0.2	.4	.7	.6	.6
Net Income	1.4	1.2	2.0	1.9	1.3
Balance Sheet					
Total Assets	15.0	37.3	38.5	41.4	43.7
Total Debt	3.0	12.3	11.1	11.7	11.7
Stockholders' Equity	6.7	16.1	17.3	19.4	21.0

[a] Disney acquired CapCities ABC on February 9, 1996.

[b] 1999 operating income includes $200 million (net) for restructuring charges and gain on sale of Starwave, not included in segment information in Exhibit 20-4b.

Source: Company Annual Reports.

Orlando, Florida. It also earned fees and royalties on Tokyo Disneyland and Disneyland Paris—opened in 1983 and 1992, respectively. In contrast to the successful U.S. and Tokyo parks, Disneyland Paris had experienced financial problems after opening due to a European recession, large initial capital expenditures, and what proved to be an overly aggressive capital structure dependent upon real estate sales for debt service (project debt accounted for 75% of project value). To avoid the theme park's bankruptcy, Disney

EXHIBIT 20-3B

THE WALT DISNEY COMPANY-RELATIVE SEGMENT PROFITABILITY, 1999 (U.S.$ BILLIONS)

Segment	Revenues		Operating Income[a]	
	Dollars	% of Total	Dollars	% of Revenues
Theme Parks and Resorts	$ 6.1	26%	$1.4	24%
Media Networks	7.5	32	1.6	21
Studio Entertainment	6.5	28	0.1	2
Consumer Products	3.0	13	0.6	20
Internet and Direct Marketing	0.2	1	(0.1)	(loss)
Total	23.3	100%	3.2	

[a] After depreciation but before amortization of intangible assets, exceptional items, corporate overhead, interest, and taxes.

Source: Company Annual Reports.

agreed to forgo some of its management and other fees while banks, some of whom were active in the Hong Kong market, restructured their loans.

In discussing Disney's strategy for the next Disney Decade, Eisner stressed the importance of international growth, saying, "The United States contains only 5% of the world's population, but it accounts for 80% of our company's revenues."[3]

Hong Kong Disneyland

In December 1999, Disney and the Hong Kong government signed a comprehensive agreement for a new theme park and resort complex to be located on the northeastern end of Lantau Island. According to the agreement, the project would have three phases. Phase I would include a Disneyland-style park offering several themed "lands" featuring Disney rides and attractions, one or two hotels, as well as a retail, dining, and entertainment complex. (Exhibit 20-4 presents an artist's rendition of the resort.) Phases II and III were less well defined, but included options to develop adjoining sites at some point in the future. Jon Headley (HBS, 1996), Disney's director of corporate finance, described the strategy this way:

> Learning from our experience with Disneyland Paris, the strategy for Hong Kong was to start small and then to add capacity over time as demand grew. In fact, Phase I included

---

EXHIBIT 20-4

ARTIST'S RENDITION OF THE HONG KONG DISNEYLAND THEME PARK

Source: Hong Kong International Theme Parks Limited Offering Circular, September 2000.

---

[3] Ibid., p. 6.

plans to double capacity within the first ten years of operations. The real keys to success are having the land available for growth and the ability to finance this growth out of operating cash flow.

Because most of the construction site was currently ocean, the first step in the project was to reclaim land. The Hong Kong government, at its expense, agreed to extend the coastline and construct the roads, utilities, and other infrastructure needed to support the park. At a cost of HK$14 billion, the land reclamation and infrastructure development was scheduled to begin at the end of 2000. Two years later, resort construction was scheduled to begin and would last until late 2005 when the park would open for business.

The government supported the project because it expected the project would generate sizable public benefits. One local economist estimated that land reclamation and construction would generate 16,000 new jobs, while the resort would generate employment for 18,000 people at opening and up to 36,000 within ten years.[4] The government stated that the expected financial rate of return on its investment was between 17% and 25% per annum and at least 6% per annum under a worst case scenario.[5]

A new corporation, Hongkong International Theme Parks Limited (HKTP), would construct, own, and operate the resort. The HK$14 billion construction cost would come from four sources (see Exhibit 20-5). The Hong Kong government and Disney would provide HK$3.25 billion (57% share) and HK$2.45 billion (43% share) of equity, re-

---

EXHIBIT 20-5

HKTP SOURCES OF CASH (HK$ IN MILLIONS)[a]

Sources of Cash		
Debt		
Bank Term Loan	$ 2,275	16.2%
HK Government Loan[b]	6,092	43.3
Subtotal	8,367	59.5
Equity		
HK Government	3,250	23.1
Walt Disney	2,449	17.4
Subtotal	5,699	40.5
Total	**$14,066**	**100.0%**

[a] Excludes the estimated HK$14 billion cost of land reclamation and infrastructure development to be contributed to HKTP by the government in exchange for nonparticipating, convertible stock.

[b] Terms included: 25-year final maturity with repayment beginning in 2016; fully subordinated to the bank loan.

Source: Hong Kong International Theme Parks Limited Offering Circular, September 2000.

---

[4] Tracy Yu of Standard Chartered Group, as reported by Knight Ridder *Tribune Bridge News*, September 11, 1999.

[5] S. Lee, "Park Still Viable If Visitors 70pc Less than Estimated," *South China Morning Post*, November 11, 1999, p. 2.

spectively. Although the government initially held a 57% share of HKTP, it received a special class of equity as compensation for the reclaimed land and infrastructure development that could be converted into HKTP common stock, which could eventually increase its equity ownership position to as much as 75%. In addition, the Hong Kong government agreed to provide HK$6.1 billion in subordinated debt with repayment starting in year 16 and ending in year 25. This left a shortfall of HK$2.3 billion.

The government wanted to fill the shortfall with some form of external finance for several reasons. A commercial bank loan would not only show that the project was viable in the eyes of the international banking community, but would also provide independent oversight of construction and monitoring of ongoing operations. Eventually, the two owners agreed to raise a HK$2.3 billion, 15-year, nonrecourse term loan for construction and a HK$1.0 billion, nonrecourse revolving credit facility for working capital needs postconstruction.

Because HKTP did not need significant construction funds until after the land reclamation was done, it had the option of waiting until 2002 before raising the bank debt. By waiting, it would save on the commitment fees charged by the banks. On the other hand, Jon Headley noted:

> Although we had two years in which to place the commercial loan, the Asian loan market was showing signs of recovery by early 2000. Knowing the structuring and syndication process could take six to nine months, we decided to start the process sooner rather than later. Our fear, given the recent volatility in the Asian banking market, was that if we waited until 2002, we might not be able to get a loan, never mind a loan with attractive pricing.

WINNING THE MANDATE

Jeff Speed (vice president, Corporate Finance, and assistant treasurer) headed the Disney deal team for the HK$3.3 billion Hong Kong Disneyland financing, supported by Jon Headley (director, Corporate Finance), Steve Dorton (manager, Corporate Finance), Carrie Ferman (senior analyst, Corporate Finance), and Sue Lai (vice president and counsel). The Disney team developed a term sheet for the bank financing and contacted the company's relationship banks as well as other banks it viewed as having expertise in the Hong Kong syndicated loan market. In these discussions, they hoped to get a preliminary expression of interest and an assessment of current conditions in the Hong Kong bank market. Disney explained that they wanted to raise a HK$3.3 billion nonrecourse loan package on a fully underwritten basis and expected to select up to three lead arrangers for the transaction. (See the Appendix for background information on syndicated bank lending.)

Chase Manhattan Bank

It was highly predictable that Disney would contact Chase. In addition to being one of Disney's top ten relationship banks, Chase was the third largest bank in the United States with more than $400 billion of assets and $175 billion of loans in 1999, and was a leader in the field of syndicated finance. In 1999, Chase was the lead arranger for 34% of total syndicated loans by dollar volume in the world's largest market, the United States, compared to 21% for the next largest competitor.[6] In the U.S. market for loans

---

[6] Market share based on bank's status as lead arranger and bookrunner (manager of syndication) for reported transactions as analyzed by Thomson Financial Securities Data.

greater than $1 billion, its dominance was even more pronounced: it led 47.5% of the deals, three times more than its nearest competitor. The financial press had recognized Chase's leadership with numerous awards: Best Loan House of the Last 25 Years 1974–1999 (*International Finance Review*), Best at U.S. Syndicated Loans—1999 (*Euromoney*), and Best Project Finance Arranger in the U.S.—1999 (*Project Finance*). Although it was not the market leader in all loan types or all locations, Chase was a formidable competitor in most markets, including Asia (see the league tables in Exhibit 20-6a, 20-6b, and 20-6c). It had over 400 professionals in its Global Syndicated Finance Group with offices in New York, London, Hong Kong, Tokyo, and Sydney. Each office had structuring and distribution teams. In its 30-person Hong Kong office, Matt Harris led the structuring team while Charles Pelham led the distribution team. As Matt Harris described it, "We have by far the largest syndicated lending platform in the Asia Pacific region. Because we have more people and greater coverage, we are able to do the largest and most difficult deals."

Making the Short List

Following an initial conference call, the Chase deal team (Harris, Pelham, Cortes, Chandiramani, and Yeo) studied Disney's term sheet and wrestled with several questions, mainly the bank's desire to win the mandate. Harris described their thought process this way:

> There are three ways to approach a deal: bid to win, bid to lose, and no bid. Although Disney was an important global client, the deal did not seem that attractive to us initially. It had a long tenor which banks don't like, we had to contend with the problems at Disneyland Paris, the sponsors wanted to mandate as many as three lead arrangers which hurts our economics, and our competitors, especially the local banks like Bank of China and Hong Kong Shanghai Banking Corporation (HSBC), were likely to bid aggressively. And so, we decided to bid to lose. Yet to protect our reputation, we wanted to bid aggressively enough to make the short list for this high-profile deal. If we happened to win the mandate, it would have to be on terms that met our earnings targets.

EXHIBIT 20-6A

BOOK MANAGER OF U.S. SYNDICATED LOANS IN 1999 (FULL CREDIT TO BOOK MANAGER)

Position	Arranger Name	Amount ($ billions)	Percent of Total
1	**Chase Manhattan Bank**	$359.6	33.8%
2	Bank America	225.6	21.2
3	Citigroup	94.7	8.9
4	JP Morgan	58.5	5.5
5	Bank One	48.9	4.6
6	Deutsche Bank AG	33.0	3.1
7	FleetBoston	31.9	3.0
8	Credit Suisse First Boston	20.2	1.9
9	First Union	19.2	1.8
10	Bank of New York	18.1	1.7

Source: Thompson Financial Securities Data.

EXHIBIT 20-6B

TOP ARRANGERS OF GLOBAL PROJECT FINANCE LOANS IN 1999

Position	Arranger Name	Amount ($ millions)	Number of Deals
1	Citigroup Inc.	$7,919.9	49
2	**Chase Manhattan Bank**	6,087.5	39
3	Bank of America	5,793.0	36
4	Deutsche Bank AG	4,715.4	44
5	Société Génerale SA	4,247.9	45
6	ABN AMRO Bank NV	3,905.6	47
7	Credit Suisse First Boston	3,345.9	18
8	Westdeutsche Landesbank Girozentrale	3,246.0	31
9	Credit Lyonnaise	2,891.9	43
10	Dresdner Bank AG	2,824.5	38

Source: Euromoney's Project Finance, July 2000.

The Disney finance team met separately with Chase and 16 other banks in Hong Kong during May 2000 to review key loan terms, including the pricing (an unknown), amount (HK$3.3 billion), maturity (15 years), and covenants. In its meeting with Disney, the Chase team emphasized its flexibility on key strategic terms, its credentials as a leading syndication bank, and its knowledge of and relationship with the local market. As for pricing, Chase indicated that it would need an underwriting fee of between

EXHIBIT 20-6C

TOP ARRANGERS OF ASIAN PROJECT FINANCE LOANS IN 1999

Position	Arranger Name	Amount ($ millions)	Number of Deals
1	HSBC	$972.7	3
2	ABN AMRO Bank NV	716.4	3
3	ANZ Banking Group Ltd.	466.3	8
4	World Bank	444.1	5
5	JBIC	363.9	2
6	Sanwa Bank Ltd.	358.1	3
7	Industrial Development Bank of India	333.0	1
8	Chang Hwa Commercial Bank Ltd.	317.7	2
9	Japan Development Bank	317.5	2
10	Citigroup Inc.	280.7	4

Source: Euromoney's Project Finance, July 2000.

100 bp and 150 bp, and that the market would probably require interest rate spreads of 135 bp to 150 bp over HIBOR to accept the deal. Although the Chase team expected ultimately to bid to lose, they agreed the deal would be much more attractive if Disney chose to award a sole lead arranger mandate.

Chase revised its outlook on market pricing in the weeks after the initial meeting in Hong Kong for two reasons. First, spreads on syndicated loans in the local market were continuing to tighten as liquidity improved (see Exhibit 20-2). Second, a senior Hong Kong government official underscored the government's commitment to the project at the Asia Pacific Loan Market Association Conference. Seeing increased potential for a successful syndication, the Chase team began to revise its objective towards winning the mandate.

On May 25, Disney notified Chase and five other banks—HSBC, Bank of China, ABN Amro, Citibank, and Fuji Bank—that they had been short-listed for the mandate, and asked them to submit final proposals by July 19.

Preparing the Final Proposal

In preparing the final proposal, the Chase team had to assess the loan's credit risk, decide whether to underwrite the full amount, commit to an underwriting fee and interest rate spread, and develop a preliminary syndication strategy. Harris also wanted the team to come up with creative features, not mentioned by Disney, which could help them win the mandate. As an example, they envisioned splitting the revolving credit facility into two parts, a HK$250 million portion that would be available for construction cost overruns and a HK$750 million portion that would not be available until completion. While the "available" portion would carry a market-based commitment fee of 37.5 bp per annum, the unavailable portion would carry a discounted fee of 15 bp per annum. Harris felt that such leeway was possible given the loan's seniority and modest size relative to HKTP's total capital.

From a credit perspective, Disney's term sheet contained several aggressive elements, particularly the 15-year final maturity and a provision that allowed repayments to start as late as three years after opening. Most bank loans, especially loans in emerging markets, were fully repayable within three to five years, and Chase expected the market to be leery of the 15-year tenor. Other credit issues were Disney's desire to use operating cash flow for expansion (capital expenditures) and its unwillingness to subordinate management fees and royalties—both features were somewhat unusual for project loans. A final concern was the fact that the borrower's principal asset, usually viewed by lenders as their fallback collateral, was oceanfront land that would not exist for nearly two years. After careful analysis, including stress testing the financial implications, Chase decided these credit issues were adequately mitigated by the borrower's conservative capital structure and the Hong Kong government's commitment to the project. As a result, Chase resolved to show maximum flexibility by making its proposal as close as possible to Disney's original request, although it would include covenants requiring minimum debt service coverage ratios.

The next issue was the commitment to underwrite the full amount. Although a fully underwritten deal exposed the bank to greater risk, the team decided to seek senior management approval for a full underwriting as requested by Disney. Such a proposal would show Chase's support for the client, signal its confidence in the deal, and provide greater profit to the firm. It might also set Chase apart from other banks that were unwilling to underwrite the deal and increase the probability of winning a sole lead mandate.

Part of the internal approval process also centered on deciding how much credit exposure Chase wanted to hold on its books after general syndication. At Chase and other major syndication banks, management differentiated between underwriting risk (the risk that the market would not buy the deal from the underwriter) and credit risk (the risk that the borrower would not be able to service the debt). As a lead arranger, Chase's general policy was to hold 10% of the loan, a percentage that declined as loan size or risk increased. Yet at times, it had to hold larger shares to signal its confidence in a particular deal. In this case, Chase decided that a final hold position of HK$300 million, slightly less than 10%, was appropriate given the 15-year maturity.

In terms of pricing, the standard procedure was to benchmark the proposed deal against recent comparable transactions with adjustments for competitive dynamics and current market conditions; the use of comparable transactions required careful analysis because no two loans were exactly alike, especially project loans. The Chase team looked at a broad universe of syndicated loans going back over several years and selected the loans in Exhibit 20-7 as the primary "comps." Based on these loans, Chase proposed an initial spread of 100 bp over HIBOR, stepping up to 125 bp in year six and to 137.5 bp in years 11 to 15. Step-up pricing, a common feature on project loans, appealed to borrowers who focused on reducing expenses in the early years and often planned to refinance the debt before the step-ups took effect. It also appealed to lending banks, which viewed the increases as compensation for longer maturities and greater future uncertainty. With regard to the underwriting fee, they still thought a number between 100 bp and 150 bp was appropriate.[7] Harris said:

> If anything, we thought our fee might be on the high end, but we didn't feel bad about this for two reasons. First, we were not afraid to lose this deal on up-front pricing— we care about deal quality and profitability, not deal volume. Second, if properly marketed, borrowers viewed the up-front fees in terms of their annual cost, not the nominal first-year cost.

Having resolved some of the key credit and pricing issues, the team turned their attention to the syndication process. Based on previous experience, they knew that clients, as well as Chase's senior management, liked to get a sense of how the syndication might unfold. Toward that end, they included two possible syndication strategies in their presentation to Disney. (Exhibits 20-8a and 20-8b present these two strategies; Exhibit 20-8c presents a third strategy, but not one that was shown to Disney.) In all three cases, Chase would fully underwrite the deal.

Under the first option (Exhibit 20-8a), Chase would be the sole mandated lead arranger (shown as the coordinating arranger in the exhibit). It would invite four banks to act as sub-underwriters with lead arranger titles in exchange for commitments of HK$660 million. By sub-underwriting the deal, Chase could reduce its exposure from HK$3.3 billion to HK$660 million. The final allocations in the general syndication would be: Chase and the four lead arrangers at HK$300 million each, four arrangers at HK$250 million each, four co-arrangers at HK$150 each, and two lead managers at HK$100 million, for the required total of $3.3 billion. The advantages of this strategy were administrative simplicity—Disney had to deal with only one lead bank, it reduced underwriting risk for Chase, and possibly easier syndication was possible given the sub-underwriter support.

Under the second option (Exhibit 20-8b), Chase and two other banks would share a joint mandate and a joint underwriting commitment, but they would skip the sub-

---

[7] While the actual fee was included in the final proposal, it has been omitted here to preserve confidentiality.

EXHIBIT 20-7
SELECTED RECENT COMPARABLE TRANSACTIONS

Borrower	Hong Kong Quasi Sovereign Deals		Regional Project Deals		Recent Corporate Deal
	Airport Authority of Hong Kong	Mass Transit Railway Corp (MTRC)	Hutchinson Telephone Corp.	Asia Container Terminals	Cheung Kong Finance Co. Ltd.
Industry	Public Utility	Public Utility	Telecommunications	Shipping	Properties
Country	Hong Kong	Hong Kong	Hong Kong	Hong Kong	Hong Kong
Rating (S&P, Moody's)	Not rated	A/A3	Not rated	Not rated	A
Guarantor	—	—	—	—	Cheung Kong (Holdings) Ltd.
Purpose	General Corporate	Working Capital / Refinancing	Build-out Financing	Project Financing	General Corporate
Facility Type	Term Loan	Term Loan	Term Loan	Term Loan	Term Loan
Amount in Transaction Currency (US$ Equivalent)	HK$6,500MM (US$837MM)	HK$3,000MM (US$386MM)	HK$4,000MM (US$514MM)	HK$3,400MM (US$437MM)	HK$2,300MM (US$296MM)
Tenor	3-year bullet/ 5-year bullet	4-year bullet	5-year/7-year	10-year amortizing	5-year bullet
Undrawn Pricing (bp)	25.0	15.0 Year 1, 25.0 Thereafter	25.0	50.0	25.0
Drawn Pricing (bp)	HIBOR + 65.0 bp / LIBOR + 85.0 bp	HIBOR + 75.0 bp	HIBOR + 110.0 bp / HIBOR + 130.0 bp	HIBOR + 170.0 bp/ HIBOR + 195.0 bp	HIBOR + 58.5 bp
Upfront Fees (bp)	(U/W) 6.0/10.0 (Top Tier) 54.0/90.0	(Club members) 25.0	(U/W) 100 /100 (Top Tier) 50.0/75.0	(Top Tier) 70.0	(Top Tier) 32.5
All-in p.a. to Top Tier (bp)	HIBOR + 85.0 / HIBOR + 105.0	HIBOR + 81.2 bp (Club members)	HIBOR + 123.9 / HIBOR + 145.6	HIBOR + 177.8 bp	HIBOR + 65.0 bp

Launch Date	May 1999	September 1999	November 1999	September 1999	November 1999
Signed Date	July 1999	September 1999	March 2000	January 2000	December 1999
Lead arrangers	Chase (books), BOC (books), HSBC, ABN, and SCB	12 banks (self-arranged)	Chase (books), ABN (books)	ABN, BofA, DG Bank, SG, NAB, WestLB, Dresdner	BofA, BOC, CEF Capital, SG
Remarks	Transaction was over-subscribed and increased from HK$4,000. Borrower is owned by the HK government and was set up to build, operate and maintain HK's new Chek Lap Kok airport.	Borrower's self-arranged club deal includes ABN, BOTM, Chase, DKB, Fuji, HSBC, BOC, BNP, Citi, DG, Hang Seng and SCB. Borrower operates the territory's mass railway system. MTRC is wholly owned by the HK government.	Lead arrangers raised over HK$12,000MM for this nonrecourse financing build-out financing. Borrower is owned by Hutchison Whampoa, Motorola and NTTMobile Communications (NTT Do Co Mo).	Sponsors are New World Infrastructure Ltd., Hong Kong Land Holdings Ltd., Sung Hung Kai Properties Ltd., and Sea-Land Orient Terminals Ltd. Transaction will finance Borrowers' 41% share in construction of Container Terminal 9 in Tsing Yi, Hong Kong.	Fully underwritten by coordinating arrangers. The transaction is over-subscribed and increased from HK$2bn to HK$2.3bn. Borrower is Li Ka Shing's property holding company

Source: Loan Pricing Corporation.

EXHIBIT 20-8A

SYNDICATION STRATEGY #1: CHASE WITH SOLE MANDATE, WITH SUB-UNDERWRITING

Titles	# of banks	Initial Under-writing Amount	Sub-Underwriting		General Syndication		
			Individual Sub U/W Amount	Total Commitment	Individual Allocation	Total Amount	Percent of Total
Coordinating Arranger (Mandated Lead Arr.)	1	$3,300	$660	$ 660	$300	$ 300	9.1%
Lead arranger (Sub-Underwriters)	4		660	2,640	300	1,200	36.4
Arranger	4				250	1,000	30.3
Co-Arranger	4				150	600	18.2
Lead Manager	2				100	200	6.1
Totals	**15**	**$3,300**		**$3,300**		**$3,300**	**100.0%**

underwriting phase. The mandated banks (coordinating arrangers) would each under-write HK$1.1 billion of the total amount and split the underwriting fee three ways. The final allocations in the general syndication would be: Chase and the two other mandated banks at HK$300 million each, four arrangers at HK$250 million each, six co-arrangers at HK$150 million each, and five lead managers at HK$100 million each. This strategy required only two additional underwriting commitments instead of four prior to the general syndication, but it meant sharing league table status as well as giving up two-thirds of the underwriting fee.

The final option was a combination of the first two (Exhibit 20-8c). In it, Chase would be the sole mandated bank and would proceed directly to the general syndication, where the final allocations would be: Chase at HK$300 million, four arrangers at

EXHIBIT 20-8B

SYNDICATION STRATEGY #2: CHASE WITH JOINT MANDATE; NO SUB-UNDERWRITING

Titles	# of banks	Initial Under-writing Amount	Sub-Underwriting		General Syndication		
			Individual Sub U/W Amount	Total Commitment	Individual Allocation	Total Amount	Percent of Total
Coordinating Arranger (Mandated Lead Arr.)	3	$3,300			$300	$ 900	27.3%
Lead arranger (Sub-Underwriters)	0						
Arranger	4				250	1,000	30.3
Co-Arranger	6				150	900	27.3
Lead Manager	5				100	500	15.2
Totals	**18**	**$3,300**				**$3,300**	**100.0%**

EXHIBIT 20-8C

SYNDICATION STRATEGY #3: CHASE WITH SOLE MANDATE; NO SUB-UNDERWRITING

Titles	# of banks	Initial Under-writing Amount	Sub-Underwriting		General Syndication		
			Individual Sub U/W Amount	Total Commitment	Individual Allocation	Total Amount	Percent of Total
Coordinating Arranger (Mandated Lead Arr.)	1	$3,300			$300	$ 300	9.1%
Lead arranger (Sub-Underwriters)	0						
Arranger	4				250	1,000	30.3
Co-Arranger	8				150	1,200	36.4
Lead Manager	8				100	800	24.2
Totals	21	$3,300				$3,300	100.0%

Sources: Chase planning documents, Casewriter estimates.

HK$250 million each, eight co-arrangers at HK$150 million each, and eight lead managers at HK$100 million each. Relative to the other two strategies, this strategy would improve Chase's compensation and league table status, but would expose it to the greatest amount of credit and syndication risk and would result in the largest syndicate as measured by the number of participating banks.

After describing the possible syndication strategies, Chase analyzed the likelihood of successful syndication based on the terms of the transaction and their knowledge of the banking market. Vivek Chandiramani described the process:

> The key to success in this business is being close to the market. This means being in touch with banks on a weekly, if not daily, basis. We started with a universe of approximately 90 banks and created a target lender list that might be interested in this deal. We then partitioned the target list into commitment size categories and assigned participation probabilities for each category. This process gives us a sense of liquidity and an indication of whether the deal will clear the market. Based on our analysis for the Disney deal, we expected it would be oversubscribed by 57%. This kind of analysis illustrates our closeness to the market and our confidence in the deal (see Exhibit 20-9).

Per Disney's request, Chase submitted its final proposal on July 19.

ARRANGING THE LOAN

After several conversations about Chase's proposal and agreements to amend certain aspects, Disney verbally awarded the sole mandate to Chase on August 10. Jeff Speed said: "We chose Chase because its pricing was competitive, it agreed to underwrite the full amount, and they showed a high degree of flexibility on structuring, particularly their willingness to permit ongoing capital expenditures without burdensome covenants."

As the next step in the process, Disney proposed a meeting in which they would execute a commitment letter with final terms, discuss the syndication strategy in greater

EXHIBIT 20-9

LIKELY PARTICIPATION IN THE HONG KONG DISNEYLAND LOAN

Tier 1: Coordinating Arrangers (@ HK$300MM)		Tier 2: Arrangers (@ HK$250MM)		Tier 3: Co-Arrangers (@ HK$150MM)		Tier 4: Lead Managers (@ HK$100MM)	
Name	Commit.	Name	Commit.	Name	Commit.	Name	Commit.
1 Chase	$300	1 ABN AMRO	$250	1 BBVA	$150	1 Banco Di Napoli	$100
2 Other Arranger	300	2 Banca Commerciale Italiana	250	2 Banca Di Roma	150	2 Bank Austria	100
		3 Banco Tai Fung (Macau)	250	3 Bank Brussels Lambert	150	3 Bank Boston	100
		4 Bank of America	250	4 Bank of Communications	150	4 Bank of Montreal	100
		5 Bank of China Macau Branch	250	5 Bank of East Asia	150	5 Bank of Nova Scotia	100
		6 Bayerische Landesbank	250	6 BNL	150	6 Bank One	100
		7 BOTM	250	7 Chekiang First Bank	150	7 CBA	100
		8 China Construction Bank	250	8 Dah Sing Bank	150	8 Emirates Bank	100
		9 Citibank	250	9 Dao Heng Bank	150	9 International Commercial Bank of China	100
		10 Commerzbank	250	10 Development Bank of Singapore	150	10 Keppel Tat Lee	100
		11 Credit Agricole Indosuez	250	11 DG Bank	150	11 Monte Dei Paschi	100
		12 Credit Lyonnais	250	12 DKB	150	12 Norinchukin Bank	100
		13 Den Danske	250	13 Erste Bank	150	13 OCBC	100
		14 Deutsche Bank	250	14 Fortis	150	14 OUB	100
		15 Dresdner	250	15 Hang Seng Bank	150	15 Taiwan Cooperative Bank	100
		16 Fuji Bank	250	16 IBA	150	16 United World Chinese Commercial Bank	100
		17 HSBC	250	17 IBJ	150	17 UOB	100
		18 Industrial and Commercial Bank of China	250	18 Liu Chong Hing Bank	150	18 Westpac	100
		19 ING	250	19 Sakura Bank	150		
		20 KBC Bank	250	20 Sanwa	150		
		21 Kincheng Banking Corp.	250	21 Shanghai Commercial Bank	150		
		22 Kwangtung Provincial Bank	250	22 Sin Hua Bank	150		
		23 Nanyang Commercial Bank, Ltd.	250	23 Sumitomo Bank	150		
		24 Natexis-BFCE	250	24 Unicredito Italiano	150		
		25 National Australia Bank	250	25 United Chinese Bank	150		
		26 Rabobank	250	26 Wing Hang Bank	150		
		27 Standard Chartered	250	27 Wing Lung Bank	150		
		28 Union Bank of Hong Kong	250				
		29 West LB	250				
		30 Yien Yieh Commercial Bank	250				
Total	$600	Total	$7,500	Total	$4,050	Total	$1,800
Prob(Participation)	100%		40%		30%		20%
Commitments	**$600**		**$3,000**		**$1,215**		**$360**

Total Commitments $5,175

% Oversubscribed 57% over the needed HK$3,300 million

Source: Company documents.

detail, and map out a syndication timetable. Agreeing on the content of the formal commitment letter would invariably require some negotiation. From experience, Chase knew their standard "market flex" provision was problematic for certain borrowers. The standard clause read:

> Chase shall be entitled, after consultation with Disney and the Borrower, to change the structure, terms, amount, or pricing of the Facility if the syndication has not been completed due to a change in the Hong Kong Dollar market and if Chase determines, after consultation with Disney and the Borrower, that such changes are advisable to ensure a successful syndication of the Facility.

Whereas borrowers disliked the provision, Chandiramani argued for its inclusion:

> Chase was the pioneer in the use of market flex terms. It makes good business sense to include this clause, even though our competitors sometimes use it against us in competitive mandates, because things can change between the time you sign a deal and the time you try to close it. Unlike the "material adverse effect" (MAE) or "material adverse change" (MAC) clauses, which allow us to pull a commitment, the market flex provision is not an out. Instead, it provides room to maneuver, to adjust key terms as with a bond issue. But to date, we have never invoked the market flex clause in Asia. Nor did we invoke the MAC clause, even during the Asian financial crisis of 1997 to 1999, and we tell this to clients.

Once they had agreed on the final terms and signed the commitment letter, Chase had to select a syndication strategy. Because Chase had committed to a fully underwritten deal, the syndication strategy was technically their decision alone. However, for relationship reasons, Chase knew it was important to accommodate Disney's priorities as much as possible, and these favored a sub-underwriting approach. Disney requested that some of the short-list banks and some other strong banks that did not participate in the bidding have senior status. Disney also wanted to keep the final bank group down to a manageable size. Jeff Speed said:

> In structuring the syndicate, we saw a tradeoff. On the one hand, a larger syndicate generates more competition for the deal and often results in better execution. The downside, however, is that we have to share confidential information with more people. In addition, it's harder to reach agreement with a larger group of banks. Because we often need to amend the project documents, a process that requires consent from banks holding at least 60% of the loan (a group known as the "Instructing Banks"), we wanted the lead banks to hold larger shares.

With Disney's preferences in mind, the Chase team had to decide whether to pursue a sub-underwriting and, if so, whom to invite as potential sub-underwriters. Should they target local banks for participation? While they did not want the syndicate to get too big and, correspondingly let the commitments get too small, they did want to give interested banks a chance to participate. Participation by Hong Kong banks, particularly at the sub-underwriter level, would bring greater political support for the deal and send stronger signals to foreign and smaller local banks about deal quality. Another reason to include local banks is that they would find it easier to fund a Hong Kong dollar loan given their ability to raise Hong Kong dollar deposits (i.e., to eliminate currency risk).

The Chase team also had to decide how much to pay in fees. According to their current thinking, they were leaning towards a sub-underwriting with fees of 95 bp for sub-underwriting commitments of HK$600 million. Of this amount, 25 bp would be on the sub-underwriting amount and 70 bp would be the closing fee on the final hold

EXHIBIT 20-10A

DESCRIPTION OF DEAL ECONOMICS SHOWN IN EXHIBIT 20-10B

Calculation of Final Hold Positions (top panel)

Number of Banks: Describes the number of banks at each syndicate tier. Chase, as the mandated Lead arranger, has agreed to fully underwrite the HK$3.3 billion loan. In this scenario, there are four other banks with Lead arranger titles with approved sub-underwriting commitments (see below). The Arrangers, Co-Arrangers, and Lead Managers represent three descending levels of participation amounts in the general syndication.

Initial Underwriting: First stage of the syndication. Commitments held by the bank(s) initially responsible for underwriting the loan. Here, Chase underwrites the full loan amount.

Sub-Underwriting (optional): An intermediate stage of syndication in which the sole underwriter(s) subdivides the full underwriting amount among a small group of banks. In Exhibit 20-10b, the four Lead arrangers each agree to sub-underwrite $660 million. The exhibit shows Chase's sub-underwriting commitment, and the total amount committed by all of the Lead arrangers collectively.

General Syndication: The final stage in which the underwriter(s) obtains commitments from additional banks in order to reduce the sub-underwriting exposures to final hold positions. The six columns show, in order from left to right:

- **Invitation Amount per bank:** Chase invites the general syndication banks to offer loan commitments in defined ranges, from a maximum of HK$250 million down to a minimum of HK$100 million. The general syndication banks must get credit approval for a specific amount and submit formal commitment letters to Chase requesting participation at a specific level.

- **Total Commitment for all banks:** Equals the number of banks times the Invitation Amount for general syndication banks; and the number of banks times the sub-underwriting commitment for Chase and the other sub-underwriters (Lead arrangers).

- **Percent Scaled Back:** In the event a deal is oversubscribed, the commitment submitted or offered by any bank may be reduced or "scaled-back" to reach the target loan amount. In this case, the HK$660 million sub-underwriter commitments are scaled back to HK$300 million final hold positions. Other banks get the requested amounts with no scale back.

- **Final Tier Allocation:** The per bank commitment amount that has been accepted for each tier in the syndicate. This amount will be reflected in the final loan documentation and is the amount on which closing fees are calculated. The final allocation equals (1-scaleback percentage) times the total commitment amount.

- **Total Allocation:** This column shows the final allocations for each tier in the syndicate.

- **Allocation per Bank:** The final allocations expressed in $US.

Calculation of Fee Income (middle panel)

- **Fees:** This example assumes that Chase charges the borrower an underwriting fee of 1.25% (total fees equal the product of the 125 bp underwriting fee times the $3.3 billion loan amount or HK$41.25 million) and allocates fees to syndicate members based on their commitment levels. As the underwriter, Chase keeps 30 bp and gives 95 bp to the sub-underwriters (including itself). The sub-underwriters keep 25 bp on their sub-underwriting allocation and give 70 bp for top-tier (arranger) commitments.

(Continued)

EXHIBIT 20-10A *(Continued)*

Calculation of Fee Income (middle panel, continued)

- **Underwriter spread:** This amount is Chase's primary compensation for acting as the sole mandated bank and underwriter. The HK$9.9 million equals the 30 bp difference between the 125 bp underwriting fee Chase receives from the borrower and the 95 bp fee it pays the sub-underwriters (25 bp sub-underwriter fee plus 70 bp closing fee), times the total loan amount (HK$3.3 billion).
- **Sub-underwriter spread:** The HK$8.25 million equals the 25 bp difference between the 95 bp sub-underwriter fee and the 70 bp closing fee paid to top-tier (arranger) banks in the general syndication, times the full loan amount of HK$3.3 billion. The five sub-underwriters (including Chase) split this fee equally providing HK$1,650 to each bank. Note: if market conditions require closing fees greater than 70 bp, then the sub-underwriter spread will be lower.
- **Closing Fee Income:** Equals the amount received by each bank based on its final commitment amount. See below for further information.
- **Pool Income:** See below.
- **Total Income per Bank (HK$000):** Equals the sum of the underwriter spread, sub-underwriter spread, closing fee income, and pool income.
- **Total Income per Bank (US$000):** Total income per bank in $US.
- **Total Income for All Banks (HK$000):** Total income across all banks in $HK.
- **Total Income for All Banks (US$000):** Total income across all banks in $US.

Calculation of Pool Income (bottom panel)

Chase agrees with the sub-underwriters to share equally in a pool consisting of any difference between the total closing fees available to be paid to member banks and the actual amount of closing fees paid member banks.

- **General Syndication Closing Fees:** The fees offered to each syndicate tier.
- **Total Available Closing Fee Income:** Equals the arranger fee of 70 bp times the full loan amount of $3.3 billion.
- **Total Payable Closing Fee Income:** Equals the actual fees paid to each tier times the final allocation amounts for that tier. All banks earn the arranger fee or less in the general syndication.
- **Pool Income:** The difference between the Total Available Fee Income and the Total Payable Fee Income is split equally among the seven sub-underwriters (HK$1.0 million divided by five banks equals HK$200,000 per bank).

Source: Casewriter.

amount. For the other tiers, they would offer up-front fees of 70 bp for arranger commitments of HK$250 million, 60 bp for co-arranger commitments of HK$150 million, and 50 bp for lead manager commitments of HK$75 million to HK$100 million. From experience, they knew that banks would need to make at least US$50,000 to cover the cost of analyzing and approving a project loan. Because the fees were paid on final allocations, Chase knew there might be a problem if the deal were substantially oversubscribed and the lower tiers got scaled back significantly.

EXHIBIT 20-10B

CALCULATION OF FEES FOR A SOLE-MANDATED DEAL WITH SUB-UNDERWRITING

Loan Amount ($HK million) = $3,300   *assumed fee*
Underwriting Fee = 1.25%
Sub-Underwriting Fee = 0.25%
Top-Tier (Arranger) Fee = 0.70%

Mandate = Sole
Sub-Underwriting = Yes
$HK/$US Exchange Rate = 7.80
Total Underwriting Fees ($HK millions) = $41.25

	Number of Banks	Initial Underwriting		Sub-Underwriting		General Syndication					
		Commitment Amount (HK$MM)	Total Commitment (HK$MM)	Allocation (HK$MM)	Invitation Amount (HK$MM)	Total Commitment (HK$MM)	Percent Scaled Back	Final Allocation (HK$MM)	Total Allocation (HK$MM)	Allocation per Bank (US$MM)
Chase	1	$3,300	$3,300	$ 660		$ 660	54.5%	$ 300.0	$ 300.0	$38.5
# Other Mandated Banks	0	$ 0	$ 0	$ 0		$ 0	0.0%	$ 0.0	$ 0.0	$ 0.0
Lead Arrangers (Sub U/W)	4					$2,640	54.5%	$ 300.0	$1,200.0	$38.5
Arrangers	4				$250	$1,000	0.0%	$ 250.0	$1,000.0	$32.1
Co-Arrangers	4				$150	$ 600	0.0%	$ 150.0	$ 600.0	$19.2
Lead Managers	2				$100	$ 200	0.0%	$ 100.0	$ 200.0	$12.8
Total	**15**		**$3,300**	**$3,300**		**$5,100**			**$3,300.0**	

Per Bank Income (HK$000)							Total Per Bank		Total for All Banks	
	Underwriting Fees	Closing Fees	Underwriter Spread	Sub-U/W Spread	Closing Fee Income	Pool Income	(HK$000)	(US$000)	(HK$000)	(US$000)
Chase	0.30%	0.70%	$9,900	$1,650	$2,100	$200	$13,850	$ 1,776	$13,850	$1,776
# Other Mandated Banks			$ 0	$ 0	$ 0	$ 0	$ 0	$ 0	$ 0	$ 0
Lead Arrangers (Sub U/W)	0.25%	0.70%		$1,650	$2,100	$200	$ 3,950	$ 506	$15,800	$2,026
Arrangers		0.70%			$1,750		$ 1,750	$ 224	$ 7,000	$ 897
Co-Arrangers		0.60%			$ 900		$ 900	$ 115	$ 3,600	$ 462
Lead Managers		0.50%			$ 500		$ 500	$ 64	$ 1,000	$ 128
Total Fees									**$41,250**	**$5,288**

(Continued)

EXHIBIT 20-10B (Continued)

Calculation of Pool Income	General Syndication Closing Fees	Final Allocation (HK$MM)	Closing Fees per Bank (HK$000)	Total Closing Fees All Banks (HK$000)
Total Closing Fee Income Available	0.70%	$3,300		$23,100
Total Closing Fee Income Payable				
Chase	0.70%	$300.0	$ 2,100	$ 2,100
Other Mandated Banks			$ 0	$ 0
Lead Arrangers (Sub U/W)	0.70%	$300.0	$ 2,100	$ 8,400
Arrangers	0.70%	$250.0	$ 1,750	$ 7,000
Co-Arrangers	0.60%	$150.0	$ 900	$ 3,600
Lead Managers	0.50%	$100.0	$ 500	$ 1,000
				$ 22,100
	Pool Income (= Total Available – Total Payable)			**$ 1,000**

Source: Casewriter.

Through an iterative process, the team had to design a combination of fees and commitment tiers that would not only garner enough commitments, but also leave adequate compensation for Chase's work as the lead arranger. Moreover, it had to provide adequate compensation for member banks commensurate with their exposure. (Exhibit 20-10a describes the calculation of deal fees as presented in Exhibit 20-10b. The latter exhibit shows the economics for a sole-mandated deal with sub-underwriting and a 125 bp underwriting fee, the midpoint of the 100 bp to 150 bp range Chase had quoted Disney. This syndicate strategy appears in Exhibit 20-8a.)

As the team worked, they were mindful of Chase's long-term strategic interest as a leader in the field. According to Harris:

> Chase takes its relationships with investor banks very seriously. We don't simply view them as "stuffee" banks, but rather partner investors with whom a close relationship built on trust is critical. While we could often keep a larger slice of the pie, we don't want to leave our investors feeling like we had gouged them on fees or denied them an opportunity to acquire a meaningful earning asset.

APPENDIX 20-1

BACKGROUND ON SYNDICATED BANK LENDING

According to Capital Data's (now Dealogic) LoanWare database, the global syndicated loan market grew from U.S.$413 billion in 1990 to U.S.$2,195 billion in 2000, making it one of the largest sources of capital in the world. The process of syndication unites a group of banks under a common set of documents for the purpose of providing credit to a borrower. The member banks share funding, repayments, and fees on a pro rata basis according to their original commitments. Usually, one bank acts as the *administrative agent* for the syndicate, keeping track of borrowings and repayments as well as serving as the clearinghouse for cash flows.

Lender compensation takes three forms. At the execution of loan documents, or *closing*, the lenders receive *closing* or *up-front* fees designed to compensate them for due diligence and credit approval. Closing fees typically range from 20 to 200 basis points (bp), with larger and/or riskier transactions commanding higher fees. After closing, borrowers pay *commitment fees* on any loan amount that was committed, but undrawn, plus interest on the amount that was drawn. Commitment fees are typically less than 50 bp per year. The loan's interest rate, at least for U.S.-dollar-denominated loans, is set in terms of a spread over published interbank rates such as six-month LIBOR (London Inter-Bank Offered Rate). For loans denominated in other currencies, bankers sometimes use local interest rates. For example, H.K. dollar loans are often based on the Hong Kong Inter-Bank Offered Rate (HIBOR). In either case, the loan rate varies over time as the benchmark rate changes, even though the loan spread remains constant.

While the majority of banks operate primarily as lenders, an increasing number of global banks are focusing on the attractive fees and higher returns on capital that come from leading the syndication process. This process consists of the following sequential events, and usually takes from one to three months to complete. First, a prospective borrower selects a *lead arranger* to advise and manage the syndication. In most cases, the *mandate* is awarded based on competitive bidding among the borrower's principal relationship banks or other banks with relevant expertise. At times, borrowers ask two or more banks to share the lead mandate (*sole* vs. *joint mandates*) to maximize the chance of a successful syndication or to reward more than one bank with lead status and compensation.

When funding certainty is critical, borrowers request *fully underwritten* bids, meaning the lead arranger (or lead arrangers) commits to provide the full amount on specific terms and pricing. The alternative is a *best efforts* fund raising in which the lead arranger agrees to underwrite less than 100% of the loan (typically the amount it is prepared to hold on its own balance sheet after general syndication) and attempts to place the remainder in the bank market. The fees and inherent risks differ between these two kinds of deals. In a best efforts deal (also known as an *arrangement*), the borrower pays the lead arranger an arrangement fee for its services and pays other lenders closing fees for their commitments. Thus, the borrower takes the risk that the market does not accept the deal and that it might have to pay higher fees or spreads to entice greater participation. In an underwritten deal, the borrower pays a single up-front fee to the lead arranger/underwriter, which retains some as compensation for its services and uses the rest as closing fees for banks participating in the syndication. Although underwritten deals can get funded faster, the underwriting fee is generally higher than the up-front fees in a best efforts deal because the underwriter faces greater credit and syndication risks.

After awarding the mandate, the borrower and lead arranger execute a *commitment letter* that confirms the amount and terms of the financing, and specifies the arranger's duties and compensation. The lead arranger then engages legal counsel to prepare an initial set of loan documents. At that point, the lead arranger and borrower usually agree on one of two basic syndication strategies: a single-stage general syndication or a two-stage syndication with sub-underwriting prior to general syndication. In a deal with sub-underwriting, the lead arranger and a small group of banks underwrite the full amount before offering participations to a broader group of banks. The two-stage process is a way to reduce the lead arranger's overall exposure more quickly and to broaden support for a deal.

The final step, known as *general syndication*, serves to distribute the loan to a group of invited banks that is large enough to commit the desired amount, but not so large as to create unattractively small loan shares or an unwieldy number of banks. Creating a supportive and cooperative syndicate facilitates making changes to loan documentation when necessary, either because ex-

(Continued)

405

ceptions arise, as they invariably do during the life of a loan, or because financial problems create a need to restructure.

Prior to general syndication, the lead arranger structures the syndicate in tiers according to commitment amounts, sets closing fees for each tier, and identifies which banks to invite to participate. Each tier has a title based on the commitment amount. The most common titles are, in descending order of commitment amount: arranger, co-arranger, lead manager, and manager. The banks invited to participate are not necessarily the borrower's relationship banks, but rather banks with syndication relationships with the lead arranger. The lead arranger prepares and sends an information memorandum containing a description of the borrower and the transaction to each bank. The lead arranger then holds a bank meeting to address questions about the deal, announce closing fees, and establish a timetable for commitments and closing.

If the total commitments received equal the amount desired, the deal is said to be *fully subscribed*; if they exceed or fail to reach the target amount, the deal is said to be *oversubscribed* or *undersubscribed*, respectively. In either case, the lead arranger, often in consultation with the borrower, determines *final allocations*. The commitments embody credit approvals from each bank, and as such, the lead arranger cannot increase the amounts. However, the lead arranger has the right to scale back commitments at its discretion. Each bank's final hold position is a matter of internal policy and varies based on factors such as the size of the bank, its internal credit policies on exposure to the particular client, country, or industry, and specific loan terms. In a general syndication, final allocations serve to reduce the underwriter(s)' exposure to a desired final hold position.

Given this process, syndicated finance groups perform two key functions: *structuring*, which involves designing and negotiating deals with borrowers, and *distribution*, which involves selling the deal into the bank market. The two functions must work closely together throughout the process because the deal that is presented to the borrower (structuring) has to reflect terms that are acceptable to the market (distribution).

Competition among banks to lead syndicated financings created a need for performance measurement. In the United States, several financial publications compile rankings known as *league tables*, which track the leadership of syndicated loans. The market places the most importance on the lead arranger and *bookrunner* titles. Usually, the lead arranger would also take the bookrunner title, which, broadly speaking, refers to the activities in the later stages of the syndication process such as managing the prospective lenders through the credit approval process, setting the closing fees, and making the final allocations. These titles appear prominently on the cover of the information memorandum, in the financial press *tombstones* after closing, and in the lucite deal mementos each lender receives.

## 21

The International Investor: Islamic Finance and the Equate Project

In August 1994, Union Carbide Corporation and Petrochemical Industries Company (PIC) began building a $2 billion petrochemical plant in Kuwait known as Equate Petro-chemicals Company (Equate). They financed construction with a $450 million bridge loan but hoped to raise $1.2 billion of permanent debt financing backed by guarantees from the United States Export-Import Bank (U.S. Exim). Despite more than a year of negotiations, they still had not worked out a deal. Having become sufficiently frustrated with process, the sponsors began exploring alternative financing structures without export credit agency (ECA) involvement. Although they were closing in on a proposal, they needed more certain commitments from various lenders before they could openly change financing structures.

One aspect of the deal that would remain the same under either structure was the inclusion of a tranche of Islamic finance, that is, funds that were invested in accordance with Islamic *Shari'a* principles (Islamic law). The sponsors had awarded a mandate to underwrite the Islamic tranche to Kuwait Finance House (KFH), Kuwait's only Islamic bank, which, in turn, had come to The International Investor (TII), an Islamic invest-ment bank, for assistance in placing the Islamic tranche. TII's chairman, Adnan Al Bahar, had asked Sulaiman Al Qimlas, Salah Nafisi, and Yahya Malik, members of TII's Structured Finance Group, to prepare a final recommendation regarding TII's involve-ment in the deal. In particular, Al Bahar wanted to know whether the proposed *ijara* structure made sense and whether TII's *Shari'a* committee was likely to accept it. In addition, he wanted to discuss how much TII should commit to place knowing that TII would not commit if it did not have investors lined up for the full amount.

Research Associate Mathew M. Millett prepared this case under the supervision of Professor Benjamin C. Esty. This case was developed from published sources. HBS cases are developed solely as the basis for class discussion. Cases are not intended to serve as endorsements, sources of primary data, or illustrations of effective or ineffective management.

PETROCHEMICAL INDUSTRIES COMPANY, K.S.C.

The State of Kuwait established the Petrochemical Industries Company (PIC) in 1963 to manufacture petrochemical products, principally fertilizer, salt, and chlorine. Exhibit 21-1 provides financial information on PIC and its parent, Kuwait Petroleum Company (KPC). PIC's creation was an important part of the government's strategy to reduce its economic dependence on oil production and refining. Exhibit 21-2 provides economic data for Kuwait. In early 1990, PIC received approval from KPC to build a large petrochemical project, a project that was abruptly stopped when Iraq invaded Kuwait on August 2, 1990. When Iraqi president Saddam Hussein refused to withdraw from Kuwait, the U.S.-led coalition launched an air campaign known as Operation Desert Storm. After three weeks of bombing and a 100-hour ground war, the coalition liberated Kuwait on February 25, 1991.

The war took a heavy toll on Kuwaiti society and infrastructure: GDP fell by more than half, oil production essentially stopped, and many citizens fled the country, not to

EXHIBIT 21-1

PIC AND UNION CARBIDE 1995 FINANCIAL SUMMARY ($ IN MILLIONS)

	Kuwait Petroleum Company (KPC)	Petrochemical Industries Company (PIC)	Union Carbide Corporation
Balance Sheet Summary			
Assets			
Cash and marketable securities	$ 5,610	$ 52	$ 449
Other current assets	5,399	89	1,747
Other assets	16,651	338	4,509
Total Assets	$27,660	$427	$6,256
Debt			
Current debt	$ 0	$ 0	$ 38
Long-term debt	$ 0	0	1,285
Total Debt	0	$ 0	$1,323
Total Liabilities (non-debt)	$ 6,346	$ 82	$2,988
Total Shareholder's Equity	21,314	345	2,045
Income Statement Summary			
Net revenues	$16,179	$142	$5,888
Operating profit	3,654	59	1,348
Income tax[a]	0	0	380
Net income	2,721	60	915
Other Data			
Number of shares (millions)	N/A	N/A	158.40
Stock price on December 1, 1995	N/A	N/A	$38.75
S&P long-term credit rating	Not Rated	Not Rated	BBB/Baa2

[a] Kuwait has no income tax. However, companies are required to make a contribution to the Kuwait Foundation for the Advancement of Sciences (KFAS) equal to 4.5% of profit before tax. As a government-owned company, PIC did not make contributions to the KFAS.

Sources: Petrochemical Industries Company 1996 Annual Report, Kuwait Petroleum Company 1996 Annual Report (KD converted to U.S.$ at 0.298 KD/U.S.$ for both PIC and KPC), Union Carbide Corporation 1995 Annual Report, and Bloomberg.

EXHIBIT 21-2

KUWAIT ECONOMIC INDICATORS

	Real GDP (KD in billions)	Inflation (%)[a]	3-month Treasury Bill Rate (%)	Government Budget Surplus or (Deficit) (KD in billions)	Exchange Rate (KD/US$)	Oil Production (millions of barrels per day)	Oil Exports (as a % of total exports)	Population (millions)	Country Credit Rating[b]	Kuwaiti Market Capitalization (US$ in million)	Number of Listed Domestic Companies
1986	KD 8.41	1.0%	—	KD (651)	0.291X	1.46	94.3%	1.79	62.3	10,108	70
1987	8.08	0.6	3.98%	(1,263)	0.279	1.39	93.1	1.87	58.3	14,196	64
1988	8.36	1.5	7.07	N/A	0.279	1.52	94.8	1.96	59.1	11,836	65
1989	8.99	3.4	8.37	(1,096)	0.294	1.79	94.5	2.05	60.2	9,932	52
1990	5.85	5.0	—	—	0.293	2.04	80.3	2.14	60.8	—	—
1991	3.51	9.1	8.73	(745)	0.284	0.19	90.7	2.07	41.8	—	—
1992	6.14	(0.5)	8.72	(5,330)	0.293	1.06	90.7	1.42	47.4	—	—
1993	7.46	0.4	6.06	(1,783)	0.320	1.87	88.1	1.46	49.2	10,049	47
1994	7.76	2.5	7.23	(977)	0.298	2.07	91.0	1.62	53.3	10,517	48
1995	7.95	2.7	7.07	(656)	0.298	2.06	88.0	1.69	53.4	13,623	52

[a] Based on the Consumer Price Index.

[b] Institutional Investor Country Credit Ratings were based on a survey of 75 to 100 international banks. Bankers were asked to grade each country on a scale of 0 to 100, with 100 representing the least chance of default. In 1995, three other Middle Eastern countries had better credit ratings than Kuwait: United Arab Emirates (60.8), Saudi Arabia (55.3), and Qatar (53.6). The United States had a credit rating of 90.7, which was fourth best in the world following Switzerland (92.2), Japan (91.6), and Germany (90.9).

Sources: Economist Intelligence Unit, *Country Reports*; International Monetary Fund, *International Financial Statistics*; Central Bank of Kuwait; The Institutional Investor, *Country Credit Ratings*; and International Finance Corporation, *Emerging Stock Markets Factbook,* 1997 and 1996, Reuters, Moneyclips, and Xinhua Overseas News Service.

Origins of GDP (% of total)	1986	1989	1994
Hydrocarbons sector	36.7%	40.9%	43.4%
Manufacturing	9.2	14.4	8.6
Transport and communications	5.4	4.0	3.5
Wholesale and retail trade	7.8	7.3	4.8
Real estate, financial, and business services	4.7	2.4	11.1
Other	36.2	31.0	28.6
Total	100.0%	100.0%	100.0%

Source: The Economist Intelligence Unit, *Country Reports for Kuwait.*

mention the extensive loss of life. What emerged from this devastation was a sense of nationalism, a commitment to rebuild as quickly as possible, and a deep sense of gratitude toward the coalition forces, especially President George Bush and the United States. To finance reconstruction, estimated to cost as much as $20 billion,[1] the Kuwaiti government issued a five-year, $5.5 billion bond priced at 50 basis points (bp) over LIBOR.[2] The Kuwaiti government also adopted a policy of developing political and commercial ties with coalition countries as a way of expressing gratitude and ensuring future domestic security.

Although Kuwait's economy recovered quite quickly, several problems remained. First, the government was running a deficit due to reconstruction costs and generous social welfare programs—the government had a history of extensive involvement in the private sector. For example, following the Suq al Manakh (stock market) crash of 1982, the government bought many private companies to prop up the ailing economy. More recently, after the Gulf War, the government purchased almost $20 billion of commercial bank loans to prop up the ailing banking system.[3]

A second problem was the country's continued dependence on oil. Following the war, the government reiterated its goal of diversifying the country's economic base. PIC, as a government-owned entity, implemented this policy by altering its plans for the new petrochemical project. Instead of acting alone, PIC established a joint venture with Union Carbide in July 1993.[4] PIC chose Union Carbide as a partner because it could provide state-of-the-art technology, access to foreign markets, and training for Kuwaiti personnel.

UNION CARBIDE CORPORATION

Union Carbide Corporation was one of the world's largest basic chemicals companies with operations in 40 countries and more than 11,500 employees in 1995 (see Exhibit 21-1 for financial information).[5] The company had two main business units: Basic Chemicals & Polymers (BC&P) and Specialties & Intermediates (S&I). The BC&P unit specialized in the conversion of hydrocarbon feedstocks (petroleum gas and naphtha) into polyethylene, ethylene, ethylene oxide, and ethylene glycol for sale to third parties and use by the S&I unit. The S&I unit took basic and intermediate chemicals and converted them into chemical and polymer products for industrial customers. The unit also licensed proprietary process technologies such as the Unipol® process—the leading technology for producing polyethylene.

Union Carbide actively developed joint ventures in key overseas markets where it could use its proprietary technologies and could source low-cost inputs for its S&I division. It had joint ventures in France, Italy, South Korea, and Canada that generated nearly $2 billion in revenues and $200 million in net income for Union Carbide in 1995.[6]

[1] Kevin Muehring, "Kuwait's Royal Refinancing Mess," *The Institutional Investor*, July 1991, p. 27.

[2] "Kuwait Repays Only Sovereign-borrowing," *Agence France Presse*, December 12, 1996, and Mariam Isa, "Kuwait Budget Gap Likely to Shrink—Central Bank," *Reuters World Service*, June 10, 1994.

[3] Pierre Tran, "Kuwait Body Calls for Reform of Investment Office," *The Reuter Library Report*, June 29, 1993.

[4] "Carbide Partner PIC Will Tap Loan," *The Arab Times*, July 18, 1994.

[5] Union Carbide Corporation 1995 Annual Report, p. 1.

[6] Calculated from data in Union Carbide Corporation's 1996 Annual Report, p. 16.

EQUATE PETROCHEMICAL COMPANY K.S.C.

PIC and Union Carbide officially formed Equate in July 1995, more than two years after signing their initial agreement.[7] They chose the name "Equate" based on the concept "Ethylene Products from Kuwait" (*Ethylene-Kuwait*). The letters E and Q also stood for *Excellent Quality*. Under the agreement, Equate would finance, construct, and operate the petrochemical plant.

The project consisted of three separate plants—one each for producing ethylene, polyethylene, and ethylene glycol—built in the Shuaiba Industrial Area near Kuwait City. Exhibit 21-3 provides an overview of the project. The first plant, an ethylene cracker, would process ethane gas fuel from a nearby PIC plant into 650,000 metric tons per year (MTY) of ethylene using known technology.[8] The Kuwaiti government guaranteed Equate's feedstock supply, while KPC agreed to subsidize its price in the early years.[9] The polyethylene and ethylene glycol plants would then use the ethylene as an input to their respective production processes. The polyethylene plant would produce 450,000 MTY of polyethylene, the most widely used plastic in the world, utilizing Union Carbide's UNIPOL® process technology. The final plant would produce 340,000 MTY of ethylene glycol, used in the production of polyester fiber, automotive antifreeze, and engine coolants, through Union Carbide's Meteor™ process technology.[10]

Each plant had its own engineering, procurement, and construction (EPC) contractor. Brown & Root of the United States, Snamprogetti of Italy, and Foster Wheeler Italiana (the Italian subsidiary of Foster Wheeler Inc., U.S.A.) would serve as the EPC contractors for the ethylene cracker, polyethylene, and ethylene glycol plants, respectively.[11] All three companies had significant construction and management experience with Middle Eastern projects. The contractors signed lump-sum, turnkey contracts requiring them to deliver fully operational plants for a set price on a given date.[12] Typically, lump-sum contracts included bonuses for early completion and penalties for late completion. PIC and Union Carbide hired Fluor Daniel, a well-known international contractor, to manage the entire project.[13] Fluor Daniel would be responsible for integrating the various facilities as well as constructing necessary utilities and related infrastructure. If built according to specification, the plants would meet the sponsors' health, safety, and environmental regulations, whichever was stricter, and fully comply with all Kuwaiti environmental regulations.

The sponsors began construction in August 1994, financed through a combination of equity and debt from a $450 million bridge loan.[14] At the time, they estimated that

[7] "Carbide Partner PIC Will Tap Loan," *The Arab Times*, July 18, 1994, and Union Carbide Corporation 1995 Annual Report, p. 15.

[8] PIC ethane supply cited in "PIC: Pointing the Way," *Middle East Economic Digest*, February 25, 1994, and "Expansion Is the Aim," *The Financial Times*, December 12, 1996, p. 3. Ethylene, polyethylene, and ethylene glycol production from Union Carbide Corporation 1995 Annual Report, p. 15.

[9] Guarantee cited in Toby Ash, "Kuwait: Bank Consortium Wins Loan Mandate," *Middle East Economic Digest*, February 9, 1996, p. 5. The subsidized feedstock prices cited in "Equate Kick-Starts New Era in Kuwaiti Industry," *Middle East Economic Digest*, December 5, 1997, p. 6.

[10] Union Carbide's technology used by Equate's plants cited in "Equate: The Right Combination," *European Chemical News*, November 24, 1997, pp. 19–20.

[11] Capital Data, Ltd.'s ProjectWare database (deal reference #271).

[12] Marilyn Radler, "Worldwide Construction Update: Petrochemicals," *Oil & Gas Journal*, September 30, 1996, p. 67.

[13] Capital Data, Ltd.'s ProjectWare database (deal reference #271).

[14] Capital Data, Ltd.'s ProjectWare database describes the $450 million bridge facility (deal reference #271). See also "Ex-Im Bank Loses in Kuwait," *Project & Trade Finance*, March 1996.

EXHIBIT 21-3

PROJECT OVERVIEW

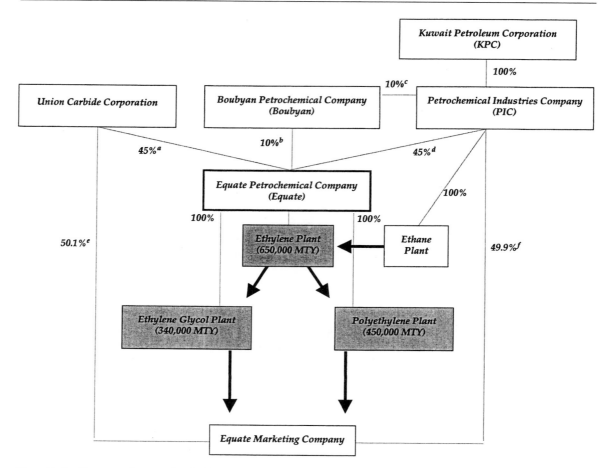

Notes: Dashed lines signify ownership; bold solid lines indicate product flow.

MTY is metric tons per year. A metric ton equals 1,000 kilograms (kg), or approximately 2,200 pounds (lb.).

Sources:

[a] Union Carbide 1996 Annual Report, p. 17.

[b] Boubyan 1998 Annual Report, p. 15.

[c] PIC 1996 Annual Report, p. 9.

[d] PIC 1996 Annual Report, p. 8.

[e] Young, Ian and Natasha Alperowicz, "Mideast Builds Export Power," *Chemicalweek*, May 14, 1997, p. 23.

[f] PIC 1996 Annual Report, p. 8.

construction costs would total nearly $2 billion (see Exhibit 21-4). By late 1995, construction was well underway, and several of the most important pieces of equipment were in place. Nevertheless, much remained undone, and the sponsors needed to replace the bridge loan with more permanent financing.

The Market for Petrochemicals

The sponsors established Equate Marketing Company, a separately owned company based in Bahrain, to market the plants' output.[15] They estimated that Equate would sell 75% of its output in the Middle and Far East and the remaining 25% in Europe, virtually all of which would be in dollar-denominated transactions.[16] Union Carbide agreed to purchase a minimum level of output at market prices as a form of project support.[17]

Like any commodity market, petrochemical prices were determined by the interaction of supply and demand, yet complicated by the fact that it took several years to build a new plant with additional capacity. The petrochemical market could be very volatile in the short-run due to temporary supply and demand imbalances. (Exhibit 21-5a shows historical prices for Equate's major products.) Although current market conditions were favorable, industry analysts differed in their predictions for the future. One analyst said, "The next recession is a long way off because the economic cycle is on the upside."[18] Yet another analyst, making a concurrent forecast, predicted the opposite, "We believe the widely held view that ethylene prices will decline only a few cents per pound over the next several months and then firm again in 1996 is incorrect. In our view the ethylene market is once again over supplied and is likely to remain so through 1996."[19]

In the longer run, industry experts predicted that world demand for Equate's products would grow between 4% and 6% per year (see Exhibit 21-5b). Growing demand would necessitate as many as 25–40 new ethylene plants, assuming an average size of 500,000 MTY, and an equal number of polyethylene plants of somewhat smaller size.[20] Although experts expected ethylene capacity to keep pace with demand, they believed polyethylene and ethylene glycol demand would exceed capacity expansion, thereby causing utilization rates to rise. Of these new plans, Equate would be a low-cost producer because of its access to cheap ethane feedstocks. One analyst noted:

> The Middle East has a large advantage on feedstock costs, and when this is combined with leading-edge Western technology, the resulting plants are extremely competitive. As long as North American companies have proper financing, their projects in the Middle East are likely to be highly successful.[21]

[15] Ian Young and Natasha Alperowicz, "Mideast Builds Export Power," *Chemicalweek*, May 14, 1997.

[16] "Kuwait Inaugurates 2-billion Petrochemical Plant," *Deutsche Presse*, November 12, 1997.

[17] Toby Ash, "Kuwait: Bank Consortium Wins Loan Mandate," *Middle East Economic Digest*, February 9, 1996, p. 5.

[18] Anne K. Rhodes and David Knott, "Ethylene Capacity Tops 77 Million mty," *Oil & Gas Journal*, April 17, 1995, p. 37.

[19] "Ethylene: Large Inventories Loom," *Chemicalweek*, August 2, 1995, p. 29.

[20] "Ethylene Building through 2000," *Chemicalweek*, November 15, 1995, p. 28.

[21] John Hoffman, "Middle East Slated for Spate of New Petchem Plants," *Chemical Market Reporter*, November 24, 1997.

EXHIBIT 21-4

SOURCES AND USES OF CAPITAL[a]

	Amount ($ millions)	Percent of Total (%)
Uses of Capital		
Construction engineering, materials and equipment	$1,500[b]	75.9%
Capitalized interest, closing/financing costs, and other costs	155[b,c]	7.8
Licensed technology	200[b]	10.1
Preliminary operating expenses	120[b]	6.1
Total Uses of Capital	**$1,975**	**100.0%**
Sources of Capital		
Petrochemical Industries Company (PIC):		
Equity capital	$ 129[d]	6.5%
Subordinated debt	220[e]	11.1
Total PIC Contribution	$ 349	17.7%
Union Carbide Corporation:		
Equity capital	$ 129[f]	6.5%
Licensed technology and subordinated debt	220[g]	11.1
Total Union Carbide Contribution	$ 349	17.7%
Boubyan Petrochemical Company:		
Equity capital	$ 29[h]	1.5%
Subordinated debt	48[i]	2.4
Total Boubyan Contribution	$ 77	3.9%
Total shareholder funding	$ 775	39.2%
Term facilities (including Islamic tranche)	$1,200[j]	60.8%
Total Sources of Capital	**$1,975**	**100.0%**

[a] Based on published sources and casewriter calculations.

[b] "Carbide Partner PIC Will Tap Loan," *The Arab Times*, July 19, 1994.

[c] Other costs serve to balance the known sources of capital ($1,975) and the known uses of capital ($1,900).

[d] PIC 1996 Annual Report, p. 8. KD 38.7 million = $129 million.

[e] PIC 1996 Annual Report, p. 9.

[f] Assumes that Union Carbide provides equity capital in the same proportion (45%) as PIC.

[g] Assumes that Union Carbide provides technology licenses and subordinated debt in the same proportion (45%) as PIC provides subordinated debt. Peter Kemp, "Special Report: Petrochemicals," *Middle East Economic Digest*, April 26, 1996, p. 9 reported that "a large portion Union Carbide's share of subordinated debt is in the form of technology licenses."

[h] Boubyan 1998 Annual Report, p. 15. KD 8.6 million = $29 million.

[i] Boubyan 1998 Annual Report, p. 16.

[j] Toby Ash, "Kuwait: Bank Consortium Wins Loan Mandate," *Middle East Economic Digest*, February 9, 1996, p. 5.

EXHIBIT 21-5A

PETROCHEMICAL PRICES FOR 1990–1995 (EUROPEAN SPOT PRICES— U.S.$ PER METRIC TON, FOB)

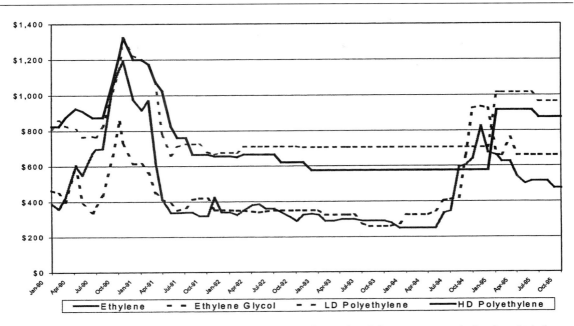

Notes: FOB means free on board. It is the price quoted to load a product on board the transporting vehicle, after which the buyer is responsible for all transportation costs. LD polyethylene means low-density polyethylene. HD polyethylene means high-density polyethylene.

Source: Chemicalweek, various issues, 1990–1995.

FINANCING THE PROJECT

Union Carbide and PIC resolved two major financing issues relatively quickly. Both wanted to use project finance but for different reasons. PIC wanted to facilitate the involvement of a foreign partner, even though it could have financed the deal on its own balance sheet. Union Carbide, on the other hand, wanted to use project finance to limit its Kuwaiti exposure. The sponsors also reached early agreement on the project's capital structure: 40% of the funding would come in the form of equity or other subordinated debt (see Exhibits 21-3 and 21-4). Of this amount, PIC would provide 45%, Union Carbide 45%, and Boubyan Petrochemical Company (Boubyan) 10%. (Boubyan was a publicly traded company formed in June 1995 to give Kuwaiti citizens a chance to invest in the project.)

A more difficult question was what kind of debt to use. The project's financial advisors, Chase Manhattan, JP Morgan, and Chemical Bank, insisted the debt would require completion guarantees from the sponsors, which they agreed to provide on a several, but not joint, basis.[22] The advisors also recommended ongoing guarantees from

[22] Union Carbide Corporation's 1995 Annual Report describes the several guarantees (p. 15).

EXHIBIT 21-5B

**PETROCHEMICAL DEMAND AND CAPACITY PROJECTIONS
(MILLIONS OF METRIC TONS PER YEAR)**

Petrochemical Product	1995	2000 (est.)	Compound Annual Growth Rate (%)
Ethylene			
Demand	71	89	4.6%
Capacity	80	104	5.4
Utilization Rate	89%	86%	
Ethylene Glycol			
Demand	7	10	6.0
Capacity	10	12	4.2
Utilization Rate	75%	82%	
Polyethylene			
Demand	37	50	6.0
Capacity	47	59	4.2
Utilization Rate	79%	84%	

Sources: Chemical Marketing Reporter, the United Nations' *Annual Review of the Chemical Industry*: 1994–1996, and casewriter estimates based on interviews with industry experts.

---

export credit agencies (ECAs), which were government-owned entities established to promote exports. ECA guarantees would protect lenders against both political (i.e., expropriation, currency inconvertibility, and war) and commercial risks of nonpayment for terms ranging from 7 to 12 years. Given the contractors' nationalities and the likely sources of plant equipment, the sponsors began negotiations with U.S. Exim, Hermes of Germany, and Sace of Italy.

Alongside the bank debt, PIC wanted to use a tranche of Islamic funds. The targeted amount of Islamic funds, though originally as high as $500 million, had been reduced to somewhere between $100 and $300 million. PIC had several reasons for wanting to use Islamic funds. First and foremost, it would give the sponsors an alternative source of funds, albeit a relatively small one given the fact that Islamic financial institutions held only $166 billion of assets in 1995.[23] At the same time, to quote a banker who worked on the project, the deal's "optics" were important. The project was in an Islamic country with a government-owned entity as one of the sponsors.

Although Islamic financial structures had existed for many years, there were few precedents for integrating Islamic and conventional funds in a single, project-financed deal. In fact, the first major co-financing was the $1.8 billion Hub River Power project in Pakistan.[24] This project used a $92 million *istisna'* (a contract commissioning and paying for the production of a specific good) during the construction phase.[25] When asked why they decided to use the *istisna'*, a banker replied, "The Islamic facility was available quickly . . . it was competitively priced and was responsive to the project's fi-

[23] International Association of Islamic Banks, *Directory of Islamic Banks and Financial Institutions*, 1997, p. 1, and Colin Barraclough, "Tough Choices for Islamic Banks," *Institutional Investor*, July 1995, p. 141.

[24] "Project Financing: Infrastructure Offers Opportunities to Combine Conventional and Islamic Finance," *Middle East Executive Reports*, July 1998, p. 7.

[25] Sara Khalili, "Unlocking Islamic Finance," *Infrastructure Finance*, April 1997, p. 19.

nancing needs."[26] Unfortunately, and somewhat unfairly, this deal tarnished co-financing as a financial structure because the closing was delayed for more than four years for political reasons.[27] Nevertheless, *Euromoney* named it "Deal of the Year" in 1994, in part because it proved the feasibility of co-financing as a financial structure.

Nevertheless, PIC wanted to incorporate Islamic funds and invited several institutions, including TII, to submit proposals to underwrite the Islamic tranche. The sponsors awarded the mandate to KFH, TII's larger and older rival, in late 1993. (Exhibits 21-6, 21-7a, and 21-7b provide KFH's financial statements.) Shortly thereafter, KFH approached TII for assistance in placing the Islamic tranche.

The International Investor (TII)

Adnan Al Bahar founded The International Investor (TII) in 1992 after spending ten years at KFH. The company's name embodied his vision of creating a financial in-

EXHIBIT 21-6

KUWAIT FINANCE HOUSE MATURITIES OF ASSETS, LIABILITIES, AND SHAREHOLDERS' FUNDS (KD IN THOUSANDS)

December 31, 1995	Total	Maturing Within One Year	Maturing After One Year
Assets			
Cash	KD 71,220	KD 71,220	KD 0
Receivables	729,602	474,574	255,028
Leased assets	19,606	11,680	7,926
Government debt bonds	345,868	60,000	285,868
Investments	189,564	82,194	107,370
Property and equipment	17,470	0	17,470
Other assets	21,956	21,956	0
Total on December 31, 1995	**KD 1,395,286**	**KD 721,624**	**KD 673,662**
Total on December 31, 1994	1,279,810	556,802	723,008
Total on December 31, 1993	1,156,010	417,413	738,597
Liabilities and Shareholders' Equity			
Due to banks and other financial institutions	KD 30,645	KD 30,645	KD 0
Depositors' accounts	1,123,713	349,089	774,624
Other liabilities and proposed cash dividends	151,470	91,875	59,595
Share capital and reserves	89,458	0	89,458
Total on December 31, 1995	**KD 1,395,286**	**KD 471,609**	**KD 923,677**
Total on December 31, 1994	1,279,810	739,268	540,542
Total on December 31, 1993	1,156,010	803,393	352,617

Note: Maturities of assets (net of provisions), liabilities and shareholders' funds have been determined on the basis of the remaining period at the balance sheet date to the contractual maturity date.

Sources: Kuwait Finance House, 1995, 1994, and 1993 Annual Reports.

[26] Ibid.

[27] Inter-American Development Bank, *Directory of Innovative Financing*, October 1995, p. 33.

EXHIBIT 21-7A

KUWAIT FINANCE HOUSE INCOME STATEMENT (KD IN THOUSANDS)

	Year Ended December 31,	
	1995	**1994**
Operating Income		
Murabaha, istisna', and leasing (*ijara*)	KD 70,682	KD 50,763
Subvention of government debt bonds	22,082	23,315
Investment income	7,230	4,148
Fees and commissions	2,646	2,224
Net gain from dealing in foreign currencies	772	841
Miscellaneous	2,747	1,157
Total operating income	KD 106,159	KD 82,448
Operating Expenses		
General and administration	KD 15,637	KD 16,267
Depreciation	2,997	2,913
Provisions	11,781	10,334
Total operating expenses	KD 30,415	KD 29,514
Profit Before Distribution to Depositors	KD 75,477	KD 52,934
Distribution to depositors	44,316	0
Total profit for the year	KD 31,428	KD 52,934
Statement of Appropriations		
Transfer to reserves	KD 18,887	KD 7,233
Distribution to depositors	0	36,600
Contribution to Kuwait Foundation for the Advancement of Sciences	784	552
Directors' fees	60	60
Proposed cash dividends of 20% (1994—14%)	8,998	5,942
Proposed issue of bonus shares of 6% (1994—6%)	2,699	2,547
Total appropriations	KD 31,428	KD 52,934

Source: Kuwait Finance House 1995 Annual Report.

---

stitution serving international users and providers of Islamic capital. TII's annual report clearly stated this objective:

> We are a financial institution that specializes in providing our clients and business partners with the knowledge, structures, strategies, and tools required to efficiently access the Islamic market.[28]

TII had two main businesses: Structured Finance and Asset Management. The Structured Finance Group helped governments, corporations, and projects raise Islamic funds, while the Asset Management Group structured financial products for investors who wished to invest according to *Shari'a* principals. Institutional investors such as

---

[28] The International Investor 1998 Annual Report, p. 1.

EXHIBIT 21-7B

KUWAIT FINANCE HOUSE FINANCING METHODS (%)

	Kuwait Finance House		Average for Islamic Banks in GCC Countries[a]	
	1995	**1994**	**1995**	**1994**
Ijara	2%	0%	15%	16%
Mudaraba[b]	0	32	7	9
Murabaha	52	32	51	45
Musharaka[c]	14	32	6	10
Others	32	4	21	20
Total	100%	100%	100%	100%

[a] The GCC (Gulf Cooperation Council) is a political, economic, social, and regional organization established in 1981 by UAE, Bahrain, Saudi Arabia, Oman, Qatar, and Kuwait to collectively meet the challenges facing the region.

[b] *Mudaraba* is a form of partnership whereby one partner contributes capital and the other contributes labor.

[c] *Musharaka* is a form of partnership whereby both partners contribute capital and labor.

Sources: The International Association of Islamic Banks, *Directory of Islamic Banks and Financial Institutions*, 1995 and 1994.

pension funds, life insurance companies, and fiduciary institutions (trust companies) made up approximately 80% of TII's investor base, while wealthy individuals made up the remaining 20%.

The company's guiding business philosophies were equality, innovation, and creativity. Equality permeated TII; it was a flat organization where no one had titles and everyone shared in effort and compensation. In fact, nobody, not even Al Bahar, had an office. Instead, they shared a common workspace known as the "kitchen" (where projects and products were "cooked"). Issam Al Tawari, a partner in the Structured Finance Group, described the business this way:

> The way to understand Islamic finance is to replace the word "Islamic" with the word "structured." Like all structured finance deals, you have constraints that must be overcome with creativity and innovation. Here, the constraints are based on the principles of *Shari'a*. The question is how to structure a deal given these constraints.

The Structured Finance Group completed its first major transaction—a $450 million airplane leasing deal for Kuwait Airways—in 1993.[29] In fact, one of the reasons the sponsors asked TII to submit an underwriting proposal for the Equate deal, even though the firm was only one year old, was because of this deal. The deal illustrated not only the growing strength of the Islamic capital market, but also TII's ability to underwrite major transactions. In this deal, TII had the dual challenge of educating both foreign and local investors on implications of *Shari'a* principles. A TII banker recalled that, while working on a similar deal at another bank, an airline executive had asked whether alcohol could be served on the leased airplanes, a reference to *Shari'a*'s prohibition of

[29] Colin Barraclough, "Tough Choices for Islamic Banking," *Institutional Investor*, July 1995, p. 141.

alcohol consumption. Because the airline's primary source of cash flow was not the sale of alcohol, TII could finance the airplanes. In contrast, Islamic financing could not be used to finance a chain of liquor stores.

The Alternative Financial Structure

The sponsors envisioned using an Islamic tranche alongside ECA-guaranteed bank debt. But after negotiating with the ECAs for more than a year without an agreement, they were frustrated with the process.[30] One of the key sticking points was the ECAs' demand for a sovereign guarantee, something the sponsors in general and PIC in particular objected to on the belief that the project was strong enough to stand on its own.[31] As a result, they began considering alternative financial structures without ECA involvement.

When a team from the National Bank of Kuwait (NBK) stepped forward and said they could raise the entire amount without ECA involvement, the sponsors greeted them with skepticism. Local banks had little experience with structuring project finance deals, never mind a deal of this size. But with Kuwaiti pride and nationalism at stake, NBK and KFH wanted to do the deal.

By the fall of 1995, the alternative structure was beginning to take shape. There would be two tranches of conventional debt, one for international banks led by Citicorp and one for local and regional banks led by NBK. Although the tranche for international banks would be bigger, it would have a shorter maturity—perhaps 8 or 9 years rather than 10 or 11 years—to limit the banks' long-term Kuwaiti exposure. To reduce this exposure, the sponsors included a debt service reserve account containing six months of principal and interest to cover any payment shortfalls.

Next, the bankers had to determine a spread for the loan reflecting the perceived sovereign and project risks (see Exhibit 21-8a and 21-8b for capital market information). Two recent deals provided some guidance on pricing. Hub River Power's $686 million, 12-year commercial loan was priced at 200 bp (escalating to 225 bp) over LIBOR in late 1994. Approximately one year later, Saudi Petrochemicals Company obtained a $700 million, 8½ year commercial loan at 125 bp over LIBOR for its Sadaf plant.[32] Two key differences between the deals help explain the pricing differential. First, Hub River Power was a new borrower while Saudi Petrochemical Company was an established credit. Second, investors perceived Saudi Arabia as an investment grade country, even though it was not rated at the time; Pakistan was rated B+/B1 at the time. Based on these transactions and current credit spreads, bankers expected the Equate deal would be priced in the range of 160 bp to 200 bp over six-month LIBOR. The banks would also charge a 50 bp commitment fee for making funds available as well as a 50 bp to 100 bp participation fee for actually disbursing the funds.[33]

While Citicorp and NBK were structuring the terms and conditions for the commercial bank tranches, KFH was structuring the Islamic tranche. Its goals were to minimize the number of complications resulting from the co-financing structure, keep the

[30] "Kuwait Petrochemicals Project to Move Forward with Private Finance," *International Trade Finance*, February 2, 1996, p. 7.

[31] Ash, "Kuwait: Bank Consortium Wins Loan Mandate," p. 5, and "Kuwait Petrochemicals Project to Move Forward with Private Finance," *International Trade Finance*, February 2, 1996, p. 7.

[32] Capital Data, Ltd.'s ProjectWare database (deal reference #2927) and "Saudi Arabia: Sadaf loan syndicate oversubscribed," *Middle East Economic Digest*, June 16, 1995, p. 29.

[33] Capital Data, Ltd.'s ProjectWare database describes the fee structure (deal reference #271).

EXHIBIT 21-8A

KUWAITI AND U.S. CAPITAL MARKET INFORMATION (DECEMBER 1995)

	Yield (percent)	Spread versus 6-month LIBOR (basis points)
6-monthLIBOR[a]	6.375%	—
Kuwaiti Interest Rates		
6-month KIBOR[b]	7.716	134.1
6-month Treasury Bills	7.631	125.6
6-month time deposit with local banks	7.230	85.5
U.S. Treasury Bills, Bonds, and Notes		
6-month	5.250	(112.5)
1-year	5.390	(98.5)
10-year	5.820	(55.5)
30-year	6.190	(18.5)
U.S. Long-term Industrial Bonds		
AAA	6.851	47.6
AA	7.051	67.6
A	7.201	82.6
BBB	7.451	107.6
BB	8.188	181.3
B	10.716	434.1
C	15.763	938.8
Broadly Syndicated Loan Grid[c]		
AA/AA−	6.570	19.5
A+	6.593	21.8
A	6.614	23.9
A−	6.621	24.6
BBB+	6.725	35.0
BBB	6.750	37.5
BBB−	6.865	49.0
BB+	7.105	73.0
BB Non-levered	7.125	75.0
BB Levered	7.875	150.0
B+	8.475	210.0
B	8.595	222.0

[a] Sterling denominated LIBOR (London Inter-bank Offered Rate).

[b] KIBOR is the Kuwaiti Inter-bank Offered Rate on KD deposits.

[c] Borrower unsecured senior debt rating. The spread over LIBOR is for all-in drawn revolving credit and term loan facilities with maturities ranging from 30 to 57 months. The pricing index uses the latest 10 to 12 transactions in each category that were not substantially under- or oversubscribed. Agent and syndication fees are not included. Also, the BB Non-levered category includes deals that were priced under 150 bp over LIBOR, while the BB Levered category includes deals that were priced over 150 bp over LIBOR.

Sources: Federal Reserve Bulletin (April 1997), Datastream, Central Bank of Kuwait, and Loan Pricing Corporation "Gold Sheets."

deal consistent with *Shari'a* principles, and ensure the deal was competitively priced to the borrowers and yet remained economically attractive to Islamic investors. Toward these ends, KFH decided that the Islamic tranche should, to the extent possible, follow the commercial bank tranches in terms of drawdown and repayment schedules, pricing, and fees.

EXHIBIT 21-8B

MONTHLY LIBOR AND KIBOR RATES, 1985 TO 1995

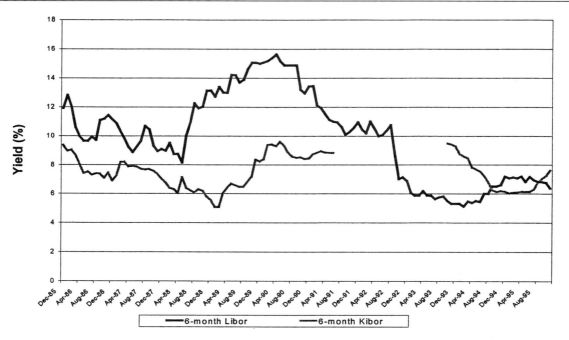

Note: There were no published KIBOR rates between August 1990 and December 1992 because of the Gulf War.

Sources: Datastream and Central Bank of Kuwait.

Structuring the Islamic Tranche

The distinguishing feature of Islamic finance was that returns had to be based on profit not interest because *Shari'a* prohibited the payment of interest, or *riba* (technically, *Shari'a* forbids making money on money). Profits were considered the just return for those who accepted the risks of ownership; the structure also promoted equality among investors. Because Islamic investors had to own the assets they financed, the bankers would have to identify specific assets for the Islamic tranche.

One approach would be to follow Hub River Power and use an *istisna'* contract (commissioned or premanufacture finance) in which one party contracts to manufacture a product for another party according to detailed time and product specifications. Analogies, which were commonly used to explain *Shari'a* principles, illustrate the importance of certainty over *gharar* (uncertainty) in these transactions. Basically, you could not sell what you did not own or could not describe accurately. Thus, you could not sell fish in the sea prior to catching them because you could not describe them in sufficient detail (i.e., in terms of type, size, and amount). On the other hand, you could describe a chair, car, or factory in great detail, thereby enabling the use of an *istisna'* contract.

Under an *istisna'* contract, the purchaser could pay in advance, at completion, or over time based on a set of predetermined completion milestones. The most common structure was known as a "back-to-back" *istisna'*, which introduced a financial intermediary such as an Islamic bank into the transaction. Under the first *istisna'* (the sale contract), a customer would agree to purchase an asset from the Islamic bank upon completion. Under the second *istisna'* (the "hire to produce" contract), the Islamic bank would agree to pay the manufacturer to build the asset in question. As an intermediary, the Islamic bank accepted the manufacturer's performance risk and the buyer's payment risk. Typically, *istisna'* contracts had maturities equal to the construction period and fixed rates that were set on the day the contracts were signed. For complex assets such as manufacturing plants, the contracts might last two or three years.

For longer-term, postconstruction financing, the sponsors could use either a *murabaha* (cost-plus financing) or an *ijara* (leasing) contract. Both structures required dedicated assets. Since construction was well underway, assets were available to "ring fence" for the Islamic tranche. In a *murabaha* contract (also known as a sale with deferred payment), an Islamic bank would purchase an asset and resell it to the project company at a higher price—hence the term *cost-plus*. While the parties would negotiate the deferred sale price in advance, the Islamic bank would collect the actual payment as a bullet at maturity or on an installment basis depending on the contract. For dollar-denominated deals, *murabaha* contracts typically lasted from one to three years, with an average of approximately two years; for dinar-denominated deals, the contracts could be longer if the investors were willing to accept the risks. Regardless of the currency, the *murabaha* contract was like investing in a fixed-rate bond, though it exposed the investor to ownership risk between the time the asset was bought and sold. Its major disadvantage, a short maturity, was indicative of lending arrangements in Kuwait. In fact, 90% of the Kuwaiti Central Bank's bills and bonds had maturities of less than two years, while none had a maturity of more than three years.

The *ijara* contract, or financial lease, was another source of permanent financing. In an *ijara*, the Islamic bank would purchase specific assets and then lease them to the project company for a period of time. To qualify for an *ijara* contract, the assets had to be separable and have economic value unto themselves. Here, Islamic scholars use the analogy of bicycle tires. You could not finance the construction of bicycle tires using an *ijara* contract because tires are not useful by themselves. In contrast, you could finance the construction of bicycles using an *ijara*. Identifying specific assets with economic value from a large, integrated project such as Equate might not be easy.

Unlike the *murabaha* structure, the *ijara* structure was a variable-rate instrument that required periodic, typically semiannual, payments. According to the contract, the payment for the following period was determined at each payment date. The standard contract set the lease profit rate based on a benchmark interest rate such as six-month LIBOR (plus a fixed spread). As with a conventional financial or capital lease, the project company would treat the leased assets as if it had purchased the asset itself. The lease obligation would appear on its balance sheet as a long-term liability offset by a depreciating fixed asset. At the end of the *ijara*, the project company would take ownership of the leased asset for a nominal charge. Thus, they were fully amortizing leases with no residual value.

Whereas all three structures—*istisna'*, *murabaha*, and *ijara*—could be used to finance Equate, the *ijara* structure was the leading contender as of December 1995, even though nothing had been set in stone. Before the sponsors could proceed, they had to resolve several issues related to the use of Islamic funds in general and to the use of co-financing in particular. For example, because the Islamic investors would own the assets, they would bear ownership risk that could be substantial for certain asset classes. For a petrochemical plant, there were equally serious environmental and third-party risks. To minimize these risks, KFH could place the assets in a special purpose vehicle

(SPV) with limited liability, but such a structure had not yet been tested in a major litigation. Thus, it was unclear whether a court might "pierce the corporate veil" and assert liability on the deal's Islamic investors.

A second issue involved the selection of assets for the Islamic tranche. The sponsors had to be willing to relinquish asset ownership. In certain circumstances, this was not easy. Some countries believed their natural resources were strategic assets and were unwilling to permit foreign ownership of those assets. If Kuwait imposed such a restriction, then the pool of available assets would shrink considerably.

A third issue involved the payment of insurance and maintenance expenses associated with the Islamically financed assets.[34] The separation of asset ownership and use could create incentive problems much the same way that drivers are less careful with rental cars than they are with their own cars—a problem known as moral hazard. In fact, even though the Islamic investors knew nothing about running a petrochemical plant, they would technically be responsible for maintaining the assets in working order and insuring them against loss. One way to solve this problem was to sign a service management contract with the sponsors, thereby obligating them to pay for insurance and maintenance.

There were also complications associated with trying to integrate Islamic and conventional funds in a single deal. Most of these issues had to be addressed in the intercreditor agreement that specified entitlements to cash flows as well as creditor rights in the event of default. There were the "simple" problems, such as which law would govern the contracts—Islamic religious law or English law? Even if they chose English law to govern the transaction, would a commercial court recognize, understand, and respect *Shari'a* principles? Another problem was how to deal with payment delays. Conventional lenders could charge penalty interest, but the Islamic investors could not. Instead, they would have to donate the penalty interest to charity or risk violating *Shari'a* principles. In the event the project experienced significant delays, this inability to collect penalty interest would be very costly to the Islamic investors.

Actual events of default introduced even more complicated issues. The standard procedure for resolving bankruptcies in the United States was to enforce an automatic stay whereby creditors could not seize assets or get paid. A judge would then supervise a liquidation in the case of Chapter 7 or a reorganization in the case of Chapter 11. In both cases, the idea was to maintain a common pool of assets to ensure maximum liquidation or going concern value. For an integrated production facility like Equate, the assets would be virtually worthless if they were liquidated piecemeal. Because the Islamic investors would own specific assets, they would have claims on those assets in a default situation. If they seized their assets, they might come out whole but could destroy the project's going concern value in the process. This kind of preferential treatment violated the standard *pari passu* treatment most conventional lenders sought in intercreditor agreements. Yet other structures that lumped the Islamic and conventional lenders into a single group ran the risk of tainting the Islamic tranche. To minimize priority issues outside of default situations, the bankers had to ensure that the drawdown and repayment of Islamic funds occurred simultaneously with the flow of conventional funds.

The complexity of co-financed deals made them potentially more costly to structure and more unwieldy to operate. Without a doubt, co-financing had its critics. One

---

[34] *Shari'a* prohibited conventional insurance because insurance contracts involved uncertainty. An alternative was to use a mutual insurance structure, or *takafol*. Under *takafol*, participants paid a defined amount into a common pool. In the event of an insured event, the participants then donated compensation to the damaged party.

EXHIBIT 21-9

EQUATE PETROCHEMICAL COMPANY FINANCIAL PROJECTIONS, 1995–2008

	1995	1996	1997	1998	1999	2000	2001	2002	2003	2004	2005	2006	2007	2008
Balance Sheet[a]														
Total Assets (given)	$644.2	$1,754.8	$2,063.8	$2,104.4	$2,168.5	$2,087.3	$2,146.2	$2,230.6	$2,343.6	$2,484.1	$2,639.3	$2,771.2	$2,909.8	$3,055.3
Other Liabilities[b]	$0.5	$0.7	$57.9	$80.4	$77.4	$37.3	$31.8	$29.0	$26.2	$34.5	$33.5	$33.5	$33.5	$33.5
Local Term Debt[c]	$0.0	$250.5	$500.0	$470.6	$411.8	$352.9	$294.1	$235.3	$176.5	$117.6	$58.8	$0.0	$0.0	$0.0
International Term Debt[d]	$1.3	$700.0	$700.0	$656.2	$604.3	$496.6	$388.9	$281.2	$173.5	$65.8	$0.0	$0.0	$0.0	$0.0
Subordinated Debt[e]	$518.9	$518.9	$518.9	$518.9	$518.9	$444.0	$438.7	$427.0	$412.1	$381.8	$319.8	$191.9	($0.0)	($0.0)
Total Debt[f]	$520.1	$1,469.3	$1,718.9	$1,645.7	$1,534.9	$1,293.6	$1,121.7	$943.5	$762.1	$565.3	$378.6	$191.9	($0.0)	($0.0)
Paid-in Capital (given)	$123.5	$286.9	$286.9	$286.9	$286.9	$286.9	$286.9	$286.9	$286.9	$286.9	$286.9	$286.9	$286.9	$286.9
Retained Earnings[g]	$0.0	($2.1)	$0.1	$91.5	$269.3	$469.6	$705.8	$971.2	$1,268.5	$1,597.5	$1,940.3	$1,972.1	$2,302.6	$2,448.1
Total Equity (given)	$123.5	$284.8	$287.0	$378.3	$556.1	$756.5	$992.7	$1,258.0	$1,555.3	$1,884.3	$2,227.2	$2,259.0	$2,589.5	$2,735.0
Income Statement														
Net Revenues (given)	$0.0	$27.7	$306.6	$613.3	$737.9	$762.1	$789.3	$815.3	$844.6	$873.2	$906.8	$943.1	$980.8	$1,020.0
Operating Profit (EBIT)[h]	$0.0	($2.4)	$150.6	$251.3	$334.2	$342.1	$361.3	$377.5	$395.3	$412.1	$409.4	$405.2	$403.1	$411.6
Interest on Term Loans	$0.0	$0.0	$88.7	$96.0	$88.4	$77.0	$63.2	$49.5	$35.7	$22.0	$10.0	$2.4	$0.0	$0.0
Interest on Sub. Debt	$0.0	$0.0	$59.7	$59.7	$59.7	$55.4	$50.8	$49.8	$48.2	$45.6	$40.3	$29.4	$11.0	$0.0
Total Interest Expense[i]	$0.0	$0.0	$148.4	$155.7	$148.1	$132.3	$114.0	$99.3	$84.0	$67.7	$50.3	$31.9	$11.0	$0.0
Profit before Taxes	$0.0	($2.4)	$2.3	$95.7	$186.2	$209.8	$247.3	$278.2	$311.3	$344.5	$359.0	$373.4	$392.0	$411.6
KFAS (taxes)[j]	$0.0	$0.0	($0.1)	($4.3)	($8.4)	($9.4)	($11.1)	($12.5)	($14.0)	($15.5)	($16.2)	($16.8)	($17.6)	($18.5)
Net Income (given)	$0.0	($2.4)	$2.2	$91.4	$177.8	$200.4	$236.2	$265.7	$297.3	$329.0	$342.9	$356.6	$374.4	$393.1
Cash Flow and Debt Service[k]														
EBIT	$0.0	($2.4)	$150.6	$251.3	$334.2	$342.1	$361.3	$377.5	$395.3	$412.1	$409.4	$405.2	$403.1	$411.6
—Depreciation			$75.0	$75.7	$77.1	$78.8	$80.5	$82.3	$84.2	$86.2	$88.1	$90.2	$92.4	$94.6
—Amortization[m,n]			$36.5	$36.5	$36.5	$36.5	$36.5	$36.5	$36.5	$36.5	$36.5	$36.5	$11.0	$11.0
—KFAS (taxes)			($0.1)	($4.3)	($8.4)	($9.4)	($11.1)	($12.5)	($14.0)	($15.5)	($16.2)	($16.8)	($17.6)	($18.5)
—Inc. in net Work. Cap.[o]			($1.5)	($3.1)	($3.7)	($3.8)	($3.9)	($4.1)	($4.2)	($4.4)	($4.5)	($4.7)	($4.9)	($5.1)
—Capital Expenditures[p]			($14.0)	($28.1)	($33.8)	($34.9)	($36.2)	($37.3)	($38.7)	($40.0)	($41.5)	($43.2)	($44.9)	($46.7)
Cash Available for Debt Service			$246.5	$328.1	$402.0	$409.3	$427.1	$442.4	$459.1	$474.9	$471.8	$467.2	$439.0	$446.9

(*Continued*)

EXHIBIT 21-9 *(Continued)*

	1995	1996	1997	1998	1999	2000	2001	2002	2003	2004	2005	2006	2007	2008
Debt Service														
Term Loan Interest[i]	($0.1)	($39.3)	($ 88.7)	($ 96.0)	($ 88.4)	($ 77.0)	($ 63.2)	($ 49.5)	($ 35.7)	($ 22.0)	($ 10.0)	($ 2.4)	$ 0.0	$ 0.0
Term Loan Principal	$0.0	$ 0.0	$ 0.0	($ 73.3)	($110.7)	($166.5)	($166.5)	($166.5)	($166.5)	($166.5)	($124.7)	($ 58.8)	$ 0.0	$ 0.0
Sub. Debt Interest[i]	($6.0)	($59.7)	($ 59.7)	($ 59.7)	($ 59.7)	($ 55.4)	($ 50.8)	($ 49.8)	($ 48.2)	($ 45.6)	($ 40.3)	($ 29.4)	($ 11.0)	$ 0.0
Sub. Debt Principal	$0.0	$ 0.0	$ 0.0	($ 0.1)	($ 0.1)	($ 74.9)	($ 5.3)	($ 11.7)	($ 14.9)	($ 30.3)	($ 62.0)	($127.9)	($192.0)	$ 0.0
Total Debt Service	($6.1)	($98.9)	($148.4)	($228.8)	($258.8)	($373.7)	($285.8)	($277.4)	($265.4)	($264.5)	($237.0)	($218.5)	($203.0)	$ 0.0
Cash Available for Dividends			$ 98.1	$ 99.2	$143.2	$ 35.6	$141.2	$164.9	$193.7	$210.5	$234.8	$248.7	$236.0	$446.9
Return on Average Assets (%)	n/a	n/a	0.1%	4.4%	8.3%	9.4%	11.2%	12.1%	13.0%	13.6%	13.4%	13.2%	13.2%	13.2%
Return on Average Equity (%)	n/a	n/a	0.8%	27.5%	38.1%	30.5%	27.0%	23.6%	21.1%	19.1%	16.7%	15.9%	15.4%	14.8%
Return on Sales (%)	n/a	n/a	0.7%	14.9%	24.1%	26.3%	29.9%	32.6%	35.2%	37.7%	37.8%	37.8%	38.2%	38.5%
Debt-to-Equity Ratio	4.21	5.16	5.99	4.35	2.76	1.71	1.13	0.75	0.49	0.30	0.17	0.08	0.00	0.00
Debt-to-Value Ratio (%)	80.8%	83.8%	85.7%	81.3%	73.4%	63.1%	53.1%	42.9%	32.9%	23.1%	14.5%	7.8%	0.0%	0.0%

a Boubyan projections have been restated using an exchange rate of KD0.2998 = US$1.00.

b Other liabilities are the difference between total assets and the sum of total debt and total equity.

c Local Term Debt is based on the Capital DATA term sheet #271, assumed rate = 8.25% = LIBOR + 175 bp.

d International Term Debt is based on the Capital DATA term sheet #271, assumed rate = 8.25% = LIBOR + 175 bp.

e Subordinated Debt is a plug to match the total given debt, assumed rate = 11.5% = LIBOR + 500 bp.

f Total Debt equals the given D/E ratio times the given shareholders' equity.

g Retained earnings is the difference between total shareholders equity and paid-in capital.

h EBIT is built up from the Net Income given in the Boubyan prospectus.

i Interest paid through 1996 is capitalized.

j KFAS tax rate is 4.5% (see case Exhibit 21-1, notes).

k Cash flows ignore the possibility of either a Capital Expenditure and/or Debt Service Reserve Funds.

l Depreciation of the plant is straight-line over a 20-year useful life. The amount is from Exhibit 21-4. (Equistar uses straight-line depreciation over 5–30 years, p. F8).

m Amortization period for the capitalized interest and preliminary operating expenses is 10 years (Equistar uses a 10-year period for capitalized expenses, p. F9). The amount is from Exhibit 21-4 and includes initial net working capital.

n Amortization period for the licensed technology is 20 years. The amount is from Exhibit 21-4.

o Assumes the change in net working capital is 0.5% of sales (based on Equistar's ratio of NWC/Sales, pp. F2–3, and Equate's growth rate).

p Assumes capital expenditures are 4.58% of sales (Equistar's ratio, p. F21).

Sources: These projections are case writer estimates based on two sources; they are *not* actual projections. The two sources are the Boubyan Petrochemical Company Offering Memorandum (4/23/95 to 5/7/95) and the financial statements contained in Equistar Chemicals, LP (Equistar Funding Corporation) Form S-4, filed 4/16/99. Boubyan is a public company whose only asset is a 10% stake in Equate. The Offering Memorandum contains summarized projections for 1995–2005—three years, 2006–2008, have been added by the case writer. Equistar is North America's largest producer of ethylene and polyethylene. Items marked as "given" come from the Boubyan Offering Memorandum.

banker claimed, "Using Islamic finance is like tying to do something with one hand tied behind your back." A lawyer from Clifford Chance, one of the leading project finance law firms, echoed a similar sentiment, "If there's no [specific tax or balance sheet] need for Islamic cash, then people won't hunt it down because of the added complexity of structuring transactions."[35]

CONCLUSION

In preparing for their meeting with Al Bahar, the deal team reviewed the current term sheet they had received from KFH. They knew Al Bahar wanted to discuss their recommendations regarding the appropriate structure, the size of the Islamic tranche, and the amount TII should commit to place. In preparation for their meeting, they studied current market data and cash flow projections (see Exhibits 21-8a, 21-8b, and 21-9). Based on their experience, they knew that equity investors would expect to earn 20% to 30% on a project like Equate, subordinated debtholders would expect 10 to 14%, and term loan providers, like TII's investors, would expect to earn 7% to 10%.[36]

In the back of their minds, they knew that TII's *Shari'a* committee would have to approve the final structure. Yet before Al Bahar could go to the *Shari'a* committee, the project had to have a more solid structure in place. What concerned him was the fact that each investor's *Shari'a* committee might also review the deal. Unfortunately, it was not uncommon for *Shari'a* committees to disagree on the permissibility of particular structures. A lawyer described the problem this way: "We have come up with a structure that has been approved by an Islamic institution and its *Shari'a* board and we have tried using the same structure for another client and it is found to be completely unacceptable."[37] While there had been attempts to harmonize *Shari'a* standards across institutions, disagreements still remained. The creation of the Bahrain-based Accounting and Auditing Organization for Islamic Financial Institutions (AAOIFI) in 1991, helped build consensus on a number of issues and narrowed the scope of disagreements on others, but complete agreement still could not be assumed.

With construction under way and the bridge loan running out, TII had to move quickly. Equate was an important deal not only for TII and the sponsors, but for Kuwait as well. It was Kuwait's first major investment since the Gulf War and the first time foreign partners had been allowed to participate in a Kuwaiti project. If done successfully, Equate would highlight the ability to finance major projects with Islamic funds. However, if something went wrong on such a high-profile transaction, Islamic finance might have a second strike against it given Hub River's problems. As advocates of Islamic finance, the members of the TII's Structured Finance Group had an incentive to participate, but only if it was going to be a successful transaction.

[35] "Newcomers Flock to the Market," *Middle East Economic Digest*, December 19, 1997, p. 7.

[36] Petrochemical firms like Union Carbide and Lyondell Petrochemicals had asset betas ranging from 0.80 to 0.90.

[37] Khalili, "Unlocking Islamic Finance," p. 9.

## 22

Introduction to Islamic Finance

Islam is the world's third monotheistic religion and comes from the same Semitic heritage as Judaism and Christianity. From the very beginning, Islam acquired its characteristic ethos as a religion uniting both spiritual and temporal aspects of life, seeking to regulate not only the individual's relationship with God, but also human relationships in a social setting. Thus, in addition to religious principles, there is Islamic law and secular institutions governing both individual behavior and societal interactions.

This note provides an introduction to Islamic Finance, one of the most important aspects of Islamic socioeconomic doctrine.[1] Because Muslims, or followers of Islam, now comprise one quarter of the world's population and Muslim countries control approximately 10% of global GNP, they represent an increasingly important segment of the global economy. Nevertheless, few people know much about Islamic finance other than the rudimentary fact that interest is forbidden. This note begins by examining the religious and legal foundations of Islamic finance, and then describes the rise of Islamic financial institutions. Although the field of Islamic banking is relatively small, with total assets of approximately $150 billion in 1997, the market is growing at 15% to 20% per year, and new developments are happening regularly. The final sections discuss some recent innovations such as Islamic project finance as well as the challenges facing Islamic banks as they seek to play a role in financing the economic development of Islamic countries.

Research Associates Fuaad A. Qureshi and Mathew M. Millett prepared this note from public sources under the supervision of Professor Benjamin C. Esty as the basis for class discussion. This note is intended to be used in conjunction with The International Investor: Islamic Finance and the Equate Project, *HBS No. 200-012. Much of the background material on Islamic finance comes from the book* Islamic Law and Finance: Religion, Risk, and Return, *by Frank Vogel and Samuel Hayes (Kluwer Law International, The Hague, The Netherlands, 1998).*

[1] Some people view the term *Islamic* as applied to banking or finance as inappropriate and even offensive based on the belief that Allah's word applies to both Muslims and non-Muslims alike. As a result, they prefer terms such as *profit bank* and *equity investor* to Islamic bank or Islamic investor (Frank Vogel and Samuel Hayes, *Islamic Law and Finance: Religion, Risk, and Return,* Kluwer Law International, The Hague, The Netherlands: 1998, p. 27).

RELIGIOUS AND LEGAL BACKGROUND OF ISLAMIC FINANCE

The Arabic term *Islam*, meaning literally "surrender," illustrates the fundamental religious aspect of Islam—that the believer accepts his or her surrender to the will of God, or *Allah* as He is known in Arabic. *Allah* is viewed as the sole God—creator, sustainer, and restorer of the world. The will of *Allah*, to which man must submit, is made known through the *Quran*, the sacred scripture that Allah revealed to his messenger, Mohammed. According to Islamic theology, the purpose of the existence of man, as of every other creature, is submission to the Divine Will. With a deep-seated belief in Satan's existence, man's fundamental role becomes one of moral struggle. For example, Satan plants the idea that man will become poor by giving to the needy. Allah, on the other hand, promises prosperity in exchange for such generosity and threatens those who hoard wealth with eternal damnation.

As this example shows, Islam governs the relationship between God and His creations. The entire body of rules guiding the life of a Muslim is known as the *Shari'a* which is derived from the word meaning path. Due to the absence of a strict delineation between the religious and secular aspects of life, Islam is more accurately described as a comprehensive code of life covering legal, ethical, and social matters. Only those believers whose lives conform to *Shari'a* will be granted entrance to heaven.

Rather than a codified body of law, the *Shari'a* is an ever-expanding interpretation of religious law. The provisions of *Shari'a* are derived through the discipline of *fiqh*, or jurisprudence. *Fiqh* is man's attempt to understand divine law based on several sources and methods:

(a) The *Quran*: Muslims believe the *Quran* is the actual word of God as transmitted to the Prophet Mohammed (570–632 A.D.).

(b) The *Sunna*: Prophet Mohammed's sayings and deeds—which are known collectively as the *Sunna*, or tradition—are codified in the *Hadith*. The *Sunna* provide further insight into the meaning of the *Quran*.

(c) *Ijma*: In essence, *Ijma* is the agreement of the Islamic community as a basis for legal decision making. The introduction of *Ijma* in the second century of Islam aided the standardization of legal theory, allowing for the resolution of individual and regional differences of opinion.

(d) *Qiyas*: *Qiyas* is the derivation of new judicial decisions through the use of strict analogy based on the texts of the *Quran* and *Hadith*. This technique is one of the main avenues for the evolution of the *Shari'a*.

(e) *Ijtihad*: *Ijtihad* is the opinion of an Islamic jurist on a particular issue based on the *Quran* and *Sunna*. It is required to find the legal or doctrinal solutions to problems not previously tackled by the *Shari'a*.

The *Shari'a* lays down four main prohibitions which serve to distinguish Islamic finance from "conventional" or "Western" finance.[2] One of the most important principles of Islamic finance is the scriptural injunction against interest, or *riba*. Instead, profit is the just return for someone who accepts the risks of ownership. This prohibition is intended to prevent exploitation and to maximize social benefits; it highlights the emphasis on social welfare over individual welfare in Islam. Interestingly, even Adam Smith noted the prohibition of interest as a hallmark of Islamic finance in his book *The Wealth of Nations*.[3]

---

[2] Allen and Overy, *Islamic Finance* (Dubai, 1993), p. 2 (Memorandum).

[3] Smith argues that even in economies where interest is proscribed, people will not lend without considering potential profits, as well as the potential cost of default. The latter is incorporated into the interest rate—and is one of the reasons he gives to explain high interest rates in Islamic economies (*The Wealth of Nations* [Chicago, IL: University of Chicago Press, 1976], Book I, Chapter IX).

In addition, the *Shari'a* declares uncertainty, or *gharar*, in contracts as un-Islamic. This concept is best illustrated by example. The sale of a building prior to construction would be forbidden due to the uncertainty of its existence at the time of the contract. However, the sale of a building for which ground has been broken would be legal. The subtle nuance here is that the former relies on the occurrence of an uncertain event for its fulfillment, namely, the commencement of construction. Islamic law also declares gambling, or *masir*, as unacceptable because it can lead to immorality (the compulsion to gamble) and other social evils such as poverty. This restriction has direct implications in the dealings of modern financial instruments such as futures and options, which may be deemed illegal due to their speculative nature. And finally, the *Shari'a* prohibits the use of certain products such as pork and alcohol, as well as commercial transactions dependent on these products.

Each of these concepts, particularly *riba*, *gharar*, and *masir*, though strictly forbidden in theory, generate a tremendous amount of debate when applied to everyday life. To resolve these debates, particularly in the presence of technological and institutional innovation, there are *fiqh* academies composed of Islamic legal and religious scholars. Through academic debate, the scholars generate *fatwas* or legal rulings on various topics.

More than the interpretive uncertainty surrounding various topics, the real issue that separates Islamic countries is the degree to which the state and government integrates Islamic principles into everyday life. Exhibit 22-1 provides a demographic breakdown of the Muslim population by country. It shows not only that Muslims comprise more than a quarter of the world's population, but also that Muslims represent the religious majority in large number of countries.

Nationalistic, cultural, and political views tend to mix with religion, resulting in varying degrees of religious intensity. Countries where the entire economic system has aligned with Islamic principles tend to be those that have an Islamic government (e.g., Pakistan, Iran, and Sudan).[4] More moderate governments (Bahrain, Brunei, Kuwait, Malaysia, Turkey, and United Arab Emirates) embrace Islamic banking, though support a dual banking system with conventional banks. Other countries such as Egypt, Yemen, Singapore, and possibly Indonesia neither support nor oppose Islamic banking. And finally, there are countries that actively discourage the creation of a separate Islamic-banking sector (Saudi Arabia[5] and Oman).

ISLAMIC FINANCIAL INSTITUTIONS

The independence of Islamic countries following World War II, combined with the renaissance of Islamic sentiment, set the stage for the modern era of Islamic finance. The first Islamic financial institution, a small Egyptian institution named Mit Ghamr Local Savings Bank, was formed in 1963. Early development was slow and did not accelerate until the oil boom in the 1970s. Prior to this time, a few ruling families and a select group of businesses controlled the majority of Middle Eastern wealth. Given limited alternatives to invest "Islamically," they chose to invest in conventional financial institutions and did so with little social recrimination. The influx of petrodollars created a larger segment of wealthy citizens looking for ways to invest their savings in confor-

---

[4] Vogel and Hayes, *Islamic Law and Finance*, p. 11.

[5] The Saudi Arabian government believes that by declaring certain financial institutions as Islamic, they would be implicitly branding other institutions as un-Islamic. For this reason, it does not distinguish Islamic banks in the chartering process.

EXHIBIT 22-1

MUSLIM POPULATION STATISTICS, 1996

Country	Muslim Population (millions)	Percent of Country's Total Population
Indonesia	196	95%
India	133	14
Pakistan	125	97
Bangladesh	104	85
Nigeria	77	75
Iran	65	99
Turkey	62	100
Egypt	59	94
Ethiopia	37	65
China	36	3
Morocco	29	99
Algeria	28	99
Sudan	26	85
Afghanistan	22	100
Iraq	20	97
Uzbekistan	20	88
Saudi Arabia	19	100
Tanzania	18	65
Syria	14	90
Yemen	13	99
Philippines	10	14
Malaysia	10	52
United States	9	4
Somalia	9	100
Cote d'Ivoire	8	60
Total of Top 25 Countries	1,259	
Total Number of Muslims	1,482	
Total World Population	5,771	
Muslim Population as a Percent of Total	**25.7%**	

Source: http://islamicweb.com/, casewriter estimates.

mance with the *Shari'a*. In response to this growing demand for Islamic financial institutions and renewed interest in Islamic principles, financial institutions began to appear throughout the Islamic world.

The greatest single boost for the resurgence of Islamic financial practices occurred in 1973, with the founding of the Islamic Development Bank (IDB) in Jeddah under the auspices of the Organization of the Islamic Conference (OIC). The purpose of the IDB was to promote economic development in the OIC's member countries, both individually and jointly, through the use of Islamic financial techniques.

By 1997, there were 176 Islamic financial institutions, with $148 billion of assets, operating in more than 50 countries. Although these institutions are collectively referred to as Islamic banks, this term is somewhat of a misnomer because there are many types of institutions, including commercial, investment, and development banks. Exhibit 22-2

EXHIBIT 22-2

FINANCIAL HIGHLIGHTS OF THE ISLAMIC MARKET, 1993–1997[a]

	1993	1994	1995	1996	1997	4-year Compound Annual Growth Rate
Number of Islamic Banks	100	133	144	166	176	15.2%
Financial Highlights ($ in thousands)						
Capital	2,390	4,954	6,308	7,271	7,333	32.3
Assets	53,815	154,567	166,053	137,132	147,685	28.7
Funds Under Management	41,587	70,044	77,516	101,163	112,590	28.3
Reserves	N/A	2,383	2,939	5,746	3,076	8.9
Net Profits	N/A	809	1,245	1,684	1,238	15.2
Sectoral Financing (%)						
Trading	31%	27%	30%	31%	32%	
Agriculture	13	13	9	8	6	
Industry	30	28	19	19	17	
Services	11	15	13	13	12	
Real Estate	N/A	5	12	12	16	
Other	15	12	17	18	16	
Total	100%	100%	100%	100%	100%	

[a] Includes other Islamic financial institutions such as Islamic investment banks.

Source: "Directory of Islamic Banks and Financial Institutions—1997," *The International Association of Islamic Banks*, Jeddah.

shows the growth of Islamic financial institutions from 1993 to 1997; Exhibit 22-3 shows the geographical distribution of these institutions as of 1997. As one might expect, the majority of the institutions and the assets are in the Middle East. Exhibit 22-4 lists the 20 largest Islamic banks, based on total assets. The largest institution, the $22 billion Bank Melli Iran, is roughly equal to the fiftieth largest U.S. bank holding company at the time.

In drawing their operating guidelines from the *Shari'a*, Islamic banks differ from their Western counterparts in several ways. First, they conduct business in an interest-free manner—to avoid *riba*. The relationship between these banks and their customers is not the standard one of creditor and debtor, but rather one of the sharing in financial risks and rewards. A second difference is the fact that profit is not the sole purpose of an Islamic bank. These banks must ensure that funds are invested in conformance with religious principles. A *Shari'a* advisory committee, comprised of Islamic jurists, oversees the operation of each institution. These committees, which range in size from one to seven members, typically meet quarterly to discuss specific products and transactions.[6] Given the evolutionary nature of business and finance, it is the committee's job to determine what is permissible, or *halal*, and what is unlawful, or *haram*. Like public accounting firms, they provide annual reports in which they assess whether an institution has "acted in compliance with the rules and regulations of the Islamic *Shari'a*." Exhibit 22-5 provides an example of a typical report by a *Shari'a* committee for The International Investor, an Islamic investment bank located in Kuwait (see Chapter 21).

[6] Vogel and Hayes, *Islamic Law and Finance*, p. 49.

EXHIBIT 22-3

REGIONAL ISLAMIC BANKING HIGHLIGHTS (1997)

Region	Number of Banks[a]	Capital Amount	%	Assets Amount	%	Deposits Amount	%	Reserves Amount	%	Net Profit Amount	%
South Asia[b]	51	884,048	12%	39,272,976	27%	25,664,913	23%	1,077,163	35%	249,792	20%
Africa	35	202,197	3	1,573,846	1	730,025	1	82,087	3	19,750	2
Southeast Asia[c]	31	149,837	2	2,332,204	2	1,887,710	2	160,136	5	45,659	4
Middle East	26	3,684,136	50	83,136,100	56	69,076,443	61	382,286	12	252,185	20
Gulf Cooperation Council[d]	21	1,787,395	24	20,449,637	14	14,088,581	13	1,353,167	44	603,642	49
Europe and America	9	616,795	8	908,922	1	1,139,541	1	20,613	1	66,707	5
Asia[e]	2	3,452	0	5,727	0	2,563	0	24	0	282	0
Australia	1	5,219	0	5,590	0	N/A	0	50	0	224	0
Total	176	7,333,079	100%	147,685,002	100%	112,587,213	100%	3,075,526	100%	1,238,241	100%

[a] Includes other Islamic financial institutions such as Islamic investment banks.

[b] South Asia includes Bangladesh, India, and Pakistan

[c] Southeast Asia includes Brunei, Indonesia, Malaysia, and the Philippines.

[d] The Gulf Cooperation Council is a political, economic, social, and regional organization established in 1981 by UAE, Bahrain, Saudi Arabia, Oman, Qatar, and Kuwait.

[e] Asia includes Russia and Kzakhstan.

Source: "Directory of Islamic Banks and Financial Institutions—1997," *The International Association of Islamic Banks,* Jeddah.

EXHIBIT 22-4

TOP 20 ISLAMIC BANKS BASED ON TOTAL ASSETS (1997)[a] (AMOUNTS IN THOUSANDS)

Name of Institution	Country	Date of Financials	Assets	Paid-in Capital	Deposits	Reserves	Net Profit	Return on Capital	Return on Assets
Bank Melli Iran	Iran	Mar-97	$ 22,415,451	$ 654,660	$ 21,709,740	$ 10,563	$ 61,153	9.3%	0.3%
Bank Sedarat Iran	Iran	Mar-97	11,771,051	309,334	7,664,060	4,105	N/A	N/A	N/A
Bank Tejarat	Iran	Mar-97	10,526,730	326,360	9,673,260	13,210	10,910	3.3	0.1
Iraqi Islamic Bank for Dev. & Invest.	Iraq	Dec-96	9,900,000	402,000	10,900,000	24,000	N/A	N/A	N/A
Al-Rajhi Banking & Investment Corp.	Saudi Arabia	Dec-97	9,369,354	400,000	6,697,177	976,460	347,188	86.8	3.7
National Bank of Pakistan	Pakistan	Dec-95	9,348,361	72,992	6,081,255	186,171	90,000	123.3	1.0
Bank Sepah	Iran	Mar-97	9,026,980	227,920	7,322,930	2,330	13,680	6.0	0.2
Bank Mellat	Iran	Mar-97	6,966,776	201,667	5,083,632	71,171	7,999	4.0	0.1
Habib Bank	Pakistan	Dec-97	5,803,520	56,265	4,800,264	218,346	(87,898)	(156.2)	(1.5)
Kuwait Finance House	Kuwait	Dec-97	5,269,317	168,503	428,110	249,497	121,813	72.3	2.3
United Bank	Pakistan	Dec-93	5,087,843	49,242	3,703,893	69,060	9,146	18.6	0.2
Muslim Commercial Bank	Pakistan	Dec-96	4,070,930	45,377	2,815,666	29,788	2,574	5.7	0.1
Agricultural Bank of Iran	Iran	Mar-96	3,023,818	233,327	1,000,990	11,817	11,239	4.8	0.4
Agricultural Dev. Bank of Pakistan	Pakistan	Dec-95	1,982,297	103,680	80,821	103,654	6,297	6.1	0.3
Dubai Islamic Bank	UAE	Dec-96	1,935,480	135,580	1,753,880	19,870	15,520	11.4	0.8
Bank of Industry & Mine	Iran	Mar-97	1,917,738	729,345	151,049	30,906	39,924	5.5	2.1
Faisal Islamic Bank of Egypt	Egypt	May-97	1,843,600	132,000	1,787,800	3,200	N/A	N/A	N/A
Citibank Pakistan	Pakistan	Dec-93	1,382,005	53,107	802,272	N/A	14,180	26.7	1.0
Bank Islam Malaysia Berhad	Malaysia	Dec-97	1,233,379	37,057	1,032,372	41,348	13,153	35.5	1.1
Bank Refah Kargaran	Iran	Mar-96	1,160,594	31,394	730,414	55,553	3,697	11.8	0.3
			$124,035,224	$4,369,810	$94,219,585	$2,121,049	$ 680,575	15.6%	0.5%
Grand Total: 176 Islamic Banks in 38 Countries			$147,685,002	$7,333,079	$112,589,776	$3,075,526	$1,238,241	16.9%	0.8%

[a] Includes other Islamic financial institutions such as Islamic investment banks.

Source: "Directory of Islamic Banks and Financial Institutions—1997," *The International Association of Islamic Banks*, Jeddah.

EXHIBIT 22-5

THE INTERNATIONAL INVESTOR 1998 SHARI'A COMMITTEE REPORT

---

report of the TII Shari'a committee

In the Name of God, the Merciful, the Compassionate

**Report of the Fatwa and Sharia Supervisory Committee
for the period 3 January 1998 through 31 December 1998**

Praise be to God, the Lord of the Worlds, and prayer and peace be upon our Prophet Mohammed, his family, companions and followers.

The Fatwa and Sharia Supervisory Committee of The International Investor held several meetings during 1998. During these regular meetings, all matters such as enquiries and contracts relating to the company's new operations of the year, which were referred to the committee by the Management of the company, were discussed and appropriate recommendations, decisions and Fatwas were made.

In the light of the statements made and submitted by the committee's secretary, the committee hereby declares that the company has acted in compliance with the rules and regulations of the Islamic Sharia in respect of all its contracts and transactions.

Ahmed Bezai'a Al-Yaseen Chairman   **Dr Khalid Al-Madhkour** Member

Dr Mohammed Fawzi Faidhulla Member   **Dr Mohammed Abdul Ghaffar Al-Sharif** Member

---

In addition to The Fatwa and Sharia Supervisory Committee, The International Investor has been privileged to be guided, since its inception, by an International Advisory Sharia Committee, outside Kuwait. This Committee has assisted with further scrutinising of the company's activities, to ensure that they are compatible with the principles of Islamic Sharia.

This committee comprises the following members:

His Eminence, Sheikh Abdulla Ibn Abdul Aziz Ibn Aqeel Chairman

His Eminence, Sheikh Saleh Ibn Abdul Rahman Al-Hussain Depty Chairman

His Eminence, Sheikh Mustafa Ahmed Al-Zarqa'a Member

His Eminence, Sheikh Abdul Rahman Ibn Abdulla Ibn Aqeel Member and Secretary

Source: The International Investor 1998 Annual Report.

ISLAMIC FINANCIAL INSTRUMENTS

Islamic banks derive their deposit base from two main sources. Transactions deposits are similar to conventional demand deposits except they do not pay interest. Islamic banks guarantee the nominal value of transactions deposits, even though most Islamic countries do not have deposit insurance funds, such as the Federal Deposit Insurance Corporation (FDIC) in the United States, to guarantee deposits. In contrast, investment deposits are like shares in a firm. Instead of paying a fixed return determined *ex ante* as interest, the bank pays a return based on any profits on its investments. For this reason, the nominal value of investment deposits is not guaranteed. Along with equity capital, deposits are the main source of liabilities for Islamic financial institutions.

Banks have a wide array of financial instruments at their disposal in which to invest these funds. As in conventional finance, these instruments may be divided into equity-like instruments (i.e., those that represent residual claims) and debt-like instruments (i.e., those that represent fixed claims). The main instruments used by Islamic institutions are as follows.[7]

Equity-like Instruments (Residual Claims)

(a) ***Modaraba* (trust financing)**: Under a *modaraba* contract, an Islamic financial institution provides the capital to finance a project, while an entrepreneur provides management skills. In financing a project, the institution does not employ its own funds—only the funds of its investors. In many respects, such contracts are very similar to Western limited partnerships. After paying for management skills, the financial institution deducts its own fee from the enterprise's profits, for managing its investor's funds. Remaining profits are distributed to investors.

(b) ***Mosharaka* (profit sharing)**: This contract is similar to a *modaraba* except that the partners are not confined to distinct roles as either financier or manager. Instead, the provision of capital and management of the enterprise are shared.

(c) **Preferred Stock**: While the *Shari'a* does not sanction the offering of different dividend payoffs to shareholders, it is legal to utilize different classes of common stock.

Debt-like Instruments (Fixed Claims)

(a) ***Morabaha* (cost-plus financing)**: In a *morabaha* contract, an Islamic financial institution purchases a commodity and then resells it to a customer at a later date for a predetermined price. The institution's profit is the difference between the price paid for the commodity and the price paid by its client. The client may opt for either immediate payment or deferred payment. Such contracts tend to come under fire for violating the prohibition of predetermined profit, but are justified by the fact that the client is not compelled to repurchase the goods from the institution. This structure creates a certain degree of risk on the part of the institution, and its profits are directly derived from that risk. In general, *morabaha* contracts tend to be short-term agreements.

(b) ***Ijara* (leasing)**: Under an *ijara* contract, an Islamic institution purchases an asset and then leases it for a rate that is periodically reviewed and possibly adjusted. The profits from the lease are justified because the financial institution owns the asset in question and, therefore, assumes risk for its performance. While the option for the lessor to purchase the asset at the end of the lease period is deemed illegal due to the uncertainty inherent in options, in some versions of *ijara* contracts the client agrees up-front to purchase the asset at the end of the lease period.

[7] See Allen and Overy, *Islamic Finance*, p. 3, and Clifford Chance, *Islamic Banking and Finance* (October 1992), p. 3 (Memorandum).

EXHIBIT 22-6

MODES OF FINANCING BY ISLAMIC BANKS, 1994–1997

	1994	1995	1996	1997
Morabaha	41.5%	45.6%	40.3%	37.0%
Mosharaka	8.2	8.7	7.2	19.0
Modaraba	12.6	15.3	12.7	6.0
Ijara	8.7	9.7	11.5	9.0
Others	29.0	21.1	28.3	29.0
Total	100%	100%	100%	100%

Source: "Directory of Islamic Banks and Financial Institutions—1997," *The International Association of Islamic Banks*, Jeddah.

(c) *Mukarada*: This instrument is similar to a revenue bond issued by an Islamic bank to finance a specific project. Investors have no voting rights, but are entitled to a proportional interest in profits and losses of the venture.

(d) *Salam* (**forward purchase**): A *salam* contract is a forward purchasing agreement in which the investor or institution directly pays the manufacturer for a commodity to be produced and delivered on a fixed date. The possibility of the lack of a market at that future date incorporates the element of risk for the lender, rendering such transactions legal. Payment is made at the time the contract is signed.

(e) *Istisna'* (**commissioned manufacture**): In an *istisna'* contract, one party agrees to buy goods made by a second party with payments occurring at some future date or dates. In some cases, an Islamic bank may represent the end user. Payments are often geared to manufacturing milestones or completion. The primary distinction between an *istisna'* and *salam* is that the former is used for goods that otherwise would not exist (see Hayes and Vogel, p. 147).

Exhibit 22-6 shows the degree to which Islamic financial institutions employ these instruments. In recent years, *mosharaka* contracts have gained significant popularity as a mode of financing, while *modaraba* and *morabaha* have experienced slight declines.

CURRENT CHALLENGES

Although the discipline of Islamic finance has progressed rapidly over the last three decades, several obstacles remain as impediments to future growth. Similar to conventional financial institutions, Islamic financial institutions face the problems of adverse selection and moral hazard. Potential bad credit risks will seek out institutions willing to lend funds on a profit-loss basis. Without the incentive to utilize the funds efficiently, or at least be accountable for a return on it, entrepreneurs may take advantage of banking institutions. As a result, the lender is at the mercy of the honest nature of the borrower. Fortunately, honesty and contractual responsibility are mandated through other religious principles.

A second, and potentially more serious, problem has to do with asset-liability management. Islamic institutions have few long-term liabilities, thereby restricting their ability to make long-term investments. If they were to invest in long-term assets, the maturity mismatch would expose them to liquidity and profit risks. This problem is exacerbated by the absence of several institutional and product innovations that exist in conventional financial systems: deposit insurance encourages long-term deposits; interest-rate swaps allow institutions to minimize interest rate exposure, interbank lending helps resolve temporary liquidity problems; and a lender of last resort helps resolve more serious liquidity problems. More importantly, it is not just a matter of time before these elements enter the Islamic financial system. Many of them, such as interest rate swaps, are forbidden according to *Shari'a*.

And finally, the proliferation of Islamic finance will be hampered by the absence of standardization both in terms the instruments that are considered legal according to religious principles and in terms of the standards for financial reporting. There are no generally accepted accounting standards for Islamic financial institutions.[8] One problem for firms conducting cross-border transactions is that certain products and services that are deemed lawful by one *Shari'a* committee may be deemed unlawful by another. This lack of interpretive consistency hampers business transactions by injecting a level of uncertainty in the process.

FUTURE DEVELOPMENTS

Given the fact that more than a quarter of the world's population is Muslim, the rising interest in Islamic finance should come as no surprise. The assets in Islamic financial institutions are growing rapidly, as is the number of Islamic institutions. To capture some of this growing market, conventional banks are opening Islamic divisions as well as "Islamic windows" in existing branches: Citbank recently opened Citi Islamic Investment bank, while ABN AMRO recently opened ABN AMRO Global Islamic Financial Services, both in Bahrain.[9] As more and more Muslims opt to invest according to *Shari'a*, opportunities are bound to grow.

Several recent developments attest to the growing interest in and importance of Islamic finance. Over the past three years, financial institutions have created several new Islamic investment funds (see Exhibit 22-7). Dow Jones, recognizing the growing investor demand for Islamic equity, recently created the Dow Jones Islamic Market Index (DJIM) which tracks 600 companies whose operations conform to *Shari'a* principles.[10]

Without a doubt, one of the biggest challenges in the Islamic world, and therefore one of the biggest opportunities, is infrastructure development. By one estimate, the potential market for infrastructure projects in the Middle East alone is $45 to $60 billion over the next ten years. In fact, there are now almost 300 infrastructure projects pending in the Middle East—not counting those in the petroleum sector.[11] Financing these projects will outstrip the capabilities of local banks and governments, especially given the fact that most of the countries with large Muslim populations are relatively poor. As

---

[8] Clifford Chance, *Islamic Banking and Finance*, p. 6.

[9] Stephen Timewell, "A market in the making," *The Banker*, February 1, 1998, p. 57.

[10] Sara Webb, "Dow Jones Plans to Launch Islamic Market Index," *The Wall Street Journal*, February 8, 1999, p. C 12.

[11] Germana Canzi, "You Cannot Afford to Wait," *Project Finance*, July 1999, p. 18.

EXHIBIT 22-7

RECENTLY ESTABLISHED ISLAMIC INVESTMENT FUNDS

Fund	Type	Year Launched	Financial Institution	Size ($ millions)
IIBU Fund II Plc.	Leasing	1994	United Bank of Kuwait	$ 51.5
Faysal Saudi Real Estate Fund	Real Estate	1995	Faysal Islamic Bank of Bahrain	27.0
GCC Trading Fund	Trading	1996	GCC Trading Fund	10.0
Oasis International Equity Fund	Equity	1996	Robert Fleming & Co. (UK)	16.6
Faisal Finance Real Estate Income Fund	Real Estate	1996	Faisal Finance (Switzerland) S.A.	100.0
Unit Investment Fund (all tranches)	*Mudaraba* syndication	1996	Islamic Dev. Bank (Saudi Arabia)	500.0
Al Safwa Int'l Equity Fund	Equity unit trust	1996	Al-Tawfeed Co. for Investment Funds	27.0
Ibn Khaldun Int'l Equity Fund	Equity	1996	PFM Group (United Kingdom)	25.0
Adil Islamic Growth Fund	Equity	1996	Faisal Finance (Switzerland) S.A.	10.0

Source: Islamic Financial Systems, Zamir Iqbal, *Finance & Development*, vol. 34, no. 2, International Monetary Fund and the International Bank for Reconstruction and Development, June 1997.

a result, economic development will require international capital. The key will be to create structures that integrate international capital with Islamic religious principles.

One such structure, known as co-financing, involves the side-by-side use of conventional and Islamic funds in a single deal. Pakistan's $1.8 billion Hub River Power project, which was signed in 1994, was the first transaction to use a co-financing structure, albeit a temporary one. Since then, there have been several other co-financed deals, including the $1.1 billion Thurayya Satellite Network, which was signed in 1998 and contained a $100 million Islamic tranche.[12] Another recent example of the attempts to combine conventional and Islamic funds is the Islamic Development Bank's infrastructure fund. The IDB plans to raise $1 billion of equity capital and another $500 million in Islamic funds for infrastructure investments in member countries; the targeted return is 18 to 20%.[13]

Interestingly, a banker working on a recent transaction in Malaysia encountered the opposite problem of not having sufficient conventional funds.

The incentive to include an Islamic finance tranche in the LR2 (Light Rail Transit System 2) project was to broaden the lender base. There was some concern that funding within the conventional market for all the projects that are coming on stream in Malaysia would

[12] Ibid., p. 20.
[13] "Islamic Institutions Plan Private Infrastructure Fund," *International Trade Finance*, October 9, 1998, p. 6.

be insufficient. There was therefore the risk that we would go to the conventional market for all of the financing and come up short.[14]

Through innovations like co-financing, Islamic countries will be able to fund development projects while simultaneously meeting the interests of Islamic investors and citizens. To do so, however, Islamic bankers will have to resolve ever more complex legal, financial, and religious issues. The continued evolution of *Shari'a* principles is necessary not only for the growth of Islamic financial institutions, but also for the efficient development of Islamic countries.

[14] Sara Khalili, "Unlocking Islamic Finance," *Infrastructure Finance*, April 1997, p. 19.

## 23

Financing PPL Corporation's Growth Strategy

Virtually all the major project acquisitions or new builds in the power sector have looked at using synthetic leases.[1]

Despite the company's beginnings as the old Pennsylvania Power & Light, the new PPL has evolved into one of the most financing savvy and innovative players in U.S. project financing, and an analyst favorite.[2]

In February 2001, Steve May, Director of Finance for PPL Corporation's PPL Global subsidiary, was preparing a report for Jim Abel, vice president—finance, and treasurer of PPL. May needed to make a financing recommendation for a $1 billion investment in peaking plants that the company had approved as part of its new growth strategy in unregulated power businesses. Several financing options existed, including corporate finance, project finance, and various leasing structures. A lease, particularly a synthetic lease, seemed to be the most promising option, but May was wrestling with whether to recommend a traditional or a limited recourse synthetic lease and how to structure the specific terms.

Both structures contained three tranches: an A tranche of debt with a corporate guarantee; a B tranche of nonrecourse debt; and a C tranche of third-party equity. In the traditional structure, the A tranche accounted for 85% of total capital, the B tranche accounted for 12%, and the C tranche accounted for the remaining 3%. In the limited recourse structure, the percentages were closer to 67%, 30%, and 3%, respectively. The

---

[1] A. Campomar, "Shape of Synthetics to Come," *Project Finance*, July 2000, p. 37.

[2] A. Healey, "Huge Volume of Structured Deals Explore Leasing Structures," *Project Finance International*, Issue 220, June 27, 2001, p. 52.

smaller A tranche in the limited recourse structure meant a smaller corporate guarantee on the assets and, therefore, greater off-credit treatment, which was particularly important given the company's growth strategy and its limited debt capacity. However, finding investors willing to accept greater project risk would take more time and cost more. But Steve May was not sure he had time to spare. Financing had to be in place before May 1, 2001, so that PPL could exercise an option to buy turbines for its peaking plants. Failure to exercise the option could delay the company's construction schedule, something PPL wanted to avoid given the nationwide race to build new generating capacity. This deadline gave May only two months to structure the lease, find investors, and close the deal.

THE ELECTRIC POWER INDUSTRY

Historically, local public utility companies generated, transmitted, and distributed electricity to designated service territories under exclusive franchises. Because governments deemed the supply of power to be a "vital public service," they granted utilities monopoly rights in exchange for regulated prices and returns. While the Federal Power Act of 1935 gave federal regulators the authority to oversee wholesale power sales and transmission, state regulators were responsible for distribution.

Beginning in the 1970s, a series of regulatory changes introduced competition to the utility industry. The first change occurred in the generation segment, with the passage of the Public Utilities Regulatory Polices Act of 1978 (PURPA). The act encouraged the creation of power plants using renewable or nontraditional fuels such as geothermal, solar, and wind power. As long as these independent generators met certain efficiency and size standards, the law required local utilities to buy all of their electrical output. In essence, PURPA created a wholesale power market (i.e., sales between power producers). Fourteen years later, Congress introduced competition into the transmission segment with the passage of the National Energy Policy Act of 1992 (NEPA). This act required utilities to make their transmission systems available to third-party users on a nondiscriminatory basis.

State regulators began experimenting with competition in the distribution segment in the mid-1990s. "Retail wheeling" legislation required local utilities to open their transmission and distribution networks to outside utilities. For example, in 1997, Montana passed the Restructuring and Customer Choice Act, which required utilities to separate their electricity generation, transmission, and distribution businesses and allowed customers to buy power from utilities other than the local monopoly supplier.

State deregulation did not always go smoothly. In September 1996, California deregulated the generation, but not transmission and distribution segments. Legislation forced the formerly vertically integrated utilities to divest their unregulated generating assets, and regulated rates on transmission and distribution assets. Furthermore, the utilities were not permitted to sign long-term supply contracts at fixed prices, at least initially. A few years later, a supply shortage coupled with a spike in gas prices led to an increase in power-generating costs that some utilities were unable to pass on to end users. One utility failed while others sat on the brink of failure. In 2001, the state was forced to use tax dollars to purchase electricity for the utilities, while angry citizens called for re-regulation.

Although deregulation opened the door for growth and expansion in the generation segment, customers were reluctant to sign long-term purchase contracts given the changes taking place in the industry. It soon became clear that unregulated generating companies would have to build power plants without the benefit of long-term purchase agreements. These plants, known as merchant power plants (MPPs), would be subject to normal supply and demand dynamics in which the low-cost producer would win.

Generating plants were categorized by the energy source used to produce electricity. Thermal plants, fueled by coal, oil, or natural gas, and nuclear plants used steam to spin turbine blades. Hydroelectric plants, in contrast, used water flow. The energy source combined with the particular production technology determined a plant's construction and operating costs. For example, coal plants were expensive to build and took a long time to start (24 hours or more) but had relatively low marginal production costs. On the other hand, gas-fired plants could be started very quickly (20 minutes to two hours) and were generally cheaper and quicker to construct. Gas, however, was a more expensive fuel than coal, which resulted in higher marginal production costs. Plants with low marginal operating costs, such as coal and nuclear plants, were known as baseload plants, while plants with high marginal costs, such as certain gas-fired plants, were referred to as peaking plants. Mid-merit plants were between baseload and peaking plants in merit (marginal cost) order.

Because power could not be stored and demand varied across the day, week, and year, generating capacity had to be available when needed. To meet fluctuating demand, energy suppliers relied on access to a mix of baseload, mid-merit, and peaking plants. Suppliers kept baseload plants running constantly to meet average expected demand. Mid-merit plants ran regularly though the winter and summer months to meet average increases in demand. And finally, peaking plants were used to meet peaks in demand and typically ran only 10% to 30% of the year. Given the nature of electricity and the industry structure, energy prices could range from $20 to $500 per MWh or more on a given day, depending on the immediacy of need.[3] Because prices were set by merit order (the highest priced energy source set the market price), peaking plants, when used, became the marginal supplier and often set market prices.

PPL CORPORATION

Headquartered in Allentown, Pennsylvania, PPL Corporation was originally incorporated as Pennsylvania Power & Light Company in 1920 as a holding company for eight regional electric companies. As of 2000, it was a Fortune 500 Company with revenues of $5.7 billion (see Exhibits 23-1, 23-2, and 23-3). The company owned steam, hydroelectric, and gas-fired generating stations in Pennsylvania, Maine, and Montana with total capacity of almost 10,000 MW. PPL sold its energy in the wholesale and retail markets in 42 states as well as Canada. In addition, PPL operated a high-quality distribution business with operations in both domestic and international markets. The company delivered energy to 1.4 million customers in Pennsylvania and Maryland and more than 4.3 million customers in the UK and Latin America. Chief Executive Officer (CEO) William Hecht noted, "Our business now truly is global—and truly competitive. And, as competitive barriers have fallen here in the United States and abroad, the fundamental building blocks in this business have changed."[4]

---

[3] MWh = megawatt hour or one megawatt of power for one hour. One MW was sufficient to power 1,000 households.

[4] Chairman's Letter, PPL 1998 Summary Annual Report, March 12, 1999, p. 2.

EXHIBIT 23-1

PPL CORPORATION BALANCE SHEET

	At December 31				
	2000	**1999**	**1998**	**1997**	**1996**
Assets					
Current assets	$ 1,945	$ 1,293	$ 948	$ 695	$ 783
Investments	1,161	695	906	605	520
Property, plant and equipment—net					
Electric utility plant	$ 5,696	$ 5,393	$4,282	$6,766	$6,905
Gas and oil utility plant	177	171	175	30	n/a
Other property	75	60	23	24	55
Total property, plant and equipment	$ 5,948	$ 5,624	$4,480	$6,820	$6,960
Regulatory and other non-current assets					
Recoverable transition costs	$ 2,425	$ 2,647	$2,819	$ 0	$ 0
Other	881	915	454	1,365	1,407
Total Assets	**$12,360**	**$11,174**	**$9,607**	**$9,485**	**$9,670**
Liabilities and Equity					
Current liabilities	$ 2,511	$ 2,280	$1,276	$ 769	$ 655
Long-term debt (less current portion)	4,467	3,689	2,983	2,585	2,802
Deferred income tax & investment tax credits	1,412	1,548	1,574	2,221	2,261
Above market NUG's contracts (less current)	581	674	775	n/a	n/a
Other non-current liabilities	976	959	862	754	741
Total Liabilities	$ 9,947	$ 9,150	$7,470	$6,329	$6,459
Minority interest	$54	$64	$0	$ 0	$0
Mandatorily redeemable securities	250	250	250	250	0
Preferred stock	97	97	97	97	466
Common equity	2,012	1,613	1,790	2,809	2,745
Total Liabilities and Equity	**$12,360**	**$11,174**	**$9,607**	**$9,485**	**$9,670**

Source: PPL Corporation Annual Reports.

PPL changed its strategy in anticipation of deregulation. In 1994, it established a subsidiary now known as PPL Global to pursue business opportunities in the unregulated electricity marketplace. Jim Abel explained:

> If we were going to become a player in this new environment, we needed to get into the market quickly or risk being locked out. To get in, we needed to identify growth opportunities and attract growth investors. The regulated energy business was conservative and mature; it was not prepared to address the challenges of deregulation. So we decided to establish a new subsidiary with a new corporate culture that could operate in a deregulated environment.

In 1996, Pennsylvania legislators enacted the Electricity Generation Customer Choice and Competition Act (Customer Choice Act) that deregulated Pennsylvania's generating markets but, unlike California, did not mandate a divestiture of the unregulated generating assets. Retail customers were permitted to select energy suppliers, which would deliver power using local transmission and distribution lines. Under the

EXHIBIT 23-2

PPL CORPORATION INCOME STATEMENT (MILLIONS OF DOLLARS, EXCEPT PER SHARE DATA)

	For the Years Ended December 31,				
	2000	**1999**[a]	**1998**[a]	**1997**[a]	**1996**[a]
Operating Revenues					
Retail electric and gas	$3,167	$2,873	$2,445	$2,397	n/a
Wholesale energy marketing and trading	2,080	1,440	1,223	650	n/a
Energy-related businesses	436	277	118	30	n/a
Total Operating Revenues	**$5,683**	**$4,590**	**$3,786**	**$3,077**	**$2,910**
Operating Expenses					
Fuel and energy purchases	$2,461	$2,031	$1,584	$ 980	$ 800
Other operating and maintenance	951	858	756	687	735
Amortization and depreciation	488	451	338	385	363
Taxes, other than income	191	161	188	204	456
Energy-related businesses	390	217	93	21	n/a
Total Operating Expenses	$4,481	$3,718	$2,959	$2,277	$2,354
Operating Income Before Extraordinary Items	$ 513	$ 504	$ 404	$ 320	$ 357
Extraordinary items (net of income taxes)	11	(46)	(948)	0	0
Preferred stock dividends	26	26	25	24	28
Net Income	**$ 498**	**$ 432**	**$ (569)**	**$ 296**	**$ 329**
Basic EPS of Common Stock					
Income before extraordinary items	$3.38	$3.14	$ 2.29	$1.80	$2.05
Extraordinary items (net of tax)	0.07	(0.30)	(5.75)	0.00	0.00
Net Income	$3.45	$2.84	$(3.46)	$1.80	$2.05
Diluted EPS of Common Stock					
Income before extraordinary items	$3.37	$3.14	$2.29	$1.80	$2.05
Extraordinary items (net of tax)	0.07	(0.30)	(5.75)	(0.00)	(0.00)
Net Income	$3.44	$2.84	$(3.46)	$1.80	$2.05
Dividends Declared Per Share	$1.06	$1.00	$1.335	$1.67	$1.67
Avg. Number of Shares Outstanding (000)	144,350	152,287	164,651	164,550	161,060

[a] Reclassified to conform to the current presentation.

Source: PPL Corporation Annual Reports.

law, PPL Electric Utilities was required to serve as a "provider of last resort" and deliver electricity at capped rates through 2009 to retail customers who did not specify alternative suppliers.[5]

The company's senior management, knowing they had to adapt to this new competitive environment, proceeded to make several strategic decisions regarding the company's position. Although PPL now had the opportunity to exit specific business

[5] "$800,000,000 PPL Electric Utilities Corporation," PPL Electric Utilities Prospectus Supplement, August 16, 2001, p. s-3.

EXHIBIT 23-3

PPL CORPORATION FINANCIAL, STATISTICAL, AND SHAREHOLDER INFORMATION, 1996–2000

	2000[a]	1999[a]	1998[a]	1997[a]	1996
Shares and Trading					
Book value per share	$13.87	$11.23	$11.37	$16.90	$16.87
Market price per share	$45.19	$22.88	$27.88	$23.94	$23.00
Price earnings ratio[b,c]	13.8x	9.7x	14.9x	12.0x	11.2x
Leverage					
Total Debt (millions)	$5,821	$5,014	$3,620	$2,870	$2,976
Debt to Total Book Capitalization	74%	76%	67%	51%	52%
Debt to Total Market Capitalization	47%	60%	45%	42%	42%
Leverage Ratio (EBITDA/total debt)[d]	3.67x	4.44x	3.11x	2.32x	n/a
Long-term Debt Ratings	BBB+	BBB+	BBB+	BBB+	BBB+
Earnings					
Basic EPS (loss)—reported	$3.45	$2.84	$(3.46)	$1.80	$2.05
Basic EPS—excluding nonrecurring items	$3.29	$2.35	$1.87	$2.00	$2.05
Dividends declared per share	$1.06	$1.00	$1.34	$1.67	$1.67
Dividend payout rate[b]	32%	43%	71%	84%	81%
Dividend yield[c]	2.35%	4.37%	4.79%	6.98%	7.26%
Profitability					
Return on average common equity (%)[d]	27.14%	16.89%	10.98%	11.69%	12.30%
Return on capital[d]	10.0%	10.4%	−6.7%	7.0%	7.7%
Implied Average Tax Rate	36%	26%	39%	43%	39%

[a] The nonrecurring items affected earnings each year, except for 1996. These adjustments affected net income and certain items under Common Stock Data.

[b] Based on diluted earnings per share excluding nonrecurring items.

[c] Based on year-end market prices.

[d] Based on earnings excluding nonrecurring items.

Source: PPL Corporation Annual Reports and Bloomberg.

---

segments, senior management decided to remain involved in each of the three power segments while actively pursuing growth opportunities in unregulated businesses such as power generation, marketing, and trading. Management believed there were advantages to remaining vertically integrated due to their experience in all three segments and their ability to balance the more volatile earnings of the nonregulated generation business with the stable earnings from the regulated transmission and distribution business. Furthermore, they saw an opportunity to add value and become a leader in the unregulated business.

PPL took a one-time restructuring charge in 1998 to reflect the market value of its generating assets. At the same time, the company also reduced its dividend and established a new target payout ratio of 45% to 55%, all in an effort to generate more cash flow to fund growth internally. Finally, the company bought back 17 million shares of common stock. One year later, Chairman William Hecht announced the company's intention to double current generating capacity from 10,000 MW to 20,000 MW by 2005 through acquisitions of existing plants and development of new plants.

In July 2000, senior management reorganized the company by separating the regulated transmission and distribution operations from the new unregulated generation operations and by creating separate financing entities to support the two distinct business strategies (see Exhibit 23-4). In 2001, PPL successfully "securitized" its electric delivery business. This first-of-its-kind transaction permitted the company to increase the financial leverage of its transmission and distribution operations without any adverse impact on PPL's Electric Utilities credit quality. Jim Abel explained:

> Electricity is a commodity, and a prerequisite to success in any commodity business is the ability to produce and deliver it at a cost that is lower than your competitors. Given the relatively large number of players in the electric generation business, we anticipate consolidation within the industry, and survivors will have to grow at a fairly rapid pace. When you add in the fact that we are in a very capital-intensive industry, the ultimate conclusion for our finance team at PPL was that a key ingredient to the long-term success of our corporate strategy lies in our ability to maintain quick access to large amounts of low-cost capital. "Securitizing" our transmission and distribution operations represented one successful element of this strategy.

Facing the need to raise potentially billions of dollars over the next five years to finance PPL's expansion strategy, Jim Abel challenged his finance team to identify new and

---

EXHIBIT 23-4

PPL CORPORATE STRUCTURE

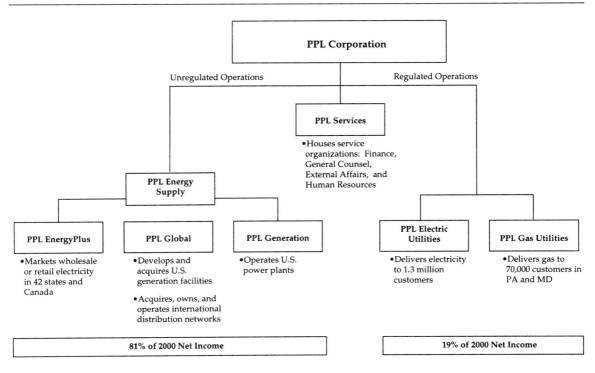

Source: Casewriter.

EXHIBIT 23-5

TRADING DATA ON U.S. POWER COMPANIES

	Price on 2/14/01	Earnings Per Share (EPS)			Price/Earnings Ratio			EPS Growth
		FY00	FY01	FY02	FY00	FY01	FY02	
AES Corp	$56.88	$1.46	$1.75	$2.40	39.0x	32.5x	23.7x	28.2%
Calpine	47.00	1.11	1.85	2.25	42.3	25.4	20.9	42.4%
Dynegy	51.23	1.43	2.00	2.45	35.8	25.6	20.9	30.9%
Enron	80.00	1.47	1.70	2.00	54.4	47.1	40.0	16.6%
Mirant	25.26	0.98	1.60	1.95	25.8	15.8	13.0	41.1%
NRG Energy	26.57	1.10	1.36	1.70	24.2	19.5	15.6	24.3%
Orion Power	25.25	0.62	1.91	2.19	40.7	13.2	11.5	87.9%
Median for Unregulated Power Companies	47.00	1.11	1.75	2.19	**42.3**	**26.9**	**21.5**	**30.9%**
Median for Power Companies w/non-regulated subsidiaries	—	—	—	—	**29.8**	**18.1**	**16.1**	**24.2%**
PPL Corporation	44.45	3.45	3.65	4.00	**12.9**	**12.2**	**11.1**	**10.4%**

Source: Adapted from D. Tulis's equity analyst report on PPL Corporation, Banc of America Securities, April 17, 2001, p. 15.

creative opportunities to raise funds. The team considered a full range of financing opportunities from equity finance to various debt finance and leasing structures, but the market valuation on the company's common stock put constraints on their options. At the time, the company's senior management believed the market was undervaluing the company's true potential and was, therefore, extremely reluctant to issue additional common stock. Many equity analysts agreed on the undervaluation and issued Buy or Strong Buy recommendations based on peer valuation analysis (see Exhibit 23-5). A Banc of America analyst initiating coverage on PPL commented:

> PPL Corporation, based in Pennsylvania, has successfully transformed itself to a growing diversified energy player that has more than 70% of earnings coming from its non-regulated generation business. . . . We believe the shares are undervalued at a P/E of 12-13X FY02 estimates. Despite its earnings visibility and attractive non-regulated generation portfolio, PPL trades at a utility multiple. . . . We believe the shares should trade at a premium to the utility group and more in line with the merchant energy group to reflect earnings momentum and value of PPL's non-regulated generation portfolio.[6]

Chairman Hecht and CFO John Biggar understood the importance of financial flexibility and ready access to the capital markets, both of which required a strong investment grade rating. Yet PPL Global, like most of its competitors in the generating sector, hoped to develop a large number of gas-fired combined-cycle plants and simple-cycle peaking plants. Unfortunately, developing peaking plants required up-front investment, created a gap of up to two years before revenues began, and produced variable cash flow streams, all of which could hurt PPL's corporate credit rating. As a re-

[6] U.S. Equity Research Report on PPL Corporation, Banc of America Securities, April 4, 2001, p. 2.

sult, the use of corporate finance, though possible, would place an enormous burden on the corporate balance sheet and could lead the rating agencies to downgrade the corporate credit rating.

The third alternative, project finance, would allow PPL Global to finance new plants with nonrecourse debt, but the assets would be on-balance sheet given its 100% ownership position. Therefore, depreciation charges would reduce the company's reported earnings per share in the short run. Moreover, the interest rate and transaction costs were high compared to corporate finance. PPL was hesitant to pay for what was effectively a walk-away put option that it was unlikely to exercise given the strategic nature of the assets. Adding to these costs was the uncertainty likely surrounding the utility industry at the time. Notwithstanding these issues, lenders were reluctant to provide much leverage to finance standalone plants with merchant risk, particularly peaker plants, given their revenue volatility and low utilization rates.

Various leasing structures presented an interesting fourth alternative as they often yielded off-balance sheet treatment and at least some off-credit treatment depending on the structure. However, like project finance, leasing structures could be expensive to implement. According to Jim Abel:

> In the unregulated division, our financial strategy grew out of necessity. We had to be creative and explore off-balance sheet financing tools because we didn't have access to a traditional corporate balance sheet. Project finance or leasing structures are not necessarily the optimal way to finance high-growth, but they were the only options available to us at the time. We had to finance new projects off their own cash flow. Our clear preference, if we could have done it, would have been to use the corporate market—it's much deeper, provides better terms and pricing, and allows for quicker execution.

In weighing the options, Abel recognized the importance of making a good, early impression on the market. He explained:

> Our goal in recent years has been to show the market that we are a serious contender in the unregulated power business. As we ventured into new businesses and new markets, we wanted to show that we could manage the businesses and deliver the earnings. We knew that the key to survival and long-term value creation was success in the early years. That success would allow us to raise more money from the capital markets down the road. Leasing transactions could play an important role in achieving these goals.

LEASING STRUCTURES IN THE POWER INDUSTRY

Noting the benefits of leasing and the corresponding interest by many U.S. power companies in leasing (for an overview of leasing in the power industry, see the Appendix), a project finance banker said:

> To an even greater extent, market participants view power plant ownership as incidental to their power and energy marketing and trading businesses. Renting or contracting for a power plant is as good as owning it, for the purpose of locking up energy and power trading volumes.[7]

Experts cited several reasons for leasing assets. First, leasing allowed the lessee to shift the residual or salvage value risk to the lessor. Second, leasing structures can

[7] D. Morash "Cash Creation," *Project Finance*, September 2000, pp. 12, 14.

result in cheaper financing for the lessee by effectively passing the lessee's tax benefits to the lessor in exchange for a lower "interest" rate. This benefit existed whenever the lessee's marginal tax rate was lower than the lessor's rate. Hence, leasing was particularly attractive to firms with low marginal tax rates (MTR) due to accumulated operating losses (NOLs), investment tax credits, or Treasury Regulation Section 861 (interest allocation) deficits. Finally, leasing can improve a company's balance sheet and income statement. A finance director from West LB explained the investment problem in the utility industry:

> U.S. power companies decided several years ago that to be a player in a changing U.S. power industry they had to engage—immediately—in a massive capital expenditure program. However, a problem was quickly foreseen with putting massive amounts of shiny new assets on the books in a short time. The exact minute a project is complete, it begins to depreciate, and this book depreciation . . . goes right to the bottom line. The multitude of revenues . . . will not arrive so promptly, however, and this creates a mismatch.[8]

A Citibank banker added:

> Leasing makes a lot of sense. In fact, if you are an earnings driven company, as most project sponsors are today, there is little reason not to do a lease. The use of leasing structures can provide for improved earnings for sponsors, which should result in increased value for shareholders in the form of higher stock prices.[9]

A managing director from CIT Structured Finance reinforced this point for high-growth companies:

> Companies that are intent on surviving the competition in the merchant power environment through a strategy of consolidation and growth are starved for capital and earnings. EPS growth is necessary to support the stock price and issue additional equity, thereby increasing debt capacity and the ability to fund more asset acquisitions and construction. Leasing enhances earnings growth and augments the capital raising process.[10]

With these considerations in mind, PPL had used leases to finance recent transactions. Unlike others in the industry, however, the company believed it should be an "asset-backed" power producer and not rely solely on leased assets.

THE MONTANA LEVERAGED LEASE

In March 1998, the Montana Power Company initiated a sealed-auction bid to divest its generating portfolio in response to Montana's 1997 Deregulation Act. The portfolio included 11 hydroelectric generating facilities with 474 MW of energy capacity, a coal-fired facility with 154 MW of capacity, and an ownership interest in the Colstrip coal-fired facility with 529 MW of capacity. PPL Global bid and won the auction in October 1998, at a cost of $760 million, not counting transaction fees. Shortly after purchase, PPL Global assigned all assets acquired in the purchase to PPL Montana, a newly formed, wholly-owned subsidiary of PPL Corporation (see Exhibit 23-6). In order to

---

[8] J. Ryan, "Extraordinary Synthetic Solution and the Madness of 07-10," *Project Finance International*, p. 11.

[9] N. Khan, J. Lindenberg, and D. Armstrong, "Leasing in Project Financing Today—An Earnings Boost," *PFI Yearbook 2000 Americas*, p. 84.

[10] D. Morash "Cash Creation," *ProjectFinance*, September 2000, pp. 12, 14.

EXHIBIT 23-6

MONTANA DEAL STRUCTURE (LEVERAGED LEASE)

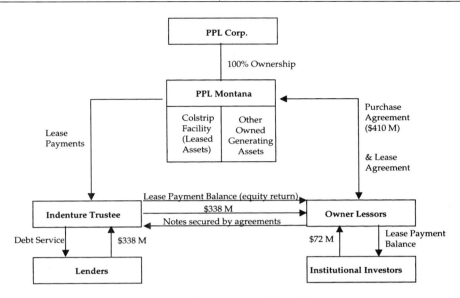

Source: Adapted from PPL Montana, LLC Offering Memorandum, July 13, 2000.

achieve an investment grade rating for the new entity, PPL Global would not be able to debt finance more than approximately 50% of the assets. Conveniently, the Colstrip interest represented a little more than half of the total value ($410 million). Within the PPL Montana entity, the company debt financed 100% of the Colstrip interest through a leveraged lease transaction, while the remaining funds came from PPL Corporation. Jim Abel explained the factors that influenced this decision:

> We viewed the Montana plants as strategic assets; they were critical to our strategy of investing in generating plants around the country. We didn't view them as a portfolio of options where we would walk away if things didn't go as planned. For that reason, straight project finance structures, and the inherent cost paid for the ability to walk away from project debt, were less attractive to us than a lease structure such as a leveraged lease. The hybrid structure gave us an opportunity to get the assets off-balance sheet and receive 100% nonrecourse debt for 50% of the financing while paying a price that was better than the traditional project finance structure.

To set up the leveraged lease, institutional investors created a special purpose entity, Owner Lessors, to represent their interests while an Indenture Trustee represented the lender's interests. The institutional investors contributed a total of $72 million in equity funds to the Owner Lessors, who issued nonrecourse debt of $338 million to lenders within the capital markets. The Owner Lessors purchased the Colstrip interests from PPL Montana for $410 million and assigned the asset title to the Indenture Trustee. Simultaneously, the Owner Lessors entered into a long-term lease (36 years) with PPL Montana and assigned the lease contract to the Indenture Trustee. The Indenture Trustee received semiannual lease payments from PPL Montana, deducted principal and interest due, and passed on the balance to the Owner Lessors for distribution to the institutional investors.

Steve May described the transaction this way:

> The leveraged lease was a good structure for this particular asset. We were able to get significant project leverage without increasing our corporate leverage or affecting our credit rating. Although we didn't get full off-credit treatment, the deal was off-balance sheet for us, and it provided lower up-front amortization than a capital lease would have. The operating lease treatment, allowing us to deduct the average lease payment over a 36-year period, gave us the opportunity to better match our costs and revenues over time and resulted in improved EPS in the early years of the lease.

LARGE-SCALE DISTRIBUTION GENERATION (LSDG) PROGRAM

In September 2000, PPL launched a $1.8 billion investment program in peaking plants. The objective of the LSDG program was to complement the company's portfolio of baseload capacity and take advantage of high-power prices during peak periods. PPL management hoped to build several plants in the West and Northeast. Plants would be sized based on a number of factors and would require 2 to 12 turbines per plant.

PPL created a $555 million revolving equipment trust that purchased 30 General Electric LM6000 gas-fired turbines (45 MW each) and related equipment [e.g., selective catalytic reduction units (SCRs) and transformers]. PPL reserved the option to buy another 36 turbines under three 12-turbine options expiring in May, June, and December of 2001. The company planned to purchase turbines from the trust as construction of new plants began. The objective was to get the financing for the first plants in place and transfer 12 of the turbines from the equipment trust before May 2001 so that the trust would have sufficient borrowing capacity to exercise the first option.

PPL had two large plant sites in the final phases of approval and one plant in late-stage development as of February 2001. These plants would cost approximately $300 million each and use 10 to 12 turbines each. Because the total construction cost would require approximately $1 billion and construction periods for several plants would be staggered, PPL split the total $1.8 billion financing into two phases. Steve May was responsible for choosing a structure to finance the first phase at a cost of $1 billion.

May and his group reviewed the financing options. Once again, the group quickly dismissed corporate finance, given the current market valuation of its common stock as well as the burden $1 billion of debt finance would put on the corporation balance sheet. As for project finance, generally a portfolio of this size would be a good candidate, but using project finance for peaking plants was problematic. May explained:

> We would have been lucky to get 30% leverage using project finance for these peakers, and the transaction would be very expensive to set up. It is very tough to raise project finance for peaking plants, especially for plants facing merchant risk. The irregular cash flows and uncertain demand simply do not appeal to most lenders. We just don't think it's the optimal way to do it.

The team also evaluated various leasing structures. May explained the process:

> First, we analyze the project returns. We look at the unlevered IRR, equity IRR, and NPV. If the project meets our hurdle rate, then we turn to the financing decision. We then compare the cost of off-balance sheet financing with the on-balance sheet alternative. In this

case, we looked at the different lease structures versus a hypothetical corporate finance deal at 50/50 leverage because that is our corporate target leverage ratio. Besides the all-in financing cost, we also analyze the impact on earnings.

May narrowed in on leasing, specifically synthetic leasing, as the best option. Because the plants would be greenfield projects, they fell within the legal and accounting constraints on synthetic leases. The structure would also provide favorable tax treatment as well as an opportunity to benefit from any asset appreciation via a purchase option. May and his team then began detailed financial analysis. (Exhibit 23-7 shows the difference between financing a hypothetical peaking plant using traditional corporate finance and a synthetic lease.) To execute a synthetic lease, PPL would create a special purpose entity (SPE) that would arrange financing for the peaking plants and purchase turbines from the revolving equipment trust. Simultaneously, the SPE would enter into a seven-year synthetic lease (two years of construction plus five years of operations) with PPL Large Scale Distributed Generation II, LLC, a newly formed, wholly-owned subsidiary of PPL Corporation.

During this period, several banks visited PPL to pitch their capabilities in structuring and financing the deal. While all said they could execute a traditional synthetic lease, several suggested an alternative structure known as a limited recourse synthetic lease. Traditional synthetic leases were structured with 97% debt, typically split into two tranches, and 3% equity (as required under EITF 90-15). The A tranche (85% of total capital) carried a parent guarantee. The B tranche (12%) was nonrecourse to the lessee; however, lenders held a first mortgage on the assets. Because the B tranche was overcollateralized (100% of the asset value against 12% of the capital), there was minimal residual risk. As a result, most lenders viewed the B tranche as a corporate credit, even though it had some project exposure. Equity shares, placed into a C tranche, assumed the residual risk (see Exhibit 23-8).

The difference between the traditional and limited-recourse synthetic lease was the size of the A and B tranches. Under the limited recourse structure, the A tranche could be decreased to as little as 35% of the total financing, while the B tranche could be increased to as much as 62% of the total. However, given the volatility of standalone peaking plant cash flows, banks were uncomfortable increasing the B tranche above 30%. Nonetheless, the smaller A tranche as compared to the traditional structure reduced the size of the parent guarantee, which decreased the corporation's overall exposure. In essence, it allowed PPL to transfer residual risk. It also provided some downside protection if the market for peaking plants did not live up to PPL's expectations. Because credit rating agencies viewed the B and C notes as project finance (i.e., non–recourse), a large portion of the debt was considered to be "off-credit," meaning it would not affect the corporation's debt capacity or debt rating. For a company with heightened sensitivity to leverage, this aspect of the deal was particularly attractive.

Unfortunately, lenders also viewed the limited-recourse structure as project finance. A leasing expert explained:

> There is no gray area for bankers. Deals are either priced on corporate risk or project risk. As the "B" tranche increases in size, the lenders take on increasing asset risk, and at some point, the deal becomes a project loan. We usually see the corporate lenders walking away when the nonrecourse debt hits 20% or more. Borrowers are then forced to seek funds in the project finance market, and that's a whole new ballgame. There are many fewer players in the market, the deal takes longer to structure, and it costs a whole lot more.[11]

---

[11] Personal interview [anonymous participation] with casewriters on September 19, 2001.

EXHIBIT 23-7

HYPOTHETICAL PROJECTIONS FOR A NEW PEAKING POWER PLANT[a] ($U.S. MILLIONS)

Financing of LSDG Project #1

Key Assumptions:

Capital Requirements		Refinance Lease in 2006 (to D/V = 50%)	
Base Investment	$300	Amount	$305
Lease costs	$ 5		
Total	$305		

	2002	2003	2004	2005	2006	2007
Operating Assumptions						
Output (GWhs)	876	876	876	876	876	876
Capacity Factor	20%	20%	20%	20%	20%	20%
Financial Assumptions (PPL Corporation)						
Expected PPL Corp. Net Income	$600.0	$630.0	$661.5	$694.6	$729.3	$765.8
Average Shares Outstanding	150.0	150.0	150.0	150.0	150.0	150.0
Earnings Per Share	$4.00	$4.20	$4.41	$4.63	$4.86	$5.11
Traditional Financed (on balance sheet with D/V = 50%)						
Project Revenue	$75.0	$77.3	$79.6	$82.0	$84.4	$86.9
Project Costs	27.0	27.8	28.6	29.5	30.4	31.3
Project EBITDA	48.0	49.4	50.9	52.5	54.0	55.6
Project Net Income (NOPAT, pre financing)	22.2	23.1	23.9	24.8	25.8	26.7
Corporate Interest Expense (after tax)	4.4	4.4	4.4	4.4	4.4	4.4
Contribution to PPL Corp. Net Income	$17.8	$18.7	$19.6	$20.4	$21.4	$22.3
Pro Form Results Including Project						
Total Net Income	$617.8	$648.7	$681.1	$715.0	$750.7	$788.1
# shares outstanding	153.8	153.8	153.8	153.8	153.8	153.8
Earnings Per Share	$4.02	$4.22	$4.43	$4.65	$4.88	$5.13
Accretion/(Dilution) ($/share)	$0.02	$0.02	$0.02	$0.02	$0.02	$0.02
Net Cash Flow (after-tax)	**22.3**	**21.8**	**22.9**	**23.9**	**25.0**	**26.1**
As Financed (100% off-balance sheet synthetic lease)						
Project Net Income (NOPAT, pre financing)	$22.2	$23.1	$23.9	$24.8	$25.8	$26.7
After tax income adjustments						
Plus: Depreciation	5.9	5.9	5.9	5.9	5.9	5.9
Plus: Corp. Debt Interest Savings	4.4	4.4	4.4	4.4	4.4	4.4
Less: Post Lease Depreciation	—	—	—	5.9	5.9	
Less: Lease payment	10.3	10.3	10.3	10.3	—	—
Less: Corp. Debt Interest Expense	—	—	—	—	8.3	8.3
Contribution to PPL Corp. Net Income	$22.2	$23.1	$23.9	$24.8	$21.8	$22.7
Pro Form Results Including Project						
Total Net Income	$622.2	$653.1	$685.4	$719.4	$751.1	$788.5
# shares outstanding	153.2	153.2	153.2	153.2	153.8	153.8
Earnings Per Share	$4.06	$4.26	$4.47	$4.69	$4.88	$5.13
Accretion/(Dilution) ($/share)	$0.06	$0.06	$0.06	$0.06	$0.02	$0.02
Net Cash Flow (theoretical, after-tax)	**20.8**	**20.3**	**21.4**	**22.4**	**25.5**	**26.7**

[a] The information in this exhibit is solely hypothetical in nature and does not represent in any way projections of operating or financial results.

Source: Casewriter estimates.

EXHIBIT 23-8

TRADITIONAL SYNTHETIC LEASE STRUCTURE[a]

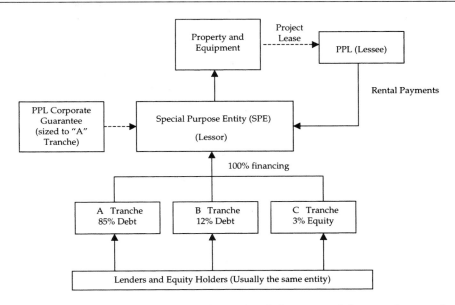

[a] In a limited recourse synthetic lease the A tranche equals as little as 35% and the B tranche as much as 62%.

Source: Casewriter.

One banker predicted it would take an additional two to four weeks of time on top of the four to six weeks it took to close a traditional synthetic lease:

> The difficulty in limited recourse structures is not getting project finance lenders comfortable with the asset risk, but rather getting them comfortable with the equity risk.[12] Generally, project finance lenders take on minimal equity risk because construction is funded pro-rata up-front. In these deals, debt pays for all the construction costs; equity only comes in at the end of the lease term in the form of a purchase option. Project finance lenders are not the company's typical relationship banks, as they are in a traditional synthetic lease, so it takes time to get them comfortable with the corporate credit.[13]

With regard to cost, the ballpark figure for the limited recourse structure was somewhere between 60 and 90 basis points more than a traditional synthetic lease for PPL (see comparison Exhibit 23-9). An investment banker explained:

> The traditional synthetic lease is priced based on corporate credit while the limited recourse synthetic lease is priced based on asset risk plus some equity risk. So the spread

[12] For clarification, the equity discussed in this quote refers to the purchase payment made by the company at the end of the five- to seven-year lease term, and not the 3% third-party equity.

[13] Personal interview [anonymous participation] with casewriters on September 19, 2001.

EXHIBIT 23-9

COMPARISON OF LEASING STRUCTURES

	Leveraged Lease[a]	Traditional Bank Synthetic[b]	Limited Recourses Bank Synthetic Lease
Investors	Lease Equity, Banks, Private Debt, 144A Investors	Banks	Banks
Percent Financing	50–80%	100%	100%
Tenor	20–40 years (75% of useful economic life— FAS 13)	5–7 years	5–7 years
Financing Cost (above corporate financing rate)	150 bps +	25–75 bps	50–110 bps
Percent Non-recourse	100%	0%–20%	20%–40%
Percent Off Balance Sheet	100%	100%	100%
Percent Off Credit Treatment	70%–80%	0%–20%	0%–60%
Asset Control	Lessee	Lessee	Lessee
Guarantees			
Rents	0%	100%	60%–80%
Residuals	0%	80%–85%	60%–80%
Transaction Costs (% of total lease cost)	3%	1.75%	2.25%
Operating Flexibility (1 = Low, 5 = High)	4	5	4

[a] This information is for a typical leveraged lease such as PPL Montana. Leveraged leases can be structured differently, for example, it is possible to provide 100% financing with a leveraged lease.

[b] Longer tenor synthetic leases have been done in the capital markets.

Source: PPL Corporation company documents.

between the two structures will vary depending on the company's credit rating and the type of asset involved.[14]

CONCLUSION

Although May was confident that a synthetic lease was the way to go, he had to decide which structure to use. On the one hand, the limited recourse synthetic lease meant greater off-credit treatment and a smaller parent guarantee. But it also meant increased costs and additional time that might jeopardize their ability to exercise the first turbine option. On the other hand, May was fairly confident the traditional structure would close on time, and it would certainly be cheaper. But the company would take an on-credit hit due to the larger parent guarantee. After deciding on a structure, he still had to convince Jim Abel that the chosen option not only made sense for this deal, but also did not hinder future efforts to raise capital.

[14] Ibid.

APPENDIX

AN OVERVIEW OF LEASING STRUCTURES

A lease contract grants one party (the lessee) the right to use an asset owned by a second party (the lessor) in exchange for a series of payments over a defined period of time. A common example is commercial real estate. Under the lease, the lessee occupies the space for a specified period while paying rent to the lessor. Leasing is not, however, limited to real estate; companies often use leasing to finance assets in which ownership or immediate ownership is not essential. Assets can include anything from office equipment to airplanes to power plants. Most commonly, a lessor uses its financial resources to buy an asset and signs a lease agreement with the lessee. Lease payments are generally equal across periods and consist of a principal payment based on the cost of the asset or some depreciation factor, and an implied interest rate. At the end of the lease, the lessee can return the asset or purchase it for a predetermined sum (known as a purchase option).

Lease financing can take many forms. From the *lessee's* standpoint, the Financial Accounting Standards Board (FASB) classifies leases in two categories: *capital* leases and *operating* leases. Capital leases are like secured loans and can be viewed as an alternative to borrowing. Similar to debt service payments, rental payments are fixed obligations. The lessee is considered to be the owner from an economic perspective because it bears all of the benefits and burdens of ownership. FASB requires the asset to appear on the lessee's balance sheet, and to be depreciated as if it had been purchased. For tax purposes, the lessee can deduct depreciation and the implied interest expense embedded in the rental payment. In contrast, the lessee is not considered to be the owner in an operating lease and, therefore, forgoes the benefits as well as the burdens of asset ownership. The asset does not appear on the lessee's balance sheet, and it expenses the contractual rental payments. Furthermore, the lessee does not record any depreciation expense, which results in earnings enhancement.

Financial Accounting Standard No. 13 (FAS 13) sets forth criteria for classifying leases. At inception, if a lease meets one or more of the following four criteria, then FASB dictates that it must be a capital lease; otherwise, it is an operating lease.

1. Title is transferred to the lessee by the end of the lease term.
2. The lease contains a bargain purchase option.[15]
3. The lease term is at least 75% of the economic useful life of the property or asset.
4. The present value of the lease payments is 90% or more of the fair market value of the property or asset, less related investment tax credits retained by the lessor.[16]

From the *lessor's* perspective, FASB has four lease classifications: *operating* leases, *sales-type* leases, *direct financing* leases, and *leveraged* leases. To categorize a lease into one of the four classifications, FASB considers two questions: (1) does the lease meet one or more of the criteria set forth in FAS 13, and (2) does the lessor receive a man-

---

[15] A bargain purchase option refers to a price that is significantly below expected fair market value.

[16] The present value is calculated using the lower of the rate implicit within the lease and the lessee's incremental borrowing rate, defined as the rate that the lessee would have incurred to borrow the funds necessary to purchase the leased asset over a similar term.

(Continued)

ufacturer or dealer profit (or loss) from the lease transaction (i.e., is the fair market value of the leased property at the inception of the lease greater or less than the lessor carrying cost)? Operating leases do not meet any of the criteria in FAS 13; but they do result in a manufacturer or dealer profit/loss, for the lessor. The other three leases meet at least one criterion in FAS 13; however, sales-type leases give rise to a lessor profit/loss, whereas direct financing and leveraged leases do not. FASB's distinction between direct financing and leveraged leases is based on how the lessor finances the asset. To qualify for a leveraged lease the lessor must acquire financing through a long-term creditor, the debt must be nonrecourse to the lessor, and the transaction must be "substantially" leveraged (interpreted to mean debt-to-capital ratio of 60% or more). Otherwise FASB deems the transaction to be a direct financing lease. A financial expert commented:

> Leveraged leasing . . . satisfies a need for lease financing of especially large capital equipment projects with economic lives of up to 25 or more years. . . . A leveraged lease is conceptually similar to a single-investor lease. However, a leveraged lease is appreciably more complex in size, documentation, legal involvement, and, most importantly, the number of parties involved and the unique advantages that each party gains.[17]

Because accounting and tax treatment affect lease terms and pricing, lessees are concerned with how lessors finance the asset in question.

The lessee's classification of leases hinges on whether it is considered to own the asset. Given the complexity of some lease structures, this distinction is not always obvious. One such structure in the market today is the synthetic lease. Synthetic leasing represents a low-cost, usually interest-only financing, that combines the accounting treatment of an operating lease with the tax treatment of a capital lease (see Appendix A-1). A financial consultant from McGuire Woods Consulting explained:

APPENDIX A-1

COMPARISON OF TAX AND ACCOUNTING TREATMENT OF VARIOUS FINANCING STRUCTURES

	Asset Purchase	Capital Lease	Operating Lease	Synthetic Lease
Tax Accounting				
Rent payments	No	No	Yes	No
Depreciation	Yes	Yes	No	Yes
Interest	Yes	Yes	No	Yes
GAAP Accounting				
Rent payments	No	No	Yes	Yes
Depreciation	Yes	Yes	No	No
Interest	Yes	Yes	No	No

Source: T. A. Dorsey, "Maximizing Profits with a Synthetic Lease," *The Appraisal Journal,* January 2000, pp. 93–96.

---

[17] P. Nevitt and F. Fabozzi, "Leveraged Leasing," Chapter 14, *Project Financing,* 7th edition, Euromoney Books, p. 147.

(Continued)

Simply stated, a synthetic lease is a financing arrangement that is classified as a lease for accounting purposes and a loan for tax purposes. This type of financing arrangement is attractive to the lessee/borrower because the lessee achieves off-balance sheet treatment for its debt but retains the tax benefits associated with ownership of property.[18]

Although synthetic leases have existed for a number of years, they became more popular in the mid-1990s as a way to finance real estate and power assets. A project finance expert at a leading investment bank commented:

Synthetic leasing has historically been used as a way for companies to finance assets off-balance sheet. However, lately the structure has received more attention. With the growing importance the market is putting on EPS performance, companies are using this structure for the earnings kick. It can't be used indefinitely: that would be counter-productive to earnings in the long-term. But if needed, this structure can produce the extra earnings boost companies are looking for.

The most effective way to structure a synthetic lease is for the lessor to create a Special Purpose Entity (SPE) to hold the asset. The SPE and the lessee enter into a short-term lease (typically five to seven years) with a purchase option at the end of the term. The SPE secures financing with the asset and the *lessee's* credit through a residual value guarantee for some fraction of the total financing (typically, it covers the A tranche only). The rental payments usually consist of the interest due on the financing, while the purchase option at the end is a balloon payment that pays back the outstanding debt and equity. At the end of the lease term, the lessee can renew the financing, purchase the asset for an amount equal to the outstanding debt and equity, or sell the asset to a third party. If the sale proceeds exceed the outstanding obligation, then the lessee may keep the difference; however, if the sale proceeds fall short, then the lessee must pay the difference up to a cap equal to its residual value guarantee. The McGuire Woods consultant noted:

The lessee's purchase option . . . permits the lessee to capture any appreciation in property. From the lessor's standpoint, the lessee retains residual risk of any decline in value of the property, contrary to a typical lease.[19]

Synthetic leases can be complex to structure, but they have important applications. They are complex to structure because numerous accounting regulations must be met for this type of structure to be deemed an operating lease. In addition to FASB 13, the major Financial Accounting Standards (FAS) and Emerging Issues Tack Force (EITF) findings that govern synthetic lease structures are:

- **FAS 98** (for sale-leaseback transactions)—Restricts operating lease treatment if a lessee demonstrates "continued involvement" in an asset that the lessee sells and then leases back. Such involvement exists if the lessee shares in the appreciation of the asset, guarantees a return to the lessor, or is obligated to purchase the asset.

---

[18] N. Little, "Financing Power Projects with Synthetic Leases," *Project Finance International*, Issue 219, June 13, 2001.
[19] Ibid.

(Continued)

—Limits synthetic leases to asset acquisitions and greenfield developments where no prior or ongoing involvement in the assets exists.

- **EITF 96-21:** Addresses "continuing involvement" in terms of payments made to the lessor.

  —Restricts the lessee from incurring significant costs before finalizing documentation of the synthetic lease (no "hard" costs and up to 10% "soft" costs)[20]

- **EITF 97-10** (in reference to greenfield projects): Addresses lessee's involvement in construction of a build-to-suit real estate transaction. If the lessee is deemed to have significant involvement or risk in construction, then the lessee will be considered the owner and the asset will receive on-balance sheet treatment.

  —Limits the value of construction guarantees, indemnities, and other payments from lessee to lessor.

- **EITF 90-15:** Outlines criteria under which a Special Purpose Entity (SPE) must be consolidated onto a lessee's balance sheet.

  —Requires the SPE/lessor to hold a minimum of 3% equity to keep the asset off the lessee's balance sheet.

- **EITF 97-1:** Restricts the circumstances in which the lessee can indemnify the lessor for pre-existing environmental conditions. Also outlines circumstances in which the lease arrangement can include defaults that are not related to the lessee's use of the property, such as defaults based on financial performance.

  —Limits indemnities by lessee to lessor and may limit lessor's recourse to lessee under certain situations.

No formal tax codes address synthetic leases. In general, however, tax regulations apply to the substance of the transaction rather than to the technical form or structure, which drives accounting treatment. Given the "interest only" nature of the lease payment and optional "bullet payment" purchase, tax authorities classify synthetic leases as a financing or, more specifically, a conditional sale. Under conditional sales, the lessee is deemed to be the owner and can, therefore, deduct interest payments (i.e., rent) and obtain tax benefits related to depreciation expense.

Because the advantages of the synthetic lease structure are based on IRS and FASB "loopholes" there is a possibility that these benefits could be lost. But for now, the structure proves a useful financial tool for the construction and/or acquisition of corporate assets, including power plants. A leasing consultant commented:

> Although synthetic leases appear to be a complicated web of accounting rules, they can be surprisingly easy and efficient to execute. It remains to be seen the extent to which energy deregulation and other changes in the industry may effect the structuring and implication of synthetic leases in the power arena. For now, the popularity of synthetic leases is undiminished, and an attractive means of providing off-balance sheet financing.[21]

---

[20] "Hard" costs are expenditures on real (physical) property used to construct the building or power plant, for example, which can include equipment purchases and building materials as well as site construction (demolition or land clearing). "Soft" costs are expenditures that are not directly attributed to construction such as interest, legal fees, or architect fees.

[21] Little, "Financing Power Projects with Synthetic Leases."

(Continued)

Besides the tax and accounting treatment, it is important to understand the way credit agencies analyze lease transactions when determining a company's debt rating. Credit ratings affect not only a company's ability to borrow, but also the rate at which it can borrow. A one-notch change in an investment-grade rating can affect a company's cost of borrowing by 30 basis points (bp) or more, and a drop to below investment-grade can affect pricing by 150 bp or more. A credit analyst at one of the leading rating agencies in the United States commented:

> A primary consideration in determining credit ratings is a company's cash flow coverage ratios. It's really the ability to cover debt obligations that we are concerned about. And by that we are talking about cash flow available for debt service. Debt to total capitalization means very little in this context. I barely look at the balance sheets anymore—they're not particularly helpful. I go right to the notes, the income statement, and the cash flow.[22]

Companies with limited debt capacity are concerned not only with on- versus off-balance sheet issues, but also with whether a credit agency views a deal as on- or off-credit. Full or 100% off-credit treatment refers to financial obligations that do not affect a company's corporate debt capacity or coverage ratios. The credit analyst explained:

> Synthetic leases are definitely a corporate obligation, and that translates into a debt obligation. The company does not receive off-credit treatment if there are guarantees on the obligations. To the extent a cash payment must be made, as is the case with synthetics, that cash payment is factored into the fixed charges, i.e., debt service.[23]

Each credit agency has its own methods and policies for analyzing various lease structure, and a fair amount of discretion is left up to the analyst. The credit analyst noted, "The best advice I can give to a company contemplating a leasing deal is to talk to us early and often."

As a financing tool, leasing is a good alternative to corporate and project debt because it contains aspects of both. Depending on the structure, a lease may be secured by corporate credit similar to corporate finance. Or it may be secured by the cash flows from an asset and offer some sort of risk mitigation, both of which are typical in project finance. Picking the "right" financing structure is a function of an asset's characteristics and the company's strategic objectives and financial position of the company (see Appendix A-2).

---

[22] Personal interview between Moody's credit analyst and casewriters on October 5, 2001.
[23] Ibid.

(Continued)

APPENDIX A-2

FINANCING DECISION TREE FOR LESSEES

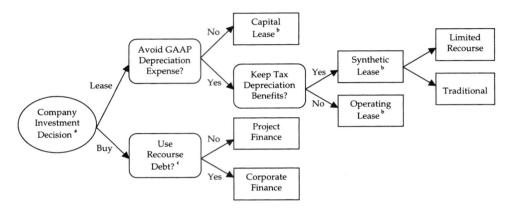

[a] The ultimate decision is for a financial manager to compare the optimal lease scenario with the optimal buy scenario.

[b] Lease choice must conform to FASB standards and tax regulations.

[c] Subject to cost, time, and risk bearing considerations as well as a company's debt capacity.

Source: Casewriter.

24

Basel II: Assessing the Default and Loss Characteristics of Project Finance Loans

The Basel II Accord poses a major threat to the project finance industry. It has the potential to drive banks out of the business of project finance, and could dramatically curtail lending in both developed and emerging markets.

—Chris Beale, Managing Director and Global Head
of Project & Structured Trade Finance, Citigroup

On August 23, 2002, the global heads of the project finance business units at ABN AMRO, Citigroup, Deutsche Bank, and Société Générale sent a letter to the Basel Committee's Models Task Force in response to the committee's assertion that project finance loans were significantly riskier than corporate loans and, therefore, warranted higher capital requirements. Nearing finalization of a new capital accord, the committee planned to impose higher risk weights on project finance loans—risk weights that would, in some cases, double or triple the capital requirements on project finance loans. The executives feared the new capital standards would have a devastating effect on project finance lending by making loan spreads uneconomic to potential borrowers and by driving business to nonbank competitors that were not subject to the same capital requirements.

To challenge the proposal, the four banks joined forces and hired Standard & Poor's Risk Solutions to analyze the default and loss characteristics of their combined project loan portfolios. The consortium had now completed the study's first two phases—assessing the historical loss given default (LGD) and the probability of default (PD)—

Professor Benjamin C. Esty and Research Associate Aldo M. Sesia, Jr. prepared this case. HBS cases are developed solely as the basis for class discussion. Cases are not intended to serve as endorsements, sources of primary data, or illustrations of effective or ineffective management.

and was including the results in its letter to the committee. The results, consortium members believed, proved that project finance loans were less risky than most corporate loans. They wondered, however, if the results would convince the committee to lower the proposed risk weights on project loans.

THE BASEL COMMITTEE

The Bank for International Settlements (BIS), headquartered in Basel, Switzerland, served as a bank for central banks and helped set international monetary policy. In 1975, the central bank governors of the G-10 countries[1] convened to form the Basel Committee on Banking Supervision. Although the committee had no supranational authority, it articulated banking standards and guidelines with the goal of closing gaps in international supervisory coverage. As part of its responsibilities, the committee developed capital adequacy standards for international banks, which served as guidelines for national bank regulators. Prior to the committee's introduction of international capital standards, national regulators established minimum capital requirements using simple capital ratios (e.g., net worth to on-balance sheet assets). In the United States, for example, regulators set the requirement for primary capital at 5.5% of total assets.

The 1988 Capital Accord (Basel I)

The Basel Committee published its first report on capital adequacy in 1988. Called the 1988 Capital Accord (Basel I), the report highlighted "dangerously low" capital levels at the world's largest banks and proposed the creation of uniform minimum capital standards. By setting minimum capital standards, the 1988 Accord protected bank owners, depositors, creditors, and deposit insurers (i.e., governments) against financial distress. The committee chose 8% as the target capital ratio (net worth to assets), though the actual amount of capital required varied as a function of a bank's asset portfolio. The Basel framework identified five broad asset categories and assigned risk weights of 0%, 10%, 20%, 50%, and 100% to them. Whereas cash had a risk weight of 0%, residential mortgages had a risk weight of 50%. Project finance and all corporate loans fell in the highest risk category with a risk weight of 100%. Thus, a bank with a $100 million project finance loan needed to hold $8 million of capital (= $100 million loan × 100% risk weight × 8% target capital ratio). National regulators adopted the accord and required banks to implement it by 1992. Simplicity, the framework's strength, was also its greatest weakness. Using five categories simplified implementation but ignored important differences between loans within a given asset category.

The New Basel Capital Accord (Basel II)

In June 1999, the Basel Committee announced plans to revise the capital standards and described its objectives as follows:

> The new framework intends to provide approaches which are both more comprehensive and more sensitive to risks than the 1988 Accord, while maintaining the overall level of regulatory capital. Capital requirements that are more in line with underlying risks will allow banks to manage their businesses more efficiently. . . . The Committee believes the

---

[1] The Group of Ten (G-10) is made up of eleven industrial countries including Belgium, Canada, France, Germany, Italy, Japan, the Netherlands, Sweden, Switzerland, the United Kingdom, and the United States.

benefits of a regime in which capital is aligned more closely to risk significantly exceed the costs, with the result that the banking system should be safer, sounder, and more efficient.[2]

The new regulatory framework consisted of three pillars. Pillar 1 (Minimum Capital Requirements) maintained the same definition of regulatory capital and the 8% target capital ratio. Pillar 2 (Supervisory Review) called for increased regulatory oversight. Pillar 3 (Market Discipline) outlined requirements for increased bank disclosure. The committee hoped to finalize the new accord by the end of 2002 and implement it by 2005.

The new proposal also focused on individual asset classes and not on a bank's entire asset portfolio or its integrated balance sheet (i.e., the combination of assets and liabilities). Rather than using just a few broad asset classes, however, the new proposal set capital requirements based on credit risk within asset classes using one of two approaches. Under the *standardized* approach, banks would use the ratings on their borrowers or loans, supplied by credit rating agencies approved by regulators, with risk weights set by the Basel Committee to determine the minimum amount of capital they needed to hold. If the borrowers or loans were unrated, banks would have to use 100% risk weights. In contrast, under the *internal ratings based* (IRB) approach, banks would classify their loans into risk categories using their own internal data, provided they could demonstrate they had accurate historical default and recovery data. Banks with PD data only, would use the *foundation* IRB approach in conjunction with supervisory estimates of LGD to determine their capital charges.[3] Banks with PD and LGD data would use the *advanced* IRB approach. In both cases, the capital requirements would be based on a framework established by the regulators, which would define the relationship between PD, LGD, and risk weights. In most cases, banks using the IRB approaches would have equal or lower capital requirements than banks using the standardized approach.

Although the IRB approaches implied there would be different standards at different banks, the committee favored the internal approaches because they incorporated a bank's specific risk profile, loan loss experience, and risk-mitigation techniques. By incorporating this information into the capital allocation process, the committee hoped to improve safety, soundness, and efficiency. Based on early feedback from the banks, the committee estimated the new accord would increase total industry capital by 14% (see Exhibit 24-1).

Besides setting capital based on subcategories of asset risk, the new accord treated project finance as an asset class distinct from corporate lending. Although the use of project finance dated back to the 1930s, if not earlier, it was a relatively small business until the 1990s, when it began to grow rapidly. By 2000, total project-financed investment exceeded $200 billion annually (see Exhibit 24-2). Given this growth, the Basel Committee's Models Task Force (MTF), formed to design the accord's IRB approaches, decided that project finance would be classified as a form of "specialized lending." Generally speaking, specialized lending involved loans secured by an asset's cash flow rather than by a corporate balance sheet and earnings (e.g., income-producing real estate).

---

[2] "The New Basel Capital Accord: An Explanatory Note," Secretariat of the Basel Committee on Banking Supervision, June 2001, p. 2.

[3] Essentially, the Basel Committee wanted banks to hold enough (regulatory) capital to cover their expected loss (EL) and unexpected loss (UL). EL was equal to PD multiplied by LGD multiplied by EAD, where PD and LGD were percentages, and EAD (exposure at default) was the loan's outstanding loan amount plus lending commitments. UL represented the volatility around the expected losses.

EXHIBIT 24-1

THE IMPACT OF BASEL II ON BANKING INDUSTRY CAPITAL

Asset Class	Percent of Total Capital Under *Current* Capital Requirements	Basel II[a]	
		Percentage Change in Required Capital by Asset Class	Change in Required Capital as a Percent of Current Total Capital Required for *All* Assets
Corporate	61%	22%	14%
Sovereign	1	238	3
Interbank	8	49	4
Retail	24	(28)	(7)
Securitization	1	108	1
Equity	3	(17)	0
Project Finance	2	22	0
Total	100%		
Total increase in capital			**14%**

[a] Percentage increase is based on the foundation IRB approach.

Source: "Results of the Second Quantitative Study," Basel Committee on Banking Supervision, November 5, 2001, p. 5.

The MTF believed specialized lending was riskier than corporate lending and, therefore, warranted higher risk weights:

> First, such loans possess unique loss distribution and risk characteristics. In particular, given the source of repayment, the exposures exhibit greater risk volatility—in times of distress banks are likely to be faced with both high default rates and high loss rates. . . . MTF's dialogue with the industry also highlighted that historical loan performance data for specialized lending exposures are scarce. Many banks therefore face difficulties in establishing credible and reliable estimates of key risk factors (including probability of default), which can be adequately validated by both the bank and its supervisor. As a result, there is no common industry standard for a rigorous, empirical, and risk-sensitive approach to economic capital estimations for specialized lending exposures.[4]

In January 2002, the Basel Committee provided further details on how project finance would be treated under the new accord. Under the standardized and the advanced IRB approaches, the risk weights for project loans would be the same as the risk weights for corporate loans with similar ratings and LGD estimates. However, the MTF said project loans would have higher risk weights than corporate loans under the foundation IRB approach because supervisory estimates of LGD for project loans were likely to be higher than LGD estimates for corporate loans. Under the foundation IRB approach, banks would classify project finance loans into four categories (strong, fair, weak, or default) and use risk weights ranging from 75% to 750% set by

---

[4] "Working Paper on the Internal Ratings-Based Approach to Specialised Lending," Basel Committee on Banking Supervision, October 2001, p. 1.

EXHIBIT 24-2

PROJECT FINANCE INVESTMENT GROWTH AND DEBT TYPE, 1994–2001

	Total Project-Financed Investment (US$ billion)								
	1994	1995	1996	1997	1998	1999	2000	2001	5-Year CAGR
Bank loans	$13.7	$23.3	$42.8	$67.4	$56.7	$72.4	$110.9	$108.5	20%
Bonds	4.0	3.8	4.8	7.5	9.8	20.0	20.8	25.0	39
Total Project Lending	17.7	27.1	47.6	74.9	66.5	92.4	131.7	133.5	23
Year-to-Year Change		53%	76%	57%	−11%	39%	43%	1%	
MLA/BLA development agencies[a]	11.3	17.6	19.0	21.9	18.5	16.6	17.7	18.8	0
Equity Financing (estimate)[b]	12.4	19.2	28.5	41.5	36.4	46.7	64.0	65.2	18
Total Private Sector Investment (including debt and equity)	$41.4	$63.9	$95.1	$138.3	$121.4	$155.7	$213.4	$217.5	18%

	Percent of Lending by Type of Debt							
	1994	1995	1996	1997	1998	1999	2000	2001
Bank loans	77%	86%	90%	90%	85%	78%	84%	81%
Bonds	23	14	10	10	15	22	16	19
Total	100%	100%	100%	100%	100%	100%	100%	100%

	Number of Projects							
	1994	1995	1996	1997	1998	1999	2000	2001
Number of projects:								
With bank loan financing	NA	NA	341	407	419	559	594	314
With bond financing	NA	22	19	25	43	78	86	79

[a] Private sector investment made by bilateral development agencies (BLAs), multilateral development agencies (MLAs), export credit agencies (ECAs), and export financing institutions. Adapted from "The Private Sector Financing Activities of International Financial Institutions: 1991–1997," IFC, January 1998. The numbers for 1994 and 2001 are casewriter estimates. Some of the reported total is for guarantees; we assume 75% of the total is for equity and debt investments.

[b] Assuming a total debt/total capitalization ratio of 70%.

Source: Adapted from *Project Finance International* (London, UK: IFR Publishing, 3/2/95, 2/28/96, 1/29/97, 1/28/98, 1/27/99, 1/26/00, 1/24/01, and 1/23/02).

the Basel Committee (see Exhibit 24-3). Given this proposal, a bank using the foundation IRB approach with a $100 million project finance loan rated "fair" would have to hold an incremental $4 million of capital under the new accord [= (150% Basel II risk weight − 100% Basel I risk weight) × $100 million × 8%]. Assuming a bank required a 20% pretax return on equity (ROE), the higher capital charge would add approximately 80 basis points to the price of the loan [= ($4 million × 20%)/ $100 million], ignoring the benefits of using less debt to fund the loan.[5] While all banks used significantly more sophisticated internal capital allocation systems—most of these systems were based on some notion of risk-adjusted return on capital (RAROC, pronounced "ray rock")—the end result was the same: spreads on low-rated project finance loans

[5] Target returns, or target returns net of funding costs, depend on many factors such as asset risk, maturity (tenor), capitalization, and current interest rates.

EXHIBIT 24-3

PROPOSED RISK WEIGHTS FOR CORPORATE AND PROJECT LOANS (FOUNDATION IRB APPROACH)

Supervisory Rating Category	Probability of Default	Risk Weights for Corporate Finance Loans	Risk Weights for Project Finance Loans		
		Basel Committee Proposal[a]	Basel Committee Supervisory Categorization	Basel Committee Proposal (Jan. 2002)	Consortium Proposal (Mar. 2002)
AAA to A−	0.03–0.09%	19–35%	Strong	75%	10–18%
BBB+ to BBB−	0.25	55	Strong	75	28
BB+	0.75	90	Fair	150	46
BB	1.00	100	Fair	150	50
BB−	2.00	130	Fair	150	65
B+	3.00	150	Fair	150	75
B to C	5–20.00	186–376	Weak	300	93–188
Default[b]	N/A	625	Default	750	313

[a] Assumes an LGD of 45% to 50% (casewriter interpretation of the Basel Committee's position).

[b] Loan ratings can migrate to the default category over time.

Source: Four Bank Consortium memorandum to the Basel Committee and national regulators, March 18, 2002, p. 2.

would have to increase. (Exhibit 24-4 shows typical terms for a project finance loan.) Because subinvestment-grade loans (BB+ and below) comprised 50% to 65% of the average bank's project loan portfolio, bankers anticipated higher capital requirements for project loans under Basel II. The Basel committee predicted that total capital for project loans would increase by 22% (see Exhibit 24-1).

Under the new accord, banks that opted to use the IRB approaches for their corporate loans would also be required to use the IRB approaches for their project loans. Banks that had historical data for their corporate loans were likely to choose the IRB approaches because they would, in most cases, reduce their capital requirements. Consequently, these banks would be obligated to use the IRB approaches for their project finance loans as well. In the event a bank did not have sufficient historical data for its project loans, it would be given a transition period to build the necessary internal systems to report the necessary data. In the interim, the bank would slot its project loans into supervisory categories using Basel Committee guidelines and apply risk weights similar to the foundation IRB approach.

INDUSTRY REACTION TO BASEL II

Project finance bankers reacted immediately to the MTF proposal. For example, Chris Beale, managing director and global head of project finance at Citigroup, said:

> As I read the proposal, alarm bells began to go off. We won't be able to price loans high enough to earn an acceptable return on capital, which means the new accord has the potential to put us out of business. Without a doubt, banks' interest in emerging market proj-

---

EXHIBIT 24-4

RETURNS ON PROJECT FINANCE LOANS

Origination Returns		
Participation/Underwriting Fees	25–75bp	Assumes loan is fully drawn (no commitment fees)
Administrative Expense	25–75bp	Credit review and underwriting expenses
Ongoing Returns		
Interest Rates (3-month Libor)	5.00%	Recent historical average
Spread (Interest Income)	Libor + 180bp	
Interest Expense	Libor	
Operating (Noninterest) Expense	10bp	
Expected Loan Loss	??	
Desired Pretax Return on Equity (ROE)	20%	= (Probability of Default × Loss Given Default)
Loan Terms		
Average Size ($ millions)	$175	Median = $70
Average Maturity (years)	8.6	Median = 8.0
Syndicate Structure		
Total number of banks	14	
Number of arranging banks	11	
Number of participating banks	3	

Source: Casewriter estimates and data contained in S. Kleimeier and W. Megginson, "Are Project Finance Loans Different from Other Syndicated Credits?" *Journal of Applied Corporate Finance* 13, (Spring 2000): 75–87.

---

ects will evaporate, while here in the U.S. borrowers will either look to corporate finance solutions or forgo their investments. The committee's key assumption—the idea that project loans are significantly riskier than corporate loans—doesn't match my personal experience, nor does it reflect the historical performance of Citigroup's project loan portfolio.

Across town at Deutsche Bank's New York office, Managing Director Sandra Bell echoed Beale's reaction:

The Models Task Force views project finance as very risky due to the perception that the probability of default is high and that it is highly [positively] correlated with loss given default. We don't believe either perception is correct and worry that the resulting capital requirements will force us to increase our loan spreads. In a market where loan pricing is important, we won't be able to price competitively with other sources of capital that are not subject to the new Basel Accord. Furthermore, the proposed changes may preclude smaller banks from participating in the syndicated loan market, thereby limiting the borrowing capacity for any single project, as the remaining project lenders won't be willing to take larger, more risky hold positions.

At ABN AMRO in Amsterdam, Managing Director Jan Prins remarked:

The Models Task Force has incorrectly assumed that project loans are riskier than corporate loans, but this is understandable given that many projects involve greenfield assets and nonrecourse lending. Moreover, the higher margins on project loans hint at greater risk. The MTF may also point to anecdotal evidence to justify their position: that is, high-profile defaults such as Eurotunnel, EuroDisney, and Iridium. But for each of these defaults, there are hundreds of successful deals that you never hear about. When you factor in all those loans, the track record is really quite impressive.

Despite the initial opposition, the Basel Committee seemed intent on establishing higher capital charges for project loans. However, some project financiers believed they could persuade the committee to do otherwise. Beale, for instance, saw the committee's request for feedback as a "call to arms." As he contemplated various responses, he had to face one reality: although most banks had long-term statistics on loan losses, few tracked the performance of project finance loans as a distinct asset class for more than a few years. Furthermore, at least at Citigroup, the reporting systems deleted loans that were prepaid or fully repaid, making it more difficult to document loan performance over the long run. Moody's Investor Service, having analyzed many bank portfolios and its own internal files, recognized this challenge:

> We believe that devising an accurate IRB approach for project finance lending is currently difficult due to one key factor: a lack of historical probability of default and loss given default data. . . . Without such data, it is difficult for any lending institution to demonstrate the accuracy of risk weights applied to a particular transaction. . . . We believe that it is currently difficult to verify whether many lending institutions can accurately predict default or losses for a project finance loan.[6]

Yet Beale remained guardedly optimistic, in part because banks were required to file detailed data on loan delinquencies and defaults with their national regulators. There was also the possibility that recent attempts to securitize project finance loans might have generated some useful data. Securitization of project loans began in 1998 when Credit Suisse First Boston issued the first collateralized debt obligation (CDO).[7] Three years later, Citigroup issued a $350 million CDO backed by 25 project loans, and other banks were trying to structure similar deals. To establish capital structures for their CDOs, particularly the size of the "first-loss" tranche, banks turned to the rating agencies to estimate the PD and LGD for their portfolios.

Despite the existence of some limited data, Beale knew it would be difficult to assemble convincing evidence, especially given the short time frame; he believed the committee wanted to finalize the new accord by March 2002. Nevertheless, he believed a quantitative study was the only way to convince the committee to change the current proposal. He hurriedly placed telephone calls to counterparts at 12 other banks, hoping they would join forces in such a study. He did not ask all of the top project finance lenders to participate, but he did contact leading banks from a wide range of countries to build a global database and to create information that would interest not only the Basel Committee but also various national regulators. He did not, for example, contact the International Finance Corporation (IFC), a member of the World Bank Group. He felt its portfolio of emerging market loans would have a different risk profile because the IFC sometimes made loans for policy reasons (e.g., to foster economic development) rather than for purely commercial reasons.

Commenting on the invitation to participate in a loan loss study, Beale said:

> Some bankers declined to participate in the study because they felt it would not benefit their banks specifically. While it is true that we [Citigroup] will likely qualify for the ad-

---

[6] Moody's Response to the Basel Committee Proposal on an Internal Rating-Based Capital Adequacy Approach for Project Finance, May 2001, p. 43.

[7] A collateralized debt obligation is a form of asset securitization in which a bank places a portfolio of project loans in a trust. Shares of the trust are then sold to investors across a range of tranches with different loss positions. Collateralized debt obligations provide capital reserve relief, create balance sheet liquidity, and allow lenders to make new loans.

vanced IRB approach with or without the study, the study will help us, and the industry, on two fronts. First, we hope to convince the Basel Committee to lower the risk weights altogether, which will reduce our capital requirements. Second, many smaller banks that participate in our loan syndicates will not qualify for the advanced IRB approach. These banks will have to use the foundation approach and, therefore, face higher capital charges. We are doing the study to benefit these smaller banks and as a way to protect the viability of our loan syndication business.

Despite these arguments, bankers declined to participate for many reasons: they did not perceive Basel II as a serious threat, they were already preparing their own replies to the Basel Committee, or they did not believe there was enough time to collect the data and respond to the committee.

THE FOUR BANK CONSORTIUM

In January 2002, four banks—ABN AMRO, Citigroup, Deutsche Bank, and Société Générale—agreed to collaborate on a loan loss study. Each bank, headquartered in a different G-10 country, was one of the top 10 project finance loan arrangers in 2001. Combined, they had originated over 25% of all project loans in 2001 (see Exhibits 24-5a and 24-5b). At their first meeting, they agreed on two objectives: first, to convince the Basel Committee to reduce the risk weights for project finance loans; and second, to build a database that participating banks (e.g., consortium members) could use to estimate PD and LGD so they would qualify for the advanced IRB approach.

To conduct the analysis, the consortium approached Risk Solutions—a division of Standard & Poor's Corporation that provided customized credit analysis, models, and data to help clients manage risk. David Keisman, a managing director, explained:

We are ideally suited to conduct the project finance loan loss study. First, having worked with corporate debt for years, we have the expertise and the experience to analyze loan losses. Second, given the collaborative nature of the project, we can provide independence and objectivity. And third, as a separate division of Standard & Poor's, our analysis and findings will be independent of the rating agency. If the study results are favorable, the

---

EXHIBIT 24-5A

VOLUME OF SYNDICATED LOANS ARRANGED BY CONSORTIUM MEMBERS (U.S.$ MILLIONS)

	1997	1998	1999	2000	2001	Total
Citigroup	$ 2,913	$ 2,514	$ 5,897	$ 11,927	$ 15,512	$ 38,763
ABN AMRO	4,512	2,350	2,302	7,875	4,019	21,058
Société Générale	754	1,998	3,218	9,616	5,301	20,887
Deutsche Bank	3,315	4,091	3,045	6,487	3,623	20,561
Subtotal	11,494	10,953	14,462	35,905	28,455	101,269
Total Market	67,425	56,651	72,392	110,885	108,478	415,831
% of Total Market	**17.0%**	**19.3%**	**20.0%**	**32.4%**	**26.2%**	**24.4%**

Source: Four Bank Consortium memorandum to the Basel Committee and national regulators, March 18, 2002, p. 6.

EXHIBIT 24-5B

GLOBAL LEAD ARRANGERS—BANK LOANS (U.S.$ MILLIONS)

2001 Rank	Name	2000 Rank	Number of Issues in 2001	Amount Underwritten in 2001	Percent of Total Lending in 2001
1	**Citigroup**	1	54	$ 15,512	14.3%
2	WestLB	7	27	8,235	7.6
3	BNP Paribas SA	9	21	6,429	5.9
4	**Société Générale**	2	17	5,301	4.9
5	CSFB	6	8	4,742	4.4
6	JP Morgan	5	18	4,333	4.0
7	Dresdner Kleinwort Wasserstein	11	17	4,038	3.7
8	**ABN AMRO**	4	19	4,019	3.7
9	**Deutsche Bank**	8	14	3,623	3.3
10	Barclays	10	18	3,612	3.3
11	Mizuho Financial Group	14	20	3,187	2.9
12	IntesaBci	24	5	2,621	2.4
13	Bank of America	3	13	2,282	2.1
14	Credit Lyonnais	17	12	2,019	1.9
15	Royal Bank of Scotland	28	16	1,911	1.8
	Other banks			36,614	33.8
	Total Market			**$108,478**	**100.0%**

Source: Adapted from *Project Finance International*, January 24, 2001 and January 23, 2002.

consortium can show them to the Basel Committee, to their national regulators, and to the rating agencies. If not, they don't have to show anyone. Our only concern is whether the banks can get us the data we need to conduct the analysis.

The consortium broke the study into three phases and set deadlines for each one, as follows: (Phase 1) analyze LGD by March 2002; (Phase 2) analyze PD by July 2002; and (Phase 3) repeat the process with six to ten additional banks by March 2003. The consortium decided to analyze LGD first because there would be fewer defaults than loans to analyze by the March deadline (the PD analysis required Risk Solutions to analyze all loans) and because the consortium was primarily concerned with changing the committee's perception that defaults on project finance loans resulted in greater losses than defaults on corporate loans. Phase 2 was needed to estimate EL, while Phase 3 was needed to bolster the study's statistical power. Before collecting any data, however, the consortium had to define project finance and determine what constituted a default to ensure consistency in data collection across the banks. Though project finance had generally accepted characteristics (e.g., repayment occurred through project cash flow), nuances in loan characteristics made consistent identification of project finance loans improbable. Prins explained the challenge:

Conceptually, project finance is very simple. It normally involves a sizeable capital investment that is financed on the merits of the asset itself. A project company is not a going concern, but rather a self-liquidating entity. The project's cash flow services its debt and provides, ideally, a good return on investment for the sponsors. In practice, however, defining a project loan is much more difficult. Basel II assumes a clear distinction between project and corporate loans, but a clear distinction doesn't really exist in practice because many loans have characteristics of both. For example, the highly structured deals in the telecom industry, the recent portfolio financings in the power industry, and the loans to project holding companies like AES highlight the many gray areas between corporate and project finance.

After much discussion, the consortium adopted the following definition for project finance:

> A project company is a group of agreements and contracts between lenders, project sponsors, and other interested parties that creates a form of business organization that will issue a finite amount of debt on inception; will operate in a focused line of business; and, will ask that lenders look only to a specific asset to generate cash flow as the sole source of principal and interest payments and collateral.[8]

The consortium then tried to define what constituted a loan default. Nathan Fox, an assistant vice president at Citigroup, explained:

> If you use a broad definition like technical defaults (e.g., the borrower violates a covenant by failing to maintain credit ratios or missing performance milestones), then a large percent of our portfolio has experienced a default. But we view these types of defaults as one of the advantages of project lending. They serve as an early warning device, a tripwire, which forces borrowers to address faltering business plans and correct problems before they become too serious. In this study, we are interested in payment default (i.e., failure to pay on time and in full), but we recognize the importance of broader definitions.

Deutsche Bank's Bell elaborated:

> The Models Task Force has taken the concept of restructuring in the project finance area as a negative. On the contrary, those of us who practice this every day view restructuring as a basis for ensuring ultimate repayment and recovery. . . . Covenant packages are deliberately designed to allow a lot of things to happen early, providing the opportunity for projects to restructure. . . . [In] the project finance world, restructuring is associated with full recovery and often includes enhanced coverage and security. And that to me is a big distinction not recognized by the committee's process.[9]

The consortium eventually adopted a broader definition of default consistent with Standard & Poor's definition, though its members realized that a broader definition would result in higher default rates, yet lower LGD estimates. According to the consortium's definition, a default occurred if:

> a borrower was unable to make a contractually scheduled payment of principal and/or interest. This would include bankruptcies that disrupt payments, including default and cure within the grace period, consensual restructuring, amendment of the credit facility's repayment terms, and/or refinancing of the facility with the original lenders in order to give the borrower more time to repay the loan.

---

[8] "Project Finance Recovery Study," Standard & Poor's Risk Solutions, March 2002, p. 5.

[9] "React or Die," *ProjectFinance*, February 2002, p. 42.

PHASE 1—RECOVERY RATES (LOSS GIVEN DEFAULT)

The first part of the analysis determined recovery rates for defaulted loans. Risk Solutions created a data template for the banks and asked them to describe each defaulted loan's original terms, cash flow history, default date, and recovery amounts. Each bank appointed a study leader to gather the necessary information. With help from colleagues around the world, they collected and reviewed internal bank files. In some cases, merger activity and reorganizations complicated the process. For example, in 1999, Deutsche Bank acquired Bankers Trust, which two years earlier had acquired Alex. Brown & Sons. In the meantime, Risk Solutions searched public records and provided the banks with a list of likely defaults.

The four banks turned in Phase I data during February 2002. Although Risk Solutions was limited in its ability to verify specific facts because it did not have direct access to company records, it was able to cross-check information to ensure consistency across the banks. The fact that most project loans were syndicated made this task significantly easier because multiple banks held positions in the same loans. Conflicting classifications and missing data forced Risk Solutions to make several, albeit conservative, assumptions. After reviewing the data, Risk Solutions calculated recovery rates. In present value terms, the recovery rate equaled the amount of the default settlement divided by the sum of the loan principal at default plus accrued interest plus interest penalties. For example, if a bank recovered $97 million on a loan with $98 million of principal due at default plus $2 million of accrued interest and penalties, it had a recovery rate of 97% (= $97 million/$100 million) and an LGD of 3% (= 100% − 97%). The calculation did not include expenses incurred to recover amounts owed.

The four banks identified 43 defaults across a range of regions and industries (see Exhibit 24-6). The mean recovery rate for project loans was 75%; the median was 100% (see Exhibits 24-7a and 24-7b). From its existing database, Risk Solutions compared project loans against four types of corporate debt: leveraged loans,[10] secured debt,

---

EXHIBIT 24-6

DISTRIBUTION OF DEFAULTED LOAN FACILITIES BY REGION AND SECTOR

Region	Number of Facilities	Percent of Total	Sector	Number of Facilities	Percent of Total
North America	18	41.9%	Power	9	20.9%
Europe	8	18.6	Oil & Gas	8	18.6
Asia Pacific	6	14.0	Infrastructure	7	16.3
Latin America	6	14.0	Metals & Mining	6	14.0
Other (incl. Africa)	5	11.6	Telecom	6	14.0
			Other	7	16.3
Total	43	100.0%	Total	43	100.0%

Source: Adapted from "Project Finance Recovery Study," Standard & Poor's Risk Solutions, March 18, 2002, p. 9.

---

[10] Leveraged loans include senior debt obligations rated BB+/Ba or lower and all unrated debt as long as the price spreads are Libor plus 150 basis points (bps) or more. Investment grade debt, real estate, securitization vehicles, and traditional project finance are not considered leveraged loans. *Source:* Loan Pricing Corporation, ⟨http://www.loanpricing.com/⟩.

EXHIBIT 24-7A

DESCRIPTIVE STATISTICS ON RECOVERY RATES BY ASSET TYPE

Asset Type	Number of Observations	Mean	Median	Standard Deviation	Maximum[a]	Minimum	Kolmogorov-Smirnov Test[b]	Rank Sum Test[b]	Kruskal-Wallis Statistic[c]
Project Finance	43	75.39%	100.00%	34.90%	100.00%	0%			
Leveraged Loans[d]	203	78.03	98.26	29.56	151.01	0	1	0	0.7424
Secured Debt	339	68.85	78.86	32.68	111.49	0	1	0	0.0829
Senior Debt	844	67.33	78.05	34.19	125.23	0	1	0	0.0567
Senior Unsecured	311	46.20	40.38	36.27	125.23	0	1	1	0.0000

EXHIBIT 24-7B

DESCRIPTIVE STATISTICS ON RECOVERY RATES: PROJECT FINANCE VS. LEVERAGED LOANS

Asset Type	Number of Observations	Mean	Median	Standard Deviation	Maximum[a]	Minimum	Kolmogorov-Smirnov Test[b]	Rank Sum Test[b]	Kruskal-Wallis Statistic[c]
Project Finance	43	75.39%	100.00%	34.90%	100.00%	0%			
Leveraged Loans[d]	203	78.03	98.26	29.56	151.01	0	1	0	0.7424
LL Rank 1[e]	182	81.66	100.00	26.55	151.01	0	1	0	0.8574
LL Rank 2[f]	19	51.29	50.85	34.33	104.36	0	1	1	0.0074
Not Classified	2	n/a	n/a	n/a	n/a	n/a	n/a	n/a	n/a

[a] Recovery rates greater than 100% can occur when a bank receives equity as part of a loan restructuring and the equity subsequently appreciates. Defaults with recoveries greater than 100% account for less than 1% of the total number of observations.

[b] A value of 1 indicates the distribution of recovery rates for this type of loan is significantly different from the distribution for project finance loans.

[c] A value near 0 indicates that the distribution for this type of loan is significantly different from the distribution for project finance loans.

[d] Leveraged loans contain secured and unsecured corporate loans of companies with over $50 million in debt at the time of default.

[e] Leveraged loans of Rank 1 are senior or *pari passu* with other existing debt.

[f] Leveraged loans of Rank 2 are subordinate to other existing debt.

Source: Adapted from "Project Finance Recovery Study," Standard & Poor's Risk Solutions, March 18, 2002, pp. 12 and 15.

senior debt, and senior unsecured debt. Although there were more observations for the various types of corporate debt, project loans exhibited higher average recovery rates than all but the leveraged loans.

Risk Solutions compared the distribution of project finance recovery rates with the distributions of recovery rates from the various types of corporate debt using three statistical tests: the Kolmogorov-Smirnov Two-Sample Test, the Wilcoxon Rank Sum Test, and the Kruskal-Wallis Test (see Appendix A for more information on the statistical tests). Based on the results, Risk Solutions concluded that the performance of project finance was most similar to the performance of leveraged loans. Risk Solutions then tested the project loans against two subcategories of leveraged loans and found they performed more like senior or *pari passu* leveraged loans (LL Rank 1) than subordinated leveraged loans (LL Rank 2).

The results essentially confirmed what the bankers had originally asserted. Beale explained:

> When I saw the results, I felt vindicated. Although we lend without the benefit of recourse to diversified corporate operations, project loans are less risky than comparably rated corporate loans. While there are many reasons for this outcome—better security, contractual mitigation of key risks, etc.—I believe the primary reasons are better information and greater transparency. In project finance you get complete access to project data and can analyze the impact of every input and output. You just can't do that in corporate lending.

On March 18, 2002, the consortium members sent a letter describing the results to the Basel Committee and to their own national bank regulators. The consortium wrote:

> The data suggests project finance loans have a significantly better LGD profile than claims on corporates. Indeed, we believe this data supports our proposal that project finance loans should receive more favorable regulatory treatment than claims on corporates across the full credit spectrum. . . . Based on the preliminary findings . . . project finance loans should require approximately half as much capital as claims on corporates under the IRB approach.[11]

The letter not only proposed reduced risk weights for project loans (see Exhibit 24-3), but it also listed 11 reasons why project finance loans were likely to outperform corporate loans (see Exhibit 24-8). Jay Worenklein, global head of project finance at Société Générale, elaborated:

> The portfolio performance of most of the major finance banks demonstrates that in crisis situations . . . banks have much higher recoveries on their project finance loans than on corporate loans. This is because of the combination of the well-structured and secured nature of most projects, the amount of equity underlying the project debt, the need for the output of the project, the sponsorship of projects by companies with a long-term commitment to their industries and to the countries involved, the careful analysis of downside scenarios relating to commodity pricing, and other factors.[12]

---

[11] Four Bank Consortium letter to national regulators and the Basel Committee on Banking Supervision Models Task Force on Specialised Lending, March 18, 2002, pp. 1–2.

[12] "React or Die," p. 42.

EXHIBIT 24-8

REASONS WHY PROJECT FINANCE LOANS OUTPERFORM CORPORATE FINANCE LOANS

Reason	Explanation
1. Control of Collateral	Perfected first-priority liens on and pledges of the project's collateral (including shares, assets, and material contracts) preserve exclusive access to repayments from a liquidation of the project or for negotiating purposes with sponsors and other lenders.
2. Strong Sponsors	Involvement of deep-pocket partners with vested interest in the projects, including central governments, sponsors, contractors, insurers, suppliers, offtakers, etc. These parties often have key stakes in the success of the project.
3. Covenant Triggers	Step-in rights and covenant triggers that serve as "early warnings" to banks to renegotiate a structure before the borrower's credit quality deteriorates beyond a curable point. While corporate loans also have these features, project finance loans are structured deliberately with tighter covenants to trigger a renegotiation of loan terms before any significant credit deterioration occurs.
4. Sponsor Interests	Sponsors often act as counterparties in the projects, giving them vested interests in the success of the project. While not contractually obligated to support a project, these groups are frequently willing to inject equity into a troubled project.
5. Restrictions	Restrictions on facility drawdowns, use of proceeds, and mandatory payments in favor of the lenders.
6. Sponsor Incentives	Contractual obligations, penalties, and remedies to influence the activities of the sponsors in favor of the lenders.
7. Cash Flow Protections	Offshore and debt service accounts to mitigate cash flow volatility where appropriate.
8. Debt Limits	Prohibition on additional indebtedness, which, when combined with the typically steady or increasing cash flows of projects, increases debt service coverages over time.
9. Transparency	Transparency of the project's performance due to its single-asset nature. In contrast, corporate borrowers frequently have diverse streams of revenues, complicated subsidiary structures and accounting treatments, and cash flow streams that are difficult to analyze.
10. Project Independence	The essential commercial value of projects allows them to survive the bankruptcy or credit deterioration of a sponsor, supplier, contractor, etc. This ability is due to the inherent independent viability of the project's value and cash flow.
11. Loan Syndication	The syndication of project financing loans encourages conservative structures that appeal to a broad retail market, limits the possibility of unsophisticated banks being able to offer aggressive bilateral loans, and ensures that all lenders benefit from a controlled recovery process in a default situation irrespective of the size or importance of their respective participations.

Source: Four Bank Consortium memorandum to the Basel Committee and national regulators, March 18, 2002, pp. 3–4.

Phase 2—Probability of Default

With time running out, the consortium quickly turned to the second phase, the PD analysis. The consortium's pooled portfolio consisted of 759 facilities and included loans from a broad range of industrial sectors and geographic locations (see Exhibits 24-9 and 24-10). Risk Solutions formed static pools at the beginning of each year to calculate *portfolio* default rates over time (see Appendix B for an explanation of this

EXHIBIT 24-9

DISTRIBUTION OF PROJECT FINANCE FACILITIES BY YEAR OF ORIGINATION

Year of Origination	Number of Facilities	Percent of Total
1988	6	0.8%
1989	11	1.5
1990	13	1.7
1991	13	1.7
1992	15	2.0
1993	23	3.0
1994	88	11.6
1995	60	7.9
1996	63	8.3
1997	99	13.0
1998	98	12.9
1999	106	14.0
2000	99	13.0
2001	65	8.6
Total	759	100.0%

Source: Adapted from "Project Finance Default Study," Standard & Poor's Risk Solutions, July 18, 2002, p. 7.

EXHIBIT 24-10

DESCRIPTION OF THE PROJECT FINANCE LOAN SAMPLE

Region	Power	Oil, Gas & Petrochem.	Infra-structure	Metals & Mining	Media & Telecom	Other	Total	Percent of Total
North America	128	22	8	6	30	10	204	26.9%
Europe	50	16	41	9	61	14	191	25.2
Asia Pacific	62	42	17	16	17	23	177	23.3
Latin America	48	25	1	15	29	8	126	16.6
Africa	9	26	1	15	10	0	61	8.0
Total	297	131	68	61	147	55	759	100.0%
Percent of Total	39.1%	17.3%	9.0%	8.0%	19.4%	7.2%	100.0%	

Source: Adapted from "Project Finance Default Study," Standard & Poor's Risk Solutions, July 18, 2002, p. 7.

methodology). Static pool analysis differed from mortality analysis, in which the rating agencies calculated *loan* default rates from origination to maturity.

Risk Solutions first analyzed the PD with default broadly defined, as it had been in Phase I. It also conducted the analysis with PD narrowly defined (i.e., excluding restructured loans with no accounting loss but with changes to amortization or maturity and defaulted loans where the borrower made payments during the cure period). Risk Solutions then compared the consortium's two PD rates with default rates on corporate loans. The definition of a corporate loan default was most similar, but not identical, to the broad default definition used for project finance loans.

The analysis suggested that project finance loans had a lower probability of default than corporate loans. The 10-year cumulative PD for project loans was 7.63% under the broader definition of default compared with 9.38% for that of corporate loans (see Exhibit 24-11). According to Risk Solutions, this result meant that project loans performed like corporate credits rated BBB− to BB, although project loans had a higher recovery rate (75% for project loans versus approximately 50% for corporate loans). Using the narrower definition of default resulted in 19 defaults (compared with 43 using the broad definition). Project loans had a PD of 3.68% and an LGD of 56%, similar to the rates of BBB+/BBB corporate loans.

EXHIBIT 24-11

DEFAULT RATES ON PROJECT FINANCE AND CORPORATE FINANCE LOANS

| | Project Finance Loans | | | | Corporate Finance Loans | |
| | Default—Broadly Defined[a] | | Default—Narrowly Defined[b] | | Default—Broadly Defined[a] | |
Year	Weighted Avg. Marginal Default Rates[c]	Cumulative Average Default Rate[d]	Weighted Avg. Marginal Default Rates[c]	Cumulative Average Default Rate[d]	Weighted Avg. Marginal Default Rates[c]	Cumulative Average Default Rate[d]
1	1.52%	1.52%	0.63%	0.63%	1.49%	1.49%
2	1.61	3.13	0.69	1.32	1.49	2.98
3	1.27	4.40	0.59	1.91	1.32	4.30
4	1.19	5.58	0.54	2.46	1.08	5.38
5	1.07	6.65	0.53	2.99	0.90	6.27
6	0.44	7.09	0.14	3.14	0.79	7.06
7	0.21	7.30	0.21	3.35	0.69	7.75
8	0.33	7.63	0.33	3.68	0.59	8.34
9	0.00	7.63	0.00	3.68	0.54	8.87
10	0.00	7.63	0.00	3.68	0.51	9.38

[a] Borrower was unable to make a contractually scheduled payment of principal and/or interest. This includes bankruptcies that disrupt payment, including default and cure within the grace period, consensual restructuring, amendment of the credit facility's repayment terms, and/or refinancing of the facility with the original lenders in order to give the borrower more time to repay.

[b] Excludes loans restructured, with no accounting loss, but with change of amortization or extension of maturity, and defaulted loans paid during the cure period.

[c] The weighted average of all static pool defaults in years 1, 2, etc.

[d] Sum of weighted average marginal default rates.

Source: Adapted from "Project Finance Default Study," Standard & Poor's Risk Solutions, July 18, 2002, pp. 10–13.

With the PD results in hand, the consortium sent a second letter to the Basel Committee on August 23, 2002. The letter stated, "This data indicates project finance loans perform better than claims on corporates, regardless of the definition of default; under a broad definition LGDs are low and PDs are average, while under a narrow definition LGDs are average and PDs are low."[13]

THE IPFA AND IFC RESPOND TO THE BASEL II PROPOSAL

In addition to the consortium, other banks and related parties responded to the Basel Committee's request for feedback. In fact, the committee received hundreds of responses on its original proposal. The International Project Finance Association (IPFA), an industry trade group, presented a working paper to the committee signed by 21 project sponsors and banks. It stated:

> An important point that IPFA would like to raise is that project finance loans enjoy a much better Loss Given Default history than Corporate Finance. . . . Based on this the proposed regulatory structure needs to be amended with terms more favourable to project finance. . . . Whilst IPFA recognizes the importance of ensuring that financial institutions maintain sound balance sheets it hopes that the new regulatory framework . . . will not impede lenders' ability to participate in project finance lending because of a disproportionate level of regulatory capital.[14]

The IFC, responsible for promoting private sector investment in developing countries, sent data on its portfolio of project loans to the Basel Committee. The IFC's portfolio of project loans had experienced a 2.1% loss rate compared with a 3.1% loss rate for all loans in its 45-year history (see Exhibit 24-12). In a letter to the committee, Suellen Lazarus, director of syndication and international securities, commented:

> In our view the specialized lending paper does not give sufficient recognition to the numerous risk mitigants that are put in place for any typical project finance transaction. By failing to do so, the proposed regulatory framework on Specialized Lending jeopardizes long-term financing for investors seeking access for their substantial long-term capital investments throughout the world, and particularly in emerging markets. . . . We strongly recommend that project finance not be included in Specialized Lending as separate from corporate lending.[15]

Lazarus also acknowledged the challenges facing the Basel Committee:

> Project finance lending is a small component of the business of most banks. For this reason, relative to its far-reaching impact, the proposal has not been at the top of most banks' Basel II agendas. . . . The Basel Committee has before it an enormous task. Its members have been impressive in their openness to ideas and patience in listening to divergent views.

---

[13] Four Bank Consortium letter to national regulators and the Basel Committee on Banking Supervision Models Task Force, August 23, 2002, p. 2.

[14] "IPFA Response to Basel Committee's Proposals (Basel II)," The International Project Finance Association, February 2001, pp. 2–3.

[15] IFC letter from Suellen Lambert Lazarus to the Secretary-General of the Basel Committee on Banking Supervision, November 16, 2001, p. 2. *Source:* International Finance Corporation, ⟨http://www.ifc.org/syndications⟩.

EXHIBIT 24-12

INTERNATIONAL FINANCE CORPORATION PORTFOLIO PERFORMANCE, 1956–2001

	Number of Projects	Total Distributions (Millions)	Average Loan Amount (Millions)	Net Losses (Millions)	Net Loss Rate
All Closed A & C Loans[a]	1,175	$9,250	$7.87	$284	3.07%
Project Finance Portfolio	675	$5,826	$8.63	$123	2.11%

[a] Loans are fixed and variable rate loans for International Finance Corporation's own account to private sector projects in developing countries; C-loans are a full range of quasi-equity products including convertible debt that impose a fixed repayment schedule also to private sector projects in developing countries.

Source: Adapted from letter from Suellen Lazarus, International Finance Corporation's director of Syndications and International Securities Department, to Daniele Nouy, Secretary-General of the Basel Committee on Banking Supervision, November 16, 2001, Attachment 1. Available from ⟨www.ifc.org/syndications/⟩.

They are grappling with highly technical issues that are not simply resolved, and yet there is the need to reduce complexity. At the same time, they are not commercial bankers and often have limited experience with the range of products they must regulate. There are few people who would want this responsibility on their shoulders.[16]

CONCLUSION

Having completed the first two phases of the loan loss study, consortium members had to decide what to do next. James Berner, an associate at Deutsche Bank, said:

At this point, I think the difficult work is done. All four banks have collected historical data, Risk Solutions has analyzed it, and we have reported the results to the Basel Committee. The results are fairly clear: project finance loans are not riskier than comparably rated corporate loans either from an LGD or PD perspective. We hope this information will convince the Models Task Force to change their original position and adopt risk weights that are equal to, if not more favorable than, the risk weights for corporate loans. In the meantime, we should try to add more banks to the study to strengthen its validity and continue to collect loan performance data for our own internal purposes.

Keisman, of Standard & Poor's Risk Solutions, concurred:

Although the results are strong, there is a need for additional analysis. We currently have data covering approximately 25% of project loan origination. I'd like to see that number closer to 50%, and I'd like to see broader geographic coverage with banks from Asia, South America, and Australia. On a more practical level, the goal is to get to the point where the addition of an incremental bank does not change the overall results. We'd also like to analyze the relationships among loan characteristics, credit behavior, and loan performance.

[16] Suellen Lambert Lazarus, "Basel II: The Project Blocker?" *Strategic Direct Investor*, March/April 2002, pp. 53–55.

In keeping with the original plan, the consortium sent letters inviting other banks to join it. While it received some expressions of interest, no other banks had yet agreed to participate in the study. One project finance banker, not involved with the consortium, conceded that project finance loans would become pricier under Basel II, but he was not convinced Basel II would have a dramatic effect on the industry. Another banker believed the industry would feel "an initial jolt" but did not believe Basel II would drive borrowers to nonbank lenders. Beale, Bell, Prins, and Worenklein, the global heads of project finance at the consortium's member banks, were less sanguine about the future under Basel II. They believed it had the potential to inflict serious damage on the industry and hoped the loan loss study would avert such a scenario.

APPENDIX A

DESCRIPTION OF STATISTICAL TESTS

	Wilcoxon Rank Sum Test (Mann-Whitney Test)	Kruskal-Wallis Test	Kolmogorov-Smirnov Two-Sample Test
Definition	A nonparametric test used to compare two independent (unpaired) groups of sampled data.	A nonparametric test used to compare N-independent groups of sampled data (typically $N \geq 3$; when $N = 2$, this test is approximately equal to the Wilcoxon Rank Sum Test).	A nonparametric test used to compare two independent groups of sampled data.
Test Procedure	Uses the average ranks of the data rather than their raw values to determine whether the two samples come from identical populations. Greater differences between the average ranks indicate the samples come from different populations.	Uses the average ranks of the data rather than their raw values to determine whether the two samples come from identical populations. Greater differences between the average ranks indicate the samples come from different populations.	Uses the empirical distribution functions to test whether two sample distributions are identical. Calculates the maximum distance between the cumulative distribution functions. Greater distances indicate different sample populations.
Test Statistic Distribution	Standardized normal	Chi-square with N-1 degrees of freedom	A specialized distribution
Key Assumptions	Samples are independent.	Samples are independent	Samples are independent and reasonably large (>30 observations); underlying distributions are continuous.
Equivalent Parametric Test	T-test	Analysis of variance (ANOVA)	Chi-square goodness-of-fit test

Definitions:

Parametric tests: When statistics are calculated under the assumption that the data follow some common distribution such as a normal (Gaussian) distribution. In this case, we can use the properties of the underlying distribution to assist in developing significance tests. Tests that do not make assumptions about the underlying population distribution are known as nonparametric or "distribution-free" tests.

Paired data: Paired data typically arise from repeated measurements on the same subject (i.e., before and after some kind of intervention) or if the subjects are matched (paired) based on some other criteria before the data are collected.

Rank: An ordinal number assigned to data after it has been arranged from the smallest to the largest (e.g., the smallest value is assigned a 1).

Source: Casewriter descriptions.

483

APPENDIX B

STANDARD & POOR'S PROBABILITY OF DEFAULT METHODOLOGY (STATIC POOL ANALYSIS)

Portfolio Analysis (Static pools by year)

Year	Total # Loans in Prior Year's Portfolio	# Loans Removed from Prior Year's Portfolio Due to: Default	Repayment	# New Loans Added to Portfolio	Total # Loans in Current Year's Portfolio	Number of Defaults (origination year, default year) Year 1	Year 2	Year 3
1990	0	0	0	100	100	$2_{90,90}$	$4_{90,91}$	$5_{90,92}$
1991	100	2	0	100	198	$3_{91,91} + 4_{90,91}$	$6_{91,92} + 5_{90,92}$	
1992	198	7	2	100	289	$1_{92,92} + 6_{91,92} + 5_{90,92}$		

Marginal Probability of Default Analysis

	Year 1	Year 2	Year 3
1990	$= (2/100) = 0.020$	$= (4/100) = 0.040$	$= (5/100) = 0.050$
1991	$= (3+4)/(198) = 0.035$	$= (6+5)/(198) = 0.056$	
1992	$= (1+6+5)/(289) = 0.042$		
Weighted Average Marginal Default Rates	$= \dfrac{(2+3+4+1+6+5)}{(100+198+289)} = 0.036$	$= \dfrac{(4+6+5)}{(100+198)} = 0.050$	$= (5)/(100) = 0.050$

Cumulative Probability of Default Analysis

	Year 1	Year 2	Year 3
Cumulative Average Default Rates	$= \mathbf{0.036}$	$= (0.036 + 0.050) = \mathbf{0.086}$	$= (0.086 + 0.050) = \mathbf{0.136}$

Source: Casewriter analysis.

25

Iridium LLC

On Friday, August 13, 1999, Iridium LLC filed for bankruptcy in the United States Bankruptcy Court in Delaware. The company, a $5.5 billion venture backed by Motorola, offered global phone, fax, and paging services via satellite, but had been having trouble attracting customers ever since it began commercial service in November 1998. In explaining the bankruptcy, some people blamed everything: "Make a list of everything you can think of—technological glitches, marketing and distribution mishaps, management turnover, etc.—and then just get to the bottom and check all of the above."[1] Others, such as Mark Gercenstein, Iridium's vice president of operations, highlighted the system's technological complexity:

> More than 26 completely impossible things had to happen first, and in the right sequence (before we could begin operations)—like getting capital, access to the marketplace, global spectrum, the same frequency band in every country of operations.[2]

Most people, however, blamed Iridium's marketing and sales efforts:

> True, Iridium committed so many marketing and sales mistakes that its experience could form the basis of a textbook on how not to sell a product. Its phones started out costing $3,000, were the size of a brick, and didn't work as promised. They weren't available in stores when Iridium ran a $180 million advertising campaign. And Iridium's prices, which ranged from $3.00 to $7.50 a call, were out of this world.[3]

Yet bankruptcy was, after all, a *financial* problem. The protection afforded by Chapter 11 would give Iridium an opportunity to rethink its competitive strategy and

Professor Benjamin C. Esty, Research Associate Fuaad A. Qureshi, and William Olson (MBA '00) prepared this case based on published sources. It is based, in part, on Scott Vuchetich's (MBA '99) Faculty Sponsored Research project. HBS cases are developed solely as the basis for class discussion. Cases are not intended to serve as endorsements, sources of primary data, or illustrations of effective or ineffective management.

[1] Peter List, "Crash and Burn," *Project Finance*, October 1999, p. 18.

[2] Peter Grams and Patrick Zerbib, "Caring for Customers in a Global Marketplace," *Satellite Communications*, October 1998, p. 24.

[3] James Surowieckipp "The Latest Satellite Startup Lifts Off. Will It Too Explode?" *Fortune Magazine*, October 25, 1999, pp. 237–254.

EXHIBIT 25-1

EXISTING AND PROPOSED SATELLITE SYSTEMS

Segment/Project	Lead Sponsor	Constellation Specifications	Estimated Cost ($billions)
Voice Transmission			
(1) Iridium, LLC	Motorola	Low orbit, 66 satellites, plus 6 spares	$ 5.5
(2) Globalstar	Loral, Qualcomm, Vodafone, Airtouch	Low orbit, 48 satellites, plus 8 spares	$ 3.3
(3) ICO	Inmarsat, TRW, Hughes, various PTTs	Medium orbit, 10 satellites, plus 2 spares	$ 4.6
(4) Ellipso	Mobile Communications Holdings	17 satellites, most in elliptical orbit	$ 1.4
(5) ECCO	Constellation Communications	Low orbit, 46 satellites, plus 8 spares	$ 3.0
(6) ACeS	Pacifik Satelit, Phillipine Long Distance	2 geosynchronous satellites	$ 0.9
(7) Thuraya	Etisalat (United Arab Emirates)	2 geosynchronous satellites	$ 1.0
		Total Cost (Voice Transmission)	**$19.7**
Data Transmission			
(1) Teledesic	Gates, McCaw, Motorola, Boeing	Low orbit, 288 satellites, plus 12 spares	$10.0
(2) Skybridge	Alcatel, Loral	Low orbit, 80 satellites	$ 4.2
(3) CyberStar	Loral	3 geosynchronous satellites	$ 1.6
(4) Astrolink	Lockheed Martin	9 geosynchronous satellites	$ 4.0
(5) Spaceway	Hughes Electronics	8 geosynchronous satellites	$ 3.2
(6) Orbcomm	Orbital Sciences	"Little LEO," 36 satellites	$ 0.3
(7) Leo One	Leo One	"Little LEO," 48 satellites	$ 0.5
		Total Cost (Data Transmission)	**$23.8**
		Total Cost (Voice & Data)	**$43.5**

Sources: Various newspaper and industry articles.

restructure its balance sheet. The restructuring process, combined with a need to convince the bankruptcy judge that the company was unlikely to go bankrupt again, required a thorough understanding of the relation between the firm's financial strategy and its demise. For example, did it have too much leverage: was its target debt-to-total capital ratio of 60% too high? If not the amount of debt, perhaps it had the wrong kind of debt, or had raised it in the wrong sequence vis-à-vis equity. Answers to these questions were critical not only to Iridium as it struggled to emerge from Chapter 11, but also to at least 14 other firms that were in the process of spending more than $40 billion on satellite communications systems (see Exhibit 25-1).

THE GLOBAL TELECOMMUNICATIONS MARKET

In 1999, the $835 billion market for telecommunications services consisted of three segments based on the mode of transmission.[4] Wireline communication systems utilized

---

[4] This figure excludes equipment revenues associated with building and supporting these services (Telecommunications Services, *U.S. Industry and Trade Outlook*, 1999).

EXHIBIT 25-2

GLOBAL TELECOMMUNICATION SERVICE SEGMENTS

Segment	1999 Size ($billions)	1990–1999 CAGR[c]	2000–2004 Est. CAGR[c]
Wireline	$609.0	8.0%	8.0%
Wireless	$206.8	14.2	15.0
Satellites			
—MSS[a]	$ 1.9	21.4	60.3
—FSS[b]	$ 17.3	31.7	28.0
Total	**$835.0**	**10.2%**	**10.1%**

[a] Mobile Satellite Services.

[b] Fixed Satellite Services.

[c] CAGR is the compound annual growth rate.

Sources: Adapted from McKinsey & Company, Telecommunications Industry Report (1999) and *U.S. Industry and Trade Outlook*, Telecommunications Services (1999).

terrestrial cable and fiber-optic technology to transmit voice and data signals. In contrast, wireless and satellite systems used radio systems and satellites, respectively, for transmission, along with wireline infrastructure to route calls. Exhibit 25-2 provides details on the size, historical growth rates, and expected future growth rates of each segment.

The satellite communications segment was further divided into Fixed Satellite Services (FSS) and Mobile Satellite Services (MSS). FSS used fixed stations on earth to transmit and receive signals, while MSS utilized mobile receivers, such as hand-held phones, and one of three types of satellites (see Exhibits 25-3a and 25-3b). *Geosynchronous Earth Orbit* (GEO) satellites maintained fixed positions relative to the earth, but were relatively inefficient at handling real-time voice and data applications because of the long time delay caused by sending signals over great distances. Located closer to earth, *Low Earth Orbit* (LEO) satellites greatly reduced the propagation loss, time delay, and power required for real-time communications, yet required significantly more satellites because orbiting satellites covered only a small fraction of the earth. *Medium Earth Orbit* (MEO) satellites were between these two systems and helped to bridge the gaps in cellular networks, in addition to handling mobile satellite telephony.

Without a doubt, the market for mobile satellite systems would be large, yet analysts disagreed on just how large it would be. For example, Leslie Taylor Associates, a telecommunications consulting firm, predicted a user base of 7 million to 12 million subscribers and revenues of $8 billion to $20 billion by 2003.[5] On the other hand, Forrester Research predicted that the global satellite market would be as much as $36 billion in 2005.[6] Given the potential size of this market, analysts were excited by the prospect of companies capturing even a small part of it. CS First Boston analyst Cynthia Motz commented:

> . . . our take is that the dream behind global mobile communications via satellite is really pretty impressive . . . why would one not consider an industry that is in its nascent stages

[5] Telecommunications Services, *U.S. Industry and Trade Outlook*, 1999, pp. 30–22.

[6] Alan Cane, "Satellite Phones Prove Their Worth," *The Financial Times*, November 13, 1997, p. 2.

EXHIBIT 25-3A

LEO/MEO/GEO SATELLITE ORBITS

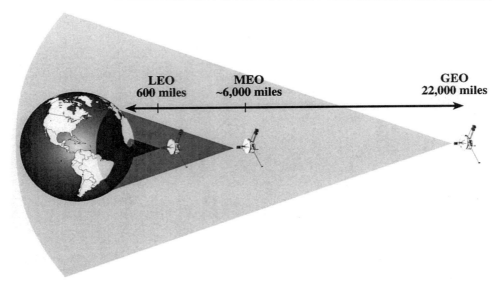

Source: Illustration by Chris Vuchetich (by permission).

EXHIBIT 25-3B

SATELLITE TECHNOLOGIES

	Low Earth Orbit (LEO)	Medium Earth Orbit (MEO)	Geosynchronous Earth Orbit (GEO)
Orbit Distance (miles)	600	6,000	22,000
Type of Orbit	Non-geosynchronous	Non-geosynchronous	Geosynchronous
Minimum number of satellites for global coverage	48	20	3–5[a]
Typical Applications	Corporate WANs Mobile Voice & Paging Rural Telephony	Corporate WANs Mobile Phones	Corporate WANs Carrier Backbones Video Broadcast
Delay Time (milliseconds)	70	120	500
Orbit Time	100–114 minutes	6 hours	24 hours
Satellite Life (years)	5–8	10–12	7–15

[a] In reality, GEO systems experienced difficulty in reaching extreme northern and southern areas. While three GEO satellites could cover the earth, five would provide better service.

Source: Adapted from data contained in Forrester Research reports, CSFB Equity Research Report, December 23, 1998 and from casewriter estimates.

of development, (or a competitor like Iridium) that can do what no other player can do right now, . . . has high barriers to entry, and 70%-90% operating cash flow margins if it works?[7]

IRIDIUM LLC

According to legend, the Iridium concept originated in 1986 when a Motorola executive and his wife were vacationing in the Caribbean and she was unable to make a cellular phone call. This predicament spurred the idea of a global telecommunications system.[8] At the time, Motorola was developing intersatellite communications systems for military applications but was searching for new, commercial applications for its communications technology. Motorola engineers began to study the feasibility of a global system in 1987. Shortly thereafter, Motorola unveiled the plans for a $3.4 billion communications system named Iridium. The name came from its proposed constellation of 77 satellites (later reduced to 66 satellites) which resembled the 77 electrons orbiting the chemical element Iridium. In addition, the system would require 12 ground stations (gateways) located around the world to link the satellites with ground lines.

The Iridium system differed from the existing, and most of the proposed, satellite systems which used "bent pipe" technology. In a bent pipe system, calls were routed along ground lines to a transmitter, beamed up to a satellite, sent down to a receiver, and then routed using ground lines to the other party. Whereas these systems kept most of their technology on the ground, Iridium put the technology in its satellites using "intrasatellite" technology. Consider a customer on top of Mt. Everest calling her children at home in New York. Her call would be transmitted directly to the nearest satellite and then passed from satellite to satellite until it reached a ground station in Arizona where it would then connect to her home in New York using existing ground lines. If she placed a call to another Iridium user, the signal would be relayed from satellite to satellite and beamed directly to the recipient's handset. A key requirement of the Iridium system was the need for direct line-of-sight connection with a satellite. Thus, the phones could not be used indoors without a special, oversized antenna to boost signal strength.

Seamless global operations were made possible by the fact that satellites transcended national boundaries. But to achieve a seamless system, Iridium had to obtain worldwide spectrum rights and negotiate royalty agreements with local phone companies. In fact, Iridium had signed 256 operating agreements with local providers in over 100 countries by July 1999.[9] While these agreements covered 90% of its targeted customer base, the company still had to negotiate agreements with another 140 countries and territories.

Iridium's Financial Projections

Iridium's target customer consisted primarily of traveling professionals, corporate executives, government employees, and rural users in both developed and developing markets. Analysts regularly cited the figure of 1% of the global cellular market as the likely

---

[7] Cynthia Motz and Robert Hordon, "The Sky's the Limit," *Credit Suisse/First Boston Analyst Report*, December 23, 1998, pp. 5, 7.

[8] Iridium web page, corporate history, (http://www.iridium.com/english/inside/comback/index.html).

[9] Chris Bulloch, "Will Mobile Satellites Fly?" *Telecommunications*, September 1999, p. 89.

initial customer base of satellite phone users.[10] Although the exact origin of this figure was not known, it quickly became the mantra of all players in the industry. If Iridium were to capture 1% of the 225 million cellular subscribers in 1998 and each one spent $1,000 annually, then Iridium would have revenues of $2.3 billion per year. If the number of cellular subscribers continued to grow at 15% per year, then 1% of the market in 2004 would equal five million customers and revenues of more than $5 billion.

Using similar analysis, Wall Street analysts made predictions about Iridium's future revenues and cash flow. Exhibit 25-4a depicts how Thomas Watts, Merrill Lynch's telecommunications/satellite analyst and the top-ranked analyst on *Institutional Investor*'s 1998 All America Research team, revised his revenue projections between 1997 and 1999.[11] As of May 1999, he was still predicting total revenues of $4.4 billion in 2006. Besides changing over time for specific analysts, revenue projections also varied across analysts. Exhibit 25-4b shows the range of revenue projections made by five analysts at approximately the same time (year-end 1998). The revenue projections for 2005 ranged from a low of $4.5 billion by CIBC Oppenheimer to a high of $6.9 billion by CS First

---

EXHIBIT 25-4A

MERRILL LYNCH'S REVENUE FORECASTS FOR IRIDIUM BY RESEARCH REPORT DATE (NOTE: PHONE SERVICE BEGAN NOVEMBER 1, 1998)

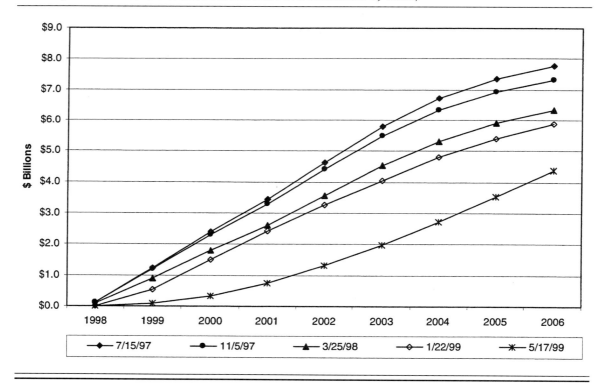

---

[10] Michael Stroud, "Motorola's $3.4 Billion Iridium Project Finds Backers," *Investor's Business Daily*, August 3, 1993, p. 4. See also the report by Motz and Hordon, "The Sky's the Limit," p. 7.

[11] Merrill Lynch was the lead underwriter for Iridium's initial public offering (IPO) in July 1997.

EXHIBIT 25-4B

ANALYST REVENUE FORECASTS FOR IRIDIUM AS OF YEAR-END 1998

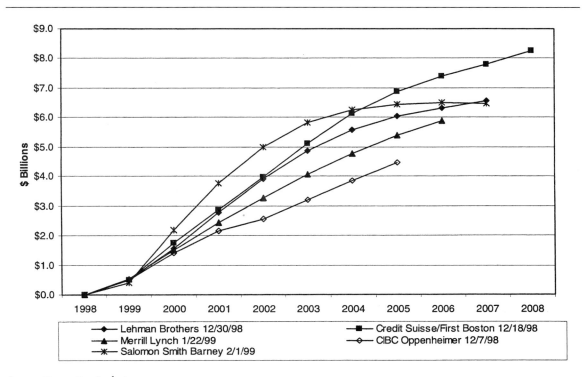

Source: Casewriter Analysis.

Boston. Exhibit 25-5 presents Iridium's cash flow projections and balance sheet data, as well as capital market data from year-end 1998.

Based on similar projections, and an assumed private market discount of 15% to 20% (only 8.5% of Iridium's shares were publicly traded at the time), four out of the five analysts surveyed had buy recommendations for Iridium: Salomon Smith Barney, CS First Boston, Merrill Lynch, and Lehman Brothers had price targets of $60, $57, $68, and $75, respectively, using free cash flow discount rates (i.e., weighted average costs of capital, WACCs) ranging from 17% to 25%. Only CIBC Oppenheimer had a hold recommendation.[12] John Coates, the bullish analyst at Salomon Smith Barney, wrote: "Iridium presents a clear investment opportunity. . . . Accordingly, we reiterate our buy rating, maintain our $60 price target, and offer 10 reasons to buy the stock immediately."[13] Coates and the other analysts cited high margins, first mover advantages, strong partnership potential, and better breadth of coverage as reasons to invest in Iridium. They also cited

[12] See the reports by Salomon Smith Barney on February 1, 1999, Credit Suisse First Boston on December 18, 1998, Merrill Lynch on January 22, 1999, Lehman Brothers on December 30, 1998, and CIBC Oppenheimer on December 7, 1998.

[13] John B. Coates, "Iridium World Communications," Salomon Smith Barney Equity Research Report, February 1, 1999, p. 2.

EXHIBIT 25-5

IRIDIUM FINANCIAL PROJECTIONS AND CAPITALIZATION, 1999–2007 ($MILLIONS)

	1998 Act.	1999	2000	2001	2002	2003	2004	2005	2006	2007
Income Statement (millions)										
# Voice Subscribers	5	600	1,475	2,525	3,675	4,550	5,275	5,900	6,525	7,150
# Paging Subscribers	0	50	125	225	325	425	525	600	650	690
Revenues	$0.2	$403	$2,183	$3,748	$4,994	$5,821	$6,249	$6,435	$6,495	$6,481
EBITDA	−436	−351	1,339	2,809	3,859	4,611	4,973	5,100	5,084	5,001
Depreciation/Amort.	552	811	966	1,213	1,333	1,084	1,109	1,020	822	605
EBIT	−988	−1,162	373	1,596	2,526	3,527	3,864	4,080	4,262	4,396
Interest Expense, net	265	387	454	424	278	59	0	0	39	92
Profit Before Tax	−1,253	−1,549	−81	1,172	2,248	3,468	3,864	4,080	4,223	4,304
Taxes @ 15%	0	0	0	176	337	520	580	612	633	646
Net Income	−1,253	−1,549	−81	996	1,911	2,948	3,284	3,468	3,590	3,658
Cash Flow Data										
Depr./Amortization	552	811	966	1,213	1,333	1,084	1,109	1,020	822	605
Capital Expenditures	716	927	1,349	1,246	1,258	1,274	385	391	413	844
Incr. (Decr.) in NWC[a]	(398)	290	63	(102)	(81)	(54)	(28)	(12)	(4)	(1)
Balance Sheet Data										
Cash	25	10	10	10	10	20	30	50	50	50
Prop., Plant & Equip.	3,584	3,215	3,597	3,630	3,555	3,745	3,020	2,390	1,981	2,103
Total Assets	3,739	3,319	3,833	3,979	3,990	4,270	3,582	2,988	2,583	2,704
Total Debt	2,854	3,930	4,437	3,352	1,266	0	0	0	450	1,155

Iridium, LLC, Capitalization as of 12/31/98

	($millions)
Debt	
Secured Bank Debt, @ Prime + 2.75%	$ 500
Guaranteed Bank Debt, @ Prime	625
Sr. Sub. Notes @ 14.5%, due 2006	323
Senior Notes A @ 13.0%, due 2005	278
Senior Notes B @ 14.0%, due 2005	480
Senior Notes C @ 11.25%, due 2005	300
Senior Notes D @ 10.88%, due 2005	348
Total Debt	2,854
Deferred payments due to Motorola	$ 218
Equity	
Preferred Partnerships (Equity—Class 2)	$ 46
Total Class 1 Equity Raised	2,114
Accumulated Losses	1,683
Net Class 1 Equity (book value)	$ 431
Debt/Total Capital (book value)	86%
Debt/Total Capital (market value)	34%
Debt/Total Capital (capital raised)	57%

Capital Market Data as of 12/31/98

Iridium Information	
Stock Price (IRIDQ)	$39.56
Equity Beta (weekly data)	1.58
Asset Beta (1998 average)	1.25
Class 1 Interests (shares)	141 million
Class 1 Interests (fully diluted)[b]	185 million
Proceeds from Class 1 warrants[b]	$220 million

Yields on US Treasury Bills, Notes and Bonds	
3-month	4.48%
1-year	4.53%
10-year	4.65%
30-year	5.09%

Prime Rate	7.75%
Yields on Corporate Bonds	
Aaa Rated	6.23%
Baa Rated	7.23%

[a] Changes in net working capital excludes cash and cash equivalents.

[b] Exercise of the outstanding Class 1 warrants would increase the number of interests from 141 to 185 million, and yield $220 million of proceeds to the company.

Sources: Salomon Smith Barney, Equity Research Report, February 1, 1999; casewriter estimates. *Federal Reserve Bulletin*; Iridium World Communications, Ltd. 1998 Annual Report.

uncertain demand, technology, competition, and regulation as the most important risks, and the company's sizable funding need as a potential threat to completion.

Competition in the MSS Segment

Although Inmarsat had been providing commercial mobile satellite service since 1982, Iridium considered three new companies as its main competition (see Table 25-A). Globalstar, a $3.3 billion joint venture between Space Systems/Loral and Qualcomm, was expected to begin service in late 1999. Its constellation would offer low-cost communication services using bent pipe technology and phones that were similar to today's cellular units. Like Globalstar, ICO Global Communications would integrate satellite technology with terrestrial networks using bent pipe technology; unlike Globalstar and Iridium, it was a MEO system that required many fewer satellites. Inmarsat and Hughes founded the $4.5 billion system in 1995 and expected it to be operational by year-end 2000.

While other systems promised global coverage, Ellipso proposed to cover only heavily populated areas. Its satellites would follow elliptical orbits, focussing on high-potential regions, thereby significantly reducing capital costs. As of 1999, Ellipso was still in early development with a target launch date of late 2002. Like Iridium, these other systems were largely limited to outdoor use.

IRIDIUM'S OPERATING AND FINANCING HISTORY

Iridium's operating and financing history prior to bankruptcy can be divided into three chronological phases: Research to June 1995, System Development to June 1998, and Commercial Launch through July 1999, ending with the bankruptcy declaration in August 1999.

Research: June 1990 to June 1995

During its start-up phase, Motorola designed the system, developed the basic technology, and raised the initial equity needed to fund early development. Motorola unveiled

TABLE A   Comparison of Mobile Satellite Service Providers

	Iridium	Globalstar	ICO	Ellipso
Total cost ($ billions)	$5.5	$3.3	$4.6	$1.4
Satellite life span	5–8 years	7–8 years	12 years	5 years
Orbit	LEO	LEO	MEO	MEO
Initial/expected cost per minute				
—Wholesale	$0.50–$1.99	$0.30	$0.30–$0.50	$0.33
—Retail	$3.00–$7.50	$2.00–$4.00	$1.50	$1.00–$1.50
Number of ground stations	12	50–80	12	6–14
Headset cost (initial)	$3,000	$750–$1500	$700	$750–$1000
Number of satellites	66	48	10	17
Market share (estimate)				
2000	72.6%	26.2%	0.9%	0.0%
2005	35.4%	26.6%	23.5%	8.3%

Source: Project Finance International, July 29, 1998, Issue 150; CS First Boston, "The Sky's the Limit," December 23, 1998; Sandra Sugawara, "Battle in the Skies," *The Washington Post*, October 18, 1993; casewriter estimates.

the project in June 1990 with simultaneous press conferences in Beijing, London, Melbourne, and New York. The following year, it incorporated Iridium as a separate company to build and operate the system. At the time, Motorola was rated AA-, and had total assets of $9.4 billion, sales of $11.3 billion, and net income of $454 million. In comparison, Iridium was initially expected to cost $3.4 billion, generate revenues of $5 billion, and have assets of $4 billion by 2002.

Between 1990 and 1993, Motorola invested $100 million in research and development. One of the company's major achievements during these early years was reserving specific radio frequencies for the system. In fact, 160 countries agreed to allocate a band of radio frequencies to LEO systems in March 1993.

To fund actual development, Motorola decided to raise the initial capital from 21 strategic partners, including major telecommunications and aerospace firms such as Nippon Iridium Ltd. (a joint venture between Kyocera and DDI Corporation), Telecom Italia, SK Telecom (South Korea), Sprint, Raytheon, and Lockheed Martin. The largest strategic partners, in terms of total investment, were entitled to board representation. Exhibit 25-6 shows the composition of Iridium's board of directors. Except for the two independent directors who received $20,000 per year, $2,500 per quarterly meeting, and 1,000 options, none of the other directors received compensation from Iridium.

According to the financing plan, Iridium would raise $1.6 billion of equity followed by $1.8 billion of debt, giving it a debt-to-total capital ratio of approximately 50%. By August 1993, Iridium had obtained commitments for $800 million from its strategic partners, including a total of $270 million from Motorola.[14] It hoped to raise another $800 million from the strategic partners in 1995, at which time Motorola's ownership share would decline from 34% to 19%.[15]

In reality, the second round of equity financing came sooner than expected. Iridium secured commitments for another $734 million of equity in September 1994.[16] Based on investor demand for the equity and general interest in the project, Iridium's bankers thought it could raise 60% of the total cost in debt.[17] The theory behind this target leverage ratio was that Iridium, once complete, would resemble a utility with high margins and steady cash flows. Exhibit 25-7 shows leverage ratios for a variety of industries as of year-end 1998. Exhibit 25-8 provides financial statistics for satellite communications companies as of year-end 1998. Exhibits 25-9a and 25-9b illustrate Iridium's capital structure in terms of total capital invested and leverage (debt as a percentage of total capital), respectively, from 1993 to 1999.

System Development: July 1995 to June 1998

By mid-1995, most of the research was done, and the company began developing the system. Motorola signed a Terrestrial Network Development Contract in 1995, under which it agreed to develop the gateway hardware and software. As part of this effort, Iridium signed 12 gateway contracts in late 1995 but needed more money before it could create and launch the first satellites—each satellite cost approximately $13 million. With revenues still more than three years away, Iridium decided to issue

[14] G. Christian Hill, "Motorola Completes the First Round of Funding for Satellite-Phone Project," *The Wall Street Journal*, August 2, 1993, p. B3.

[15] Michael Stroud, "Motorola's $3.4 Billion Iridium Project Finds Backers," *Investor's Business Daily*, August 3, 1993, p. 4.

[16] "Iridium Inc. Completes Its Equity Financing," *The Wall Street Journal*, September 21, 1994, p. B7.

[17] G. Christian Hill, "Iridium Hopes to Line Up Its Financing Soon," *The Wall Street Journal*, January 29, 1993, p. B2.

EXHIBIT 25-6

IRIDIUM LLC BOARD OF DIRECTORS AS OF MARCH 31, 1999

Name of Director	Age	Director Since	Company	Title	Designated by	IWCL Director?	IWCL Shares[a]
1) Aburizal Bakrie	51	7/97	The Bakrie Group	Chairman	South Pacific Iridium		
2) Hasan M. Binladin	50	1/96	Saudi Binladin Group	Senior VP	Iridium Middle East		
3) Herbert Brenke	61	9/98	E-Plus Mobilfunk	Chairman (retired)	Vebacom Holdings		
4) Gordon J. Comerford	61	7/93	Motorola, Inc.	Senior VP (retired)	Motorola		
5) Atilano de Oms Sobrinho	55	6/96	Inepar S.A.	President	Iridium SudAmerica		
6) Stephen P. Earhart	50	3/99	Motorola, Inc.	SVP, Dir. of Finance	Motorola		
7) Robert A. Ferchat	64	1/95	Iridium Canada, Inc.	Chairman	Iridium Canada, Inc.		
8) Alberto Finol	64	7/93	Iridium SudAmerica	Chairman	Iridium SudAmerica	Yes	127,900
9) Edward Gams	51	7/93	Motorola, Inc.	VP, Dir. Inv. Relations	Motorola		
10) Durrell Hillis	58	6/98	Motorola, Inc.	Senior VP	Motorola		
11) Kazuo Inamori	67	7/93	DDI Corporation	Founder & Chairman	Nippon Iridium		
12) Georg Kellinghusen	51	1/99	o.tel.o communications	Chief Financial Officer	Vebacom Holdings		
13) S.H. Khan	60	10/94	Credit Analysis & Research	Chairman	Iridium India		
14) Robert W. Kinzie, **Chairman**	65	10/91	Iridium LLC	Chairman	Iridium LLC	Yes	108,382
15) Anatoly I. Kiselev	59	7/93	Khrunichev State Research	Director General	Khrunichev		
16) Richard L. Lesher, **Vice Chairman**	65	6/97	US Chamber of Commerce	President (retired)	**Independent Director**	Yes	9,367
17) John F. Mitchell	71	7/93	Motorola, Inc.	Vice Chairman	Motorola		
18) Giuseppe Morganti	66	4/96	Iridium Italia S.p.A	CEO	Iridium Italia		
19) J. Michael Norris	52	7/96	Motorola, Inc.	Senior VP	Motorola		
20) Yusai Okuyama	67	7/96	DDI Corporation	President	Nippon Iridium		
21) Moon Soo Pyo	45	1/99	SK Telecom Co., Ltd.	Senior VP	SK Telecom		
22) John A. Richardson	56	3/98	Iridium Africa Corp.	CEO	Iridium Africa		
23) Theodore H. Schell	54	7/93	Sprint Corp.	Senior VP	Sprint		
24) William A. Schreyer	70	6/97	Merrill Lynch & Co.	Chairman (emeritus)	**Independent Director**	Yes	10,367
25) Edward F. Staiano, **Vice Chairman**	62	10/94	Iridium LLC	CEO	Iridium LLC	Yes	387,400
26) Sribhumi Sukhanetr	66	7/93	Thai Satellite Telecom. Co.	Chairman	Thai Satellite		
27) Tao-Tsun Sun	49	1/94	Pacific Electric Wire & Cable	President	Pacific Iridium		
28) Yoshiharu Yasuda	58	1/96	Nippon Iridium Corp.	President	Nippon Iridium	Yes	2,000
29) Wang Mei Yue	57	10/95	Iridium China	Chairman & President	Iridium China		

[a] As of March 1, 1999, there were 20,223,000 IWCL shares outstanding including shares that could be acquired within 60 days pursuant to the exercise of options (19,725,986 shares not including share equivalents). Officers of IWCL and Iridium LLC (the parent) collectively held 768,480 shares.

Source: Iridium LLC, Form 10K Annual Report for the year ended December 31, 1998.

EXHIBIT 25-7

FINANCIAL STATISTICS FOR SELECT INDUSTRIES, DECEMBER 31, 1998

	1998			
S&P Industry Group	**Debt to Total Capital (Book Value)**	**Times Interest Earned**	**Return on Assets**	**Projected Growth in Sales[c]**
Retail (General Merchandise)	60%	5.8X	7.96%	6.5%
Retail (Food Chains)	59	4.0	6.08	7.5
Telephone (Local Service)	59	4.5	8.09	4.5
Tobacco	57	8.5	9.88	9.0
Electric Utilities[a]	57	2.6	2.86	4.5
Natural Gas Utilities[a]	53	2.9	3.65	9.4
Lodgings-Hotels	53	9.9	9.75	9.0
Airlines	53	5.9	7.09	7.2
Water Utilities[a]	52	3.1	3.04	5.8
Hardware & Tools	50	−1.4	−11.96	NA
Aerospace/Defense	50	6.1	3.66	2.4
Railroads	45	2.9	2.56	5.6
Household Products	40	6.9	11.26	8.7
Restaurants	38	4.4	8.03	11.7
Publishing (Newspapers)	38	8.1	9.09	7.9
Iron & Steel	38	14.8	6.92	10.9
Personal Care	36	11.5	9.43	9.4
Chemicals (Specialty)	36	46.8	7.93	5.2
Telecommunications (Long Distance)	33	3.6	3.60	8.0
Textiles (Apparel)	28	5.8	9.01	7.4
Health Care (Drugs)	25	25.1	15.16	10.3
Leisure Products	25	5.0	6.60	10.0
Telecommunications (Cellular)	24	4.0	2.17	14.5
Retail (Specialty)	23	8.7	6.20	10.7
Textiles (Home Furnishing)	19	2.5	2.60	8.6
Electronics (Semiconductors)	15	33.0	15.03	10.1
Electronics (Components Distribution)	11	27.6	11.34	12.0
Biotechnology	8	30.6	23.51	18.0
Computer (Software/Services)	3	16.3	18.25	23.5
Computers (Networking)	1	112.3[b]	13.58	44.5
Mean	**36**	**14.1**	**7.75**	**10.4**
Median	**38**	**6.0**	**7.95**	**9.0**

[a] Data from S&P Compustat database.

[b] 1996 data used instead of 1998 data.

[c] Three to five year projected compound annual growth rate from Value Line Investment Survey.

Source: S&P Analyst's Handbook, Standard & Poor's Corp., New York, 1999, and Value Line.

EXHIBIT 25-8

FINANCIAL STATISTICS FOR SATELLITE COMPANIES AS OF DECEMBER 31, 1998

Company	Sales ($ millions)	Assets ($ millions)	Debt/Total Capitalization[a] Book Value	Market Value	Interest Coverage	Provision for Taxes ($ millions)	Net Income ($ millions)	Current Debt as % of Total Debt	Current Ratio	Cash as % of Assets	Equity Beta	S&P Senior Debt Rating
(1) Iridium, LLC	$ 0.2	$3,738.9	86%	34%	0.72	$ 0.0	−$73.6	4%	0.19	0.7%	1.58	CC[b]
(2) Globalstar L.P.	$ 0.0	$2,670.0	79%	29%	−1.28	$ 0.0	−$50.6	15%	0.59	2.1%	1.70	B[b]
(3) ICO Global Communications	$ 0.1	$2,659.4	24%	21%	N/A	$ 3.8	−$110.7	0%	4.84	20.6%	1.36	B
(4) Gilat Satellite Networks	$155.3	$ 410.3	26%	32%	−15.70	$ 0.3	−$81.6	2%	1.60	1.8%	1.71	N/A
(5) PanAmSat Corp.	$767.3	$5,890.5	22%	12%	3.04	$95.9	$124.6	1%	2.36	3.0%	0.96	A−
(6) Comsat Corp.	$616.5	$1,790.8	41%	20%	1.72	$ 5.8	$26.4	3%	1.41	1.7%	1.47	A−
(7) Orbital Sciences Corp.	$734.3	$ 962.7	29%	11%	0.70	$ 4.5	−$6.4	13%	1.21	2.8%	1.35	BB

[a] Debt/Total Capitalization is calculated as the ratio of total debt to the sum of debt, equity, and preferred stock.

[b] S&P Long-Term Debt Rating for 12/98 used in lieu of S&P 1998 Senior Debt Rating.

Company Descriptions:

(1) Iridium employed a network of 66 satellites to provide handheld global satellite telephone and paging network. It was based in Washington, D.C.

(2) Globalstar was a joint venture between Space Systems/Loral and Qualcomm. It used a constellation of 48 satellites and was based in New York, New York.

(3) ICO Global Communications, based in the Cayman Islands, would provide mobile and cellular services via a system of 12 satellites.

(4) Gilat Satellite Networks, based in Israel, employed VSAT (Very Small Aperture Technology) for telecommunications and data transmission.

(5) PanAmSat, with 20 satellites, was the leading commercial provider of satellite-based communications services. It was based in Greenwich, Connecticut.

(6) Comsat provided global telecommunications using the 19 Inmarsat satellites (the INTELSAT system). It was based in Bethesda, Maryland.

(7) ORBCOMM, the satellite division of Orbital Sciences, had total sales of $0.8 million, an operating loss of $4.0 million, and identifiable assets of $241.5 million in 1998. ORBCOMM used a constellation of 28 LEO satellites for global data transmission, and was based in Dulles, Virginia.

Sources: Company Annual Reports, S&P Compustat, *S&P Bond Guide,* Bloomberg.

EXHIBIT 25-9A

IRIDIUM CAPITALIZATION (DOLLARS), 1993–1999

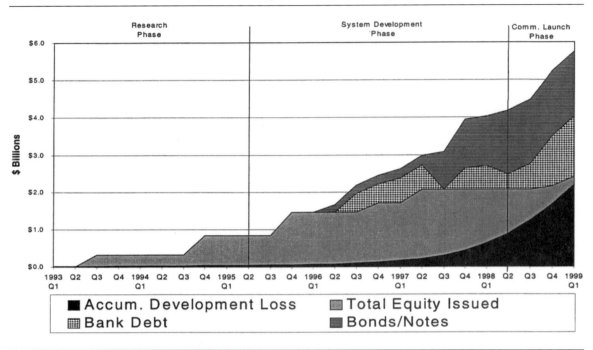

$300 million of zero coupon bonds. Although zero coupon bonds were more expensive than cash-pay bonds by anywhere from 100 basis points (bp) to 300 bp depending on their rating and market conditions, they were attractive to highly leveraged firms with limited cash flow.

When Iridium tried to market the bonds, however, it encountered resistance. Investors wanted the bonds to come with warrants, thereby raising the effective yield to approximately 25%, and a completion guarantee from Motorola.[18] These demands, combined with Standard & Poor's CCC+ rating on the issue, prompted Iridium to cancel the offering in September 1995 because it undervalued the company and its prospects. And so, Iridium proceeded with development funded by its initial equity.

Development proceeded at a steady pace throughout 1996, highlighted by an organizational change, a new chief executive officer (CEO) named Edward Staiano, and additional fund raising. Iridium converted from a corporation to a limited liability company named Iridium LLC, which meant its income would not be subject to U.S. taxation, but it would still provide limited liability for the strategic partners. With money running out and a failed public offering behind it, management decided to raise debt from the strategic partners instead of the public markets. It sold $238 million of ten-year bonds with warrants in April 1996. For the first five years, the bonds accrued

[18] Quentin Hardy, "Iridium Pulls $300 Million Bond Offer; Analysts Cite Concerns about Projects," *The Wall Street Journal*, September 22, 1995, p. A5.

EXHIBIT 25-9B

IRIDIUM CAPITALIZATION (PERCENT), 1993–1999

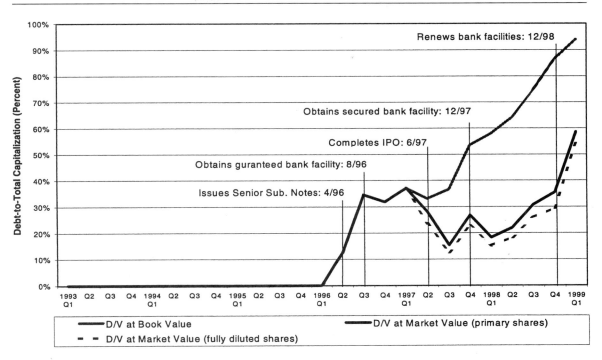

Source: Iridium Annual Reports and 10K Statements.

interest at a rate of 14.5%; for the last five years, beginning in September 2001, they paid cash interest.[19] But this was still not enough money, and so Iridium signed a $750 million bank facility in August 1996. Because Motorola, by then a AA-rated company, had agreed to guarantee this facility in exchange for Class 1 warrants, the banks priced the loan at the prime rate technically, the interest rate was a function of several indicator rates, of which the prime rate was the best known.

Iridium used the funds to pay for satellites and the first launch, which occurred on May 5, 1997. Over the next 12 months, it deployed a total of 47 satellites aboard U.S., Russian, and Chinese rockets. As Iridium was deploying satellites, it also began developing the handheld phone units through an agreement with Kyocera of Japan. One observer described the original phones as "a brick with a baguette sticking out of it."[20]

In addition to being a critical year for Iridium in terms of system development, it was also a critical year in terms of raising badly needed capital. Prior to 1997, Iridium had only been able to raise capital from its strategic partners and banks. Yet in 1997 alone, it issued $240 million of equity through an initial public offering (IPO), issued

[19] Iridium World Communications Ltd., Class A Common Stock Prospectus dated January 21, 1999, p. F29.
[20] Henry Goldblatt, "Just a Few Customers Shy of a Business Plan," *Fortune Magazine*, March 29, 1999, p. 40.

three tranches of high-yield debt totaling $1.1 billion, and signed a $1 billion secured bank facility.

Its first foray into the public markets occurred in June 1997, when Iridium World Communications Ltd. (IWCL), a Bermuda corporation, sold 12 million shares at $20.00 each. These shares represented 8.5% of Iridium's total outstanding shares (technically, the shares were called Class 1 "interests"). IWCL's creation, like Iridium LLC's creation, was done for tax reasons: it precluded U.S. taxation of dividends paid to IWCL shareholders. Unlike its previous attempt to sell public bonds, investor demand was strong, prompting management to increase the offer size from $200 million to $240 million. According to one source, Iridium could have sold $1 billion of equity.[21]

The IPO's success encouraged Iridium to issue $800 million of high-yield debt in two tranches, under Rule 144A, in July 1997. The Series A senior notes were priced to yield 13.00% and came with warrants to purchase IWCL shares; the Series B senior notes required a higher yield (14.00%) because they did not come with warrants. Both were semiannual, cash-pay bonds with an eight-year maturity; they were due in 2005. Initially rated B-, these bonds sold at an effective yield of almost 700 bp over Aaa rated bonds. Exhibit 25-10 depicts Iridium's stock and bond prices since the IPO.

Continued strength in the bond market allowed Iridium to issue a third series of senior notes in October 1997. The Series C notes sold at par with a coupon of 11.25%, a spread of 400 bp over Aaa-rated bonds. A banker commented on Iridium's second trip to the high-yield debt market in just over three months: "The high yield market runs hot and cold. When it is available and pricing aggressively, you go for it. In a project this size, you get money whenever and wherever you can."[22]

Following this advice, Iridium established a two-year senior secured line of credit with a syndicate of banks in December 1997. The line consisted of a $350 million term loan and a $400 million revolving line of credit, with an additional $250 million available on the revolving line in September 1998, if Iridium achieved certain operating milestones. Prior to signing the loan agreement, Iridium conducted an "asset drop-down transaction" in which Iridium LLC transferred all of its assets and liabilities to a wholly-owned subsidiary known as Iridium Operating LLC (see Exhibit 25-11). The purpose of this transaction was to pledge all of Iridium's assets to the lending syndicate as security for the loan. In addition, the line was secured by a $243 million capital call on the strategic partners. In other words, the banks could require the strategic partners to invest up to $243 million if default were imminent. While the pledge of assets and the capital call made the secured debt cheaper than the public notes, it was, nevertheless, significantly more expensive than the guaranteed line of credit. It had a variable interest rate equal to prime plus 2.75%. Both lines matured in September 1998, the scheduled commercial launch date, but could be extended until June 30, 1999, by mutual agreement.

Having created the gateways, deployed the first satellites and tested the system, Iridium began to prepare for commercial launch. It deployed the remaining 19 satellites in early 1998. Iridium's perfect record in satellite deployment impressed industry experts who cited a 10% to 15% failure rate as typical, and pleased investors as the stock price soared to over $70 per share.[23] Globalstar, in contrast, suffered a major setback in September 1998, when it lost 12 satellites in a single, failed launch. Iridium also began to court prominent customers for the launch. Its first major customer was the U.S.

---

[21] Chris Donnelly, "Debt issuance puts Iridium in orbit," *Project Finance International Yearbook* 1998, p. 74.

[22] Anonymous conversation between the casewriter and a banker who worked on the deal, February 17, 2000.

[23] Motz and Hordon, "The Sky's the Limit," p. 27.

EXHIBIT 25-10

STOCK AND BOND PRICES, JULY 1997–SEPTEMBER 1999

Source: Datastream and Bloomberg.

government, which purchased a high-capacity connection for military use.[24] Also in preparation for the launch, Iridium issued a fourth series of senior notes ($350 million of Series D notes) in May 1998. Like the previous high-yield issues, this one was rated B− and was due in 2005, but had a lower interest rate of 10.88%.

Commercial Launch: July 1998 to July 1999

Iridium announced the new service in July 1998, with a $140 million advertising campaign in 16 languages across 45 countries with the slogan "Freedom to Communicate. Anytime, Anywhere."[25,26] Unfortunately, Iridium quickly ran into trouble: it failed to

[24] Quentin Hardy, "Iridium Gets U.S. Military as First Big Customer," *The Wall Street Journal*, January 26, 1998, p. B7.

[25] Despite the quote on page one, the advertising campaign cost approximately $140 million, not $180 million.

[26] Christopher Price, "Iridium: Born on the Beach But Lost in Space," *Financial Times*, August 20, 1999, p. 22.

EXHIBIT 25-11

IRIDIUM ORGANIZATIONAL STRUCTURE, DECEMBER 31, 1998

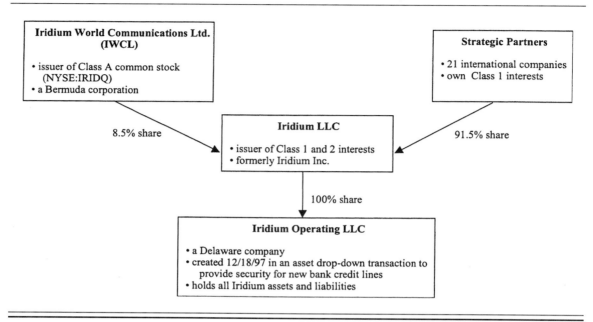

answer over one million sales inquiries due to internal confusion, and it experienced logistical problems trying to distribute phones.[27] These problems forced Iridium to delay the start of commercial service by two months. Nevertheless, commercial service began on November 1, 1998, with a phone call from Vice President Albert Gore at the White House to Alexander Graham Bell's great-grandson in Virginia.[28]

Within weeks, it became clear that Iridium was not attracting as many customers as it had expected, a fact that concerned the bankers and forced Iridium to negotiate new bank facilities in December 1998. Unfortunately, it was not a good time to raise capital in the wake of the financial crisis in Russia, turmoil in Asia, and collapse of the Long-Term Capital Management (LTCM) hedge fund. Rather than replacing the bank loans with long-term debt as planned following launch, Iridium was forced to renew its bank facilities. At the time, the banks reviewed the company's strategic plans, hired independent consultants to review the projections, and conducted their own market analysis. Feeling satisfied with the results, the banks provided a new guaranteed facility and a new secured line of credit. The new guaranteed facility consisted of a $475 million term loan due in December 2000, and a $275 million revolving credit facility expiring in December 2001. Once again, Motorola guaranteed the full $750 million in exchange for warrants and cash payments based on the spread between the bank loans and Iridium's Series A and B bond rates.[29] This guarantee allowed Iridium to borrow at the prime rate.

---

[27] Leslie Cauley, "Losses in Space: Iridium's Downfall," *The Wall Street Journal*, August 18, 1999, p. A1.

[28] Vice President Gore greeted Gilbert M. Grosvenor with the famous words Bell uttered to his assistant in 1876: "Mr. Watson, come here, I want you" (Iridium World Communications Annual Report 1998, p. 1).

[29] Iridium Annual Report, 1998, p. 59.

TABLE B   Covenants on the New Secured Bank Facility, December 1998

Date	Cumulative Cash Revenue ($ millions)	Cumulative Accrued Revenue ($ millions)	Number of Satellite Phone Subscribers	Number of System Subscribers[a]
March 31, 1999	$ 4	$ 30	27,000	52,000
June 30, 1999	50	150	88,000	213,000
September 30, 1999	220	470	173,000	454,000

[a] Total system subscribers includes users of Iridium's phone, fax, and paging services.

Source: Iridium World Communications Ltd., 1998 Annual Report.

Iridium also signed a new $800 million secured credit facility. The facility provided $800 million in cash priced at prime plus 2.75%.[30] In an effort to increase their security, the banks included a number of new covenants on the loans that established quarterly milestones in terms of revenues and subscriber levels. Table 25-B provides details on the new covenants.

With new bank loans, but lower than expected cash flow, management began to search for ways to conserve cash. For 1999, the firm projected aggregate cash needs of $1.65 billion to cover system operation, financing costs, working capital, and software development; the firm would need similar amounts annually for the next three years. Beginning in 2000, the firm would have to increase system capacity; the following year it would have to start replacing the satellite constellation assuming a five-year useful life for the satellites. These two activities would require more than $6 billion of capital expenditures between 2000 and 2004 (see Exhibit 25-5). To reduce its immediate cash requirements, Iridium reached an agreement with Motorola to defer up to $400 million in contract payments. Exhibit 25-12 documents Iridium's previous payments and future obligations to Motorola. In an effort to raise cash, Iridium conducted a secondary equity offering in January 1999, which raised an additional $240 million at a price of $37.38 per share. After this offering, IWCL's executive officers and directors owned 3.8% of IWCL, which, in turn, owned 13.3% of Iridium LLC (see Exhibit 25-6).

Although these steps temporarily solved the cash flow problems, Iridium continued to stumble in terms of execution. In March 1999, it was unable to fill 15,000 orders for satellite phones because the manufacturer could not ramp up production fast enough. This and other distribution problems made it clear that Iridium would miss its first quarter targets on both revenues and the number of subscribers. In fact, Iridium announced that it had only 7,188 satellite subscribers, 10,294 total service subscribers, and cumulative cash revenues of $195,000 as of March 31, far short of the required 27,000 satellite subscribers, 52,000 total subscribers, and $4 million of cash revenues.[31]

The banks, however, granted a 60-day extension to the end of May. Shortly thereafter, Roy Grant, the company's chief financial officer (CFO), announced his resignation. The next month, John Richardson, head of Iridium's African gateway, replaced Staiano as CEO, and Leo Mondale became CFO. In May, the banks waived the covenants until the end of June. When Iridium missed the June targets as well, the bankers extended the deadline one more time until August 11, 1999. The only bit of positive news during this time, at least from Motorola's perspective, came when Teledesic announced

---

[30] Iridium form 8-K, dated December 19, 1997, p. 6.

[31] Iridium LLC, form 10-Q, March 31, 1999, p. 24.

EXHIBIT 25-12

PAYMENTS TO MOTOROLA FROM IRIDIUM LLC ($ MILLIONS), 1995–2003

	System Development			Operations and Maintenance	Total
Year	Support Agreement	Space System	Terrestrial Network		
1995	$0.6	$ 802			$ 803
1996	0.9	836	64		901
1997	0.7	577	74		652
1998		589	139	129	857
1999 est.			6	537	543
2000 est.				558	558
2001 est.				581	581
2002 est.				605	605
2003 est.				472	472
Total	**$2.1**	**$2,804**	**$283**	**$2,882**	**$5,871**

Source: Iridium World Communications Ltd. Class A Stock Prospectus, January 21, 1999.

that Motorola had been selected as the prime contractor for its $10 billion "internet in the sky" system.

In an attempt to save the company, Iridium took increasingly more drastic measures. The new management fired 15% of the workforce in June 1999 and revamped the company's marketing strategy. They cut the usage charge from as high as $7.00 per minute to $1.89, and slashed the advertising budget to $12 million.[32] But even these actions were not enough, as Iridium missed the scheduled interest payments on its notes on July 15. When asked whether Iridium might declare bankruptcy, CFO Mondale stated that bankruptcy was not a realistic option because "Our investors, partners, and distributors do not feel that Iridium will quickly, if ever, recover from a bankruptcy."[33]

DEFAULT AND BANKRUPTCY

By August, Iridium had still not attracted enough customers or generated sufficient revenue to meet the covenants on its secured credit facility. As a result, it was in technical default when the August 11 deadline arrived. Two days later, a group representing the public bondholders filed an involuntary bankruptcy petition based on cross-default provisions in the notes. Later that same day, Iridium filed a voluntary Chapter 11 bankruptcy petition to protect itself from creditors. Iridium's CEO, John Richardson, explained: "The action is the most efficient way to conclude Iridium's restructuring negotiations. . . . We are confident that Iridium will emerge from this process as a stronger

---

[32] Quentin Hardy, "Iridium, in Bid to Bolster Ailing Service, Cuts Staff and Prices, Shifts Marketing," *The Wall Street Journal*, June 14, 1998, p. B8.

[33] Leslie Cauley, "A Bankruptcy-Court Filing by Iridium Isn't a Realistic Option, Says Official," *The Wall Street Journal*, July 19, 1999, p. A4.

and more vibrant company in the telecommunications marketplace."[34] Twelve days later, *The Wall Street Journal* published a letter from Richardson to the public in which he wrote:

> We recognize our missteps and are working diligently to correct them. Our single most important goal is to provide world-class service to our customers. To meet our goal, we must get our financial house in order. . . . I want to assure our customers, investors, and partners worldwide that Iridium will continue to provide its pioneering, high-quality global telecommunications service without interruption. We are still in business, and it is business as usual.[35]

[34] Iridium LLC Press Release, August 13, 1999.
[35] Open letter published in *The Wall Street Journal*, August 25, 1999, p. B7.

Project Finance Research, Data, and Information Sources

This note documents the major sources of project finance research and data, and is intended to be used as a reference guide for researchers interested in the field of project finance. The note is divided into nine sections:

1. Books and Monographs
2. Trade Magazines and Journals
3. Articles, Notes, and Book Chapters
4. Rating Agency Analysis and Publications
5. Related Finance Books and Articles
6. Project Finance Software
7. Project Finance Data Sources
8. Export Credit Agencies (ECAs)
9. Multilateral Development Banks and Agencies

The information contained in this note is also available on the HBS Project Finance Portal (http://www.hbs.edu/projfinportal) (see Exhibit 1).

1. BOOKS AND MONOGRAPHS

This section contains information on books in three areas: (1.A) Project Finance Books, (1.B) Books Related to Project Finance, and (1.C) Books on Specific Projects.

This note updates a previous version prepared by Research Associate Fuaad A. Qureshi, under the supervision of Professor Benjamin C. Esty as the basis for class discussion

EXHIBIT 1

HBS PROJECT FINANCE PORTAL

Project Finance Portal (www.hbs.edu/projfinportal/)

 Project Finance Portal | RESEARCH, DATA, AND INFORMATION SOURCES

This portal is intended to be a reference guide for students, researchers, and practitioners seeking to obtain information about project finance. In addition to bibliographical references for books, articles, and case studies, the site contains more than 900 links to related sites.

Research and Publications

Articles, Notes, and Book Chapters
Books and Monographs
Case Studies and Notes
Courses
Rating Agency Information
Related Finance Books and Articles
Trade Magazines and Journals
Software
Legal and Regulatory Issues
Glossary of Terms

Project Finance Links

General Project Finance Sites
Project Finance Data
Rating Agency Information
Publications
Country Data
Emerging Markets Data
Development Banks
Export Credit Agencies (ECAs)
Law Firms
Private Finance Initiative (PFI/PPP)
Bankers and Advisors
Project Sites
Related Finance Sites

If you have any suggestions for additional content, please contact Professor Benjamin C. Esty.
Last updated March 20, 2003.

This material, content, and organization is copyright protected. It comes from the Harvard Business School note entitled, "Project Finance Research, Data, and Information Sources," HBS #201-041, ©2000.

| HBS Home | Search | Index | Faculty |

1.A. Project Finance Books

BEENHAKKER, H.L., 1997, *Risk Management in Project Finance and Implementation*, Quorum Books (Westport, CT).

BENOIT, P., 1996, *Project Finance at the World Bank: An Overview of Policies and Instruments* (World Bank Technical Paper Number 312), The World Bank (Washington, DC).

BULJEVICH, ESTEBAN C., and YOON S. PARK, 1999, *Project Financing and the International Financial Markets*, Kluwer Academic Publishers (Norwell, MA).

FABOZZI, F., and P. NEVITT, 2000, *Project Financing* (7th ed.), Euromoney Publications (London, UK).

FINNERTY, J.D., 1996, *Project Finance: Asset-Based Financial Engineering*, John Wiley & Sons (New York).

FITZGERALD, P.F., and B.N. MACHLIN, 2001, *Project Financing: Building Infrastructure Projects in Developing Markets (2001)*, Practicing Law Institute (NY, NY).

HOFFMAN, S.L., 1998, *The Law and Business of International Project Finance*, Kluwer Law International (Boston, MA).

International Finance Corporation, 1999, *The Private Sector Financing Activities of International Financial Institutions 1991–1997* (Washington, DC).

International Finance Corporation, 1999, *Project Finance in Developing Countries* (Lessons of Experience Number 7), The World Bank (Washington, DC).

KHAN, M.F.K., and R.J. PARRA, 2003, *Financing Large Projects: Using Project Finance Techniques and Practices*, Pearson Education Asia Pte Ltd, Prentice Hall (Singapore).

LANG, L.H.P., 1998, *Project Finance in Asia* (Advances in Finance, Investment, and Banking), Vol. 6, Elsevier Science Ltd. (North-Holland).

LEVY, S.M., 1996, *Build, Operate, Transfer: Paving the Way for Tomorrow's Infrastructure*, John Wiley & Sons (NY, NY).

MERRO, EDWARD W., LORRAINE McDONNELL, and R. YILMAZ ARGUDEN, 1988, *Understanding the Outcomes of Megaprojects: A Quantitative Analysis of Very Large Civilian Projects*, The Rand Corporation (Santa Monica, CA).

MILLER, J.B., 2000, *Principles of Public and Private Infrastructure Delivery*, Kluwer Academic Publishers and the American Infrastructure Consortium (Boston, MA).

NEVITT, P., 1983, *Project Financing* (4th ed.), Euromoney Publications (London, UK).

POLLIO, G., 1999, *International Project Analysis & Financing*, University of Michigan Press (Ann Arbor, MI).

RAZAVI, H., 1996, *Financing Energy Projects in Emerging Economies*, PennWell (Tulsa, OK).

SADER, F., 2000, *Attracting Foreign Direct Investment into Infrastructure: Why Is It So Difficult?*, Foreign Investment Advisory Service (FIAS), Occasional Paper number 12, World Bank and International Finance Corporation (IFC) (Washington, DC).

SQUIRE, L., and H.G. VAN DER TAK, 1975, *Economic Analysis of Projects*, Johns Hopkins University Press (Baltimore, MD).

The World Bank and International Finance Corporation, 1996, *Financing Private Infrastructure*, (Washington, DC).

1.B. Books Related to Project Finance

ALTSHULER, A., and D. LUBEROFF, 2003, *Mega-Projects: The Changing Politics of Urban Investment*, The Brookings Institution Press (Washington, DC).

CAUFIELD, CATHERINE, 1996, *Masters of Illusion: The World Bank and the Poverty of Nations*, Henry Holt and Company (New York).

EASTERLY, WILLIAM, 2001, *The Elusive Quest for Growth: Economists' Adventures and Misadventures in the Tropics*, MIT Press (Cambridge, MA).

FLYVBJERG, B., N. BRUZELIUS, and W. ROTHENGATTER, 2003, *Megaprojects and Risk: An Anatomy of Ambition*, Cambridge University Press (Port Chester, NY).

HIRSCHMAN, ALBERT O., 1967, *Development Projects Observed*, The Brookings Institute (Washington, DC).

MACAULAY, DAVID, 2000, *Building Big* (A Companion to the PBS Series), Houghton Mifflin Company (Boston, MA).

MILLER, R., and D.R. LESSARD, 2000, *The Strategic Management of Large Engineering Projects*, MIT Press (Cambridge, MA).

MORAN, T.H. (ed.), 1998, *Managing International Political Risk*, Blackwell Business (Malden, MA).

MORAN, T.H. (ed.), 2001, *International Political Risk Management*, The World Bank Group (Washington, DC).

MORRIS, PETER W.G., 1988, *The Anatomy of Major Projects: A Study of the Reality of Project Management*, Chichester/Wiley (New York).

Multilateral Investment Guarantee Agency (MIGA), *Investment Guarantee Guide*, The World Bank (Washington, DC).

O'LEARY, A.F., and J. ACRET, 2001, *Construction Nightmares: Jobs from Hell and How to Avoid Them* (2nd ed.), Building News Books.

PETTINGER, R., 2000, *Investment Appraisal: A Managerial Approach*, St. Martin's Press (New York).

PRS Group, 1998, *The Handbook of Country and Political Risk Analysis*, PRS Group (East Syracuse, NY).

VENEDIKIAN, H.M., and G.A. WARFIELD, 1996, *Export-Import Financing* (4th ed.), Wiley Frontiers in Finance (New York).

WAGNER, DANIEL, 1999, *Political Risk Insurance Guide*, International Risk Management Institute (Dallas, TX).

World Bank, 1997, *The World Bank Guarantees Handbook* (Washington, DC).

World Commission on Dams, 2000, *Dams and Development: A New Framework for Decision Making: The Report of the World Commission on Dams*, Earthscan Publications Ltd (London, UK).

1.C. Books on Specific Projects

DAVIS, H., 1996, *Project Finance: Practical Case Studies*, Euromoney Books (London, UK).

FETHERSTON, D., 1997, *The Chunnel: The Amazing Story of the Undersea Crossing of the English Channel*, Times Books (New York).

HUGHES, THOMAS P., 1998, *Rescuing Prometheus: Four Monumental Projects That Changed the Modern World*, Pantheon Books (New York).

MEHTA, ABHAY, 1999, *Power Play: A Study of the Enron Project* (Dabhol in India), Orient Longman Ltd. (Hyderabad, India).

2. TRADE MAGAZINES AND JOURNALS

Finance and Development: a quarterly publication published by the International Monetary Fund (IMF).

Global Finance: each year publishes *Best Project Finance Deals* (in February) and *Best Banks in Project Finance* (in October).

Global Project Finance and Privatization: a quarterly newsletter from Cadwalader, Wickersham & Taft.

The Journal of Structured and Project Finance: a quarterly journal published by Institutional Investor.

Project Finance: a quarterly newsletter published by Milbank, Tweed, Hadley, & McCloy LLP.

ProjectFinance: a monthly trade journal published by Euromoney Publications. Annual publication: Project Finance Yearbook.

Project Finance International: a biweekly magazine published by Thomson Financial. Annual publication: Project Finance International Yearbook (January).

3. ARTICLES, NOTES, AND BOOK CHAPTERS

This section contains information in six areas: (3.A) Project Finance Overviews and Theoretical Articles, (3.B) Structuring Projects, (3.C) Valuing Projects, (3.D) Managing Project Risk, (3.E) Financing Projects, and (3.F) Negotiating Projects.

3.A. Project Finance Overviews and Theoretical Articles

BREALEY, R.A., I.A. COOPER, and M.A. HABIB, 1996, Using Project Finance to Fund Infrastructure Investments, *Journal of Applied Corporate Finance* 9:3, pp. 25–38.

BUCKLEY, A., 1996, Project Finance, appears in *International Capital Budgeting*, Chapter 14, pp. 335–363, Prentice Hall.

CHEMMANUR, T.J., and K. JOHN, 1996, Optimal Incorporation, Structure of Debt Contracts, and Limited-Recourse Project Financing, *Journal of Financial Intermediation* 5, pp. 372–408.

CLIFFORD CHANCE, 1991, Project Finance, London, UK (February).

ESTY, B.C., 2002, Returns on Project-Financed Investments: Evolution and Managerial Implications, *Journal of Applied Corporate Finance*, Spring, pp. 71–86.

ESTY, B.C., and I. CHRISTOV, 2002, Recent Trends in Project Finance: A 5-Year Perspective, *Project Finance International*, Special 10th Anniversary Issue, Issue #249, September 18, pp. 74–82.

JOHN, T.A., 1991, Optimality of Project Financing: Theory and Empirical Implications in Finance and Accounting, *Review of Quantitative Finance and Accounting* 1, pp. 51–74.

KENSINGER, J.W., and J.D. MARTIN, 1988, Project Finance: Raising Money the Old-Fashioned Way, *Journal of Applied Corporate Finance*, Fall, pp. 69–81.

SHAH, S., and THAKOR, A.V., 1987, Optimal Capital Structure and Project Financing, *Journal of Economic Theory* 42, pp. 207–243.

SMITH, R.C. and I. WALTER, 1990, Global Financial Services: Strategies for Building Competitive Strengths, appears in *International Commercial and Investment Banking* (New York: Harper Business). Chapter 9, pp. 214–219.

WYNANT, L., 1980, Essential Elements of Project Finance, *Harvard Business Review*, May–June, pp. 165–173.

3.B. Structuring Projects

BUEHRER, T.S., J.J. EMERY, M.T. SPENCE, JR., and L.T. WELLS, JR., 2000, Administrative Barriers to Foreign Investment: Reducing Red Tape in Africa, Foreign Investment Advisory Service (FIAS), Occasional Paper No. 14, International Finance Corporation-Multilateral Investment Guarantee Agency (Washington, DC).

FOWKES, D., N. KAHN, and D. ARMSTRONG, 2000, Leasing in Project Finance, *Journal of Project Finance*, Spring, pp. 21–31.

KLEIN, MICHAEL, 1998, Bidding for Concessions—The Impact of Contract Design, Viewpoint Note No. 158, The World Bank Group, November.

KLEIN, MICHAEL, JAE SO, and BEN SHIN, 1996, Transaction Costs in Private Infrastructure Projects—Are They Too High?, Viewpoint Note No. 95, The World Bank Group, October.

McPHAIL, KATHRYN, and AIDAN DAVY, 1998, Integrating Social Concerns into Private Sector Projects, World Bank Discussion Paper No. 384, World Bank (Washington, DC).

PFEFFERMANN, GUY, 2000, Paths Out of Poverty: The Role of Private Enterprise in Developing Countries, International Finance Corporation (Washington, DC).

SAHLMAN, W.A., 1988, Aspects of Financial Contracting in Venture Capital, *Journal of Applied Corporate Finance*, Vol. 1, No. 2, Summer, pp. 23–36.

WELLS, L.T., and T.S. BUEHRER, 2000, Cutting the Red Tape: Lessons from a Case-Based Approach to Improving the Investment Climate in Mozambique, appears in *Administrative Barriers to Foreign Investment*, International Finance Corporation and The World Bank (Washington, DC).

3.C. Valuing Projects

ANG, J.S., and T. LAI, 1989, A Simple Rule for Multi-national Capital Budgeting, *Global Finance Journal* 1, pp. 71–75.

ESTY, B.C., 1999, Improved Techniques for Valuing Large-Scale Projects, *Journal of Project Finance* 5, Spring, pp. 9–25.

FOWKES, D., N. KAHN, and D. ARMSTRONG, 2000, Leasing in Project Financing, *Journal of Project Finance*, Spring, pp. 21–31.

IMAI, J., and M. NAKAJIMA, 2001, A Real Option Analysis of an Oil Refinery Project, *Financial Practice and Education*, Fall/Winter, pp. 78–91.

KARMOKOLIAS, YANNIS, 1996, Cost Benefit Analysis of Private Sector Environmental Investments: A Case Study of the Kunda Cement Factory, International Finance Corporation Discussion Paper #30 (Washington, DC), June.

KOPELIC, S.A., and D.S. FOGEL, 1996, Project and Investment Valuation with Regards to Emerging Markets, Katz Graduate School of Business, University of Pittsburgh, case #298-001, available through ECCH Collection.

LESSARD, DONALD R., 1979, Evaluating Foreign Projects—An Adjusted Present Value Approach, MIT Working Paper no. 1062-79 (Boston, MA), April.

MASON, S.P., and C.Y. BALDWIN, 1988, Evaluation of Government Subsidies to Large-Scale Energy Projects, *Advances in Futures and Options Research* 3, pp. 169–181.

MASON, S.P., and R.C. MERTON, 1985, The Role of Contingent Claims Analysis in Corporate Finance (see the application of contingent claims analysis to a pipeline project in the appendix) in *Recent Advances in Corporate Finance*, E.I. Altman and M.G. Subrahmanyam, eds., Richard D. Irwin (Homewood, IL).

MERTON, R.C., and Z. BODIE, 1992, On the Management of Financial Guarantees, *Financial Management*, Winter, pp. 87–109.

ROSE, S., 1998, Valuation of Interacting Real Options in a Toll Road Infrastructure Project, *Quarterly Review of Economics and Finance* 38, pp. 711–723.

SAVVIDES, S., 1994, Risk Analysis in Investment Appraisal, *Project Appraisal Journal*, Vol. 9, No. 1, March, pp. 3–18.

SMIT, H.T.J., 1997, Investment Analysis of Offshore Concessions in the Netherlands, *Financial Management* 26, Summer, pp. 5–17.

WACHS, M., 1990, Ethics and Advocacy in Forecasting for Public Policy, *Business & Professional Ethics Journal* 9: 1 & 2, Spring/Summer, pp. 141–157.

WELLS, L.T., 1975, Social Cost/Benefit Analysis for MNCs, *Harvard Business Review*, March/April, pp. 40–154.

WHITE, D.E., R.S. POATS, and M.J. BORCHI, 2000, The Role of Volatility Value in Power Plant Financing, *Journal of Project Finance*, Summer, pp. 23–31.

WOOLDRIDGE, S.C, M.J. GARVIN, Y.J. CHEAH, and J.B. MILLER, 2002, Valuing Flexibility in Private Toll Road Development: Analysis of the Dulles Greenway, *The Journal of Project and Structured Finance*, Winter, pp. 25–36.

3.D. Managing Project Risk

BAIN, R., and M. WILKINS, 2002, Road Risk, *Project Finance Transport Report*, September, pp. 2–5.

BANERJEE, S., and T. NOE, 2002, Exotics and Electrons: Electric Power Crises and Financial Risk Management, Tulane University working paper, January.

BEALE, C., M. CHATAIN, N. FOX, S. BELL, J. BERNER, R. PREMINGER, and J. PRINS, 2002, Credit Attributes of Project Finance, *Journal of Structured and Project Finance* 8: 3, Fall, pp. 5–9.

DAILAMI, M., and R. HAUSWALD, 2001, Credit Spread Determinants and Interlocking Contracts: A Clinical Study of the Ras Gas Project, University of Maryland working paper, November.

DYMOND, C., and J. SCHOENBLUM, 2002, Targeted Risk Capital, *Journal of Structured and Project Finance*, pp. 32–39.

ESTY, B.C., 1999, Petrozuata: A Case Study on the Effective Use of Project Finance, 1999, *Journal of Applied Corporate Finance* 12: 3, Fall, pp. 26–42.

FORTIN, R. JAY, 1995, Defining Force Majeure, *Project and Trade Finance*, Euromoney Publication, January.

FROOT, K.A., D.S. SCHARFSTEIN, and J.C. STEIN, 1994, A Framework for Risk Management, *Harvard Business Review*, November/December, pp. 91–102.

HEADLEY, J.S., and P. TUFANO, 1994, Why Manage Risk?, Harvard Business School Case no. 294-107.

International Finance Corporation, 1999, Mitigating Major Project Risks, Chapter 4 in *Project Finance Lessons from Experience* #7 (Washington, DC).

International Finance Corporation (IFC, a member of the World Bank Group), Policy on Environmental Assessment (OP 4.01, October 1998).

International Finance Corporation (IFC, a member of the World BankGroup), Policy on Indigenous Peoples (OP 4.20, September 1991). An Operational Directive from the World Bank Operational Manual.

KLOMPJAN, R., and M.J.R. WOUTERS, 2002, Default Risk in Project Finance, *Journal of Structured and Project Finance* 8: 3, Fall, pp. 10–21.

LEVEY, D.H., and V.J. TRUGLIA, 2002, Revised Country Ceiling Policy, *Moody's Sourcebook: Project & Infrastructure Finance* (original article published June 2001), December, pp. xci–xcii.

MARSHELLA, TOM, 2001, Three R's: Risk, Return, Rating, *ProjectFinance*, Latin America Report, June, pp. 5–8.

MARTI, STEPHAN, and LOWELL KEITH, 2000, Cash Flow Volatility as Opportunity: Adding Sophisticated Insurance Capital to the Project Finance Mix, *Journal of Project Finance*, Fall, pp. 9–13.

MILLER, R., and D. LESSARD, 2000, Understanding and Managing Risks in Large Engineering Projects, *International Journal of Project Management* 19: 8, pp. 437–443.

Moody's Corporation, 2000, Heightened Construction Risk for Complex Projects: Welcome to the Billion Dollar Club!, February, in *Moody's Project Finance Sourcebook*, October, pp. 146–154.

MORAN, THEODORE H., 1973, Transnational Strategies of Protection and Defense by Multinational Corporations: Spreading the Risk and Raising the Cost for Nationalization in Natural Resources, *International Organization* 27: 3, Spring, pp. 273–287.

PENROSE, J., and P. RIGBY, 2000, Debt Rating Criteria for Energy, Industrial, and Infrastructure Project Finance, *Standard & Poor's: 2000–2001 Infrastructure Finance: Criteria and Commentary*, October, pp. 15–65.

RIGBY, P.N., 1999, Merchant Power: Project Finance Criteria, *Standard & Poor's: 1999 Infrastructure Finance Criteria and Commentary*, October, pp. 24–39.

RASMUSSEN, KAREN, 1999, Mitigating Currency Convertibility Risks in High-Risk Countries, Viewpoint Note No. 180, The World Bank Group, April.

RUSTER, JEFF, 1996, Mitigating Commercial Risks in Project Finance, Viewpoint Note No. 69, The World Bank Group, February.

WALSH, R., 1999, Pacific Rim Collateral Security Laws: What Happens When the Project Goes Wrong?, *Stanford Journal of Law, Business and Finance* 115, pp. 115–147.

WELLS, L.T., and E. GLEASON, 1995, Is Foreign Infrastructure Investment Still Risky?, *Harvard Business Review*, Reprint 95511, September/October, pp. 1–12.

WEST, G., 1996, Managing Project Political Risk: The Role of Investment Insurance, *Journal of Project Finance*, Winter, pp. 5–11.

World Bank, 1998, The World Bank Guarantee: Catalyst for Private Capital Flows, Project Finance and Guarantees Department.

3.E. Financing Projects

BAVARIA, S.M., 2002, Syndicated Loans—A Rated Market, at Last!, Standard & Poor's Corporation, February 12, 2002.

CASTLE, G.R., 1975, Project Financing-Guidelines for the Commercial Banker, *Journal of Commercial Bank Lending* 57, April, pp. 14–30.

ESTY, B.C., 2001, Structuring Loan Syndicates: A Case Study of the Hong Kong Disneyland Project Loan, *Journal of Applied Corporate Finance* 14: 3, pp. 80–95.

ESTY, B.C. and W.L. MEGGINSON, 2003, Creditor Rights, Enforcement, and Debt Ownership Structure: Evidence from the Global Syndicated Loan Market, *Journal of Financial and Quantitative Analysis* 38: 1, pp. 37–59.

FORRESTER, J. PAUL, 1995, The Role of Commercial Banks in Project Finance, *Journal of Project Finance*, Summer, pp. 53–58.

FRUHAN, W.E., 1979, Freeport Minerals Company, appears in *Financial Strategy*, Chapter 5, Irwin (Homewood, ILL).

KLEIMEIER, S., and MEGGINSON, W.L., 2000, Are Project Finance Loans Different from Other Syndicated Credits?, *Journal of Applied Corporate Finance*, Spring.

KUNKLE, J.W., J.L. SOLTZ, L. MONNIER, and C. JOASSIN, 2002, Layer It On—The Essentials of Rating Project Subordinated Debt, Fitch Ratings Criteria Report, September 9, 2002.

McKEON, P., 1999, High-Yield Debt: Broadening the Scope of Project Finance, *Journal of Project Finance*, Fall, pp. 62–69.

PARRA, R.J., and M.F.K. KHAN, 2001, Layered Finance, *Journal of Structured and Project Finance*, Fall, pp. 49–60.

PHILLIPS, P.D., J.C. GROTH, and R.M. RICHARDS, 1979, Financing the Alaskan Project: The Experience at Sohio, *Financial Management*, pp. 7–16.

SIMPSON, P., and N. AVERY, 1995, The Role of Capital Markets in Project Financings, *Journal of Project Finance*, Spring, pp. 43–48.

3.F. Negotiating Projects

KOLO, A. and T.W. WÄLDE, 2000, Renegotiation and Contract Adaptation in International Investment Projects, *Journal of World Investment*, Vol. 5, pp. 5–57.

RILEY, HANNAH C., and JAMES K. SEBENIUS, 1995, Stakeholder Negotiations over Third World Natural Resource Projects, *Cultural Survival Quarterly* 19: 3, pp. 39–43.

SALACUSE, JESWALD W., 2001, Renegotiating International Project Agreements, *Fordham International Law Journal* 24: April, pp. 1319–1370.

SALTER, M.S., and S. HALL, 1994, Block 16: Conoco's "Green" Oil Strategy (A, B, C, & D), Harvard Business School cases no. 394-001, no. 394-005, no. 394-006, and no. 394-007.

SEBENIUS, J.K., and H.C. RILEY, 1997, Stone Container in Costa Rica (A & B), Harvard Business School cases no. 897-140 and no. 897-141.

SEBENIUS, J.K., and H.C. RILEY, 1997, Stone Container in Honduras (A & B), Harvard Business School cases no. 897-172 and no. 897-173.

WHEELER, M., 2001, North East Solid Waste Committee—NESWC (A, B, & C), Harvard Business School cases no. 801-067, no. 801-068, and no. Draft.

4. RATING AGENCY ANALYSIS AND PUBLICATIONS

Each year, the rating agencies publish summaries of their most important research reports and guidelines on ratings methodologies. These reports are available from the rating agencies directly or, in some cases, are available online.

Moody's

Project and Infrastructure Finance Sourcebook, December 2002.
Project and Infrastructure Finance Sourcebook, December 2001.
Project Finance Sourcebook, October 2000.
Project Finance Sourcebook, October 1999.

Power Company Sourcebook, October 1999.
Project Finance Sourcebook, October 1998.
Project Finance Sourcebook, October 1997.

Standard and Poor's (S&P)
Ratings criteria by type of project
Books

Project and Infrastructure Finance Review (Criteria/Commentary), October 2002.
Project and Infrastructure Finance Review (Criteria/Commentary), October 2001.
Infrastructure Finance (Criteria and Commentary), October 2000.
Infrastructure Finance (Summary Analyses), September 1999.
Infrastructure Finance (Criteria and Commentary), September 1999.
Infrastructure Finance (Summary Analyses), September 1998.
Infrastructure Finance (Criteria and Commentary), September 1998.
Global Project Finance, September 1997.
Global Project Finance, September 1996.

Fitch IBCA, Duff & Phelps (report discontinued in 2000)

Global Project Finance, October 1999.
Global Project Finance, October 1998.

5. RELATED FINANCE BOOKS AND ARTICLES

This section contains information in five subject areas: (5.A) Real Options Analysis, (5.B) General Valuation Analysis, (5.C) Emerging Markets Research, (5.D) Valuation in Emerging Markets, and (5.E) Risk Management and Financial Engineering.

5.A. Real Options Analysis

AMRAM, M., and N. KULATILAKA, 1999, *Real Options: Managing Strategic Investment in an Uncertain World*, Harvard Business School Press (Boston, MA).

BRENNAN, M., and E. SCHWARTZ, 1985, A New Way of Evaluating Natural Resource Investments, *Midland Journal of Corporate Finance* 3, pp. 78–88.

COPELAND, T., and V. ANTIKAROV, 2001, *Real Options: A Practitioner's Guide*, Texere LLC (New York).

COPELAND, T., and P. KEENAN, 1998, Making Real Options Real, *The McKinsey Quarterly*, No. 3, pp. 128–141.

DIXIT, A.K., and R.S. PINDYK, 1994, *Investment under Uncertainty*, Princeton University Press (Princeton, New Jersey).

DIXIT, A.K., and R.S. PINDYK, 1995, The Options Approach to Capital Investment, *Harvard Business Review*, May/June, pp. 105–115.

KEMNA, A.G.Z., 1993, Case Studies on Real Options, *Financial Management*, Autumn, pp. 259–270.

KULATILAKA, N., and A. MARCUS, 1992, Project Valuation under Uncertainty, *Journal of Applied Corporate Finance*, Fall, pp. 92–100.

LESLIE, K., and M. MICHAELS, 1997, The Real Power of Real Options, *The McKinsey Quarterly*, No. 3.

LESLIE, K., and M. MICHAELS, 1998, The Real Power of Real Options, *Corporate Finance* 158, January, pp. 13–20.

MAJD, S., and R.S. PINDYCK, 1987, Time to Build, Option Value, and Investment Decisions, *Journal of Financial Economics* 18, pp. 7–27.

MCDONALD, R., and D. SIEGEL, 1986, The Value of Waiting to Invest, *The Quarterly Journal of Economics* 101, November, pp. 707–727.

MYERS, S.C., and S. MAJD, 1990, Abandonment Value and Project Life, *Advances in Futures and Options Research* 4, pp. 1–21.

SIEGEL, D., J. SMITH, and J. PADDOCK, 1987, Valuing Offshore Oil Properties with Option Pricing Models, *Midland Journal of Corporate Finance* 5, pp. 22–30.

TRIGEORGIS, LENOS, 1996, Interactions Among Multiple Real Options, Chapter 7 in *Real Options: Managerial Flexibility and Strategy in Resource Allocation*, The MIT Press (Cambridge, MA).

TRIGEORGIS, LENOS, 1996, *Real Options: Managerial Flexibility and Strategy in Resource Allocation*, The MIT Press (Cambridge, MA).

5.B. General Valuation Analysis

COPELAND, T., T. KOLLER, and J. MURRIN, 2000, *Valuation* (3rd ed.), John Wiley & Sons (New York).

EHRHARDT, E.R., 1994, *The Search for Value*, Harvard Business School Press (Boston, MA).

FAMA, EUGENE F., and KENNETH R. FRENCH, 1997, Industry Costs of Equity, *Journal of Financial Economics* 43, pp. 153–193.

FRUHAN, W.E., 2002, Note on Alternative Methods for Valuing Terminal Value, Harvard Business School Case no. 298-166.

FRUHAN, W.E., 2002, Note on the Equivalency of Methods for Discounting Cash Flows (valuing equity through either equity cash flow or free cash flow methods), Harvard Business School Case no. 202-128.

KESTER, W. C., R. P. MELNICK, and K.A. FROOT, 1994, Note on Fundamental Parity Conditions, Harvard Business School Case no. 288-016.

KESTER, W.C., J. MORLEY, 1992, Note on Cross-Border Valuation, Harvard Business School Case no. 292-084.

LESSARD, D.R., 1979, Evaluating Foreign Projects—An Adjusted Present Value Approach, in *Frontiers of International Financial Management*, Warren, Gorham, and Lamaont (Boston, MA).

PEREIRO, LUIS E., 2002, *Valuation of Companies in Emerging Markets: A Practical Approach* Wiley-Finance/John Wiley & Sons (New York).

RUBACK, R.S., 1995, An Introduction to Cash Flow Valuation Methods, Harvard Business School Case no. 295-155.

RUBACK, R.S., 1995, A Note on Capital Cash Flow Valuation, Harvard Business School Case no. 295-069.

RUBACK, R., 2002, Capital Cash Flows: A Simple Approach to Valuing Risky Cash Flows, *Financial Management*, Summer, pp. 85–103.

5.C. Emerging Markets Research

BEIM, DAVID O., and CHARLES W. CALOMIRIS, 2001, *Emerging Financial Markets,* McGraw-Hill Irwin (New York).

BEKAERT, G., and C.R. HARVEY, 2002, Research in Emerging Markets Finance: Looking to the Future, *Emerging Markets Review* 3, December, pp. 429–448.

DIAMONTE, R., J. LIEW, and R. STEVENS, 1996, Political Risk in Emerging and Developed Markets, *Financial Analysts Journal*, May–June, pp. 71–76.

ERB, C., C. HARVEY, and T. VISKANTA, 1996, Political Risk, Economic Risk, and Financial Risk, *Financial Analysts Journal* 52, November–December, pp. 29–46.

ERB, C., T. VISKANTA, C.R. HARVEY, 1997, The Making of an Emerging Market, *Emerging Markets Quarterly* 1, pp. 14–19.

HARVEY, CAMPBELL R., 1995, Predictable Risk and Returns in Emerging Markets, *Review of Financial Studies* 8, Fall, pp. 773–816.

HARVEY, CAMPBELL R., 2000, Drivers of Expected Returns in International Markets, *Emerging Markets Quarterly*, Fall, p. 17.

International Finance Corporation, 1998, *Financial Institutions* (Washington, DC).

International Finance Corporation, *Emerging Stock Markets Factbook*, Annual (Washington, DC).

5.D. Valuation in Emerging Markets

ABUAF, NISO AND QUYEN CHU, 1994, The Executive's Guide to International Capital Budgeting: 1994 Update, Salomon Brothers Corporate Finance, August.

ABUAF, NISO, QUYEN CHU, et al., 1997, The International Cost of Capital—The Empirical Evidence, Salomon Brothers Corporate Finance, June.

BEKAERT, GEERT, and CAMPBELL R. HARVEY, 1995, The Cost of Capital in Emerging Markets, Duke University mimeo, November 19.

ERB, CLAUDE B., CAMPBELL R. HARVEY, and TADAS E. VISKANTA, 1996, Expected Returns and Volatility in 135 Countries, *The Journal of Portfolio Management*, Spring, pp. 46–58.

ESTRADA, J., 2001, The Cost of Equity in Emerging Markets: A Downside Risk Approach (II), *Emerging Markets Quarterly*, Spring, pp. 63–72.

ESTRADA, J., 2002, Systematic Risk in Emerging Markets: the D-CAPM, *Emerging Markets Review* 3, December, pp. 365–379.

GODFREY, S., and R. ESPINOZA, 1996, A Practical Approach to Calculating Costs of Equity for Investments in Emerging Markets, *Journal of Applied Corporate Finance*, Fall, pp. 80–89.

HARVEY, CAMPBELL R., 2000, Drivers of Expected Returns in Emerging Markets, *Emerging Markets Quarterly*, Fall, pp. 1–17.

JAMES, M., and T.M. KOLLER, 2000, Valuation in Emerging Markets, *The McKinsey Quarterly*, no. 4, pp. 78–85.

KECK, T., E. LEVENGOOD, and A. LONGFIELD, 1998, Using Discounted Cash Flow Analysis in an International Setting: A Survey of Issues in Modeling the Cost of Capital, *Journal of Applied Corporate Finance*, Fall, pp. 82–99.

KESTER, W. CARL, and K.A. FROOT, 1997, Cross-Border Valuation, Harvard Business School Note no. 295-100.

LESSARD, DONALD R., 1996, Incorporating Country Risk in the Valuation of Offshore Projects, *Journal of Applied Corporate Finance*, Fall, pp. 52–63.

MARISCAL, J., and K. HARGIS, 1999, Emerging Markets Discount Rates, Goldman Sachs Portfolio Strategy, March 22, pp. 1–18.

MARISCAL, J., and K. HARGIS, 1999, A Long-term Perspective on Short-term Risk: Long-term Discount Rates for Emerging Markets, Goldman Sachs Portfolio Strategy, October 26, pp. 1–23.

STULZ, RENÉ M., 1995, Globalization of Capital Markets and the Cost of Capital: The Case of Nestlé, *Journal of Applied Corporate Finance*, Fall, pp. 30–38.

ZENNER, MARC, and ECEHAN AKAYDIN, 2002, A Practical Approach to the International Valuation & Capital Allocation Puzzle, Salomon Smith Barney Financial Strategy Research, July 26.

5.E. Risk Management and Financial Engineering

FITE, D., and P. PFLEIDER, 1995, Should Firms Use Derivates to Manage Risk? Ch. 7 in Beaver and Parker, eds., *Risk Management Problems and Solutions*, McGraw-Hill (New York), pp. 139–170.

SMITHSON, C.W., C.W. SMITH, and D.S. WILFORD, 1995, *Managing Financial Risk, A Guide to Derivative Products, Financial Engineering, and Value Maximization*, Irwin Professional Publishing (Burr Ridge, IL).

6. PROJECT FINANCE SOFTWARE

NOTE: *The presence of a product on this list does not constitute an endorsement of its use.*

Decisioneering, Inc.: Forecasting and risk analysis software—maker of Crystal Ball.

Fundman Series (Softcare Software Services): Software that performs financial and credit analysis on infrastructure projects.

INFRISK: Risk management simulation software. The World Bank Institute developed the software to assist with measuring and managing project risks.

Mofinet.com: Offers Excel spreadsheets for financial applications in the fields of project finance and corporate valuation.

Palisade: Risk analysis, decision analysis, Monte Carlo simulation, and optimization software.

ProFinTools Project Finance: Valuation software. It provides a standardized approach to project evaluation and simulation analysis to test the robustness of project design.

Promoter: A tool for evaluating and appraising projects. It predicts the revenues, costs, and cash flows, and calculates IRRs, NPVs, DSCR, and other key criteria.

RiskEase and RiskMaster: The software provides risk analysis to help with evaluating and appraising projects.

7. PROJECT FINANCE DATA SOURCES

Asia Infrastructure Database: Data on energy, power, telecommunications, and transport markets in Asia.

Centre for Monitoring Indian Economy (CMIE): Comprehensive database of over 5,000 projects.

Construction Industry Institute: Data and research reports on the construction industry.

Dealogic ProjectWare: The ProjectWare database includes more than 9,000 transactions from 1994 to the present; the Loanware database includes more than 120,000 transactions (loan facilities including project loans) since 1980. Project Finance Review gives readers news on the project finance market as well as market rankings, project volumes, and market/sector reports (subscription based).

Global Infrastructure Projects Database: The Infrastructure Division of the International Trade Association (U.S. Commerce Dept.) maintains this database. The database describes projects to assist U.S. companies seeking business with large-scale infrastructure projects around the world.

International Finance Corporation (IFC) Project Document Database: Provides information about existing and proposed IFC projects.

Latin American Power Projects Database: Data on Latin American power projects.

Loan Marketing Association (LMA): Pricing data and information from the secondary market for loans.

Loan Pricing Corporation (LPC): Project finance loan data and Deal Scan database (historical database of project finance loans).

MBendi: Information on African projects.

MZ Project Finance: Information on project finance and public private partnerships (PPP). The KnowledgeBank section provides information and data about project finance.

Portfolio Management Data: Data on syndicated loans and credit loss information.

Sustainable Energy & Economy Network (SEEN): A political interest group with the goal of educating people about the problems associated with fossil fuel investments. Has a database of energy projects.

Thomson Financial Securities Data: Financial data and research reports on companies, industries, and markets worldwide in the SDC Platinum database. The project finance database covers more than 1,700 transactions since 1992.

World Bank Private Participation in Infrastructure (PPI) Database: Contains information on 1,900 projects in developing countries worth almost U.S.$580 billion. Infrastructure projects are in four sectors: telecommunications, energy, transportation, and water/sanitation. Data run from 1990 to 2000.

World Bank Project Finance & Guarantees Group: Information on the World Bank Guarantee Program.

World Bank Project Search: Database of World Bank projects by country and sector.

World Development Federation: WDF's goal is to improve global quality of life through the implementation of "super projects"—billion dollar projects that enhance economic development. Has a database of more than 1,600 projects.

World Mine Cost Data Exchange: This site is a one-stop source of mine cost spreadsheet models and operating cost information based on verifiable engineering and production data and peer review by mining industry analysts from around the world.

8. EXPORT CREDIT AGENCIES (ECAS)

Country	Institution Name	Acronym	Web Address
Argentina	Compañia Argentina de Seguros de Credito a la Exportación SA	CASC	www.casc.com.ar
Australia	Export Finance and Insurance Corp.	EFIC	www.efic.gov.au
Austria	Oesterreichische Kontrollbank Aktiengesellschaft	OeKB	www.oekb.at
Belgium	Ducroire/Delcredere, The Belgian Export Credit Agency	OND	www.ducroire.be www.delcredere.be
Bermuda	Sovereign Risk Insurance LTD	Sovereign	www.sovereignbermuda.com
Brazil	Seguradora Brasileira de Crédito à Exportação S/A	SBCE	www.sbce.com.br
Canada	Export Development Canada	EDC	www.edc.ca
China	China Export & Credit Insurance Corporation	Sinosure	www.sinosure.com.cn
Cyprus	Export Credit Insurance Service	ECIS	n/a
Czech Republic	Exportní Garanční a Pojišťovací Společnost, A.S.	EGAP	www.egap.cz
Denmark	Eksport Kredit Fonden	EKF	www.ekf.dk
Finland	Finnvera PLC		www.finnvera.fi
France	Coface		www.coface.com www.cofacerating.com
Germany	HERMES Kreditversicherungs-AG PwC Deutsche Revision Aktiengesellschaft Wirtschaftsprüfungs Gesellschaft	HERMES PwC	www.hermes-kredit.com n/a

Country	Institution Name	Acronym	Web Address
Greece	Export Credit Insurance Organisation	ECIO	www.oaep.gr
Hong Kong	Hong Kong Export Credit Insurance Corporation	HKEC	www.hkecic.com
Hungary	Hungarian Export Credit Insurance LTD	MEHIB	www.mehib.hu
India	Export Credit Guarantee Corporation of India LTD	ECGC	n/a
Indonesia	Asuransi Ekspor Indonesia	ASEI	www.asei.co.id
Israel	Israel Foreign Trade Risks Insurance Corporation LTD	IFTRIC	www.iftric.co.il
Italy	SACE Institute for Export Credit Insurance Services	SACE	www.isace.it
	Società Italiana Assicurazione Crediti SPA	EULER-SIAC	www.eulergroup.com
Jamaica	National Export-Import Bank of Jamaica LTD	EXIMJ	www.eximbankja.com
Japan	Nippon Export and Investment Insurance	NEXI	http://nexi.go.jp
Republic of Korea	Korea Export Insurance Corporation	KEIC	www.keic.or.kr
Malaysia	Malaysia Export Credit Insurance BHD	MECIB	www.mecib.com.my
Mexico	Banco Nacional de Comercio Exterior, SNC	Bancomext	www.bancomext.gob.mx
The Netherlands	Gerling NCM Credit and Finance AG	GERLING NCM	www.ncmgroup.com
Norway	Guarantee Institute for Export Credits	GIEK	www.giek.no
Poland	Export Credit Insurance Corporation	KUKE	www.kuke.com.pl
Portugal	Companhia de Seguro de Créditos S.A.	COSEC	www.cosec.pt
Singapore	ECICS Credit Insurance LTD	ECICS	www.ecics.com.sg
Slovenia	Slovene Export Corporation, Inc.	SEC	www.sid.si
South Africa	Credit Guarantee Insurance Corporation of Africa LTD	CGIC	www.creditguarantee.co.za
Spain	Compañia Española de Seguros de Crédito a la Exportación, SA	CESCE	www.cesce.com
	Compañia Española de Seguros y Reaseguros de Crédito y Caución, SA	CyC	www.creditoycaucion.es
Sri Lanka	Sri Lanka Export Credit Insurance Corporation	SLECIC	www.slecic.lk
Sweden	Exportkreditnämnden	EKN	www.ekn.se
Switzerland	Swiss Export Risk Guarantee Agency	ERG	www.swiss-erg.com
Chinese Taipei	Taipei Export-Import Bank of China	TEBC	www.eximbank.com.tw
Turkey	Export Credit Bank of Turkey	Türk Eximbank	www.eximbank.gov.tr
United Kingdom	Export Credits Guarantee Department	ECGD	www.ecgd.gov.uk
	Euler Trade Indemnity PLC	ETI	www.eulergroup.com
United States	Export-Import Bank of the United States	Ex-Im Bank	www.exim.gov
	FCIA Management Company, Inc.	FCIA	www.fcia.com
	Overseas Private Investment Corporation	OPIC	www.opic.gov
	American International Group, Inc.	AIG	www.aig.com
	Zurich Emerging Markets Solutions	ZEMS	www.zurichna.com/politicalrisk
Zimbabwe	Credit Insurance Zimbabwe LTD	Credsure	n/a
World Bank Group	Multilateral Investment Guarantee Agency	MIGA	www.miga.org

Source: Adapted from Berne Union Yearbook 2003.

9. MULTILATERAL DEVELOPMENT BANKS AND AGENCIES

Institution Name	Acronym	Web Address
African Development Bank	ADB	www.afdb.org
Asian Development Bank	ADB	www.adb.org
European Bank for Reconstruction and Development	EBRD	www.ebrd.com
European Investment Bank	EIB	www.eib.org
Inter-American Development Bank	IDB	www.iadb.org
Inter-American Investment Corporation	IIC	www.iadb.org/iic
International Monetary Fund	IMF	www.imf.org
Islamic Development Bank	IDB	www.isdb.org
Nordic Investment Bank	NIB	www.nibank.org
United Nations Development Program	UNDP	www.undp.org
World Bank Group		www.worldbank.org
International Finance Corporation	IFC	www.ifc.org
Multilateral Investment Guarantee Agency	MIGA	www.miga.org

Source: Casewriter.

Project Finance Glossary*

This glossary contains three parts: a list of more than 300 definitions for terms commonly used in the field of project finance; a list of more than 150 acronyms for official institutions and other project finance terms; and a description of various coverage ratios used by project finance lenders.

PART I: PROJECT FINANCE TERMS AND DEFINITIONS

A

Acceleration: A remedy available to lenders following an event of default that causes a borrower's indebtedness to become immediately due and payable in full.

Acceptance: The positive response to an offer seeking participation in a credit facility.

Accrued Interest: The interest earned on a loan or note between two interest payment dates.

Administrative Agent: The arranger of a syndicated loan.

Ad Valorem Tax: A tax or duty based on the value of a good or service (Latin: "according to value").

Affiliate: A corporation that directly (or indirectly) controls or is controlled by another corporation.

Agency Agreement: A legal agreement between a borrower, a group of lenders, and one or more agent banks governing the rights and responsibilities of the agent(s) in the transaction. The agency agreement is an integral part of a syndicated loan.

Agent: The bank responsible for administering a project financing.

All-In Rate: The interest rate, including the loan spread, commitment fees, and other up-front fees.

All Risks Insurance: Insurance against physical damage to the project during operations.

A-Loan: A loan from a multilateral agency such as the International Finance Corporation (IFC) where it is the lender of record and where it books the loan for its own account.

American Depository Receipt (ADR):   A certificate of ownership issued by a U.S. bank representing a claim on underlying foreign securities. ADRs may be traded in lieu of trading in the actual underlying shares.

Professor Benjamin C. Esty prepared this note as the basis for class discussion.

* For a list of references, see page 542.

Amortization: The periodic reduction of principal, capitalized expense, or goodwill.

Annual Debt Service Coverage Ratio (ADSCR): The ratio between operating cash flow and debt service during any one-year period. This ratio is used to determine a project's debt capacity.

Arbitrage Pricing Theory (APT): An asset pricing model based purely on arbitrage arguments. The APT implies that multiple risk factors determine an asset's required rate of return. In contrast, the Capital Asset Pricing Model (CAPM) uses a single risk factor (beta) to determine required rates of return.

Arrangement Fee: A fee paid to a mandated bank or group of banks (lead arrangers) for arranging a transaction. It includes fees to be paid to participating banks.

Arranger: A bank or other financial institution responsible for originating and syndicating a loan transaction. The arranger always has a senior role, is often the agent, and usually participates in the transaction at the most senior level (it holds the largest share of the loan).

Assignment: A transfer of legal title to an asset for security purposes.

Availability Factor: A measure of how much a power plant is available to produce power, usually expressed as the ratio (a percentage) of a power plant's available hours to the total number of hours in such a period.

Availability Period: The period during which a loan is available for drawdown.

Average Debt Service Coverage Ratio (Average DSCR): The average annual debt service coverage ratio (ADSCR) calculated over the life of a loan.

Average Loan Life: The average maturity for all repayments weighted by the principal outstanding.

Avoided Costs: Incremental costs that a utility would incur to purchase or generate electricity if it did not purchase electricity from an independent power project (IPP).

B

Backcast: The use of historical rather than predicted information (a forecast) in a financial model. Often done to test the robustness of a project's capital structure to changes in underlying conditions.

Backwardation: A market condition in which futures prices are lower in the distant delivery months than in the nearest delivery month. This condition may occur when the costs of storing the product until delivery are effectively subtracted from the price today. The opposite of contango.

Balance of Payments: A system of recording all of a country's economic transactions with the rest of the world for a certain period. The balance is typically broken into three accounts: capital, current, and gold.

Balloon Payment: A final debt repayment that is substantially larger than the preceding repayments.

Bankable: Capable of being financed.

Base Case: A cash flow projection with variables measured at their expected values.

Base Load Plant: A power plant that runs all the time, as opposed to a plant that is used only in times of peak electricity requirements (a peaking plant).

Base Rate: On a variable rate loan, it is the key underlying rate to which lenders add a spread to come up with a total lending rate for the borrower.

Basis Point (bp): One-hundredth of 1 percent (1/100 * 1%, or 0.0001).

"Behind-the-Fence" (project or transaction): A project that derives all of its revenues from a local customer such as a mine mouth power plant (i.e., a project that is fully integrated in some kind of manufacturing process). For power projects, the "fence" refers to the boundary between the power grid and the industrial facility. See also "Inside the Fence."

Berne Union: The Berne Union was established in 1934 to determine sound principles for export credit and foreign investment insurance. As of 2002, the Berne Union had 51 members from 42 countries.

Best and Final Offer (BAFO): A second-stage bid in a public procurement.

Best Efforts Arranger: A bank or other lender that agrees to syndicate a loan but is unwilling to guarantee successful completion of the deal.

Bilateral Agency (BLA): An institution established by one country to promote trade with other countries, such as an export-import agency or an export credit agency (ECA).

Black-Scholes Option Pricing Model: A model for pricing call options based on arbitrage arguments developed by Fischer Black and Myron Scholes (with insights from Robert Merton) in 1973. The model uses the stock price, the exercise price, the risk-free interest rate, the time to expiration, and the expected standard deviation of the stock return.

Boilerplate: Standardized terms and conditions in legal contracts or other documents.

B-Loan: A loan syndicated by a multilateral lender, such as the IFC, that acts as the lender of record on behalf of the funding participants (commercial banks and other institutional investors).

Book Runner: The bank that extends invitations for a syndication and is responsible for determining the composition of the lending group and the final hold positions.

Brady Bonds: Bonds issued by developing countries under a debt-reduction plan.

Bridge Financing: Interim or temporary financing.

British Thermal Unit (Btu): The quantity of heat needed to raise the temperature of 1 pound of water by 1°F at or near 39.2°F.

Builders-All Risk: The standard insurance package used during construction.

Build-Lease-Transfer (BLT): The situation when a private owner builds an infrastructure facility, leases it for use, and then transfers it to another entity after a specified period.

Build-Own-Operate-Transfer (BOOT): The situation when a private owner builds, owns, and operates an infrastructure facility and then transfers it to another entity after a specified period.

Build-Own-Transfer (BOT): The situation when a private owner builds, owns, and then transfers an infrastructure facility to another party, often at no cost, after a specified period.

Build-Transfer-Operate (BTO): The situation when a private owner builds an infrastructure facility, transfers it to another entity, and then operates it on a contractual basis for a specified period.

Bullet Loan: A term loan with periodic installments of interest only with the entire principal due at the end of the term as a final payment. The final payment on a balloon loan is sometimes referred to as a bullet.

Bullet Repayment: Repayment of a loan in a single installment at its maturity.

Buydown: A single payment by a project contractor to reflect future cash flow losses from anticipated and sustained underperformance; the amount is typically paid out of liquidated damages.

Buyer Credit: An arrangement under which a bank in the supplier's country lends to a buyer, or a bank, in the buyer's country that enables the buyer to purchase certain goods or services.

C

Call Option: The right to *buy* a given asset at a fixed price during a particular period.

Capital Account: That portion of the balance of payments that measures international lending and investment.

Capital Expenditures (CapEx): Long-term expenditures for property, plant, and equipment.

Capitalized Interest: During the pre-completion period, a project company can borrow to repay current interest obligations. By capitalizing interest, the principal balance outstanding increases by an amount equal to the interest due.

Cash Available for Debt Service (CADS): The amount of cash available to service debt after all essential operating expenses have been met.

Cash Deficiency Guarantee: A guarantee that requires the project sponsor(s) to contribute additional capital to the project company in the event cash deficiencies materialize due to pre-agreed causes.

Cash Flow Cascade: The order of priorities under the financing documentation for the application of the project's cash flow. See also cash waterfall.

Cash Waterfall (or Cash Flow Waterfall): The order of priority for project cash flows as established under the loan and financing documents.

Charge: A fixed charge refers to a defined set of assets and is usually recorded in an official registry. A floating charge refers to other assets, which change from time to time (e.g., cash accounts, inventory, or receivables) but which become fixed charges after a default.

Civil Law: Law inspired by old Roman law and associated with the Napoleonic code (French civil law). The primary feature of civil law systems is that laws are codified rather than determined by judges based on precedent, as in common law.

Claw Back: The ability to recover prior project cash flows that may have been distributed to the sponsors. A claw back is used if there is a shortage of funds to meet defined operating expenses such as maintenance or debt service.

C-Loan: A full range of quasi-equity products with both debt and equity characteristics (e.g., convertible debt and subordinated loans) offered by the IFC or other multilateral agencies.

Club: A group of underwriters who do not need to proceed to syndication as part of a fund raising.

Cofinancing: The situation where different lenders agree to fund under the same documentation and security packages and yet may have different interest rates, repayment profiles, and terms. The lenders typically hold different debt tranches.

Cogeneration: The production of energy from the waste heat of industrial processes.

Coinsurance: The phenomenon whereby a surplus of cash flows from one or more assets or divisions is used to cover the financial obligations of another asset or division.

Collateral: Assets pledged as security under a loan to assure repayment of debt obligations.

Collateralized Bond Obligation (CBO): Securities issued against a portfolio of bonds with different degrees of credit quality.

Collateralized Debt Obligation (CDO): Securities issued against a portfolio of debt instruments with different degrees of credit quality.

Collateralized Loan Obligation (CLO): Securities issued against a portfolio of loans with different degrees of credit quality.

Commercial Interest Reference Rates (CIRR): The interest rates charged by export credit agencies on their subsidized export credits.

Commercial Operations Date (COD): The date on which the independent engineer (IE) certifies that a facility has completed all required performance tests and/or is built to the specifications outlined in the engineering procurement and construction (EPC) contract.

Commercial Risks: The various risks that can affect a project during operations, such as changes in input and output prices, fluctuations in demand, or failures in mechanical processes.

Commitment Fee: A per annum fee applied to undisbursed balances that lenders are committed to lend; the fee is charged until the end of the availability period.

Common Law: The legal system of England and former English colonies. A body of law based on custom and general principles that serves as a precedent or is applied to situations not covered by statute.

Complementary Financing: Where different lenders agree to fund a project under similar yet parallel documentation and a pro-rata security package.

Completion: The date on which the project's cash flows become the primary method of repayment. It occurs after a completion test typically involving both financial and physical performance criteria. Prior to completion, the primary source of repayment is usually from the sponsors or from the contractor.

Completion Guarantee: A guarantee that ensures a project will achieve physical and/or financial completion. A turnkey contractor guarantees physical completion (achievement of certain operating performance). The guarantees are normally secured by performance bonds and/or penalties in the form of liquidated damages. Alternatively, project sponsors sometimes provide lenders with completion guarantees by agreeing to pay the scheduled debt service in the event the project company does not or cannot pay.

Completion Test: A test of the project's ability to perform as planned and generate the expected cash flows. In a limited-recourse deal, it is the time when the project moves from a full recourse to a nonrecourse financing.

Compound Interest: Interest resulting from the periodic addition of simple interest to principal; the sum then serves as the principal for the computation of interest owed during the following period.

Concession Agreement: An agreement made between a host government and a project company or sponsor to permit the construction, development, and operation of a particular project.

Conditions Precedent (CPs): A set of preconditions that must be satisfied before the borrower can request drawdown or other credit facilities be made available under a lending agreement.

Constant Dollar: Dollars from a base year that are used to adjust the dollars of other years in order to ascertain purchasing power. The goal is to remove the effects of inflation and other forms of price escalation.

Consumer Price Index (CPI): An index measure of inflation equal to the sum of prices of a number of assets purchased by consumers weighted by the proportion each represents in a typical consumer's budget.

Contango: A market condition in which futures prices are higher in the distant delivery months than in the near-term months. The opposite of backwardation.

Contingent Equity: A standby commitment involving a specific amount of money callable by lenders for the purpose of covering cost overruns until completion.

Cost, Insurance, and Freight (CIF): A quoted price, including the cost of packaging, freight, insurance, and other charges paid from the time of loading to the arrival at a specified destination.

Counter-Party: The other participant to a project agreement or a swap contract.

Country Risk: Narrowly defined, it refers to cross-currency and foreign exchange availability risks. More broadly defined, it can also include the political risks of doing business in a given country.

Coupon: The interest amount or rate payable on a bond.

Covenant: An agreement by a borrower to undertake (a positive covenant) or not to undertake (a negative covenant) a specific action. Breaching a covenant is considered an event of default.

Covered: When a loan or a tranche of a loan is protected by political risk insurance (PRI).

Covered Interest Rate Parity: The principle that the yields from interest-bearing foreign and domestic investments should be equal when the forward currency market is used to predetermine the domestic currency payoff from a foreign investment.

Credit Enhancement: A guarantee issued by a third party assuring the payment or performance obligations of a major project participant. Credit enhancement can include other assets pledged as security for an obligation, guarantees from a project sponsor or host government, letters of credit payable to the project company as security for a project participant's contractual undertakings, a debt service reserve fund, and/or contingent equity commitments.

Creeping Expropriation: A series of acts that have an expropriating effect on a project's value.

Cross-default Provision: A provision under which default on one debt obligation triggers default on all other debt obligations.

Cure Period: A period during which a borrower is allowed to remedy a default under a contract.

Current Account: The portion of the balance of payments that tracks the import and export of goods and services.

Current Dollar: Actual or real prices and costs at each point in time. Includes the effects of inflation and other forms of price escalation.

D

Debenture: A debt obligation secured by the borrower's general credit rather than being backed by a specific lien on property. In other words, the debt obligation is not collateralized.

Debt Capacity: The total amount of debt a company can prudently support given its earnings expectations, equity base, and asset liquidation value.

Debt Service: Principal repayments plus interest payable; usually expressed as the annual amount due per calendar or financial year.

Debt Service Coverage Ratio (DSCR):   A quantitative measure used by lenders to determine whether a project's prospective net cash flow from operations can support (make timely service payment on) a given amount of debt at the indicated potentially available terms. For any given debt service period, the debt service coverage ratio is defined as the cash available for debt service (CADS) divided by the total amount of debt service.

Debt Service Reserve Account (DSRA):   A reserve account set up to ensure the timely payment of principal and interest.

Default: When a covenant has been broken or an adverse event has occurred. A monetary default occurs when a repayment is not made on time. A technical default occurs when a project parameter is outside defined or agreed-upon limits, or a legal matter is not yet resolved.

Default Interest: A higher interest rate payable on principal amounts after an event of default.

Defeasance: The prepayment of financial obligations, often through a third party, in circumstances where the third party assumes the responsibility to discharge the financial obligations. When it occurs, the lender has no recourse to the original obligor.

Deficiency Agreement: Where cash flow, working capital, or revenues are below agreed levels or are insufficient to meet debt service, then a deficiency or make up agreement provides the shortfall to be provided by the sponsor or another party, sometimes to a cumulative limit.

Devaluation: Either a formal reduction in the spot price of a currency or a gradual reduction due to market forces.

Developing Countries: Defined by the World Bank in terms of gross national income per capita in 2000 as follows: (a) low-income, U.S.$755 or less; (b) lower-middle income, from U.S.$756 to U.S.$2,995; and (c) upper-middle income, from U.S.$2,996 to U.S.$9,265.

Development Bank: A lending agency that provides funds to encourage the creation or expansion of productive facilities in developing countries.

Development Finance Institution (DFI):   A financial institution that provides debt and equity investments for projects in developing countries.

Disbursement: An accounting and financial term used to describe the actual payout or drawdowns of cash under a loan agreement.

Discount Rate: The annual percentage rate used to determine the present value of future cash flows.

Dispatch: The schedule of production for all the generating units on a power system, generally varying from moment to moment to match the production with power requirements. As a verb, to dispatch means to direct the plant to produce power.

Dividend Trap: A restriction on a project company's ability to pay dividends, despite having cash available to do so, because of current or accumulated losses.

Drawdown: An actual takedown of money by the borrower under the terms of a loan facility.

E

Enclave Project: A project whose products are exported, for which payment is received outside the host country.

Equity Cash Flow (ECF):   Cash flow available to equityholders. It is equal to net income plus depreciation less capital expenditures less increases in net working capital (NWC) less principal repayment plus new debt proceeds.

Escrow Account: A deposit held in trust by a third party to be turned over to the grantee on specified conditions. In project finance, an escrow account is often used to channel funds needed to pay debt service.

Event of Default: Any event that entitles the lender to cancel a debt facility, declare all amounts owed by the debtor to become immediately due and payable, and/or enforce security.

Evergreen: A contract that rolls over after each agreed period until canceled by one party.

Execute: Formally sign documentation or implement a required action.

Export Credit Agency (ECA):   An organization that assists in supporting exports from its country through the use of direct loan and guarantee mechanisms provided to importers.

Export Credits: Credit facilities or guarantee programs made available by a country for the benefit of exporters of goods or services in an effort to promote exports.

Expropriation: A forced transfer of ownership or value from a private owner to a government entity.

F

Face Value: The maturity value of a debt instrument. Also known as par value or nominal value.

Feedstock: The raw materials supplied to a processing or refining plant.

Final Take: The fractional amount of a syndicated loan allocated to a particular bank. Because of oversubscription, the amount may be less than the commitment the bank offered to take.

Financial Close: The date on which all project contracts and financing documentation are signed and conditions precedent to initial drawing of the debt have been satisfied or waived.

Financial Viability: The ability of a project to provide acceptable returns to equityholders and to service its debt on time and in full.

Fiscal Year (FY): Accounting period covering 12 consecutive months over which a company determines earnings and profits. The fiscal year serves as a period of reference for the company and does not necessarily correspond to the calendar year.

Fixed Exchange Rate: Foreign exchange rate set and maintained by government support.

Floating Charge: A security interest created over variable or unascertainable assets such as receivables, inventories, spare parts, bank accounts, and so on.

Floating Exchange Rate: A country's decision to allow its currency value to change freely. The currency is not constrained by central bank intervention and does not have to maintain its relationship with another currency in a narrow band. The currency value is determined by trading in the foreign exchange market.

Floating Rate: An interest rate that is reset periodically.

Force Majeure: An excuse for contractual nonperformance due to events beyond the control of either party. These events are either "acts of God" (floods, fires, or other natural disasters) or political risks (war, strikes, riots, expropriation, breach of contract, etc.). Contractual performance is forgiven or extended by the period of *force majeure* (French: "superior force").

Forward Contract: A contract between two parties to exchange a commodity at a set price on a future date. Differs from a futures contract in that most forward commitments are not actively traded or standardized and carry the risk from the creditworthiness of the other side of the transaction.

Free Cash Flow (FCF): Cash available for capital providers. It is defined as earnings before interest payments adjusted for taxes (EBIAT); plus depreciation, amortization, and other noncash charges; less capital expenditures; less increases in net working capital.

Free On Board (FOB): A transportation term in which the seller's quoted price includes the cost of delivering the goods to a specified location. The buyer assumes responsibility for all transportation costs from that point onward.

Full Cover: Guarantees or insurance for both political and commercial risks provided to a lender by an export credit agency or international finance institution.

Full Recourse: No matter what risk event occurs, the borrower agrees to repay the debt. By definition, this is not a project financing unless the borrower's sole asset is the project.

Funding Risk: The impact on project cash flow from higher funding costs or lack of availability of funds.

Futures Contract: A legal agreement between a buyer (seller) and an established exchange or its clearing house in which the buyer (seller) agrees to take (make) delivery of something at a specified price at the end of a designated period. The price at which the parties agree to transact in the future is called the futures price. The designated date at which the parties must transact is called the settlement or delivery date. These contracts are usually tradable on exchanges.

G

Gearing: A measure of leverage such as the ratio of debt to equity or debt to total capitalization.

Generally Accepted Accounting Principles (GAAP): The set of standardized rules established for the reporting of a project or company's financial results for accounting purposes. These rules are established by independent accounting organizations in each country worldwide.

Golden Share: A shareholding interest entitling the holder to exercise a degree of control over certain activities of the company.

Governing Law: The law used to interpret a contract's terms and conditions, as set forth in the contract or as applied by a court.

Grace Period: The period within which a default is resolved without incurring penalty interest or other charges. A period during which interest or principal is not yet payable; it usually occurs after start-up, commissioning, and completion in a project financing.

Greenfield: Refers to a project being conceived and executed where no project company, assets, or operations exist. A greenfield site or project location is one where no infrastructure exists to support the project.

Guarantee: An agreement to repay a loan or ensure performance. It may be limited in time and amount.

Guarantor: A party who agrees to guarantee repayment or performance.

H

Hard Currency: A currency that is likely to maintain its value against other currencies over time and not likely to be eroded by inflation. In contrast, a soft currency is likely to lose purchasing power over time. Hard currencies are usually freely convertible.

Heat Rate: The amount of fuel required to generate a kilowatt hour (kwh) of electricity.

Hedging: A strategy that eliminates a risk through the spot sale of the risk or through a transaction in an instrument that represents an obligation to sell the risk in the future. The goal is to ensure that any profit or loss on the current sale or purchase will be offset by the loss or profit on the future purchase or sale.

Hell-or-High-Water Clause: An absolute commitment to perform an action with no contractual defense.

Host Country: The country in which a project is located.

Hurdle Rate: A minimum acceptable internal rate of return (IRR). Projects generating returns in excess of the corporate hurdle rate are viable candidates for implementation.

I

Inconvertibility: The inability to exchange a local currency for a foreign currency.

Indemnity: A legal obligation to cover a liability.

Independent Engineer (IE): A consulting firm that helps lenders by evaluating the technical aspects of a project (e.g., completion schedule, technical feasibility, etc.). See also Lenders' Engineer.

Industrialized Countries: The World Bank defines an industrialized country as one having in 2000 gross national income per capita of U.S.$9,266 or more.

Information Memorandum: A document that describes the project and the financing details; issued in connection with a loan syndication.

Infrastructure Project: A project in one of the following industrial sectors: power (electricity and gas), telecom, transportation, or water/sewage.

"Inside the Fence" (project or transaction): A project that derives all of its revenues from a local customer such as a mine mouth power plant (i.e., a project that is fully integrated in some kind of manufacturing process). For power projects, the "fence" refers to the boundary between the power grid and the industrial facility. See also "Behind the Fence."

Inter-Creditor Agreement: An agreement between lenders, or classes of lenders, describing the rights and obligations in the event of default.

Interest Rate Parity Theorem: An expression that assumes the interest rate differential between two countries is equal to the difference between the forward foreign exchange rate and the spot rate.

Internal Rate of Return (IRR): The discount rate that makes the net present value equal to zero. Multiple IRRs occur mathematically if the periodic cash flows change signs more than once.

International Center for Settlement of Investment Disputes (ICSID): A member of the World Bank Group that helps to encourage foreign investment by providing international facilities for conciliation and arbitration of investment disputes.

International Swap and Derivatives Association (ISDA): An organization that produces standard documentation for interest rate swaps.

Investment Grade: An investment rating level of BBB− or better from Standard & Poor's Corporation or Baa3 or better from Moody's Corporation.

Irrevocable Letter of Credit: A letter of credit that cannot be changed or canceled without the consent of all parties involved.

J

Joint and Several Liability: Each party is liable for the full amount of the liability, but performance by one discharges the obligations for all the parties.

Junk Bond: A bond with a subinvestment-grade credit rating of BB+ or lower from Standard & Poor's Corporation or Ba1 or lower from Moody's. Also known as speculative or high-yield debt.

K

Keepwell Letter: A form of guarantee in which the guarantor agrees to keep the recipient of the guarantee covered by injecting capital as needed.

L

Lead Arranger: The senior tier of arrangers in a syndicated loan facility.

League Tables: A ranking of lenders and advisors according to the underwriting, final take, or number of project finance loans or advisory mandates completed during a given period.

Lease: The owner of an asset (the "lessor") agrees to receive lease payments from the user (the "lessee"). The lessor receives the benefit of depreciation as a tax deduction and has the asset as security.

Legal Opinion: Opinions provided by the legal advisors on the validity and enforceability of all project and finance documents, including security documents.

Legal Risk: The risk that a party to a contract will not be able to enforce security arrangements, enforce foreign judgments, have a choice of law, or refer disputes to arbitration.

Lenders' Engineer: An engineering firm that advises lenders on technical matters. See also **Independent Engineer.**

Lessee: The user of a leased asset.

Lessor: The owner of a leased asset.

Letter of Credit (L/C): A financial instrument issued by a financial institution for the benefit of a customer under which the financial institution agrees to pay money to the beneficiary thereof upon demand or upon the occurrence of specified events.

Letter of Intent (LOI): A letter from one company to another acknowledging a willingness and ability to do business.

Lien: A legal security interest on property to secure the repayment of debt and the performance of related obligations.

Limited Recourse: Under certain conditions (related to legal, financial, or operating conditions), lenders have access to the sponsors' credit or other legal security to fulfill a project's debt obligations. There is usually recourse in the event of fraud, misrepresentation, or nondisclosure. For this reason, and because lenders often have some kind of recourse prior to completion, nonrecourse is often described as "limited-recourse" financing.

Liquid: Easily traded or converted to cash.

Liquidated Damages (LDs): Specific and limited amounts that a contracting party is required to pay to another contracting party in the event an agreed-upon area of performance is not achieved.

Loan Amortization: The scheduled repayment of loan principal. A loan amortization schedule specifies the amounts of principal to be repaid and the dates on which repayments are to be made.

Loan Life Cover Ratio (LLCR): The net present value of cash available for debt service (CADS) from the calculation date to the final maturity of the debt facilities divided by the principal outstanding on the calculation date.

London Club: The London Club has evolved as an *ad hoc* forum for restructuring sovereign debt. Each London Club is formed, usually by a group of commercial banks, at the initiative of the debtor country and is dissolved when a restructuring agreement has been signed.

M

Maintenance Reserve Account: A reserve account that builds up cash balances sufficient to cover a project's maintenance expenses.

Majority Banks: A group of banks within a syndicate holding a specified percentage of the commitments (typically 66.67%) with the power to bind the syndicate as a whole in calling events of default and agreeing to certain amendments or waivers.

Mandate: The formal appointment to advise on or arrange a project financing.

Mandated Bank: The bank given the authority to proceed into the marketplace on behalf of the borrower, on the basis of the terms and condition set out in the mandate letter. The mandated bank is often referred to as the arranger in the Euromarkets and the administrative agent in the United States.

Margin: The amount expressed as a percent per annum above the interest rate basis or cost of funds. For hedging and futures contracts, the cash collateral deposited with a trader or exchange as insurance against default.

Market Flex: The unilateral right reserved for underwriters to vary the structure and conditions of a mandate if the syndication process does not raise sufficient funds. Borrowers may negotiate restrictions on this unilateral right limiting variations to price only (called "price flex").

Material Adverse Change (MAC): Prior to closing, an event or occurrence that allows the lender to adjust the terms (e.g., rate) of a loan agreement. After closing, an event that gives lenders the right to refuse further drawings or to require immediate debt repayment.

Material Adverse Event (MAE): Any event or circumstance that affects a party's ability to perform or comply with any of its material obligations under the transaction documents. Such an event may allow the party to change some aspect of the contractual agreement.

Maturity: The final date a project finance loan is repayable.

Merchant Power Plant (MPP): A power plant that sells electricity without a long-term power purchase agreement.

Minemouth: Usually refers to a power-generating plant located next to a coal mine.

Mini-perm: A loan for the construction period and first few years of operations taken with the intent of refinancing with more permanent (long-term) debt at a future date.

Modeling Bank: The institution responsible for creating the lenders' base case financial model.

Monoline Insurance: Insurance of an individual financial risk (rather than general casualty insurance).

Monte Carlo Simulation: The use of a random number generator to quantify the effects of uncertainty in a financial model.

Multilateral Agency (MLA): An institution organized by a group of countries to promote development (e.g., the World Bank, the IFC, and the Inter-American Development Bank).

N

Negative Arbitrage: The loss of interest caused by having to draw the full amount of a bond financing and then redeposit the funds until they are required at a later date. Because borrowing rates are typically higher than deposit rates, the deposited funds earn a negative spread.

Negative Covenants: Promises by the borrower in a loan agreement to abstain from undertaking certain actions.

Nonrecourse: The lenders rely on the project's cash flows and security over the project vehicle's assets as the only means to repay debt service.

Notional Principal: In an interest rate swap agreement, notional principal mirrors the principal outstanding under a loan agreement at any point during the loan life.

Novation: The transfer of rights and obligations from one contracting party (which is released of those obligations) to a third party, with the agreement of each of the other contracting parties.

O

OECD Consensus: Guidelines created by the Organization for Economic Cooperation and Development (OECD) that are intended to prevent distortions in price competition among manufacturers of different countries. The OECD Consensus is derived from an OECD agreement, "Arrangement on Guidelines for Officially Supported Credits" (1978), which limits export credit to 85% of the contract value and holds interest rates to a minimum of the OECD interest rate matrix, which is revised semiannually.

Off-Balance-Sheet Liability: A corporate obligation that does not appear as a liability on the company's balance sheet or is not required to appear by the applicable accounting standards.

Offering Circular: A document that describes the terms and conditions of securities being offered for sale and provides financial information relating to the borrower and any guarantor. Also called a prospectus.

Offshore Entity: A term for any entity located outside the boundaries of a given country.

Offtake Agreement: An agreement to purchase all or a substantial part of the product produced by a project, which typically provides the revenue stream for a project financing.

Offtaker (Offtake Purchaser): The purchaser of a project's output.

Onlending: The process by which a multilateral agency or other government agency lends funds to a financial institution (or possibly another government agency) with the expectation that those funds will be used to fund loans to ultimate borrowers (also called relending).

Operations and Maintenance (O&M) Agreement: A contract obligating a party to operate and maintain a project.

Oversubscription: The situation when the underwriting commitments from a syndication exceed the amount sought by the borrower.

P

Par: Face value.

***Pari Passu*:** Literally, "with equal treatment among themselves." A legal term that refers to financial instruments that rank equally in right of payment with each other and with other instruments of the same issuer. Applies to both the right to be paid from available operating cash flow and the rights in the event of liquidation.

Paris Club: Since 1956, countries facing default have negotiated debt-restructuring arrangements with bilateral official creditors in the Paris Club, an informal body created for the purpose of maintaining strict standards for rescheduling or reducing debt.

Partial Credit Guarantee (PCG): An instrument designed to cover private lenders against all risks during a specified period of the financing term of debt for a public investment. These guarantees are designed to extend maturities and improve commercial terms.

Partial Risk Guarantee (PRG): An instrument designed to cover private lenders against the risk that a government or a government-owned agency fails to perform its contractual obligations vis-à-vis a private project.

Participant: A party to a funding agreement. It usually refers to the banks at the lower levels of a syndicate.

Payment Cascade: See Cash Waterfall.

Performance Bonds: Guarantees purchased by the project developer issued by commercial banks or insurance companies to guarantee full and successful implementation of a contract according to prespecified performance guidelines.

Political Risk: Eight risks associated with cross-border investment and financing: currency inconvertibility, expropriation, war and insurrection, terrorism, environmental activities, landowner actions, nongovernmental activists, and legal and bureaucratic approvals. The first three are insurable. It overlaps with the political component of *force majeure* risk.

Portfolio Financing: A financing transaction involving multiple projects or assets. Because the financing incorporates elements of both corporate and project finance, it is known as a hybrid financing.

Positive Covenants: Promises made under a loan agreement by the borrower to undertake certain actions.

Power Purchase Agreement (PPA): A contract for a large customer to buy electricity from a power plant. This is usually the most important contract underlying the construction and operation of a power plant.

Praecipium: The amount of the front-end fee that is not distributed to syndicate members.

Preferred Creditor Status: A designation given to the International Monetary Fund (IMF), all World Bank Group member institutions, and many of the regional multilateral banks. These institutions are only able to lend to member countries if there is recognition that in the event of a foreign exchange crisis, the preferred lenders have first call on available foreign exchange.

Prepayment: Repayment of greater than the scheduled principal amount. If a project company is forced to prepay principal with excess cash flow, then it is referred to as a mandatory prepayment.

Present Value Factor: A factor used to calculate the present value of an amount to be received at a future point in time. If the opportunity cost of funds is 10% over next year, then the present value factor is equal to 0.909 $[1/(1 + 0.10)]$.

Prime Rate: The rate at which U.S. banks lend U.S. dollars to their most creditworthy customers.

Private Placement: A private placement occurs when a security is not registered with the U.S. Securities and Exchange Commission (SEC). Disclosure requirements for private placements are less stringent, though no less complete than for a public placement.

Proceeds Account: The account into which all advances under the loan facilities, proceeds of base equity and contingent equity, and all project revenues are paid. The borrower is permitted to make withdrawals from the proceeds account only to make payments in connection with project costs and transfers to other accounts in accordance with prescribed cash waterfall.

Production Loan: A project financing where the repayment is linked to some kind of production.

Pro Forma: A financial projection based on a set of assumptions.

Project Appraisal Report: A formal assessment of the viability of the proposed undertaking and the robustness and predictability of revenue generation.

Project Company: A special-purpose entity created to develop, own, and operate a project.

Project Completion: Occurs when a defined set of technical and financial tests have been met as stipulated in the financing documents.

Project Finance: Involves a corporate sponsor investing in and owning a single-purpose industrial asset (usually with a limited life) through a legally independent entity financed with nonrecourse debt.

Project Funds Agreement: Agreement, usually by sponsors, to provide additional funds as needed until project completion or other agreed date.

Project Life Cover Ratio (PLCR): The net present value of a project's cash available for debt service (CADS) over the project's defined life divided by the amount of principal outstanding at the time of calculation.

Project Holding Company: A company that owns and finances several standalone projects. Because some of the corporate liabilities are secured by multiple assets, it represents a hybrid form of financing with elements of both project and corporate finance.

Pro Rata: Shared or divided according to a ratio or in proportion to their participations.

Prospectus: A document that describes the terms and conditions of securities being offered for sale and provides financial information relating to the borrower and any guarantor. Also called an offering memorandum.

Purchasing Power Parity: The notion that the ratio between domestic and foreign price levels should equal the equilibrium exchange rate between domestic and foreign currencies.

Put Option: An option to sell an asset at a given price.

Put-or-Pay Agreement: An agreement whereby a supplier undertakes to supply an agreed quantity of materials to the project company and to make payments sufficient to enable the company to obtain alternative supplies in the event of supplier failure.

Q

Qualified Institutional Buyer (QIB): An institutional investor that is qualified to buy unregistered or private-placement (e.g., Rule 144A) securities.

Quasi-equity: A type of deeply subordinated debt security or senior equity security (e.g., preferred shares) whose holders are paid before ordinary shareholders but after senior debtholders. Other forms of quasi-equity can include various kinds of convertible debt.

R

Rating: An evaluation of creditworthiness provided by a rating agency such as Standard & Poor's Corporation or Moody's.

Rating Agency: A company providing an independent view on the creditworthiness of the project company or some other security.

Refinancing: Prepayment of the existing debt and substitution of new debt on more attractive terms (e.g., at a lower cost, with a longer maturity, or with fewer or less restrictive covenants).

Representations: A series of statements of fact or law made by one party to an agreement on the basis of which the other party undertakes to enter into the agreement. The representations will typically cover such matters as the legality and enforceability of documentation, the financial condition of the borrower, and the absence of any material litigation or other proceedings against the borrower. Material inaccuracies in the representations will normally constitute default under the loan agreements.

Request for Proposals (RFP):   An invitation to bid on a public procurement.

Reserve Account: A separate cash account used to meet future payment obligations such as debt service, maintenance, or capital expenditure.

Reserve Tail: Proven reserves available after the final maturity of the debt; applies to projects involving natural resources.

Retention: An amount held back from construction contract payments to ensure that the contractor completes the construction before the retention (typically 5 to 15% of the contract price) is returned to the contractor.

Revocable Letter of Credit: A letter of credit that can be changed or canceled by the issuing bank or by any party involved until payment is made.

Revolving Credit Agreement: A legal commitment on the part of a bank to extend credit up to a maximum amount for a definite term. The notes evidencing debt are short term, such as 90 days. As notes become due, the borrower can renew the notes, borrow a smaller amount, or borrow amounts up to the specified maximum throughout the term of commitment.

Risk Contamination: The phenomenon whereby a failing division (or asset) drags an otherwise financially healthy division into default.

Royalty: A share of revenue or cash flow to the government or grantor of the concession or license.

Rule 144A: An SEC rule that provides an exemption from the registration requirements of the Securities Act of 1933 for certain securities sold to qualified institutional buyers.

S

Secondary Market: After the initial distribution of bonds or securities, additional trades occur between investors in what is known as the secondary market.

Senior: The highest ranking for repayment, security, or action.

Sensitivity Analysis: Analysis of how changing an input variable in a financial model affects the value, performance, or solvency of a given project.

Set-off: A claim made by someone who allegedly owes money that the amount should be reduced because the other person owes him or her money.

Several Liability: A legal term that conveys the meaning that nonperformance by one entity of its obligations will not affect or alter the obligations of the other parties.

Shadow Tolls: Tolls based on project use but payable by the government or other contracting authority rather than the general public.

Shareholders Agreement: The generic term for any contract between two or more shareholders governing their conduct in relation to the corporation, or partnership, in which they own shares.

Share Retention Agreement: An agreement, usually by sponsors, not to sell their shareholding(s) in the project company (or to maintain an agreed-percentage shareholding).

Sources and Uses Statement: A document showing where a company intends to get its cash and where it intends to spend the cash over a specific period.

Sovereign Guarantee: A government guarantee of its obligations under project documents.

Sovereign Risk: The risk that the host country government will default in its contractual undertaking with the project or another project participant, such as under guarantees, indemnity agreements, or input and offtake contracts.

Special Purpose Entity (SPE):   See Special Purpose Vehicle.

Special Purpose Vehicle (SPV):   An entity established for a particular purpose, such as obtaining off-balance sheet financing or isolating the sponsors' other assets from the project's creditors.

Sponsor: A party wishing to develop and finance (with equity) a project. Shareholders of project companies are known as sponsors.

Spot Market: The market for buying and selling a specific commodity, foreign currency, or asset at the prevailing price for immediate delivery.

Spot Price: The current market price of the actual physical commodity. Also called the cash price.

Standby Letter of Credit: A letter of credit that provides for payment to a beneficiary when that beneficiary provides certification that certain obligations have not been fulfilled.

Step-in Rights: The right of lenders to assume sole or principal responsibility for carrying out all or part of the project's contractual responsibilities or to make arrangements for carrying them out. Step-in rights are designed to ensure continuity of the project and its ability to operate following a default by the sponsor.

Structural Subordination: Occurs when a bank or other institution lends to a holding company that uses the loan proceeds to infuse capital, in the form of equity or deeply subordinated shareholder loans, into one or more newly purchased operating companies. The holding company lender is structurally subordinated in right of payment relative to third-party lenders that may be extending credit directly to the operating subsidiaries.

Subordinated: The subordinated party accepts a lower priority of repayment and/or security than the senior party.

Sub-sovereign Risks: Risks relating to a public sector entity other than the central government (e.g., local and state governments).

Supply-or-Pay Contract: A contract in which the supplier agrees to provide goods or services to a project over time for a negotiated fee. If it is unable to do so, it must either provide the goods or services from an alternative source at its own expense or pay damages to the project for expenses incurred by the project in securing the goods or services itself.

Surety Bond: A form of guarantee to ensure contractual performance. For example, an insurance company can guarantee that a contractor will complete a project by issuing a surety bond payable in the event the contractor fails to complete the project.

Swap: An arrangement in which two entities lend to each other on different terms, for example, in different currencies or at different interest rates, fixed or floating.

Sweep: Typically a covenant that requires all or a specified fraction of available cash flow to be used for debt service, including prepayments of principal.

Syndicated Loan: A commercial banking transaction in which two or more banks participate in making a loan to a borrower.

Synthetic Lease: A kind of lease that combines the tax treatment of a capital lease with the accounting treatment of an operating lease. Thus, the lessee can deduct depreciation and interest expenses for tax purposes but does not record those expenses on its GAAP accounting statements.

T

Take-and-Pay Contract: A contract that requires the buyer to take and pay for the good or service only if it is delivered.

Take-or-Pay Contract: A contract that creates an unconditional obligation on the part of the buyer (offtaker) to pay for the good or service even if it is not produced or available from the seller.

Takeout: A new financing to refinance an existing loan.

Tax Holiday: A benefit granted to a project that provides project owners an exemption from taxation for a negotiated or statutory period.

Tenor: The number of years a loan is outstanding (i.e., the final maturity or term).

Term: The loan life or tenor; the period to a loan's final maturity.

Term Loan: A loan with an original or final maturity of more than one year, repayable according to a specified schedule.

Term Sheet: A document that outlines in general terms the key agreements to be contained in a legal document; other terms loosely associated and often used interchangeably are a letter of understanding (LOU) and a memorandum of understanding (MOU).

Third-party Liability Insurance: Insurance against damage or injury caused by the project to third parties.

Throughput Agreement: A throughput agreement is a hell-or-highwater contract to put and pay for material through a facility.

Tolling Agreement: An agreement under which a project company imposes tolling charges on each project user as compensation for processing raw material.

Tombstone: An advertisement describing some kind of capital raising that lists the sponsor, amount raised, participants, and key roles played by the participants.

Tranche: A separate portion of a project financing, perhaps with different lenders, margins, and terms.

Trustee: An independent or nominated third party who administers corporate or financial arrangements.

Turnkey Contract: A construction contract that provides for the complete engineering, procurement, construction, and start-up of a facility by a certain date, for a fixed price and at guaranteed performance levels.

U

Undersubscription: The situation when the underwriting commitments from a syndication are less than the amount sought by the borrower.

Underwrite: An arrangement under which a financial house agrees to buy a certain agreed amount of securities of a new issue on a given date and at a given price, thereby assuring the issuer the full proceeds of the financing.

Underwriting: The commitment to fund is not contingent upon successful syndication.

Unsecured: The financier has no security other than a legal commitment by the borrower to repay the loan.

Unwind: To reverse a swap or hedge.

V

Vendor Finance: Debt provided by a supplier of equipment or services to the project company.

W

Warranty: A guarantee that a given fact will exist at some future date, as promised.

Withholding Tax: A tax on interest, royalty, or dividend payments, usually those paid overseas.

Wrapped Bonds: Bonds guaranteed by a monoline insurance company.

Y

Yankee Bonds: Foreign bonds denominated in U.S. dollars and issued in the United States by foreign banks and corporations. These bonds are usually registered with the SEC.

PART II: PROJECT FINANCE ACRONYMS

ACRS	Accelerated Cost Recovery System
ADB	Asian Development Bank
ADR	American Depository Receipt
ADSCR	Annual Debt Service Coverage Ratio
AfDB	African Development Bank
AfDF	African Development Fund
APT	Arbitrage Pricing Theory
APV	Adjusted Present Value
AWA	Amendment and Waiver Agreement
BAFO	Best and Final Offer
BAR	Builders' All Risk (insurance)
BBSY	Refers to a screen (i.e., a page name) on the Reuters Monitor System that shows benchmark interest rates used to price variable rate loans
BIPS	Basis Points
BIS	Bank for International Settlements
bl	Barrel (equal to 42 U.S. gallons)
BLA	Bilateral Agency (e.g., U.S. Export-Import Bank)
BLT	Build-Lease-Transfer
bp	Basis point (1/100 of 1%, or 0.0001)
BOO	Build-Own-Operate
BOOT	Build-Own-Operate-Transfer
BOT	Build-Own-Transfer
BTO	Build-Transfer-Operate
Btu	British thermal unit
CADS	Cash Available for Debt Service
CAGR	Compound Annual Growth Rate
CAMENA	Central Asia/Middle East/North Africa
CapEx	Capital Expenditure
CEN	Confiscation, Expropriation, and Nationalization (collectively, "CEN" perils)
CAPM	Capital Asset Pricing Model
CBO	Collateralized Bond Obligation
CCF	Capital Cash Flow
CCGT	Combined Cycle Gas Turbine
CDC	Commonwealth Development Corporation (United Kingdom)
CDO	Collateralized Debt Obligation
CfD	Contract for Differences
CIF	Cost, Insurance, and Freight
CIP	Covered Interest Parity
CIRR	Commercial Interest Reference Rates
CLO	Collateralized Loan Obligation
COD	Commercial Operation Date
COFACE	Compagnie Française d'Assurance pour le Commerce Exterieur (French export credit agency)

CPI	Consumer Price Index
CPs	Conditions Precedent
CTA	Capacity and Tolling Agreement
CUP	Cooperative Underwriting Program
DCF	Discounted Cash Flow
DCR	Drawdown Cover Ratio
DFI	Development Finance Institution
DIS	Delay-in-Startup (insurance)
DOD	Debt Outstanding and Disbursed
DSCR	Debt Service Coverage Ratio
DSPA	Debt Service Payment Account
DSRA	Debt Service Reserve Account
EA	Environmental Assessment
EBIAT	Earnings Before Interest but After Taxes
EBIT	Earnings Before Interest and Taxes
EBITDA	Earnings before Interest, Taxes, Depreciation and Amortization
EBRD	European Bank for Reconstruction and Development
EC	European Community
ECA	Export Credit Agency
ECF	Equity Cash Flow
ECGD	Export Credit Guarantee Department (UK export credit agency)
ECU	European Community Unit
EDC	Export Development Canada (Canadian export credit agency)
EFIC	Export Finance and Insurance Corporation (Australian export credit agency)
EIA	Environmental Impact Assessment
EIB	European Investment Bank
EIS	Environmental Impact Statement
EIU	Economist Intelligence Unit
EOD	Event of Default
EPC	Engineering, Procurement, and Construction
EPS	Earnings per Share
ESA	Equity Support Agreement
EU	European Union
FASB	Financial Accounting Standards Board
FCF	Free Cash Flow
FDI	Foreign Direct Investment
FERC	Federal Energy Regulatory Commission
FIAS	Foreign Investment Advisory Service (part of the World Bank Group)
FM	*Force Majeure*
FOB	Free on Board
ForEx	Foreign Exchange
FRB	Federal Reserve Board (Washington, D.C.)
FSU	Former Soviet Union

FX	Foreign Exchange
FY	Fiscal Year
GAAP	Generally Accepted Accounting Principles (e.g., U.S. GAAP)
GDP	Gross Domestic Product
GNP	Gross National Product
ha	Hectare
HDSCR	Historic Debt Service Cover Ratio
HIBOR	Hong Kong Inter-Bank Offered Rate
HIPC	Heavily Indebted Poor Country
HoldCo	Holding Company
IBRD	International Bank for Reconstruction and Development (a member of the World Bank Group)
ICB	International Competitive Bidding
ICRG	International Country Risk Guide
ICSID	International Center for Settlement of Investment Disputes
IDA	International Development Association
IDB	Inter-American Development Bank
IDC	Interest During Construction
IE	Independent Engineer
IFC	International Finance Corporation
IMF	International Monetary Fund
IPP	Independent Power Producer (or Independent Power Plant)
IRR	Internal Rate of Return
ISDA	International Swap and Derivatives Association
IsDB	Islamic Development Bank
ITC	Investment Tax Credit
JBIC	Japan Bank for International Cooperation
JEXIM	Japan Export-Import Bank
KExim	Korean Export-Import Bank
KfW	Kreditanstalt für Wiederaufbau
km	Kilometer
kWh	Kilowatt-Hour
LIBOR	London Inter-Bank Offered Rate
L/C	Letter of Credit
LDs	Liquidated Damages
LLC	Limited Liability Company
LLCR	Loan Life Cover Ratio
LME	London Metals Exchange
LNG	Liquefied Natural Gas
LOC	Letter of Credit
LOI	Letter of Intent
LOU	Letter of Understanding

LPG	Liquefied Petroleum Gas
LSTK	Lump-sum Turnkey Contract
MAC	Material Adverse Change
MACRS	Modified Cost Recovery System
MAE	Material Adverse Event *or* Material Adverse Effect
MDB	Multilateral Development Bank
MIGA	Multilateral Investment Guarantee Association (a member of the World Bank Group)
MITI	Ministry of International Trade and Industry (Japan)
MLA	Multilateral Agency (e.g., International Finance Corporation)
MNC	Multinational Corporation
MOF	Ministry of Finance (Japan)
MOU	Memorandum of Understanding
MPP	Merchant Power Plant
MSCI	Morgan Stanley Capital International
MW	Megawatt (1,000 Watts)
NGO	Nongovernmental Organization
NPV	Net Present Value
NWC	Net Working Capital
OECD	Organization for Economic Cooperation and Development
OM	Offering Memorandum
O&M	Operation and Maintenance
OPEC	Organization of Petroleum Exporting Countries
OPEX	Operating Expenses
OPIC	Overseas Private Investment Corporation
p.a.	Per Annum (annually)
PCG	Partial Credit Guarantee
PDSCR	Projected Debt Service Cover Ratio
PFA	Project Funds Agreement
PFI	Private Finance Initiative
PLCR	Project Life Coverage Ratio
PPA	Power Purchase Agreement
PPI	Private Participation in Infrastructure (Note: can also be the Producer Price Index)
ppm	Parts Per Million
PPP	Public-Private Partnership *or* Purchasing Power Parity
PRG	Partial Risk Guarantee
PRI	Political Risk Insurance
PUC	Public Utilities Commission
PUCHA	Public Utility Holding Company Act (of 1935)
PURPA	Public Utilities Regulatory Policy Act (of 1978)
PV	Present Value
QIB	Qualified Institutional Buyer

RECs	Regional Electricity Companies
RFP	Request for Proposals
ROA	Return on Assets
ROE	Return on Equity
ROI	Return on Investment
ROIC	Return on Invested Capital
ROW	Right of Way
SACE	Istituto per i Servizi Assicurativi del Commercio Estero (Italian export credit agency)
S&P	Standard & Poor's Corporation
SCR	Sovereign Credit Rating
SEC	Securities and Exchange Commission (United States)
SIC	Standard Industrial Classification
SOE	State-owned Enterprise
SPV	Special-purpose Vehicle
T&D	Transmission and Distribution
UNCITRAL	United Nations Commission on International Trade Law
UNCTAD	United Nations Conference on Trade and Development
UNDP	United Nations Development Program
UNEP	United Nations Environmental Program
USAID	United States Agency for International Development
USEXIM	Export-Import Bank of the United States (U.S. export credit agency)
VAT	Value-added Tax
VPD	Vehicles Per Day
WACC	Weighted Average Cost of Capital
WTO	World Trade Organization

PART III: PROJECT FINANCE COVERAGE RATIOS

Definitions

CADS
= Cash Available for Debt Service
CADS equals pretax operating income (revenues minus operating expenses) plus interest income from reserve accounts minus mandatory capital expenditures minus investments in net working capital minus required contributions to reserve accounts (maintenance, capital expenditures, etc.). Notes: (1) depreciation should not be subtracted from the operating expenses; and (2) certain taxes such as property taxes and sales taxes should be subtracted from operating income, but income taxes should not. Although proceeds from a debt service reserve account are available to pay debt service in the event of a cash flow shortfall, they are not typically included in the cash available for debt service.

DS
= Debt Service
DS includes interest payments and principal repayments due on a given date.

DSRA
= Debt Service Reserve Account

EBIT
= Earnings Before Interest and Taxes

EBITDA
= Earnings Before Interest and Taxes plus Depreciation and Amortization

FCF
= Free Cash Flow
Free cash flow equals EBIT after taxes, plus depreciation and amortization, minus capital expenditures and increases in net working capital (NWC).

K_D
= The cost of debt (i.e., stated interest rate); if there are multiple debt tranches or instruments, then it is the weighted average cost of debt where the weights are based on principal amounts.

Coverage Ratios

1. **Interest Coverage Ratios (e.g., Times Interest Earned, or TIE)**

$$TIE = EBIT \, / \, \text{Interest Due}$$

The traditional interest coverage ratios commonly used in corporate finance are rarely used in project finance. Because most projects have limited lives, their debt capacity falls over time. As a result, project lenders require projects to use fully amortizing debt. In contrast, corporations with theoretically infinite lives refinance or roll over existing debt. For this reason, project lenders care more about the ability to cover total debt service than interest payments alone.

2. **Debt Service Coverage Ratio (DSCR) or Annual Debt Service Coverage Ratio (ADSCR)**

$$DSCR = CADS \, / \, DS$$

The **Minimum Debt Service Coverage Ratio (Minimum DSCR)** provides a measure of financial risk by highlighting the year with the lowest coverage ratio. Typical ranges for the minimum DSCR are:
   a. $2.0\times$ for a merchant power plant (MPP) with full market risk
   b. $1.8\times$ for natural resources project with commodity pricing risks

    c. 1.5× for an infrastructure project with some market risk

    d. 1.3× for an independent power plant (IPP) with a power purchase agreement

The **Average Debt Service Coverage Ratio (Average DSCR)** equals the average of the annual debt service coverage ratios calculated over the life of the loan. (*Note:* This measure can be distorted in later years if cash flow is high and debt service is relatively low.) It provides an indication of whether the project, over some defined period, generates sufficient cash flow to repay its debt. It does not, however, guarantee that the project can pay its debt service in all years. To the extent the Average DSCR is high, it is an indication that principal amortization can be shifted through time to cover periods of tight coverage.

3. **Loan Life Coverage Ratio (LLCR)**

   The LLCR equals the net present value of CADS from the calculation date through the final maturity date (discounted at the weighted average interest rate on all debt facilities and tranches) divided by the total principal outstanding at the calculation date. The ratio measures a project's ability to service all of its debt while outstanding but does not indicate whether there are shortfalls in any given year.

   $$\text{LLCR} = \frac{NPV(CADS \text{ during loan life @ } K_\text{D})}{\text{Total Debt}}$$

4. **Project Life Coverage Ratio (PLCR)**

   The PLCR is the same as the LLCR except that the net present value of CADS is calculated over the life of the project rather than the life of the loan. For infrastructure and other kinds of projects, project life is defined as the concession or offtake period (contractual period). In contrast, for extractive industries (e.g., mining, oil, etc.), project life is determined as the time until a specified fraction of total reserves is left. In natural resources projects, this ratio is sometimes referred to as the reserve coverage ratio (RCR). The ratio measures a project's ability to service all of its debt but does not indicate whether there are shortfalls in any given year.

   $$\text{PLCR} = \frac{NPV \ (CADS \text{ during project life @ } K_\text{D})}{\text{Total Debt}}$$

5. **Drawdown Coverage Ratio (DCR)**

   The DCR is a forward-looking coverage ratio that is relevant in the early stages of a project's life, before it has drawn down the full loan amount. In contrast to the LLCR, which analyzes current indebtedness, the DCR analyzes coverage relative to the maximum expected debt level.

   $$\text{DCR} = \frac{NPV \ (CADS \text{ during loan life @ } K_\text{D})}{(\text{Maximum Amount to Be Borrowed})}$$

REFERENCES

Many of the definitions contained in this glossary come from or were created from one or more of the following sources. The definitions have been revised to make them current and consistent across the glossary.

Davis, H. *Project Finance: Practical Case Studies*. London, UK: Euromoney Books, 1996.

Development Bank of Southern Africa Web site, ⟨www.dbsa.org/privatesector/project_finance.htm⟩.

Harvey, C. Website, ⟨http://www.duke.edu/~charvey/Classes/wpg/glossary.htm⟩, Hypertextual Finance Glossary.

Hoffman, Scott L. *The Law and Business of International Project Finance*. London, UK: Kluwer Law International, 1998.

Khan, M.F.K., and R.J. Parra. Financing Large Projects: Using Project Finance Techniques and Practices. Prentice Hall (Pearson Education Asia Pte Ltd) Singapore 2003.

MZ Project Finance Web site, ⟨www.mzprojectfinance.com/project_finance/glossary.htm⟩. Produced by Mauro Zajec.

Nevitt, P.K. and F.J. Fabozzi. *Project Financing*, 7th ed. London, UK: Euromoney Books, 2000.

Pollio, G. *International Project Analysis and Financing*. Ann Arbor, MI: University of Michigan Press, 1999.

"Project Finance in Developing Countries." Lessons of Experience, Number 7, International Finance Corporation, Washington, DC, 1999.

Razavi, H. *Financing Energy Projects in Emerging Economies*. Tulsa, OK: PennWell Books, 1996.

Rhodes, T. *Syndicated Lending: Practice and Documentation*, 3rd ed. London, UK: Euromoney Books, 2000.

Yescombe, E.R. *Principles of Project Finance*. London, UK: Academic Press—an imprint of Elsevier Science, 2002.

Index

A

L

M